Library of
Davidson College

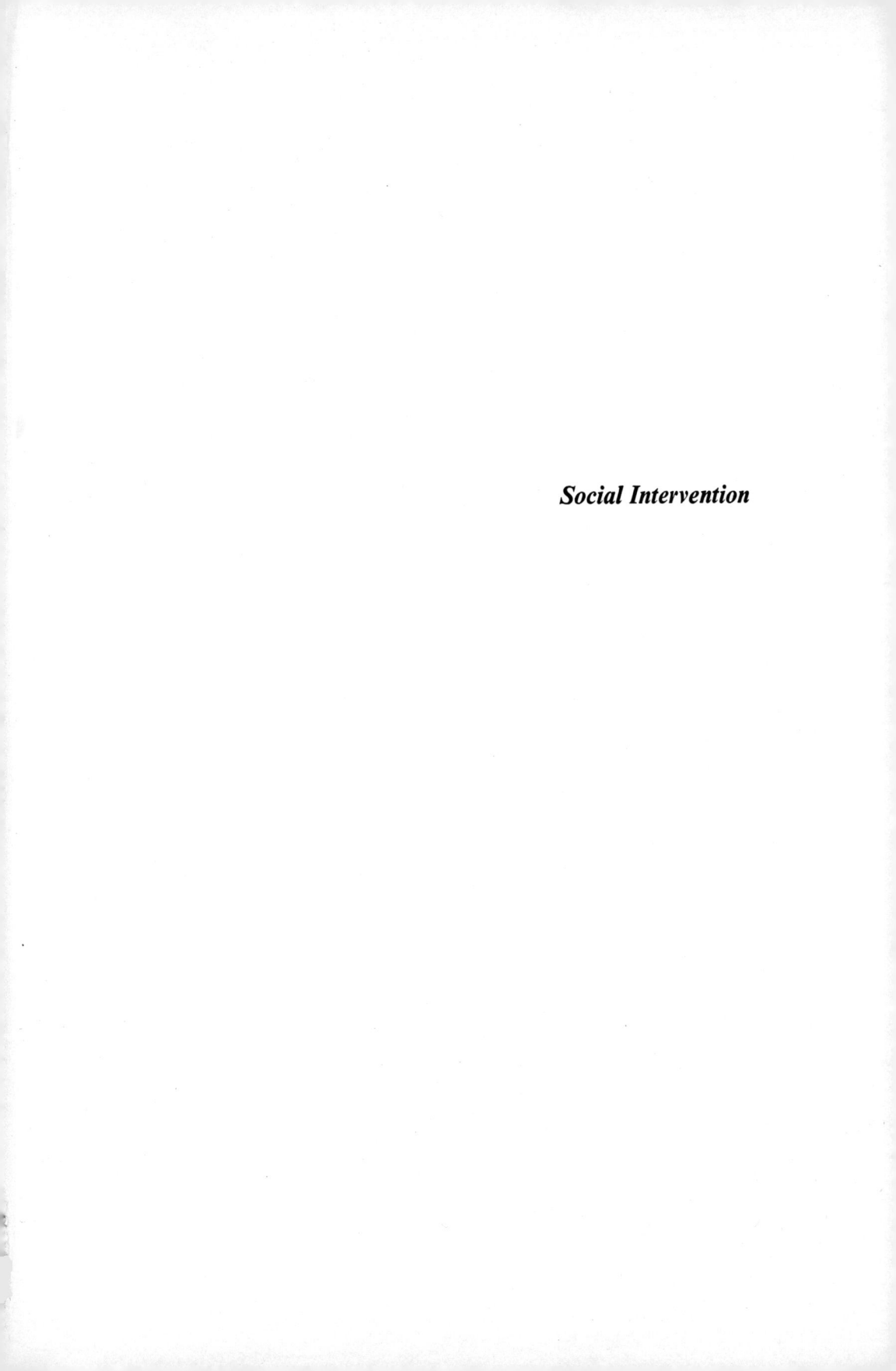

Social Intervention

*Edited and with
introductions by*
HARVEY A. HORNSTEIN
BARBARA BENEDICT BUNKER
W. WARNER BURKE
MARION GINDES
ROY J. LEWICKI

Social Intervention

A BEHAVIORAL SCIENCE
APPROACH

[Fp]

THE FREE PRESS, *New York*
COLLIER-MACMILLAN LIMITED
London

Copyright © 1971 by The Free Press
A DIVISION OF THE MACMILLAN COMPANY

Printed in the United States of America

All rights reserved. No part of this book may be reproduced or transmitted in any form or by any means, electronic or mechanical, including photocopying, recording, or by any information storage and retrieval system, without permission in writing from the Publisher.

The Free Press
A Division of The Macmillan Company
866 Third Avenue, New York, New York 10022

Collier-Macmillan Canada Limited
Toronto, Ontario

Library of Congress Catalog Card Number: 77-143509

printing number
1 2 3 4 5 6 7 8 9 10

Contents

INTRODUCTION   1

part one
Individual Change Strategies of Social Intervention   9

1. CHRIS ARGYRIS
   T-Groups for Organizational Effectiveness   31

2. ARTHUR H. KURILOFF and STUART ATKINS
   T-Group for a Work Team   44

3. JOHN P. CAMPBELL and MARVIN D. DUNNETTE
   Effectiveness of T-Group Experiences in Managerial Training and Development   61

4. DOUGLAS R. BUNKER and ERIC S. KNOWLES
   Comparison of Behavioral Changes Resulting from Human Relations Training Laboratories of Different Lengths   91

5. A. K. RICE
   From Learning for Leadership   103

6. ROBERT R. BLAKE and JANE SRYGLEY MOUTON
   Some Effects of Managerial Grid Seminar Training on Union and Management Attitudes Toward Supervision   114

7. CHARLES H. KEPNER and BENJAMIN B. TREGOE
   Developing Decision Makers   122

8. NORMAN R. F. MAIER and LESTER F. ZERFOSS
   MRP: A Technique for Training Large Groups of Supervisors and Its Potential Use in Social Research   134

part two
Techno-Structural Strategies of Social Intervention 143

9 **A. K. RICE**
   Productivity and Social Organization in an Indian Weaving Shed: An Examination of Some Aspects of the Socio-Technical System of an Experimental Automatic Loom Shed   157

10 **LEONARD R. SAYLES**
   The Change Process in Organizations: An Applied Anthropology Analysis   185

11 **FRANCES TORBERT**
   Making Incentives Work   195

12 **RICHARD BECKHARD**
   The Confrontation Meeting   213

13 **FRED E. FIEDLER**
   Engineer the Job to Fit the Manager   223

14 **ROBERT SOMMER**
   Small Group Ecology   234

15 **FRED I. STEELE**
   Physical Settings and Organizational Development   244

part three
Data-Based Strategies of Social Intervention 255

16 **D. W. ADAMS and A. E. HAVENS**
   The Use of Socio-Economic Research in Developing a Strategy of Change for Rural Communities: A Colombian Example   270

17 **RICHARD BECKHARD**
   Helping a Group With Planned Change: A Case Study   286

18 **FLOYD C. MANN**
   Studying and Creating Change: A Means to Understanding Social Organization   294

19 **M. B. MILES, H. A. HORNSTEIN, P. H. CALDER, D. M. CALLAHAN, and R. STEVEN SCHIAVO**
   Data Feedback: A Rationale   310

20 **CLAIRE SELLTIZ**
   The Use of Survey Methods in a Citizens Campaign Against Discrimination   316

Contents   vii

    21   **GEORGE W. FAIRWEATHER**
           Experimental Social Innovation Defined   330

part four

Organization Development: Cultural Change as a Strategy of Social Intervention   343

    22   **WARREN G. BENNIS**
           Changing Organizations   361

    23   **W. WARNER BURKE** and **WARREN H. SCHMIDT**
           Primary Target for Change: The Manager or the Organization?   373

    24   **PAUL C. BUCHANAN**
           Crucial Issues in Organizational Development   386

    25   **ROBERT R. BLAKE** and **JANE SRYGLEY MOUTON**
           Grid OD: A Systems Approach to Corporate Excellence   401

    26   **RICHARD BECKHARD** and **DALE G. LAKE**
           Short- and Long-Range Effects of a Team Development Effort   421

part five

Violence and Coercion as Strategies of Social Intervention   441

    27   **LEONARD BERKOWITZ**
           The Study of Urban Violence: Some Implications of Laboratory Studies of Frustration and Aggression   468

    28   **RALPH W. CONANT**
           Rioting, Insurrection and Civil Disobedience   476

    29   **IRVING HOWE**
           From The Politics of Confrontation   487

    30   **NITISH R. DÊ**
           Gherao as a Technique for Social Intervention   493

    31   **ZBIGNIEW BRZEZINSKI**
           Revolution and Counterrevolution (But Not Necessarily About Columbia!)   502

    32   **JERRY RUBIN**
           What the Revolution Is All About, or We Are All Vietcong and We Are Everywhere   507

    33   **WILLIAM GORING**
           Bang: An Anarchist Approach to Social Intervention   512

34 **GEORGE L. PEABODY**
Power, Alinsky, and Other Thoughts 521

part six
Nonviolence and Direct Action as Strategies of Social Intervention 533

35 **GENE SHARP**
Mechanisms of Change in Nonviolent Action 546

36 **MARTIN OPPENHEIMER and GEORGE LAKEY**
Direct Action Tactics 558

37 **MORTON DEUTSCH**
Conflicts: Productive and Destructive 566

38 **VICTORIA M. OLDS**
Freedom Rides: A Social Movement as an Aspect of Social Change 577

Index 587

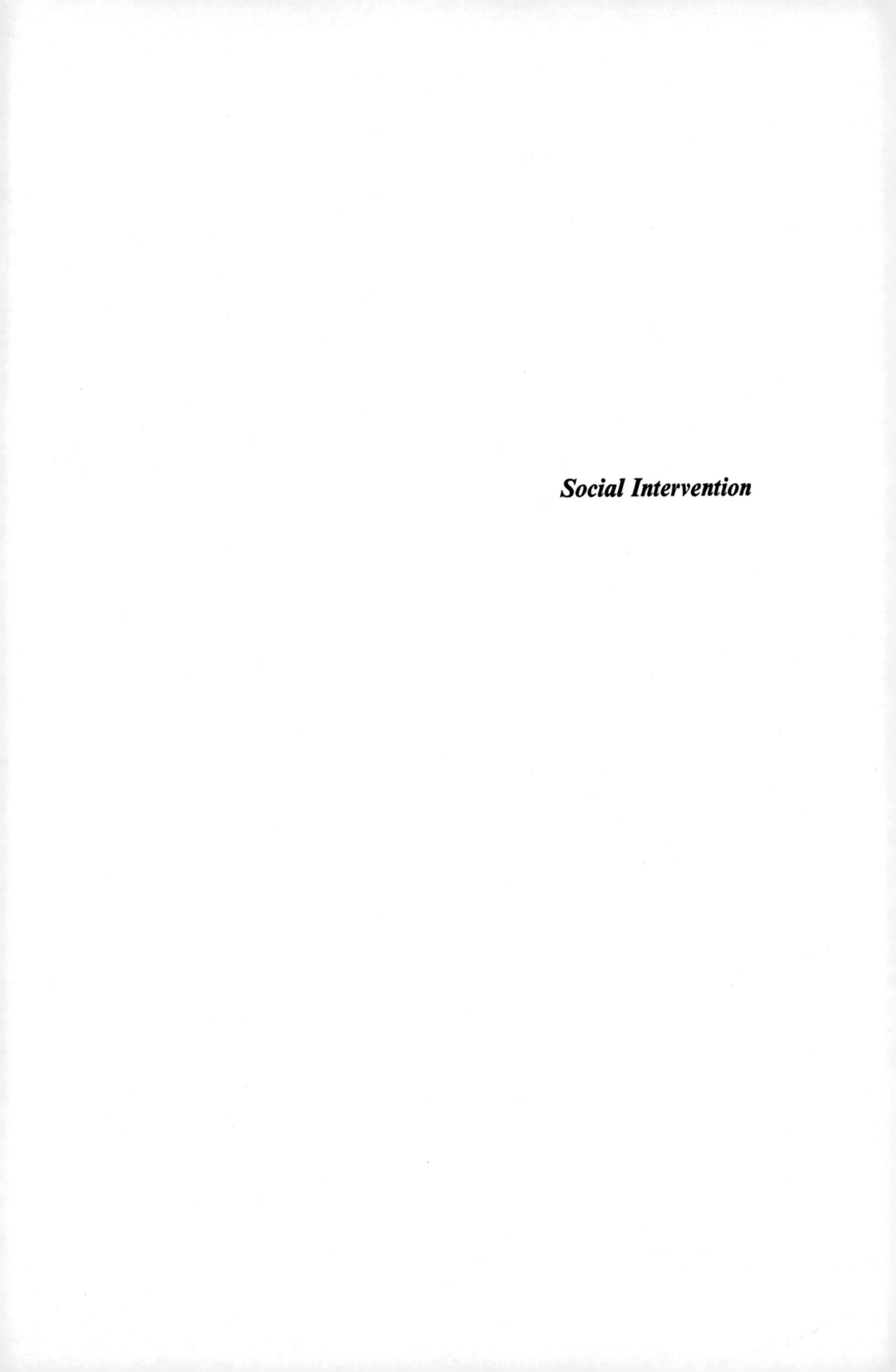

Social Intervention

Introduction

a while ago, the efficacy of the more militant aspects of the black civil rights movement was explained to one of this book's authors by a New York cab driver. "With Luther King," the driver said, "when there was nonviolence and all, then whites would feel sorry; no one likes to see defenseless people hurt. But now, with all the threatening, and fighting, and burning, everyone just wants to protect themselves. That's the wrong way. It just frightens your friends away."

"Well," his passenger responded as they bumped along New York's West Side Highway, "what if you were to assume that your friends couldn't do very much because those in power—those who really control decisions around the city and country—profited by keeping things just the way they are?"

"That's different," he acknowledged, "then it's like business. If you make it worthwhile for the guy to do what you want, he'll do it. Take my boss, for instance—if I aggravate the hell out of him, he gives me what I want just to get rid of me."

In his own way, the cab driver is a student of social change. His comments reflect his understanding that there are different strategies for changing social systems and that the effectiveness of the various strategies is altered by various situational contingencies. This book attempts to expand on these thoughts. To do this we present six approaches to social intervention and identify some of the psychological and sociological assumptions underlying each of them. Thus the book should be of interest to our discerning cab driver as well as to practitioners of social change and scholars interested in studying the theoretical and experimental issues associated with different strategies of changing social systems.

Every day the media of mass communication report attempts to change social systems. Programs for the introduction of economic incentives in industry, human relations training, and even armed rebellions are all examples. The objective of this book is to consider an array of social interventions, all of which have the same ultimate purpose: altering the behavior and functioning of a social system. We also hope to group these interventions into meaningful categories by identifying common organizing principles, which include implicit and explicit assumptions made by change agents about (1) the psychological and sociological phenomena mediating change efforts, (2) the nature of social systems, and (3) the rules of contingency which define the conditions under which a strategy is likely to achieve its objectives.

That this book and similar ones are being written in increasing numbers reflects a current view of planned social intervention: It is essential, feasible, and demands systematic study. Other viewpoints have not given as much support to the practice or study of planned social intervention. The Calvinist view of a social order which was preordained and immutable gave way during the Enlightenment when the "rationalists" endorsed one strategy of social change. They believed that change could be accomplished simply by presenting the "truth." (See part one of this book, "Individual Change Strategies of Social Intervention" for further discussion of this view.) The rationalists' strategy is less important than the notion implicit in their view: That social systems *could* yield to planned social interventions. That belief is a necessary requisite for the development and study of the technology of social intervention.

By engaging in this pursuit, however, one runs the risk of being accused of social tinkering. Some argue that social organizations are self-regulatory and that for optimum conditions to develop the only intervention should be that of an "invisible hand." To plan a social intervention is to violate the process of natural law—a Sisyphean, if not immoral, task. Others argue that individual rights to self-determination are abrogated by such interventions. (Such reasoning seems to be by persons who indulge themselves in the notion that the functioning of social organizations is a consequence of accumulated individual decisions, freely made.)

Despite the views of these critics, a casual reading of newspapers suggests that planned social intervention is widespread (albeit, sometimes unskillful) and is generally viewed as being both necessary and feasible. There is undeniable evidence that some groups within our society are trying to remedy the injustices of history and technological progress by the use of various social interventions. The change agents who are organizing and guiding these interventions represent many segments of society—Martin Luther King, Ralph Nader, the Black Panthers, the federal government, labor unions, NTL, and Yippie leader Jerry Rubin. Their goals vary, as do the kinds of intervention that they use in order to change social systems.

A different approach to social intervention is considered in each of the book's six parts. These approaches are labeled as follows:
(1.) Individual Change Strategies of Social Intervention.
(2.) Techno-Structural Strategies of Social Intervention.
(3.) Data-Based Strategies of Social Intervention.
(4.) Organizational Development: Culture Change as a Strategy of Social Intervention.
(5.) Violence and Coercion as Strategies of Social Intervention.
(6.) Nonviolence and Direct Action as Strategies of Social Intervention.

Introduction

Although an attempt is made to maintain clear distinctions with regard to the organizing principles underlying each approach there is necessarily some overlap. This overlap is analogous to the one that exists when strategies for social intervention are employed in reality.

An introductory section at the beginning of each part presents these organizing principles, as well as the research and theories from the behavioral and social sciences which are relevant to each approach.

Admittedly, with only a few exceptions, social interventions have developed in an atheoretical fashion. Nevertheless, implicit within them are a number of psychological and sociological assumptions. By articulating these assumptions and their interrelationships, we hope to begin building systematic conceptual frameworks for describing the dynamics of social intervention. The understanding of social process provided by these frameworks may allow the practitioner to be more effective in his application of an intervention approach, and the theoretician to be more aware of gaps in his knowledge of social process.

Following the introductory sections, each part contains several papers which describe social technology representing the approach considered in that section. Generally speaking, the papers can be categorized as case studies and descriptive expositions, theoretical essays, or research studies. Both the differences and the similarities in the technology presented in these papers are discussed in the introductory sections.

In selecting papers that describe social intervention technology, two broadly stated criteria have been used. First, excluded are technologies that are solely or primarily concerned with changing *individuals*, and that are not at all, or are only indirectly, concerned with changing *social systems*.* For example, individual psychotherapy is not discussed unless it is part of a plan to change a social system. Second, social interventions that are not *planned*, deliberate attempts to change social systems are excluded. Hence, technological advances such as automation, which have had profound effects on social systems are not considered.

One final word—a precaution—before presenting brief summary statements of each part. In this book, social intervention techniques are grouped according to their common adherence to a set of related organizing principles. These principles, along with the exigencies of the social context within which a technique was developed and the ethical values of the change agent, have all influenced the style and application of each technique. Hence, some strategies tend to be idiosyncratic: They are used by some groups in some social contexts, but not by other groups in other contexts. The selections included in this book naturally reflect this idiosyncratic application of social intervention technology. Readers should not, however, be misled into believing that the intervention

---

* No attempt will be made to provide a rigorous definition of such terms as social system, social organization, or organization, which are used synonymously throughout this text. Excellent discussions of these concepts can be found in Etzioni (1964), Katz and Kahn (1966), March and Simon (1958), and Parsons (1960). Suffice it to say that our definition of these terms should be interpreted to include formal and informal, voluntary and involuntary, industrial, governmental, and educational systems.

techniques are appropriately used only in settings in which they have been commonly used. To gain flexibility in the use of social interventions, readers are urged to consider the principles underlying their use. For example, our New York cabbie applied an assumption underlying the use of violence: People will yield to demands if the costs for not doing so are greater than the rewards. Or, as he said, "... you make it worthwhile for the guy to do what you want...." Our cabbie did not threaten or commit mayhem; he simply applied the principle in a manner befitting his social context. He "aggravated the hell" out of his boss to get what he wanted. We hope that the systematic application of these principles will be as successful for all of us.

A brief abstract of the contents of each of the book's six parts follows. The introductory sections in each part contain an overview of the papers in that part.

INDIVIDUAL CHANGE STRATEGIES OF SOCIAL INTERVENTION

The common premise shared by the strategies in this part is that individual change is the primary mediator of social or organizational change. Although the central focus of these strategies is upon changing various aspects of the individual, this is regarded as a stepping stone to the major, though perhaps indirect, target of the change strategy—the organization.

The part begins with an examination of four theoretical frameworks which have had a significant influence on how change is conceptualized and which are reflected in the articles selected to represent the range of individual change strategies. They are the analytic model, the social–psychological model, the behaviorist model, and the Socratic-rational model. It is proposed that these theoretical frameworks lead to focusing on different aspects of the personality as targets for change. Feelings, values, attitudes, perception, and skills and actions are discussed as typical change targets representing varying degrees of centrality to the personality. Whenever possible, behavioral science research is presented to amplify the discussion of the relationship between personality and behavior change.

The strategies are further described in terms of the degree of explicit goal definition provided to the individual in the process of changing. The degree of explicitness on this dimension is seen as closely related to the target within the personality which is selected for change. Finally, four major issues raised by the use of individually oriented strategies are discussed:

(1.) What is the relationship between improved individual functioning and organizational effectiveness?
(2.) How much transfer of training can be anticipated from the learning situation to the job situation?
(3.) How many individuals must be changed in any system to improve system functioning?
(4.) What is the role of group norms in either facilitating or hindering individual change, and what social influence process must be taken into account?

Introduction

TECHNO-STRUCTURAL STRATEGIES OF SOCIAL INTERVENTION

The intervention strategies in this group share the assumption that technology and environment constrain the design of organizational structure, but these constraints do not fully determine its form. Therefore, the formal structure of any organization represents only one of several possible alternative structures. A goal of techno-structural intervention is to determine the alternative that is most satisfying and efficient. Such intervention strategies can be divided into two groups: (1) those that are directed at changing the organizational structure in order to provide greater congruence between technological and environmental demands and the organizational structure; and (2) those that attempt to alter technological or environmental conditions in order to achieve this congruence. Several strategies are reviewed, and related theory and research are presented.

DATA-BASED STRATEGIES OF SOCIAL INTERVENTION

The major concern of this part is with the procedures that the "affiliated" and "unaffiliated" change agents have developed for coping with nonrational (psychological) factors that influence the success of data-based strategies for social intervention. "Affiliated change agents" are actually members of the system in which they are trying to produce change, or they have entered into a mutually agreed-upon contractual relationship with the system. In contrast, "unaffiliated change agents" are not members of the target system nor are they a party to any mutually agreed-upon contractual agreement with the system.

Four technologies commonly used by affiliated change agents are discussed —diagnostic surveys, survey feedback, evaluative research, and action research. In varying degrees these social intervention technologies emphasize one or the other of two different aims: (1) *Initiatory aims* have the primary objective of collecting and presenting data in order to initiate problem-solving discussions among system members; and (2) *pragmatic aims* have the primary objective of using scientific procedures in order to collect data which will provide policy-makers with a rational, scientific basis for decision-making and problem-solving.

By placing different emphasis on these aims, data-based strategies differ in the procedures that they have developed for data collection and design, presentation and interpretation of data, formulating action steps, and dissemination of findings.

Social intervention techniques of unaffiliated change agents are also discussed and it is suggested that some of these techniques have political rather than initiatory or pragmatic aims. Their objective is to use data to create an influential constituency which will seek to effect changes in a designated social system. The effect of political aims on the tactics of unaffiliated change agents is considered.

ORGANIZATIONAL DEVELOPMENT: CULTURAL CHANGE AS A STRATEGY OF SOCIAL INTERVENTION

An organizational development process is defined as "the creation of a culture which supports the institutionalization and use of social technologies to facilitate diagnosis and change of interpersonal, group, and intergroup behavior, especially those behaviors related to organizational decision-making, planning, and communication."

It is argued that the characteristic social norms of modern organizations are based upon value systems which are inconsistent with the full use of modern social technology. Hence, before this social technology can be systematically employed, organizations must be culturally predisposed toward their use. Three steps aimed toward changing the culture of an organization precede the institutionalization of these social intervention techniques: (1) *entry* in which the aim is to create a felt need for change; (2) *normative change* aimed at exposing increasingly large numbers of system members to the new norms; and (3) *structural change*, an attempt to place OD advocates in positions that provide them with the flexibility, prestige, and protection necessary to conduct OD projects. Examples are cited, and relevant research and theories are discussed.

VIOLENCE AND COERCION AS STRATEGIES FOR SOCIAL INTERVENTION

The strategies reviewed in this part are concerned with the role of violence and coercion in social intervention. These strategies have received little systematic, interdisciplinary study by social scientists, although there are a number of popular descriptions of violent social change in the literature of history, sociology, anthropology, and political science.

This part reviews a number of the more popular variables in violent intervention, grouped into four major categories: (1) *intraindividual* and *personality variables* (biological, personality and socialization factors that lead to aggressive or violent behavior); (2) *social-structural variables* (economic and political conditions that spark social violence); (3) *cultural influences* (social class, nationality, etc.); and (4) *social–psychological variables* (power, social deviance, and the effect of interpersonal and intergroup conflict). After presenting the theory and research related to each of these variables, the implications for planned violent social intervention are explored. Strategies and tactics are suggested to aid the interventionist in the use of violent means, and evaluations of each strategy are discussed.

NONVIOLENCE AND DIRECT ACTION AS STRATEGIES FOR SOCIAL INTERVENTION

The use of nonviolence in social intervention represents an attempt by interventionists to change the attitudes and/or behavior of a target person or group. A major assumption underlying this approach is that nonviolent tactics will beget a nonviolent response, and that, in some instances, nonviolence will arouse the social conscience of attackers or third parties. It is not assumed that the target initially feels a need for change. Following a description of nonviolent action in history, and the issues surrounding the definition and characterization of nonviolent action, the typical interventionist's personality and belief systems are examined.

Introduction 7

The strategy and tactics of nonviolence are divided into two approaches to changing the other—indirect and direct. The indirect approach disconfirms the other's expectations by using nonviolent techniques; the direct approach challenges the other's power, and attempts to alter his attitudes and/or behavior toward the interventionist and his group. Both approaches are examined in detail, and suggestions are made to the interventionist for the design and implementation of nonviolent action.

References

Etzioni, A. *Modern Organizations*. Englewood Cliffs: Prentice-Hall, 1964.
Katz, D., and R. L. Kahn. *The Social Psychology of Organizations*. New York: Wiley, 1966.
March, J. G., and H. A. Siman. *Organizations*. New York: Wiley, 1958.
Parsons, T. *Structure and Process in Modern Societies*. New York: The Free Press, 1960.

PART ONE

Individual Change Strategies of Social Intervention

*t*he premise shared by the strategies presented in this part is that individual change is the primary mediator of social or organizational change. This central focus—the changing of various aspects of the individual—is regarded as a stepping stone to the major, though perhaps indirect, target of the change strategy—the organization. Since social organizations are artificial structures devised by individuals, it should follow that individuals can bring about change in the systems of which they are members. Thus, in theory at least, any positive change on an individual level can be evaluated in terms of its usefulness to the system. In practice, however, the system is often so psychologically distant from the intervention experience that the effects of any individual change may be dissipated.

We begin this part by exploring the theoretical assumptions of these strategies as they have been influenced by a number of psychological models. Then, we describe the strategies with regard to that aspect of individual functioning which is to be changed. In the course of this discussion, overviews of relevant research literature are presented. It should be noted that although it is possible to find support in the psychological literature for most of these strategies, their development, with few exceptions, did not occur directly in response to the results of behavioral science research. One may, however, choose to use the research literature as a justification, on a *post hoc* basis; and this is the procedure we have adopted here. The strategies are further characterized in terms of the degree of goal-definition which they provide. Some strategies provide individuals with clearly defined and behaviorally specific goals, whereas others provide a situation in which individuals participate in goal-setting and in devising methods of working on change. As a conclusion to this introduction we discuss some of the problems inherent in all individual-change strategies which intend to have organizational effects.

THEORETICAL MODELS

Many models of human behavior offer notions about individual change that are relevant to the subject matter here. We describe four theoretical frameworks which have had a significant influence on how change is conceptualized. They are the analytic model, the social–psychological model, the behaviorist model, and the Socratic-rational model.

ANALYTIC MODEL

The influence of analytic concepts throughout the behavioral sciences has been far-reaching. Many analytic notions, such as the existence of the unconscious, are so commonly accepted that they serve as implicit bases for several intervention strategies. On the other hand, there are some strategies that are explicitly derived from analytic theory. These strategies share the assumption that the process underlying individual behavior and the therapeutic techniques for changing it are applicable to the normal individual in the group setting. The Tavistock approach to individual change and Gerald Caplan's (1964) approach to mental health consultation are presented as illustrations of the application of the analytic model to intervention strategies.

There are two features of the analytic model—resistance and transference cure—that are particularly pertinent to change strategies. The analytic notion of *resistance* is of special importance in any attempt to change an individual. In therapy, patients express a desire to get well; similarly, in the various change interventions participants want to learn from the experience, become more competent on an interpersonal level, and increase their effectiveness. Movement toward change, however, does not always proceed smoothly or easily. People arrive late for sessions, forget what they were going to say, omit important information, or announce that they have nothing to talk about. These are some of the external manifestations of resistance. Menninger (1958) interprets such resistance as strong forces within each individual which serve "to defend himself against any change in his life adjustment . . . uncomfortable though it may be in many respects (p. 101)." In this sense, resistance reflects the ambivalence of the individual toward change potential. At the same time that he desires change, he also must protect himself from the anxiety and threat associated with a loosening of the ego's defense structure.

Although resistance may occur on a conscious level, such as intentionally withholding information, the most crucial and most difficult aspects of resistance are unconscious. A primary goal of the therapeutic situation is, in fact, to make the patient aware of the process of resistance itself. Awareness of this conservative tendency to maintain the psychological status quo does not, however, resolve the difficulty. The individual may be aware of the presence of resistance in general, but may not be aware of his specific manifestations of resistance. Moreover, resistance recurs throughout the process of change (Watson, 1967). Thus, any analytically-oriented change agent not only must acknowledge the presence of resistance, but also must constantly deal with it if significant change within the individual is to occur.

The idea of a *transference cure* is also relevant to the various change strategies (including those that do not derive from analytic theory). "Transference cure" can be defined as an apparently positive change which occurs in the individual and derives from the patient–therapist relationship. Such a change usually occurs during a period of positive transference when the patient may experience a desire to please the therapist, may see the therapist as someone who can gratify his needs, or may view the therapist as someone who has great knowledge and magical power with regard to his problems. Wolstein (1954) regards a therapeutic success, or transference cure, during this period of positive transference as being based on the suggestion of the therapist which may lead to a temporary removal of symptoms. Thus, the individual may "guess" at what kind of behavior the therapist considers to be healthy and modify his own behavior in that direction. For example, in a therapeutic situation, the patient may learn to become aware of his feelings but he may not be able to do this once the therapeutic relationship is terminated or when he is outside of the therapeutic session. Analogously, in a group setting the individual may conform to group norms, such as openness, but he may not be able to sustain them without the presence of the group. Thus, a focal question for all change strategies is whether the observed change represents true internal or intrapsychic change, or whether it represents a more superficial adaptation to the situation.

Tavistock Approach. The Tavistock approach to training in group process represents the most significant of the analytically based strategies. In *Learning for Leadership*, Rice (1965) says that "individual behavior is affected by unconscious forces, and as a corollary, that individuals and groups of individuals always behave in ways that are not wholly explicable in terms of their rational and overt intentions (p. 90)." In this training method, the consultant treats the group as an individual; he interprets the process of the group much as a therapist interprets for an individual patient, focusing first on resistance and transference and then on other issues. The consultant's primary obligation is to point out what is going on as well as what may be learned if the members so choose. In the typical Tavistock study group, members have the opportunity to examine and learn as a group from their own and other members' behavior.

According to Bion (1961), all members in a new group share certain basic assumptions which hinder the development of a reality-oriented work group. Initially, the members react affectively with anxiety and with defensive styles of behavior (such as "dependency on the leader," "pairing," and "fight–flight"), rather than by examination of the processes. These forms of resistance are the first subject of learning for the group. Moreover, the special and clearly defined role of the consultant in relation to the learning task leads most groups to focus on relationships with authority during the early stages of the group. After this examination takes place, other issues (such as member responsibility and competence, fears of the irrational, and interpersonal relations between members) can be subjects for learning. In addition to the study group, Tavistock conferences also emphasize process in larger group settings, intergroup phenomena, and the application of these learnings to concrete work settings.

Mental Health Consultation. Another application of analytic theory to organizational change through the individual is found in mental health consultation, as described by Gerald Caplan (1964). He discusses four types of consultation activities ranging from working with an individual consultee about a particular client or patient (of the consultee) to working with a group of administrators on such issues as planning of mental health programs or the interpersonal aspects of the agency operation. Thus, while some mental health consultation does focus on effecting broad change through the individual members of the system, other mental health consultation is concerned only indirectly with organizational change.

Caplan not only relies on analytic concepts as the theoretical base for his work, but also sees analytic training as appropriate, perhaps vital, training for consultation. The consultant uses his knowledge of personality dynamics to diagnose and interpret the consultative dilemma, the dilemma being the reason for the request for consultation and the cause of the work difficulty. The solution of this dilemma is derived from the consultant's analysis of "theme interference." This is seen as a distortion in perception and judgment which results from the intrusion of an underlying problem into the individual's functioning. According to Caplan, this problem derives from some longstanding personality difficulty which is exacerbated by some aspect of his work. Thus, he may respond in terms of his particular problem rather than to the reality of the situation. This results in a decrease in the effectiveness with which he uses his professional skill. The notion of theme interference, which is central in Caplan's consultation model, is similar to the processes underlying Sullivan's description of parataxic distortion and of transference in psychotherapy.

A weakness of Caplan's approach is that, although he attempts to differentiate between therapy and consultation in theory, the line is difficult to maintain in practice as long as consultation is considered to be an extension of the traditional, one-to-one analytic approach.

SOCIAL–PSYCHOLOGICAL MODEL

Perhaps the notions that have had the most pervasive influence on change strategies derive from the work of Kurt Lewin (1947). His description of the role of the peer group in group discussion and decision-making and of the change process in individuals provides the foundation for the laboratory method of training or re-education. Within the peer group, equality of status and power distribution encourages discussion, free decision-making, and internalization of the decisions (Katz and Kahn, 1966). The classical demonstration of this is provided by Lewin's experiment in changing food buying habits of women during World War II (Lewin, 1943). In this study, participation in group discussion was more effective than were lectures in changing group (and individual) readiness to purchase unusual cuts of meat. In laboratory training, the group is treated as a peer group even though back-home roles may not be of equal status. The group's characteristics, norms, and value systems are not preplanned but emerge through discussion within the group. This procedure facilitates the internalization of individual change by increasing the likelihood that an individual not only will adhere to such standards but also will regard them as his own. Here Lewin's three-stage change process is most relevant to describing the individual changes that occur.

The first of the three stages is the *unfreezing* of old attitudes, values, or behavior patterns. Perhaps the best definition of the term "unfreezing" is simply a decrease in the stability or strength of one's old attitudes or values. This occurs in settings where old approaches may not be effective or may be subject to scrutiny, where one receives information that is discrepant with one's own self-perceptions, and where one is confronted with a new and ambiguous situation. In this situation, there is a certain degree of anxiety and a breakdown of the usual social structure. This occurs in laboratory training where individuals are confronted with groups that lack an agenda or common rule of behavior. The second stage is the *change* itself, or the acquisition of new attitudes, values, norms, and behaviors which emerge through the group process. The third stage is *refreezing*—securing the change as an integral, internalized part of the individual. When the norms of the temporary system are strong, change within the setting is relatively easily achieved. In contrast, maintaining the change outside of the group setting is more difficult since the norms which facilitated the original change may not be in force in the individual's natural peer or work group.

BEHAVIORIST MODEL

The behaviorist point of view presents a third relevant mode for change strategies. The primary assumption is that present, conscious, overt behavior is the appropriate focus of change. Thus, there is little need to hypothesize about or to be concerned with internal or unconscious processes. What is important is to bring about change in the person's actual performance or behavior; any internal changes that may occur are more or less secondary by-products. This view is, of course, in direct contrast to the view espoused by analytically oriented change specialists. The controversy between the behaviorist and the analytic point of view has been especially highlighted with regard to psychotherapeutic intervention. The analytically oriented change specialists (whether they be psychotherapists or trainers) contend that dealing with unconscious processes and producing insight and understanding are vital in order to bring about significant change within the individual (Ford and Urban, 1967).

In contrast, Hobbs (1966) suggests that insight may follow behavior change, and that prior awareness is not necessary. The experimental evidence on operant conditioning (Krasner and Ullmann, 1965), desensitization (Wolpe, 1958) and other behavior modification techniques supports the notion that change in at least some kinds of behavior can indeed occur without the individual's insight. Hastorf (1965) describes a study using reinforcement procedures in which he changed an individual's behavior in a group whose task was to discuss human relations problems. The most interesting aspect of this study was not, however, that they could get an individual to talk more and to be more active in a group, but rather that the individual's satisfaction with his own behavior increased and that others' perceptions of this target individual altered as well. These changes were without any apparent "insight" as to the reinforcement contingencies.

SOCRATIC-RATIONAL MODEL

The Socratic-rational model, which came to prominence with the Enlightenment but which has long been present in Western culture, represents the notion that men are eminently rational and behaviorally responsive to new information. According to this view, change comes about as persons are exposed to knowledge; when one knows the truth, one acts accordingly. There are two types of assumptions or premises which are used to explain why men are behaviorally responsive to knowledge. One assumption based on a hedonistic premise is that knowledge can be used in the service of self-interest: The individual's own interests are best served by doing what is rational. In fields like economics and psychology this point of view has led to a study of rational approaches to decision-making and to the calculation of strategies for "the rational game-player," the person who is guided by his head and self-interest and who can resist the encroachments of other motivations.

The other assumption explains the assumed responsiveness of men to knowledge by affirming that there is something motivationally compelling about the "truth" which commands appropriate changes in both feeling and behavior. Prejudice, for example, can be ameliorated when confronted by knowledge which disallows biased belief. Thus, social progress occurs as more and more people become exposed to "true knowledge." The commitment in this country by Horace Mann and others to a broad system of public education reflects this view of social progress.

The Socratic-rational framework is a marked contrast to one which emphasizes the irrationality of men and which sees the irrational forces both within persons and outside of them as difficult to control. The history of Western culture has seen an interweaving of both views, with one sometimes much more dominant than the other. In this century with Freud's emphasis on the importance of the irrational and with Dewey's stress on the rational permeating the educational system, we live in a period when both views are strongly in evidence.

The same differential blending of assumptions about the importance of the rational and irrational is found in the various strategies represented in this section. At least one (Blake and Mouton, in this part) depends heavily on the assumption that actions flow from rational attitudes and that when attitudes are changed, behavior is affected. Others (for example, T-groups) use cognition as a way of identifying and conceptualizing learning after it has taken place emotionally. Cognitive understanding is assumed to be a means of facilitating transfer of learning to other, non-training contexts. This is in contrast to the Tavistock approach where the task is to use the ego (the rational) to look at the irrational and control it by understanding it.

TARGETS FOR CHANGE

One or another of the theoretical models discussed above provides the conceptual framework for most of the strategies presented in this section. In part, the theoretical model limits which aspect of individual functioning can be the target for change. Even within these limits, however, different targets may be selected by various strategies which share a common theoretical framework. For example, it would be unusual for an analytically based strategy to focus on changing verbal behavior, but it would not be unusual for one analytically based strategy to emphasize value change while another emphasizes feeling change. The important commonality would be that both strategies attempt to mediate change by dealing with unconscious motivation, resistance, or transference phenomena.

If one looks at the various change techniques, one finds that they attempt to modify the different aspects of the individual's functioning. For the purposes of this section, we have selected for elaboration five aspects of individual functioning which are frequent or common targets of the change strategies: feelings, values, attitudes, perceptions, and skills and actions (overt behavior). It is important to emphasize that these are not necessarily the only possible foci of change strategies. Rather, they are significant in terms of their relationship to the underlying theoretical notions and to their application in the field.

It seems to us that a continuum ranging from *internal* to *external* with regard to personality would provide a meaningful framework along which to contrast and differentiate the various aspects of the individual which are enumerated above. The focus of change can be an aspect that is central to the intrapersonal structure of the individual or it can be peripheral to his intrapersonal structure. This internal–external continuum is not proposed as a precise, quantitative one, but rather as a dimension for the differentiation of the targets. (For another approach, see Harrison, n.d.) A number of criteria and illustrations may be helpful in order to clarify further the dimensions of this continuum. For example, changes that are considered to represent the internal end of the continuum are not easily measured because they are usually not directly observable and must be inferred from behavior. Moreover, they are often difficult to describe in verbal terms because they deal with intrapsychic properties, such as feelings. In contrast, changes representing the external end of the continuum are more visible behaviorally and thus more easily subject to measurement. Additionally, one often finds greater agreement in defining or describing the more external aspects such as skills and actions.

FEELINGS

A focus on modifying the feelings of individuals is found in a number of change strategies. Feelings, as we are using the term, are considered to be the person's subjective affective responses in relation to himself and to others. Feelings certainly represent the most internal of the targets. In our culture, at least, feelings are not only inadequately translated into verbal, conscious terms but individuals often have difficulty interpreting their own feelings. The complexity of this process is illustrated by Schacter's (1964) work which suggests that physiological arousal is not the sole determinant of the individual's interpretation of his emotional state. His studies indicate that the label attributed to the feeling state is a function of the individual's cognitive interpretation of the external situation.

The primary assumption of intervention strategies that focus on feelings is that people function better if they are aware of their feelings and have the opportunity to express them. However, since feeling change is not always accompanied by visible behavioral changes, it may occur without any clear or overt impact.

Generally, those strategies that emphasize change in individual feelings are less directly concerned with the implications of such change for the organization as a whole. They do assume, however, that better functioning individuals will contribute to the development of a better functioning organization. Various psychotherapeutic techniques and group approaches, such as the personal growth group or the encounter group, fall within this category of strategies. The latter groups focus on freeing a person's feelings and ventilation of such feelings. The process of change includes initial awareness of one's feelings, an opportunity to express them in a permissive environment, and finally understanding one's feelings about oneself and with regard to one's relationship with others. Needless to say, concern with feelings is not the exclusive domain of the intrapsychically oriented strategies. Other strategies also attend to feeling change although it is usually regarded as a secondary or even indirect goal rather than a primary one.

The difficulties inherent in a focus on feeling change are as numerous as they are apparent. Three particular problems are most relevant.

(1) *Identification of desirable changes.* Because of the nature of affective experience it may be difficult to identify what kind of change is to be sought. The simplest approach to this problem has been to specify that feelings should become more positive. Thus in studies of people who had completed psycho-

therapy, it was anticipated that their feelings about themselves and their general well-being would be more positive than at the beginning of therapy (Strupp, Wallach, and Wogan, 1962) or than patients who had not yet begun therapy.

(2) *Measurement of feeling change.* Since feelings are not visible but must be inferred or reported, the question of appropriate measures is of major import. Most studies of psychotherapeutic change rely on self-report of observations by others (therapists or friends). The methodological inadequacies of these are well-known and need not be elaborated here. Lipkin (1954) in his study of client-centered therapy, measured feeling change by asking the client to describe his feelings at the end of each interview. These descriptions were then analyzed for positive, negative, and ambivalent statements. Balkin (1968) had his subjects fill out the Personal Feeling Scales devised by Wessman and Ricks (1966). One positive aspect of both these studies, in contrast to others (e.g. Strupp *et al.*, 1962) was that the reports by the subjects were ongoing rather than retrospective.

(3) *Relevance of feeling change for behavioral change.* This is the most crucial issue for strategies that focus on feeling change. No one has yet demonstrated adequately that feeling change by itself has specific behavioral consequences. In order to arrive at this conclusion, it is necessary to combine the findings of two types of studies. In the first type of study, the usual approach is to relate feeling change to outcome of therapy. Such studies generally find that change in a positive direction is associated with successful therapeutic outcome (Lipkin, 1954; Strupp *et al.*, 1962; Balkin, 1968). In the second type of study, the psychotherapeutic process is related to external criteria changes in behavior. For example, patients receiving psychotherapy included a higher percentage of full-time employed than patients who received no therapy (Fairweather, 1960). In another study an increase in grade-point average was found for students who had counseling but not for a control group (Kircheimer, Axelrod, and Hickerson, 1949). Since feeling change is assumed to be an important component of psychotherapy—specifically successful psychotherapy—and psychotherapy is related to more effective functioning one might reason that feeling change is also an important ingredient in increased effectiveness. This line of reasoning necessitates making many assumptions that have not been experimentally demonstrated. Psychotherapy includes many other processes in addition to feeling change which may actually account for the behavioral change observed. Moreover, the studies in this area are generally correlational in nature and do not indicate a causal relationship. It may be, for example, that when people have successes in other aspects of the therapeutic situation they then feel better about themselves and others.

Although most of the studies cited are concerned with psychotherapeutic processes, they are most relevant to other change strategies that emphasize feelings. A conservative conclusion about the significance of feeling changes to behavior change might be that, although there is considerable emphasis on feelings and such an emphasis is subjectively gratifying, there is no clear evidence that it results in significant behavioral change.

VALUES

The next most "internal" target on our continuum would be values. According to Katz (1969) and other theoreticians, values are hierarchial systems of attitudes having affective loadings which cause them to be rather central to personality and thus difficult to change. Others (McGuire, 1969) prefer to think of values as components of attitudes. From the analytic point of view, values are internalized aspects of superego development.

Although the definitional question is an important one, it is a much debated one. Some of those interested in social change (including Argyris, in this part) see values as assumptions about human nature and particularly about the nature and control of motivation to which individuals are cathected and which govern their interactions with others. For others, values are most often seen as internalized social norms which require social support and therefore are situationally modifiable.

Douglas McGregor (1960) has been a major articulator of this point of view. He points out that much management behavior rests on assumptions about human behavior which are at best only partially true and which derive from organizational models (such as the military and the Catholic Church) which are of doubtful usefulness to contemporary institutions. This view which he calls Theory X assumes that men are hedonistic, lazy, motivated to work only from survival needs, and ultimately rational. McGregor also espouses another view, Theory Y, which assumes that men work because of multiple gratifications and that behavior is affected by emotional and social events as well as by material incentives. He appeals to management to "become more sensitive to human values and to exert self-control through a positive ethical code (p. 12)."

A more comprehensive statement of what such an approach would mean is made by Argyris (1962) who sees value change as the important first step to increasing interpersonal competence. He asserts that certain commonly held contemporary values lead to ineffective interpersonal functioning. For example, he points out that the assumption that feelings are not an important part of any working relationship and should not be openly acknowledged and dealt with is a very dysfunctional value to hold in many situations. Argyris sees T-groups as a means of helping people change values and try out new behaviors which will be more effective in work settings. Rather than attempt to measure value change, he assumes that value change will, with training, be reflected in increased interpersonal competence. In his research he has developed a method of evaluating interactions in terms of interpersonal competence. Therefore, his major research concern has been to identify changes in interpersonal competence among those who have been exposed to individual training.

While there have been a number of important studies on value change, few of these have also focused on measuring behavior change. In an historically important study Newcomb (1943, 1963) found that those Bennington College graduates whose political values had gradually become more liberal during their years in a liberal college tended to maintain these changed values 25 years later. Philip Jacob (1957), who studied the factors in higher education leading to value change, found that the most important influences were frequently individual relationships of students with particular faculty members.

ATTITUDES

Attitudes have often been the focus of change strategies. Traditionally, attitudes have been viewed as having three elements—an affective or feeling core, a cognitive or belief element, and a connotative or action implication. Organized into hierarchical systems, these attitudes form value systems. Resistance to changing an attitude will clearly depend on its intensity, its specificity, and how it is linked into the value hierarchy to which it is connected—that is, how many links it makes with that system and how strong these links are.

The implicit or explicit assumption of those interested in changing attitudes is that such change is desirable because it will lead to subsequent adjustments in behavior in the direction supporting the change in attitudes. Blake and Mouton (in this part), for example, begin their attitude change program by measuring the current attitudes of managers and encouraging change toward an optimal standard. It is assumed that because a person's "actions are rooted in, and flow out of his own basic attitudes," (p. 8) change in the direction of an ideal attitude will lead to more effective job functioning.

This assumption has recently been the subject of critical consideration among behavioral scientists. Festinger (1964) in an article in the *Public Opinion Quarterly* soberly announced that he had only been able to find three studies in the literature that could possibly be seen as support, and somewhat dubious support at that, for such a notion. In fact, he pointed to a number of studies which seem to demonstrate quite the opposite conclusion—that attitude and behavior are very uncertainly linked. These supporting studies (Mann, 1959; Saeger and Gilbert, 1950) go back to La Piere's (1934) excursion across this country during which he assessed racial discrimination in hotels and restaurants. He found that many proprietors who "said" they would not accommodate Orientals did in fact do so when faced with the actual decision. A problem with this type of study is, of course, that it says more about the effect of already held attitudes on behavior in particular situations than about the effect of *changed* attitudes on concurrent behavior. (For a study of previously held attitudes which demonstrate a more positive relation between attitude and behavior, see deFleur and Westie, 1958.)

However, there are some studies now available which indicate a more positive connection between attitude and behavior change. Several studies by reinforcement theorists demonstrate measured or implied attitude change leading to changes in behavior. In one (Krasner, Ullmann, and Fisher, 1964) subjects whose attitudes towards medical scientists had been reinforced and changed did a repeated task significantly better for a "medical scientist" than an unreinforced control group. In another experiment (Hare, Hislop, and Lattey, 1964) subjects who were being reinforced in either a positive or negative direction in a choice task changed their behavior in the direction of the reinforcement only if they were aware that they were being reinforced. Although these studies do not give us any new information about the connections between attitude and behavior, they are interesting to consider when one examines the role which reinforcement plays in the learning of new behaviors and especially as one thinks about the change agent as reinforcer.

Three studies which deal with *changed* attitudes and behavior are relevant. The first, by Festinger (1964), is a re-analysis of some data of Maccoby (1962) and concerns attitudes toward toilet training. In the study mothers agreed to delay toilet training for their children. Despite this agreement, they actually began training their children earlier than a control group of other mothers.

The other two studies deal with the effects of human relations training and behavior change. In one (Fleishman, Harris, and Burtt, 1955), supervisors who had a two-week human relations training course aimed at increasing trust, warmth, and consideration changed significantly on the attitude measure of considerateness but did not differ from a control group on an on-the-job behavioral measure. The other study (Dyer 1967) had judges observe the interaction of groups of T-group-trained students and non-trained control groups. As predicted, the trained group both changed attitudes in the desirable direction and, according to the rates, ranked higher on interpersonal behavior measures.

With such minimal and mixed evidence it is not surprising that during the past few years there has been an interest in looking more closely at the assumed relation between attitudes and behavior. Festinger concludes that a key issue which is being ignored is the relation of recently changed attitudes to the environmental or behavioral supports which stabilize the change: "otherwise the same factors that produce the initial opinion and behavior will continue to nullify the effect of the opinion change (p. 416)." Support for this emphasis would come from the work of several psychologists. Schein (1962) points out in his examination of brainwashing that there are two conditions for successful attitude-behavioral change: (1) the weakening or undermining of the supports for the old patterns of behavior or attitudes and (2) the reinforcement of the new attitudes exclusively. Daryl Bem (1965; 1967; Bandler, Madaras and Bem, 1968) has advanced the thesis that attitudes are formed in the process of observing one's own behavior. In other words, we see ourselves behave in a certain way and we infer our attitude on the basis of this self-observed behavior. Finally, Fishbein (1969) has been emphasizing the need to look more closely at behavior itself and at how situational determinants or individual differences may lead to behavior change.

PERCEPTION

We use perception (or *person perception*, as it is variously called) to mean the process whereby a person makes observations and inferences with regard to psychological characteristics of himself, others, or a social situation. One may take the view that aspects of perception (for instance, the ability to integrate complex phenomena) may be of primary significance. However, we have limited our discussion to the type of approach most frequently reported in the literature —attempts to increase the accuracy of a person's perception *vis-a-vis* himself, others, and social situations. This is a commonly stated goal of change strategies. This point of view implies that the more you know about others in terms of their attitudes, interests, likes, dislikes, and personality structure, the more effectively you can interact with them. Groups have also been regarded in these terms. If a group is composed of individuals who have accurate social perception, then the group is assumed to be more effective than one which is composed of individuals who have less accurate social perception (Steiner, 1955).

This definition of perception seems to place it near the internal side of our continuum. Certainly, the object of the process is something that is within the person who is being observed. A change in one's perception of another or a situation is not necessarily visible to others, yet it is often very apparent to the perceiver himself. Moreover, it may be that if a person is able to use the data presented by a given situation more adequately in terms of interpreting it, one might assume that the same process would be applicable to other situations. This issue is relevant to whether accuracy of perception is a general or specific trait, which is discussed later in this part.

Much research has been conducted in the area of perception in the last 20 years. This has ranged from a focus on the conditions under which accurate perception is facilitated, the personality traits associated with it, and the relationship between accurate perception and effective functioning. It is this latter area that is most relevant to this paper. If perception is to be considered a legitimate or worthwhile target for change strategies, then one must have some indication that it is associated with or brings about more effective functioning.

A position of leadership within a group is generally considered to indicate that the leader is effective in interpersonal relations. The view that leaders have more accurate social perceptions than nonleaders has been studied in a variety of group situations. A study by Hites and Campbell (1950) found leaders to be no more accurate in estimating opinions of group members than nonleaders. In contrast, many other studies do indicate some positive relationship between leadership and sensitivity (Chowdhry and Newcomb, 1962; Talland, 1954; Bell and Hall, 1954; Greer, Galanter, and Nordlie, 1954).

Similar contradictory results have been reported in slightly different settings. Gage and Exline (1953), using T-group members, found no significant correlations between individual accuracy in predicting group opinion or individual satisfaction and perceived effectiveness in the group. In contrast, Gage (1953) reported that accuracy of perception of strangers was related to interpersonal effectiveness as measured by sociometric status. In view of these conflicting findings, Exline (1960) has proposed that accuracy and sociometric status are more likely to be related when both of the measures are relevant to the accepted goals of the group.

One may conclude from the relevant literature that there is a low but positive relationship between accuracy of perception and effectiveness of the individual or group. However, this conclusion is tempered by the numerous theoretical and methodological problems that beset the study of accuracy of perception. For example, *stereotype accuracy* (ability to judge the average other) is often a large component of the accuracy of perception (Lindgren and Robinson, 1953; Cronbach, 1958). Another question that has been raised is whether accuracy of perception is based on *assumed similarity* (that is, if one's judgment is based on the assumption that the other person is similar, then accuracy depends on degree of actual similarity rather than acuity of perception). Fiedler (1964) has extensively investigated assumed similarity from a slightly different perspective. He has examined the relationship between effective leadership (as measured by group performance) and the degree to which the leader sees his least preferred co-worker as similar to himself. The leader who assumes little similarity between himself and his least preferred co-worker (low LPC) tends to be task-oriented, controlling, and active whereas the leader who views his least preferred co-worker favorably (high LPC) is generally permissive, passive, and considerate. According to Fiedler, the low LPC leader is most effective when he has power and a well-structured task to accomplish or when the group is so weak that it will deteriorate without his control. In contrast, the high LPC leader does better when the group is faced with an ambiguous task.

Another significant issue is whether accuracy of perception is a *general or specific skill*. The two studies most frequently cited (Crow and Hammond, 1957; Cline and Richards, 1960) present opposing results. Perhaps the only reasonable conclusion is that accuracy of perception may be a general trait under some conditions; however, these conditions are not yet clearly understood.

These three issues of stereotype accuracy, assumed similarity, and generality of perceptual accuracy have far reaching implications for change strategies. One must raise the question of whether the learning that occurs in a T-group, for example, reflects an increase in stereotype accuracy. In situations where the observed persons are indeed similar one may find accuracy of perception as well as generality of accuracy. This may obtain, however, without true accuracy. Fiedler's studies suggest that a specific type of assumed similarity (LPC) may, in fact, be a hindrance to effective functioning in certain kinds of work groups although not in others.

SKILLS AND ACTIONS

The last target of change, and the one we consider to represent the external end of the continuum, can be called skills and actions, or perhaps more generally *overt behavior*. The change, if it occurs, is directly visible not only to the individual but also to any other observers. Moreover, the desired behavior can be specified in advance and can be measured. The changed behavior is presumably applicable to situations other than the training one. A familiar example would be learning to drive a car. The learner is given the relevant information about the operation of the car and the opportunity to practice the skill. The degree to which the learner has mastered the skill is easily measured and it is assumed that he can then drive any other car with equal skill.

Strategies which focus on altering such overt behavior or actions of an individual discount the need for some intervening process. The assumption is that you can focus on the desired behavior and train people to a particular criterion level. No assumptions are made about changing anything other than the particular predetermined behavior. This is in direct contrast to strategies which focus on the other targets which have been discussed. These other strategies assume that changes in values, for example, are necessary prerequisites for initial behavioral change and maintenance of the change. In these strategies many of the behaviorist assumptions seem to provide the best theoretical explication of this kind of training.

The overt behavior which is to be changed may be as *specific* and discrete as learning how to operate a particular machine or it may be as *general* as improving one's problem-solving skills. Kuriloff (1966) discusses the importance of training programs for specific skills to improve work and increase production. He cites one example where such training not only led to better performance but also led to a change in organizational structure. In this instance, assembly teams were taught how to adapt the usual equipment to include special design features. The result of this was to upgrade the performance of the routine assembly team. The special engineering group which had previously been responsible for this work was then able to attend to work of a more complex nature.

Although any kind of specific skill training has the potential to lead to organizational change, there are some strategies which are directly relevant to organizational functioning. These are the strategies which focus on improving problem-solving, decision-making, and communications skills. A variety of methods are used by these strategies to facilitate training. Kepner and Tregoe (1960) review a number of these techniques such as case study, coaching, lecture, and role-playing. Their own technique is to construct situations similar to the ones encountered by the trainees in the real work situation and ask the trainees to solve the constructed problem. Maier and Zerfo attend to problem-solving skills and provide cases to be worked out by the trainees using a methodology which emphasizes role-playing. Overt behavior is then evaluated, and trainees practice those behaviors which do not meet the criterion.

Although these strategies change behavior itself, it is still possible to raise the question of transfer into the actual job situation. How effective is role-playing as a way of changing behavior? There are several interesting studies, (Janis and Mann, 1965; Mann, 1967; Mann and Janis, 1968) which have examined the effectiveness of "emotional role-playing" as a vehicle for changing attitudes and behavior about cigarette smoking. These studies do appear to demonstrate changes which persist over an 18-month period. The role-playing technique has greater effectiveness than the other more cognitive techniques with which it is compared. However, it would be premature to use these studies to justify role-playing as a job training technique since other factors (in this case, fear of lung cancer) are clearly part of their effectiveness.

DEGREE OF STRUCTURE OF CHANGE STRATEGIES

We have discussed some strategies of individual change on an internal–external continuum, where we can observe the level at which the change occurs and the focus of the specified target of change within the person. It is also possible to concentrate on the strategies themselves and to attempt to characterize them. A major difference between the various strategies represented in this section lies in the degree of explicit goal definition provided to the individual. Some strategies predetermine the change goal for the individual, whereas others feature the individual participating in the decisions both about the focus and the direction of the change. In general, those strategies where the target of change is more internal (feelings or values) tend to exhibit a collaborative model of goal-setting, while those strategies where the change target is more external (skills and actions) tend to specify specific goals in advance.

The assumption on which many of the goal-specific strategies rest is that there is a standard of excellence against which a person may be measured and toward which he should move. The discrepancy between what the trainee actually does and what is presented as effective behavior or attitudes is expected to provide the motivation needed for change in the normative direction. The reason that these strategies can be so precisely predetermined is, of course, that the target and the direction of the change can be very specifically identified in advance. For example, Blake and Mouton hope to move trainee attitudes in the direction of a specified point of view about management. Maier wishes to develop problem-solving and diagnostic abilities. The training event is usually structured to provide practice, critique, and more practice of the desired new behavior to some criteria. What is characteristic of all these strategies is that they require prior decisions by the trainers about what knowledge, attitude, or skills shall be learned by participants.

Other strategies whose goals are more general (such as improving interpersonal competence or developing general understanding of group processes) are less explicit about individual change goals. This is necessarily so since the goals are relative. For example, in order to be more interpersonally competent some people may need to express themselves more freely while others may need to place limits on self-expression. Within these strategies the participant or group must identify learning goals and then decide how to implement them. This is not to say that these events are without structure. In sensitivity training groups, for example, feedback is the mechanism through which participants help other participants to discover areas of discrepancy between their intentions toward others and their actual behavioral communications. These discrepancies can become goals for personal change which are worked on in the group. In the Tavistock study group, the consultant's role and his interpretations provide material from which the group may learn. In both cases, however, the structure provides the participant with the opportunity to learn but does not identify specific learning goals for him. The assumption appears to be that collaboration in setting the change goal is a prerequisite to effectively changing the more internal aspects of the person.

SOME ISSUES RAISED BY INDIVIDUAL-ORIENTED STRATEGIES

This part will focus on those issues which are relevant to the use of individual change strategies as a way of increasing organizational functioning. The four major issues which are discussed below are (1) the individual vs. organizational functioning; (2) the transfer of training problem; (3) the critical mass problem; and (4) the social influence problem.

THE PROBLEM OF INDIVIDUAL VS. ORGANIZATIONAL FUNCTIONING

The self-actualization of individuals is seen by some, such as Maslow and Argyris, as both valuable to the person and productive for the employing organization. According to this view, if individuals are challenged and stimulated in their overall development and thus experience the job situation as satisfying, then their job performance will be more effective, efficient, and innovative. A number of the individual-oriented strategies do indeed have the effect of stimulating personal development. In an article included in this part, Campbell and Dunnette (1968) describe the subjective personal changes which participants in T-groups generally report. However, much of the evidence regarding the relationship between satisfaction on the job and effective job functioning is complex and far from clear (Likert, 1961). The question of how much personal learning organizations are willing to support appears to be a function of that organization's goals, assumptions, and value commitments to worker development and satisfaction rather than a function of a clear understanding of the relationships between personal development and system change.

THE TRANSFER OF TRAINING PROBLEM

Since individual-oriented approaches typically create individual change in a temporary system away from work settings, a central issue for system change is whether characteristics of the temporary system are sufficiently similar to those of the work setting to provide for generalization of learning.

A major question in the transfer of training issue is "What has the person learned about the applicability and the relevance of his learning to other settings?" One possibility is an *undergeneralization* of the applicability. For example, a person may learn that a new behavioral alternative is only possible in a T-group or with his consultant, or that it is desirable when endorsed and solicited by peers. *Overgeneralization* of the applicability is the second possibility. In this instance a person may learn that a new behavioral alternative should be taken into any situation, disregarding any qualifying contingencies. A third possibility is that a person learns to produce the new behavioral alternative only when some *specific combinations of situational conditions* are present. Unfortunately, the research literature has not provided any statement about what individual-oriented training teaches people about the applicability of new behavioral alternatives, although there is some indication that the learnings are transferable from human relations "labs" to other settings (Bunker, 1965; Miles, 1965). The same issue arises with other types of learnings which occur in individual change. What does the learner do with his new intellectual awareness of group processes; how and when does he use it? The most straightforward attempt to meet this issue has been made by those who insist on close simulations as a method for skills training (see Maier, and Kepner and Tregoe in this part). Despite these attempts this problem remains a major area of concern and uncertainty for most of these strategies.

THE CRITICAL MASS PROBLEM

In applying individual-oriented approaches to organizations, one is also faced with the problem of critical mass. That is, if changing aspects of individuals is the primary *modus operandi* of system change, how many individuals must be changed before system change occurs. If one were to risk calculating an equation for critical mass, he would immediately be involved in such issues as: Should all individuals be considered equivalent, or are some more heavily weighted because of their position in the system? For example, should decision-makers be more heavily weighted than their subordinates; and, if such weighting seems reasonable, what dimensions shall be used to determine the weighting? A number of dimensions seem intuitively plausible, including decision-making power (formal and informal), status, esteem, and access to resources—not to mention the subtleties of the calculus of interpersonal attraction and effectiveness.

THE SOCIAL INFLUENCE PROBLEM

Finally, individual-oriented approaches tend to overlook (or, in the case of the social–psychological model, misunderstand) an essential notion: Behavior which is regulated by social norms remains unchanged. Thus, persons may change in a temporary system which is the site of the intervention and then be unable to function in a similar way "back home." Lack of attention to the discrepancies between the norms of the change culture and of the home culture as well as failure to develop methods of dealing with this issue has been and continues to be a major criticism of the efficacy of individual-oriented change strategies.

OVERVIEW

The eight selections included in this part represent a variety of technologies for accomplishing individual change as well as a diversity of targets of change.

The first two selections use the T-group as the technology of choice for improving organizational functioning. It should be noted, however, that the T-group can be employed in the service of change directed at different aspects of personality. For example, Argyris, in his article "T-groups for Organizational Effectiveness," is concerned primarily with value change which occurs during the unfreezing–refreezing process described by Lewin. The Argyris selection, which is an excellent overview of the functions of laboratory education, also discusses the usefulness of this method of training for an organizational setting. On the

Introduction

other hand, Kuriloff and Atkins, in "T-Groups for a Work Team," focus on improved person perception as the basis for change. This selection includes a descriptive account of the life of one T-group which may be useful to readers who have not been participants themselves.

Because the T-group is such a widely used technology we have included two selections which assist the reader in making his own evaluations of this method. The third selection, "Effectiveness of T-Group Experiences in Managerial Training and Development," by Campbell and Dunnette, is a comprehensive review of research on T-groups. It should be noted that despite its title the review includes studies of T-group training with a variety of populations. This review will help the reader to conceptualize the types of changes claimed by T-group practitioners. After this review, we present an excellent example of a research study by Bunker and Knowles, "Comparison of Behavioral Changes Resulting from Human Relations Training Laboratories of Different Lengths," which is of interest because it is one of only a few studies which have attempted to measure behavioral transfer to the home work setting.

A brief excerpt from A. K. Rice's *Learning for Leadership* follows the four pieces on the T-group. The Tavistock "study group" described by Rice is both similar and dissimilar to the T-group. Although the group is unstructured, the role of the consultant and the focus on group processes are carefully specified. It exemplifies a blending of the analytic and rational assumptions.

The selection by Blake and Mouton, "Some Effects of Managerial Grid Seminar Training on Union and Management Attitudes Toward Supervision," adopts attitude change as the aspect of personal functioning selected for change. The technology used ("instrumented groups") is noteworthy because the groups have assigned tasks. In addition, unlike the T-groups or study groups, they function without "trainers."

The last two selections in this part represent attempts to change behavior directly via skills training. Kepner and Tregoe in "Developing Decision Makers" use a simulated situation to train participants in decision-making skills, while Maier in "MRP: A Technique for Training Large Groups of Supervisors and Its Potential Use in Social Research" uses "multiple role playing" to improve organizational functioning.

Thus the selections provide a broad spectrum of technologies arising from several theoretical assumptions which are used to structure change at different levels of centrality to the personality.

References

Argyris, C. *Interpersonal Competence and Organizational Effectiveness.* Homewood, Illinois: Dorsey Press, 1962.

Balkin, J. L. "Once More, with Feeling: Psychotherapy Revisited." Unpublished doctoral dissertation, Columbia University, 1968.

Bandler, R. J., Jr., G. R. Madaras, and D. J. Bem. "Self-Observation as a Source of Pain Perception," *Journal of Personality and Social Psychology,* 9 (1968): 205–209.

Bell, G. B., and H. E. Hall. "The Relationship Between Leadership and Empathy," *Journal of Abnormal and Social Psychology*, 49 (1954): 156–157.
Bem, D. J. "Reply to Judson Mills," *Psychological Review*, 74 (1967a): 536.
Bem, D. J. "Self-Perception: An Alternative Interpretation of Cognitive Dissonance Phenomena," *Psychological Review*, 74 (1967b): 183–200.
Bem, D. J. "An Experimental Analysis of Self-Perception," *Journal of Experimental Social Psychology*, 1 (1965): 199–218.
Bion, W. R. *Experience in Groups*. New York: Basic Books, 1961.
Bunker, D. R. "Individual Applications of Laboratory Training," *Journal of Applied Behavioral Science*, 1 (1965): 131–148.
Caplan, G. *Principles of Preventive Psychiatry*. New York: Basic Books, 1964.
Chowdry, Kalma, and T. M. Newcomb. "The Relative Abilities of Leaders and Non-Leaders to Estimate Opinions of Their Own Group," in P. Hare, E. F. Borgatta, and R. F. Bales (eds.). *Small Groups: Studies in Social Interaction*. New York: Knopf, 1962, 235–245.
Cline, V. B., and J. M. Richards, Jr. "Accuracy of Interpersonal Perception—A General Trait?", *Journal of Abnormal and Social Psychology*, 60 (1960): 1–7.
Cronbach, L. J. "Processes Affecting Scores on 'Understanding of Others' and 'Assumed Similarity,'" *Psychological Bulletin*, 52 (1955): 177–193.
Crow, W. J., and K. R. Hammond. "The Generality of Accuracy and Response Sets in Inter-Personal Perception," *Journal of Abnormal and Social Psychology*, 54 (1957): 384–390.
deFleur, M. L., and F. R. Westie. "Verbal Attitudes and Overt Acts: An Experiment on the Salience of Attitudes," *American Sociological Review*, 23 (1958): 667–673.
Dyer, R. D. "The Effects of Human Relations Training on the Interpersonal Behavior of College Students." Unpublished doctoral dissertation, University of Oregon, 1967.
Exline, R. V. "Interrelations Among Two Dimensions of Sociometric Status, Group Congeniality and Accuracy of Social Perception," *Sociometry*, 23 (1960): 85–101.
Fairweather, G. W., R. Simon, M. E. Gebhard, E. Weingarten, J. L. Holland, R. Sanders, G. B. Stone, and J. E. Reahl. "Relative Effectiveness of Psychotherapeutic Programs: A Multi-criteria Comparison of Four Programs for 3 Different Patient Groups," *Psychological Monographs*, 74, No. 5 (Whole No. 492) (1960).
Festinger, L. "Behavior Support for Opinion Change," *Public Opinion Quarterly*, 28 (1964): 404–417.
Fiedler, F. E. "A Contingency Model of Leadership Effectiveness," in L. Berkowitz (ed.), *Advances in Experimental Social Psychology*. New York: Academic Press, 1964, 49–80.
Fishbein, M. "Attitude and the Prediction of Behavior," in Martin Fishbein (ed.), *Readings in Attitude Theory and Measurement*. New York: Wiley, 1967, 472–477.
Fleishman, E., E. Harris and H. Burtt. "Leadership and Supervision in Industry: An Evaluation of Supervisory Training Program." Columbus: Ohio State University, Bureau of Educational Research, 1955.
Ford, D. H., and H. B. Urban. "Psychotherapy," in P. R. Farnsworth, Olga McNemar, and Q. McNemar (eds.). *Annual Review of Psychology*, 18 (1967): 333–372. Palo Alto: Annual Reviews, Inc.
Gage, N. L. "Accuracy of Social Perception and Effectiveness in Interpersonal Relationships," *Journal of Personality*, 22 (1953): 128–141.
Gage, N. L., and R. V. Exline. "Social Perception and Effectiveness in Discussion Groups," *Human Relations*, 6 (1953): 381–396.
Greer, F. L., E. H. Galanter, and P. G. Nordlie. "Interpersonal Knowledge and Individual and Group Effectiveness," *Journal of Abnormal and Social Psychology*, 49 (1954): 411–414.
Hare, R. D., M. W. Hislop, and Christine Lattey. "Behavioral Change Without Awareness in a Verbal Conditioning Paradigm," *Psychological Reports*, 15 (1964): 542.
Harrison, Roger. "Some Criteria for Choosing the Depth of Organizational Intervention Strategy." (Mimeographed.)
Hastorf, A. H. "The 'Reinforcement' of Individual Actions in a Group Situation," in L. Krasner and L. P. Ullmann (eds.). *Research in Behavior Modification: New Development and Implications*. New York: Holt, Rinehart and Winston, 1965, 268–284.
Hites, R. W., and D. T. Campbell. "A Test of the Ability of Fraternity Leaders to Estimate Group Opinion," *Journal of Social Psychology*, 32 (1950): 95–100.
Hobbs, N. "Sources of Gain in Psychotherapy," in E. F. Hammer (ed.). *Use of Interpretation in Treatment: Technique and Art*. New York: Gruen and Stratton, 1968, 13–21.
Jacob, P. E. *Changing Values in College*. New York: Harper, 1957.

Introduction 29

Janis, I. L., and L. Mann. "Effectiveness of Emotional Role Playing in Modifying Smoking Habits and Attitudes," *Journal of Experimental Research in Personality*, 1 (1965): 84–90.
Katz, D. "The Functional Approach to the Study of Attitudes," *Public Opinion Quarterly*, 24 (1960): 163–204.
Katz, D., and R. L. Kahn. *The Social Psychology of Organizations*. New York: Wiley, 1966.
Kepner, C. H., and B. B. Tregoe. "Developing Decision Makers," *Harvard Business Review*, 38 (1960): 115–124.
Kircheimer, B. A., D. W. Axelrod, and G. X. Hickerson, Jr. "An objective Evaluation of Counselling," *Journal of Applied Psychology*, 33 (1949): 249–257.
Krasner, L., and L. P. Ullmann. (eds.) *Research in Behavior Modification: New Developments and Implications*. New York: Holt, Rinehart and Winston, 1965.
Krasner, L., L. P. Ullmann and D. Fisher. "Changes in Performance as Related to Verbal Conditioning of Attitudes Toward the Examiner," *Perceptual and Motor Skills*, 19 (1964): 811–816.
Kuriloff, A. H. *Reality in Management*. New York: McGraw-Hill, 1966.
LaPiere, R. T. "Attitudes vs. Actions," *Social Forces*, 13 (1934): 230–237.
Lewin, K. "Forces Behind Food Habits and Methods of Change," *Bulletin of the National Research Council*, 108 (1943): 35–65.
Lewin, K. "Group Decision and Social Change," in T. Newcomb and E. Hartley (eds.). *Readings in Social Psychology*. New York: Holt, Rinehart and Winston, 1947, 330–344.
Likert, R. *New Patterns of Management*. New York: McGraw-Hill, 1961.
Lindgren, H. C., and Jacqueline Robinson. "An Evaluation of Dymond's Test of Insight and Empathy," *Journal of Consulting Psychology*, 17 (1953): 172–176.
Lipkin, S. "Clients' Feelings and Attitudes in Relation to the Outcomes of Client-Centered Therapy," *Psychological Monographs*, 68, No. 1 (Whole No. 372) (1954).
Maccoby, N., A. K. Romney, J. S. Adams, and E. E. Maccoby. "Critical periods in seeking and accepting information," Paris-Stanford Studies in Communication, Stanford, California Institute for Communication Research, 1962.
Mann, J. H. "The Relationship Between Cognitive, Behavioral, and Affective Aspects of Racial Prejudice," *Journal of Social Psychology*, 66 (1959): 223–228.
Mann, L. "The Effects of Emotional Role Playing on Smoking Attitudes and Behavior," *Journal of Experimental Social Psychology*, 3 (1967): 334–348.
Mann, L., and I. L. Janis. "A Follow-up Study on the Long-Range Effects of Emotional Role Playing," *Journal of Personality and Social Psychology*, 8 (1968): 339–342.
Maslow, A. H. *Eupsychian Management*. Homewood, Illinois: Dow-Jones-Irwin, 1965.
McGregor, D. *The Human Side of Enterprise*. New York: McGraw-Hill, 1960.
McGuire, W. "The Nature of Attitudes and Attitude Change," in Lendzey and Aronson (eds.). *The Handbook of Social Psychology*. Reading, Mass.: Addison Wesley, 1969, 136–314.
McGuire, W. "Attitudes and Opinions," *Annual Review of Psychology*, 17 (1966): 475–514.
Menninger, K. *Theory of Psychoanalytic Technique*. New York: Basic Books, 1958.
Miles, M. B. "Learning Processes and Outcomes in Human Relations Training: A Clinical Experimental Study," in E. H. Schein and W. G. Bennis, *Personal and Organizational Change Through Group Methods: The Laboratory Approach*. New York: Wiley, 1965, 244–254.
Newcomb, T. M. "Persistence and Regression of Changed attidues: Long-range Studies," *Journal of Social Issues*, 19 (1963): 3–14.
Newcomb, T. M. *Personality and Social Change: Attitude Formation in a Student Community*. New York: Dryden, 1943.
Rice, A. K. *Learning for Leadership*. London: Tavistock Publications, 1965.
Saenger, G., and E. Gilbert. "Consumer Reactions to the Integration of Negro Sales Personnel," *International Journal of Opinion and Attitude Research*, 4 (1950): 57–76.
Schachter, S. "The Interaction of Cognitive and Physiological Determinants of Emotional State," in L. Berkowitz (ed.). *Advances in Experimental Social Psychology*. New York: Academic Press, 1964, 49–80.
Schein, E. A. "Man Against Man," *Corrective Psychiatry and Journal of Social Therapy*, 8 (1962): 90–97.
Steiner, I. D. "Interpersonal Behavior as Influenced by Accuracy of Social Perception," *Psychological Review*, 62 (1955): 268–274.
Strupp, H. H., M. S. Wallach, and M. Wogan. Psychotherapeutic Experience in Retrospect:

Questionnaire Survey of Former Patients and Their Therapists," *Psychological Monographs*, 76, No. 43 (1962).

Talland, G. A. "The Assessment of Group Opinion by Leaders, and Their Influence on its Formation," *Journal of Abnormal and Social Psychology*, 49 (1954): 431–434.

Watson, Goodwin. "Resistance to Change," in Goodwin Watson (ed.). *Concepts for Social Change*. Washington: The National Training Laboratories, NEA, 1967, 10–25.

Wessman, A. E., and D. F. Ricks. *Mood and Personality*. New York: Holt, Rinehart and Winston, 1966.

Wolpe, J. *Psychotherapy by Reciprocal Inhibition*. Stanford, California: Stanford University Press, 1958.

Wolstein, B. *Transference: Its Meaning and Function in Psychoanalytic Therapy*. New York: Gruen and Stratton, 1954.

1

CHRIS ARGYRIS

T-Groups for Organizational Effectiveness

What causes dynamic, flexible, and enthusiastically committed executive teams to become sluggish and inflexible as time goes by? Why do they no longer enjoy the intrinsic challenge of their work, but become motivated largely by wages and executive bonus plans?

Why do executives become conformists as a company becomes older and bigger? Why do they resist saying what they truly believe—even when it is in the best interest of the company?

How is it possible to develop a top-management team that is constantly innovating and taking risks?

Ask managers why such problems as these exist and their answers typically will be abstract and fatalistic:

"It's inevitable in a big business."
"Because of human nature."
"I'll be damned if I know, but every firm has these problems."

Statements like these *are* true. Such problems *are* ingrained into corporate life. But in recent years there has evolved a new way of helping executives develop new inner resources which enable them to mitigate these organizational ills. I am referring to *laboratory education*—or "sensitivity training" as it is sometimes called. Particularly in the form of "T-groups," it has rapidly become one of the most controversial educational experiences now available to management. Yet, as I will advocate in this article, if laboratory education is conducted competently, and if the right people attend, it can be a very powerful educational experience.

Reprinted by special permission. Vol. 42, No. 2, pp. 60–74, *Harvard Business Review*. Copyright © 1964 by the President and Fellows of Harvard College.

How does laboratory education remedy the problems I have mentioned? By striving to expose and modify certain values held by typical executives, values which, unless modified and added to, serve to impair interpersonal effectiveness. As Exhibit 1 explains, these values are ingrained in the pyramidal structure of the business enterprise. The exhibit summarizes several basic causes of management ineffectiveness as isolated by three studies: a large corporate division —30,000 employees, grossing $500 million per year; a medium-size company—5,000 employees, grossing in excess of $50 million per year; and a small company—300 employees. The results of these studies are reported in detail elsewhere.[1]

EXHIBIT 1. THE PYRAMIDAL VALUES

There are certain values about effective human relationships that are inherent in the pyramidal structure of the business organization and which successful executives (understandably) seem to hold. Values are learned commands which, once internalized, coerce human behavior in specific directions. This is why an appreciation of these values is basic in understanding behavior.

What are these "pyramidal" values? I would explain them this way.

(1.) The important human relationships—the crucial ones—are those which are related to achieving the organization's objective, i.e., getting the job done.

(2.) Effectiveness in human relationships increases as behavior becomes more rational, logical, and clearly communicated; but effectiveness decreases as behavior becomes more emotional.

(3.) Human relationships are most effectively motivated by carefully defined direction, authority, and control, as well as appropriate rewards and penalties that emphasize rational behavior and achievement of the objective.

If these are the values held by most executives, what are the consequences? To the extent that executives believe in these organizational values, the following changes have been found to happen.

(1.) There is a *decrease* in receiving and giving information about executives' interpersonal impact on each other. Their interpersonal difficulties tend to be either suppressed or disguised and brought up as rational, technical, intellectual problems. As a result, they may find it difficult to develop competence in dealing with feelings and interpersonal relations. There is a corresponding decrease in their ability to own up to or be responsible for their ideas, feelings and values. Similarly there is a dropping off of experimentation and risk-taking with new ideas and values.

(2.) Along with the decrease in owning,[2] openness, risk-taking, there is an *increase* in the denial of feelings, in closeness to new ideas, and in need for stability (for example, "don't rock the boat"). As a result, executives tend to find themselves in situations where they are not adequately aware of the human problems, where they do not solve them in such a way that they remain solved without deteriorating the problem-solving process. Thus, if we define interpersonal competence as being aware of human problems, and solving them in such a way that they remain solved, without deteriorating the problem-solving process, these values serve to decrease interpersonal competence.

(3.) As the executives' interpersonal competence decreases, conformity, mistrust, and dependence, especially on those who are in power, increase. Decision making becomes *less effective*, because people withhold many of their ideas, especially those that are innovative and risky, and organizational defenses (such as management by crisis, management by detail, and through fear) *increase*.

If this analysis is valid, then we must alter executives' values if we are to make the system more effective. The question arises as to what changes can and *should* be made in these values.

But since executives are far from unknowledgeable, why have they clung to these pyramidal values? First, because they are *not necessarily wrong*. Indeed, they are a necessary part of effective human relationships. The difficulty is that alone they are not enough. By themselves they tend to lead to the above consequence. What is needed is an additional set of values for the executives to hold. Specifically there are three.

(1.) The important human relationships are not only those related to achieving the organization's objectives but those related to maintaining the organization's internal system and adapting to the environment, as well.

(2.) Human relationships increase in effectiveness as *all* the relevant behavior (rational and interpersonal) becomes conscious, discussable, and controllable. (The rationality of feelings is as crucial as that of the mind.)

(3.) In addition to direction, controls, and rewards and penalties, human relationships are most effectively influenced through authentic relationships, internal commitment, psychological success, and the process of confirmation. (These terms are clarified in the body of the article.)

CHANGE THROUGH EDUCATION

But how does one change an executive's values? One way is by a process of reeducation. First there is an unfreezing of the old values, next the development of the new values, and finally a freezing of the new ones.

In order to begin the unfreezing process, the executives must experience the true ineffectiveness of the old values. This means they must have a "gut" experience of how incomplete the old values are. One way to achieve this is to give them a task to accomplish in situations where their power, control, and organizational influences are minimized. The ineffectiveness of the old values, if our analysis is correct, should then become apparent.

A second requirement of reeducation arises from the fact that the overwhelming number of educational processes available (for example, lecture, group discussion, and the like) are based on the pyramidal values. Each lecture or seminar at a university has clearly defined objectives and is hopefully staffed by a rational, articulate teacher who is capable of controlling, directing, and appropriately rewarding and penalizing the students. But, as I have just suggested, these represent some of the basic causes of the problems under study. The educator is in a bind. If he teaches by the traditional methods, he is utilizing the very values that he is holding up to be incomplete and ineffective.

To make matters more difficult, if the reeducational process is to be effective, it is necessary to create a *culture* in which the new values can be learned, practiced, and protected until the executives feel confident in using them. Such a culture would be one which is composed of people striving to develop authentic relationships and psychological success. Briefly, *authentic relationships* exist when an individual can behave in such a way as to increase his self-awareness and esteem and, at the same time, provide an opportunity for others to do the same. *Psychological success* is the experience of realistically challenging situations that tax one's capacities. Both are key components of executive competence.

AIMS OF PROGRAM

The first step in a laboratory program is to help the executives teach themselves as much about their behavior as possible. To do so they create their own laboratory in which to experiment. This is why the educational process has been called "laboratory education." The strategy of an experiment begins with a dilemma. A dilemma occurs when, for a given situation, there is no sound basis for selecting among alternatives, or there is no satisfactory alternative to select, or when habitual actions are no longer effective.

What do people do when confronted with a dilemma? Their immediate reaction is to try out older methods of behaving with which they are secure, or else to seek guidance from an "expert." In this way, the anxiety so invariably associated with not knowing what to do can be avoided. In the laboratory, then, the anticipated first reactions by participants to a dilemma are to try traditional ways of responding.

Only when conventional or traditional ways of dealing with a dilemma have been tried—unsuccessfully—are conditions ripe for inventive action. Now people are ready to think, to shed old notions because they have not worked, to experiment, and to explore new ways of reacting to see if they will work. The period when old behavior is being abandoned and when new behavior has yet to be invented to replace it is an "unfrozen" period, at times having some of the aspects of a crisis. It is surrounded by uncertainty and confusion.[3]

Fullest learning from the dilemma-invention situation occurs when two additional types of action are taken.

One is feedback, the process by which members acquaint one another with their own characteristic ways of feeling and reacting in a dilemma-invention situation. Feedback aids in evaluating the consequences of actions that have been taken as a result of the dilemma situation. By "effective" feedback I mean the kind of feedback which minimizes the probability of the receiver or sender becoming defensive and maximizes his opportunity to "own" values, feelings, and attitudes. By "own" I mean being aware of and accepting responsibility for one's behavior.

The final step in the dilemma-invention cycle is generalizing about the total sequence to get a comprehensive picture of the "common case." When this is done, people are searching to see to what extent behavior observed under laboratory conditions fits outside situations. If generalization is not attempted, the richness of dilemma-invention learning is "lost."

T FOR TRAINING

The core of most laboratories is the T (for training) Group.[4] This is most difficult to describe in a few words. Basically it is a group experience designed to provide maximum possible opportunity for the individuals to expose their behavior, give and receive feedback, experiment with new behavior, and develop everlasting awareness and acceptance of self and others. The T-Group, when effective, also provides individuals with the opportunity to learn the nature of effective group functioning. They are able to learn how to develop a group that achieves specific goals with minimum possible human cost.

ROLE OF EDUCATOR

In these groups, some of the learning comes from the educator, but most of it from the members interacting with each other. The "ground rules" the group establishes for feedback are important. With the help of the educator, the group usually comes to see the difference between providing help and attempting to control or punish a member; between analyzing and interpreting a member's adjustment (which is not helpful) and informing him of the impact it has on others. Typically, certain features of everyday group activity are blurred or removed. The educator, for example, does not provide the leadership which a group of "students" would normally expect. This produces a kind of "power vacuum" and a great deal of behavior which, in time, becomes the basis of learning.

There is no agenda, except as the group provides it. There are no norms of group operation (such as *Robert's Rules of Order*) except as the group decides to adopt them. For some time the experience is confusing, tension-laden, frustrating for most participants. But these conditions have been found to be conducive to learning. Naturally, some individuals learn a great deal, while others resist the whole process. It is rare, however, for an individual to end a two-week experience feeling that he has learned nothing.

Usually the T-Group begins with the educator making explicit that it is designed to help human beings to

... explore their values and their impact on others;

... determine if they wish to modify their old values and develop new ones;

... develop awareness of how groups can inhibit as well as facilitate human growth and decision making.

Thus a T-Group does not begin without an objective, as far as the educator is concerned. It has a purpose, and this purpose, for the educator, is emotionally and intellectually clear.

However, the educator realizes that the purpose is, at the moment, only intellectually clear to the members. Thus, to begin, the educator will probably state that he has no specific goals in mind for the group. Moreover, he offers no specific agenda, no regulations, no rules, and so on. The group is created so its members can determine their own leadership, goals, and rules.

There is very little that is nondirective about a T-Group educator's role. He is highly concerned with growth, and he acts in ways that he hopes will enhance development. He is nondirective, however, in the sense that he does not require others to accept these conditions. As one member of the T-Group, he will strive sincerely and openly to help establish a culture that can lead to increased authentic relationships and interpersonal competence.

However, he realizes that he can push those in the group just so far. If he goes too far, he will fall into the trap of masterminding their education. This is a trap in which group members might like to see him fall, since it would decrease their uncomfortableness and place him in a social system similar (in values) to their own. In other words, his silence, the lack of predefined objectives, leadership, agenda, rules, and so on, are not designed to be malicious or hurt people. True these experiences may hurt somewhat, but the hypothesis is that the pain is "in the service of growth."

At this point, let me assume that you are a member of such a T-Group, so that I can tell you what you are likely to experience.

ACTION AND REACTION

At the outset you are likely to expect that the educator will lead you. This expectation is understandable for several reasons:

(1.) An educator in our culture tends to do precisely this.

(2.) Because of the newness of the situation, the members may also fear that they are not competent to deal with it effectively. They naturally turn to the educator for assistance. It is common in our culture that when one member of a group has more information than the others as to how to cope with the new, difficult situation, he is expected by the others, *if he cares for them*, to help them cope with the new situation.

(3.) Finally, the members may turn to the educator because they have not as yet developed much trust for each other.

The educator may believe it is helpful, during the early stages of a T-Group, to tell you that he understands why you feel dependent on him. But he will also add that he believes that learning can take place more effectively if you first develop an increasing sense of trust of one another and a feeling that you can learn from one another.

In my case, when I act as the educator for a T-Group, I freely admit that silence is not typical of me and that I need to talk, to be active, to participate. In fact, I may even feel a mild hostility if I am in a situation in which I cannot participate in the way that I desire. Thus, anything you (members) can do to help me "unfreeze" by decreasing your dependence on me would be deeply appreciated. I add that I realize that this is not easy and that I will do my share.

Typically, the members begin to realize that the educator supports those individuals who show early signs of attempting to learn. This is especially true for those who show signs of being open, experimentally minded, and willing to take risks by exposing their behavior. How are these qualities recognized?

There are several cues that are helpful. First, there is the individual who is not highly upset by the initial ambiguity of the situation and who is ready to begin to learn. One sign of such an individual is one who can be open about the confusion that he is experiencing, He is able to own up to his feelings of being confused, without becoming hostile toward the educator or the others.

Some members, on the other hand, react by insisting that the educator has created the ambiguity just to be hostile. You will find that the educator will encourage them to express their concern and hostility as well as help them to see the impact that this behavior (i.e., hostility) is having on him. There are two reasons for the educator's intervention: to reinforce (with feelings) the fact that he is not callous about their feelings and that he is not consciously attempting to be hostile; and to unfreeze others to explore their hostility toward him or toward each other. Such explorations can provide rich data for the group to diagnose and from which to learn.

PROBLEM OF MIMICKING

As the group continues, some members begin to realize that the educator's behavior now may serve for what it is. That is, it may be as valid a model as the educator can manifest of how he would attempt to help create an effective group, and to integrate himself into that group so that he becomes as fully functioning a member as possible. The model is his; he admits owning it, but he is *not* attempting to "sell" it to others or in any way to coerce them to own it.

You may wonder if viewing the educator as a source of "model behavior" would not lead you simply to *mimic* him.

Although this may be the case, we should not forget that as you begin to "unfreeze" your previous values and behavior, you will find yourself in the situation of throwing away the old and having nothing new that is concrete and workable. This tends to create states of vacillation, confusion, anxiety, ambivalence, and so on.[5] These states in turn may induce you to "hang on" to the old with even greater tenacity. To begin to substitute the new behavior for the old, you will feel a need to see that you can carry out the new behavior effectively, and that the new behavior leads to the desired results.[6]

Under these conditions the members usually try out any bit of behavior that represents the "new." Experimentation not only is sanctioned; it is rewarded. One relatively safe way to experiment is to "try out the educator's behavior." It is at this point that the individual is mimicking. And he should feel free to mimic and *to talk about the mimicking and explore it openly*. Mimicking is helpful if you are aware of and accept the fact that you do not *own* the behavior, for the behavior with which you are experimenting is the educator's. If the educator is not anxious about the mimicking, the member may begin safely to explore the limits of the new behavior. He may also begin to see whether or not the educator's behavior is, for him, realistic.

INDIVIDUAL VS. GROUP

At the outset the educator tends to provide that assistance which is designed to help the members to

... become aware of their present (usually) low potential for establishing authentic relationships,

... become more skillful in providing and receiving nonevaluative descriptive feedback,

... minimize their own and others' defensiveness,

... become increasingly able to experience and own up to their feelings.

Although interpersonal assistance is crucial, it is also important that the T-Group not be limited to such interventions. After the members receive adequate feedback from one another as to their inability to create authentic relationships, they will tend to want to become more effective in their interpersonal relationships. It is at this point that they will need to learn that group structure and dynamics deeply influence the probability of increasing the authenticity of their interpersonal relations.

An example of the interrelationship between interpersonal and group factors may be seen in the problems of developing leadership in a group. One of the recurring problems in the early stages of a T-Group is the apparent need on the part of members to appoint a leader or a chairman. Typically, this need is rationalized as a group need because "without an appointed leader a group cannot be effective." For example, one member said, "Look, I think the first thing we need is to elect a leader. Without a leader we are going to get nowhere fast." Another added, "Brother, you are right. Without leadership, there is chaos. People hate to take responsibility and without a leader they will goof off."

FURTHER COMPONENTS

Laboratory education has other components. I have focused in detail on T-Groups because of their central role. This by no means describes the total laboratory experience. For example laboratory education is helpful in diagnosing one's organizational problems.

Diagnosing Problems. When a laboratory program is composed of a group of executives who work in the same firm, the organizational diagnostic experiences are very important. Each executive is asked to come to the laboratory with any agenda or topic that is important to him and to the organization. During the laboratory, he is asked to lead the group in a discussion of the topic. The discussion is taped and observed by the staff (with the knowledge of the members).

Once the discussion is completed, the group members listen to themselves on the tape. They analyze the interpersonal and group dynamics that occurred in the making of the decision and study how these factors influenced their decision making. Usually, they hear how they cut each other off, did not listen, manipulated, pressured, created win–lose alternatives, and so on.

Such an analysis typically leads the executives to ask such questions as: Why do we do this to each other? What do we wish to do about it, if anything?

On the basis of my experience, executives become highly involved in answering these questions. Few hold back from citing interpersonal and organizational reasons why they feel they have to behave as they do. Most deplore the fact that time must be wasted and much energy utilized in this "windmilling" behavior. It is quite frequent for someone to ask, "But if we don't like this, why don't we do something about it?"

Under these conditions, the things learned in the laboratory are intimately interrelated with the everyday "real" problems of the organization. Where this has occurred, the members do not return to the organization with the same degree of bewilderment that executives show who have gone to laboratories full of strangers. In the latter case, it is quite common for the executive to be puzzled as to how he will use what he has learned about human competence when he returns home.[7]

Consultation Groups. Another learning experience frequently used is to break down the participants into groups of four. Sessions are held where each individual has the opportunity both to act as a consultant giving help and as an individual receiving help. The nature of help is usually related to increasing self-awareness and self-acceptance with the view of enhancing interpersonal competence.

Lectures. As I pointed out above, research information and theories designed to help organizational learning are presented in lectures—typically at a time when it is most clearly related to the learnings that the participants are experiencing in a laboratory.

Role-Playing of "Real" Situations. As a result of the discussions at the laboratory program, many data are collected illustrating situations in which poor communications exist, objectives are not being achieved as intended, and so on. It is possible in a laboratory to role-play many of these situations, to diagnose them, to obtain new insights regarding the difficulties, as well as to develop more effective action possibilities. These can be role-played by asking the executives to play their back-home role. For other problems, however, important learnings are gained by asking the superiors to take the subordinates' role.

Developing and Testing Recommendations. In most organizations, executives acknowledge that there are long-range problems that plague an organization, but that they do not have time to analyze them thoroughly in the back-home situation (for example, effectiveness of decentralization). In a laboratory, however, time is available for them to discuss these problems thoroughly. More important, as a result of their laboratory learnings and with the assistance of the educators, they could develop new action recommendations. They could diagnose their effectiveness as a group in developing these recommendations—have they really changed; have they really enhanced their effectiveness?

Intergroup Problems. One of the central problems of organizations is the intergroup rivalries that exist among departments. If there is time in a laboratory, this topic should be dealt with. Again, it is best introduced by creating the situation where the executives compete against one another in groups under "win–lose" conditions (for example, where only one can win and someone must lose).

IMPACT ON ORGANIZATION

The impact of laboratory education on the effectiveness of an organization is extremely difficult to isolate and measure.[8] Organizations are so complex, and their activities influenced by so many factors, that it is difficult to be precise in specifying the causes of the impact.

In one study that I conducted of the 20 top executives of a large corporate division, I did find a significant shift on the part of the experimental group toward a set of values that encouraged the executives to handle feelings and emotions, deal with problems of group maintenance, and develop greater feelings of responsibility on the part of their subordinates for the effectiveness of the organization. This shift is quantified in Exhibit 2.

Exhibit 2. *Before and After Values of 11 Executives Who Experienced Laboratory Education*

In an administrative situation, whenever possible ...	Before T-Group	Six Months After
1a. The leader should translate interpersonal problems into rational intellective ones	100%	10%
1b. The leader should deal with the interpersonal problems	0	81
2a. The leader should stop emotional disagreement by redefining the rational purpose of the meeting	90	10
2b. The leader should bring out emotional disagreements and help them to be understood and resolved	6	81
3a. When strong emotions erupt, the leader should require himself and others to leave them alone and not deal with them	100	18
3b. When strong emotions erupt, the leader should require himself and offer others the opportunity to deal with them	0	82
4a. If it becomes necessary to deal with feelings, the leader should do it even if he feels he is not the best qualified	100	9
4b. The leader should encourage the most competent members	0	90
5a. The leader is completely responsible for keeping the group "on the track" during a meeting	100	0
5b. The group members as well as the leader are responsible for keeping the group "on the track"	0	100

As the exhibit shows, the impact of laboratory education continued at a high level for a period in excess of six months. However, during the tenth month a fade-out began to appear. *This was studied and data were obtained to suggest that the executives had not lost their capacity to behave in a more open and trustful manner, but they had to suppress some of this learning because the corporate president and the other divisional presidents, who were not participants in the laboratory, did not understand them.*

This finding points up two important problems. Change is not going to be effective and permanent *until the total organization* accepts the new values. Also, effective change does *not* mean that the executives must lose their capacity to behave according to the pyramidal values. They do so whenever it is necessary. However, now they have an additional way to behave, and they use it whenever possible. They report that irrespective of the problem of acceptance by others, they find the pyramidal values are effective when they are dealing primarily with *routine, programed* decisions. The new values and manner of leadership seem to be best suited for decisions that are *unprogramed, innovative*, and require high commitment.

It is important to emphasize that laboratory education does *not* tell anyone what type of leadership to select. It does not urge him always to be more "democratic" or "collaborative." A successful laboratory helps the executives realize the unintended costs of the "old," develop "new" leadership behavior and philosophies, and become competent in utilizing whatever leadership style is appropriate in a given situation. A laboratory helps an individual increase his repertory of leadership skills and his freedom to choose how he will behave. If it coerces the executive, it is for him to become more *reality-centered*.

Another way of describing the impact of a laboratory program on an organization is for me to offer you excerpts from a tape of a meeting where the executives discussed the difficulties as well as successes that they were having 30 days after the program. The first part of the tape contains a discussion of examples of concrete changes which the members felt were a result of the laboratory. Here is a sample of the changes reported:

1. Executives reported the development of a new program for certain pricing policies that could not be agreed upon before, and laid part of the success to their new ability to sense feelings.

2. One executive stated, "We are consciously trying to change our memos. For example, we found a way to decrease the 'win–lose' feelings and 'rivalries.' "

3. The personnel director reported a distinct improvement in the sensitivity of the line managers to the importance of personnel problems, which before the laboratory seemed to have a second-class status. He said he was especially pleased with the line executives' new awareness of the complexity of personnel problems and their willingness to spend more time on solving them.

CONCLUSION

While I do not hold up laboratory education as a panacea to remedy all organizational problems, I do feel that six conclusions can fairly be drawn:

1. Laboratory education is a very promising educational process. Experience to date suggests that it can help some organizations to *begin* to overcome some of their problems.

2. Laboratory education is *not* a panacea, nor is it a process that can help every organization. Furthermore, it must be followed by changes in the organization, its policies, managerial controls, and even technology. Not all organizations can profit from it; nor do all organizations need similar amounts of it. All these factors should be carefully explored before becoming involved.

3. Not all laboratory programs are alike. Some focus more on interpersonal learning, some on intellectual problem solving, some on small groups, some on intergroups, and some on varying combinations of all of these. Again a careful diagnosis can help one to choose the right combination for the organization, as well as the appropriate educators. Nor are all laboratory programs equally effective. The competence of the educators can vary tremendously, as well as the receptivity of those who attend. The best thing to do is to attempt to attend a laboratory program conducted by competent professionals.

4. Openness, trust, commitment, and risk-taking grow only where the climate is supportive. A one-shot program, even at its best, can only begin the process of unfreezing the executive system. For optimum results, repeat or "booster" programs will be necessary.

5. Although I personally believe that a laboratory program with the "natural" or actual working groups has the greatest probable payoff, it also has the greatest risk. However, one does not have to begin the process this way. There are many different ways to "seed" an organization, hoping to develop increasing trust and risk-taking. The way that will be most effective can best be ascertained by appropriate study of the executive system.

6. Finally, if you ever talk to an individual who has had a successful experience in a laboratory, you may wonder why he seems to have difficulty in describing the experience. I know I still have difficulty describing this type of education to a person who is a stranger to it.

I am beginning to realize that one reason for the difficulty in communication is that the meaningfulness of a laboratory experience varies enormously with each person. Some learn much; some learn little. I find that my learning has varied with the success of the laboratory. Some can hardly wait until it is over; others wish that it would never end. Anyone who understands a laboratory realizes that all these feelings can be real and valid. Consequently, to attempt to describe a laboratory (especially a T-Group) to an individual who has never experienced one is difficult because he may be one of those persons who would not have enjoyed the process at all. Therefore, an enthusiastic description may sound hollow.

Another reason why it is difficult to communicate is that the same words can have different meanings to different people. Thus one of the learnings consistently reported by people who have completed a laboratory is that the trust, openness, leveling, risk-taking (and others) take on a new meaning—a meaning that they had not appreciated before the laboratory. This makes it difficult for a person who found laboratory education meaningful to describe it to another. He may want very much to communicate the new meanings of trust, risk-taking, and so on, but he knows, from his own skepticism before the laboratory, that this is a difficult undertaking and that it is not likely to succeed.

The point to all this is that the results of laboratory education are always individualistic; they reflect the individual and the organization. The best way to learn about it is to experience it for one's self.

Notes

1. Argyris, Chris, *Interpersonal Competence and Organizational Effectiveness*. Homewood, Illinois: Richard D. Irwin, Inc., 1962; *Understanding Organizational Behavior*. Homewood, Illinois: The Dorsey Press, Inc., 1960; and *Explorations in Human Competence*. Manuscript, Department of Industrial Administration, Yale University, New Haven, 1964.

2. Defined on page 36.

3. See Blake, Robert K. and Jane S. Mouton, *The Managerial Grid*. Houston, Texas: Gulf Publishing Co., 1963.

4. For a detailed summary of research related to laboratory education, see Dorothy Stock, "A Summary of Research on Training Groups," in Leland Bradford, Kenneth Benne, and Jack Gibb (eds.), *T-Group Theory and Laboratory Method; Innovation in Education*. New York: Wiley, 1964.

5. Barker, Roger, Beatrice A. Wright, and Mollie R. Gonick, "Adjustment to Physical Handicap and Illness," *Social Science Research Council Bulletin*, 55 (1946), 19–54.

6. Lippitt, Ronald, Jeanne Watson, and Bruce Westley, *The Dynamics of Planned Change*. New York: Harcourt, Brace & World, Inc., 1958.

7. For an example, see Argyris, *Interpersonal Competence and Organizational Effectiveness*, *op. cit.*, Chapter 9.

8. Blake, Robert K. and Jane S. Mouton, "Towards Achieving Organization Excellence," in Warren Bennis (ed.), *Organizational Change*. New York: Wiley, 1964. As this article went to press, I read an excellent manuscript of a speech evaluating the effectiveness of laboratory education, "The Effect of Laboratory Education Upon Individual Behavior," given by Douglas R. Bunker before the Industrial Relations Research Association in Boston on December 28, 1963.

2

ARTHUR H. KURILOFF AND STUART ATKINS[1]

T-Group for a Work Team

INTRODUCTION

*T*his is the account of a successful training group session in a small manufacturing organization. It involved a vertical section of people from different departments: supervisors and their subordinates. And it included the boss, the general manager.

The company, Delta Design, Inc., affiliated with a West Coast electronic manufacturing firm, was offered an order for special equipment which for years had been furnished by a competitor. Dissatisfied with previous quality and delivery time, the customer asked Delta to deliver this difficult job in one-third the normal production time and offered a large bonus if the deadline were met. Key men at Delta eagerly accepted the challenge which just two months earlier would have been *impossible* to consider had it not been for their unusual training experience—a T-Group for a work team.

The aim of the training session was to improve the abilities of the people to resolve interpersonal difficulties which were impeding the effective solution of many problems important to the conduct of the business.

To the trainers and the boss who participated, there were several elements, novel in their experience, which can be hypothesized as predisposing T-Group training in business toward a successful outcome:

(1.) A substantial level of trust built up in the participants before the T-Group facilitates the training activity. The participants had learned to speak somewhat freely without fear of recrimination.

(2.) Presence of the boss during all sessions reduces the participants' concern about the possibility of the trainers' carrying tales to him.[2]

Abridged and reprinted by special permission. Vol. 2, No. 1, pp. 63–93, *The Journal of Applied Behavioral Science.* Copyright © 1966 by the National Training Laboratories, National Education Association of the United States, Washington, D.C.

T-Group for a Work Team

(3.) Training should be intensive, with meetings on consecutive days, but with part of each day spent at work.

(4.) Reinforcement of the new behavior patterns arising from the training is more effective when there is immediate application of the learning on the job.

(5.) Training in business should be primarily focused on improving interpersonal relations and communications *for the sake of the business*, not necessarily for the personal development of the individuals.

(6.) Interpersonal relationships and communication among the participants are improved on the job by reducing the mass and multiple ignorance about people's true feelings for one another.

(7.) Acceptance of company data transmitted between people depends in large part upon acceptance of each other as people, and upon how much each respects, trusts, and likes the other.[3]

PART I—THE COMPANY

Delta Design, Inc., is a small manufacturing firm which produces environmental testing chambers, a technical product involving mechanical and electronic engineering design. It is affiliated with a parent company ten times the size of Delta. The president of the parent company is also president and principal stockholder of Delta. I came to Delta from the parent company five months prior to the T-Group sessions.

Before my arrival Delta had been run by another executive from the parent company. Having primarily a financial background, he had to rely on Rod, the chief engineer; Hans, the production manager; and Earl, the purchasing manager, for decisions relating to the product line and its manufacture. A lack of trust and confidence existed among these three men for many reasons stemming from prior history of the company. The psychological warfare that grew out of the distrust between Rod and Hans tended to distort or destroy their objectivity about technical matters. Decisions reached by the former boss, based on the tangled information from Hans and Rod, sometimes led to improper actions by the company, but more often to stalling and delaying of decisions until the particular opportunity for creative action had disappeared.

Between Hans and Earl, tensions had gradually increased. Earl, an experienced production man, had developed the habit of carping at Hans about what he saw as ineffective and wasteful methods of running the shop. Earl took pains to point out apparent discrepancies in shop operations and incidents in which shop people had complained to him about Hans's dictatorial actions and behavior.

Hans, in turn, blamed failures to meet schedules and production delays on Earl's inability to cope with the purchasing problems. He blamed Earl for recurring critical shortages of items needed to finish the jobs, for not knowing how to schedule his buying, for antagonizing vendors, for being rough and crude with vendors' salespeople so that they were indifferent to doing a good job of supplying Delta. When Hans had used to do the buying, he claimed, the company did not have critical shortages; he got along well with the vendors, and they went out of their way to render special service to Delta.

In March, I was asked by the parent company to take charge at Delta. As a mechanical engineer with extensive practical experience, I had more than once been in charge of engineering and production operations and had suffered the pains of similar organizational problems during my career. At the parent company I had been responsible for management training and development. During the year prior to my move to Delta, I had run a management training session once a week for their key people. Thus, when I took over, I was known to the men casually, if not intimately.

Recognizing that Delta employees would be fearful of the new order, at first I made no drastic changes. I instituted meetings attended by Rod, Hans, Jim, manager of standard engineering, Earl, and Bob, a new man, in charge of sales coordination between field and factory. Meetings were unstructured, but at first essentially problem-centered. Each man was encouraged to talk about problems relating to the business as he saw them. Tentative solutions were considered. I encouraged more openness and adopted the procedure of halting the discussion of a particular problem to encourage the men to consider the discussion and interaction process itself. By my words and responsive attitude, I tried to communicate the idea that feelings could be talked about openly, with safety—that it was important for the success of the business operation to consider feelings, their underlying causes, and to resolve conflicts so the group could get on to constructive solutions of the problems plaguing the business.

Though there was noticeable improvement in the ability of key men to deal with one another, I felt, after five months, that the time was ripe for a more intensive and powerful attempt to resolve the problems of interpersonal conflict. By a fortunate chance, through the parent company it was possible to schedule a T-Group for key men and supervisors, with professionally skilled trainers.[4]

What follows, then, are significant excerpts from a day-by-day account of the T-Group experience. This experience ended the psychological warfare that had distorted and destroyed the objectivity and cooperation of the key men at Delta.

PART II—THE T-GROUP

A great deal of emotion and sentiment will be described in the account. What may make it seem odd to some is the strangeness of openly expressed emotion in a place of business. Its very absence, however, is a contributing cause to difficulties in communication.

Simply stated, communication between people on a job involves more than words, more than passing on technical and nontechnical information. *Acceptance or rejection of company data transmitted between people often depends upon the acceptance or rejection of each other, as people, and upon how much the people respect, trust, and like each other.*[5] Acceptance or rejection of information also depends upon the degree to which people operate on untested opinions and assumptions about each other and how they use these inaccurate assessments to determine the urgency and importance, or accuracy, of what is communicated. Seldom, if ever, are these assumptions explicitly stated in words.

One of the revelations of the T-Group experience is the mass and multiple ignorance about each other that exists between people who work side by side, day in and day out.[6] One of the things people do not know is that they all want to know the same things—how to get through to one another more effectively, how to be better liked, respected, appreciated, and understood—the very basis for the acceptance or rejection of much communication! What people who work together have not known about one another fills the hours of a T-Group. This personal ignorance, in spite of physical proximity, is one of the paradoxes of business life and one of the costliest factors in operating a business. This lack of knowledge causes confusion, duplication, conflict, apathy, and avoidance of responsibility.

On the other hand, when people come to disclose their personal feelings, voice their assumptions—when they make themselves more fully known as persons, no matter how embarrassing it may be at first—they provide many new possibilities for being understood, liked, respected, and trusted.[7] In short, they are more approachable and understandable, are seen to be more the kinds of persons with whom one could like to communicate, the kinds of persons to be trusted with one's technical and nontechnical information.

When people feel this way about each other, the information that passes between them is more accurate, complete, and frequent. Business decisions are far more likely to be made on the basis of fact instead of emotion! Strangely enough, to get more facts flowing in a company, people's emotions must be given full reign, as in the special framework of a T-Group. The highly personal account of the Delta T-Group, which follows, is one attempt to demonstrate the advantages of encouraging more open emotional expression in business.

Table 2-1.   *Members of the T-Group*

Art		Vice-President and General Manager
Hans		Production Manager
	Jules	Supervisor of special assembly group
	Ross	Supervisor of special assembly group
	George	Supervisor of standard assembly group
	Chuck	Supervisor of door assembly group
	Chester	Supervisor of tray group
Earl		Purchasing Manager
Rod		Manager of Custom Engineering
Jim		Manager of Standard Engineering
	Ted	Engineer, working for Jim
Bob		Manager of Distribution
Helen		Office Manager
Stu		Trainer
Jack		Trainer

DAY 1—THE WARM-UP

It was 3:00 p.m. The circle was formed. Fifteen assorted chairs had been pulled from various offices of the company. The room was cool and quiet, and the irregular shapes of the assorted chairs were a striking physical reminder to me of the psychological differences that would soon be expressed here.

Fifteen brave people would be confronting one another in this circle, finding it very difficult to hide, even behind silence or bright, facile talk. The wide space in the center of the circle would be the dumping ground for people's misconceptions, for untested assumptions about one another that caused confusion, for unstated resentments that had slowed down working effectiveness, making people avoid one another when they should have been working together.

All these personal feelings would be the facts of our group. This would be our agenda: that feelings are facts, the facts of business life that can hinder or help the enterprise.

People who were lingering in the hall began leisurely to drift into the circle. There was chatter and laughter about things on the job, topics of personal interest—anything but the fact that they were in a strange and frightening situation. We trainers said nothing, but we felt the excitement and apprehension involved in facing the same unknown, establishing many new relationships, and becoming a member of the group with all its risks and rewards.

Finally Art called the meeting to order. A hush descended. With the silence pressure built up on the inside. Someone finally asked, "What are we supposed to do?"

Jack, the co-trainer, a tall, slow-speaking, mild-mannered man of few words, explained that the purpose of our getting together was to explore our feelings and relationships. Projecting a quiet strength, he said, "It's important to express feelings about one another, including us trainers. No holds are barred." He added, "However, everyone should also feel free *not* to respond if it becomes too difficult or too uncomfortable. Openness is valued, but so is the right of privacy."

Then slowly it began. People talked about petty irritations such as not being able to get parts, exasperating delays in schedules, not being able to complete necessary paperwork, and what had happened in the companies for which they had previously worked. No one began to explore the existing relationships within the present group. Even though most of the comments were directed to Earl, the purchasing manager, emphasis was on procedures, not personal feelings. It was dull. Then it happened.

Jim, the young project engineer, who was formerly second-in-command under Rod, voiced his concern about his relationship with him. With an eager, expectant look, he turned to Rod and asked, "What's happened to us? Lately we can't seem to get anywhere on design problems."

"Strange," Rod replied, in his cool, composed way, "I've noticed it, too."

They began talking as if they were just getting to know each other. Groping to pin down this uneasiness in their relationship, they discovered the turning point. It was the time of acquisition of the company, when Jim was given a design group of his own, and Rod was made manager of custom engineering instead of chief engineer over all engineering operations—and Jim.

Jack asked Rod, "How did you feel about your loss of status?"

Smiling, Rod replied, "Of course I didn't like it." He went on in a matter-of-fact tone. "You know, the usual things happened. I sent out some résumés. But things seemed to straighten out here after a while, and good jobs weren't easy to find." Rod went on to relate that it appeared to him that now that Jim had a design group of his own, he had done a turnabout in his philosophy of working and solving engineering problems. In fact, Rod said that Jim seemed downright dishonest, that he had agreed with Rod's philosophies formerly only because Rod was the boss at the time.

Jim was puzzled and disclaimed the accusation of dishonesty. Talking across the circle, Rod and Jim became deeply enmeshed in trying to clarify this misunderstanding. Occasionally their intense exchange was interrupted by questions and opinions from other people who were acting as psychological negotiators to help them come to terms with their relationship.

At the most heated points in their exchange, Rod smiled continuously. Jack finally commented to Rod, "I've noticed you always smile when you're expressing resentment. It's difficult to tell that you're really bothered. This can confuse people. I know, I do the same thing."

At first Rod denied being resentful. Then he said he was unaware of his smiling. The group could not understand why Rod would not be resentful under the circumstances and made this very clear to him. Finally, Rod admitted his resentment. But he smiled. The group pointed this out, too. Rod found it difficult not to accept the consistent and concerted opinions of thirteen other people.

"If you had only let me know how you felt," Jim implored, "we could have straightened this out long ago."

"Well, I got the message that you didn't much care what I thought," Rod countered. "When you invited the engineering people to your house for that barbecue, you didn't invite me. I assumed you wanted the opportunity to solidify your position with your new people."

"Wait a minute!" Jim protested. "I swear that wasn't an intentional slight. Someone told me you were going on a trip and leaving that Sunday afternoon. And as for being dishonest with you about what I told you when I worked for you—well, I *did* mean what I said. But I never had a design group before, and we've never had a design problem like we've had on the new line. I had to change my point of view on some things."

I used this experience to point out the curious way untested assumptions can lead us so far from the reality of a situation and from contact and closeness with people. I stated, too, that Rod's failure to express his resentment had only made it swell inside—so much so that he had to attribute the same feelings to Jim and interpreted many things along these lines.

The first session ended, and during the coffee break Rod and Jim stood in the hall, drinking coffee and talking busily. Excited, Rod said, "I'm sure glad we could clear the air! I feel a lot better now that I got it out in the open. I think I can sit down and work with you now. My feelings won't be standing between us." Rod extended his hand. He did not smile.

In the evening, after the supper break, Bob, the sales co-ordinator between the field and the factory, began reminiscing about the company for which he had worked previously. He spoke about the ten-year close relationship he had had with an engineer and how well he had complemented the engineer's genius with his own ability to get things done. Unaware, he seemed to be lamenting the loss of his friend and the great feeling of accomplishment he had gotten from working with him.

Bob, with his crisp, musical New England accent, turned to Jim and said wistfully, "How lucky you are, lad, to have your youth and to have the clean, bright spark of a good engineer." There was a note of sadness in Bob's affection for Jim. His head hanging, Bob looked like an old man. He sounded as if his career were ended. Mournfully, he talked about lost opportunities to study engineering. Peering over his round-rim glasses, his thin face drawn tight, he confessed to Jim, "If I could do it over, I would want to be like you. You're a fine young man."

Deeply moved, Jim said, "I never knew you felt that way about me. I appreciate it. Thank you."

Then people in the group began to tell Bob how they had sensed a change in him over the past months, the loss of spriteliness, vigor, and the growing sourness when he approached them with his coordinating activities. They described his abruptness and curtness. They expressed the feeling of being like little children with an impatient father. But the group left it there, as if they were not prepared to press it further, after seeing Bob's sadness.

Then the youthful office manager, Helen, leaned her attractive red head forward and gaily announced, "I have a communications problem! Maybe we can straighten it out." She related how difficult it was for her to get through to a certain person whom she kept nameless. "What do you do when you try to please someone and nothing seems to work?" Her voice began to tremble. Though she continued to describe her situation in general terms, it appeared as if the group knew to whom she was referring. The tension in her voice increased. She was anxious.

Jack commented, "It seems you're talking about someone in this room." There was silence.

The group knew, but they waited for Helen. "All right!" she blurted out, with forced courage. "You probably all know anyway. It's Bob." Again there was silence. "Bob, I don't know what to do to please you," her voice pleaded. "You make me feel everything I do is wrong."

Bob responded defensively at first, but with white-haired kindness tempering his criticism of her inefficiency with certain procedures. He gave reason after reason to support his case against Helen.

"That's not true!" Helen insisted. Heatedly, she raced through her counter arguments. They interrupted each other. There was anger in their voices.

"Look here, young lady!" Bob snapped. "You can't talk to me that way. Didn't anyone ever teach you to respect your elders? When you've had as much experience as I—when you've lived through what I have, when you've seen the things I have, then I'll listen to you!"

The group chided Bob for invoking his age and experience as a reason to shut Helen out.

T-Group for a Work Team

"Bob, I give up," Helen said, painfully and with deep puzzlement. "What do you want from me?" she begged. Bob did not respond. Perhaps the group had shut him up. Perhaps he could not answer. He listened. Her voice shaking, Helen explained that they had gotten along well when they both started with the company a year ago, when she worked for him. What had happened?

With the former sadness in his voice, Bob finally replied, "Every time I get someone trained to help me, they're taken away."

Bob described the mounting paperwork, the pressure from the field for answers on technical applications and delivery dates. He evoked a picture of a man drowning in responsibility.

Noticing that Helen was fighting back tears, mixed with her anger, I commented, "I have the feeling that you've been wanting to cry."

"I wish I could," she mumbled. "I'm afraid I'll look foolish."

"We won't laugh," I promised.

She began to weep. The group was quiet, apprehensive.

We waited.

She stopped.

Then softly, as she wiped her eyes, she said, "I feel much better. Thank you for being patient."

"See what you've done," Bob snapped accusingly at me. "I suppose you'll blame me, laddie."

I asked Bob why he felt so responsible for everyone—Helen, the men in the field, production, engineering. Giving my further impression, I said to Bob that it appeared to me that he had a strong fear of failure and shouldered responsibility that was not rightfully his. "Why do you try to make everything perfect?" I asked.

"That's enough, laddie, I've said my piece," Bob concluded with finality. "No more. I have to leave for school in a few minutes and now I'm all upset."

I backed off.

There were a few disconnected comments from people, and then Bob left.

PART II—LOVE AND HATE

Silence closed in. People stared. Time was at a standstill. The silence was eerie to me—like a quiet town before a shattering earthquake breaks loose.

Jim's face grew more serious, then peevish-looking. "I feel there's a cloud over the group." Folding his hands across his chest, he added, "What's more, I don't think we're very honest."

"Well, I'll say what's on my mind," George said emphatically. Accepting Jim's challenge, George turned to his boss, Hans, and said, "I've never had the feeling you liked my work the six months I've been here. What do you think of my work, Hans?"

Hans twisted in his seat. People leaned into the circle to watch. Hans hesitated, then apologized, "I find it hard to speak because of the language. I think something in my head with one language and try to say it in English."

Art told Hans not to worry about the words, that he would help him out if he needed it. "Just say what you feel," Art encouraged him.

Hans's pink-skinned, porcelain-clean face seemed soft even though it appeared tired. It seemed an effort for him to speak. "I think, George, you work good. I know I should tell you before."

But, of course, what else could he say? It sounded sincere, but nevertheless I could sense the group's distrust—as if its feeling were: What do you *really* think?

Hans carefully phrased his thoughts. "George, I like when you get things done. I don't have to tell you too much."

Still the group seemed skeptical of his sincerity.

"On the other hand," he continued, "sometimes you run around, jump up and down to get what you want. You make some people upset by being always in a hurry. But I never say anything to you because you work good. And usually I do not hire people like you, but you do not seem like that when you came for the job. But I got used to you now."

George was rapt, listening to Hans. He looked puzzled and seemed to be suppressing his pleasure.

"You are different from me, George. I have been slow, careful to do things. You have to understand my methods. For many years I work with my father in his factory in Switzerland—I am Swiss, but people think I am German. Even when I was six years old, I help my father in the shop. I hand my father the tools. If I hand him the wrong wrench, he hits me with it. You become careful. You learn not to make a mistake."

I winced for Hans, as the image of the child being struck by his father with a wrench settled into my awareness.

"One time, I make a mistake. He had a lighted torch in his hand. He hits me with it in the chest." Hans looked down at his chest. "It burns my shirt. It burns my chest all over."

"I never take my eyes off the work. I watch everything," Hans said. "I dare not make a mistake."

More silence.

Jack leaned forward and spoke softly, "Hans, did you ever feel that you could please your father?"

"No," Hans said. Then tears came to his eyes. He began to relive the awful feelings of his childhood. Soon he was crying openly. He sobbed.

I hoped that the little child inside all of us would understand. For me, his self-disclosure and his feelings had catapulted me into his world. It happened so fast. I thought how long he must have wanted, more than anything, to be known and understood.

Silence.

It was time to end the session, but it was hard to break the mood. Finally people stood up. Few could leave, and they huddled quietly. Eventually they went out into the hall.

Jack whispered to me, "Let's quit when we're ahead."

For a few minutes I walked through the halls alone, thinking about my own father. I wandered accidentally into the shop. There were Rod and Jim, George and Chuck, and several other supervisors who work under Hans. They were gathered around an assembly bench, stunned. In an almost reverent tone, Jim said, "I've never experienced anything like this in my life. I find it hard to believe." The others agreed. "Did you know this would happen?" Jim asked.

"We hoped something would happen," I answered, "but we couldn't predict what. I'd like to take credit, but I can't. A group of people can do more for one another by accepting one another's feelings than any one individual—when they have it in mind. Our job is to help them want to." I caught myself going into a lecture. I stopped. I didn't want to spoil their feeling of solemnity. They needed to feel.

Chuck broke the silence. "Look at Hans's office at the end of the shop, and that big glass window. He can see the whole shop through it. I used to see him looking out and I'd wonder what he was thinking. Now I know. Can you imagine, now I know!" His delight was painful. Then, with utter disbelief, he added, "To think that I was working so close to him and I never knew how lonely he was."

We walked slowly out of the shop together, saying nothing. . . .

DAY 4—THE PEACEFUL AND LONELY SEA

There was excitement in the group. People seemed intoxicated. They shared a big secret—a joke on the rest of the company.

Rod said, "Everybody in the shop is confused. They saw Hans and me working on a problem and laughing together!" Others reported stories. People not in the group were wondering what was happening. They were describing a new zest and energy loose in the shop.

Art, we agreed, was not one to let himself be known. It was possible that he would never open his world more to the outside. But, we concluded, maybe he should arrive at this decision with more understanding of the puzzlement he posed for people. Like all of us, he would have to make the choice between the loneliness of concealment and the vulnerability of exposing more of his self.

The break ended and the group returned to the circle. I appealed to the group. "Frankly, I'm frustrated with Art. Are there any suggestions on how to get him to come out more, to be more responsive with us, to let us in a little?"

Bob looked across the circle at Art, studying him for a moment and then he spoke, with lyric rhythm in his New England lilt. "I think I understand Art. What it is about him, I'm not sure. I think . . . I think he must be very much like me, in some ways."

Bob closed his eyes. He was concentrating, as if he were going into a trance to divine some feelings deep in his soul. "I have known this man, at times. . . . The time he told me about violins—the labor, the patience, the craftsmanship to make them. He makes them, you know. He loves that—to hear the beautiful sounds made by the strength and power of his hands. For a moment then—only for a brief moment—I felt this man. He opened the door—just a crack—

and I saw inside." Bob paused. "And I saw myself inside. I saw . . . a loneliness."

The room was still. "It's like being out on my boat, alone, surrounded by the sea. I go out at night when it is pitch black, with only the moon on the water to light the way."

"Don't think I wasn't frightened when I first went out. It's dark and quiet, and the only sound is the water splashing against the side of the boat. A clean, cool spray hits my face. All around me darkness. Nothing. . . . At first the sea is rough, but then—far out—the sea is calm. I'm not frightened anymore. 25 miles—I'm following the stars. 35 miles—the moon glistens on the water. 45 miles—a fish jumps out of the sea—I'm startled! . . . It's quiet again. 55 miles—I can feel the excitement in me. I'm almost there—65 miles. I made it. I stand up in the boat and stare into the darkness, then up to the sky. Something surges over me. I throw my arms open wide and scream into the darkness. . . . I wait . . . listen. . . . Nobody hears me."

People were crying for the lonely old man. There was the look of peace on Bob's face and slowly, somehow, the loneliness was leaving. He looked young, strong.

Softly, I said, "Do you realize you've taken us with you? You've given us the privilege of being the first on your boat."

People said, "Thank you, Bob," "You're a poet." "You've got great courage." "I could listen to you all night." "I've never known what a wonderful person you are."

Jim asked, "How old are you, Bob?"

"Forty-nine," Bob replied.

Jim exclaimed, "Is that all! You've been acting like you're an old man—like your life's over, like your career with the company was finished. You've even looked old."

Jack said, "You're a young, powerful person, Bob. Look at yourself."

Bob's smile was young. He seemed to be overwhelmed with the adulation of the group—with the love that came by letting people in. . . .

DAY 5—BIG WORDS AND LITTLE BOYS

Jack and I were late, but the group had been waiting quietly in the circle. On the floor, in the center, was a 12-inch-tall polystyrene object, shaped like a large mushroom. The group watched the trainers curiously. No one said why the object was there or what it was. They laughed and enjoyed their prank.

Jack and I looked at each other. We knew how difficult last days were. We felt the same desire to be distracted from the sadness of saying goodbye.

Finally Hans pulled the object from the center of the circle. Jim confessed he had put it there.

Bob turned more serious and said, "I'd like to tell you how good I feel. It's like . . ."

Jim interrupted, "You must! I heard you on the 'phone this morning. You were really firing up those field people to sell."

"That's nothing," Helen laughed. "The door between Bob's office and mine is open for the first time in six months. We actually talked together!" The group laughed.

"What will I tell my wife when she gets back from vacation?" Bob asked. "She'll never believe what's happened here."

"Bob, I have a suggestion for you," Rod said. "The second night, I could see my wife's reaction. With all my enthusiasm, she was getting a little annoyed at hearing about the group. I'm sure she must have felt left out. So I took it easy and just told her a little at a time. It was a lot easier for her."

I added, "It's like going to sea. Take your wife out a few miles at a time. In fact, the same thing holds true about the purpose of T-Groups. The journey is going deeper into ourselves and becoming closer with people. We have to go a little at a time. Test how far we can go—how far the limit is. And it's very frightening at first. The sea's the roughest when you start, but when you find your 65-mile limit, you're the master—and the sea is the calmest."

One of the shop supervisors said, "Driving to work the other morning, I heard this song on the radio—probably for the fifteenth time. But it's the first time I ever really heard the words. I think it's called 'People.' It goes, 'People who need people are the luckiest people in the world.' It really got to me."

Jack joined in, "There's another line in that song I remember, 'We're children needing other children, and yet, letting our grown-up pride hide all the need inside, acting more like children than children.'"

Helen looked cautiously at Art and said, "And there's not one big word in it, either."

"All right, all right," Art protested. "I still say words and sentences should be designed for the job, much the same as sheet metal in our temperature chambers. Words are things, to be worked and shaped. Our language is the only thing that makes us uniquely different from animals. We should use it, develop it. And that's what I believe. You'll just have to accept it."

"Maybe Art can meet us halfway," I posed. "He could use smaller words and we could learn some bigger ones. Maybe we would all benefit."

"Look," Art said, beginning to stir. "You've got to understand one thing. I've been an intense reader all my life—all kinds of things with all kinds of words. When I was a kid, they skipped me three grades in school. I was nine and the other kids were 12. They didn't want to have anything to do with me. I was too little. So I'd go home and read and learn more words. I've learned them, and I like to use them. That's me."

Art didn't seem so different after all. The group seemed more comfortable knowing something about the man inside the "good manager."

"Art brought his violin," Bob announced, "as we asked."

Everyone encouraged Art to play. He went to his office to get the violin and returned with the long black case. He opened it and walked into the center of the circle. "I'm still learning to play," he apologized. "I figured if I'm going to make them, I should have the fun of hearing the results."

Finally, with the violin tucked comfortably under his chin, Art began to play. No one seemed bothered by his musicianship—he went right on when he made a mistake. People seemed pleased at just being let in on something so important to him. When he finished, the group applauded and thanked him.

It became quiet again. Some people were looking at the floor; others were staring thoughtfully. They were deep in the silence.

I commented how difficult it was to say goodbye. Then each person told of his way of avoiding a goodbye. There were laughter and sadness.

"Do you have any suggestions how to carry this on?" Bob inquired. "After you leave, how often should we meet?"

"It's something you can decide together," I replied. "It depends on how often you want to, how often you think there's a need."

"What about trainers?" Rod asked.

"Work together yourselves," I recommended. "If the group seems at a standstill, don't give up and run for a trainer. Stay with it—confront one another with your feelings. Then, if you're still hung up, you can get a trainer or you can get a trainer when you want to get checked out or tie things together."

Jack was slumped slightly in his chair. Then he engaged several people who had not participated much, giving them a last opportunity to express themselves. This unfinished business continued right through to the evening.

Occasionally someone would comment on the time left before the end of the T-Group. There was one hour left. Some people became more quiet, more thoughtful. A half-hour remained. They began telling what the week's experience had meant to them personally—what it meant to them in their work.

Someone said, "When you get to know the people you work with, it just seems you work better together. You understand what's going on. You don't waste a lot of time and energy trying to second-guess them."

There were only a few minutes left. We sat together in the circle. The room was still. Someone coughed. Another sighed. It was quiet again.

Jack stood up in front of his chair. Other people stood up, slowly. Some moved a few feet into the center of the circle. Soon everyone was in the center, mingling quietly and expressing their appreciation.

One by one, people maneuvered toward Jack and me and each expressed thanks in his own way. We huddled together in two's and three's. We looked into each other's eyes as though we were getting used to a new kind of closeness. We could reach each other more directly now, in a way that was impossible before. . . .

CONCLUSION

To the profit-minded businessman, the intensely personal nature of the disclosures made by the people in the training sessions may seem strange and unrelated to business. However, in such disclosures lies the strength of T-Group training, for then the person behind the job emerges. Treating one another as people, with similar and understandable needs, fears, and concerns, makes the business relationship smoother and easier. People are less fearful of one another and more approachable. They talk more freely and openly about problems, are less afraid of showing ignorance, and less concerned about what people will think of them. They become more concerned about solving the problems of the business. Thus the intensely personal experience of the T-Group removes the mystery and fear of personal feelings which often block the accomplishment of the job.

To many, first exposure to expression of emotion in business may make them uncomfortable. This stems from the strangeness of the experience, which is contrary to our social custom of not revealing our feelings. In the Delta T-Group it took some time for the members to become accustomed to the experience. The discomfort came about from the members' fear of losing control of their emotions. In these Delta sessions this never happened. Rather, the members, once the strangeness had worn off, were relieved and grateful not to have to struggle with concealed feelings that interfered with their work.

This cannot be accomplished at first without the assistance of professional trainers. The trainers lend reassurance to the group that feelings will not get out of hand. Furthermore, they set up the acceptability of expressing feelings. It seems more appropriate for a trainer to encourage feelings at first than for a boss to do so, for the latter is seen mainly in his authority role.

In addition, the trainers can confront people with their feelings because of their objectivity as outsiders. Also they do not operate under the same degree of risk about being liked and accepted as those inside the company. Acting as a model, they often encourage the expression of feelings by disclosing their own.

Finally, the trainers employ their skill in pointing out the group's processes, that is, when they are evading important issues or avoiding expression of feelings. They also lend support and protection to those who find it difficult to function in a group.

Another question which might bother the business manager is the possible loss of authority by self-disclosure as a member of the training group. The fact of life is that the moment the manager sits down behind his desk he automatically re-establishes the authority of his role. The signs and symbols of his position are all around him, making him remote and unapproachable. The revelation of the person behind the authority, as disclosed in the T-Group, improves use of communication by diminishing the fear induced by the authority symbols. It does not in any way reduce the authority. Authority is like love: the more you give away, the more you receive in return.

As noted in the beginning of this paper, the acid test of the practical value of this T-Group came two months after the sessions, when Delta was offered a special bonus by a new customer. In order to earn the bonus offered for meeting the critical and almost impossible deadline, Delta had to use every resource at its command with maximum effectiveness. Confusion, miscommunication, or duplication of effort would have been disastrous.

Under conditions existing when he took over, Art would not have considered taking this job. Having watched Delta's key people work together for two months since the T-Group, he felt the risk now lay only in the technical problems and not in the people's ability to work together. Art had seen the key people concentrate more on their work and worry less about what others were up to. They were paying attention to their own jobs, and that is what made the business begin to move.

Once this special order had been planned with the key people, Art felt confident enough to leave the plant for a two-week trip to develop new business. He returned in time to see the job tested, crated, and shipped as scheduled. The bonus on this job alone paid for the time and money spent in the training sessions, several times over. The open expression of feelings paid off in many ways, not the least of which was dollars and cents.

In the months that have passed since the Delta T-Group training sessions, there has been considerable evidence that the ability of the people to communicate effectively has reached and remains at a level substantially higher than before training. Problem solving has been and remains at a much more effective level.

On more than one occasion, Rod and Jim, both engineering managers, have talked out frictional differences arising from divergent viewpoints on solutions for technical problems or conflicts on scheduling of work in the common laboratory.

While the boss was away on an extended trip, Jim, Rod, and Hans, the production manager, together saw the need for a line of new environmental chambers. They established specifications, agreed on the basic design, set a price range, and completed building and testing of a prototype model before the boss got back. Such cooperative and expeditious effort would have been impossible a year prior to that time. Nor would they have dared to proceed without an okay from the boss. There are numerous instances of this kind.

But, beyond these kinds of operational improvements, there has been and remains a feeling of buoyancy in the organization. There is an exciting sense of possibility for accomplishment, a good feeling of vitality difficult to put into words.

In conclusion, it seems to us that several of the hypotheses stated in the introduction have been substantiated by the limited experience of the Delta training group:

(1.) Depth of feeling and openness of expression came early in the training, indicating a high level of trust before the T-Group sessions.

(2.) Testing of the boss's reactions proved in the early sessions that it was safe to be open in front of him about dissatisfactions of all kinds without fear of recrimination. Thus the presence of the central power figure removed the blocks to full expression as we have experienced them in other T-Groups.

(3.) The successive sessions of six hours each on consecutive days kept the productivity of the group at a continuously high level. In contrast, we have seen slippage in productivity in other groups because of the long intervals between sessions scheduled on a once-a-week basis.

(4.) Working a part of each day, between T-Group sessions, the participants had the opportunity to apply and test their new behavior on the job. With positive reinforcement on the job, individuals were stimulated to deeper involvement in the T-Group and thus encouraged other members to test out new behavior on the job.

(5.) The test of the value of the T-Group method in business lies in the improvement of ability to achieve economic and organizational goals. Keeping this as the central target in the Delta T-Group intensified the effectiveness of applying the learning in the real world. That this happened in the Delta experience is clear and evident.

(6.) The reduction in conflict and improvement in communication now apparent among Delta personnel started with the elimination in the T-Group of the multiple ignorance about one another's true feelings. Organizational channels of communication were opened as the blocks to personal communication were removed.

(7.) The cooperative solution of many different kinds of problems at Delta since the training experience was made possible by continuing transmission of more complete and accurate data of various kinds. This had not happened prior to the T-Group because of distrust, dislike, and lack of respect among key personnel. The T-Group reversed this condition, allowed the data to flow, and facilitated the solution of problems.

Notes

1. Although this paper is the collaborative effort of the two authors, the section on the company was written by Mr. Kuriloff, the section on the T-Group by Mr. Atkins, and the introduction and conclusion by both together.
2. Bradford, L. P., J. R. Gibb and K. D. Benne (eds.). *T-Group Theory and Laboratory Method*. New York: Wiley, 1964. *Note:* Superiors and subordinates together attended the sessions. This has not been usual in T-Groups. See Ch. 2, 20, by Benne, Bradford, & Lippitt.
3. *Ibid.* "Climate for Trust Formation," by Jack R. Gibb, 279–309.
4. This was part of a seminar in T-Group methods for professionals, under joint sponsorship of the National Training Laboratories and the Western Training Laboratory, directed by Dr. James V. Clark, of the Graduate School of Business Administration, U.C.L.A. The Delta training group, as well as two similar groups, was made available by Delta's parent company, Non-Linear Systems, Inc., in August 1964.
5. Bradford, Gibb, & Benne (eds.). *op. cit.* Ch. 10.
6. Lippitt, R., Jeanne Watson, & B. Westley. *Dynamics of Planned Change*. New York: Harcourt, Brace & World, 1958, 42–44.
7. Jourard, S. M. *The Transparent Self*. Princeton, N.J.: Van Nostrand, 1964, Part II, The Importance of Self-Disclosure in Human Experience, 19–55.

References

Argyris, C. *Interpersonal Competence and Organizational Effectiveness*. Homewood, Ill.: Dorsey Press, 1962. *Note:* For comments on the advisability of the "natural" work group in sensitivity training, see Ch. 12, p. 278, by Roger Harrison.

Argyris, C. "T-Groups for Organizational Effectiveness," *Harvard Business Review*, March–April 1964.

Blake, R. J., and Jane S. Mouton. *The Managerial Grid*. Houston: Gulf, 1964.

Blake, R. R., A. C. Bidwell, and J. J. Farrell. "Team job Training: A New Strategy for Industry," *Journal of the American Society of Training Directors*, October 1961, 15 (10).

Blake, R. R., Jane S. Moutin, and M. G. Blansfield. "How Executive Team Training Can Help You," *Journal of the American Society of Training Directors*, January 1962, 16 (1).

Blansfield, M. G. "Depth Analysis of Organizational Life," *California Management Review*, 5 (1962): 29–36.

Bradford, L. P., J. R. Gibb, and K. D. Benne, (eds). *T-Group Theory and Laboratory Method*. New York: Wiley, 1964.

Clark, J. V. "A Healthy Organization," *California Management Review*, 4 (Summer 1962) (4).

Jourard, S. M. *The Transparent Self*. Princeton, N.J.: Van Nostrand, 1964.

Leavitt, H. J. *Managerial Psychology*. Chicago: The University of Chicago Press, 1958.

Lippitt, R., Jeanne Watson, and B. Westley. *Dynamics of Planned Change*. New York: Harcourt, 1958.

Marrow, A. J. *Behind the Executive Mask*. New York: American Management Association, 1964.

Tannenbaum, R., I. R. Weschler, and F. Massarik. *Leadership and Organization: A Behavioral Science Approach*. New York: McGraw-Hill, 1961.

3

JOHN P. CAMPBELL AND MARVIN D. DUNNETTE

Effectiveness of T-Group Experiences in Managerial Training and Development[1]

At the fifth meeting the group's feelings about its own progress became the initial focus of discussion. The "talkers" participated as usual, conversation shifting rapidly from one point to another. Dissatisfaction was mounting, expressed through loud, snide remarks by some and through apathy by others.

George Franklin appeared particularly disturbed. Finally pounding the table, he exclaimed, "I don't know what is going on here! I should be paid for listening to this drivel? I'm getting just a bit sick of wasting my time here. If the profs don't put out— I quit!" George was pleased; he was angry, and he had said so. As he sat back in his chair, he felt he had the group behind him. He felt he had the guts to say what most of the others were thinking! Some members of the group applauded loudly, but others showed obvious disapproval. They wondered why George was excited over so insignificant an issue, why he hadn't done something constructive rather than just sounding off as usual. Why, they wondered, did he say their comments were "drivel"?

George Franklin became the focus of discussion. "What do you mean, George, by saying this nonsense?" "What do you expect, a neat set of rules to meet all your problems?" George was getting uncomfortable. These were questions difficult for him to answer. Gradually he began to realize that a large part of the group disagreed with him; then he began to wonder why. He was learning something about people he hadn't known before. ". . . How does it feel, George, to have people disagree with you when you thought you had them behind you? . . ." Tannenbaum, Wechsler, and Massarik, 1961, p. 123.

This article is an abridged version of a comprehensive review of the literature published in *Psychological Bulletin*, Vol. 70, No. 2 (1968): 73–108. Reprinted by special permission. Copyright © 1968 by the American Psychological Association, Inc. Readers interested in a complete review of the literature should consult the original article.

*t*his short episode taken from a management-development session illustrates many of the features of an educational technique referred to as the T-Group method of sensitivity training. When integrated with other techniques such as lectures and group problem-solving exercises, the complete program is usually relabeled "laboratory education."

This paper is devoted to an analysis and appraisal of the application of this technique (T-Group) to problems of managerial development. The focus is on the published literature surrounding the topic and not upon the authors' personal experiences. The authors are academic psychologists interested in organizational behavior and not T-Group or laboratory-education practitioners.

In brief, this paper attempts to: (1) identify and summarize the crucial elements of the T-Group method; (2) call attention to some of the difficulties in researching both the dynamics and the effects of the method; and (3) summarize in some detail the research evidence bearing on the utility of T-Groups for training and development purposes.

It is acknowledged at the outset that no single explicitly defined set of experiences can be labeled the laboratory method. There are many variations, or "training designs," depending upon the characteristics of certain parameters. However, at the heart of most efforts is a common core of experience known as the T-Group, usually regarded as the crucial part of the program (Bradford, Gibb, and Benne, 1964, p. 2; Schein and Bennis, 1965, p. 15). It is this common core which receives most of the attention from practitioners, researchers, and critics and which is the focus of this review.[2]

FORM AND NATURE OF THE T-GROUP METHOD

Two elements used to distinguish the T-Group from other training methods are the learning goals involved and the processes used to accomplish these goals. Advocates of T-Groups tend to focus on goals at two different levels (Buchanan, 1965; Schein and Bennis, 1965). Flowing from certain scientific and democratic values are several metagoals, or goals which exist on a very general level. Schein and Bennis mentioned five, which they asserted to be the ultimate aims of all T-Group training: (1) a spirit of inquiry or a willingness to hypothesize and experiment with one's role in the world; (2) an "expanded interpersonal consciousness" or an increased awareness of more things about more people; (3) an increased authenticity in interpersonal relations or simply feeling freer to be oneself and not feeling compelled to play a role; (4) an ability to act in a collaborative and interdependent manner with peers, superiors, and subordinates rather than in authoritative or hierarchical terms; and (5) an ability to resolve conflict situations through problem solving rather than through horse trading, coercion, or power manipulation.

According to Schein and Bennis (1965), these metagoals are seldom articulated, but are implicit in the functioning of most T-Groups. A number of more proximate objectives usually are made explicit and are regarded by most authors as the direct outcomes of a properly functioning T-Group. It is true that not *all* practitioners would agree that *all* T-groups try to accomplish *all* of these aims, but they are sufficiently common to most discussions of the T-group method that the authors feel relatively few qualms in listing them as the direct or proximate outcomes desired. The list is drawn from a variety of sources (Argyris, 1964; Bradford et al., 1964; Buchanan, 1965; Miles, 1960; Schein and Bennis, 1965; Tannenbaum et al., 1961):

(1.) Increased self-insight or self-awareness concerning one's own behavior and its meaning in a social context. This refers to the common aim of learning how others see and interpret one's behavior and gaining insight into why one acts in certain ways in different situations.

(2.) Increased sensitivity to the behavior of others. This goal is closely linked with the above. It refers first, to the development of an increased awareness of the full range of communicative stimuli emitted by other persons (voice inflections, facial expressions, bodily positions, and other contextual factors, in addition to the actual choice of words) and second, to the development of the ability to infer accurately the emotional or noncognitive bases for interpersonal communications. This goal is very similar to the concept of empathy as it is used by clinical and counseling psychologists, that is, the ability to infer correctly what another person is feeling.

(3.) Increased awareness and understanding of the types of processes that facilitate or inhibit group functioning and the interactions between different groups—specifically, who do some members participate actively while others retire to the background? Why do sub-groups form and wage war against each other? How and why are pecking orders established? Why do different groups who may actually share the same goals, sometimes create seeming insoluble conflict situations?

(4.) Heightened diagnostic skill in social, interpersonal, and intergroup situations. Achievement of the first three objectives should provide an individual with a set of explanatory concepts to be used in diagnosing conflict situations, reasons for poor communication, and the like.

(5.) Increased action skill. Although very similar to No. 4, it was mentioned separately by Miles (1960) and refers to a person's ability to intervene successfully in inter- or intragroup situations so as to increase member satisfactions, effectiveness, or output. The goal of increased action skill is toward intervention at the interpersonal rather than simply the technological level.

(6.) Learning how to learn. This does not refer to an individual's cognitive approach to the world, but rather to his ability to analyze continually his own interpersonal behavior for the purpose of helping himself and others achieve more effective and satisfying interpersonal relationships.

The T-Group learning experience has as its focal point the small, unstructured, face-to-face group, usually consisting of 10 to 15 people. The success of the venture depends on the crucial process of feedback. Thus, the participants must be able to inform each other how their behavior is being seen and interpreted and to describe the kinds of feelings generated. This is the primary process by which the delegates "learn." They must receive articulate and meaningful feedback about their own behavior, including their own feedback attempts (feedback on feedback) and their efforts to interpret group processes. (For example, did the other group members think Individual X was correct when he observed that Y and Z were forming a clique because they both felt rejected?)

For the feedback process to contribute to the goals of the training, at least two additional elements are believed necessary. First, a certain amount of anxiety or tension must be generated, particularly in the early part of the group's life. Anxiety supposedly results when an individual discovers how deficient his previous role-bound methods of interacting are for successful functioning in this new type of group situation.

A possible explanation for this type of anxiety generation flows from some of the stimulus-response formulations of Dollard and Miller (1950). Almost every individual has an established self-image protected by a number of defense mechanisms. Such mechanisms have become resistant to change because of their repeated association with the reinforcing properties of anxiety reduction; that is, they protect the self-image from threat. Thus, in the T-Group when an individual's usual mode of interacting is thwarted and his defense mechanisms are made a direct topic of conversation, considerable anxiety results. Such anxiety then constitutes a force for new learning because, if the group experience is a successful one, new methods of anxiety reduction will be learned. If the T-Group is successful, these methods will be more in line with the goals of the training and will have more utility for the individual in coping with his environment than his old methods which may indeed have been dysfunctional. Thus, anxiety serves the purpose of shaking up or jarring loose the participant from his preconceived notions and habitual forms of interacting so that feedback may have its maximum effect. Without such "unfreezing," feedback may be ineffectual (Schein, 1964).

The second element necessary for assuring effective feedback is what Schein and Bennis (1965) referred to as a climate of "psychological safety" and Bradford et al. (1964) called "permissiveness." That is, no matter what an individual does in a group or what he reveals about himself, the group must act in a supportive and nonevaluative way. Each individual must feel that it is safe to expose his feelings, drop his defenses, and try out new ways of interacting. Such an atmosphere has its obvious counterpart in any constructive clinical or therapeutic relationship.

The role of the trainer also constitutes a dominant technological element bearing on the group's effectiveness for giving feedback and promoting psychological support. The trainer serves as a model for the participants to imitate; that is, he absorbs feelings of hostility and frustration without becoming defensive, provides feedback for others, expresses his own feelings openly and honestly, and is strongly supportive of the expression of feelings in others. In short, he exhibits for consideration the very processes deemed necessary for maximum learning to occur.

However, in the so-called "instrumented" T-Group (Berzon and Solomon,

1966; Blake and Mouton, 1962) there may be no trainer. The function of a behavior model is accomplished by a series of questionnaires requiring the participants to rate themselves and each other on how supportive they are, how freely they express feelings, and how skillfully they give feedback.

SOME ASSUMPTIONS

The training technology just described seems to make a number of assumptions, both explicitly and implicitly. The authors offer the following list for consideration:

(1.) A substantial number of group members, when confronted with others' behaviors and feelings in an atmosphere of psychological safety, can produce articulate and constructive feedback.

(2.) A significant number of the group members can agree on the major aspects of a particular individual's behavior exhibited in the group situation. Certainly a complete consensus is not to be expected, but neither must the feedback go off in all directions. A certain degree of communality is necessary if the feedback is to be helpful for the individual.

(3.) Feedback is relatively complete and deals with significant aspects of the individual's behaviour.

(4.) The behavior emitted in the group is sufficiently representative of behavior outside the group so that learning occurring within the group will carry over or transfer.

(5.) Psychological safety can be achieved relatively quickly (in the matter of a few hours) among either complete strangers or among associates who have had varying types and degrees of interpersonal interaction.

(6.) Almost everyone initially lacks interpersonal competence; that is, individuals tend to have distorted self-images, faulty perceptions, and poor communication skills.

(7.) Anxiety facilitates new learning.

(8.) Finally, transfer of training occurs between the cultural island and the "back home" situation.

Little can be said about the validity of such assumptions since they involve extremely complex processes with as yet only a very thin research context.

PROBLEMS FACING T-GROUP RESEARCH

Before reviewing research results, the authors shall comment on some of the problem faced by investigators who wish to conduct research on the T-Group and its effects. Many of these difficulties are certainly not peculiar to the T-Group, but it is believed that T-Group research faces certain unique problems which severely constrain any effort to explicate the effects of the method.

One of the major difficulties mentioned by Schein and Bennis (1965) is the lack of an explicit theory of learning for use in specifying the relation between learning experiences and learning outcomes. Nine individuals presented their formulations of the T-group change process in Bradford et al. (1964), and all were very different. Schein and Bennis attributed this diversity of theory to the wide range of learning outcomes seen as possible. Outcomes may include increased awareness, increased knowledge, changes in values, changes in attitudes, changes in motivation, or changes in actual behavior. Organizing all these into a single coherent system specifying relationships between training elements and learning outcomes is difficult indeed—probably more difficult for laboratory education than for other training methods. Presently, it is unclear what kinds of outcomes to expect from any specific T-Group effort.

A second problem, not unique to T-Groups, is the ever-present question of transfer of learning from the training group to the individual's life outside the group. More specifically, does what is learned in a T-Group transfer to the organizational setting? Assuming that transfer does occur, the problem of observing and measuring it remains. The measurement problem involves two major steps: assessing what changes have occurred over the course of the training, and determining how such changes are manifested in the organizational setting. For example, do people really become more sensitive to the feelings of others during the course of the T-Group, and are they then also more sensitive to the feelings of others on the job? Both these questions must be examined empirically.

Any assessment or measurement of what goes on in T-Group training must first cope with the problems involved in measuring this elusive phenomenon called interpersonal sensitivity. The problems are many, and they have already been well documented by Cronbach (1955), Gage and Cronbach (1955), Cline (1964), and H. C. Smith (1966). The major difficulty grows out of the plethora of strategies available to anyone who seeks to discern accurately the attributes, feelings, and reactions of others. Unless the various components and strategies involved in interpersonal sensitivity are taken into account during the design of measuring instruments and during the design and implementation of research investigations, little new knowledge concerning T-Group training effects or the likelihood of transferring skills back to the work setting will accrue. So far (as will be seen in subsequent sections), most investigators have not attempted to cope with the serious measurement and design problems inherent in this area.

A REVIEW OF THE EMPIRICAL LITERATURE

Three reviews (Buchanan, 1965; House, 1967; Stock, 1964) of the T-Group literature have previously appeared. The present review is focused primarily on studies of the usefulness of the T-Group technique for influencing the behavior of people in organizations. That is, of principal interest here is the relationship of T-Group training to appropriate criterion measures. In addition, studies bearing on the viability of the assumptions underlying the method and investigations showing how successful the technique has been in capitalizing on the essential features of its technology have also been included. For example, investigations of the utility of interpersonal feedback in a group or studies of the effects of different trainer styles are relevant. The authors have also tried to limit citations to studies employing subjects who have some sort of management or supervisory responsibility. However, in the interest of including all potentially relevant research, the authors have also reviewed studies using students in business administration or related fields that imply an interest in management or administrative careers.

The discussion is organized according to the type and quality of criteria used. Martin's (1957) distinction between internal and external measures of training effects has been adopted. *Internal criteria* are measures linked directly to the content and processes of the training program, but which have no direct linkage to actual job behavior or to the goals of the organization. Examples of internal criteria include measures of attitude change, performance in simulated problem-solving situations, and opinions of trainees concerning what they thought they had learned. Obviously, changes in internal criteria need imply no necessary change in job behavior; for example, a change in attitudes toward employees may or may not be accompanied by different behavioral patterns back on the job.

External criteria are those linked directly with job behavior. Superior, subordinate, or peer ratings, unit production, or unit turnover are examples of external criteria that have been used. Neither of these two classes of criteria is regarded as more important than the other. It will subsequently be argued that a thorough knowledge of both is essential for a full understanding of training effects. The relationship between internal and external criteria is the essence of the problem of transfer to the organizational setting.

EXTERNAL CRITERIA

Studies by Boyd and Elliss (1962), Bunker (1965), and Miles (1965) are the three research efforts most frequently cited in support of the ability of the T-Group experience to change job behavior. Valiquet (1964) carried out a similar study, All four investigations used a "perceived change" measure as the basic external criterion. This measure is an open-ended question asking a superior, subordinate, or peer of the subject to report any changes in the subject's behavior in the job situation during some specified period of time. The specific question used in the Bunker (1965), Miles (1965), and Valiquet (1964) studies is as follows:

Over a period of time people may change in the ways they work with other people. Do you believe that the person you are describing has changed his/her behavior in working with people over the last year as compared with the previous year in any specific ways? If YES, please describe:

Estimates of change were usually obtained from several (three to seven) observers for each subject. In the Boyd and Elliss (1962) study, the observers were interviewed by the researchers, while in the other three studies, data were obtained by including the above question in a mailed questionnaire. Observers were not asked to judge the positive or negative aspects of the behavior changes, but merely to describe those which had occurred. In all four studies the perceived-change data were obtained several months after completion of training.

All studies used at least one control group, and in the Bunker, Miles, and Valiquet studies they were chosen in a similar, but unusual, fashion. Controls were matched with experimental subjects by asking each person in the experimental group to nominate a "control" individual who was in a similar organizational position and who had never participated in a T-Group. It is not clear from the report how the control subjects were chosen in the Boyd and Elliss study.

Subjects in the Miles (1965) and Bunker (1965) studies were participants in NTL programs. Miles used 34 high school principals as an experimental group and two groups of principals as controls. One "matched" group of 29 was chosen via the nomination procedure, and a second group of 148 was randomly selected from a national listing. Responses to the perceived-change measure were solicited from six to eight associates of each experimental and control subject and from the subjects themselves approximately eight months after the training. Returns were obtained from an average of five observers per subject.

Two other external criterion measures also were used: the Leadership Behavior Description Questionnaire (LBDQ—Stogdill and Coons, 1957), which was completed by observers, and the Group Participation Scale, a peer-nomination form originally developed by Pepinsky, Siegel, and Van Alta 1952) as a counseling criterion measure. Data from both these instruments were collected before and after the training for one-half of the experimental group and the matched-pair control group. To check any Treatment × Measurement interaction effects, data for the second half of the experimental group were collected posttraining only. There were no interactions.

A large number of other measures were also included in the study. Ratings of various training behaviors (internal criteria) were obtained from trainers, peers, and the participants themselves. These ratings were analyzed via the multitrait, multimethod (Campbell and Fiske, 1959) technique and subsequently collapsed into an overall "trainee effectiveness" score. More importantly, five measures of the individual's organizational situation were obtained: (1) security, as measured by length of tenure in present job; (2) power, as measured by the number of teachers in the participant's school; (3) autonomy, as measured by length of time between required reports to the immediate superior; (4) perceived power, as measured by a Likert-type scale; and (5) perceived adequacy of organizational functioning, as measured by a Likert-type scale. In addition, a number of personality measures were administered, including items intended to assess ego strength, flexibility, and self-insight. The participants were also asked to rate their "desire for change" before starting the training.

No significant results were found with the LBDQ or the Group Participation Scale, and the personality measures were not predictive of anything. However, results obtained with the perceived-change measure were statistically significant. The observers reported perceived behavioral changes for 30 percent of the experimentals, 10 percent of the matched controls, and 12 percent of the randomly selected controls. The corresponding percentages for self-reported changes are 82 percent, 33 percent, and 21 percent for the three groups. The participants tended to report considerably more changes than the observers. An informal content analysis was carried out, and Miles (1965) concluded that the nature of the changes reported included increased sensitivity to others, heightened equalitarian attitudes, greater communication and leadership skills, and patterns of increased consideration and relaxed attitudes in their jobs. No details are given as to how the content analysis was performed.

Bunker's (1965) experimental group included 229 people from six different laboratories conducted at the NTL during 1960 and 1961. The participants were presumably rather heterogeneous, but a substantial proportion had leadership or managerial responsibilities. The matching-by-nomination procedure yielded 112 control subjects. Perceptions of behavior change were obtained from each experimental and control subject and from five to seven associates of each subject approximately a year after the training period. The 229 experimentals and 112 controls represented return rates of approximately 75 percent and 67 percent. Eighty-four percent of the observers returned questionnaires.

Bunker presented a list of 15 inductively derived categories that were used for content analyzing the perceived-change data. The 15 categories were grouped within three major classes labeled: (1) overt operational changes, that is, communication, relational facility, risk taking, increased interdependence, functional flexibility, self-control; (2) inferred changes in insight and attitudes, that is, awareness of human behavior, sensitivity to group behavior, sensitivity to others' feelings, acceptance of other people, tolerance of new information, self-confidence, comfort, insight into self and role; and (3) global judgments, really a catchall for changes with no specific referent. No details were given concerning how this classification scheme was developed. However, an agreement rate of 90 percent was reported when trained independent judges used the categories to classify the responses. Eleven of the 15 subcategories yielded statistically significant differences between experimental and control groups with the trained group showing greater change in each category. The greatest differences (ranging up to 20 percent to 25 percent) were in areas related to increased openness, receptivity, tolerance of differences, increased operational skill in interpersonal relationships, and improved understanding of self and others. Again, about one third (ranging up to 40 percent) of the members of the experimental group were reported to have changed in comparison with 15 per cent to 20 percent in the control group. Categories showing no differences between the groups reflected such things as effective initiation of action, assertiveness, and self-confidence. However, Bunker (1965) emphasized that changes among the trainees differed greatly from person to person and that actually there was "no standard learning outcome and no stereotyped ideal toward which conformity is induced [p. 42]."

Both the Boyd and Elliss (1962) study and Valiquet's (1964) investigation used managerial personnel from a single organization. Boyd and Elliss employed an experimental group of 42 managers selected from three different T-Groups conducted during 1961 at a large Canadian public utility. Their two control groups consisted of 12 control individuals who received no training and 10 managers who received a conventional human-relations training program employing lectures and conference techniques. Perceived changes were collected by interviewing each manager's superior, two of his peers, and two of his subordinates. The percentages of observers reporting changes for the laboratory-trained group, the conventionally trained group, and the no-training group were 65 percent, 51 percent, and 34 percent, respectively. The percentage of subjects showing changes "substantially" agreed upon by two or more observers was 64 percent for the experimental group and 23 percent for the two control groups taken together. All the above differences are statistically significant. For all subjects a total of 351 statements of perceived change was reported, but only 137 changes were agreed upon by two or more observers. Of twenty-two reported changes judged to be unfavorable (for example, an increase in irritability or loss of tolerance) by the researchers, 20 were attributed to members of the laboratory-trained group. The observers were also asked to Q-sort a deck of 80 statements describing different kinds of job-behavior changes. No significant differences were found with this instrument. In their conclusions, Boyd and Elliss emphasized the great heterogeneity among the trainees in their behavioral outcomes. They also argued that no particular pattern could be regarded as a typical training outcome.

Valiquet (1964) randomly selected 60 participants from an ongoing laboratory-type training program conducted in certain divisions of a large multiproduct corporation. The program was a continuing one and included T-Group meetings at various management levels and follow-up meetings designed to promote the effective use of interpersonal skills for solving current organizational problems and planning future activities. Difficulties encountered in choosing an appropriate control group coupled with a low rate of response to the questionnaire resulted in a serious loss of subjects. Final results were available for 34 trained subjects and only 15 matched control-group subjects. On the average about five observers were nominated by each experimental and control subject. The change categories developed by Bunker were used to content analyze the descriptions obtained from each observer. Statistically significant differences were obtained between experimentals and controls on total number of changes observed, total changes agreed upon by two or more observers, and total number of changes reported by the subjects themselves. Results by category were much the same as in the Bunker study except that differences were greater in this study for the categories of "risk taking" and "functional flexibility," defined as the ability to accept change and to be an effective group member. Valiquet believes these differences occurred because the program involved in-plant training conducted with co-workers, and the trainers were from within the firm, thereby facilitating the transfer of actual behavior to the work situation.

The above investigations, primarily the first three, seem to form the backbone of the evidence used to support the utility of the T-Group method for the development of individuals in organizations. Certain summary statements can be made. In all the studies, between two and three times as many "changes" were reported for the experimental groups as for the control groups. In absolute terms about 30 percent to 40 percent of the trained individuals were reported as exhibiting some sort of perceptible change. The percentage was somewhat higher in the Boyd and Elliss (1962) study where the observer opinions were gathered by means of an interview rather than by questionnaire. Within the limits of the method, the types of perceived changes which seem to discriminate best between experimentals and controls have to do with increased sensitivity, more open communication, and increased flexibility in role behavior.

The studies suffer from a number of obvious methodological limitations: The observers responding to the criterion measures apparently knew whether or not the individual they were describing had been through T-Group training. Several of the authors suggested that the effects of such contamination were probably not serious, arguing that the variance in the types of changes was always greater for the experimental groups than for the control groups and that the proportion of changes verified by more than one observer was always higher for the trained group. Such arguments may or may not soothe the stomachaches of those who worry about this type of bias. There is a second potential source of error in that the multiple describers for each subject were nominated by the subject and probably had varying degrees of interaction with each other. It is not known to what extent the observers might have discussed the fact that they had been asked to describe a particular individual and thus contaminated each other's observations. Also, no before measures were used, and the estimation of change depended solely on recollection by the observers. The pervasive influence of perceiver bias on what is remembered and reported is a well-documented phenomenon in psychological research. Further, it is difficult even to speculate how the above potential biases might interact with the practice of having individuals in the experimental groups suggest subjects for the control group who in turn nominate their own observers. A suggestion of such a troublesome interaction is reported in the Valiquet (1964) study. The group of subjects for whom the least changes were reported had originally nominated a significantly higher percentage of peers as describers, rather than superiors or subordinates.

Moreover, it is important to remember that the kinds of changes reported in these four studies have no direct or established connection with job effectiveness. Even if an individual does actually exhibit more "sensitivity" or "functional flexibility" on the job, one still knows nothing about how these constructs may be related to performance effectiveness. The relationship between such measures and job effectiveness constitutes an additional research question which has yet to be examined.

Underwood (1965) did ask observers to rate behavior changes according to their effects on job performance, but his study used fewer subjects and describers than those discussed above. Fifteen volunteers from a group of 30 supervisors who had participated in 30 hours of inplant T-Group training were assigned to the experimental group. The control group consisted of 15 supervisors who had not been in the course, but who were matched on department, organization level, and age with those in the experimental group. Each subject was asked to recruit one observer who was then given a sealed envelope containing instructions for observing and reporting on any behavioral changes in the subject's "characteristic behavior pattern." Thirty-six reports of behavior change were gathered over a 15-week period. Some observers made no reports; several made more than one.

Nine individuals in the experimental group were reported to have changed in some fashion versus seven in the control group; however, there were nearly $2\frac{1}{2}$ times as many changes reported for the experimental group as for the control group. Although the frequencies are small, it is interesting to note that in the control group the ratio of changes judged to increase effectiveness was 4 : 1, while in the experimental group the ratio was only 2 : 1. In other words, the suggestion is that while the T-Group produced more observable changes in its members' job behavior it also produced a higher percentage of unfavorable changes with respect to their rated effects on job effectiveness. This is the only study of its kind, and it is unfortunate that the Ns are so small and the sources of observer bias so prevalent.

$N = 1$ STUDIES

Another type of external criterion study might be labelled the $N = 1$ (Dukes, 1965) investigation. Its distinguishing feature is that the criteria used to evaluate the effectiveness of the training consist of summary data reflecting the overall performance of the organization or organizational subunit. For example, changes in the firm's profit picture or changes in a subunit's turnover rate over the course of the training period might be used as criterion measures. Such a procedure is probably most appropriate for T-Group and laboratory programs aimed at increasing organizational effectiveness by means of inplant training sessions and the incorporation of actual organizational problems as topics of discussion during the latter stages of the program.

The most frequently cited study relevant to T-Group training was reported by Blake, Mouton, Barnes, and Greiner (1964). The training experience was the Management Grid program which progresses in several stages. Initially, a series of T-Group-like sessions is conducted for the purpose of exploring interpersonal relationships among peers and giving managers feedback about their particular management styles. A certain amount of structure and theory is also introduced in an attempt to move individual managers toward what Blake and Mouton (1964) called the 9,9 style of management, a style roughly akin to a maximum concern for both interpersonal relations and production problems. Over the course of a year or more, other training phases consisting of group examination of authority relationships between managements levels, practice in the resolution of intergroup conflict, and collaborative problem solving are implemented. The program is intended to involve all managerial personnel from a particular firm.

Blake et al. (1964) presented the first phases of the grid program to all 800 managers in a 4,000-employee division of a large petroleum corporation. A large number of evaluation criteria were used with some being applied both before and after training and others only after the program had been completed. The measures obtained after completion of the program were such things as perceived changes in work-group performance (for example, "boss' work effort," "quality of group decisions," and "profit and loss consciousness"), perceived changes in working relationships, and a number of items concerning attitudes toward specific management values and techniques. The above data were gathered from approximately 600 managers, and each respondent also was asked to estimate the change in his perceptions from 1962 to 1963, the year that included the grid program. The before-and-after measures included indexes of net profit, controllable operating costs, unit production per employee, frequency of management meetings, management-promotion criteria, frequency of transfers, and relative success in solving a number of persistent organizational problems (for example, high maintenance costs, high utility costs, plant safety, and management communication). The data concerning the effectiveness of problem solutions were quite subjective and largely anecdotal in nature.

In general, the results were interpreted positively. For example, over the course of the training program the firm experienced a considerable increase in profits and a decrease in costs. The investigators attributed 56 percent of the profit increase to noncontrollable factors, 31 percent to a reduction in manpower, and 13 percent (amounting to several million dollars) to improved operating procedures and higher productivity per man-hour. The substantial increase in productivity per employee was said to have been achieved without increased investment in plant and equipment. Other criterion changes cited were an increased frequency of meetings, increased transfers within the plant and to other parts of the organization, a higher frequency of promotion for young line managers as opposed to staff men with more tenure, and a greater degree of success in solving the organizational problems discussed above. Besides these summary criteria, the individual measures of values and attitudes suggested a shift toward the attitudinal goals of the grid program, and the perceptual measures indicated a change toward the 9,9 style of managing. Recall, however, that these individual measures were obtained posttraining only, and the respondent was asked to estimate the amount of change that had taken place over a year's time.

QUESTIONNAIRE MEASURES OF INDIVIDUAL PERCEPTIONS

Most of the criterion measures used in these investigations are individual perceptions obtained by means of standardized questionnaires. In some cases it is stretching a point to classify them as external criteria. For example, a measure of job satisfaction may have little or no relationship to measures of job behavior, but it is still a job-centered rather than a training-centered measure. A number of other ambiguities will be evident.

Beer and Kleisath (1967) studied the effects of the laboratory phase of the Management Grid program on the 230 managerial and professional personnel in one corporate division. Several questionnaire measures of perceptions of organizational functioning were obtained before and approximately a year after the 1-week grid program. Other questionnaire measures were used to assess changes in perceptions of group processes, perceptions of intergroup processes, perceptions of communication patterns, job satisfaction, and commitment to the organization. Voluntary turnover was also included as a criterion measure.

The questionnaires provided a total of 41 scales with which to assess perceptual changes, and the authors pointed out that 37 of these changed in the predicted direction. However, only 14 of the 37 were statistically significant, and a number of significant differences were quite small. The change in turnover is difficult to interpret in that the index decreased over the experimental period, but only back to the level it had been two years before. Turnover had increased prior to the implementation of the grid program.

In sum, the results of the study tend to be in the predicted directions, but not overwhelmingly so. Unfortunately, there are competing explanations. No control groups were used, and the grid cannot be isolated as the cause of the changes. Even if it were, the same criticism applies here as with the Blake et al. (1964) study regarding Hawthorne-type effects. Perhaps any kind of group human-relations program would produce similar outcomes.

Some of the difficulties involved in using perceptual data as criteria are illustrated in a study reported by Taylor (1967). The primary criterion measures were 20 semantic differential scales used to describe the trainee, 25 pairs of statements defining scales for describing the trainee's work group, and the eight-item Likert scale for measuring the trainee's orientation toward Theory Y or Theory X (Haire et al., 1966).

All the measures were completed before and six months after a one-week T-Group laboratory conducted for 32 managers in a single organization. Some of the measures were also administered one month after the T-Group. An average of four associates of each subject also responded to the criterion measures with the aim of describing the participants' observed behavior. While the results tended to show a number of significant changes in the participants' own responses, corresponding changes were not observed by the trainees' associates. This general result was also true regarding the Theory Y-Theory X measure (McGregor, 1960).

Buchanan and Brunstetter (1959) used trainees' perceptions of how their work units changed as a measure of the effects of an intraorganizational laboratory program directed at organization development. All the managers in one large department ($N = 224$) were used as an experimental group, and all the managers in a second department ($N = 133$) constituted a control group. Three to seven months after the completion of the training, the participants were asked via a questionnaire to rate changes in the effectiveness of various functions occurring in their own subunits during the previous year. No before measure was used. On those functions judged by the researchers to be under the control of the manager, the experimental group reported a greater number of effective changes. Unfortunately, it is difficult to draw conclusions from the results of such a study. There is no way to estimate how comparable the two departments were before the training began. Also, the trainees were actually being asked to judge what kind of an effect they themselves had had on the department, since it was only through them that the training could have an impact.

While the questionnaire studies cited above have yielded a relatively vast amount of data, the results are quite mixed and are open to numerous alternative explanations. Statistically significant differences are not abundant, and even these tend to be quite small. Over it all hangs the constant threat of response biases that have no parallel in actual behavior change.

INTERNAL CRITERIA

PERCEPTIONS OF SELF

Several investigations have focused on the change in an individual's self-perception occurring during training. Such a criterion flows directly from one of the major aims of T-Group training—increasing the clarity and accuracy of individuals' perceptions of their own behavior. Studies by Bass (1962a), Bennis, Burke, Cutter, Harrington, and Hoffman (1957), Burke and Bennis (1961), Clark and Culbert (1965), Gassner, Gold, and Snadowsky (1964), Grater (1959), and Stock (1964) are relevant. A number of these were designed to assess discrepancies between descriptions of "actual self," "ideal self," and "others" (either a specific or some generalized other) and to measure any changes in these discrepancies produced by the T-Group experience.

Two such studies are the ones by Burke and Bennis (1961) and Gassner et al. (1964). Burke and Bennis asked 84 participants from six different NTL groups to use 19 bipolar, adjectival rating scales to describe three concepts: (1) "The way I actually am in this T-Group," (2) "The way I would like to be in this T-Group," and (3) "Each of the other people in this group." The series of ratings of others was used to develop a pooled (or average) description of each subject on each of the 19 scales. The rating scales were administered during the middle of the first week and readministered at the next-to-last session of the third week. Changes were in the direction of greater agreement between actual and ideal self-descriptions and toward subjects' seeing themselves more nearly as others described them. The changes were statistically significant on all rating scales for all groups combined, but not for each of the six groups. No control group was used.

The results by Gassner et al. (1964) illustrate the dangers of making inferences from studies without control groups. They conducted three experiments using undergraduate students at CCNY as subjects, and each of the experiments employed a control group which received no training. Sample sizes were 45–50 for the experimental groups and 25–30 for the controls. The principal measure was the Bills Index of Adjustment and Values (a checklist of 40 descriptive adjectives). It was completed by each subject for each of three sets: (1) "This is most characteristic of me;" (2) "I would like this to be most characteristic of me;" and (3) "Most CCNY students my age would like this to be characteristic of them." As in the previous study, members of the experimental groups reduced their discrepancies between actual and ideal self-descriptions. They also tended to see themselves as being more similar to the average student. However, the control groups showed similar changes, and there were no differences between the two groups on the postmeasures.

Significant changes in the self-image are not always found. The Bennis et al. (1957) study was carried out on 12 business-administration students participating in a semester-long T-Group, and changes in perceptions of actual self and ideal self were assessed by means of a 34-item inventory of possible role behaviors. The items were culled from a wide variety of sources and represented such role behaviors as, "tries hard to understand the contributions of others . . .," "uses group setting to express nongroup oriented feelings . . .," etc. The subjects rated each of the possible role behaviors on a 7-point scale according to how descriptive they felt it was of their real or ideal self. Over the course of the T-Group, there was no significant change in the discrepancy between actual and ideal self-descriptions. However, the authors pointed out that the study was intended to be exploratory, and only 12 subjects were used.

A study by Stock (1964) serves to muddy the waters a bit more. On the basis of her own data, she suggested that individuals who change the most in terms of their self-percept actually become more variable and seem less sure of what kinds of people they really are. Again, however, no control group was employed.

In summary it seems relatively well established that the way in which an individual sees himself may indeed change during the course of a T-Group. However, there is no firm evidence indicating that such changes are produced by T-Group training as compared with other types of training, merely by the passage of time, or even by the simple expedient of retaking a self-descriptive inventory after a period of thinking about one's previous responses to the same inventory.

INTERPERSONAL SENSITIVITY

In spite of the complex measurement problems involved, several studies have attempted to assess how a T-Group affects the accuracy of interpersonal perception.

In the Bennis et al. (1957) study cited above, a measure of "social sensitivity" was derived by first computing the discrepancy between an individual's prediction of another subject's response and the subject's actual response. For each individual the discrepancies were then summed over all the items and all the other group members. While there was a slight tendency for the accurate predictors to be predicted more accurately themselves, no changes occurred in this measure over the course of the T-Group.

Gage and Exline (1953) also attempted to assess how well T-Group participants could predict the questionnaire responses of the other group members. Two NTL groups of 15 and 18 persons, respectively, responded to a 50-item questionnaire before and after a 3-week laboratory. The items were opinion statements concerning group processes, leadership styles, the scientific study of human relations, and so on. To control for the effects of taking the same items twice, two 50-item forms judged to be "equivalent" by the researchers were administered before and after. The subjects were asked to give their own opinions and also to predict how they thought the group as a whole would respond. An accuracy score for each person was obtained by correlating his predictions on each of the 50 items with the group's composite response on each of the items. Thus, each correlation, or accuracy index, was based on an N of 50. In addition to the accuracy measure, a "similarity" index was obtained by correlating the actual responses of each subject with the group response. The actual responses of the subjects were also correlated with their predictions of the group response to yield a measure of "assumed similarity." None of these three indexes changed significantly over the course of the training.

In a study employing a larger sample ($N = 115$) but no control group, Harrison (1966) used a modified version of Kelly's Role Construct Repertory Test to secure self-descriptions and descriptions of ten associates before, three weeks after, and three months after participation in NTL training. The modified form of the Kelly test asks the describer to respond to triads of individuals by selecting a word or phrase that discriminates one member of the triad from the other two and then to gives its opposite. The concepts used by the subjects were coded into two categories—concrete-instrumental, and inferential-expressive. The former included such bipolar terms as man-woman, has power-has little power, and knows his job-incompetent. Some examples from the latter category are: afraid of people-confident, tries to get personal-formal and correct, and warm-cold. Interrater agreement for coding terms was 94 percent, and 83 percent of the bipolar terms used by the subjects were classified into one of the two categories, 29 percent as concrete-instrumental and 54 percent as inferential-expressive. In sharp contrast to the usual finding of an effect shortly after training with a subsequent drop off over time, Harrison found significant increases in the frequency of subjects' use of interpersonal concepts to describe associates three months after training, but no short-term (three-week) differences.

Oshry and Harrison (1966) asked 46 middle managers to evaluate some possible causes of unresolved interpersonal work problems, and the resources available for dealing with them, before and after they participated in a two-week NTL program. The problems were actual situations faced by the subjects in their back home work situation. The subjects were given a standard set of 45 items which listed a number of antecedent causes and possible ways of dealing with such problems. According to Oshry and Harrison, the managers, after training, viewed their work as more "human" and less impersonal, and they saw more distinct connections between getting work done and the satisfaction of interpersonal needs than before training. Moreover, after training the managers tended more often to see themselves as the most significant cause or contributor to their own work problems, but they failed to see how these new views of problem causes could be translated into managerial action.

In a similar study, Bass (1962b) showed the film *Twelve Angry Men* to 34 executives before and after two weeks of T-Group training. The subjects were asked to finish a series of incomplete sentences describing the behavior of the characters portrayed in the film. Bass concluded that the training resulted in participants becoming more sensitive to the interpersonal relationships exhibited in the film. Although no control group was used, two other groups of trainees were shown the film only after training in order to assess possible effects of seeing the film twice. All groups responded similarly on the posttraining questionnaire, suggesting that the increased sensitivity to interpersonal relations was due to the training and not merely to seeing the film twice.

In contrast to the negative findings regarding perceptual accuracy scores, the studies cited above establish fairly well that people who have been through a T-Group describe other people and situations in more interpersonal terms. However, there is still the more important question of whether this finding actually represents increased sensitization to interpersonal events or merely the acquisition of a new vocabulary.

ATTITUDE CHANGE

Turning to another type of internal criterion, the authors were surprised to find relatively few studies relating T-Group experiences to attitude changes. This is in contrast to recent reviews of other areas of management-development research (J. P. Campbell, 1966; Miner, 1965) which have shown a rather heavy reliance on attitude measures as criteria. P. B. Smith (1964), Schutz and Allen (1966), and Baumgartel and Goldstein (1967) used the Fundamental Interpersonal Relations Orientation-Behavior questionnaire (FIRO-B; Schutz, 1958) as the primary dependent variable to assess the impact of T-Group training. FIRO-B includes a series of attitude items designed to measure six relatively homogeneous dimensions related to three major types of an individual's behavior in groups—control (that is, attempting to influence the proceedings), inclusion (that is, initiating contacts with others in a group), and affection (that is, moving toward others in a close and personal way). The questionnaire contains a pair of scales for each behavior category: one to assess the respondent's own tendency or desire to show the behavior, and the other to assess how much he wants others in the group to show it.

Using only the four scales measuring attitudes toward affection and control, P. B. Smith (1964) obtained responses from 108 English managers and students before and after they had been trained in T-Groups (11 groups in all) and compared them with responses obtained from a control group of 44 students (six groups in all) who merely took part in a series of discussions. The overall disparity between one's own behavioral tendencies and that desired in others decreased for the T-Group trainees, but showed no change for those in the control group. The largest changes occurred for those who initially showed strong control and weak affection tendencies and who desired low control and high affection from others in the groups. These changes are consonant with the aims of the T-Group method.

Schutz and Allen (1966) used FIRO-B to study possible attitude changes among 71 persons of widely varied backgrounds who participated in a Western Training Laboratories sensitivity program. Thirty students in an education class at the University of California (Berkeley) were used as a control group. FIRO-B was administered before training, immediately after the two-week sessions, and again by mail six months after the session had been completed. Correlations between pre- and posttest scores for the various FIRO-B scales were much lower for the experimental group than for the control group, indicating that the training induced greater changes in the attitudes measured by FIRO-B. The lowest correlations on all six scales (that is, most change) were obtained between the pretest and six-month posttest scores obtained by the trainee group. This outcome reinforces Harrison's results showing that T-Group effects may be manifested only after some time. Unfortunately, the investigators did not report the specific nature or direction of the changes occurring on the various scales of the FIRO-B.

Baumgartel and Goldstein (1967) also used FIRO-B as a criterion measure, in addition to the Allport-Vernon-Lindzey Study of Values (Allport, Vernon, & Lindzey, 1960). Subjects were 100 students (59 male, 41 female) in five sections of a semester-long human-relations course (including T-Group experiences) conducted at the University of Kansas. The two criterion instruments were administered pre and post, and the results were analyzed for males versus females and for high-valued versus low-valued participants identified by peer nominations. The data for the latter dichotomy were gathered at the conclusion of the course. No control group was used. The researchers predicted changes in the direction of more expressed control, lower religious values, and higher political values—especially for the participants who were seen as high valued by their peers. Only the prediction for the religious scale was supported; however, there were a number of significant results not predicted by the investigators. Overall, there was a significant increase in wanted control and a significant decrease in wanted affection. Most of the changes could be attributed to the high-valued females and low-valued males. The statistical significance of these interactions was not subjected to a direct test; however, the implication is clear that taking account of individual differences is a necessity when evaluating the effects of such training experiences.

The Baumgartel and Goldstein (1967) study illustrates another serious difficulty in evaluating T-Group research. In a large number of the studies cited in this review the training program presented the T-Group in conjunction with other learning experiences such as reading assignments, lectures, simulated problem exercises, and the like. Thus, it is difficult to attribute any positive or negative results unequivocally to the influence of the T-Group, although this is often the implication given by investigators. The difficulty is compounded by descriptions of training programs which are usually so incomplete as to preclude any careful assessment of the role played by these other methods.

An attitude measure derived from the goals of the Management Grid program was used by Blake and Mouton (1966) to assess changes in union and management attitudes toward supervisory practices. Only the first phase (the part most analogous to a T-Group) of the grid program was evaluated, and the researchers' attention was concentrated on changes in attitudes toward five "distinct" managerial styles: maximum concern for both production and people (9,9), minimum concern for both production and people (1,1), maximum concern for production and minimum concern for people (9,1), maximum concern for people and minimum concern for production (1,9), and a moderate but balanced concern for both production and people (5,5). The analysis consisted of examining mean scores on all the alternatives pertaining to a particular management style. Significant differences in the predicted directions were obtained between the two groups on the pretest. Managers scored higher than union members on the styles with a high production orientation and lower on those with a low production orientation. No initial differences were found on the 5,5 style. Relative to the before and after comparisons, the managers tended to exhibit more shifts than the union personnel although both groups tended to move in the same direction. The management group increased on 9,9 (the largest difference), decreased on 5,5 and decreased on 1,9. The differences for the other two styles were not significant. Union members increased on 9,1 and decreased on 1,9.

While these results are encouraging, several problems remain. There were no comparison groups, and the strong possibility that any one of a number of other human-relations training methods would produce similar results cannot be entirely discounted. Also, the items appeared to be geared to the stated goals and content of the training program. Thus, the "correct" answer was apparent to the respondent, and a positive response bias may have been elicited which would account for the results.

Kernan (1964) used the Leadership Opinion Questionnaire (LOQ—Fleishman, Harris, and Burtt, 1955) to study possible attitude changes resulting from T-Group training. The LOQ yields scores labeled "Consideration" and "Initiating Structure," corresponding roughly to a concern for employee human relations and a concern for getting the work out. It was administered before and after a three-day laboratory-training program conducted within a single organization. Experimental and control groups consisted of 40 and 20 engineering supervisors, respectively. No significant before-after differences were obtained for either group on either of the scales of the LOQ.

In contrast, significant before and after differences were found on the LOQ in the previously cited study by Beer and Kleisath (1967). Recall, however, that no control group was used.

Finally, Kassarjian (1965) attempted to assess changes in inner- versus other-directedness in four student and six adult extension T-Groups ($N = 125$) and observed no significant differences. His criterion measure was a 36-item forced-choice inventory, which had yielded predicted relationships with other variables in previous research. The items, generated from Riesman's formulations (Riesman, Glazer, and Denny, 1950), yielded a test-retest reliability of .85 and on previous occasions had discriminated significantly (and in the expected direction) between foreign-born and native-born United States citizens, urban and rural groups, occupational categories, and age groups. In addition, the inventory yielded significant and expected correlations with the Allport-Vernon-Lindzey Study of Values. Control groups ($N = 55$) similar in composition to the experimental groups were also used, and no significant differences were observed.

Again, the scarcity of research relating laboratory education to attitude change is disappointing and rather hard to understand.

PERSONALITY CHANGE

An internal criterion which so far has yielded completely negative results is the standardized personality measure. Massarik and Carlson (cited in Dunnette, 1962) administered the CPI (Gough, 1957) before and after a relatively long sensitivity-training course conducted with a group of students ($N = 70$) at UCLA. No significant changes were observed. Kernan (1964) also administered the F scale (Adorno, Frenkel-Brunswik, Levinson, and Sanford, 1950) before and after the 3-day T-Group laboratory. Again, no significant differences were obtained between scores before and after training for the 40 engineering supervisors. However, as the authors of both these studies are quick to point out, changes in such basic personality variables may be just too much to expect from such a relatively short experience, even if the T-Group is a "good" one.

SIMULATIONS

The last class of criteria to be considered is the situational test or artificial task which is intended to simulate job activities or job behavior. Performance in a business game or on a case problem is an example of this kind of dependent variable.

Bass (1967) used the Carnegie Institute of Technology Management Game (Cohen, Dill, Kuehn, & Winters, 1964) to study the effects of T-Group training on the simulated managerial behavior of a number of University of Pittsburgh graduate students in business administration. The Carnegie Tech game is extremely complex and is designed to simulate the activities of several firms in a multi-product industry. A number of students compose each firm, and they must interact effectively if the company is to prosper. Nine T-Groups (without trainers) met for 15 weeks. At the end of the 15 weeks three of the groups were divided into thirds and reformed into three new groups, three of the groups were split in half and reassembled, and three of the nine groups remained intact. The nine teams then competed with one another in the game. The splintered groups broke even or made a profit, but the intact groups lost an average of 5.37 million dollars over the 15-week trial period even though the intact groups gave the most positive descriptions of their openness, communication, and cooperation. On the basis of his own subjective observation, Bass attributed the lower performance of the intact groups to their neglect of the management-control function. In his opinion, the members of the intact groups never bothered to ask each other if they were carrying out their respective assignments. These results are somewhat difficult to assimilate into an evaluation of the T-Group experience per se since both the splinter and intact groups had identical training. However, the study does demonstrate the danger of assuming relatively straightforward transfer from the T-Group to another setting.

Argyris (1965) used a case discussion as a situational task and then attempted to measure, via observational techniques, the changes in interpersonal competence over the course of a laboratory program conducted for executives in a university setting. On the basis of previous work, an extremely complex method for content analyzing sound tape recordings of group sessions was developed such that scores on various dimensions of interpersonal competence could be assigned to each individual. The dimensions were originally derived by rationally grouping discrete individual verbalizations and were given such labels as "owning up vs. not owning up," "experimenting vs. rejecting experimentation," "helping others to be open vs. not helping others be open," etc. Certain logically defined group norms such as trust versus conformity are also scored. The dimensions are all bipolar, and rationally assigned integers carrying pluses and minuses are used to represent magnitude. Behaviors are also categorized according to their expression of cognitive ideas versus feelings, and the feelings component is given much greater weight. Case discussions were scored before and after the T-Group experience, which was part of a six-week "living-in" executive development program. There were 57 managers in the experimental group and 56 in the control group. In general, the results were mixed and fell short of what the author considered to be success. As reflected in the content analysis, the norms which evolved in the experimental groups seemed to reflect greater overall competence than the controls. However, differences on the individual dimensions were much more difficult to interpret and seemed to offer no clear pattern. One frustrating aspect of the article is that the nature of the difference between the experimental and control groups is never actually described. Such an oversight was obviously unintentional, and the joint probability of such an error by both author and editor must be fantastically small; however, the effect is to leave the definition of experimental and control to the interpretive powers of the reader.

There are, of course, many other studies purporting to evaluate the effectiveness of laboratory training by using trainee opinion gathered at the conclusion of the training program. Almost without exception such studies are favorable. However, in the absence of at least a control group or before and after measures, such studies are not reviewed here.

INDIVIDUAL DIFFERENCES

So far research focused on the "average" effects of T-Group or laboratory training has been considered. That is, the crucial question has been whether or not the training makes a difference for the group as a whole. Such a generalized interpretation may cover up important interactions between individual differences and training methods. Given a particular kind of outcome, certain kinds of people may benefit from T-Group training while others may actually be harmed. The same reasoning may be applied to the interaction of differences in situational and organizational variables with the training experience. However, very few studies have investigated interactive effects.

The previously mentioned study by Bennis et al. (1957) used standardized personality measures to make differential predictions about the possible influences of T-Group training. The personality measures included Cattell's 16 PF, the EPPS, and Harrington's Self-Sort Test. Schutz' FIRO-B was also administered. Relationships between these variables and the perceptual data were negligible.

Essentially negative results were also found by Steele (in press) who used the Sensation-Intuition (S-N) scale from the Myers-Briggs Type Indicator (Myers, 1962) to predict changes for 72 participants in an NTL program, 39 middle managers in a two-week Managerial Grid laboratory, and 45 students in a course employing a T-Group. The S-N scale is conceptualized as measuring a preference for basic modes of perceiving or becoming aware of the world, with the sensation end of the scale corresponding to preferences for facts, realism, practicality, and thoroughness, while intuition represents preferences for multiple causation, abstractness, experimentation with stimuli, and a chance to generate individualistic ideas and association about stimuli.

The criteria were trainer ratings and a questionnaire consisting of seven open-ended items designed to measure interpersonal values by posing a hypothetical conflict situation and asking for a course of action. In general, the S-N scale was related to the value orientation of the participants and to their general style of group behavior, as rated by the trainer. However, it was not related to changes on any of these variables.

Still in the personality realm, Mathis (1958) developed an index of T-Group trainability using a sentence-completion format. From the theories of group development formulated by Bion (1959) and Lewin (1947), he reasoned that the existence of intrapersonal conflicts and tendencies toward the open communication of both aggression and affection would signify greater receptivity to the training, and the sentence-completion scale was scored to reflect these factors. The scale was then administered to 50 people at the beginning of a T-Group, and the 10 highest and 10 lowest scorers were interviewed at the conclusion of the sessions. The individuals scoring high on the trainability index were rated higher on sensitivity, sophistication, and productivity. Again, it must be remembered that these ratings were based on what the subject said in an interview immediately following the T-Group program. There was no control group and no interviews before training.

Finally, Harrison and Lubin (1965) divided 69 people in a 1962 Western Training Laboratories program into two categories based on their orientations toward people versus tasks expressed via a questionnaire. Judgments of learning during training were made by the trainers. The investigators concluded that while the person-oriented members were more expressive, warm, and comfortable the task- or work-oriented members learned the most over the course of the laboratory program. However, the authors did not report if the work-oriented participants were still judged to be less effective than the person-oriented individuals, in spite of what they had learned, or were equal or superior to the person-oriented group after training. They were only "observed" to exhibit more "change." The data are quite subjective.

SUMMARY AND CONCLUSIONS

Argyris (1964) has commented that probably more research has been conducted on the effects of the T-Group method than on any other specific management-development technique. A comparison of the present paper with a recent review of evaluation research on all types of management-development methods (J. P. Campbell, 1966) supports the validity of Argyris' statement. Thirty-seven of the 44 studies cited in the present review were focused on evaluating the outcomes of T-Groups. Of these 37, the majority (23) used internal criteria. Based on the results of these studies, the following comments seem warranted:

1. The evidence, though limited, is reasonably convincing that T-Group training does induce behavioral changes in the "back home" setting. This statement is based primarily on results from the first five studies reviewed. However, the subjective probability estimate of the truth of this generalization is not 1.00 because of the confounding elements already discussed, namely, the manner of choosing control groups, and the fact that most observers probably knew who had or had not received the T-Group experience.

The $N = 1$ studies can contribute very little to any general conclusions. Their lack of control, zero degrees of freedom, and susceptibility to contaminating influences such as the Hawthorne effect cast considerable doubt on the utility of their results.

Given the fact of actual behavioral changes attributable to the T-Group method, there remains the vexing problem of specifying the nature of these changes. Here the data are even less conclusive. Several researchers (for example, Boyd and Elliss, 1962; Bunker, 1965) strongly resisted discussing the nature of any "typical" training effect; they implied that each trainee's pattern of change on various behavioral dimensions is unique. If this is true, the present lack of knowledge about how individual difference variables interact with training-program variables makes it nearly impossible for anyone to spell out ahead of time the outcomes to be expected from any given development program. That is, if training outcomes are truly unique and unpredictable, no basis exists for judging the potential worth of T-Group training from an institutional or organizational point of view. Instead, its success or failure must be judged by each individual trainee in terms of his own personal goals.

However, in spite of this strong focus on uniqueness, it is true that group differences have been obtained which seem to be compatible with some of the major objectives of laboratory training.

Still another problem in evaluating the back home changes is that the perceived-change measures have not usually related observed changes to actual job effectiveness. Observers have been asked to report changes in behavior, not changes in performance. The only study to attack this problem directly was Underwood's (1965). His results lead to the suggestion that while laboratory training seems to produce more actual changes than the simple passage of time the relative proportion of changes detrimental to performance is also higher for the laboratory method.

2. Results with internal criteria are more numerous but even less conclusive. For example, evidence concerning changes in self-perceptions remains equivocal.

The special problems of measuring changes in sensitivity and accuracy of interpersonal perception have already been touched upon. People who have been in a T-Group do apparently use more interpersonally oriented words to describe certain situations, but this says nothing about their general level of "sensitivity" or the relative accuracy of their interpersonal perceptions.

Again, the authors lament the small number of studies using well-researched attitude measures and/or situational measures as criteria. If such criteria were more widely used, one might have a clearer idea of exactly what kinds of attitudes and skills are fostered by laboratory education. As it is, no conclusions can be drawn.

NEEDED RESEARCH APPROACHES

Since the research results for both external and internal criteria tend to be equivocal, one might properly speculate on how research *should* proceed if one is to gain a better understanding of what the effects of T-Group training are. Only with such an understanding can one judge the relative worth of T-Group training as a personnel-development technique. Hopefully, future research will take into account at least seven major considerations:

(1.) Researchers must devote more effort to specifying the behavioral outcomes they expect to observe as a result of T-Group training.

(2.) More measures of individual differences must be incorporated in future T-Group studies. Quite simply, the question is, for what kinds of people are particular training effects observed?

(3.) More attention must be given to interactions between organizational characteristics, leadership climates, organizational goals, and training outcomes and effects.

(4.) The effects of T-Group training should be compared more fully with the behavioral effects stemming from other training methods.

(5.) A corollary to the above is the need to explore the *interaction* of T-Group training and other learning experiences. This has immediate relevance because of the frequent practice of combining the T-Group with other methods in a laboratory program.

(6.) It is imperative that the relative contributions of various technological elements in the T-Group method be more fully understood.

(7.) Finally, more effort should be directed toward forging the link between training-induced behavior changes and changes in job-performance effectiveness.

To sum up, the assumption that T-Group training has positive utility for organizations must necessarily rest on shaky ground. It has been neither confirmed nor disconfirmed. The authors wish to emphasize again that utility for the organization is not necessarily the same as utility for the individual.

It should also be strongly emphasized that many if not all the points leading to the above statement can be applied equally to other methods of management development. The entire field suffers from a lack of research attention. However, the objectives of the T-Group method are considerably more far-reaching than other techniques, and the types of behavior changes desired are, by their very nature, more difficult to observe and measure. These two features serve to place greater research demands on the T-Group method than on other techniques dealing with more restricted, and perhaps less important, behavior domains. For the time being, the T-Group must remain a very interesting and challenging research area, which is where the energies of its proponents should be applied.

AN ADDENDUM

In the opinion of the present authors, one cannot come away from an examination of the T-Group literature without a strong impression of its humanistic and sometimes existential flavor, even when the intended focus is the development of individuals in their organizational roles. This impression is fostered by a sometimes heavy reliance on anecdotal evidence (for example, Argyris, 1962, 1964; Blake and Mouton, 1963; Foundation for Research on Human Behavior, 1960), by the emphasis often placed on purely personal development (Bugental and Tannenbaum, 1963), and by explicit attempts to conceptualize T-Group learning in an existential framework (Hampden-Turner, 1966). To practitioners with this sort of bias, the present treatment of the research literature probably seems unduly mechanistic and sterile.

There are at least two possible replies to the perceived sterility of controlled systematic research. On the one hand, it is an unfortunate fact of scientific life that the reduction of ambiguity in behavioral data to tolerable levels demands systematic observations, measurement, and control. Often the unwanted result seems to be a dehumanization of the behavior being studied. That is, achieving unambiguous results may generate dependent variables that are somewhat removed from the original objectives of the development program and seem, thereby, to lack relevant content.

On the other hand, negative feelings about the sterility of research results may reflect a rejection of both the scientific and organizational points of view. That is, it may be argued that the crucial factor in T-Group training is how each *individual* feels at the end of the training program, and that investigating hypotheses concerning human behavior or assessing performance change is of little consequence. This view is quite legitimate so long as the T-Group assumes a status similar to that enjoyed by other purely individual events such as aesthetic appreciation or recreational enjoyment—events from which each individual takes what he chooses.

The danger in all of this is that the scientific and existential orientations may not be kept distinct. Argyris (1967) and Bass (1967) argued strongly that the distinction has become blurred at a number of key points, to the detriment of laboratory education. The present authors' view is that a normative or scientific orientation definitely cannot be used to argue against an individual's positive feelings about his own experiences in a T-Group, and it is hoped that any such connotation has been avoided. However, it is equally inappropriate to claim that a program has utility for accomplishing organizational goals and then to justify such a statement on existential grounds.[3]

Notes

1. This investigation was supported in part by the National Institute of Mental Health, United States Public Health Service (Research Grant 5 RO1 MH 08563-04), and in part by a behavioral science research grant to the second author from the General Electric Foundation.
2. See also the "debate" between Argyris and Odiorne reported in the *Training Directors Journal*, 17 (10) (1963): 4-37.
3. For further discussion of these points the reader should consult the responses to the Argyris and Bass articles published in the *Journal of Applied Behavioral Science*, 2 (3) (1967).

References

Adorno, T. W., E. Frenkel-Brunswik, D. J. Levinson, and R. M. Sanford. *The Authoritarian Personality*. New York: Harper, 1950.
Allport, G. W., P. E. Vernon, and G. Lindzey. *Manual Study of Values*. (3rd ed.) Boston: Houghton-Mifflin, 1960.
Argyris, C. *Interpersonal Competence and Organizational Behaviour*. Homewood, Ill.: Irwin, 1962.
Argyris, C. "T-Groups for Organizational Effectiveness," *Harvard Business Review*, 42 (2) (1964): 60-74.
Argyris, C. "Explorations in Interpersonal Competence—II," *Journal of Applied Behavioral Science*, 1 (1965): 255-269.
Argyris, C. "On the Future of Laboratory Education." *Journal of Applied Behavioral Science*, 3 (1967): 153-182.
Bass, B. M. "Mood Changes During a Management Training Laboratory," *Journal of Applied Psychology*, 46 (1962): 361-364. (a)
Bass, B. M. "Reactions to *Twelve Angry Men* as a measure of sensitivity training," *Journal of Applied Psychology*, 46 (1962): 120-124. (b)
Bass, B. M. "The Anarchist Movement and the T-Group," *Journal of Applied Behavioral Science*, 3 (1967): 211-226.
Baumgartel, H., and J. W. Goldstein. "Need and Value Shifts in College Training Groups," *Journal of Applied Behavioral Science*, 3 (1967): 87-101.
Beer, M., and S. W. Kleisath. "The effects of the Managerial Grid lab on organizational and leadership dimensions." In S. S. Zalkind (Chm.), *Research on the impact of using different laboratory methods for interpersonal and organizational change*. Symposium presented at the meeting of the American Psychological Association, Washington, D. C., September 1967.
Benne, K. D. "History of the T-Group in the Laboratory Setting," in L. D. Bradford, J. R. Gibb, and K. D. Benne (eds.). *T-Group Theory and Laboratory Method*. New York: Wiley, 1964.
Bennis, W., R. Burke, H. Cutter, H. Harrington, and J. Hoffman. "Note on Some Problems of Measurement and Prediction in a Training Group," *Group Psychotherapy*, 10 (1957): 328-341.
Berzon, B., and L. N. Solomon. "Research Frontier: The Self-Directed Therapeutic Group—Three Studies," *Journal of Counseling Psychology*, 13 (1966): 491-497.
Bion, W. R. *Experiences in Groups*. New York: Basic Books, 1959.
Blake, R. R., and J. S. Mouton. "The Instrumented Training Laboratory," in I. R. Wechsler

and E. H. Schein (eds.). *Issues in Human Relations Training.* Washington, D. C.: National Training Laboratories-National Education Association, 1962.

Blake, R. R., and J. S. Mouton. "Improving Organizational Problem Solving Through Increasing the Flow and Utilization of New Ideas," *Training Directors Journal,* 17 (9) (1963): 48–57.

Blake, R. R. and J. S. Mouton. *The Management Grid.* Houston: Gulf, 1964.

Blake, R. R., and J. S. Mouton. "Some Effects of Managerial Grid Seminar Training on Union and Management Attitudes Toward Supervision," *Journal of Applied Behavioral Science,* 2 (1966): 387–400.

Blake, R. R., J. S. Mouton, L. B. Barnes, and L. E. Greiner. "Breakthrough in Organization Development," *Harvard Business Review,* 42 (6) (1964): 133–155.

Blansfield, M. G. "Depth Analysis of Organizational Life," *California Management Review,* 5 (1962): 29–42.

Boyd, J. B., and J. D. Elliss. *Findings of Research Into Senior Management Seminars.* Toronto: Hydro-Electric Power Commission of Ontario, 1962.

Bradford, L. P., J. R. Gibb, and K. D. Benne. *T-Group Theory and Laboratory Method.* New York: Wiley, 1964.

Buchanan, P. C. *Organizational Development Following Major Retrenchment.* New York: Yeshiva, 1964. (Mimeo)

Buchanan, P. C. "Evaluating the Effectiveness of Laboratory Training in Industry," in *Explorations in Human Relations Training and Research.* No. 1. Washington, D. C.: National Training Laboratories-National Education Association, 1965.

Buchanan, P. C., and P. H. Brunstetter. "A Research Approach to Management Development: II," *Journal of the American Society of Training Directors,* 13 (1959): 18–27.

Bugental, J. R. T. and R. Tannenbaum. *Sensitivity Training and Being Motivation.* Los Angeles: University of California, Institute of Industrial Relations, 1963.

Bunker, D. R. "Individual Applications of Laboratory Training," *Journal of Applied Behavioral Science,* 1 (1965): 131–148.

Bunker, D. R., and E. S. Knowles. "Comparison of Behavioral Changes Resulting from Human Relations Training Laboratories of Different Lengths," *Journal of Applied Behavioral Science,* 2 (1967): 505–524.

Burke, H. L., and W. G. Bennis. "Changes in Perception of Self and Others During Human Relations Training," *Human Relations,* 14 (1961): 165–182.

Campbell, D. T., and D. W. Fiske. "Convergent and Discriminant Validation by the Multi-Trait, Multi-Method Matrix," *Psychological Bulletin,* 56 (1959): 81–105.

Campbell, J. P. *Management Training: The Development of Managerial Effectiveness.* Greensboro, N. C.: The Richardson Foundation, 1966.

Clark, J. V., and S. A. Culbert. "Mutually Therapeutic Perception and Self-Awareness in a T-Group," *Journal of Applied Behavioral Science,* 1 (1965): 180–194.

Cline, V. B. "Interpersonal Perception," in B. A. Maher (ed.). *Progress in Experimental Personality Research.* New York: Academic Press, 1964.

Cohen, K. J., W. R. Dill, A. A. Kuehn, and P. R. Winters. *The Carnegie Tech Management Game: An Experiment in Business Education.* Homewood, Ill.: Irwin, 1964.

Cronbach, L. J. "Processes Affecting Scores on 'Understanding of Others' and 'Assumed Similarity,'" *Psychological Bulletin,* 52 (1955): 177–193.

Deese, J. *The Psychology of Learning.* New York: McGraw-Hill, 1958.

Dollard, J., and N. E. Miller. *Personality and Psychotherapy: An Analysis in Terms of Learning, Thinking, and Culture.* New York: McGraw-Hill, 1950.

Dukes, W. F. "$N = 1$," *Psychological Bulletin,* 64 (1965): 74–79.

Dunnette, M. D. "Personnel Management," *Annual Review of Psychology,* 13 (1962): 285–314.

Fleishman, E., F. F. Harris, and H. E. Burtt. *Leadership and Supervision in Industry.* Columbus: Ohio State University, Personnel Research Board, 1955.

Foundation for Research on Human Behavior. *An Action Research Program for Organization Improvement.* Ann Arbor, Michigan: Author, 1960.

French, J. R. P., Jr., J. J. Sherwood, and D. L. Bradford. "Changes in Self-Identity in a Management Training Conference," *Journal of Applied Behavioral Science,* 2 (1966): 210–218.

Friedlander, F. "The Impact of Organizational Training Laboratories Upon the Effectiveness and Interaction of Ongoing Work Groups," *Personnel Psychology,* 1968.

Gage, N. L. and L. J. Cronbach. "Conceptual and Methodological Problems in Interpersonal Perception," *Psychological Review,* 62 (1955): 411–422.

Gage, N. L., and R. V. Exline. "Social Perception and Effectiveness in Discussion Groups," *Human Relations*, 6 (1953): 381–396.
Gassner, S., J. Gold and A. M. Snadowsky. "Changes in the Phenomenal field as a Result of Human Relations Training," *Journal of Psychology*, 58 (1964): 33–41.
Gough, H. *California Psychological Inventory Manual*. Palo Alto, Calif: Consulting Psychologists Press, 1957.
Grater, M. "Changes in Self and Other Attitudes in a Leadership Training Group," *Personnel and Guidance Journal*, 37 (1959): 493–496.
Haire, M., E. E. Ghiselli, and L. W. Porter. *Managerial Thinking*. New York: Wiley, 1966.
Hampden-Turner, C. H. "An Existential 'Learning theory' and the Integration of T-Group Research," *Journal of Applied Behavioral Science*, 2 (1966): 367–386.
Harrison, R. "Import of the Laboratory on Perceptions of Others by the Experimental Group," in C. Argyris, (ed.). *Interpersonal Competence and Organizational Behavior*. Homewood, Ill.: Irwin, 1962.
Harrison, R. "Cognitive Change and Participation in a Sensitivity Training Laboratory," *Journal of Consulting Psychology*, 30 (1966): 517–520.
Harrison, R., and B. Lubin. "Personal Style, Group Composition, and Learning," *Journal of Applied Behavioral Science*, 1 (1965): 286–301.
House, R. J. "T-Group Education and Leadership Effectiveness: A Review of the Empirical Literature and a Critical Evaluation," *Personnel Psychology*, 20 (1967): 1–32.
Kassarjian, H. H. "Social Character and Sensitivity Training," *Journal of Applied Behavioral Science*, 1 (1965): 433–440.
Kernan, J. P. "Laboratory Human Relations Training: Its Effect on the 'Personality' of Supervisory Engineers," *Dissertation Abstracts*, 25 (1964): 665–666.
Kimble, G. A. *Hilgard and Marquis' "Conditioning and Learning."* (2nd ed.) New York: Appleton-Century-Crofts, 1961.
Klaw, S. "Two Weeks in a T-group," *Fortune*, 64 (8) (1961): 114–117.
Kuriloff, A. H. and S. T. Atkins. "T-Group for a Work Team," *Journal of Applied Behavioral Science*, 2 (1966): 63–94.
Lewin, K. "Group Decision and Social Change," in T. Newcomb and E. Hartley (eds.). *Readings in Social Psychology*. New York: Holt, 1947.
Lohman, K., J. H. Zenger, and I. R. Weschler. "Some Perceptual Changes During Sensitivity Training," *Journal of Educational Research*, 53 (1959): 28–31.
Martin, H. O. "The Assessment of Training," *Personnel Management*, 39 (1957): 88–93.
Maslow, A. H. *Eupsychian Management: A Journal*. Homewood, Illinois: Irwin, 1965.
Mathis, A. G. "Trainability as a Function of Individual Valency Pattern," in D. Stock and H. A. Thelen (eds.). *Emotional Dynamics and Group Culture*. Washington, D. C.: National Training Laboratories-National Education Association, 1958.
McGregor, D. *The Human Side of Enterprise*. New York: McGraw-Hill, 1960.
Miles, M. B. "Human Relations Training: Processes and Outcomes," *Journal of Counseling Psychology*, 7 (1960): 301–306.
Miles, M. B. "Changes During and Following Laboratory Training: A Clinical-Experimental Study," *Journal of Applied Behavioral Science*, 1 (1965): 215–242.
Miner, J. B. *Studies in Management Education*. New York: Springer, 1965.
Morton, R. B. and B. M. Bass. "The Organizational Training Laboratory," *Journal of the American Society of Training Directors*, 18 (10) (1964): 2–15.
Myers, I. B. *Manual for the Myers-Briggs Type Indicator*, Princeton, N.J.: Educational Testing Service, 1962.
National Training Laboratories. *21st Annual Summer Laboratories*. Washington, D. C.: Author, 1967.
Oshry, B. I. and R. Harrison. "Transfer from Here-and-now to There-and-then: Changes in Organizational Problem Diagnosis Stemming from T-Group Training," *Journal of Applied Behavioral Science*, 2 (1966): 185–198.
Pepinsky, H. B., L. Siegel, and E. L. Van Alta. "The Criterion in Counseling: A Group Participation Scale," *Journal of Abnormal and Social Psychology*, 47 (1952): 415–419.
Riesman, D., N. Glazer, and R. Denny. *The Lonely Crowd*. New Haven: Yale University Press, 1950.
Schein, E. H. "Management Development as a Process of Influence," in H. J. Leavitt and L. R. Pondy (eds.). *Readings in Management Psychology*. Chicago: University of Chicago Press, 1964.

Schein, E. H., and W. G. Bennis. *Personal and Organizational Changes Through Group Methods: The Laboratory Approach.* New York: Wiley, 1965.
Schutz, W. C. *FIRO: A Three-Dimensional Theory of Interpersonal Behavior.* New York: Holt, 1958.
Schutz, W. C., and V. L. Allen. "The Effects of a T-Group Laboratory on Interpersonal Behavior," *Journal of Applied Behavioral Science,* 2 (1966), 265-286.
Skinner, B. F. *Science and Human Behavior.* New York: Macmillan, 1953.
Smith, H. C. *Sensitivity to People.* New York: McGraw-Hill, 1966.
Smith, P. B. "Attitude changes Associated with Training in Human Relations," *British Journal of Social and Clinical Psychology,* 3 (1964), 104-113.
Solomon, R. L. "Punishment." *American Psychologist,* 19 (1964), 239-253.
Steele, F. I. "Personality and the 'Laboratory Style'," *Journal of Applied Behavioral Science* (in press).
Stock, D. A. "Survey of Research on T-Groups." in L. P. Bradford, J. R. Gibb, and K. D. Benne (eds.). *T-Group Theory and Laboratory Method.* New York: Wiley, 1964.
Stogdill, R. M., and A. E. Coons. *Leader Behavior: Its Description and Measurement.* (Business Research Monograph No. 88) Columbus: Ohio State University, Bureau of Business Research, 1957.
Tannenbaum, R., I. R. Weschler, and F. Massarik. *Leadership and Organization: A Behavioral Science Approach.* New York: McGraw-Hill, 1961.
Taylor, F. C. "Effects of Laboratory Training upon Persons and Their Work Groups," in S. S. Zalkind (Chm.). *Research on the Impact of Using Different Laboratory Methods for Interpersonal and Organizational Change.* Symposium presented at the meeting of the American Psychological Association, Washington, D. C., September, 1967.
Underwood, W. J. "Evaluation of Laboratory Method Training," *Training Directors Journal,* 19(5) (1965), 34-40.
Valiquet, I. M. "Contribution to the Evaluation of a Management Development Program," Unpublished Master's Thesis, Massachusetts Institute of Technology, 1964.
Wagner, A. B. "The Use of Process Analysis in Business Decision games." *Journal of Applied Behavioral Science,* 1 (1965), 387-408.
Weschler, I. R., and J. Reisel. *Inside a Sensitivity Training Group.* Los Angeles: University of California, Institute of Human Relations, 1959.
Yates, A. J. *Frustration and Conflict.* New York: Wiley, 1962.
Zand, D. E., F. I. Steele, and S. S. Zalkind. "The Impact of an Organizational Development Program on Perceptions of Interpersonal, Group, and Organizational Functioning," in S. S. Zalkind (Chm.). *Research on the Impact of Using Different Laboratory Methods for Interpersonal and Organizational Change.* Symposium presented at the meeting of the American Psychological Association, Washington, D. C. September 1967.

4

DOUGLAS R. BUNKER AND ERIC S. KNOWLES

Comparison of Behavioral Changes Resulting from Human Relations Training Laboratories of Different Lengths

*r*ecent developments in methods of measuring training outcomes have permitted the accumulation of respectable evidence that enduring changes in behavior and cognitive orientation are induced by laboratory methods of training. Miles (1960, 1965), Boyd and Elliss (1962), Bunker (1963, 1965), and Valiquet (1964) have reported studies of on-the-job changes in working style and interpersonal relations in which groups experiencing laboratory training were perceived by co-workers as having changed significantly more than control groups.

Although broad individual differences in response to training are observed both within particular laboratories and across somewhat different training programs, general consistencies in the kinds and directions of changes reported are also apparent. The descriptions of change are overwhelmingly positive, though performance decrements are also observed. Those subjects who are reported as having changed are seen typically as being more understanding of the social situations within which they work and more able to control their own behavior according to an increased awareness of their impact upon others. The work of Boyd and Elliss and of Valiquet, in particular, indicates that these changes tend to be adaptive for both the individual and the organization to which he belongs.

While these findings may be generally confirming for the laboratory training practitioner, they provide little substantive information to guide his efforts. Further systematic inquiry is necessary to develop and test a theory of laboratory training and learning, and to inform the decisions trainers must make relating to laboratory design, participant selection, group composition, duration, setting, cognitive inputs, and myriad other practical matters.

This paper reports part of the findings of a study of long-term behavior changes among participants in four human relations training laboratories conducted at Bethel, Maine, during the summers of 1960 and 1961 (Bunker, 1963, 1965). The original design of this project involved the extension to a heterogeneous population of an evaluation methodology developed by Miles with an occupationally homogeneous group of participants. At the same time, the study was conceived as a natural field experiment in which the effect of duration of training upon measures of long-term change could be assessed. For several years prior to 1961 the regular summer training programs conducted by the National Training Laboratories (NTL) had been three weeks long. In November of 1960, the governing board of NTL voted to reduce the length of the summer programs in 1961 from three to two weeks. This created a unique opportunity for the study of variable duration. Although strict experimental control was impossible due to both the complex nature of the variable and the variety of other factors operating, appropriate statistical procedures were used to cope with the uncontrollable aspects of the environment.

RESEARCH DESIGN AND METHODS

In summary, the principal independent variable is the length of the laboratory experience; the dependent variable is the amount of change in relations with others in a work setting. The raw data for measures of the dependent variable consisted of retrospective change descriptions obtained from subjects and their work associates. The data collection was initiated by soliciting three kinds of information from each participant: (1) the name of a control subject occupying a parallel role in his organization; (2) the names of ten other associates who could be asked to describe changes in the subject's behavior; and (3) a self-change description. After a similar panel of describers was nominated by each responding control subject, a sample of seven describers was selected for every subject and questionnaires were mailed with a letter soliciting cooperation.

The ease of the task requested and the persistent follow-up resulted in a very satisfactory rate of return. Fewer than one-third of the subjects did not reply or refused to cooperate. After a further paring of the sample by the researchers in order to control for job changes and other contaminating intervening experiences such as additional training, about 50 percent of the original experimental and control groups were included in the study. Describer response rates were even more satisfactory. Eighty-four percent of those receiving the questionnaire replied.

These data were obtained about ten to twelve months following training.

Comparison of Behavioral Changes

By waiting for this period we tapped only those effects durable enough to have survived the waning of immediate posttraining enthusiasm and erosive organizational pressures. The separation of training and inquiry also had the advantage of reducing contamination of data from awareness of the training activity on the part of describers. The time lag also permitted other events to intervene, some of which had the effect of reducing the sample, while others likely affected the the criterion about the same way for all samples.

The subjects and describers completed a very simple open-end behavior change questionnaire. In addition to a few items concerning the nature of the describer's relation to the subject, they were asked a question which for the describers took the following form:

Over a period of time, people may change in the ways they work with other people. Since May of 1960 (or 1961), do you believe that the person you are describing has changed his/her behavior in working with people in any specific way, as compared with the previous year?

Yes——— No———

If yes, please describe.

Table 4-1. *Inductively Derived Categories for Content Analysis**

A. *Overt Operational Changes—Descriptive*
   1. Communication
      S. Sending—shares information, expresses feelings, puts ideas across
      R. Receiving—more effort to understand, listens attentively, understands
      U. Unspecified—communicates better, communication skills improved
   2. Relational facility—cooperative, tactful, less irritating, easier to deal with, able to negotiate
   3. Risk taking—willing to take stand, less inhibited, experiments more
   4. Increased interdependence—encourages participation, involves others, greater leeway to subordinates, less dominating, lets others think
   5. Functional flexibility—more flexible, takes group roles more easily, goes out of way, contributions more helpful, less rigid
   6. Self-control—more self-discipline, less quick with judgment, checks temper.

B. *Inferred Changes in Insight and Attitudes*
   1. Awareness of human behavior (intellectual comprehension)—more conscious of why people act, more analytic of others' actions, clear perceptions of people
   2. Sensitivity to group behavior—more conscious of group process, aware of subcurrents in groups
   3. Sensitivity to others' feelings—more capacity for understanding feelings, more sensitive to needs of others
   4. Acceptance of other people—able to tolerate shortcomings, considerate of individual differences, patient
   5. Tolerance of new information—willing to accept suggestions, considers new points of view, less dogmatic, less arbitrary
   6. Self-confidence
   7. Comfort—relaxed, at ease (must be specific as to setting or activity)
   8. Insight into self and role—understands job demands, more aware of own behavior, better adjusted to job.

C. *Global Judgments*
   1. Gross characterological inferences, noncomparable references to special applications of learning, and references to consequences of change.

* Scoring depends upon an explicit statement of qualitative or quantitative difference. Changes may be positive or negative, reflecting increases or decreases in quantity and greater or less utility. Precise category fit according to scoring conventions required for sets of categories A and B.

The content of the change descriptions obtained was analyzed by a presence-absence method for each of the 17 specific categories listed in Table 4-1. The classification system was sufficiently comprehensive to cover the full range of descriptions, and the scoring process was objective enough to permit the achievement of interscorer reliabilities about 90 percent agreement. Protocols were stripped of group identification to ensure blind scoring.

Two different measures of perceived behavior change were obtained for each subject by combining scores from the several descriptions for each man. The total change score is simply the sum of the perceived changes reported in all categories by all describers for each man. It is the basic measure derived from the descriptions, and the one which provides the most liberal estimate of change. The second measure is a verified change score that consists of a count of those scoring instances in which two or more describers' reports are congruent in their specific mentions of change. This score is a more conservative estimate of change and is less subject to describer bias. In addition to these composite scores, a set of individual category scores is obtained for each subject. These scores define the dimensions along which change has taken place. They permit the qualitative analysis of individual differences and the discrimination of differential effects which follow various training interventions.

SAMPLE COMPARABILITY

Though we advocate the strict control of subject sophistication as a variable, coping with this problem is extremely difficult. Within this study, sophistication was controlled to the extent that subjects were excluded if they had ever attended a laboratory other than the one under consideration. Bernoulli's law of large numbers (with samples in this case of 52 and 101) and the fact that pairs of samples were drawn in successive years support the assumption that these samples are comparable on relevant psychological dimensions.

The data upon which we can base a comparison of the samples come from the subject's responses to demographic questions. Table 4-2 reports the percentages for response rates, sex, mean age, and occupation. Matched control

Table 4-2. *Response and Background Data for Three-Week, Two-Week, and Control Samples*

	Per Cent Participating	Per Cent Cooperating	N	Per Cent Male	Mean Age
3-Week	50.6	73.9	53	73.6	37
2-Week	51.2	69.4	102	72.3	40
Control	49.7	64.0	72	79.2	38

	OCCUPATION (BY PERCENTAGE)					
	Business	Religion	Government	Education	Social Service	Other
3-Week	13.2	24.5	11.3	13.2 ($p<.05$)*	28.3	9.4
2-Week	14.8	19.8	10.9	27.7	21.8	4.9
Control	16.9	22.1	7.8	26.0	18.2	7.8

* Two-tailed χ^2 test

subjects were combined and are shown as the control group. The samples are similar in their proportion of responses, in their male-female composition, in the mean age, and in the distribution of ages (not shown). The differences between the proportion of subjects in each of the general occupational categories are within the normal range of change, except for the educational classification ($p < .05$; two-tailed). Included under education are teachers, principals, interschool administrative personnel, special education personnel, college and adult teachers, and representatives of professional education associations. There were disproportionately fewer of these people undergoing the three-week laboratory than either the two-week laboratory or control condition. This difference in the number of educational subjects, however, did not significantly contribute to the overall differences in the change score (Table 4-9).

RESULTS

The total change score provides the most powerful test of differences among the various samples. The means and distributions of the total change scores for the various samples are reported in Table 4-3. The total number of changes mentioned

Table 4-3.   *Total Change Score (number of changes mentioned)*

	3-Week	2-Week	Control
19–20	3	1	
16–18	3	5	
13–15	4	7	
10–12	13	15	6
7– 9	14	29	6
4– 6	10	25	27
1– 3	4	15	22
0	0	4	11
minus	1	0	0
$\bar{X}$	9.14	7.38	4.01
n	52	101	72

ranged between minus three (three changes for the worse) and plus twenty. While both laboratory-trained samples evidence many more changes than the control sample, there is also a significant difference between the distributions of three- and two-week samples. Significantly more changes were ascribed to people attending a three-week laboratory than to participants in two-week programs (Table 4-4).

This finding is confirmed by the results for verified change scores. The distribution of the number of verified changes for each sample is presented in Table 4-5, and a chi-square test of the significance of the difference between three- and two-week laboratories with respect to the number of subjects for whom one or more verified changes were reported is in Table 4-6. The two three-week programs in our sample produced verified changes in a significantly greater proportion of their participants than did the two-week laboratories.

It should be pointed out, however, that the distributions of verified changes for the two samples are not significantly different; this indicates, perhaps, that it is the number of people attaining the "threshold of visible change," rather than the magnitude of the change, that differentiates the two- from the three-week laboratory. The concept of a threshold of change is inferred from the fact that the percentage of people who show verified changes is very much greater for the three-week (76.9 percent) laboratory than it is for the two-week laboratory

Table 4-4. *Means and Significance Levels of Differences Between Sample Distribution as Tested by a Two-Tailed Mann-Whitney U-Test*

	Mean	2-Week	Control
3-Week	9.14	$p < .05$	$p < .0001$
2-Week	7.38		$p < .0001$
Control	4.01		

LEVEL OF SIGNIFICANCE

Table 4-5. *Number of Verified Changes*

	3-Week	2-Week	Control
6	2		
5	2	1	
4	1	5	
3	5	7	1
2	11	20	4
1	19	26	16
0	12	42	51
$\bar{X}$	1.58	1.11	0.40
n	52	101	72
Percentage of subjects changing	76.9	58.4	30.6

Table 4-6. *A Comparison of Verified Changes Made by Subjects in 3-Week and 2-Week Programs*

VERIFIED CHANGE OBSERVED

	3-Week Program	2-Week Program	Total
One or more	40	59	99
None	12	42	54
N	52	101	153

$\chi^2 = 5.15$
$p(\chi^2 = 5.15) < .05$ (two-tailed)

(58.4 percent) (Table 4-5). The elevated total change score for the three-week laboratory can be attributed to more people showing significant changes rather than the same number of people changing in more ways. Since this measure is based upon describer agreement, there is the possibility that subjects with higher verified scores may differ from other subjects in that their changes are more visible and therefore more open to observation.

In reviewing laboratory differences, it is important to note that there were no significant differences between laboratories of the same length on the criterion measures. In addition, as may be seen in Table 4-7, the change scores for the 30

Comparison of Behavioral Changes

Table 4-7. *One-Way Analysis of Variance in Verified Change Scores Among 30 T-Groups in Four Training Laboratories*

Source	Sum of Squares	d.f.	M.S.	F Ratio
Among T-Groups	45.46	29	1.57	.838*
Error	226.41	121	1.87	
Total	271.87	150		

* Not significant

different T-Groups from the four conferences are not significantly different. There is as much variability in scores among members of the same T-Group as there is among groups. The only significant source of variation in the training setting is common to laboratories of the same length.

An examination of the differences between the two samples in the distribution of scores for particular content categories indicates the particular ways in which the three-week samples differed from those of two weeks. Table 4-8 summarizes the percentage of subjects in each sample described as having changed in each category. Clearly, some categories make a greater contribution to the total difference between the two samples than do others. Both "increased interdependence" (A-4) and "improved communication (unspecified)" (A-1-U) are

Table 4-8. *Differences Between Samples in the Per Cent of Subjects Described as Changing in Specific Content Categories*

Category	PER CENT OF SUBJECTS			DIFFERENCES IN PER CENT OF Ss		
	3-Week	2-Week	Control	3-Week −2-Week	3-Week −Control	2-Week −Control
A. Actional changes						
A-1-S Sending communication	40	29	24	11	16*	5
A-1-R Receiving communication	26	35	15	−9	11	20**
A-1-U Unspecified communication	18	5	7	13*	11*	−2
A-2 Relation facility	36	38	22	−2	14	16*
A-3 Risk taking	36	33	26	3	10	7
A-4 Increased interdependence	40	23	19	17*	21*	4
A-5 Functional flexibility	33	20	8	13	25***	12*
A-6 Self-control	27	25	12	2	15*	13*
B. Cognitive changes						
B-1 Awareness of human behavior	36	31	19	5	17*	12
B-2 Sensitivity to group behavior	24	23	10	1	14*	13*
B-3 Sensitivity to others' feelings	46	35	8	11	38***	27***
B-4 Acceptance of other people	40	46	26	−6	14	20*
B-5 Tolerance of new information	35	39	25	−4	10	14
B-6 Self-confidence	40	30	12	10	28***	18**
B-7 Comfort	29	37	25	−8	4	12
B-8 Insight into self and role	44	29	18	15	26**	11

* p (two-tailed chi-square) < .05
** p (two-tailed chi-square) < .02
*** p (two-tailed chi-square) < .01

significantly higher for the three-week laboratory than for the two-week or control samples. The first of these two categories includes statements in which the behavior of the subject is described as involving subordinates more in decisions affecting them, letting others do more thinking and experimenting, and acting less dogmatically toward others. The communication (unspecified) category difference cannot be interpreted unless it is considered in relation to the differences observed in the "sending" and "receiving" categories. Although neither of these discriminates between the two laboratory-trained samples beyond chance, we note that "sending" for the three-week program and "receiving" for the two-week program are significantly higher than for the control group. If we assume that the general statement that a person communicates better refers to his own communicative arts, or improved message sending, the three-week outcome appears to be more active in contrast to the receptive emphasis of the two-week result. Though the evidence for this interpretation is not compelling, it receives some additional support from both the size and direction of the difference for "increased interdependence," "functional flexibility," and "insight into self and role." The first two of these involve active, overt behavior changes in which the subject exercises the initiative. The third is attitudinal, but it indicates that the subject's behavior is more integrated, conscious, and purposive.

Looking at the other side, we note that in addition to being higher in changes categorized as "receiving," the two-week sample is higher in "acceptance of other people," "tolerance of new information," and "comfort." None of these categories reflects an orientation toward action or implementation. They primarily involve cognitive reorientations and seem to be predominantly intrapsychic rather than interpersonal in focus. Although this entire analysis is tenuous, given its post hoc character, the consistency of the pattern of differences suggests that while the two laboratory-trained samples are not markedly different in the insight and sensitivity categories, the three-week sample generally evidences more relational and practical effects.

DISCUSSION

The results reveal several areas of difference between the three-week and two-week samples studied. First, the three-week laboratory fostered more behavioral changes as indicated by the total change score and the verified change score. Second, the analysis of changes by content categories indicates that the changes resulting from three-week and two-week laboratories were qualitatively different. The participants in a three-week laboratory made changes toward more proactive and interactive behavior.

Having demonstrated the differences between the different-length laboratories in the amount and kinds of enduring changes reported, we must now attempt to account for these differences. If duration of training were the only independent variable, we might well invoke a moratorium concept to explain the results. In contrast to the two-week laboratory, the three-week program may be experienced by participants as a more complete break from their back-home environment and a more compelling confrontation with their membership in the laboratory community. According to this conception, the middle week of the longer program is significant as a period during which the participant is psychologically neither arriving nor departing, but is thoroughly present. Under these circumstances, his involvement as a member and learner is more intense and complete, and thus facilitates the entire learning process.

The interpretation might rest if all other factors save duration were constant and if the results revealed only quantitative differences in outcomes between two- and three-week programs. Since the T-Group is the major feature of the laboratory approach, the number of sessions and the amount of time devoted to T-Group experience should vary directly with laboratory duration, if the time variable is to operate alone. Otherwise, differences in training design and content would distinguish the two lengths of programs and become a principal source of variation in outcomes. A detailed examination of the content of the training programs is thus required if we are to understand and account for the obtained results.

Table 4-9. *Differences in Laboratory Program*

	TOTAL NUMBER OF HOURS		HOURS PER WEEK		NUMBER OF MEETINGS	
	3-Week	2-Week	3-Week	2-Week	3-Week	2-Week
Training group	40.0	38.0	13.3	19.0	24.0	22.5
Information sessions	17.6	13.9	5.9	7.0	15.0	12.0
Discussion of back-home problems	12.0	0.0	4.0	0.0	7.5	0.0
Exercise	4.5	4.2	1.5	2.1	2.5	2.5
Other programs	4.8	1.6	1.6	0.8	3.0	1.0
Total	78.8	57.9	26.3	28.9	52.0	37.0

In making the change from three-week to two-week laboratories, the planners had to apply either a proportional reduction of all activities or a selective reduction of program elements considered expendable. Table 4-9 presents a synopsis of the programs that were run under the three-week and two-week formats. It is apparent that the T-Group was deemed the core of the program; the total time in the T-Group remains nearly constant in the transition. This emphasis on the T-Group was maintained with a sharp reduction of back-home problem discussion and other program features. While the three-week laboratory spent 12 hours of program time dealing with the application of training to the back-home situation, often with direct attention to an individual's specific problems, the two-week laboratory excluded this activity.

It is apparent that the duration variable in this study was not the only variable operating. The two-week laboratory was not simply a shorter version of the three-week laboratory; the two-week program was qualitatively different, including a greatly reduced emphasis on the application of laboratory learnings to the participant's ongoing organizational situation.

Since the two variables are confounded, the differences in the enduring changes made by the laboratory participants may be due to the duration variable or to the program differences or to some interaction between these two variables. While we cannot parcel out the effects of duration from those of program content, we must point out that the qualitative differences in the content of the learnings are consistent with the program differences. Overt, pro-active changes in the back-home setting following training are associated with training experiences which deal directly with application planning and practice. While one would expect quantitative differences in outcome to result from differences in the duration of training, the qualitative differences we found tend to emphasize the importance of the differences in program content. The specific program activities concerned with the transfer of training appear to have fulfilled a particularly important training function.

Edgar Schein's (Bennis, Schein, Berlew, and Steele, 1964; Schein and Bennis, 1965) analysis of the training process into unfreezing, changing, and refreezing components, based on the Lewinian (1958) model of change, provides a framework into which the results of this study can be integrated. Refreezing, or the stabilization and integration of changes, is postulated to occur primarily through two mechanisms: (1) integrating new responses into the personality; and (2) integrating new responses into significant ongoing relationships. The first mechanism is a legitimate one for the T-Group to foster. New behaviors, once tried and found advantageous, can be tested and interfused with other behaviors and aided by open and facilitative interpersonal relationships.

Although the T-Group is a significant factor in integrating new responses into the personality, it is often antithetical to the integration of new responses into the back-home situation. The emphasis on the immediate interpersonal relationships and the negation of outside social forces preclude the discussion of back-home problems. In addition, Schein and Bennis (1965) remind us that "the vulnerable point in maximally heterogeneous laboratories, as in the long residential laboratories, is that the learning produced may be personally meaningful but difficult to integrate back home." Organizationally relevant learning is not necessarily the same as personally relevant learning and in some cases they may not be compatible. Schein and Bennis (1965) offer the specific hypothesis that "the longer the laboratory, the greater the likelihood that what is learned will be out of line with back-home norms and values, hence the less the likelihood of its being relationally refrozen."

The specific position a person holds within the organization is another factor affecting the ease with which a laboratory participant will initiate changes. Matthew Miles (1965) found that a perceived change score correlated with the security and the power of the position a participant held in his home organization. Rather than being entrenched and committed to the extant structure and traditions of their organizational relationships, people who had secure and powerful positions were able to feel free enough to attempt new behaviors. Their position allowed them to be less pressured by the organizational demands for conformity to prelaboratory behavior. Merton's (1940) concept of the bureaucratic emphasis on reliability of behavior is a particularly important one for the designers of laboratory training to consider. For members of conventional complex organizations, the laboratory experience may be so different as to seem isolated and irrelevant to their organizational experience. When this happens, the impact of training is likely to be washed out upon their re-entry into the organization. The data presented in this study suggest that the participartion in specific back-home planning activities helps the trainees to cope with the organizational requisites for behavior consistency.

The findings of this research have important implications for the design of human relations training laboratories. Since 1961, when the two-week sample investigated here was drawn, the trend in laboratory design has been toward more emphasis upon the self-awareness and personal-growth aspects of the training experience. Cognitive inputs, skill exercises, and application practice and planning sessions have been sharply reduced, while the balance has shifted further toward T-Groups and other activities involving the exploration of the self. It follows that either the implicit objectives of training have shifted or that current practitioners assume that job-situated changes in behavior can be mediated sufficiently by the acquisition of insights and changed attitudes toward the self. Our analysis of these data tends to support Hobbs's (1962) well-reasoned argument that insight is not enough; at least not enough relative to the potency of direct application planning. These findings are also consonant with Bennett's (1955) conclusion that a clear decision to take a future action, along with consensual group support, increased the probability of implementation.

This paper does not report the final, definitive experiment on these issues. The fact that the independent variable of duration was drastically confounded by the differences in program content requires that we make the conventional caveat that further research is needed. The present evidence, however, strongly suggests that planning and action-practice lead to behavior change. If learning is to be transferred and integrated into the participant's organizational relationships, a program activity separate from the T-Group and aimed directly at facilitating the application of laboratory learning to the back-home setting should be included in training designs.

References

Bennett, Edith B. "Discussion, Decision, Commitment, and Consensus in Group Decision," *Human Relations*, 8, No. 3 (1955).
Boyd, J. B., and J. D. Elliss. *Findings of Research into Senior Management Seminars*. Toronto: Personnel Research Department, the Hydro-Electric Power Commission of Ontario, 1962.
Bradford, L. P., J. R. Gibb, and K. D. Benne. *T-Group Theory and Laboratory Method*. New York: Wiley, 1964.
Bunker, D. R. "The Effect of Laboratory Education Upon Individual Behavior," *Proceedings of the 16th Annual Meeting*, Industrial Relations Research Association, December 1963.
Bunker, D. R. "Individual Applications of Laboratory Training," *Journal of Applied Behavioral Science* 1, No. 2 (1965): 131–148.
Hobbs, N. "Sources of Gain in Psychotherapy," *American Psychologist*, 17, No. 11 (1962).
Lewin, K. "Group Decision and Social Change," in Eleanor E. Maccoby, T. M. Newcomb, and E. L. Hartley, *Readings in Social Psychology* (3rd ed.). New York: Holt, 1958, 197–211.

Merton, R. K. "Bureaucratic Structure and Personality," *Social Forces*, 18 (1940): 560–568.
Miles, M. B. "Human Relations Training: Processes and Outcomes," *Journal of Consulting Psychology*, 7, No. 4 (1960): 301–306.
Miles, M. B. "Learning Processes and Outcomes in Human Relations Training: A Clinical Experimental Study," in E. H. Schein and W. G. Bennis, *Personal and Organizational Change Through Group Methods: The Laboratory Approach*. New York: Wiley, 1965, 244–254.
Schein, E. H. "Personal Change Through Interpersonal Relationships," in W. G. Bennis, E. H. Schein, D. E. Berlew, and F. I. Steele. *Interpersonal Dynamics*. Homewood, Illinois: Dorsey Press, 1964, 357–394.
Schein, E. H., and W. G. Bennis. *Personal and Organizational Change Through Group Methods: The Laboratory Approach*. New York: Wiley, 1965.
Valiquet, M. I. "Contribution to the Evaluation of a Management Training Program." Unpublished Master's Thesis, Alfred P. Sloan School of Management, M.I.T., 1964.

A. K. RICE

From *Learning for Leadership*

There is an extensive literature on small-group characteristics and behaviour. I am concerned here with those aspects of group behaviour that arise from the unconscious forces contributed by the group members. A major contribution to the understanding of these forces has been made by Bion (1961). He has suggested that a group always behaves simultaneously at two levels. At the manifest level a group meets to perform a specific task; at the same time it behaves as if it had made one of three discrete assumptions: to reproduce itself: to obtain security from one individual upon whom its members can depend; or to preserve itself by attacking someone or something, or by running away. He distinguished these characteristics of group life as the *work group*, the group met to perform its specific task; and the *basic group*, the group acting on one of the discrete assumptions. The basic group met to reproduce itself he called *pairing*, the group met to obtain security from one person, *dependent*, and the group met to fight or to run away, *fight-flight*.[1]

A basic assumption is a tacit assumption; and members of a group behave *as if* they were aware of it, even though it is unconscious. Not only is participation in a basic assumption unavoidable, but in involves each member's sharing in the emotions to which he contributes. Bion postulated that the individual member of a group is affected disagreeably whenever he thinks or behaves in a manner at variance with the prevailing assumption.

In a group behaving simultaneously as a work group and as a basic group, conflict is therefore found between:
(1.) the basic group and the individuals who compose it;
(2.) the work group and the basic group;

Excerpts reprinted by special permission from *Learning for Leadership* by A. K. Rice. London: Tavistock Publications, 1965, pp. 12–13, 57–68. Copyright © The Tavistock Institute of Human Relations, 1965.

(3.) the work group suffused with the emotions associated with one basic assumption and the other repressed or denied basic assumptions.

The more a group manages to maintain a sophisticated level of behaviour, the more it uses the emotions with one basic assumption to suppress and control the emotions associated with the other two. Thus for a group involved in a fight the appropriate assumption that should be mobilized is "fight-flight," and the group uses this assumption to suppress and control "pairing" and "dependence." But if casualties mount the group may no longer be able to suppress the emotions associated with either reproduction or security, and its members may lose their stomach for the fight and the basic assumption may change.

The "internal world" of the small group is made up, then, of the contributions of its members to its work task and to its basic assumptions. At the level of task performance members take part as rational mature human beings; at the level of the basic assumption they go into an unconscious collusion that may support or resist performance of their manifest task. The resulting pattern of interpersonal relations is therefore one of cooperation and conflict between the members of the group as individuals and between them and the group culture they produce. The external environment of the group includes other individuals, groups, and institutions with which the group, as a group, has relationships. Leadership, however transient and changing, is required to control transactions between the group and its environment. If the prevailing basic assumption is appropriate to task performance, the work leader may also lead the basic group; but if the basic group is in conflict with the work group, a different internal leader may be required to give expression to the emotions associated with the prevailing assumption.

THE PRIMARY TASK OF THE STUDY GROUP

The purpose of the study group is to "provide an opportunity to learn about the interpersonal life of a group as it happens." The group's task is therefore defined as the study of its own behaviour in the "here and now."

Members of study groups are selected from heterogeneous backgrounds. So far as is possible, the members of a group do not already know each other, nor do they know the consultant, nor do they do the same kind of job. The intention behind the heterogeneity is to avoid importing into the study group any of the conventions or traditions that are characteristic of a particular way of life, or any predetermined relationships that would, at least in the beginning, affect the life of the group. The intention, in short, is that members of the group should all start from scratch in getting to know each other and in building an interpersonal life. It is seldom possible today to compose study groups of complete strangers each from a different kind of job. Experience indeed suggests that heterogeneity is perhaps less important than we once thought it, and we, as well as others, have worked with groups of close colleagues.[2] However, in a short conference in which time for any one series of events is severely limited, the greater the differences of age, sex, and job among the members of a group, the easier it is for them to find common ground in the task they have been set.

The consultant's job is to help the group to study its own behaviour as a group. He is not concerned with individual behaviour as such, except in so far as it is a manifestation of group behaviour. By this I mean that the consultant is concerned with what the group is doing—how it is using its members to further its own ends, be it to work at its task or to avoid it. The consultant's leadership is task-orientated; he, if nobody else, must keep to the task defined.

Experience of conferences shows that what is to happen in study groups is usually the major preoccupation of most members on arrival. It is the event that causes them most anxiety. Until they have dealt with this anxiety by testing the reality of study-group experience against their fantasy of it, they find it difficult to pay much attention to other events. Moreover, on entering any new situation, most individuals try to find some small group with which they can identify themselves while they come to terms with their human and physical environment. For these reasons the first study-group session is timed to take place as soon after the opening of the conference as possible. The second and when possible the third sessions then precede the introduction of any other event. Equally, however, because study groups are constructed specially for the purpose of studying group behaviour and hence have few, if any, parallels in everyday life, they are stopped before the end of the conference.

DISCUSSION IN THE STUDY GROUP

In spite of all that has been written and said about study groups, most members appear surprised and even embarrassed when, at the beginning of the first session of the group, they find that the consultant does not behave like a traditional discussion group leader. In the opening plenary the consultant has been introduced by name to the conference; the task of the group and his role have been defined, and both have been described in the literature sent out in advance. Members nevertheless appear to expect some kind of introduction from him, even if it is only an announcement that the session should start.

Though there are, of course, individual variations, most consultants start as they intend to continue. That is, they study the behaviour of the group, which includes their own contribution to it, and intervene only when they think that their intervention will illuminate what they believe to be happening. They therefore seldom speak until they have some evidence of behaviour on which to base what they have to say. At the beginning of a series of study groups, they can have little or no evidence about the behaviour of the specific group. Hence, they remain silent.

At the first session of one study-group series the group, most of whose members had heard or read about consultant behaviour in study groups, arrived, more or less together, a few minutes before the session was due to begin. I arrived as the last members were going in, and went straight to one of the armchairs that I had previously arranged in a circle. There were two or three low tables in the circle on which ashtrays had been placed. There was a lively chatter as the members sat down, moved the tables to more convenient places, asking each other if they smoked, moved again to allow two friends to sit next to each other (it was not completely heterogeneous). Gradually, the chatter died down, until at the time the session was due to start there was complete silence. It was as though everyone had not only been looking at his watch (I did not observe anybody doing so), but had previously synchronized it with every other one. The members turned to me. I remained silent. After a few seconds, the member sitting on my right suggested that everybody should introduce himself. He announced his name and the organization from which he came. He was followed by the member on his right, and so on round the group until the introductions finished with the member on my left. Before I could work out—and still less have time to say—what this meant in terms of group behaviour, in such a way that any comment I made could help the group to understand why it had ignored my non-participation in this way, two members started to discuss a particularly brutal murder that had taken place two days before, and was still front-page news in the daily press. Gradually, other members joined in, and the discussion, which was very serious, ranged over other similar crimes and on to capital punishment.

After fifteen minutes the discussion started to falter, contributions appeared to become forced, various attempts to revive the discussion by introducing new aspects of the incident and its implications were not taken up. Embarrassment grew, members found it difficult to look at each other, and started to look at me again. After about twenty minutes there was a silence and I made my first comment. I said that I felt that so far as the group was concerned I was the one who had been "murdered," in that I had been prevented from getting on with my task. I pointed out that the group had been discussing an external event and had paid little attention to what was happening "here and now," but that by their serious discussion they had made it difficult for me to intervene. I added that I felt that the faltering and embarrassment arose because members were feeling guilty about what they had done to me; but that they had done it to escape from the task they had met to perform. This comment was greeted with scorn and derision:

"We certainly haven't murdered you—what a way to talk!"
"I've never heard such nonsense. I'd just forgotten you were there."
"You were perfectly free to join in the discussion."

But I was not free to join in the discussion, except in so far as I believed that my contribution would be pertinent to the study of group behaviour. In Bion's terms, the prevailing assumption at the beginning was dependent; when I failed to take the role of leader of the dependent group, the member on my right stepped in; when that failed, a pair of members took over and the assumption was "pairing", but the lead they gave produced "flight." My comment turned this into "fight," with myself as the object of the hostility.

On another occasion at the start of a series of study groups the same lead was given—that is "let us introduce ourselves"—but at the end of the introductions there was another awkward and embarrassed silence. And while I was wondering what to say:

"Well, we didn't learn much from that—in fact I've forgotten most of the names already. I seldom do pick them up the first time."

So the members went round the group again, but not so systematically, asking each other questions: how to spell names, what each other's organizations did. This conversation died as the other had done, in embarrassed silence. Slapping his hands on the table (on this occasion we were in upright chairs round a table) a member said loudly:

"Well, that's cleared the decks!"

I commented that they had perhaps been cleared for a fight and that the fight was going to be against me for not doing what was expected of me—for not giving the kind of leadership they expected. I pointed to their hostility, shown by lack of support, to others who had tried to take a lead. The members individually and collectively denied they had any such feelings:

"*I* don't feel hostile, but I do feel afraid of what is going to happen. If only we had a clear purpose."
"We need to establish formalities to enable us to discuss."
"We're trying to find a common denominator. This is an unnatural situation. The trouble is that nothing is happening. There is nothing to study. We're not competing for a job or anything . . . (*a pause, in which tension in the group could be felt to mount*). We all look at Mr Rice . . . (*then another pause*). For God's sake somebody else talk!"

And the tension was broken by laughter.

Even though members have been told what their task is, they find the absence of the traditional leader, who will instruct them in how to tackle it—a task that is in reality difficult—worrying and even frightening. They feel as though they are being threatened by their lack of progress. Most groups struggle with this situation, and in the struggle seem able only to unite in hostility towards the consultant because he does little to relieve their distress. The assumption seems to be that he could help, if he would, and that it is only perversity on his part—or a trick, or manipulation—that stops him. He does not care enough for them, but when he suggests that they hate him for this:

"I don't understand what all this talk of hatred is about. I don't feel hatred for anybody here, not even for the consultant."
"It's nonsense, I don't hate him, but I think he should speak more often. After all he's paid to do that and we've paid to listen to him."

Later these expressions modify:

"I don't understand all this talk of hatred and hostility, but I certainly get irritated with the way he keeps on harping on the subject. I'd forgotten he was here. I was interested in the topic."
"He said he's not here to teach. I think he's here to enrich the Tavvy's experience."
"Hell, I didn't pay for that!"

These exchanges lead usually to more overt discussion of "leadership" and the qualities required of a leader. Invariably, the discussions become more abstract and intellectual:

"The leader has to personalize himself."
"A leader has to be a man of integrity; he has to create an organization."
"He has to see that the group gets on with its job, and provide the necessary equipment and knowledge to do it. If the group hasn't got it, it's his job to see that it is obtained."

If the consultant intervenes, as he does, to suggest that it is his leadership that is found wanting, he is in the early stages, either ignored or reassured. He is told that they are trying hard, but just have not got the knowledge. He is accused of holding back, or he is asked to elucidate some difficult point. Although it is not often said directly, he gets the impression that if only he would relent and give just a short dissertation on leadership, all would be well. Members show distress more openly, and when this happens others look at him with a "There, see what you have done." If he points out that the group is behaving as if it only had to produce a sufficiently moving case to make him try to do what he knows to be impossible, the group either gets angry with him or displays still more distress.

At some stage, particularly when he has prefaced some intervention with "I feel that . . .", he is brusquely told that his feelings are his own concern and that the group is not interested in them. As the sessions follow each other, there is occasionally an attempt, usually short-lived, to create a more familiar type of organization. Somebody suggests that a chairman and a secretary should be appointed, agenda and minutes prepared. Only one group that I have worked with has ever got to the point of electing members to these roles, and on that occasion only one said that he would accept office, but even he changed his mind before taking it:

"Don't we need a chairman to organize our discussions? He could bring out people and keep order."
"He could fertilize our discussion and direct it so that it doesn't wander."
"I was scared stiff when you suggested me for chairman. I knew just what you'd do to me if I accepted."
"How do you mean 'what we would do to you?'"
"You'd treat me as you've—I mean we've—treated Mr Rice, or anybody else who has tried to get us to work at our job."

With the failure of the members to sustain intellectual discussions either of group problems in general or of leadership problems in particular, and with their inability to arrive at any acceptable form of organization, there frequently follows a period of depression and hopelessness. There is nothing to be learnt from this exercise; "It is a waste of time" and "It was a mistake to come" are common remarks. Members often deal with the depression by making jokes and by maintaining a strenuous belief that silences are no longer disturbing:

"I visited the shrine of Cardinal Wolsey this afternoon."
"Well, we're not interested."

"Do psychiatrists put the price up when there is silence?"
"Would it be useful if I suggested . . ."
A chorus of "No!"
"It's strange, but I don't find it nearly so difficult to tolerate silence as I did at the beginning. I feel more at home with you all."
And when one member who had been silent for an unusually long time was asked why:
"I'm practising to be a consultant!"

Gradually, this kind of joking behaviour, interspersed with long and often discursive discussions about group process, about leadership in other situations, well-known leaders, religious conversions, the bringing up of children, usually leads to a more hopeful discussion about what has been learned: the toleration of silence, the relief at being able to express feelings more openly, the reassurance that their expression need not be destructive, that there is meaning in the study group:

"Let's list some of the things we've got from this group. For example, we know what we mean when we say a group fights or runs away; that it is dependent on its leader; that we let pairs try to find solutions for us; the group splits in different ways about different things, and different people take the lead, not necessarily those who should do. These very things happen back home in our boardrooms, departments, schools, and committees. If we have these things pointed out when we're experiencing them, they really mean something, they really come home."

At this stage I am accepted, even praised, as the "leader" who has brought this about. But this phase invariably takes place long before the end of the series. My refusal to go into collusion with the group in assessing how well it has done, and my interpretation of the "stock-taking" as an attempt to escape the end of the group before the end has been reached, frequently lead, after denials, to a discussion of the techniques of running groups. If I go on to point out that the group appears to be assuming that, because we know that "projection" takes place, we shall avoid it in future, the group tends to turn to an examination of my "skill" in taking groups. If I then take this up as an attempt to make me once more into the "good" leader, who will not let them go away empty-handed, there is either more joking or a further period of depression:

"What were we talking about that we were so keen to get on with?"
(*Silence*)
"We were talking about why we attacked and ran away, and why we didn't seem able to control it."
(*Silence*)
"Something about groups and individuals who make them up."
(*Silence*)

And even irritation and anger seem useless. The depression comes from the realization that there is no escape from work if group behaviour is to be understood. A renewed attack on me or on the conference as a whole is normal, but by now the attacks are more sophisticated, and the inquiry into their origin and form is more deliberate and penetrating. Members who take a lead are not "destroyed" so briskly and the reasons for dissatisfaction with their leadership are examined more closely. In one group a member said:

"I feel everything I thought I'd learnt has been useless; even what I thought I knew when I came seems of little value now."
—and she burst into tears. But when other members of the group tried to comfort her and to reassure her that she was good at her job:
"Don't be such fools. I can at least cry here and look at why I'm crying."

Not only is the group preoccupied with its ending, but feelings about it are the more intense because the group will finish before the end of the conference. By this time it is always difficult for members to accept the special nature of the study group and hence the reality of the need to finish it early; to acknowledge that it has only a limited value within the context of the conference. In this dilemma it is not unusual for members to say that the experience has been useless and has no value outside the conference setting, and that therefore the group can be disbanded without compunction or regret. But they find it difficult to accept that it can have been entirely useless when they have spent so much time in it. If by contrast, they believe it to have been a wonderful experience, then it should not end before it has to, that is, at the end of the conference. Hence, its ending is either a major act of hostility on the part of the staff of which the consultant is a member, or the members have been misled by the staff into thinking the group would be more productive than it has been—and this too has been the consultant's fault for not making it better. Study groups usually end with members having feelings both of relief at the end of a trying experience and of regret and mourning for something valuable that has been lost. But if, mixed with these feelings, there can be some work at what ending means, then perhaps the study group has achieved its aim.

CONSULTANT TO A STUDY GROUP

Most members of study groups attend them to learn about what happens in groups. They know that this means the study of their own as well as of others' behaviour. They know that their own behaviour will be exposed to the scrutiny of the consultant and of their fellow members. They suspect that, though the consultant will not comment on them as individuals, what he says will refer to them and may imply criticism of their past behaviour.

In the group the consultant has only his own observations and feelings to guide him. He can feel worried, rejected, angry, confused, and embarrassed; or he can feel calm, wanted, happy, and relaxed. He can ask himself why he is feeling as he is feeling, and judge what arises from within himself as part of his own personality make-up and what comes from the group, what the group is projecting upon him. He can ask himself what these expressions of feeling mean in terms of group behaviour, and why the group is treating him in this way. If he can explain his feelings, and why they have arisen, he may then be able to help the group to understand its own behaviour.

Inherently, the members of any study group must at times feel hostile to their consultant. By becoming members of a study group and by accepting his role, they are consciously or unconsciously accepting that they need to understand more about their own behaviour towards others and about others' behaviour towards them. Inevitably they must hope that their learning will be largely about others, and that any change they may feel they have to make in their own behaviour will not reflect on themselves, but only suggest ways of accommodating to the foibles of others. But whatever the rationalization, unconsciously they have to accept that they might have failed in the past. This acceptance in itself, as it is realized, can be felt as an affront to their self-respect. They are not likely to let it go without challenge. The consultant's job is to confront the group, without affronting its members; to draw attention to group behaviour and not to individual behaviour; to point out how the group uses individuals to express its own emotions, how it exploits some members so that others can absolve themselves from the responsibility for such expression.

As a group fails to get its consultant to occupy the more traditional roles of teacher, seminar leader, or therapist, it will redouble its efforts until in desperation it will disown him and seek other leaders. When they too fail, they too will be disowned, often brutally. The group will then use its own brutality to try to get the consultant to change his task by eliciting his sympathy and care for those it has handled so roughly. If this manoeuvre fails, and it never completely fails, the group will tend to throw up other leaders to express its concern for its members and project its brutality onto the consultant. As rival leaders emerge it is the job of the consultant, so far as he is able, to identify what the group is trying to do and to explain it. His leadership is in task performance, and the task is to understand what the group is doing "now" and to explain why it is doing it. Drawing attention to interesting phenomena without explanation is seldom used.

THE STUDY GROUP IN THE CONFERENCE

The only overt constraints placed on the study group are the definition of its task and the consultant's persistent attempt to refuse to do anything else. Members can do what they like. They frequently ask:

"Why don't we go and watch a football match, or talk about racing?"
"Why don't we take a walk in the country?"
"Why do we even bother to sit in this room?"

Nothing but group pressures and their own conscience is stopping them from doing anything they wish. No sanctions can be imposed. The only discipline is imposed on the consultant, who will not, if he is able to avoid it, go into collusion with the group to do anything other than study the behaviour of the group, and that only for the time laid down in the programme. He "controls the boundary" of the group, and thus provides security for the members in three ways: he stays in role; he starts and stops on time; and he maintains confidentiality.

In practice, members of study groups discuss almost anything from leadership as an abstract concept to the kind of leadership they are getting in their own group; from external events that have nothing whatever to do with their task to their own feelings for each other. Gradually, during the course of the conference, they learn that it is possible, in the study group, to express their feelings more openly and frankly than is usual in other groups; to question assumptions about value systems that it is difficult, if not impossible, to question in more conventional settings; and to build up a feeling of intimacy and security that here, in this group, they can be themselves without fear of the consequences. This is what usually gives rise to the euphoric feeling, part way through, of having learnt so much.

The first crack in this euphoria comes with the realization that the group will end, that death and coming to terms with it by adequate mourning are an essential part of any living experience. Members realize that after the end of the conference some of them may meet each other again, but that the group, as a group, will not survive the conference. If it is so valuable then some means should be found of making it live on. The reality that it will not calls into question the process by which such intimacy and such reassurance have been achieved:

"I'd never have believed this kind of feeling was possible—but what is it? I feel I know you all well, and you me, but to what end? Haven't we really been fooled all along?"

"I'll be glad when this session is over. The first time I've really felt like this."

"I think the (coffin) lid is down and screwed home, but are we right about the identity of the corpse?"

"It may be the consultant but I'm afraid it's the group."

"It's going to be a difficult grave to arrange. Whoever lies next to . . . will have an uncomfortable time. He's bound to turn."

"This feeling is as hard as a wall. Nobody dares to make a serious remark."

"There's not much time. Why do we stay here to the bitter end? There's good clean air outside."

In the study group members are face to face with a leadership that is neither destroyed by hatred nor rendered impotent by love. The consultant accepts a task responsibility and an authority that imposes no discipline on the members. He cannot impose any sanctions for failure to cooperate in task performance, nor, perhaps more importantly, can he reward good performance. Learning is its own reward; lack of learning its own punishment. It is for many members a new task, a new kind of authority, and a new kind of leadership, whose strength they can experience for themselves. They can defend it or attack it, imitate it or denounce it; they can learn from it.

The whole experience is within their grasp; nothing that happens outside the group is relevant to the task they have to perform. As a group they have no external environment to contend with; as individuals they have only each other and themselves. It is the most simple, and at the same time the most primitive and direct, experience of the forces that impinge on them when they lead and that they bring to bear on those who lead them.

In most conferences there are between twelve and fifteen study-group sessions, two or three of which take place before any other event is started. Thereafter members have to contend with an increasing number of different events. By contrast with experience of other events, study groups, when they are not in session, are frequently said to be warm and secure:

"You know where you are in a study group. You are intimate with everybody in it. It's safe to express your feelings there."

Thus, in spite of its impact, it is one of the conference events that provide protection for experiment in other situations. It is for this reason that, though study groups finish before the end of the conference, they continue beyond the ending of other "here and now" experiences. Ending them before the end of the whole is an attempt to ensure that if they have gained a false value—as comforting and secure—the test of the reality, the "let down," is taken in the conference itself, while members are still there, and have the staff and each other to help them to cope.

Notes

1. My own experience in groups, which started when I was a member of a Bion training group, makes me feel that pairing and dependence are, like "fight-flight," opposite poles of the same assumption. The dependent group has met to obtain security from an individual who can never satisfy the demands made on him; the pairing group in the hope of producing the new magical dependent leader, a hope that is always vain.

2. Chris Argyris, *Interpersonal Competence and Organizational Effectiveness*. Homewood, Illinois: Dorsey Press, 1962.

6

ROBERT R. BLAKE AND JANE SRYGLEY MOUTON

Some Effects of Managerial Grid Seminar Training on Union and Management Attitudes Toward Supervision[*]

a union is a significant variable in an organization's success in achieving production. Because union leaders must concern themselves with problems arising from supervision, it is important that union leaders and management understand each other's attitudes toward work. Even better is the situation where members of both reference groups hold in common a single set of values regarding sound supervision. Yet what little experimental work is available on differences in attitudes between union and management toward work demonstrates a lack of common outlook (Haire, 1955). For example, union leaders and managers differ in their attitudes on issues of industrial relations (Rim and Mannheim, 1964). Out of 17 items on a questionnaire concerned with socioeconomic ideology, supervisory and personnel policy, motivation of workers, and union role, there were significant differences between union and management attitudes on 11 of the items.

Many descriptions have been written of wage earner or union member attitudes toward management as the opposing force to labor, on the one hand, and on management as supervisors, on the other. Fewer descriptions seem to be available that reflect situations where union members and managers, through use of a commonly shared cognitive framework, have examined their own values about concepts of management.

Where discrepancies in attitudes toward the same thing exist between two

Abridged and reprinted by special permission. Vol 2, No. 4, pp. 387–400. The Journal of Applied Behavioral Science. Copyright © 1966 by National Training Laboratories, National Education Association of the United States, Washington, D.C.

groups who must work together, a key issue is how such attitudes can be changed if change is desired. The purpose of this study was to evaluate similarities and differences in attitudes between union and management members toward supervisory practices and the effects of a Managerial Grid Seminar (MGS) on these differences.

An objective of the MGS is, through study of the Managerial Grid, to assist managers to solve problems of achieving production through more effective use of people. Some effects of this training on management branches of several organizations have been studied (Blake and Mouton, 1963; Blake, Mouton, Barnes, and Greiner, 1964). Conclusions suggest that two important results are being obtained. First, organization profit is increased, probably to a significant degree. Second, individual managers find greater reward from their personal contributions to organization objectives, both in their dealings with other individuals and in their work as members of teams. As yet, training of those who are the recipients of supervision at the wage level has not been attempted. Logic compels the view, however, that a true organization integration of people and production occurs best when both those who are responsible for supervision and those who are supervised have a common set of ideas about sound supervision.

THE STUDY

An experiment was conducted in which the participants in two Seminars were from the management and union leadership of the same plant. A common frame of reference that would aid cooperation of the two groups was being sought. The purpose of the Seminars was to aid management personnel and union officers in gaining a fundamental understanding of modern behavioral science concepts concerning sound production-people relationships. This paper has to do with that experiment.

THE MANAGERIAL GRID

As a basis for appreciating the conceptual aspects of the training, the Managerial Grid is presented in Figure 6-1. It identifies five theories of managerial behavior based on two key variables found in organizations. One variable reflects concern for production or output (horizontal axis); the other, concern for people (vertical axis).

The 1,1 style represents minimum concern for production and people 1,9 denotes high concern for people at the expense of concern for production, and 9,1 denotes a high concern for production at the expense of people. 5,5 is a compromise style where people and production needs are balanced, while 9,9 represents maximum, integrated concern for both human relationships and production (Blake and Mouton, 1964).

HYPOTHESES

Discrepancies in Union-Management Perspectives Regarding Sound Supervision. Prior to training, union and management members are expected to hold

116   Individual Change Strategies of Social Intervention

different attitudes toward sound supervision. Managers are expected to score higher on 9,9 and 9,1 (high production orientations) than union officials; the union is expected to score higher on 1,9 and 1,1 (low production orientations) than management. No differences are predicted between union and management members in the size of the 5,5 scores.

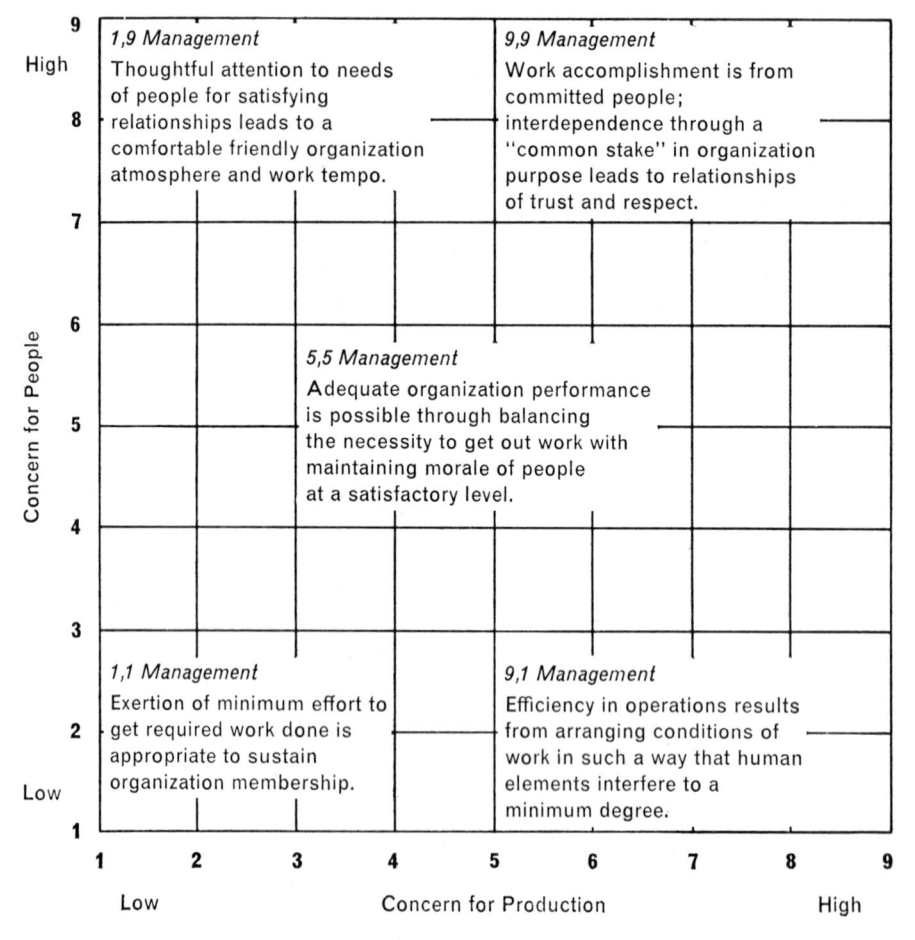

Figure 6-1. The Managerial Grid

The rationale is as follows. Management, having as its key responsibility the attainment of production, is more likely to support theories of supervision which have a high production orientation. These are 9,9 and 9,1. Union leadership, having as its key responsibility the representation of people rather than production, is likely to have a lower production orientation than management and thereby to embrace more strongly theories of supervision which do not have a high concern for production, i.e., 1,9 and 1,1. Since 5,5 is midway along these two dimensions, no logical basis of difference is afforded. Thus the prediction is one of no difference in scores.

Changes in Perspective. Both union and management members are expected to shift their attitudes toward supervision in the same directions in connection with the Seminar experience. The predicted directions of shift for both union and management members are increases in scores that contain a heavy emphasis on production (9,9 and 9,1) and decreases in scores for those styles which do not (5,5; 1,9; and 1,1). After the Seminar, participants are expected to prefer the integrated 9,9 Grid style to compromise or "either-or" solutions. Both management and union are also expected to see 9,1 in a more favorable light. For the union, the predicted change is based on the assumption that the pre-Seminar attitude of the union members is based on mistrust and misunderstanding of management goals which causes them to reject strongly management's production-centered goals and attitudes. The Seminar is expected to help clear up this and similar kinds of misunderstandings and mistrusts.

These predictions relate to what people think constitutes sound supervision. They do not relate to the kind of style characteristic of the individual completing the test.

METHOD

SUBJECTS

Of the 56 participants, 33 were management personnel and 23 union representatives. All key union executives such as president, secretary, or board members, plus additional union personnel such as stewards, with responsibilities beyond those of the average union member, were included. Managers were selected because of their core responsibilities for the management's side of the union-management relationship. They included the general manager, the assistant general manager, all department managers reporting to the general manager, and other line managers drawn from lower levels of supervision. Management and union each assumed responsibility for the selection of their own participants.

TRAINING

The design and execution of each of the two Seminars were identical. The prework distributed prior to the formal training calls for participants to complete a number of instruments of self- and organization examination as well as to read *The Managerial Grid* (Blake and Mouton, 1964). The learning situation was like that pioneered by NTL (National Training Laboratories, 1953). The significant changes from conventional laboratory training included (1) all activities as structured learning experiments and (2) heavy emphasis on learning to understand and use Grid theory as the basis for managing production-people relationships.

INSTRUMENT

The instrument used in the present study is entitled, *A Comparison Study of Personal Managerial Styles* (PMS) (Scientific Methods, Inc., 1962). The purpose of this forced-choice questionnaire is to assess beliefs concerning supervisory practices. Each of 40 items represents a problem situation of supervision. The two alternatives to each item describe different managerial attitudes toward the use of people in a production setting. To obtain these alternatives, each of the five prime Grid styles (9,9; 5,5; 9,1; 1,9; and 1,1) was paired with every other Grid style four times. Thus, every style is an alternative 16 times.

Three points are available to be distributed between the two alternatives so as to weight the degree of preference felt for one over the other. Equal weighting cannot be given to both. This instrument yields five scores, one for each of the Grid styles. Test-retest reliability is .86, and there is no correlation between subscores higher than $\pm.10$.

A sample item is:

When a subordinate disagrees, the manager should
    a—shift his position to maintain cooperation (1,9)
    b—see to it that the subordinate follows orders (9,1)

RESULTS

Similarities and differences in attitudes toward Grid styles are shown in Table 6-1 with pre and post means and standard deviations presented for both union and management. A horizontal reading points out differences between union and management for each Grid style.

DISCREPANCIES IN UNION AND MANAGEMENT PERSPECTIVES REGARDING SOUND SUPERVISION

The first hypothesis is that management makes higher scores on 9,9 and 9,1 than the union and that the union scores higher on 1,9 and 1,1 than the management. No differences in 5,5 scores are predicted.

Differences between union and management preferences for all styles were in the predicted direction. The average pretraining 9,9 score for management members (36.5) was significantly greater, than that for union members (31.7) ($p<.01$). The significance of the 9,1 trend, with the means being 24.1 for management and 22.2 for union, though not high ($p<.10$), is in the predicted direction.

On 1,9, the average union score of 22.1 versus the average of 19.5 made by the management ($p<.05$) is in the predicted direction. The average 1,1 score made by the union of 12.2 was significantly higher than the 1,1 average of 8.3 for the management respondents ($p<.05$).

A final confirmation of predictions is with respect to the 5,5 scores. Means for management and union were almost identical (31.5 versus 31.8), with the differences not significant. An interesting and unexpected difference in the 5,5 scores is the following. The SD for the union was almost twice as large as that for management. This pretraining difference is significant at the .01 level, suggesting that there was far more uniformity of attitude toward 5,5 among management members than among union personnel.

The first hypothesis is supported by these data. Management members

Table 6-1. Union and Management Attitudes Toward Various Managerial Grid Styles

GRID STYLE	TEST	MANAGEMENT[a] M	SD	UNION[b] M	SD	DIFF	T/
9,9	Pre	36.5	5.8	31.7	5.7	4.8	2.98**
	Post	42.4	5.3	33.7	5.3	8.7	6.20**
	Shift M	5.9	4.7	2.0	5.8	3.9	2.75**
	SD	4.7		5.9			
	t	7.20**		1.65			
5,5	Pre	31.6	3.5	31.8	6.7	−0.2	0.16
	Post	29.8	5.5	31.4	5.4	−1.6	1.10
	Shift M	−1.8	5.5	−0.4	5.4	−1.4	0.95
	SD	5.5		5.5			
	t	1.88*		0.34			
9,1	Pre	24.1	3.7	22.2	5.7	1.9	1.48
	Post	25.0	5.4	24.3	5.6	0.7	0.44
	Shift M	0.9	4.6	2.1	5.2	−1.2	0.93
	SD	4.7		5.5			
	t	1.08		1.87*			
1,9	Pre	19.5	5.0	22.1	3.7	−2.6	1.89*
	Post	15.6	3.6	19.4	3.6	−3.8	3.96**
	Shift M	−3.9	5.7	−2.7	4.7	−1.2	0.87
	SD	5.8		4.8			
	t	3.90**		2.67**			
1,1	Pre	8.3	4.4	12.2	7.4	−3.9	2.45*
	Post	7.2	3.3	11.1	6.9	−3.9	2.77**
	Shift M	−1.1	3.7	−1.1	7.1	0.0	0.03
	SD	3.7		7.3			
	t	1.62		0.75			

[a] N = 33   [b] N = 23   *p < .05   **p < .01

score higher than the union on Grid styles with a high production orientation (9,9 and 9,1) and lower than the union on Grid styles with a low production orientation (1,9 and 1,1). As predicted, 5,5, which is an intermediate or middle-of-the-road theory, was found to be accepted equally by both groups. These kinds of differences in viewpoint as to what constitutes sound supervision lie at the very core of the union-management relationship. In all probability they constitute significant barriers to union-management problem solving.

CHANGES IN PERSPECTIVE

Given the differences in outlook present before training, the next question is, "Were the shifts in attitude toward supervision production by the Seminar training consistent with the hypothesis regarding changes in perspective?"

The character of changes in outlook toward supervision can be seen by an examination of the columns of Table 6-1. In all ten comparisons, the trend of change is confirmed. Both management and union increase their scores on the production theories, 9,9 and 9,1. Both groups decrease their scores on the posttraining data for supervisory styles which do not place high emphasis on production—5,5; 1,9; and 1,1.

Generally, the magnitude of shifts in the management data is greater than that in the union data. The most significant shift for management is toward 9,9 with a *t* of 7.20. The next most significant is away from 1,9 with a *t* of 3.90. The most significant shift for the union is away from 1,9 with a *t* of 2.67, while the next most significant shift is toward 9,1 with a *t* of 1.87. The only significant difference between the management and the union was in 9,9. The management shift of 5,9 toward 9,9 was significantly larger than the union shift of 2.0 (p<.01). The conclusion that seems warranted from these findings is that while both groups had demonstrated a similar pattern in terms of direction of change, the absolute magnitude of change in the one most conspicuous area, that is, toward 9,9, was far greater for the management than for the union.

The item changes concur strongly with the results and conclusions drawn from an analysis of the total scores. Table 6-2 exhibits results from the item-by-item analysis of direction of change on items of significant change (p<.10) by management and union.

Table 6-2. *Significant Item Shifts Made By Union and Management*

Changes away from Grid styles	Changes toward Grid styles					Total number of changes from Grid styles*
	9,9 U M	5,5 U M	9,1 U M	1,9 U M	5,1 U M	U M
9,9	——					0 0
5,5	1 2	——	1 1			2 3
9,1	0 2		——			0 2
1,9	2 4	0 2	1 1	——		3 7
1,1	0 2	1 0	2 1	1 0	——	4 3
Total Number of Changes Toward Grid Styles	3 10	1 2	4 3	1 0	0 0	Total Number of Changes 9 15

* The maximum number of shifts in one style (toward plus away from any style) is 16.

The general trend of results was consistent with the predictions. Of the 24 changes, 22 were away from 1,9; 5,5; and 1,1; and 20 were toward 9,9 and 9,1. As predicted, the items which received the greatest increases were first, 9,9 and second, 9,1. The managerial theories which underwent the greatest reduction in preference were first, 1,9 and second, 1,1.

SUMMARY

Two one-week Seminars were participated in by 33 managers and 23 union members from the same plant. A forced-choice questionnaire assessed union and management beliefs concerning supervisory practices.

Each of the major findings of this investigation is presented below:
(1.) Management and union views differed significantly both before and after training. Managers scored higher on styles of supervision with a high emphasis on production (9,9 and 9,1) and lower on styles with a low concern for production (1,9 and 1,1) than did the union.

(2.) Both union and management attitudes changed as a result of the Seminar.
   a. Both groups moved toward 9,9 and 9,1 supervisory attitudes and away from 5,5; 1,9; and 1,1.
   b. The management's attitudes changed more as a result of training than did the union's.

The general conclusion may be drawn from the results of the experiment that there are basic differences between union and management points of view about what constitutes sound supervision. These provide a potential source of friction when the two groups confer on their common problems. Both groups did change their views in the same direction as a result of the MGS. The character of change is toward increased endorsement of the production orientation and increased rejection of the people orientation, except under the integrated 9,9 style. The Seminars, then, served as a means of attitude change. They also provided the union and management participants with a constructive cognitive framework within which to understand and attempt to improve their relationship.

Note

* Assistance in the preparation of this selection was provided by Linda Green Bell.

References

Blake, R. R., and Jane S. Mouton. "Improving Organizational Problem Solving Through Increasing the Flow and Utilization of New Ideas," *Training Directors Journal*, 17, No. 9 (1963): 48–57; No. 10: 38–54.

Blake, R. R., and Jane S. Mouton. *The Managerial Grid*. Houston, Texas: Gulf, 1964.

Blake, R. R., Jane S. Mouton, L. B. Barnes, and L. E. Greiner. "A Managerial Grid Approach to Organization Development: The Theory and Some Research Findings," *Harvard Business Review*, 42, No. 6 (1964): 133–155.

Haire, M. "Role Perception in Labor-Management Relations," *Industrial and Labor Relations Review*, 8, No. 2 (1955): 204–216.

National Training Laboratories. *Explorations in Human Relations Training*. Washington, D. C.: the Laboratories, 1953.

Rim, Y., and B. F. Mannheim. "Factors Related to Attitudes of Management and Union representatives," *Personnel Psychology*, 17 (1964), 149–164.

Scientific Methods, Inc. *A Comparison Study of Personal Managerial Styles*. Austin, Texas: The Company, 1962.

7

CHARLES H. KEPNER AND BENJAMIN B. TREGOE

Developing Decision Makers

In this article we are going to describe a new and different approach to developing decision-making abilities. This approach has been practiced and refined in a wide variety of companies. If you could sit in on one of the training sessions, you would not at first notice executives and managers doing anything very different from what they usually do on the job. They would be sitting in the same offices and at the same desks where they usually sit. They would be getting information over the telephone, in the mail, and in conference. They would be discussing problems with many of the same men they ordinarily talk with. And, as always, they would be making decisions.

But after a while you would notice that there are differences. For example, while the particular problem under consideration would be *like* the problem managers have every day, it would not actually have come up in company operations, having been created for the special purpose of an exercise in decision making. Moreover after reaching a decision on it, the managers would go into special session with a course leader (who would have been monitoring their conversations) to review what they did and analyze how they could have done it better. Later on, they would go on to tackle another problem in very much the same way.

Since this approach is such a new one in concept, we shall first examine the need for it. What is the object of training? What kinds of experiences make for real learning? Why do not other methods *fill* the need, even though they may help a great deal? After looking at questions like these, we shall then turn to the principles and mechanics of the new approach as it is being practiced today in a number of firms.

Abridged and reprinted by special permission. Vol. 38, No. 5, pp. 115–124, *Harvard Business Review*. Copyright © 1960 by the President and Fellows of Harvard College.

PRESSING NEED

When an executive makes a decision, he commits his organization in some degree to a course of action. If the decision is a poor one, his company will suffer accordingly. All of his art in working with people to implement his poor decision will only extend and perpetuate the effects of his inadequacy as a manager. Nothing that he can do will change the situation much until the decisions themselves are improved.

Can an executive develop his abilities to make effective management decisions except through the process of making good ones and bad ones over a long period of time? Many managers are emphatic in saying that they doubt it. And they can point to good evidence to back them up. Short cuts and easy ways to executive excellence in decision making have been notably unsuccessful. Experience still appears to be the best teacher of this most basic management skill.

EXPERIENCE AS A TEACHER

Most managers agree that they have learned their most important lessons from experience, rather than from being told what to do or from talking or reading about decision making. Why is experience such as effective teacher?

For one thing, something learned from experience is seldom recalled as an isolated and unique insight. Because the lesson is learned from a concrete situation it is easier to see how it might apply in similar situations. Also, lessons from experience are incontrovertible: this event actually took place, this actually was done, and these were the results. Something else *might* have been done but this is what *did* happen.

But these things are true only of experiences which have made their point. Not all experiences produce such outstanding effects. If they did, one week of normal management activity would make a past master out of any man—and, of course, this is definitely not so. Much experience seems to be flat and unprofitable.

Look back on your own experiences that were helpful. Chances are you will find that each of them involved a decision which had to be made. You were in a position to take action and you did. And, most important, you found out the results of your actions so that you could analyze and evaluate what you had done, what went right and what went wrong. You could then modify your approach to the problem and improve on it. You had evidence on which to base your assessment of success.

Now look back on your experiences which did *not* give you new insight into the decision-making process. The trouble may have been that you were not ready for the experience. You were caught by surprise. As a result, you were unprepared to bring any new ideas to bear on the problem but dealt with it just as you had in the past. Or the situation itself may have been so confused that you could not take immediate decisive action. Lines of authority and responsibility were not clear. And even when you did take action, there was no feedback to tell you the results of your performance. You did what you thought appropriate, and it was like dropping a feather down a well in the dark—no splash, no sound, no way of knowing what effect, if any, your best-intentioned action might have produced.

Unfortunately, most real-life decision-making experiences are of this latter sort. Feedback on the results of action taken is extremely slow in coming and never very clear even when available. *Moreover, when there is feedback at hand to tell us that a decision was inadequate, it is usually next to impossible to determine the specific weakness in procedure that was responsible for the failure.*

ESSENTIAL CONDITIONS

We might generalize about all this as follows. Looking at good and poor learning experiences, and *considering any learning situation*, there are three essentials which must be present:

(1.) New ideas, new skills, or new ways of approaching old ideas and skills.
(2.) An opportunity to put these innovations into practical action.
(3.) Feedback as to the results of the actions taken, and the relationship between what was done at each step of the way and the end result.

To put it in another way, there can be no learning if there is nothing new to be learned. Given new ideas, there can be no learning of any consequence if there is no opportunity to put these into practice. And having put them into practice, there can be no learning about the appropriateness and utility of the ideas if there is no feedback as to the results of having used them. The kind of feedback provided is critical, for it will determine the kind of learning that takes place. It is not enough to know that the end results were poor. The feedback provided must also enable the learner to see how the specific procedures and actions contributed to the final outcome.

Stated positively, the best approach to learning of any kind will be the one which provides all three essentials in the greatest degree for the least expenditure of time, effort, and money.

MAKING EXPERIENCE WORK

We must try to create realistic situations in which the manager can learn new ideas, practice putting them to work, and see the results quickly.

This kind of experience *can* be made to order. To illustrate what can be done, here is a telephone conversation between two of four men who are beginning to deal with a fairly typical crisis situation—defective products in the field. This situation has been created as the practice phase of a training program embodying the three essentials of learning. The four men involved have taken on the responsibilities of the division general manager of a company and his heads of production, of sales, and of purchasing and shipping. Each has a number of intra- and inter-departmental memos, letters, reports, forecasts, and other data on his desk in his office, such as he might normally receive. These pose the crisis which the man must correct. The following exchange takes place between the division chief and the production head:

"Hello, production. This is the general manager. Say, what's the story on those rejects on line 1?"

"We've had an increase in rejects but not enough to account for the customer complaints which sales has been on my back about."

"Customer complaints! What complaints? You mean some of the rejects have gotten past quality control out into the field?"

"Sales just called in a panic. He said he just got word that some of the product is defective in the California area and sales have fallen off as a result. Complaints are that the thing is buckling and sagging, and dealers want replacements. It could be tied in with the reject problem, but we've got that licked now. Definitely."

"We'll play hell making replacements out of inventory. I got a report from the warehouse. Some inventory levels are critically low as a result of the rejects from your production changeover. You better call purchasing and shipping and see how you can get those inventories up. I'm going to get hold of sales and get the whole story. On second thought, maybe the four of us had better get together in my office and nail this thing down so we can see what has to be done about it."

This is not play-acting, and it is not a game. The men are working in a real business setting, on a problem that is just like a real one, and with information in the same form in which it comes in real life. The participants must use every bit of skill and understanding they have to make the best decisions they can. Each of them is working under an impelling sense of urgency which will not let up until the matter has been settled one way or another.

What is more, they must use the channels of communication normally open to them—inter-office telephone and face-to-face meetings. They need not guess at a hidden theory of business but rather must use the information provided them about a concrete situation concerning specific products and events. Their task is to use this information as efficiently as possible to analyze the situation and recognize the problems facing them, to determine what is wrong, and to resolve the difficulty.

FEEDBACK SESSIONS

After the crisis is over and they have made their decisions and set the necessary courses of action into being, they can examine their performance in a critique session in a way that is never possible on the job. They can analyze their decisions and the information and assumptions that went into them in light of all of the information that was available. This feedback can be provided by the course leader, who has monitored their conversations and who knows all of the information that is available to the four of them.

The feedback critique session is the heart of this method for providing controlled experience. The management situation with which they have dealt is essentially what might be called a "closed" system of information about the company and the crisis which has arisen. What has gone into the situation is known, and also what has come out of it as decisions made and courses of action selected is a matter of record.

It is therefore possible to lay bare what was done by the managers to arrive at these decisions and actions. The information used and how it was used stand in sharp contrast to the total information available and complete knowledge

of the situation. The decisions made were either based on an adequate assessment of the situation and a complete use of the information, or they were not. Questions like these are discussed in the critique session:
- What were the assumptions that were made about the situation?
- What information was not used and why not?
- How efficiently was the available information communicated?
- How did the general manager go about co-ordinating the efforts of his people, and what were the effects of his actions?
- What might he have done?
- Were procedures for handling the crisis adequately set out, or did things just happen?
- Were the consequences of the decisions made properly considered?

In other words, the experience is systematically turned inside out to provide the managers with complete feedback on their performance.

ASSIGNMENTS ROTATED

In the next session these four men will be facing other management problems, perhaps an organizational problem, or one of inventory control, or one involving the choice of a new product line. A top staff function may be represented on the team next time. Each man will be responsible for operating a different functional area of the business in the next session, and another one of the four will take over as general manager. By rotating through various functional positions in the company during a series of controlled experience sessions, each man has an opportunity to look at typical management problems and decisions from a number of different points of view which complement his normal on-the-job responsibilities.

THE APEX COMPANY

We shall turn at this point to the program that we have been helping a number of companies to carry out. Because it has been tested in such a wide variety of situations, it offers the best opportunity to see the new approach "in action."

The managers are given a short briefing just prior to the beginning of the problem. The concepts that apply to this case are stressed, and ground rules are gone over in detail. The managers go into the session knowing what they are expected to learn from it and what they will be required to do. They are as fully set and prepared to gain from the experience as possible.

The managers then receive the exercise material, which sets out what has happened in Apex over the last few days. There are memos from within their own departments, from other departments, or from outside the company. There are policy directives, requests for information, financial statements, production and sales records, and other information which would realistically come their way on the job. For example:

- The sales manager might have the latest sales forecasts, a report on last week's finished product inventory from distribution, a "wire" from one of his district managers in the field, cost estimates on a new product line for pricing purposes, and other relevant information.

• The production manager may know nothing about sales forecasts but would have the latest quality control reports, manufacturing cost break-downs, and overtime records.

Of course, some of the information of division-wide interest would be routed to all the managers. Such data would describe the immediate situation confronting each man and pose the problems to be solved.

Each man takes this material to his own or to an assigned office. He reads through the information, organizes it, takes notes, or does whatever he normally would do in a similar real-life situation. The men cannot expect to find a slip of paper neatly labeled, "This is a problem, solve here." Problems do not appear this way in real life or in the Apex Company. Most problems appear first as seemingly unrelated bits of information which take on meaning as these pieces are put together. And this is the way they appear to the four members of the Apex management team.

ORGANIZATIONAL SETUP

Two years ago we created the "Apex Company" as a vehicle for the controlled experience approach to developing decision-making skills. It is a company of about 400 people. It has two divisions, commercial and military products. It is small enough to be readily grasped by the managers assigned to it, yet large enough to embody the kinds of business problems faced by much bigger organizations. Its products are easily visualized. Its plan of organization is relatively clear-cut and provides both line and staff functions.

Our purpose is not to present an organization in complete detail. It is not our aim to indoctrinate managers in the particular methods and philosophies of the Apex Company as a model business. Unlike the computer game, it is not the business itself which is of interest but the way in which managers use the information provided them in making their decisions. Almost any business, conducted according to almost any set of policies, would serve as the necessary setting within which to solve problems.

Four managers work in the Apex Company at one time and manage either the commercial products division or the military products division in the various sessions. Each of the four is assigned to a different functional position in the division and is responsible for the operation of that area. Some of the positions to which the men are assigned are division manager, production manager, sales manager, distribution manager (a function including purchasing, shipping, and inventory control), finance, and industrial relations. They include both line and staff. The four positions to be filled in each session are not the same; however, there is always a general manager.

HOW MANAGERS PREPARE

Each session consists of two groups of four men. Each group is confronted with the same information and is working on the same situation but independently of each other. Each man receives a chapter of study materials to absorb on his own time before taking part in each problem session. These materials provide him with a set of concepts and techniques which he will use in the experience. Each man also receives in advance background information on the company, the division which he will be operating, and the department he will manage.

GOING INTO ACTION

As the managers go through the materials, they begin to see their part in the crisis facing Apex. They become aware of the actions called for by them in dealing with the crisis situation. When they have assimilated the information, they reach for the interoffice telephone and begin the task of managing Apex.

They talk over the phone with the other department managers, ask for or give information, set procedures, coordinate activities, give orders, make decisions, and do anything else they feel is appropriate to the situation. They may decide to call a conference if they wish and use it as they normally would in the course of day-to-day operations. They draw on whatever skill and understanding of management they can muster.

Moreover, because they have only one and a half hours, they work under a real time pressure and sense of urgency. This means that each step in dealing with the information must be carefully approached and well thought out. They must coordinate their actions and communicate effectively. If they have a conference, they must use it well or valuable time is lost. As in every crisis situation, they must get the most out of the information they have available within a limited amount of time if they are going to make the best decisions. (They cannot have access to more information than is initially provided.) This is never an easy task. It takes the urgency of a crisis to put the spotlight on decision-making deficiencies.

The controlled experience situations are put together so that the cause of the major problems confronting Apex can be determined *if the information is used effectively.* As in real life, if the decision is based on an inadequate analysis of the problem and its cause, the decision will be effective only through chance. If it is based on a good analysis, management has done all that can be asked of it (even though in actuality chance may later upset the decision).

This is not to say that there is only one possible decision that is adequate. The situation is too complex for that. Given a satisfactory determination of the cause of the problem, there are any number of courses of action available to the group depending on such factors as long and short-range considerations, or their estimate of potential consequences. They must use their experience, judgment, and skill in evaluating the courses of action available to them.

By the time the exercise is terminated, after about an hour and a half or two hours, the men have pretty well decided what to do, how to do it, and what instructions to issue.

RECONSTRUCTION AND REVIEW

The eight members of the two Apex management teams then return to the conference room for a critical evaluation of their performance. In the critique, conducted by the course leader, the men probe into their own performance and that of their whole management team also. They reconstruct the situation and trace out their decisions step by step. They examine the assumptions they have made and the ways in which they interpreted and used the information available to them. They uncover the information they did not use but should have used. The emphasis is on how good the decisions they made were in light of the total situation. What facts *might* they have seen that were not seen? What improvements *might* have been made that were overlooked?

The course leader can help in this reconstruction and provide feedback on the information that was available but not used since he knows all the facts. He also has the advantage of having monitored the telephone calls during the session and having sat in on any meetings that were called. He is in a good position to spot that behavior which may have stood in the way of effectively getting out and using the information in the team's approach to the problem.

When the data come out in the critique discussion and the managers see the actual cause of the problem they were tackling, they have a yardstick against which to compare their own use of the information and the approach they took. They can assess what actually was done against what might have been and what should have been done.

NEW INSIGHTS FOR MANAGERS

It often comes as a shock to seasoned managers to realize how unsystematic their approach has been to a complex managerial problem. They find, for instance, that they have tended to jump to conclusions without examining all of the information available to them. They find that they have tended to move toward setting corrective action before they are sure exactly what the problem is with which they should be concerned. They find that their efforts usually end in an impasse when their approach to the information has not been rational.

Robbed of their customary crutch of "experience in the job" and precedent, they see that perhaps they have been trying to manage without getting all the information out or without thinking through what the problem is that must be solved, what is causing the problem, and what it is they hope to achieve with corrective action. Indeed, they are likely to find the first exercise a somewhat shattering experience. From that point forward they tend to become much more thoughtful in their approach to the management of Apex. They become more aware of the assumptions they make, of the procedures they use in arriving at decisions, and of the consequences which those decisions bring into being. They begin to look more shrewdly over their shoulders at their own methods as they go through the decision-making process, and they begin to become critically, aware of how they are performing.

It invariably turns out that the two management teams have approached an identical situation in different ways. Different information has been considered or overlooked and different assumptions have been made. Very frequently someone on one of the two teams will ask, "Are you sure that we were working on the same problem that they were? It can't be, because the outcome looks so different!"

It is very revealing to see such a divergence. Comparing the two approaches helps in getting a more complete picture of all the information available. It highlights differences in procedure, in setting objectives, in the assignment of importance to items of information. It also reveals interesting differences in the way each general manager operated in the situation. Did he delegate, coordinate, or take over the solving of the problem? Just what *was* his function, and just what *were* the responsibilities of his subordinates to him?

Feedback in the critique is direct and unequivocal. The managers have done their best in a difficult situation. They have drawn on their full range of skill and ability. If their performance has been anything less than perfect, it seems clear that they need to improve the *way* they are managing. By examining how they arrived at any imperfect decisions they have made, they can see the kind and amount of change that is necessary if they are to be more effective. It is common to hear a participant wryly say, "Now I know why I have that trouble on the job," or "This is what I do all the time, but I never knew it before."

Best results are obtained if the focus can be changed somewhat from session to session in a company. In the Apex program, for example, in one session major stress will be on recognizing problem situations and getting out the information to specify these problems adequately. In another the focus will be on the process of determining the problem's cause as a basis for action. Another one highlights the procedures for effectively working with complex quantitative and qualitative data in the weighing and evaluating of alternative courses of action. Still another requires that controls be established for the successful implementation, the maintenance, and the potential modification of a decision that has been made.

PROGRESS ON THE JOB

What difference does the new approach make in the way a manager carries out his job? Are the insights he gains at the critique sessions of such a nature that they can—and will—be *applied* in his later work?

Follow-up evaluations reveal that participants believe they have practiced what they learned. They report that they applied the gains at once in their operations. More specifically:

• *Managers report that they have become acutely aware of how they deal with information in solving problems and making decisions.* Habits of dealing with information, built up over many years, come in for close scrutiny in the review sessions. The detailed feedback allows the managers to study implications of their methods of operation for the first time, and the results are sometimes painfully dramatic. Here are two reactions from executives:

"I suddenly realized in the session that I was doing exactly the same thing on the job—I was tending to include an assumption of the cause of the problem right in the statement of the problem. I would overlook other possible causes until too late."

"For years I have been saying, 'We need more information before we can make that decision.' And I said the same thing while working through this Apex problem. But in the feedback session I discovered that we *did* have enough information to make a good decision—and we simply hadn't used it efficiently. I wonder how many times I've made that same mistake on the job."

• *Managers report a greater awareness of their methods and procedures of approaching decisions on the job.* Here is a typical comment:

"I find myself asking a lot more questions. Do I really know what the problem is? Do I have all the information I need, or am I overlooking something?"

Still others mention that they frequently catch themselves thinking: "Wait a minute. That's just where I fell on my face in Apex. I'd better make sure I've really assessed the consequences of this."

• *As a result of this more critical approach, executives think they now manage with less backtracking and greater efficiency.* One general manager reported that when his men who have participated come to him with a matter which calls for his review, they have all the information ready and organized in a way they never had before.

• *Because they have a clearer conception of problem solving and decision making, many managers mention that they are able to make more efficient use of their subordinates.* They are in a better position to coach their people and to help them improve their procedures on the job. And this makes sense, because it is difficult to point out to a man how he approaches a problem and decisions if there is no recognition of what goes into decision making.

• *A great number of the comments in follow-up evaluations deal with improved communications and abilities to work with other managers.* To quote a few comments:

"I have had much better communications with [the others who participated in the same training] than I have ever had before. Things have gone much more smoothly as a result."

"Rotating through various spots in the Apex organization has given me a better feeling for the need for information of the guy on the other side of the fence. This has helped me in communicating on the job."

• *Many managers, even those in small, closely knit organizations, are impressed by how much better they get to know the other managers with whom they work.* They feel that this increased knowledge provides the basis for improved working relationships on the day-to-day job.

A number of companies have also credited the intensive Apex experience with leading to improvements in methods and products. A set of important production controls was developed in one firm as a result of rethinking a problem which had been plaguing management for some time. Conscious application of the methods developed in the discussions resulted in a marked reduction of overhead costs in another instance, in the designing of some universal tooling device in another, and in the reduction of a bid by 30 percent in still another.

CONCLUSION

To put the new approach in perspective, now that its content is clear, let us compare it with some of the other training concepts that have proved themselves:

How does it compare with the case method? There are some obvious similarities. For example, both the new approach and the case method focus on concrete situations. Also, both stress what the participant can teach himself from the experience.

But in the Apex approach the managers do not analyze what is going wrong and what should be done from the position of the outsider. They are themselves part of the case. They are there. What is more, the decisions they make are reviewed, soon after the making, against the decisions that they could have made if they had had a better grasp of the situation and had fully used what was available to them. And the impact of one decision over the telephone or in conference can be seen on other decisions and actions leading up to the final disposition of the problem. (How that final decision would have affected the company cannot, of course, be known for sure—but the managers can make some good guesses in the critique sessions.) This feedback information comes while the live case is still fresh in the executive's mind, so that there is the greatest possible opportunity to learn.

How does the new approach compare with role playing? The fact that each participating manager may be responsible for an area of the business other than his normal one may suggest to some that this is a role-playing session. However, the fact that a man is responsible for a job different from the one he normally holds does not really make his action role playing any more than job rotation could be termed role playing.

The major distinction has to do with limits on the use of information. In real life *and in Apex*, a manager can only use the information he has available to him, that which he can gain from someone else or which he has available from experience. He cannot make up information as he goes along. By contrast, in role playing the stage is set for the participants and they act out the situation, bringing in as much information as their imaginations will allow.

This distinction is critical because of its implications for the critique of performance. Since the information is generated during the session in role playing, it is not possible to have a grasp of the total body of information available and to consider how effectively it was used. There is no control over what goes into the session. It is only possible to discuss the feelings of the participants. This limitation does not hold for the Apex approach. The latter allows analytical discussion of communication and the process of decision making *as well as* of the feelings of the participants in the situation.

In sum, all these management development techniques are designed to give the executive something he can take back to his work and use. The critical questions are: What happens back at his desk? How much does he take back with him? How usable is it? How long does it last?

Our experience leads us to believe that the executive will carry away permanently useful and usable knowledge from a management development experience only to the extent that the experience gives him all three essentials for learning—

new ideas and skills, practice in using them, and feedback on the results and how his specific actions contributed to them.

FUEL FOR SELF-IMPROVEMENT

The approach described in this article was designed as a highly efficient way of combining these three essentials of learning into a controlled experience for the improvement of decision-making abilities. While the combination seems to be a very effective one, it does not, of course, constitute a cure-all. There are no panaceas in management development. Old managers do not change into paragons of executive virtue overnight.

What the Apex series does is provide a set of situations from which the manager can gain illuminating insights into decision making and the quality of his own performance. Continued development must come through coaching and on-the-job analysis of his daily performance. The series of controlled experiences in which he has taken part does not remove from him the responsibility for self-evaluation and self-development. But it does provide him with the kind of information that makes his further progress more assured.

8

NORMAN R. F. MAIER AND LESTER F. ZERFOSS

MRP: A Technique for Training Large Groups of Supervisors and Its Potential Use in Social Research

*h*uman relations skills are difficult to learn merely through reading or by hearing lectures. To be effective, training in the skills must be accompanied by attitude and feeling changes. A supervisor who does not respect his employees will have difficulty in practicing effective methods because his approaches will not hide his basic attitude. It is because skills and attitudes are so interdependent in personnel work that training methods must incorporate both.

One of the important approaches in the improvement of supervisors is that of increasing their employees' participation in the solving of some of the day-to-day problems. Many employees are distrustful of changes in the job, and there frequently is a feeling that the supervisor plays favorites and discriminates against others. Techniques of selling employees on changes that affect them, and the usual procedures designed to develop fair practices, usually fail to solve these attitudinal problems (Coch and French, 1948; Lewin, 1947). It is exactly in these areas that employee participation seems to be most valuable and for which the group decision method (Bradford and Lippitt, 1945; Lewin, 1947; Lewin, Lippitt and White, 1939; Maier, 1948) (in which the supervisor shares his problem with his group) has been developed.

Reprinted by special permission. Vol. 5, No. 2, pp. 177–186, *Human Relations*. Copyright © 1952 The Tavistock Institute of Human Relations.

However, there is a great deal of resistance on the part of supervisors to sharing work problems with their groups because they feel they are giving up something in the process (Maier, 1949). In order to overcome this resistance, new types of training methods are needed. These new methods require that supervisors learn through participation because they, like rank and file employees, also shy away from changes that effect them.

Discussion meetings (Coch and French, 1948; Maier, 1948; Maier, 1949) and role-playing procedures (Bavelas, 1947; Bradford and Lippitt, 1945; Lippitt, Bradford, and Benne, 1947) are two of the best participation training methods. However, their nature is such as to limit their uses to training in small groups. In training large groups it has been necessary to confine one's procedures to lectures, visual aids, movies, and demonstrations. None of these approaches permits active participation and practice. An audience participation technique, recently developed by Donald Phillips (Lippitt, Bradford and Benne, 1947), has received a high degree of acceptance in industry. It is one of the first methods to permit small group discussions within the general framework of an audience situation. The procedure, often referred to as "Phillips 66," accomplishes general participation by dividing the audience into committees of six, each of which holds a discussion for six minutes on some specific question previously put to them. The major limitation of the Phillips 66 method is that the subject-matter to be used for discussion is limited in scope, and it can only be adapted to certain types of situations.

Recently, we have tested a procedure at The Detroit Edison Company which combines the role-playing approach with Phillips 66, and which may be described as Multiple Role Playing (MRP). This method permits role-playing to be carried out in such a manner that all members of a large audience can participate. The purpose of the technique is to give each member of an audience a first-hand experience in the group decision method. It permits the training of supervisors in skills of leading discussions and at the same time gives them an experience of the way things appear to employees, by finding themselves placed in the employee's position. Training supervisors to use group decision requires that they develop: (1) confidence in the way employees behave when given an opportunity to solve job problems, and (2) skill in putting a problem to the group. The MRP method serves in both of these capacities. The experiences obtained in these group discussions give the participants an opportunity to discover that the way employees behave depends greatly upon the kind of situation the supervisor creates. Thus, both the attitude of the supervisor and his skill in leading the discussion directly determine the outcome of the conference. Participants who function as employees see the errors that the supervisor makes and discover how their own reactions are influenced by the situation he creates. Participants who serve as supervisors can discover how conflicts in groups become resolved and find ways to help the process along. All can experience some of the emotional loadings that attach themselves to matters of prestige and fair play. The few participants who function as observers can discover how lifelike a role-playing process might become, and they can observe how the discussion process leads to attitude changes. As an observer, a person can have a disinterested attitude and objectively evaluate the process.

In repeating this method, different persons can function as observers, supervisors, and employees and thus gain a variety of experiences from these exchanges in function.

In order to make the group decision experience a success with untrained leaders, it is important that the problem be so structured that the leader is likely to do a good job and that the group will readily participate in the discussion. To accomplish good discussion leadership, the problem used for our demonstration was one for which the supervisor is unlikely to have a ready-made solution. In having no preferred solution himself, he is inclined to act permissively, and thus encourage free and frank discussion instead of imposing or selling his own views. To produce a lively discussion, the problem that is used must be one which creates a conflict in attitudes. In order to solve the problem these attitudes have to become reconciled.

The work situation described in this paper is based on an actual case in industry and raises the type of problem that a crew can solve more satisfactorily than a supervisor. As such, it readily lends itself to a group decision rather than an autocratic decision which is imposed on the crew by the supervisor. In the real life situation the foreman had a new truck to distribute. He realized that his decision would not meet with approval since each man would feel he had a claim. He therefore put the problem to the crew. The crew solved the problem in such a way that there was a general exchange of trucks, so that each man got a different truck and at the same time the poorest truck was discarded. Everyone was satisfied with the solution.

In setting up this problem for role-playing, we have given each participant a personal attitude, so that a typical set of life-like conflicts would be created. This is the usual procedure in role-playing. The deviation from the usual procedure is that the same roles are simultaneously played by many groups, each without the guidance of a trainer. This absence of specific guidance during the role-playing process makes standardization more essential and requires the use of clear-cut problems. However, we find that these limitations are not serious.

SETTING UP THE ROLE-PLAYING PROCEDURE

(1.) The first step in the procedure is for the trainer or the person in charge of the meeting to request the audience to divide itself into groups of six, with three persons in one row turning around to meet with three persons directly behind them. Assistants can be an aid to help persons in odd seats join others in making up these groups. By arranging the seating rows in multiples of three, the task of organizing the groups is simplified. (In our situation the seats themselves could be turned around and this made for more comfort.)

Since the number of persons required in a group is six, there may be a remainder of from one to five persons. Each of those extra persons is asked to join one of the discussion groups and serve as an observer.

(2.) When the audience has been divided into groups, the trainer announces that each group will receive a set of instructions. The persons who pass out the material will hand these instructions to one member of each group. This member will play the part of Walt Marshall, the foreman of a crew of repairmen. The other five members of the group will be repairmen who report to Walt Marshall. The foreman is to keep this material until instructed further. In the meantime he may look over the top page, labelled "Walt Marshall—Foreman of the Repair Crew."

(3.) The trainer then asks the crew members of all groups to give their attention while he reads them their instructions.

General Instructions for Crew:
You are repairmen for a large company and drive to various locations in the city to do your work. Each of you drives a small truck, and you take pride in keeping it looking good. You have a possessive feeling about your trucks and like to keep them in good running order. Naturally, you like to have new trucks, too, because a new truck gives you a feeling of pride.

Here are some facts about the trucks and the men in the crew who report to Walt Marshall, the supervisor of repairs:

George—17 years with the company, has a 2-year-old Ford truck.
Bill—11 years with the company, has a 5-year-old Dodge truck.
John—10 years with the company, has a 4-year-old Ford truck.
Charlie—5 years with the company, has a 3-year-old Ford truck.
Hank—3 years with the company, has a 5-year-old Chevrolet truck.

Most of you do all of your driving in the city, but John and Charlie cover the jobs in the suburbs.

In acting your part in role-playing, accept the facts as given as well as assume the attitude supplied in your specific role. From this point on let your feelings develop in accordance with the events that transpire in the role-playing process. When facts or events arise which are not covered by the roles, make up things which are consistent with the way it might be in a real life situation.

The names of the five men, years of service, age, and make of truck should then be placed on an easel-chart or black board, so that ready reference to them can be made.

(4.) The foreman is then asked to pass out the material he has been given, which consists of six sets of instructions, one for each person in the group. He should keep the top set for himself and pass out one set of instructions, beginning on his left, to each of his five crewmen. The sequence of the instructions should be George, Bill, John, Charlie, and Hank so that the seating order corresponds to the order to seniority as listed on the easel.

The content of the specific instructions for each member of the group is as follows:

Walt Marshall—Foreman of Repair Crew
You are the foreman of a crew of repairmen, each of whom drives a small service truck to and from his various jobs. Every so often you get a new truck to exchange for an old one, and you have the problem of deciding to which of your men you should

give the new truck. Often there are hard feelings because each man seems to feel he is entitled to the new truck; so you have a tough time being fair. As a matter of fact, it usually turns out that whatever you decide, most of the men consider wrong. You now have to face the issue again because a new truck has just been allocated to you for distribution. The new truck is a Chevrolet.

Here are some brief facts about your situation:

George—17 years with the company, has a 2-year-old Ford truck.

Bill—11 years with the company, has a 5-year-old Dodge truck.

John—10 years with the company, has a 4-year-old Ford truck.

Charlie—5 years with the company, has a 3-year-old Ford truck.

Hank—3 years with the company, has a 5-year-old Chevrolet truck.

All of the men do city driving, making fairly short trips, except for John and Charlie who cover the suburbs.

In order to handle this problem you have decided to put the decision up to the men themselves. You will tell them about the new truck and will put the problem in terms of what would be the most fair way to distribute the truck. Avoid taking a position yourself because you want to do what the men think is most fair.

George: When a new Chevrolet truck becomes available, you think you should get it because you have most seniority and don't like your present truck. Your own car is a Chevrolet, and you prefer a Chevrolet truck such as you drove before you got the Ford.

Bill: You feel you deserve a new truck. Your present truck is old, and since the senior man has a fairly new truck, you should get the next one. You have taken excellent care of your present Dodge and have kept it looking like new. A man deserves to be rewarded if he treats a company truck like his own.

John: You have to do more driving than most of the other men because you work in the suburbs. You have a fairly old truck and feel you should have a new one because you do so much driving.

Charlie: The heater in your present truck is inadequate. Since Hank backed into the door of your truck, it has never been repaired to fit right. The door lets in too much cold air, and you attribute your frequent colds to this. You want a warm truck since you have a good deal of driving to do. As long as it has good tires, brakes, and is comfortable you don't care about its make.

Hank: You have the poorest truck in the crew. It is five years old, and before you got it, it had been in a bad wreck. It has never been good, and you've put up with it for three years. It's about time you got a good truck to drive, and you feel the next one should be yours. You have a good accident record. The only accident you had was when you sprung the door of Charlie's truck when he opened it as you backed out of the garage. You hope the new truck is a Ford since you prefer to drive one.

Members are asked to study their roles until they have a feeling for them. It is perhaps necessary to caution them not to show their roles to each other, but to put them aside when they have finished with them.

(5.) When everyone is ready, the trainer gives the signal for the foreman to take the responsibility of starting their meetings. Each foreman should assume that he has called his men together and that he is seated with them to discuss a problem.

(6.) Less than half an hour is adequate for most groups to solve the problem. (If the leader and his assistants observe the groups they can pretty well judge when most of the groups have reached a solution.) Before interrupting the discussion, it is desirable to announce from the floor that three more minutes will be allowed the groups to settle on some arrangement.

MRP: A Technique for Training Supervisors

(7.) At the end of the three-minute period, the members are asked to break off their discussions and join in the analysis of the results.

ANALYZING THE RESULTS

The extent of the analysis need not be confined to the points discussed below, but the analysis should cover the following points:

(1.) Determination of the number of groups arriving at a solution. (In obtaining this figure, only the foreman should vote.)

(2.) Determination of the number of men who are satisfied with the solution. (In this case only the repairmen of crews which reached a solution should raise their hands.) This figure is important because it indicates the degree of satisfaction obtained from the procedure. The chairman may ask how this degree of acceptance compares with what would have been obtained if the foreman had supplied the solution.

(3.) Determination of number of crews which discarded Hank's truck. (In this case only the foremen should raise their hands.) The proportion of the number of times that Hank's truck was discarded to the number of groups becomes a measure of the quality of the solution. The fear that men might fail to discard the poorest truck would constitute one of the reasons why a foreman might hesitate to put such a problem to them. If the proportion of crews discarding the poorest truck is very large, it indicates the danger of not having the poorest truck discarded is more imagined than real.

(4.) Determination of the number of crews in which the new truck went to various members of the crew. (In this case only the foremen should vote on the five alternatives.) This analysis brings out the variety of solutions obtained and shows that the same problem with the same roles produces different solutions. Under such circumstances it becomes clear that a company could not work out a policy that would be satisfying to all crews.

This analysis might also be followed by questions such as, "In how many cases did George use his seniority and make a strong demand for the new truck?" "How often did he get it when he was that kind of a George?" "How often did George get the new truck when he did not throw his seniority around?" Such questions frequently reveal that George is more likely to get the new truck when he is a reasonable person and considerate of men with less service than when he is demanding.

5. Determination of the number of crews in which:
(a) All men obtained a different truck.
(b) 4 men obtained a different truck.
(c) 3 men obtained a different truck.
(d) 2 men obtained a different truck.
(e) No exchange in old trucks were made and only the man receiving the new truck benefited.

(Only the foreman should vote on these alternatives.) This analysis gives an idea of the extent to which all men were given consideration. If time is taken to analyze these data, it might be found that the foreman's conduct of the meeting determined the number of men who benefited by the addition of a new truck to the crew.

Following the analysis of the crews, the persons serving as observers should be asked to give their evaluations of the discussion meetings they observed. Their report may include: the way foreman put the problem; the extent to which he hampered the discussion; the extent to which he imposed his own ideas; and evaluation of things he did which helped things along. These reports not only involve the observers in the procedure, but add supplementary material on the different approaches various foremen may have used.

SOME SAMPLE RESULTS

We have tested the case in three audiences. In one of these, 17 groups were formed and in 14 of these, all persons were satisfied with the solution they had reached. A total of five individuals out of 102 were dissatisfied with the solutions of their groups. In the second group tested, six groups were used and two persons (in two different groups) out of 42 were dissatisfied. In the third audience, 19 out of 21 groups had time to reach a decision and only one person in each of two groups was dissatisfied. If we combine our groups, we find that 42 out of 44 groups reached a decision and only nine out of 220 repairmen (4.1 per cent) were dissatisfied.

In each of three tests of the method, all persons participating readily agreed that anything approaching the degree of satisfaction shown could not have been obtained if supervisors had supplied the solution.

In 41 out of the 42 groups, Hank's truck (the poorest one) was eliminated. This result clearly shows that the group decisions were in accordance with the interests of good management. Thus, the fear that group decisions might lead to poor-quality decisions was not supported.

The new truck went to George, the senior man, in 20 of the 42 groups. In 16 cases out of 28 he got it when he did not insist on it because of his seniority, and in 4 cases out of 10 he got it by defending his rank. Thus George gained most when he acted least in his own selfish interests.

A great variety of solutions developed in these groups. The new truck went to each of the individuals in one group or another; the frequency being in the order of George, John, Hank, Bill and Charlie. In most instances there was a general exchange of trucks. All men got a different truck in four groups; four men got a different truck in ten groups; three men in sixteen groups; two in eight groups; and only one got a different truck (the new one) in four groups.

From descriptions of the discussion process, there seemed to be a trend in which the general exchange of trucks was greatest when the leader was permissive. The first part of the discussion develops a conflict of interests, and if the leader is permissive at this stage, the idea of exchanging trucks develops. Many men who played the part of the supervisor were surprised at this development because most of them went into the discussion with the idea of getting the new truck assigned to some particular individual and getting the rest of the group to agree on who was most needy. It is this emphasis on the leader's part which prevents the general exchange which usually develops out of the free discussion. Thus, the idea that all can profit when the crew gets a new truck emerges as a new idea, and it is a group product.

GENERAL EVALUATION

The technique of MRP has some distinct advantages over ordinary role-playing. When many groups of persons engage in role-playing at the same time, the process is facilitated since all of them enter into it without the embarrassment that comes from feeling that they are being observed. Thus groups which have never experienced role-playing quickly get the spirit of the procedure and go into the process in a natural and interested manner. The feeling that the situation is unreal and artificial, which non-participants frequently report, is eliminated because all become involved. Because this method reduces self-consciousness, it is particularly helpful for initiating role-playing techniques in supervisory training.

A second value that emerges is the fact that real live data are obtained from the subsequent analysis. A single role-playing case raises questions which have to do with the fact that a certain individual determined the outcome and so the result may not be typical. In being able to draw upon various groups, one is able to make comparisons and generalizations which could not be made without a rich background of experience. The idea that solutions are tailored to fit a particular group of personalities is clearly brought home by the fact that solutions vary even when the problem and the roles are identical.

Thus we find that in the process of attempting to induce into a large group some of the benefits of small discussion and role-playing, we not only succeeded in achieving some of these advantages, but captured some entirely new ones.

The MRP method can be used for all types of role-playing which are so effective for attitude change and the development of skills. One must however structure the roles so as to conform to the purpose of the training and the experience of the participants. Thus, if one wishes to emphasize (1) leadership skills in putting a problem to a group, (2) discussion leading skills, (3) sensitivity to the feelings of others, (4) ways for dealing with hostile persons, (5) skills to up-grade the quality of decisions, and (6) methods to cause a group to feel responsible for reaching decisions acceptable to all, one must design role-playing situations which will highlight these performance areas.

References

Bavelas, A. "Role-playing and Management Training," *Sociatry*, 1 (1947): 183–191.
Bradford, L. P., and R. Lippitt. "Building a Democratic Work Group," *Personnel*, 22 (1945): 2–13.

Coch, L., and J. R. P. French, Jr. "Overcoming Resistance to Change," *Human Relations*, Vol. I, No. 2 (1948): 512–532.
Lewin, K. "Group Decision and Social Change," in T. M. Newcomb and E. L. Hartley (eds.). *Readings in Social Psychology.* New York: Holt, 1947, 330–344.
Lewin, K., R. Lippitt, and R. K. White. "Patterns of Aggressive Behavior in Experimentally Created Social Climates," *Journal of Social Psychology*, 11 (1939): 271–299.
Lippitt, R., L. P. Bradford, and K. D. Benne. "Sociodramatic Clarification of Leader and Group Roles," *Sociatry*, 1 (1947): 82–91.
Maier, N. R. F. "A Human Relations Program for Supervision," *Industrial and Labor Relations Review*, 1 (1948): 443–464.
Maier, N. R. F. "Improving Supervision through Training," in A. Kornhauser (ed.). *Psychology of Labour-management Relations.* Champaign, Illinois: Industrial Relations Research Association, 1949, 27–42.
Phillips, J. D. "Report on Discussion 66," *Adult Education Journal*, 7 (1948): 181–182.

PART TWO

Techno-Structural Strategies of Social Intervention

*t*echnological and environmental influences on organizational structure are the main concern of the intervention techniques in this section. These strategies, which we have labeled "techno-structural strategies of social intervention," generally assume that technology and environment constrain the design of organizational structure, but these constraints do not fully determine its form. Therefore, the formal structure of any existing organization represents only one of several possible alternative structures. The goal of techno-structural interventions is to determine the alternative that is most satisfying and efficient.

Such intervention strategies can be divided into two groups: (1) those that are directed at changing the organizational structure in order to provide greater congruence between technological and environmental demands and the organizational structure (for example, either centralizing or decentralizing managerial decision-making) and (2) those that propose to alter technological or environmental conditions in order to achieve this congruence (for example, attempts to redesign machines or architecture). These strategies do not try primarily to change individual behavior directly or through the alteration of peer group norms and values. Rather, they follow the widely shared assumption that individual psychological states and behavior will change in response to new demands arising from changes in organizational structure, technology, or environment. This assumption is supported by research in the behavioral sciences and by the observations of noted economist John Kenneth Galbraith in his book *The New Industrial State*: "The imperatives of technology and organization, not the images of ideology, are what determine the shape of economic society."

Psychological research provides more direct evidence to support the contention that individual satisfaction and behavior, as well as group effectiveness, are influenced by *structural properties* of organizations (such as communication channels, participation in decision-making, and status hierarchy); and *environmental conditions* (such as spatial relations among group members). Some of these research findings are presented prior to a discussion of the common characteristics of techno-structural interventions.

CHANNELS OF COMMUNICATION

Research in this area has focused on the effects of two variables—*patterns of communication* and *position centrality*—on such outcome measures as accuracy and speed of problem-solving, morale and satisfaction of group members, and leader nomination (Christie, *et al.*, 1952; Gilchrist, *et al.*, 1955; Leavitt, 1951; and Shaw, 1954). Typically, in these experiments each person in the communication network is given some of the information needed to solve a problem. The group's task is to use whatever communication channels are available to organize the information in order to arrive at a correct solution.

Patterns of communication have been varied by channeling communications which ordinarily are in the form of written messages. For example, in an *all-channel* pattern, each member has a communication channel with every other member and can communicate with every other member on a one-to-one basis; in a *circle* pattern, each member has a communication channel to two other members who, however, cannot communicate with one another; and, in a *wheel* pattern, one member has communication channels to all of the members but they cannot communicate with one another. "Position centrality" refers to the number of communicative links which a person occupying one position must use in order to send a message, by the shortest route, from his position to other positions.

These studies have demonstrated the following:

(1.) The ease of solving simple problems is associated with the degree of network centralization, that is, the degree to which there is one position closely linked to all the others (Leavitt, 1951);

(2.) Complex problems tend to be solved most effectively in networks with relatively high connectivity. "Connectivity" can be defined as the number of members who are linked through a communication channel (Shaw, 1954; Gilchrist, *et al.*, 1955). Thus, all-channel networks, in which each member can communicate with all other members, tend to be most efficient (in terms of time and errors) in solving complex problems.
(3.) Group satisfaction tends to be greater with higher levels of connectivity.
(4.) The likelihood of emerging as a group's leader increases with centrality of position in a network.
(5.) Centrality of position in a network is associated with individual satisfaction.

In actual organization settings (*i.e.* outside of experimental laboratories), the relationship between formal channels of communication and group process is likely to be mitigated by the existence of informal channels of communication. In some instances, these informal channels may be more flexible than the prescribed channels and network members may be able to organize themselves in ways that are more responsive to the exigencies of unfamiliar problems. One of the selections in this part, Beckhard's report of the "confrontation meeting," describes a deliberate attempt to provide an organization with a temporary all-channel network.

Beckhard's report, as well as previous research, suggests that no simple communication network is ideally suited to the resolution of all problems. Communication networks are required that allow participants to make appropriate variations in their use of communication channels. As Guetzkow and Simon (1955) have said, "The imposition of certain restrictions on the communication channels available to a group affects the efficiency of the group performance, not *directly* by limiting the potential efficiency of task performance with optimal organization in the given net, but *indirectly* by handicapping its ability to organize itself for efficient performance."

PARTICIPATION IN DECISION MAKING

Lewin's early distinction between "own" and "induced" motivation has stimulated a continuing interest in the question of why people are more satisfied and more productive when they participate in making decisions that affect their activities (Coch and French, 1948; Hornstein, *et al.*, 1968; Likert, 1961; Morse and Reimer, 1956; Smith and Tannenbaum, 1963; and Tannenbaum, 1962). It is generally assumed that participation in goal-setting is more likely to create self-induced motivation toward the goal, thereby limiting the need for close surveillance, continuous social influence in the direction of the work goal, and restraining forces to prevent people from withdrawing. These assertions have been supported when participation is the consequence of a leader's interpersonal style (Lippitt and White, 1943) and structural change (Coch and French, 1948).

Although the principle of participation has been widely supported by the results of various investigators, there is reason to believe that under certain conditions, *restriction of participation* is more effective than participation.

Fiedler's (1964) investigations of the relative effectiveness of styles of leadership rather than rules of organizational structure provide evidence for this qualification. His findings indicate that controlling, authoritarian leaders tend to be most effective either in very favorable or relatively unfavorable task conditions while permissive, considerate democratic leaders are most effective in situations which are intermediate in favorableness. Favorable situations are defined as those in which (1) leader–member relations are positive; (2) the task is clear and well-structured; and (3) the leader has clear authority to reward and punish. As Deutsch and Hornstein (1970) suggest, "In terms of own and induced motivation, Fiedler's findings might be reinterpreted as indicating that under conditions where motivations of the leader and the members are highly congruent and where the task is clearly defined, the leader is not 'imposing' his motivation on the others and there is nothing to be gained by a belabored discussion of the obvious."

STATUS HIERARCHY

In common parlance "status" refers to prestige. The term "status hierarchy" implies the ranking of individuals or groups along one or more dimensions. In some instances the dimensions reflect individual characteristics such as age, height, weight, and intelligence. More interesting for our purposes, however, is when individual or group status is attributable to the position that the individual or group occupies in a social structure.

When groups have a task to perform, it is common to find that they allocate different aspects of the task to various members. This process, called *specialization of function*, produces distinguishable positions in group structures, each with its own rights and responsibilities. In small, informal groups, specialization of function and a subsequent status hierarchy may evolve in an unnoticed and unplanned way. In formal organizations, however, there are deliberate attempts to formulate rules which specify for each position its function, responsibility, authority, and location in a communication network. Moreover, status hierarchies can be considered a part of formal organization structure insofar as positions are deliberately distinguished by endowing them with desirable outcomes, such as material rewards, control over one's fellows, wider latitude in freedom of choice, access to resources, and a central position in the communication network.

Experimental research on the effects of status hierarchies on behavior is characterizied by a focus on the effect of occupying a low status position and by a dearth of work in formal organizations. Nevertheless, some findings have received consistent support in experiments conducted in both natural settings and experimental laboratories. For example, low status members tend to direct their communications upward, toward high status members, rather than toward peers. Moreover, the low status members who cannot advance in the hierarchy send relatively more communications that are irrelevant to the immediate task (Thibaut, 1950; Kelley, 1951). These findings have been interpreted as suggesting that communication serves as a substitute for actual upward movement in the status hierarchy, and that low status members attempt to placate those in more desirable positions through the communications. Other findings are as follows: (1) low status members tend to attribute positive characteristics to their high status counterparts; (2) high status members are relatively unlikely to communicate dissatisfaction with their jobs to low status members; and (3) both high and low status members avoid public criticism of persons at other status levels.

By analogy, these findings suggest that status hierarchies will influence the effectiveness of work groups by reducing necessary critical evaluation across status lines and by stimulating irrelevant communication from low status members. These possibilities have not passed unnoticed by techno-structural interventionists. One group (Rice, 1958; Trist *et al.*, 1963) has suggested that work groups be composed of members who are each capable of performing all the tasks assigned to their work group. Such an arrangement minimizes structurally induced status differences in groups. However, it does not remedy the problems caused by status hierarchies that are socially, rather than structurally, determined, such as those that are a consequence of friendship patterns or relative skill in performance. Presumably, status hierarchies that develop along these social dimensions produce effects similar to those that are attributed to formal status hierarchies.

SPATIAL RELATIONS

There is said to be an area at the United Nations accessible to delegates and staff that was deliberately designed to provide opportunities for intimate, out-of-earshot conversations. In creating such a space, it is almost certain that the architect, implicitly or explicitly, assumed some correspondence between the design of physical space and behavior. At the United Nations, the architectural plan in this one area might have been developed to stimulate and to facilitate *sub rosa* conversation.

Psychological ecology is the label applied to the study of the regularities that people show in their use of physical space and the effects of physical space on behavior. In part, the research suggests that use of space is mediated by interpersonal relations. For example:

(1.) Over time, leaders in small discussion groups tend to move to the head position at rectangular tables (Sommer, 1959).
(2.) At rectangular tables, members of cooperating pairs tend to sit side-by-side; members of conversing pairs sit corner-to-corner; and members of competing pairs sit opposite one another (Sommer, 1965; Norum, 1966).
(3.) Members of discussion groups tend to direct their comments to people sitting opposite them when the group has less controlling leadership, but direct them to people sitting adjacent when the group has more controlling leadership; this effect has been attributed to the restriction of eye contact to adjacent peers in the presence of a strong leader (Hearn, 1957).

Other studies suggest that physical space has a more direct effect on individual and group behavior.

(1.) Physical proximity increases the likelihood of affiliation. Festinger, Schachter, and Back (1950) in their study of a housing community found that friendship groups were more often composed of next-door neighbors; moreover, the most popular persons were those who lived in apartments that maximized their contact with others (for instance, those next to stairwells).
(2.) Members of experimental juries who sat at end positions tended to participate more and have greater influence (Strodtbeck and Hook, 1961).
(3.) People tend to maintain some physical distance between themself and others. They resist encroachment upon their physical space and may withdraw when such encroachment occurs (Felipe and Sommer, 1966).

The importance of research in this area is evident in a statement made by Sommer (1968), which we paraphrase: If we can learn the spatial arrangements that foster and impede patterns of behavior, we shall be able to design spaces to fit task group functions.

STRATEGIES OF SOCIAL INTERVENTION

The central components of techno-structural strategies of social intervention are identified in the following paragraph: The specific design of the *work-flow* in any social system is determined by the *goals* of the system in combination with available *technology* and *environment*. (Work-flow can be defined as a series of tasks that must be performed in a regular predetermined order by separate individuals or groups.) *Organizational structures* are created to control, regulate, and facilitate maintenance of the desired work-flow. As Rice (1959) has said, organizations are dispensible means to an end; as such they should be changed when necessary. Techno-structural advocates identify two general categories of problems that indicate need for change in organizational structure: the organizational structure may produce psychological by-products which adversely affect organizational effectiveness and individual satisfaction; the organizational structure may be inconsistent with work-flow demands.

In the next section here we will discuss the problems of identifying technological and environmental constraints as they are manifest in the work-flow, review the characteristics of organizational structure that are common targets of change for techno-structural strategies, and conclude with an examination of some principles of organizational structure that have been proposed by one group of techno-structural interventionists.

THE IDENTIFICATION OF TECHNOLOGICAL AND ENVIRONMENTAL CONSTRAINTS

Analysis of the relationship between work-flow (inasmuch as it represents some consequences of underlying technological and environmental constraints) and organizational structure is guided by the principle of organizing by discrete task. In fact, work-flow can be defined as a series of discrete tasks which are performed in a predetermined order. These discrete tasks and their relationships to one another are assumed to be a most efficient basis for designing organizational structure. Hence, the first step is to identify discrete tasks, which have been called "unit-work-flow" by Sayles (1964) and "primary task" by Rice (1958), and Trist *et al.*, (1963). A subsequent step is to change the organizational structure in order to optimize the structural positions of the control and service functions required by each discrete task.

Although there are no clear or certain criteria for identifying a discrete task, there is some consensus that a discrete task includes the input, conversion, and output functions of the productive process. *Input* refers to the acquisition of "raw" material. ("Raw" is defined as the state of material when it is received by some individual or work group. The material might be administration forms, people, steel, or food.) *Conversion* refers to the changing of the raw material into products, and *output* refers to the disposal of products to the next step in the work-flow.

Discrete tasks are not necessarily recognized by organization planners and may not be represented on charts of organizational structure, job description, or work-flow. The consultant's job is to identify discrete tasks and suggest appropriate changes in organizational structure. Chapple and Sayles (1961) have proposed the use of time as a basic diagnostic measure in the determination of discrete tasks. By this procedure, recordings are made of what a person does, when, where, with whom, how long, and how often. These data, along with information gleaned from work-flow charts and the geographical positioning of people and technology, provide a basis for segmenting work-flow into discrete tasks. Chapple and Sayles further propose that each of these tasks be placed under the control of a single supervisory unit.

The objective of this process is to design an organizational structure which is responsive to the discrete components of the entire work-flow. It assumes that efficient task performance is most likely when supervisory units can maintain control over the behavior of all individuals or groups whose activities are part of a simple discrete task.

TARGETS OF CHANGE

Supervisory control is one component of organizational structure that can be changed in the service of technological demand. Other components of organizational structure that are common targets of change are (1) social characteristics—including group size and composition in terms of identifiable individual features (for example, intelligence, manual dexterity, authoritarianism), structure of authority, status hierarchy, incentive systems, and formal channels of communication; (2) environmental characteristics—including spatial relations among group members and other features of the physical setting; and (3) task characteristics—including special task demands (for example, manual skill, knowledge, or creative ability), task difficulty, and the degree to which the task is specific or vague in prescribing behavior necessary for its completion.

The selection included in this part provides a number of examples of attempts to change these and similar variables for the purpose of producing change in individual satisfaction and behavior, and organizational efficiency.

PRINCIPLES OF ORGANIZATIONAL STRUCTURE—
A PROPOSAL FROM TAVISTOCK

Rice (1958) and his colleagues at Tavistock have based their efforts to induce social change on three assumptions about the way a task should be organized to provide gratification to those engaged in the task:

(1.) Tasks should be organized so that those involved complete the whole task. This proposal is supported by experimental evidence which demonstrates that interrupted activity lacks closure and is therefore recalled more frequently than completed activity (Zeigarnik, 1927). To experience a sense of completion, however, an individual need not complete the task himself; it can be completed by a cooperatively linked work partner (Lewis and Franklin, 1944).

(2.) Tasks should be organized so that those engaged in them control their own activities.

(3.) Related tasks should be organized so that those engaged can have satisfactory relationships. Evidence supporting these second and third principles can be found in Argyris (1964) and Katz and Kahn (1966).

Two additional assumptions from Tavistock are made about work group organization. These are presented with references to relevant research literature, but without any further comment:

(1.) The most efficient work group is one containing the smallest number of people necessary to perform a "whole" task.

(2.) Stability is highest with fewest differences in status and when needed skills are understood and aspired to by all members of a group (Thibaut, 1950; Kelley, 1951).

SOCIAL NORMS AND TECHNO-STRUCTURAL INTERVENTIONS

The causal chain assumed by techno-structural interventions can be portrayed as follows: Technological and environmental demands impose constraints on an organization's structure; in turn, organizational structure influences a number of individual and group factors which affect satisfaction and performance. This sequence is not invariable. Evidence exists to support the contention that individual satisfaction and performance as well as an array of psychological variables influence and constrain patterns of organizational structure, rather than vice versa. For example, Strauss (1954) describes the way in which social relationships contributed to the failure of a change in job structure; segregation of blacks as a structural arrangement in parts of the United States and Africa can be interpreted as partly determined by the attitudes and values of white residents; and the bussing of school children, an attempted change in that segregated structure, is resisted for some of the same attitudinal reasons. At the moment that this volume is being prepared, the Vietnam peace negotiations in Paris are stalemated because antagonists cannot agree on the shape of a conference table. In part, their inability to reach accord on environmental design can be attributed to their feelings of competition, belligerence, and mistrust of each others' motives.

These events provide support for an obvious assertion: As men live together in groups they develop social norms to organize and regulate their dealings with one another. These norms may be influenced by organizational structure as well as by technological and environmental conditions, but these conditions are not the sole determinants of social norms. For some time, anthropologists such as Arensberg and Niehoff (1964) have noted that cultural systems with similar social norms survive in different environments and vice versa. Other influences in the development of group culture include needs and personality of group members (Schutz, 1958), special events not arising from the organizational structure (for example, the death of a group member or an accident), and common interests of group members (Newcomb, 1943; and Newcomb *et al.*, 1967).

The development of different social norms under similar structural conditions has been noted by Orth (1963). He studied two sections of students at the Harvard Graduate School of Business. These sections, which were deliberately composed of individuals with similar backgrounds and ability, developed two very different sets of norms. One section had norms which were non-academically oriented; the other's were more compatible with academic success. These norms affected performance: At the close of the year, the former section had a greater number of under-achievers, while the latter had a greater number of over-achievers.

Some years ago, the role of social norms as mediators of change was commented on by Lewin, who said, "As long as group standards are unchanged, the individual will resist changes more strongly the further he is expected to depart from group standards. If the group standard itself is changed, the resistance which is due to the relation between individual and group standards is eliminated" (Lewin 1958, p. 210). Direct attempts to change group standards and individual adherence to group standards are discussed in two of the parts of this book: "Individual Change Strategies of Social Intervention" and "Organizational Development: Cultural Change as a Strategy of Social Intervention." Techno-structural interventions present two alternatives for overcoming potentially obstructive social norms.

The first alternative admonishes change agents to fit the change into existing social norms. Sibley (1960) describes a change effort which failed because the attempt was unnecessarily incongruent with existing beliefs and neglected to make use of existing social structures. Specifically, he reports an attempt to introduce improvement in sanitary conditions in a Philippine village. The program divided the village into zones. Zonal boundaries were established by using existing streets and a sugar mill railway for guidelines. Within each zone, three officers were selected under "supervision" of the change agents (apparently their influence was more than supervisory). These officers tended to be young, unmarried, and educated. The program for improvement failed. Its errors were that traditional demarcation of the village, especially for cooperative work efforts, had been along kinship lines, not by streets and the sugar mill railway;

and that traditional village leaders had always been older, not so well educated, and married. Sibley concludes, " . . . for planned change efforts to be successful they must be congruous with existing cultural beliefs (or at least not in conflict with them) and must be presented in a manner which makes full use of existing social structural arrangements."

Fitting the change into existing norms and beliefs may be a sound principle, but it is one that is difficult to put into practice. Unhappily, there are few clearly defined criteria for identifying social norms and for determining what constitutes a "good fit" between norms and proposed changes. Consequently, successful use of this alternative depends on the skill and intuition of the individual change agent. (For a useful resource in using this approach the reader is directed to C. M. Arensberg and A. H. Niehoff, *Introducing Social Change: A Manual for Americans Overseas*.)

The second alternative to changing social norms directly attempts to produce change in behavior or attitude by introducing structural changes which use compelling force or which satisfy strongly felt needs of group members. The reliance on compelling force is demonstrated by the frequent manipulation of two structural components—*administrative controls* and *incentives*. Both have the capacity to forcefully control behavior. Administrative controls provide more rapid detection of deviation from authorized work-flow and more complete control over all individuals and groups affecting completion of a discrete task. In circumstances where behavior can be linked to identifiable outputs, manipulating rewards and punishments contingent on outputs provides strong pressure to behave in a manner likely to yield rewards. One group of studies supporting the assumptions of cognitive dissonance theory (Festinger, 1957; Brehm and Cohen, 1962), provides an interesting principle in the use of force and incentive to gain compliance. It suggests that compliance accompanied by a favorable change in attitudes is most likely when the force or incentive used to obtain compliance is the minimum necessary. Minimum force provides individuals with insufficient justification for having engaged in unpalatable behavior. Recognizing that they have engaged in behavior which they view as undesirable arouses dissonance, a state of tension. To reduce the tension that they experience, individuals change their view of the compelled behavior and see it more favorably. Once again, there are no clear standards for determining what constitutes "minimum necessary force or incentive." Employment of this principle relies upon experimenter and change agent intuition.

The Deutsch and Collins (1951) study on interracial housing demonstrates another condition when structural change has attitudinal and behavioral consequences. Their study compared the attitudes and behavior of whites living in integrated and segregated housing projects. The results were clear: Living in integrated projects produced favorable changes in feelings, beliefs, and action tendencies toward blacks. We can assume that a crucial factor in producing these changes was the lawful *requirement* that the projects be integrated and the resident's voluntary decision to live in an integrated project. We can also assume that contact with blacks provided residents with positive experiences and in-

Introduction 153

formation contrary to their prejudiced beliefs. Thus, structural change may produce desired psychological and behavioral changes under conditions of enforcement when participants choose to accept the imposed constraints and/or when subsequent experiences are positively evaluated and disconfirm earlier suspicions.

Structural changes may also overcome constraints of social norms when these changes alleviate adverse conditions, without significantly increasing psychological distress. For example, building badly needed cesspools might be readily accepted if the location, use, and care of the cesspools did not violate any local taboos and if the indigenous population recognized the need for such a change. Often the groups involved are not so accommodating as to experience and accept the need for change. Under these conditions, change agents are faced with creating a felt need where none exists. This is an area in which intervention technology seems particularly limited. A review of the literature suggests that commonly used devices for creating needs are (1) demonstration projects which provide unequivocal evidence of the value of an innovation; (2) introduction of beneficial innovations to a competing group; and (3) provision to the target group of indisputable data that evidence a need and provision of a means to satisfy that need.

To summarize, social norms, once they have been established, not only influence the development of social structure, but also act as obstacles to change in the existing social structure. Three responses to such resistance have been discussed:—direct change of norms, fitting the change to the norm, and planning structural changes that use compelling force or satisfy strongly felt needs of group members.

OVERVIEW

Both groups of techno-structural intervention strategies are represented by the selections included in this section—those that are directed at changing the organizational structure, and those that attempt to alter technological or environmental conditions. A classic representative of the first group is a paper by A. K. Rice entitled, "Productivity and Social Organization in an Indian Weaving Shed." The intervention strategy described by Rice focuses on diagnosing the change of the relationship between the technical and social–psychological characteristics of a production system. The changes are guided by six assumptions about small-work-group organization. Rice's description of the intervention and its success is carefully documented with data on actual work productivity. The relationship between social and technological systems is also a major concern in Sayles' paper, "The Change Process in Organizations: An Applied Anthropology Analysis." In this paper, Sayles depicts managers as a kind of internal change agent whose job it is to detect and correct disturbances in these two systems. He says "External pressures and internal problems require constant 'changes,' but the manager endeavors to accomplish this as he returns the system to equilibrium." To effect these changes and restore equilibrium, Sayles asserts that it is not enough to use persuasion and influence; one must change major organizational constraints including work flow, job incumbents, authority structure, incentive systems, channels of communication, and job structure.

Diagnosis and change of the last three of these constraints are the focus of articles by Torbert, Beckhard, and Fiedler.

In his article, "Making Incentives Work," Torbert describes three major incentive plans, those of Scanlon, Rucker, and Nunn. He also discusses the assumptions underlying these plans and the social conditions that are necessary for their success. What is immediately obvious is that a group monetary incentive plan can be an *additional* device for enhancing organizational effectiveness by engendering cooperation; by itself, however, it is insufficient to produce cooperative relationships within a social system. Torbert says, "Unless management and workers.... undertake to create a built-in structure for listening to each other and working together, old habits of thought and attitudes of mutual doubt and fear are bound to continue."

Beckhard's paper, "The Confrontation Meeting," is concerned with altering another major organizational constraint, namely, channels of communication. Beckhard observes that in crisis periods, such as those that follow major organizational changes, there tends to be "much confusion and an expenditure of dysfunctional energy that negatively affects both productivity and morale." These periods, he continues, are often characterized by a reduction in communication between levels of management. The reduced communication affects people's feelings of influence and control and further aggravates the situation. The confrontation meeting is an intervention that temporarily increases the level of communication while allowing work on the causes of a current crisis.

Changing jobs, not men, is the theme in Fiedler's article, "Engineer the Job to Fit the Manager." Using his own research for evidence, Fiedler argues that people have leadership styles that interact with three dimensions of a job: the power invested in the leadership position, the task structure, and leader–member relations. He suggests that these dimensions are more easily altered than a person's leadership style. Hence, system effectiveness can be improved by altering these dimensions in order to provide for an optimum interaction between them and leadership style.

The remaining two selections in this part, one by Sommer and the other by Steele, deal with environmental change as a means of diagnosing and altering social systems. These two articles are especially concerned with the effect and significance of spatial arrangements and architectural design on social behavior. Both articles suggest that the use of space reflects the state of various social and psychological factors such as task structure, personality, interpersonal familiarity, and intergroup conflict. Moreover, the use of space affects communication, friendship, and perceived status.

It is important to note that space limitations required omitting representation of at least two significant techno-structural strategies of social intervention—operations research and human engineering. Their technical complexity and their comprehensive presentation in other sources influenced our decision to omit them from this text. A full understanding of techno-structural strategies, however, requires an acquaintance with these two approaches.

References

Arensberg, C. M., and A. H. Niehoff. *Introducing Change: A Manual for Americans Overseas.* Chicago: Aldine, 1964.
Argyris, C. *Integrating the Individual and the Organization.* New York: Wiley, 1964.
Brehm, J. W., and A. R. Cohen. *Explorations in Cognitive Dissonance.* New York: Wiley, 1962.
Chapple, E. D., and L. R. Sayles. *The Measure of Management.* New York: Macmillan, 1961.
Christie, L. S., R. D. Luce, and J. Macy, Jr. *Communications and Learning in Task Oriented Groups.* Cambridge, Massachusetts: Research Laboratory of Electronics, 1952.
Coch, L., and J. R. P. French. "Overcoming Resistance to Change," *Human Relations*, 1 (1948): 512–532.
Deutsch, M., and M. E. Collins. *Interracial Housing: A Psychological Evaluation of a Social Experiment.* Minneapolis: University of Minnesota Press, 1951.
Deutsch, M., and H. Hornstein. "The Social Psychology of Education," in S. Ball and J. Davitz (eds.). *Psychology and Education.* New York: McGraw-Hill, 1970.
Felipe, N., and R. Sommer. "Invasions of Personal Space," *Social Problems*, 45, No. 2: 206–214.
Festinger, L., S. Schachter, and K. Bach. *Social Pressures in Informal Groups: A Study of Human Factors in Housing.* New York: Harper, 1950.
Festinger, L. *A Theory of Cognitive Dissonance.* Evanston, Illinois: Row Peterson, 1957.
Fiedler, F. E. "A Contingency Model of Leadership Effectiveness," in L. Berkowitz (ed.). *Advances in Experimental Social Psychology.* New York: Academic Press, 1964.
Galbraith, J. K. *The New Industrial State*, Boston: Houghton Mifflin, 1967.
Gilchrist, J. E., M. E. Shaw, and L. C. Walker. "Some Effects of Unequal Distribution of Information in a Wheel Group Structure," *Journal of Abnormal Social Psychology*, 51 (1955): 119–122.
Guetzkow, H., and H. A. Simon. "The Impact of Certain Communication Nets Upon Organization and Performance in Task-Oriented Groups," *Management Service*, 1 (1955): 233–250.
Hearn, G. "Leadership and the Spatial Factor in Small Groups," *Journal of Abnormal and Social Psychology*, 54 (1957): 269–272.
Hornstein, H., D. M. Callahan, E. Fisch, and B. A. Benedict. "Influence and Satisfaction in Organizations: A Replication," *Sociology of Education*, 41, No. 4 (Fall, 1968).
Katz, L., and R. L. Kahn. *The Social Psychology of Organizations.* New York: Wiley, 1966.
Kelley, H. H. "Communication in Experimentally Created Hierarchies," *Human Relations* (1951): 39–56.
Leavitt, H. J. "Some Effects of Certain Communication Patterns on Group Performance," *Journal of Abnormal Social Psychology*, 46 (1951): 38–50.
Lewin, K. *Field Theory in Social Science.* New York: Harper, 1959.
Lewis, H. B., and M. Franklin. "An Experimental Study of the Role of the Ego in Work: II. The Significance of Task Orientation in Work," *Journal of Experimental Psychology*, 34 (1944): 195–215.
Likert, R. *New Patterns of Management.* New York: McGraw-Hill, 1961.
Lippitt, R., and R. White. "The 'Social Climate' of Children's Groups," in R. G. Barker, J. Kounin and N. Wright (eds.). *Child Behavior and Development.* New York: McGraw-Hill, 1943.
Morse, N. C., and E. Reimer. "The Experimental Change of a Major Organization Variable," *Journal of Abnormal Social Psychology*, 3 (1956): 120–129.
Newcomb, T. M. *Personality and Social Change.* New York: Dryden Press, 1943.
Newcomb, T. M., L. E. Koenig, K. Flacks, and B. P. Warwick. *Persistence and Change: Bennington College and its Students after Twenty-Five Years.* New York: Wiley, 1967.
Norum, C. A. "Perceived Interpersonal Relationships and Spatial Arrangements," Unpublished Master of Arts Thesis, University of Chicago, Davis, 1966.
Orth, C. *Social Structure and Learning Climate: The First Year at the Harvard Business School.*

Boston: Division of Research, Graduate School of Business Administration, Harvard University, 1963.
Rice, A. K. *Productivity and Social Organization: The Ahmedabad Experiment.* London: Tavistock Publications, 1958.
Sayles, L. *Managerial Behavior.* New York: McGraw-Hill, 1964.
Shaw, M. E. "Some Effects of Problem Complexity upon Problem Solution Efficiency in Different Communication Nets," *Journal of Experimental Psychology*, 48 (1954): 211–217.
Shutz, W. *FIRO: A Three Dimensional Theory of Interpersonal Behavior.* New York: Rinehart, 1958.
Sibley, W. B. "Social Structure and Planned Change: A Case Study for the Philippines," *Human Organization*, 19 (Winter, 1960–61): 209–211.
Smith, D. G., and A. S. Tannenbaum. "Organizational Control Structure: A Comparative Analysis," *Human Relations*, 16 (1963): 299–316.
Sommer, R. "Studies in Personal Space," *Sociometry*, 22 (1959): 247–260.
Sommer, R. "Small Group Ecology," *Psychological Bulletin*, 67, No. 2 (1967): 145–152.
Strodback, F. L., and L. H. Hook. "The Social Dimensions of a Twelve-man Jury Table," *Sociometry*, 24 (1961): 397–415.
Tannenbaum, A. S. "Control and Effectiveness in a Voluntary Organization, *American Journal of Sociology*, 66 (1961): 33–46.
Thibaut, J. W. "An Experimental Study of the Cohesiveness of Underprivileged Groups," *Human Relations*, 3 (1950): 251–278.
Trist, B. L., G. W. Higgin, H. Murray, and A. B. Pollock. *Organizational Choice.* London: Tavistock Publications, 1963.
Zeigarnik, B. "Das Behalten erledigter Handlungen," *Psychologische Forschung*, 9 (1927): 1–85.

A. K. RICE

Productivity and Social Organization in an Indian Weaving Shed: An Examination of Some Aspects of the Socio-Technical System of an Experimental Automatic Loom Shed

The tendency to treat the technological and social organizations of an industrial unit as separate systems has sometimes led to difficulty when technological change has been introduced without adequate appreciation of its social repercussions. In their account of the Hawthorne Studies, Roethlisberger and Dickson described an industrial organization as a social system and drew attention to the interdependence of the technological and human organizations. In the human organization they included the formal and informal structure of groups. Trist and Bamforth in a study of coalmining showed that the introduction of the three shift longwall cycle into British coalmining resulted in the breakdown of an established social system, and in the formation of maladaptive mechanisms as defences against the social and psychological consequences of the technological organization. Rice and Trist in investigating change in labour

Reprinted from *Human Relations*, 6 (1953): 297–329. Used with permission. Copyright © 1953. The Tavistock Institute of Human Relations.

turnover used a method of analysis which suggested that an understanding of the whole system—the socio-technical system, containing both technical and social dimensions—was necessary to explain both kind and direction of change in labour turnover when either technological or social change occurred.[1]

This paper describes a preliminary analysis of the socio-technical system of an experimental automatic loom shed, weaving cotton cloth, on the basis of which the methods of working were reorganized and an increase in productivity achieved. The analysis was made during recent work by the Tavistock Institute in the Ahmedabad Manufacturing and Calico Printing Company Limited in Ahmedabad, India. The company, known more familiarly as the "Calico Mills," manufactures finished cloth from raw cotton and employs approximately eight thousand workers. The author visited the mills in the capacity of professional consultant. The purpose of his visit, which was exploratory, was to allow both the company and the institute to discover whether it was possible to establish a collaborative relationship in which the institute could make a contribution to the solution of the general social and production problems of the mills. The analysis was made in collaboration with a development group in which the author worked with the chairman, the mill manager, and works manager of the company. (The works manager was the direct executive subordinate of the mill manager, who reported directly to the chairman. The works manager also acted, however, as a technical staff officer to the chairman.) The members of this group and the author collaborated closely, working as a group, in pairs or singly as the situation demanded, until each was satisfied, from his own point of view, of the validity of the analysis. They reported as a group to the other members of senior management at all stages. The decision to initiate the reorganization was taken by the chairman at a meeting which was attended by all senior managers. At that meeting the weaving master of the mill concerned was called in. He listened with evident enthusiasm to the proposals and began at once to produce from his own experience arguments in their favour. The works manager, as the senior executive responsible for the experimental loom shed, then discussed the proposals with the top supervisor of the shed. Thereafter the supervisors and worker in the loom shed took over the proposals as their own; and within a few hours, to the surprise of management, the workers had organized their own working groups. The chairman, the mill manager, the works manager, and the author did not attend any of the discussions with supervisors or workers, nor did they visit the loom shed again until the reorganization had been implemented. The author returned to London on the seventh day of the experimental period and the results reported in this paper have been sent to him by the works manager. The paper has, however, been discussed in detail with the chairman of the company on a recent visit to England. His help with the paper and his permission to publish it are gratefully acknowledged.[2]

The paper is divided into three parts. First, there is a brief description of the loom shed before reorganization; second, this organization is analysed and the reorganization is described; and finally, the results of the reorganization are reported.

THE EXPERIMENTAL AUTOMATIC LOOM SHED

THE ACTIVITIES OF THE LOOM SHED

Automatic looms had been introduced into one of the mills of the Ahmedabad Manufacturing and Calico Printing Company in June 1952. By March 1953 an experimental shed containing 224 looms had been set up. It was designed eventually to hold 304 looms but, at the time of reorganization, a part of the shed was still under construction.

The operations of automatic weaving are carried out by bobbins containing *weft* yarn (threads across the length of cloth) and *beams* containing *warp* yarn (threads along the length of cloth). An automatic loom is prepared for weaving by *loading*. A beam is *gated* into brackets at the back of a loom and each warp thread is passed through the eye of a *heald*, then through a *reed* or comb, to keep it in place and is finally connected to a roller on the front of the loom which takes the woven cloth. A bobbin containing weft yarn is placed in a *shuttle* from which it is automatically ejected when it is empty or the weft thread breaks. Empty bobbins are automatically replaced by full bobbins stored in a *battery*. When the loom is weaving the shuttle is knocked backwards and forwards through a *shed* formed by the separation of the warp threads by the rise of some healds and the fall of others. As the shuttle travels through the shed it leaves behind it a weft thread which is wound from the bobbin within the shuttle. Each weft thread so inserted is banged into place by the reed. The weaving ceases when the warp yarn on the beam has all been converted into cloth on the roller. The loom is then *unloaded*, the finished cloth is taken from the loom (this may occur at intervals during weaving by cutting off the finished cloth) and the empty beam is removed. During weaving, stops of short duration occur whenever a warp thread breaks. A loom is restarted when the broken ends have been joined together (knotted). The looms are fitted with mechanical stops which halt the loom automatically whenever a warp thread breaks.

The activities of a single loom are, therefore, cyclic—load, weave, unload. But since weaving time (including stops for yarn breaks) always greatly exceeds loading and unloading time, the total activities of a loom shed containing a number of looms are continuous, only a small proportion of the looms being stopped for loading and unloading at any one time. During stops for the loading and unloading of looms, general loom maintenance, automatic device maintenance, tuning, and oiling activities are carried out, and all accumulated fluff is removed from under the loom.

The length of yarn which can be wound on a beam or on a bobbin depends upon the size of the beam or bobbin and upon the fineness of the yarn (the *count*—the finer the yarn, the higher the count). The kind of cloth woven (*sort*) depends upon the count of the yarn, and upon the number of threads to the inch in both warp and weft. The rate of weaving depends, therefore, upon the speed and continuity of loom run and upon sort.

Under the climatic conditions in Ahmedabad relative humidity in the loom shed has to be artificially maintained at 80–85 percent to enable yarn to stand

Table 9-1. *Occupational Roles, Tasks, Social Organization and Rates of Pay of Supervisors and Workers on One Shift of Experimental Automatic Loom Shed*

Occupational Role	Number per Shift	Task	Social Organization	Position on Scale Based on Rate of Pay*
Top Supervisor	1	Is responsible for the quality of production of cloth by the shed. Co-ordinates work of two Shifts.	Responsible to Weaving Master of Mill; has as direct subordinates Work Supervisor, Erection Supervisor, and Humidification Fitter.	8.0
Erection Supervisor	1	A specialist temporarily provided by the loom manufacturers during installation of looms.	Responsible to Top Supervisor; no subordinates.	8.0
Work Supervisor	1	Co-ordinates and controls all workers in loom shed except the humidification fitter; allocates work and manages relationships between different kinds of workers.	Responsible to Top Supervisor. All workers other than humidification fitter comprise his command.	3.5
Jobber	2	Maintains looms and adjusts them when running; prepares loom for weaving after beam is "gated"; adjusts healds, threads reed, and tunes loom.	Responsible to Work Supervisor; forms a pair relationship with Assistant Jobber; makes relationships with weavers, oilers, sweepers and gaters, over whom he exercises directive authority.	2.3
Feeler-Motion Maintenance Fitter	1	Maintains automatic device which starts mechanical process of ejecting empty bobbins and replacing them with full.	Responsible to Work Supervisor, works by himself, informed of need for services by Supervisor, Jobber or Weaver.	2.2
Weaver	8	Joins broken ends of yarn by knotting; restarts loom after stops. Responsible for 24 or 32 looms depending on the degree of training received.† Depends upon services of all other workers, in particular gater, jobber, smash-hand, feeler-motion maintenance fitter and battery filler.	Responsible directly to Work Supervisor, and to jobber, and exercises some directive authority over smash-hands who rank as assistant weavers.	1.6–2.0
Humidification Fitter	1	Maintains humidification plant and keeps a constant check on humidity.	Responsible to Top Supervisor. Works by himself.	1.8
Assistant Jobber	2	Assists jobber on complex tasks and performs simple jobber's tasks under supervision.	Responsible to jobber with whom he makes a pair relationship.	1.4–1.8

Productivity and Social Organization

Occupational Role	Number per Shift	Task	Social Organization	Position on Scale Based on Rate of Pay*
Gater	2	Removes empty beam and places new beam with healds in brackets at back of loom. (Warp threads are already drawn through healds.) May assist jobber in preparing loom for weaving.	Responsible to Work Supervisor; works partly by himself and partly with jobber; informed of need for services by Supervisor, jobber or weaver.	1.6
Battery Filler	5	Keeps batteries charged with filled bobbins.	Responsible to Work Supervisor; works by himself but can be called upon by the weaver.	1.2
Oiler	1	Oils looms.	Responsible to Work Supervisor but instructed to oil loom by jobber.	1.1
Smash-hand	3	Joins broken ends of yarn after a smash, i.e., when a large number of threads break at once through some major fault.	Responsible to Work Supervisor and to weaver by whom he is informed of need for services (in training as a weaver).	1.0
Cloth Carrier	1	Removes woven cloth from looms and transports to Inspection department.	Responsible to Work Supervisor. Works by himself but has to approach weaver to stop loom so that he can carry out his task.	1.0
Bobbin Carrier	2	Transports full bobbins from Spinning department to loom shed. Removes empty bobbins ejected by automatic device and returns them to Spinning department.	Responsible to Work Supervisor. Works by himself.	1.0
Sweeper	1	Removes dirt and fluff from shed.	Responsible to Work Supervisor. Works by himself except when called to clean under loom by jobber during loading.	1.0
Total	32‡			

* The positions on the scale are determined by taking the wage of the lowest paid workers as 1 and showing other rates of pay in proportion. Actual rates are not given to avoid complications of comparison with British and American standards of living. The pay rates are related to status.

† The standard number of looms per weaver had started at 12, had been increased successively to 18, 24 and 32, and the provisional target was 64.

‡ The total number of workers in the shed was considered to be adequate ultimately for 240 looms instead of the 224 then in the shed.

up to the strain put on it in the weaving process. For this purpose a plant is installed which humidifies the whole shed.

Two eight-hour shifts were worked, the day shift from 7.00 a.m. to 3.30 p.m. with a half-hour break from 11.00 a.m. to 11.30 a.m., and the night shift from 3.30 p.m. to midnight with a half-hour break from 7.30 p.m. to 8.00 p.m.

Productivity is measured by two figures—efficiency and damage. Efficiency is the number of *picks* (weft threads) inserted in any shift, expressed as a percentage of the number of picks which would have been inserted had the loom run continuously for the whole shift—no allowance is made for loading, unloading or for any other stops. Damage is the percentage of cloth not accepted as of standard quality by the inspectors and viewers after weaving. The higher the efficiency and the lower the damage, the greater the productivity.

THE OCCUPATIONAL ROLES AND TASKS

Current British and American practice had been followed in the organization of the shed. The total task of weaving had been broken down into component operations, and each component was performed by different workers. The number of workers allocated to the various tasks had been based upon British, American, and Japanese[3] standards modified by time studies of work under Indian conditions and based upon yarn breakage rates existing in the mill at the time of installation. The experimental shed started working when twelve looms had been installed. Neither management nor workers had had experience of modern working methods with automatic looms. During the first eight months looms were brought into production as they were erected and workers trained to use them. By March 1953 relatively stable conditions has been established, and further loom erection had been halted pending the completion of the building. The numbers of workers on a shift, their tasks, and their positions on a scale based on differential rates of pay during March 1953 are shown in Table 9-1.

A first examination of Table 9-1 shows that, although all the tasks of the shed were interdependent, only the jobbers and assistant jobbers had any form of stable work group structure and that the other workers formed an aggregate of individuals some of whom were virtually independent of each other. The jobbers had some authority over most other workers and weavers had some authority over smash-hands, but the lines of authority were confused and undefined. For example, the oiler could be directed by a jobber, but the relative authority of the two jobbers was not established; in the same way the smash-hands could be given orders by a weaver, but the order in which the eight weavers could demand their services was not defined.

THE WORK ORGANIZATION

Because the production process of a loom shed, in contrast to that of a single loom, is continuous rather than cyclic all activities in the shed were directed to maintaining the *steady state* of multiple loom weaving. Production in the shed, therefore, depended upon the simultaneous carrying out of all the activities of

Productivity and Social Organization

Table 9-2. *The Number of Looms per Worker and the Number of Workers in Each Occupational Role in the Experimental Automatic Loom Shed*

Activity	Task	Occupational Role	Number of Looms per Worker	Number of Workers
Weaving	Knotting broken yarn	Weaver	24–32	8
	Battery filling	Battery Filler	40–50	5
	Removing empty bobbins	Bobbin Carrier	224	1
	Knotting broken yarn	Smash-hand	60–80	3
Loading and Unloading	Replacing empty beams	Gater	112	2
	Removing woven cloth	Cloth carrier	112	2
Loom Maintenance	Fitting and tuning	Jobber	112	2
	Fitting	Assistant Jobber	112	2
	Specialized fitting	Feeler-Motion Fitter	224	1
	Oiling	Oiler	224	1
Cleaning	Sweeping and cleaning	Sweeper	224	1
Humidifying	Specialized fitting	Humidification Fitter	224	1
Totals	12	12	—	29

the shed. The activities were carried out by workers who performed tasks and took occupational roles. The tasks performed by the workers related their occupational roles to the activities of the shed. Because the activities of the shed had been broken down into their component tasks and the number of workers required to perform the tasks had been determined by work studies of the separate components, workers in different occupational roles worked on different numbers of looms. For example, weavers operated twenty-four or thirty-two looms depending upon their skill, while battery fillers charged the batteries of from forty to fifty looms and smash-hands served on average seventy-five looms. This method of determining the number of workers required to carry out a total production process is the normal production engineering corollary of job-breakdown and work study. Katz and Kahn have included it as

Table 9-3. *Differentiation of Experimental Automatic Loom Shed into Loom Groups*

Kind of Loom Group	Number of Loom Groups	Number of Tasks in Each Loom Group	Number of Workers in Kind of Loom Group	Occupational Roles
I (24–32)	8	1	8	Weaver
II (40–50)	5	1	5	Battery Filler
III (60–80)	3	1	3	Smash-hand
IV (112)	2	4	8	Gater Cloth Carrier Jobber Assistant Jobber
V (224)	1	5	5	Bobbin Carrier Feeler-Motion Fitter Oiler Sweeper Humidification Fitter
Totals	19	12	29	

a major factor in their concept of the machine theory of organization. The analysis of the loom shed showing the number of workers and the number of looms per worker related to activities, tasks and occupational roles is shown in Table 9-2.

In Table 9-2 it can be seen that each task was allocated to one occupational role, and that the twelve tasks were, therefore, performed by twenty-nine workers who, between them, took twelve occupational roles. It may also be seen that the looms in the shed were divided into five different kinds of loom-group which varied as to the number of looms, the number of tasks performed, and the number of workers engaged in each group. This analysis is shown in Table 9-3, from which it can be seen that the twelve tasks performed by twenty-nine workers were performed in a total of nineteen overlapping loom groups of five kinds. The differentiation of the looms into loom groups is also shown in Figure 9-1.

MANAGEMENT HIERARCHY OF THE LOOM SHED

One consequence of the different kinds of loom groups and of the allocation of one component task to one occupational role was that the workers could not conveniently be grouped for supervision. Thus, in spite of the directive responsibility of the jobbers for all other workers and of the weavers for some, the work supervisor was directly responsible for twenty-six different individuals. A chart of the management organization is shown in simplified form in Figure 9-2 (it was not possible to represent all lines of communication).

The overall picture of loom shed organization is a confused pattern of relationships among an aggregate of individuals for whom no stable internal group structure could be discerned. This picture may be both compared and contrasted with that found by Trist and Bamforth in the longwall system of coalmining. The effect of job-breakdown and task allocation led there, especially on the filling shift, to a similar aggregate of individuals with no discernible stable internal group structure; but the sequential nature of the process led to splitting and isolation, and the segregation of those engaged on component tasks of the total process both between and within shifts. In the experimental automatic loom shed the continuous nature of the process and the simultaneous performance of all component tasks led to confusion.

CHANGE OF SORT

A change of sort—kind of cloth woven—may change the work-load of some of the workers. Thus a change of sort involving a change to a higher reed (greater number of threads per inch in the warp) may require an increase in the number of weavers, because the greater number of threads may cause more frequent breaks, but a change involving a yarn of finer count may require a decrease in the number of battery fillers, gaters, and bobbin carriers, because more yarn could be wound on bobbins and beams. Without necessarily requiring an alteration in the total number of workers, a change of sort involved, therefore, either a change in individual work loads or change in the kinds of workers employed. Each change

Productivity and Social Organization

I. Eight Groups of **24-32**:

1 Weaver	1 Weaver	1 Weaver	1 Weaver	1 Weaver	1 Weaver	1 Weaver	1 Weaver
24-32 LOOMS	24-32 LOOMS	24-32 LOOMS	24-32 LOOMS	24-32 LOOMS	24-32 LOOMS	24-32 LOOMS	24-32 LOOMS

II. Five Groups of **40-50**:

1 Battery Filler	1 Battery Filler	1 Battery Filler	1 Battery Filler	1 Battery Filler
40-50 LOOMS	40-50 LOOMS	40-50 LOOMS	40-50 LOOMS	40-50 LOOMS

III. Three Groups of **60-80**:

1 Smash Hand	1 Smash Hand	1 Smash Hand
60-80 LOOMS	60-80 LOOMS	60-80 LOOMS

IV. Two Groups of **112**:

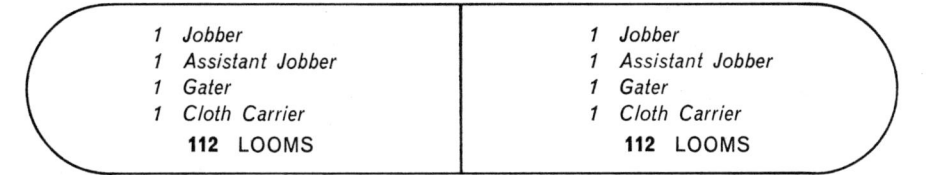

1 Jobber 1 Assistant Jobber 1 Gater 1 Cloth Carrier **112** LOOMS	1 Jobber 1 Assistant Jobber 1 Gater 1 Cloth Carrier **112** LOOMS

V. One Group of **224**:

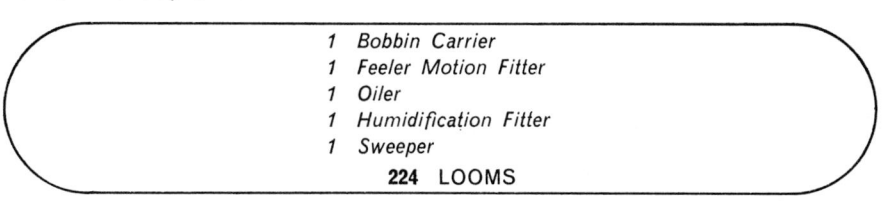

1 Bobbin Carrier
1 Feeler Motion Fitter
1 Oiler
1 Humidification Fitter
1 Sweeper
224 LOOMS

Figure 9-1.   Organization of Loom Shed in Overlapping Loom Groups

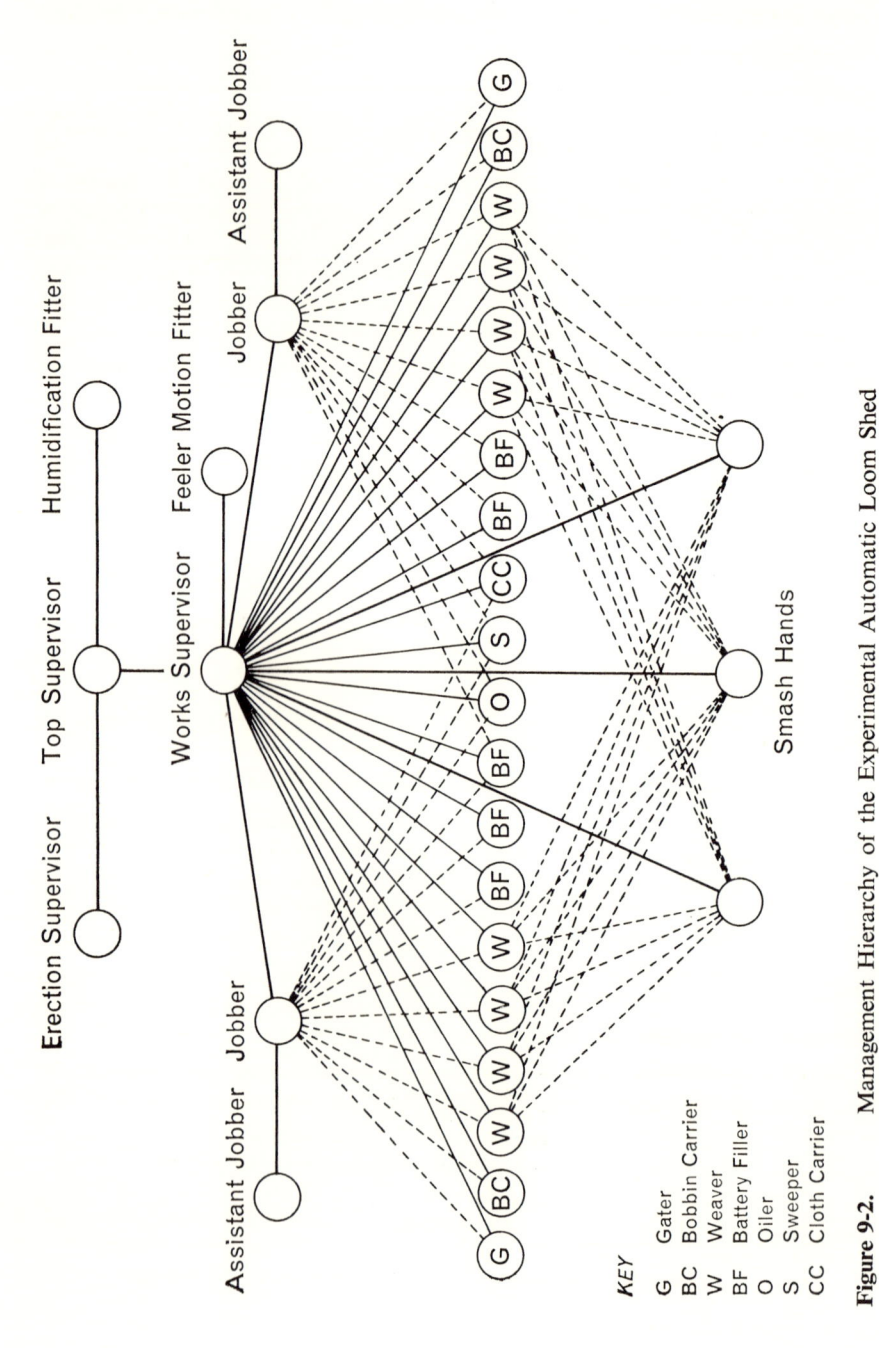

166   Techno-Structural Strategies of Social Intervention

Figure 9-2. Management Hierarchy of the Experimental Automatic Loom Shed

KEY
G   Gater
BC   Bobbin Carrier
W   Weaver
BF   Battery Filler
O   Oiler
S   Sweeper
CC   Cloth Carrier

altered the relationships between interdependent tasks and restructured some of the loom groups. Any change of sort was, therefore, likely to add to the confusion of task and worker relationships.

THE GOVERNMENT OF THE SHED

The work supervisor had so much to do in the handling of work allocations and of worker relationships that the top supervisor had to assist him by dealing directly with jobbers and other workers. Indeed, had not the top supervisor so helped the work supervisor, it is difficult to see how he could usefully have filled his time. In the same way the jobbers' technological tasks were so many and their supervising responsibility so undefined that the work supervisor had to assist them by giving direct orders to their nominal subordinates.

This breakdown of the hierarchical structure placed a high premium on the quality of the relationships between the supervisors and between the work supervisor and the workers. That the breakdown had led to no overt relationship difficulties was undoubtedly due in part to the high quality of the relationships, but it was also due to the considerable attention which had been given to the experimental shed by the chairman, mill manager, and works manager ever since its opening. The lack of internal structure had been counterbalanced by a strong management structure external to the workers. In practice the *governing system*[4] of the shed included members of higher management in addition to those shown on the organization chart.

In spite of this strong governing system, however, the current figures for efficiency were lower and the percentage of damaged cloth was higher than budgeted targets. Faced with this short-fall in expected productivity there were, apart from technological improvements, two possibilities: still further to strengthen the external structure of the governing system by increasing the number of supervisors and tightening inspection, or by reorganization, to create and stabilize an internal structure of the working-group. The danger of increasing the number of supervisors and of tightening inspection was that the workers would not only continue to experience the discomfort of the internally unstructured confusion but would feel further coerced and policed, and in consequence might increase their resistance to greater effort and productivity. In addition, the presence of higher management in the governing system of the shed could only be temporary, and their withdrawal would leave gaps in the governing system which would need still more supervisors as replacements, thus enhancing any feelings the workers had of being regarded as untrustworthy.

THE SOCIO-TECHNICAL SYSTEM OF THE LOOM SHED[5]

INTERDEPENDENCE OF TASK AND INDEPENDENCE OF WORKERS

All tasks in the shed were interdependent, but many of the individual workers performing the tasks were virtually independent, in the sense that they were only linked through the work supervisor, while those who had interdependent relationships had varying degrees of interdependence in overlapping loom groups. Thus each weaver, depending upon the sort on his looms, had on average the services of one quarter of the time of a dependent pair consisting of jobber and assistant jobber; five-eighths of that of a battery filler; three-eighths of a smash-hand, and so on. Any change of sort altered the proportions of the services he could command. Battery fillers each served, on average, one and three-eighths weavers; each smash-hand two and two-thirds weavers. With some sorts the time of a particular battery filler might be completely filled in serving the looms of two weavers and there was then opportunity for the two weavers and their battery filler to build interdependent relationships consistent with the interdependence of their tasks, but this was not a common pattern.

Generally, it may be said that the area of the shed and the number of workers were both too large and task relationships too confused for there to be much opportunity to build stable, cohesive relationships between the members of the total work group, and the confused loom groups precluded the formation of small, internally structured and internally led work-groups consistent with task relatedness.

JOB BREAKDOWN, MULTIPLE GRADES AND WORKER MOBILITY

Job breakdown and consequent specialization had reduced the quality and range of skills required for performance of tasks in the loom shed. A weaver no longer had to service his looms, tune them, refill shuttles, or stop the loom to prevent damage. Indeed, the loom itself had become the weaver and all the workers in the loom shed now serviced this mechanical weaver. In spite of the persistence of the title of weaver for one of the occupational roles the weaver's task may be more accurately described as *loom-end-knotting*. The similarity of his task to that of a *piecer* in ring spinning will be recognized by all who are familiar with the textile industry.

In general, specialization of task had restricted the possibilities of task or role rotation. Because of low labour turnover only the prospect of completion of the shed and the installation of more looms, an isolated event, held out any real hope of promotion or transfer. Even such an event only offered the opportunity of transfer from one specialized task to another.

Mobility was further restricted by the many different status grades and, since the status grades were allied to rates of pay, almost any exchange of tasks would have involved a change of pay—a change only easy to accomplish in one direction. In short, the workers were chained to their roles and tasks.

SMALL WORK GROUP ORGANIZATION

Six assumptions were made about work-group organization, that:
(1) when individual tasks are interdependent the relationships between those performing the tasks will have important effects on productivity;
(2) groups of workers engaged in the same loom group are more likely to form

internally structured stable and cohesive group relationships than those in overlapping groups;
(3) interchangeability of tasks (role rotation) gives greater freedom of movement to workers;
(4) the coincidence of obvious physical and loom-group boundaries enables a working group to realize itself and identify itself with its "territory";
(5) the fewer differences there are in work-group status (and pay) consistent with offering opportunities for promotion, the more likely is the internal structure of a group to stabilize itself and the more likely are its members to accept internal leadership;
(6) when individual members of small work-groups become disaffected to the extent that they can no longer fit into their work-group, they need to be able to move to other small work-groups engaged on similar tasks if group stability is to be maintained.

None of the conditions made in these assumptions were satisfied by the existing socio-technical system. The tasks of the loom shed were therefore re-examined. The smash-hands were already accepted as weavers in training; and the weaver depended to a considerable extent on the efficiency with which the battery filler performed his task. The battery fillers, in their turn, had aspirations to become weavers. Bobbin carriers fetched all bobbins from the Spinning department for the battery fillers. Assistant jobbers were already members of a pair, and gaters sometimes assisted jobbers to get looms running after a stop to replace an empty beam. The feeler-motion maintenance fitter was responsible for a specialist part of general loom maintenance. The oiler was under the nominal control of both jobbers, and although the sweeper and the cloth carrier each had his special task and were not considered interchangeable, they and the oiler were all graded as unskilled.

SHORT AND LONG LOOM STOPS AS A BASIS FOR ANALYSIS

Cloth is only woven when the loom is running; all tasks in the shed are, therefore, directed to keeping the loom weaving. Loom stops are of two kinds: *short stops* caused by simple yarn breaks (half minute to one minute); and *long stops* for gating (one to one and a half hours), meal breaks (half an hour) and intervals between the second and first shifts (seven hours). During actual shift hours workers could be divided into those whose tasks were directed to keeping the looms running through short stops and those whose tasks were to get the looms weaving again after a long stop. Thus weavers, battery fillers, smash-hands, and bobbin carriers were concerned with the weaving loom, while gaters and cloth carriers were concerned when the loom was stopped for loading new beams at the back or for removing finished cloth from the front. At the same time, the jobber, assistant jobber, feeler-motion fitter and oiler had to use the opportunity of a long-stop to obtain access to the loom for maintenance work. Even the sweeper had to use that time as his only opportunity to get under the loom to remove accumulated fluff. Only the humidification fitter was not concerned directly with looms and was, therefore, ignored in the subsequent analysis. The

Table 9-4. *Temporal Analysis of Occupational Roles and Tasks*

	SHORT STOPS	Tasks Connected With LONG STOPS		
Occupational Roles	Weaving	Loading-Unloading	Loom Maintenance	Departmental Duties
Weavers	×			
Battery Fillers	×			
Smash-hands	×			
Bobbin Carrier	×			
Gaters		×		
Cloth Carrier		×		
Jobbers			×	
Assistant Jobbers			×	
Feeler-Motion Fitter			×	
Oiler			×	
Sweeper			(×)	×
Humidification Fitter				×

temporal analysis of the occupational roles and tasks in terms of short and long stops is shown in Table 9-4.

The re-examination of shed tasks and the temporal analysis of occupational roles and tasks suggested that two sub-groupings were possible—a short-stop sub-group and a long-stop sub-group which would include those concerned with loading and unloading and with loom maintenance.

VARIATION IN NUMBERS REQUIRED WITH CHANGE OF SORT

Change of sort demanded change in the number of weavers, battery fillers, and

Table 9-5. *Theoretical Number of Looms per Worker By Sorts*

Sort Number	Short-Stops per Loom Hour*	LOOMS PER Weaver	Battery Filler	Gater
1	1.4	38	28	80
2	1.4	38	33	116
3	1.2	42	50	96
4	1.4	38	66	114
5	1.4	38	66	114
6	1.6	35	69	114
7	1.6	35	69	80
8	1.6	35	69	98
9	2.0	32	84	80
10	2.0	32	84	115
11	1.6	35	110	300
12	1.8	33	110	360
13	1.8	33	120	300
14	1.8	33	120	360
15	1.8	33	138	360
16	2.0	32	138	360

* The figures for short-stops per loom hour in this column were based on existing performances; in addition to the figures shown in this and subsequent tables, other figures based on the carrying out of technical improvements which would reduce the rate of yarn breakage were also calculated.

Table 9-6. Number of Variable Workers for 960 Looms

Sort		Weavers	Battery Fillers	Total Weavers and Battery Fillers	Gaters
Coarse	1	26	34	60	12
	2	26	29	55	9
Medium	3	23	19	42	10
	4	26	15	41	9
	5	26	15	41	9
	6	27	14	41	9
	7	27	14	41	12
	8	27	14	41	10
	9	30	12	42	12
	10	30	12	42	9
Fine	11	27	9	36	3
	12	29	9	38	3
	13	29	8	37	3
	14	29	8	37	3
	15	29	7	36	3
	16	30	7	37	3

gaters, less change in the number of cloth carriers and bobbin carriers, and virtually no change in the number of other workers. To examine the limits of the changes required, the theoretical number of looms which could be attended by weavers, battery fillers, and gaters was calculated for each sort likely to be woven in any loom shed in the mill. These theoretical numbers are shown in Table 9-5.

The results of Table 9-5 were then converted to show the number of workers who would theoretically be required to work 960 looms for all varieties of sort. (The figure 960 was chosen arbitrarily to give a large enough number to avoid too much approximation.) These results are shown in Table 9-6, in which it will be seen that although there are considerable variations in the number of weavers, battery fillers, and gaters over the whole range they can be grouped into three main sorts in which comparatively little variation occurs in the total number of weavers and battery fillers or in the number of gaters. These main sorts correspond to the coarse, medium, and fine counts.

Variation in the numbers of cloth carriers and bobbin carriers with change of sort was found to be too small to merit consideration. It appeared, therefore,

Table 9-7. Varying Number of Workers Required for 960 Looms

Occupational Roles	Numbers Required for Each Main Sort		
	Coarse	Medium	Fine
Weavers } Battery Fillers }	60	42	38
Gaters	12	12	3
Totals	72	54	41

Table 9-8. *Number of Other Workers Required for 960 Looms*

Occupational Roles	Number Required For All Sorts
Jobbers	8
Assistant Jobbers	8
Feeler-Motion Mechanics	4
Oilers	4
Sweepers	4
Bobbin Carriers	4
Cloth Carriers	8
Smash-hands	12
Total	52

that, provided weavers and battery fillers could be regarded as partly interchangeable tasks, two kinds of workers would be required whose numbers varied with change of sort. The figures are summarized in Table 9-7, in which the greatest numbers in the columns of total weavers and battery fillers and of gaters for each of the three main sorts was taken.

The numbers of other workers required for 960 looms based on the numbers in the shed are shown in Table 9-8.

THEORETICAL WORK GROUP ORGANIZATION

The results of the analyses shown in Tables 9-4, 9-7, and 9-8 were then combined with the results of the re-examination of related occupational roles. The combined result is shown in Table 9-9.

Inspection of the loom shed showed that the looms were installed in rows of sixteen and that wide gangways separated off two blocks of sixty-four. That is to say that a block of sixty-four looms was an easily recognizable territory separated from other looms by wide gangways and pillars. The outline plan of the shed is given in Figure 9-3. Further constructional work and the installation

Table 9-9. *Theoretical Numbers of Workers Required for 960 Looms*

Sub-Group	Occupational Roles	Coarse	Medium	Fine
Short Stop	Weavers / Battery Fillers	60	42	38
	Smash-hands	12	12	12
	Bobbin Carriers	4	4	4
	Totals	76	58	54
Long Stop	Jobbers and Assistants / Gaters / Feeler-Motion Fitters	32	32	23
	Cloth Carriers / Oilers / Sweepers	16	16	16
	Totals	48	48	39
	Grand Totals	124	106	93

Productivity and Social Organization

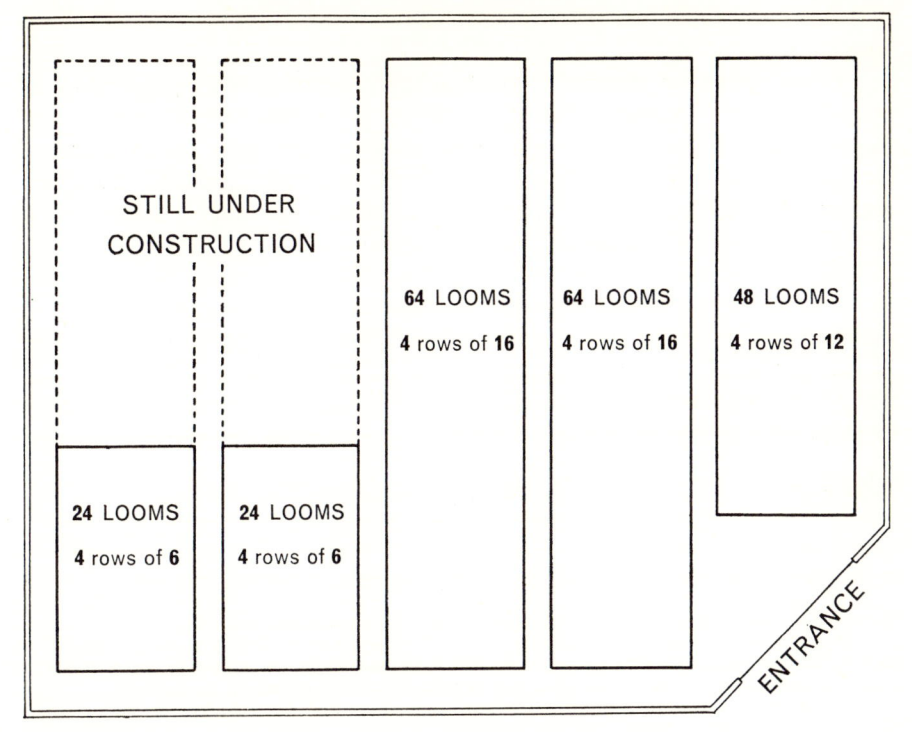

```
┌─────────────────────────────────────────────────────────────┐
│  ┌ ─ ─ ─ ─ ┐  ┌ ─ ─ ─ ┐  ┌─────────┐ ┌─────────┐ ┌────────┐ │
│  │         │  │       │  │         │ │         │ │        │ │
│  │ STILL UNDER        │  │64 LOOMS │ │64 LOOMS │ │48 LOOMS│ │
│  │ CONSTRUCTION       │  │         │ │         │ │        │ │
│  │         │  │       │  │4 rows   │ │4 rows   │ │4 rows  │ │
│  │         │  │       │  │of 16    │ │of 16    │ │of 12   │ │
│  └ ─ ─ ─ ─ ┘  └ ─ ─ ─ ┘  │         │ │         │ │        │ │
│  ┌─────────┐  ┌───────┐  │         │ │         │ │        │ │
│  │24 LOOMS │  │24 LOOMS│ │         │ │         │ │        │ │
│  │4 rows of 6│ │4 rows of 6│                              │ │
│  └─────────┘  └───────┘  └─────────┘ └─────────┘ └────────┘ │
│                                                    ENTRANCE │
└─────────────────────────────────────────────────────────────┘
```

Figure 9-3.   Plan of Experimental Automatic Loom Shed

Table 9-10.   *Theoretical Numbers of Workers Required for 64 Looms*

		\multicolumn{3}{c}{NUMBERS REQUIRED FOR EACH MAIN SORT}
Sub-Group	Occupational Roles	Coarse	Medium	Fine
Short Stop	Weavers ⎱ Battery Fillers ⎰	4.0	2.8	2.5
	Smash-hands ⎱ Bobbin Carriers ⎰	1.1	1.1	1.1
	Totals	5.1	3.9	3.6
Long Stop	Jobbers and Assistants ⎱ Gaters Feeler-Motion Fitters ⎰	2.1	2.1	1.5
	Cloth Carriers ⎱ Oilers Sweepers ⎰	1.1	1.1	1.1
	Totals	3.2	3.2	2.6
	Grand Totals	8.3	7.1	6.2

of more looms would turn the two blocks of twenty-four into two more blocks of sixty-four.

It was, therefore, decided to start an experimental group on one block of sixty-four looms, to extend this, if successful, to the other block of sixty-four looms, and ultimately to use the block of forty-eight near the entrance of the shed as a training group. The figures for the theoretical numbers of workers required for 960 looms were, therefore, reduced to the number required for sixty-four looms and the results are given in Table 9-10.

STATUS DIFFERENCES AND TITLES

An examination of the status grades showed that there appeared to be three natural grades of which one would provide the group leader. These, together with their positions on the same scale based upon wages as in Table 9-1, are shown in Table 9-11. It will be seen that for the group leader the new grade involved a

Table 9-11. *Status Grades for The Experimental Small Work Group*

Grade	Status	Rank
A	Group leader who would also be the working head of the long-stop sub-group	2.4
B	Fully experienced members of either the short-stop sub-group or the long-stop sub-group	2.0
D	Those engaged almost entirely on the "unskilled" jobs of battery filling, sweeping, oiling or carrying, but which should nevertheless be higher than that of a new unskilled entrant once they had been accepted as integral members of a working group	1.2

small rise in pay, and that for some previously designated "unskilled" the rise was larger. At the same time, whereas previously only jobbers and weavers were paid piece rates,[6] it was proposed that all members of the experimental group should participate. It was hoped that any increased cost incurred by these changes would be offset by eliminating the need for extra supervision and inspection, and by greater efficiency.

The wide difference between Grades B and D led to the interpolation of a sub-grade C (rank 1.6) for those who had earned promotion from Grade D but had not yet acquired sufficient experience to qualify for Grade B.

It was recognized that the current titles given to occupational roles would not necessarily be appropriate to any form of reorganized internally-led small work-group, since more of the tasks would be interchangeable. Various possible titles were suggested, but the danger of expressing, consciously or unconsciously, hopes or expectations led to a decision to await discussion with the supervisors and workers before trying to define either the new grades or the new roles.

OTHER ASPECTS OF THE ANALYSIS OF THE SOCIO-TECHNICAL SYSTEM

The repeated examination of the occupational roles and tasks in the loom shed raised a number of other questions to which answers could not immediately be obtained or solutions, if obtainable, could not be immediately implemented. Some of these questions concerned the uniformity of the level of mechanization in the various shed operations, others would have involved analyses of other parts of the total textile manufacturing process. Time was not immediately available for the investigation of other parts of the process and changing the level of mechanization in some operations required the solution of engineering problems and the invention or development of further mechanical devices. Some alterations—for example, those related to the removal of fluff—were awaiting the arrival of equipment already ordered.

One outstanding question was that of the long loom stops caused by meal breaks and by intervals between shifts. Apart from insisting that in general the purpose of an automatic machine was to run without attention, it was decided not to suggest at once any alteration in the current practice during meal breaks. The question of intervals between shifts was complicated by trade union agreements and Indian Industrial Court awards and was left for future consideration.

RESULTS OF THE EXPERIMENT

SPONTANEOUS ACCEPTANCE OF REORGANIZATION

At a meeting of the chairman, and mill, works, and personnel managers and the author it was decided to discuss the analysis with the weaving master, the supervisors, and workers at once, and with their approval to start an experimental group on the one block of sixty-four looms. The weaving master was called into the meeting and as soon as he heard of the notion of a *group of workers for a group of looms*, he spontaneously accepted the proposed reorganization. This spontaneous acceptance by the weaving master provided for higher management a first validation of the "goodness of fit" of the proposed reorganization with the felt needs of those working in the experimental loom shed. The works manager started discussions with the supervisors on the same evening. It had been expected that it would probably take some time for the discussions to be held, first with the supervisors of each shift and then with the workers, and that the experimental group would then be chosen by the supervisors in consultation with the works manager and a suitable date for starting chosen. In the event, the supervisors and workers immediately took possession of the system and by the next day, by a complex sociometric process which there was no time to investigate, the workers had themselves organized two experimental groups. By the following day groups had been organized by the workers for the two blocks of sixty-four looms for both shifts, making four small work-groups (experimental groups a, b, c and d). That the actual members of the groups so spontaneously chosen were not those who would have been picked by the works manager was considered (with some misgiving perhaps) less important than that the grouping was spontaneous and that the number in each group had been spontaneously fixed at seven. There were only medium counts on the particular looms and each spontaneously chosen work-group consisted of a long-stop sub-group of one Grade

A, one Grade B, and one Grade D, and a short-stop sub-group of two Grade B and two Grade D. The composition of each group is shown in Table 9-12.

It was decided to allow the groups so chosen to work for an experimental period whose length would be determined by events.

Table 9-12. *Composition of Each Experimental Group*

	NUMBER IN EACH SUB-GROUP		
Grade	Short Stop	Long Stop	Total
A (leader)		1	1
B	2	1	3
D	2	1	3
Totals	4	3	7

THE MANAGEMENT OF THE SHED AFTER REORGANIZATION

The immediate effect on management after the shed had settled down to this reorganization was that the number of individuals reporting directly to the work supervisor was reduced. Although those workers not included in the experimental groups still continued as before reorganization, those in the experimental groups were now responsible to their group leaders. In addition workers requiring training, instead of being spread over the whole shed, could now be concentrated in one loom group of forty-eight where they could receive more direct attention from the supervisors. It was decided that, as soon as the building was completed and the full complement of 304 looms installed, the other two blocks of sixty-four looms would be organized in the same way as the experimental groups. This organization would leave the work supervisor with four group leaders reporting directly to him and would free the top supervisor to give special attention to the training loom group. Instead of the shed's needing more supervision it appeared that there was every chance that the present supervisors would be under-employed.

The sophistication of higher management in permitting the shed to reorganize itself was followed by the beginning of their withdrawal from the governing system of the shed, not so much as part of a consciously determined plan but as the result of increased confidence in the ability of those in the shed to solve their own problems. In August the chairman of the company reported that "Whereas I always spent some time in the experimental shed every time I went to the mill (on average twice a week), I don't think I've been in it more than two or three times since it was reorganized, not because I've lost any interest in it, but because I know it is going well."

So far as the group leaders and workers are concerned, there has been no noticeable change in their attitude to the reorganization since their first spontaneous acceptance, and there have been requests from the workers not included in the experimental groups to be allowed to organize themselves in the same way. In discussion with the supervisors, the workers expressed a positive desire to avoid the old titles of their jobs but no enthusiasm for any other titles than the "A", "B" and "D" grade designations. In August (the latest information) experimental group tasks were still known by all those in the shed as "A", "B" and "D" jobs and those in occupational roles as "A", "B" and "D" workers.

In general it can be said that, as far as can be ascertained, the assumptions made about small work group organization have been proved correct.

FOUR PHASES OF THE EXPERIMENTAL PERIOD

A detailed consideration of the experimental period shows that it may be described in four phases:

First Phase—the eleven working days immediately after reorganization. During this phase there was an increase in the efficiency of the experimental groups but at the cost of an increase in the percentage damage and of neglect of loom maintenance.[8] This was discussed by the works manager with the supervisors, group leaders, and workers who expressed themselves as willing to cooperate in the attempt to reduce the damage and improve maintenance, but as unable adequately to keep down damage and keep up maintenance while maintaining the rate of working with short loom-stops at 1.5–2.0 per hour, the current rate.

Second Phase—three working days, during which the top supervisor took over the group leadership of one of the groups to investigate the possibility of maintaining efficiency while avoiding increased damage and decreased maintenance. As a result of this investigation during which efficiency fell considerably in all four groups, extra help at the rate of half an extra Grade D worker was given to each group (based on theoretical needs with loom stops per hour of 1.75).

Third Phase—eight working days of resettlement following the damage and maintenance investigation. In this phase efficiency climbed, damage remained less than it had been before the experiment started and loom maintenance was restored to its former level. Discussions took place between the works manager, supervisors, group leaders, and workers about the running of looms during meal intervals.

Fourth Phase—the remaining thirty-seven working days of the experimental period. As a result of discussions during the third phase, looms were not stopped by the workers at the beginning of the meal break but were allowed to run on until they stopped automatically when yarn broke. The extra help given in the third phase was withdrawn.[9] After thirty-seven days a partial third shift was started working on one of the experimental blocks of sixty-four looms and on one of the groups of forty-eight. Results thereafter are not, therefore, strictly comparable with those of the experimental period.

FIGURES OF EFFICIENCY AND DAMAGE

The results of the comparison of the mean percentage efficiencies of the experimental groups with the mean percentage efficiency of the shed before reorganization are given in Table 9-13. Standard deviations of the distributions of percentage efficiencies are given in Table 9-14. (All figures are based on an eight-hour shift.)

The results show a significant difference between the mean percentage efficiencies of each experimental group in the fourth phase, and the shed efficiency before reorganization, and between the mean percentage efficiency of the combined groups in the fourth phase, and the shed efficiency before reorganization.

Table 9-13. *Mean Percentage Efficiencies of Four Experimental Groups Compared with Shed Efficiency Before Reorganization*

Phases of Experimental Period	EXPERIMENTAL GROUP				
	a	b	c	d	Combined
1st. March 30–April 10 11 working days	87.7	87.9	86.5	86.4	87.1
2nd. April 11–April 14 3 working days	67.7	69.6	73.2	79.8	72.6
3rd. April 15–April 23 8 working days	84.0	86.4	83.0	86.3	84.9
4th. April 24–June 6 37 working days	95.9	96.2	94.0	94.1	95.0
Shed Efficiency Before Reorganization* March 1–March 28 23 working days	(79.8)	(79.8)	(79.8)	(79.8)	79.8

* The range of individual weaver's efficiencies before reorganization was 74.4–85.0.

Table 9-14. *Standard Deviations of Distributions of Percentage Efficiencies*

Phases of Experimental Period	EXPERIMENTAL GROUP				
	a	b	c	d	Combined
1st. March 30–April 10 11 working days	2.4	4.9	1.8	4.0	3.6
2nd. April 11–April 14 3 working days	2.7	3.7	.7	1.8	5.2
3rd. April 15–April 23 8 working days	5.3	3.2	6.8	1.6	4.9
4th. April 24–June 6 37 working days	2.6	2.3	2.6	2.4	2.7
Standard Deviation Before Reorganization March 1–March 28 23 working days	(3.1)	(3.1)	(3.1)	(3.1)	3.1

Except in the second phase (three days) they show no significant difference between the mean percentage efficiencies of the experimental groups or in the fourth phase between the standard deviations of the distributions of percentage efficiencies of the experimental groups. The standard deviations of the distributions of the experimental groups are less for each group than that of the distribution for the whole shed before reorganization.

The results of the comparison of mean percentage damage of the experi-

Productivity and Social Organization

mental groups with the mean percentage damage of the shed before reorganization are given in Table 9-15. No daily damage figures were available for the period before reorganization or for the experimental groups for the first six days of the experimental period. Because there was no night shift in the inspection department, the damage of the experimental groups a and b and of c and d had to be combined. The standard deviations of the distributions of the damage of groups a and b and of c and d are shown in Table 9-16.

Table 9-15. *Mean Percentage Damage of Four Experimental Groups Compared with Shed Damage Before Reorganization*

Phases of Experimental Period	EXPERIMENTAL GROUP		
	a & b	c & d	Combined
1st. April 6–April 10 5 working days	37.8	45.5	41.6
2nd. April 11–April 14 3 working days	31.2	36.2	33.7
3rd. April 15–April 23 8 working days	18.8	25.7	22.3
4th. April 24–June 6 37 working days	17.8	21.9	19.9
Shed Damage Before Reorganization March 1–March 28 23 working days	(31.8)	(31.8)	31.8

Table 9-16. *Standard Deviations of Distributions of Damage of Four Experimental Groups*

Phase of Experimental Period	EXPERIMENTAL GROUP	
	a & b	c & d
1st. April 6–April 10 5 working days	3.2	4.8
2nd. April 11–April 14 3 working days	7.1	3.8
3rd. April 15–April 23 8 working days	3.5	4.3
4th. April 25–June 6 37 working days	3.2	3.3

The results show a significant difference between the mean percentage damage of each of the pairs of experimental groups and that of the shed before reorganization. They also show significant differences between the means of the experimental groups in all phases. The differences between the means of experimental groups can be accounted for by difficulties with humidification during construction, which affected the sixty-four looms near the new building more than the others. The boundary of the affected area was, however, difficult to define, and other factors (at present unkown) may have affected performance.

It may also be noted that in the period before reorganization the proportion of looms to workers (excluding the humidification fitter) was in the proportion of 8 : 1; that if eventually the number of workers in the shed had been found adequate to man 240 looms, the proportion would then be 8.6 : 1; and that in the experimental groups the proportion was 8.5 : 1 during the period when extra help was given, and 9.1 : 1 after it was withdrawn.

LIMITATIONS OF THE FINDINGS

The findings of the experiment are those of operational research. It was not possible, within the circumstances of the experiment, to relate the findings to the ecological background of economic, industrial, or cultural conditions in India nor, because of language difficulties, was it possible to relate them to the attitudes and relationships of the supervisors and workers of the loom shed itself. The only evidence of the "goodness of fit" of the analysis was its spontaneous acceptance, rapid implementation and continuity. It may, however, be inferred that, by being permitted to implement their own reorganization, the workers were given a first experience of their own capacity to create an internal structure; and that management, in its turn, was able to accept the internal structuring of small work groups as a method of management and as an alternative to additional imposed external structure.

An examination of the efficiency and damage results in the rest of the shed, that is, the looms other than those included in the experimental groups, strongly suggests the effects of forces of induction from the experimental groups. Theoretically the rest of the shed continued with the previous form of organization during the experimental period. The formation of the experimental groups, however, had an inevitably disturbing effect on the whole shed and involved a reallocation of tasks and work loads among the rest of the workers. This disturbance, apart from any of the effects of being left out of the experiment, would have led to the expectation of induced negative forces in the experimental period. These expectations were confirmed by the results but only in the first three phases of the experimental period. During the fourth phase the mean percentage efficiency of the rest of the shed was 81.4 (shed efficiency before reorganization 79.8), and the mean percentage damage was 23.0 (shed damage before reorganization 31.8). The full figures are given in Table 9-17. The view that this improvement was a reflection of the success of the experimental groups was supported by a request from the workers in the rest of the shed to be allowed to reorganize themselves in the same way as had the experimental groups. Action was deferred until the end of the experimental period.

There is, as yet, no adequate information about the effects and repercussions in the rest of the mill. There have been no known adverse effects and some favourable interest has been shown. As far as can be ascertained, social, economic, and technological conditions both outside and inside the mill and loom shed remained constant throughout the period for which results are reported in this paper. The only known change is that of climate which grew steadily hotter from the beginning of March to the end of July.

On June 7th a partial third shift was started on one of the experimental

Productivity and Social Organization

Table 9-17. *Efficiency and Damage Figures for Rest of Loom Shed During Experimental Period*

Phases of Experimental Period	Efficiency Percent	Damage Percent
1st. April 6–April 10 5 working days	71.0	42.7
2nd. April 11–April 14 3 working days	66.6	40.5
3rd. April 15–April 23 8 working days	68.9	26.6
4th. April 25–June 6 37 working days	81.4	23.0
Shed Before Reorganization March 1–March 28 23 working days	79.8	31.8

groups of sixty-four looms and on one of the groups of forty-eight. The shift was started with new and comparatively inexperienced workers. It provided the opportunity for the upgrading of some of the members of the experimental groups and the reallocation of some tasks. The results since June 7th are not, therefore, comparable with those of the experimental period. The mean percentage efficiency of the whole shed for all shifts for the period June 8th–August 22nd (the latest figures available) was, however, 90.3 (before reorganization 79.8) and the mean percentage damage was 24.5 (before reorganization 31.8). The works manager comments, ". . . these results have coincided with the most difficult part of the year, working conditions are severe and absenteeism maximum . . .".

SUMMARY AND CONCLUSIONS

(1.) An experimental automatic loom shed which contained 224 looms was manned by 29 workers, of whom 28 were concerned directly with the manufacture of cloth and one with artificial humidification.

(2.) The activities of a single automatic loom are cyclic—load, weave, unload—and require the successive performance of tasks to carry them out. The activities of a loom shed containing a number of looms are continuous, and require the simultaneous performance of tasks to maintain the continuity.

(3.) The weaving process had been broken down into component tasks and the number of workers allocated to different tasks had been determined by work-studies of the separate components.

(4.) The looms in the shed were differentiated into nineteen different loom groups of five kinds which overlapped in different degrees. Each kind of loom group contained a different number of looms—groups which were manned by a different number of workers. There were eight loom groups of 24–32 looms manned by one weaver to each group; five loom groups of 40–60 looms manned by one battery filler to each group; three loom groups of 60–80 looms manned by one smash-hand to each group; two loom groups of 112 looms, manned by one jobber, one assistant jobber, one gater and one bobbin carrier to each group; and one loom group of 224, manned by one feeler-motion fitter, one cloth carrier, one oiler, one sweeper and one humidification fitter.

(5.) All tasks of the manufacturing process were interdependent, but the workers performing them worked in different kinds of loom-groups and had, therefore, different degrees of interdependence. Some were virtually independent of each other. Thus a weaver had on average the services of one-quarter of a pair consisting of jobber and assistant jobber, five-eighths of a battery filler, three-eighths of a smash-hand, and so on.

(6.) The resultant pattern was of an aggregate of individuals with confused task and worker relationships and with no discernible internal group structure. This resultant was compared and contrasted with the longwall method of coal-mining in which job breakdown in a predominantly cyclic process had led to a similar lack of internal work-group structure but with splitting and segmentation rather than confusion.

(7.) Change of sort (kind of cloth woven) led to a restructuring of some kinds of loom group and in consequence to a change in the pattern of relationships.

(8.) Higher management had provided reinforcement for the governing system of the shed. This, and the high quality of the relationships between supervisors and between supervisors and workers, had prevented any overt difficulties resulting from the lack of group structure, but in the shed efficiency was lower and damage was higher than target figures.

(9.) In spite of the persistence of "weaver" as a title for an occupational role the weaver was the loom, and all workers, including the "weavers," serviced the machines. The tasks performed were found to be differentiated into two main groups: those concerned with short loom stops (after a simple yarn break) and those concerned with long loom stops (for loading and unloading and loom maintenance, for meal intervals and between shifts). During shift hours two worker sub-groupings appeared possible—the short-stop sub-group and the long-stop sub-group.

(10.) An analysis of changes in the numbers of workers with change of sort showed that relatively stable numbers could be obtained for each of three main groups of sorts—coarse, medium, and fine—and that provided some tasks could be considered interchangeable no changes in worker groups would be required for changes within the main sort. The theoretical numbers required for blocks of sixty-four looms, into which the loom shed was divided by physical boundaries, were calculated.

(11.) Three natural grades within a worker group for sixty-four looms were found. They were designated by letters only, rates slightly in excess of existing rates were fixed for these grades and it was decided to pay piece rates to the whole group.

(12.) It was decided by higher management to discuss with mill and shed management and the workers the organization of one experimental work group for a group of sixty-four looms.

(13.) Shed supervisors and workers spontaneously took possession of the reorganization, and the workers themselves immediately organized four experimental groups. Higher management took no part in the discussions with supervisors and workers and permitted the experimental groups so chosen to start work.

(14.) The results of the experiment were:
(*a*) The creation of internally-structured and internally-led small work-groups.
(*b*) A reduction in the number of those reporting directly to the supervisors and a consequent strengthening of the executive command.
(*c*) The beginning of the withdrawal of higher management from the governing system of the shed.
(*d*) Old occupational role titles were abandoned but new titles were not chosen. Five months afterwards both tasks and roles were still known by the letters designating the grades.
(*e*) After an immediate increase in mean efficiency in the experimental groups at the cost of increased damage and inadequate maintenance, a settling down at a new level of performance in which efficiency was higher and damage lower than before reorganization.

(15.) These results could not, in the time available, be related to the general ecological background of economic, industrial or cultural conditions in India, nor because of language difficulties could any direct evidence of the workers' attitudes and feelings be obtained. The only evidence of "goodness of fit" was the spontaneous acceptance, implementation, and continuation by the workers, and the withdrawal from the governing system of the shed by higher management.

(16.) The rest of the shed showed some evidence of the incidence of forces of induction, but this evidence could not be followed up in the time available. The experimental period finished when a partial third shift was started. No adequate information was available of repercussions in the rest of the mill.

(17.) Although, therefore, all the effects cannot at present be related to their causes, and the analysis has not yet been followed completely through, it seems fair to conclude that the findings reported had a direct relationship to the event of reorganization.

Notes

1. E. L. Trist of the Tavistock Institute, who collaborated with the author in the writing of this paper, first used the concept of *socio-technical* system when studying the socio-psychological and technical problems of the introduction of increased mechanization in coal-mining. The term has since been extended to designate a general field of study concerned with the interrelations of the technical and socio-psychological organizations of production systems.
2. Members of the Ahmedabad Manufacturing and Calico Printing Company: development group—Gautam Sarabhai, Chairman of the Company, J. A. Gandhi, Mill and Sales Manager, and J. C. Thaker, Works Manager; other members of the senior management concerned—S. A. Kher, Finance and Purchasing Manager, and W. H. Date, Personnel Manager; members of mill and shed Management—T. M. Desai, Weaving Master, C. P. Caprihan, Top Supervisor, and M. M. Bhatt, S. R. Rajguru and B. B. Dave, Work Supervisors.

3. The looms in the shed are of Japanese manufacture and figures of worker allocation of similar installations in Japan were supplied by the manufacturers.

4. The system, external to the production system which services, co-ordinates, and controls the production system. Rice and Trist, "Institutional and Sub-Institutional Determinants of Change in Labour Turnover," *Human Relations*, 5, No. 4, 348.

5. The principles used in making this analysis were formulated by E. L. Trist in studying the development in continuous mining in No. 1 Area, East Midlands Division of the National Coal Board, especially the type of organization that seems to be emerging in relation to the machine faces.

6. Piece rate was based upon an average standard efficiency of 85 percent per month, higher or lower efficiencies resulting in proportional increase or decrease in the amount of pay excluding "dearness" (cost of living allowance) which, on the scale given in Tables 9-1 and 9-2, was approximately 0.75, e.g., for an average monthly percentage efficiency of 87, the bonus equalled 2/85ths of the basic monthly rate (total pay less dearness allowance). For percentages over ninety-two the proportional increase was doubled; i.e., ninety-three was paid as ninety-four, etc.

7. Since, as yet, this was a purely theoretical exercise based on current work-studies, the numbers were not rounded off.

8. On the second day of the experimental period, a breakdown in the humidification plant flooded a part of the shed, spoiled twenty-five beams in the experimental groups and halted the whole shed for just over an hour.

9. This was found possible, although checks showed the loom stops still at the rate of 1.6 per hour.

References

Katz, Daniel, and Robert L. Kahn. "Human Organization and Worker Motivation," in L. R. Trip (ed.). *Industrial Productivity*. Industrial Relations Research Association, 1951, 146–71.

Rice, A. K., and E. L. Trist. "Institutional and Sub-Institutional Determinants of Change in Labour Turnover," *Human Relations*, 5, No. 4 (1952).

Roethlisberger, F. J., and William J. Dickson. *Management and the Worker*. Cambridge, Massachusetts: Harvard University Press, 1939.

Trist, E. L., and K. W. Bamforth. "Some Social and Psychological Consequences of the Longwall Method of Coal-Getting," *Human Relations*, 4, No. 1 (1951).

10

LEONARD R. SAYLES

The Change Process in Organizations: An Applied Anthropology Analysis[1]

*U*nfortunately, the subject of change in organizations (or of community or culture) is typically dealt with as a distinct, separate process, apart from the normal functioning of the system. Change is apparently viewed as something that is imposed on an unwilling, unresponsive audience or consumer. The problem of change, therefore, is usually one of gaining consent or acceptance through cajoling, force, participation, spotting the most likely sources of resistance and, occasionally, identifying gate-keepers or possible allies.

In other words, it is the difficulty of *introducing change* into a resistant system which has captured the attention of most students of the subject. However, if one observes the behavior of managers or leaders it will be noted that this aspect of the problem does not account for a significant amount of the total amount of time and energy expended on administration. Our purpose here, then, is to broaden the analysis to include the total process of change. This means viewing change as an intimate, integral part of the administrator's task of managing—really *stabilizing*—a system of human relations. Change, then, is not a special, for holidays only, activity. It is part and parcel of the normal administrative process of assessing how the system is operating, determining where *significant* deviations are occurring, identifying the source of the disturbances, taking administrative actions to eliminate the source of the instability (what we will call short-run change) and, finally, where the disturbance or

Reprinted from *Human Organization*, 21 (1962): 62–67. Used with permission Copyright © 1962 The Tavistock Institute of Human Relations.

deviation is recurring—the introduction of long-run change and its implementation and control.

What follows is an exposition of the stages in this process and their interrelationship. This analysis also represents our view of the job of the administrator in operational or interactional terms. It is an effort to depart from subjective, unquantifiable variables that have usually been associated with the analysis of all management processes (not just change) often quasi-psychological variables like the degree of personal security or sensitivity of the leader, the degree of "consideration" he generates and his ability to give assignments which equate authority and responsibility (parenthetically, a most unrealistic and unlikely possibility).

One last point to the introduction and approach. It is naive to assume that the administrator-leader suddenly commits himself to the accomplishment of change and then devotes all his efforts to this objective. Change must be accomplished simultaneously with the continued operations of an organization or system of work relationships. There is no "breathing spell," typically, where the organization can go all-out in the effort to pull itself up by its boot straps. This, of course, is another reason for considering change as part of the total organizational process.

THE PARADOX: CHANGE AND STABILITY

Paradoxically, the manager's job is to accomplish both stability and change. In order to maximize both the productivity of the processes under his jurisdiction *and* maintain high motivation among subordinates (which in turn facilitates productive efforts), he must endeavor to minimize the frequency with which the patterns of work flow and coordination are disturbed. In fact, the frequency with which such actual or potential interruptions to the work patterns occur, as we have described in a recent book,[2] are the prime determinants of the work load of the manager. It is the development and maintenance of work flow routines which is his major objective, and these "predictable and repeated patterns of interaction" are the source of morale or the absence of debilitating stress and its concomitant: destructive emotional reaction (what we have called compensatory behavior).[3]

In a situation requiring cooperative endeavors, whether it is a work group, employees and managers, or staff and line officials, each tries to develop a stable pattern of work, of interaction. When these stable patterns are disturbed, individuals experience stress or an uncomfortable feeling of pressure and dissatisfaction. A breakdown in the flow creates opposition as the individuals struggle to restore it. The expected responses from the individuals in the sequence prove inadequate, and new coordination problems arise.

The regularities of actions and interactions disappear when this stress occurs, and erratic variation takes over. The difference is obvious between a smoothly running operation and one with a problem. Under stress, people react emotionally, and, because more than one individual is involved, the reactions usually conflict with each other.

Thus, a vicious circle is established. Something happens in the work situation that causes the relationship of individuals to change or to depart from the normal pattern. This creates a stress, either of opposition or nonresponse, that is further complicated by higher levels of supervision and staff specialists whose unexpected interactions, i.e., outside the usual organization pattern, irritate the disturbed work-flow relations. People get upset; they become angry with each other and, depending on their individual characteristics, react temperamentally. These personality conflicts have direct ramifications in the work process because the emotional reactions change the pattern of contact and interaction. Joe is angry with Bill, so he does not check with him before starting a new experimental run. Consequently, a special test that should have been included in the run is left out, and the whole thing has to be done over. To complete the circle, these emotional disturbances damage the work-flow sequence, which causes additional personality stresses.[4]

But, of course, as we "sophisticated" observers know, the achievement of this stability—which is the manager's objective—is a never-to-be-attained ideal. He is like a symphony orchestra conductor—endeavoring to maintain a melodious performance in which the contributions of the various instruments are coordinated and sequenced, patterned and paced—while the orchestra members are having various personal difficulties, stage hands are moving music stands, alternating excessive heat and cold is creating audience and instrument problems, and the sponsor of the concert is insisting on irregular changes in the music to be played.

In other words, the manager faces constant internal and external interruptions. As we shall see, some of these require mere palliatives—readjustments —in order to bring the system of relationships back to stability, for example, a disciplinary action (which is one type of change). Other disturbances require more drastic action if the system is to be stabilized, for example, the introduction of new methods or personnel as a result of a change in market conditions or the demands of some other part of the organization.

Presumably we might call this a moving equilibrium. External pressures and internal problems require constant "change," but the manager endeavors to accomplish this as he returns the system to equilibrium.

DETECTING DISTURBANCES OR DEVIATIONS

Thus, an important element in the manager's job is the detection of disturbances or deviations in the system of human relationships which comprise his workflows. This is the control function of the manager: developing methods of detection whereby he can assess and appraise how and where he should devote his managerial efforts, perhaps supplemented by the assistance of other specialists.

We need to be aware that a manager's scarcest resource is (or ought to be) his own time and energy, and that of other members of management. Therefore, he needs to devote his attention to what are indeed problems and avoid spending time in areas which are functioning well.

How does the manager "check" or control? He looks at statistical reports of quality, quantity, turnover, and what have you. He "inquires around" as to how people are doing and he endeavors to "sense" when people are acting differently. Unfortunately, some of this is usually done intuitively and there is little systematic attention to an integrated control system.[5] In a well-developed theory of organization change, we would expect to set forth the actual pattern of control: how frequently and with whom or what the manager checks. We would also expect to see an integrated series of controls involving technical measures of performance (e.g. quality, quantity, etc.) embodied in relatively automatic data processing systems combined with measures of organizational relationships.

Among others, F. L. W. Richardson, Jr., has shown that one can interrelate variations in the technical performance of a system with variations in the human relations dimensions.[6] In other words, there are correlations between such things as output and changes in internal work group interactions, manager-subordinate interactions and subordinate-outside group interactions. These provide the new materials of an effective and objective monitoring system. The manager need not be able to "smell trouble."

ASSESSING THE SIGNIFICANCE OF THE DEVIATION

The next step in the process is the manager's assessment of the significance of the deviations he is observing. It is likely that Parkinson's Law could be stated more realistically in terms of managers making work for themselves and others by going into action to deal with a problem that is not a problem—in other words, to introduce a change in a system which is operating within *expected limits of variation*.

The mathematical statisticians have begun to work on just this problem—noting that management can introduce serious instabilities into inventory maintenance systems, that is, can really amplify variations—by endeavoring to overcorrect for variation. We see the same thing in human relations terms—where the supervisor contacts his own subordinates and others to discuss "mutual problems," where the contact itself creates the problem, and none existed before. The foolishness is never detected, of course, because the endeavor to overcorrect the system *does create a problem* which in turn justifies the supervisor's attention and energy expenditure.

Of course, the opposite is the more traditionally identified difficulty: the failure to detect quickly enough or to move quickly enough to quench a real fire. Thus the manager requires as part of his control apparatus a theory of significant differences which will enable him to place certain "limits" on the occurrence or amplitude of the phenomenon he is observing. This requires a knowledge of the limits on normal or expected variation, given the nature of the system. He then hoards his managerial actions for the significant deviations in the system—and avoids becoming himself a source of upset where none existed before.

It may be well to repeat here that this theory of change encompasses deviations or disturbances in the system that are imposed by superior fiat or environment change as well as internal malfunctioning. We could expect that instabilities from the "outside" would be transmitted through his contacts with his own superior and other managers as well as through the flows of relationship in which his subordinates participate with "outsiders" in their job activities.

From the point of view of organization design and the specification of managerial actions, it thus becomes possible to set forth explicitly (and thus control and check the performance of) managerial surveillance actions. These would include operationally definable patterns for what to check, how and how often, as well as techniques of data analysis to ascertain significant differences. This becomes another step in the process of making managerial actions less art and intuition and more science, but within the realm of human relationships. For example, we can distinguish those checks that require the manager to initiate, those initiated to him, and those that come from reports. All, however, require organizational analyses, that is, a knowledge of the time dimensions of the work-flow system which are to be controlled, prior to the elaboration of the "checking" and "evaluation" procedures.

CORRECTIVE OR STABILIZING ACTION

In moving toward a science of administration we would view the next task of the manager in the control-change sequence as taking corrective actions where significant deviations have been revealed. Here, too, we can be explicit about the interaction pattern required. These are the "short-run" changes. This area is the one usually encompassed by the human relations literature when it deals with getting a behavior change. This means the traditional techniques of order-giving, criticism, discipline, training, communication and persuasion (of course, we would insist that these can all be described in operational, interaction terms[7]).

We can, in fact, write sequences of remedial action which the supervisor takes (or should take) in endeavoring to bring the work flow system back to a stable state. Some of these patterns involve outside contacts as well which may serve to bring the system back to normal. For example, the unsatisfactory pacing of the activities of a service department may be creating internal problems. The manager may move through his superior or other channels in seeking to bring the tempo of these activities more in alignment with his needs. Or additional personnel may have to be secured through recruitment channels or permission to work overtime secured from higher management in order to adjust to pressures for increased output. From the point of view of the organization as a whole, the manager operating these controls also must be required to alert his manager and others who may be affected by the departures from equilibrium of his system. This enables them to take complementary actions to avoid having the disturbance spread from the jurisdiction of this manager through the entire organization. All of these actions can be prescribed and quantified interactionally.

ANALYZING RECURRING OR CONTINUING SOURCES OF DEVIATION AND STRESS

Some of the problems with which the supervisor must cope will not be solved by the administrative actions to which we have referred. These are the ones we distinguish as recurring problems. They are the cause of comments like this:

I am always having to go down to engineering and have a battle over specifications—hardly a week goes by in which there isn't an argument here and probably a big meeting as well.

Some are not recurring, they are just never solved. We have referred to these in our recent book as "spiralling" or cumulating deviations.[8] Figuratively an initial source of infection in the organizational system "spreads" to other flows and these, in turn, may react back on the original source, thus adding to the disturbance at that point. These are the so-called major crises or explosions. In either case the detection by the supervisor that such a problem exists should bring into action additional remedial measures.

The first of these may well be an investigatory pattern. After all, these are the problems which consume inordinate amounts of supervisory time and create major losses to the organization. Their occurrence suggests that some more significant and far reaching change is required than an adjustment in the attention of the immediate activity pattern of the supervisor. So-called staff groups, or consultant-specialists, unfortunately even task force committees, may be used to assess the situation. They come into action, or should be mobilized *only* when the controls maintained by the manager identify this type of problem or when the auditing mechanisms of the staff group themselves so indicate. It is well to note at this point that large, complex organizations frequently assign to staff groups the responsibility for accumulating some of the data that the manager uses for control purposes.[9]

As part of the investigatory process, the manager needs to be intellectually aware of the likely structural sources of stubborn instability. At some future time control mechanisms may be developed which will identify the source as well as the problem. The applied anthropologist has contributed a great number of "classic cases" for such an analysis:

(1.) Heavily "unbalanced" interaction patterns such as some of the jobs in Whyte's restaurants,[10] and as exhibited by poor supervisors and conflict-laden union-management relations.[11]

(2.) Unstable or irregular patterns (e.g. Whyte's time-study-man analysis[12]), also other staff positions.

(3.) Contacts where there is an inadequate frequency of contact (e.g. see Sayles' discussion of "Erratic Groups"[13] and Tavistock studies of the Longwall coal-getting method[14] and the Indian Weaving Shed[15]).

The applied anthropologist has identified these as typical sources:

(1.) Locations where the manager's jurisdiction has been poorly conceived such that "unit work flows" are broken by the organization. These are

The Change Process in Organizations

interrelated work positions between which a constant "rhythm" needs to be maintained, that is the parameters of the flow are identical.
(2.) Service groups outside of these flows which become "scarce resources."
(3.) Work positions where the requirements of the job are incompatible with personality of the incumbent.
(4.) Employees in positions which have undergone transformations to which they have not yet adjusted (e.g. the "succession" problem, the change in "status" and power of the nurse or the first line supervisor, and see also the many examples in H. O. Ronken and P. R. Lawrence, *Administering Changes*).[16]
(5.) "Men in the middle."
(6.) The impact of organizational innovations such as staff groups or incentives.

This then is an interim requirement for the change process—technical diagnoses of potential organizational trouble spots which can drain managerial time and energy. Beyond the diagnosis the manager has a great deal of work to do. This is the implementation process.

Usually we find that the manager must spend a great deal of time convincing superiors in the organization that a structural or "long-run" change is necessary, even before he gets an opportunity to engage in the difficult job of establishing the change in the organization. Many managers—or leaders—are kept so busy "putting out fires" that they never take on the job of seeking to find the source of recurring blazes. In a sense a rather great capital investment, in terms of time and energy, is necessary to provide a more permanent solution. The manager must take time away from his regular activities to undertake lengthy "selling" contacts with superiors and others plus the major problems of coping with affected subordinates. Many lack the energy and the ability to do this, and this is the major reason why "change" is not introduced at an appropriate rate in the organization, *not* the recalcitrance of subordinates, unions and habits!

IMPLEMENTING THE CHANGE

The traditional human relations literature has also concentrated on the problem of gaining acceptance for structural changes. Here is where one reads about participation and timing, the use of informal leaders, etc. Arensberg, however, again from the point of view of the applied anthropologist, has provided the only clearly operational description of the implementing process.[17]
(1.) First an increase in managerial initiative to subordinates.
(2.) Opportunity for increased inter-worker contacts (presumably informal group activity).
(3.) Followed by an increase in redressive contacts or initiations to the manager (and in turn the manager must be prepared time-wise to accept these).
(4.) Rewarding managerial responses to these subordinate initiations (often the change period is such a hectic one that time is not available for this step).
In our terminology both (1) and (3) represent compensatory behavior-reactions

of the individuals to the stress of changed jobs, managerial contact patterns, etc.

Again these are time-consuming patterns of administration and detract from the other commitments of the supervisor. In addition, the organization typically may neglect the more formalized accommodation patterns identified by the anthropologist as easing major dislocations in human patterns of interaction. We have in mind the *rites de passage* and symbolic ceremonies which the community has evolved for such crises.

VALIDATING THE CHANGE

The manager cannot afford to assume that a change he has introduced has actually become part of the operating system. We know that human relations systems tend to return to previous equilibria when pressures are removed which have shifted them away from that position. However, it would be a mistake to assume that all changes are imposed on "comfortable" equilibria, although these are the ones which are grist for the case writers. There are many situations in which people are under substantial stress and tension; the organization is not providing them with personal satisfactions, and they welcome change. Whether initially welcomed or not, the manager must utilize methods of appraisal to validate that the change has become stabilized. Essentially this means checking to see that the flow, sequence and co-ordinating patterns are as planned.

ORGANIZATION CHANGE VS. CONVERSION

It should now be evident that the applied anthropologist's theory of change and administration encompasses both traditional methods of persuasion and influence, usually emphasized in social psychological terms but operationally definable in behavioral, interaction terms, and more long-run or permanent alterations in the organizational constraints. In another work we have chosen to call the former "conversion" by which we meant simply that the manager seeks to convince or persuade a subordinate to shift his behavior in some way and thus eliminate a source of disturbance.[18]

Obviously, this type of administrative activity is important and constantly used. It is involved in the giving of brief orders and lengthy disciplinarian sessions. But the administrator who relies solely on this type of change is ignoring one of the most important parts of his job: seeking out and remedying the persisting and compounding problems. These require, as we have endeavored to illustrate, the introduction of changes in the organizational constraints: the flow of work, the components of jobs, the incumbents on jobs, the structure of authority, the incentives and even the controls themselves that are used.

CONCLUSION

We have endeavored to write an operational description of the change process as an integral part of the manager-leader's day-to-day administrative activities.

This analysis lends itself to behavioral quantification and objective validation so that the organization can provide for change within its structure and appraise the success of its members in carrying forth these patterns. Rather than a "last straw," when all else has failed, change, in the applied anthropologist's view, can precede serious crises. Further, administrators can be trained in terms of unambiguous behavioral skills to carry forth such programs.

In our view, the process of change has consisted of these interrelated sequences of managerial action:

(1.) Specific organizational and technical checks (of prescribed characteristics and frequency) on the stability of the system under the jurisdiction of the manager.
(2.) Established criteria for evaluating significant deviations from the desired stable state.
(3.) Prescribed administrative patterns of corrective action to bring the system back to equilibrium. (Short-run change.)
(4.) Appraisals of recurring or continuing instabilities in the system with provision for staff (or specialist) assistance in investigating potential structural sources of organization stress and remedial measures.
(5.) Administrative patterns for implementing "long-run" organizational structural change.
(6.) Administrative action to validate the change.

We have purposely ignored the usual shibboleths about starting at the top of the organization and getting "grass roots" support, etc., etc. In our view of change as part of every manager's operational job requirement, this pattern is repeated at each level with adjustments in controls to view the processes below. There is no starting or ending point as such—change is an integral and essential part of all organizational behavior.

What is the implication for this description of the change process in organizations for the growing social concern with the impact of large hierarchical structures on initiative and creativity? It would seem to me that this type of analysis presents a far different prognosis for the role of the individual than the usual political science view of delegated and strictly delimited authority or the psychologists' emphasis on palliatives to reduce the sting of hierarchical power.

In our recent research we have viewed the actual behavior of managers in a very large organization and we find that their organizational positions give them much "leeway" in utilizing their personality skills and energies in meeting the challenges of constant restabilization requirements and the need to initiate to introduce change. The notion that the lower level manager deals passively as a transmitter of orders from higher ups and a feed-back mechanism, reporting what is going on below, is just not reality, except where the manager's personality is inadequate to taking the initiative. We would not want, however, to minimize the number in the latter category.

When the organization is viewed as a complex series of interlocking patterns of human relationships, work flow patterns and control patterns, the opportunity for the individual to innovate and shape his own environment becomes apparent. Creativity and innovation are a product of the individual's ability to extract the time and energy from the "fire fighting" preoccupations of the moment, in order to modify the pressures and stresses which are being showered on himself and on his subordinates. The hierarchy is no barrier to this—it is, as it has been in every culture—the challenge to the able.

Notes

1. Copyright by L. R. Sayles, 1961. Part of a larger work, *Managerial Behavior*. New York: McGraw-Hill, 1964.
2. Eliot D. Chapple and Leonard R. Sayles. *The Measure of Management*. New York: Macmillan, 1961, 46–68.
3. *Ibid.*, 114–141.
4. *Ibid.*, 37–38.
5. There has been inadequate attention paid to the development of a theory of systems control outside of some of the recent efforts of the mathematical statisticians. Eliot Chapple is also concerned with this problem, and his remarks may concentrate on this area.
6. F. L. W. Richardson, *Talk*, *Work*, and *Action*, Monograph No. 3, Society for Applied Anthropology, 1961.
7. Cf. Chapple and Sayles, *op. cit.*, 48–64.
8. *Ibid.*, 161.
9. The so-called staff-line problem is usually the result of a failure to organize on this basis. Staff groups go into action and initiate to the supervisor in areas and at times when the supervisor has not agreed there is a significant deviation. Then his dealing with the staff itself becomes a stressful relationship and a time-consuming one. In turn, this is partially the result of the failures of traditional administrative management theory in conceptualizing the staff "role." Apart from its audit functions the staff ought to be measured on its success in bringing deviating systems back to equilibrium—which, in turn, would minimize their conflicts with line managers. For a fuller discussion of this problem see G. Strauss and L. Sayles, *Personnel*. Prentice-Hall, New York, 1960, 399–417.
10. William F. Whyte, *Human Relations in the Restaurant Industry*. McGraw-Hill, New York, 1948.
11. William F. Whyte, *Pattern for Industrial Peace*. Harper & Bros., New York, 1951.
12. William F. Whyte, *Money and Motivation*. Harper & Bros., New York, 1955.
13. Leonard R. Sayles, *Behaviour of Industrial Work Groups*. Wiley, New York, 1958, 78–79.
14. E. L. Trist and E. W. Bamforth, "Social and Psychological Consequences of the Longwall Method of Coal-getting," *Human Relations*, IV (1951) 8.
15. A. K. Rice, "Productivity and Social Organization in an Indian Weaving Shed," *Human Relations*, VI (1953) 297–329.
16. Harvard University, Division of Research, Graduate School of Business Administration, Boston, 1952.
17. Cf. Conrad Arensberg and Geoffrey Tootell, "Plant Sociology: Real Discoveries and New Problems," in Mirra Komarovsky (ed.)., *Common Frontier of the Social Sciences*. The Free Press, Glencoe, Illinois, 1957.
18. Chapple and Sayles, *op. cit.*

11

FRANCES TORBERT

Making Incentives Work

• Are there incentive plans which increase acceptance of the goals of business, reduce resistance to change, and maintain high productivity?
• How many companies overrate the effectiveness of their piecework incentive programs?
• Do most incentive plans distort earnings in relation to employee skill and effort?
• What is automation doing to the concept of piecework?
• Can we study pay practices without examining management, worker, and union attitudes and behavior?

"*I*f you read the surveys and listen to some industrial engineers, you think piecework is still *the* answer," said a plant manager recently, "but I'm betting that in less than five years 60 percent of piecework plans will be dead and buried." The speaker, who used to be enthusiastic about individual incentives, is sure that in two years management in his firm will have shifted to some other program.

Interviews with many executives, especially in smaller companies, suggest that stability in incentive programs may be more apparent than real. Predictions on the two- to five-year picture in automation tend to confirm the forecast, without regard to company size.

Piece rates and similar *individual* incentives may continue in more than 40 percent of present applications; in a few aspects of semiautomated work, there may be areas of usefulness for them. But in a period of rapid technological change and shifts in labor-management relations, perhaps we should take another look at piecework and the advantages of some of its possible alternatives—

Reprinted from *Harvard Business Review*, 37, 5 (September/October, 1959): 81–92. Used with permission. © 1959 by the President and Fellows of Harvard College; all rights reserved.

particularly *group* incentive plans. Once heralded as the solution to all labor-management problems, group plans still have their enthusiasts as well as their skeptics. What progress have these programs made?

PIECEWORK PROBLEMS

Even without automation, which in its advanced forms makes individual piece rates absurd, many things are happening which reduce the usefulness of individual incentives. The increased percentage of indirect labor, the variety of tasks performed by indirect workers, and the blurring of the distinction between direct and indirect work have presented a major problem. Much time and money have gone into attempts to set standards for indirect work, and a few large companies claim success in this venture. But attempts to use individual incentives for these employees have not often succeeded in smaller firms. Most attempts at piece-rate and similar programs for indirect workers have had poor results.

Even in direct labor areas the amount of trouble appears to be greater than many managers admit. Loose rates, maintenance costs for standard revision and clerical work, grievances, worker resistance to change, whipsawing union pressures on rates and base pay, and related problems are causing some employers to pay more to get work done under incentives than competitors are paying under daywork. Further, companies which pay time wages more often have retained proper relationships between pay and skill. Maintenance men and other skilled workers are particularly likely to find their pay "out of whack" when semi-skilled workers have been able to maintain high earnings under incentives.

RESTRICTION OF OUTPUT

And what about the worker who does not respond—who does not *want* to respond—to incentives? Researchers have not neglected him, either.

Whiting Williams and others described restrictive behavior in the early part of this century, and the Hawthorne studies, made at Western Electric Company in the 1920's, documented output restriction unforgettably. A flood of information on restrictions comes every year from workers and ex-workers; yet claims regarding the power of incentives continue.

Perhaps the most interesting recent report of incentive responses is from Melville Dalton. He studied a group of 84 experienced machine-shop workers. Output figures for these men were kept for two years. Only 9 men—less than 11 percent—made an all-out response to the piece-rate incentive, and 25 percent did not respond at all. The rest responded unevenly, but kept a ceiling on their efforts at all times. Many of the men in this group showed feelings of distress about the incentives. The other two groups of workers had resolved their conflicts. According to Dalton, "the rate busters renounced the group; the bottom producers renounced the incentives."

The rate busters were "lone wolves," who were highly money-conscious. They not only were anxious to earn as much as possible; they also saved their money and were reluctant and niggardly contributors to charity drives. The all-out restrictors, with the lowest incomes, led active social lives inside and outside the shop.

The men in the middle included nine with ulcers or incipient ulcers—an illness often associated with tension. None of the other men were thus afflicted. Said one of the men in the middle group:

"Nobody gets any good out of an incentive system. It makes bad feeling among the workers, between the workers and the checkers, and between workers and the bosses. Now you take that son-of-a-bitch over there (nodding toward a rate buster), the incentive system made him what he is. He's got a bad principle and the system brought it out. . . .

"The thing that's so damn aggravating is that one job pays twice as much as it should and the next only one fourth what it should. What you make you lose. . . ."[1]

Dalton and Whyte agree that these men may not be typical of experienced incentive workers. Yet the study yields results which resemble those in other analyses. Indeed, as a whole this group appears to have responded to incentives with somewhat *more* effort than groups described in other studies.

WORKER CONNIVANCE

All of this raises some very practical questions for management. How many firms want to settle for adroit fooling of time-study men by cynical workers, large numbers of grievances (20 percent or more) growing out of rate complaints, and divisive feelings between workers and the company? How many want to encourage featherbedding? Pressure by workers for more service from tool cribs, more runners, shop clerks, and other accessory employees "so we won't have to do nonincentive work" is exerted even when direct workers are actually holding a ceiling on effort.

Herbert R. Northrup, who reports such practices, gives interesting evidence of a production increase to suit a special purpose:

"Success in converting the incentive system into a featherbedding device is revealed annually during the first two weeks in May. Earnings during this period determine vacations (in a certain company). Curiously enough, earnings generally spurt about 30 per cent above the average for the previous six weeks."[2]

One foreman told me that, harried by workers, industrial engineers, and cost accounting people, he often connives with his men to get and keep loose rates. He commented:

"Piecework brings out the worst in men. They decide that the company plays dirty, so they play dirty, too. And these managers who think workers are so dumb are actually being out-smarted every day of the year. They brought it on themselves."

IN PERSPECTIVE

But all is not black with piecework. It has worked fairly well, especially in firms with records of outstanding fairness and competence. Moreover, piecework has certain advantages to workers besides possible monetary gains. Incentive systems may free men from supervision: "I've made my quota; now I can loaf or talk." Again, the operative on a repetitious job may find that time passes less slowly when he is thinking about making his quota—if he decides to make the effort. Also, there are the amusements of organized goldbricking, of "deals" with tool-crib men, of figuring out improved hiding places for "kitties," of working out a slow timing for a fast job, and so on.

On balance, however, it is difficult to recommend piecework for many companies. If it solves problems, it tends to solve them in the short run only to multiply them in the long run. And in a dynamic society in which productivity *and* cooperation are needed, piecework tends to destroy the will to cooperate. Group incentive programs—which stimulate both effort and cooperation—may be better (though not, of course, perfect) alternatives.

GROUP INCENTIVES

In "Life in the Automatic Factory," Charles R. Walker has reported that conventional individual incentives are inappropriate for automated work.[3] In a pipe mill he studied:

> The operators of highly automatic machinery complained that incentive coverage was too narrow. They wanted maintenance men included, even if the result were a reduction in their own pay. Down time is a major problem under automation; hence the relationship of maintenance to production is an intrinsic one.
>
> When asked for comments about their new work, the men requested "a chance to help solve mill problems." They also observed that unless the work performed by each man was properly related to that of everyone else costly troubles developed.

This suggests the advisability of group incentives, combined with production committees or employee meetings to aid in solving scheduling and operating difficulties under automation. Some managements report that group incentives have got them out of serious economic difficulties even with conventional technology.

One California company with departmental and subdepartmental group incentive plans found that production almost doubled when a deteriorated piece-rate system was discarded in favor of the group bonuses. Base rates in this firm are kept carefully in line with area wage rates. Transferability of workers between departments now is readily accepted. Average bonuses have ranged from 15 percent to 20 percent of base pay. Self-policing by group members is excellent, and low production workers have been discharged because of pressure from other employees for their elimination.

EMPLOYEE-INITIATED ACTION

Group incentives do not always work so well, but chances for success usually increase when a management adds the ingredient of interaction. To illustrate how a group bonus can fail to motivate until changes of this kind are introduced, let us take another illustration from Whyte:

> In the paint room of a company which manufactured wooden toys, women

spray-painted the toys, then hung them on hooks which carried them into a drying oven. The girls were on a group learners' bonus for six months. Industrial engineers had estimated that workers would reach standard performance at the end of this time.

But things went badly. Absenteeism, turnover, and complaints were serious. Many hooks went into the oven empty. The girls said that time-study men expected the impossible, and complained of heat from the oven, of fumes, and of the messy nature of the work.

A consultant was brought in. The foreman decided, after having a talk with him, to meet with the girls to discuss their work. At the meeting, the girls complained that the room was poorly ventilated and hot. The foreman volunteered to seek a solution to this problem, and suggested a later meeting to report results. At the second meeting the girls asked for some large fans. Management agreed to this, and three fans were installed.

The employees' attitude seemed enough improved so that the foreman ventured another meeting. It had barely started when the girls complained that time-study men had set the conveyer speed too fast. Then they asked to be allowed to control its speed themselves. They said they could keep up with the conveyer part of the time, but not all day long.

This heretical request was at first turned down. But after meetings between standards men and the foreman, there finally came an admission that some latitude on conveyer speed was possible. The decision was made to try the girls' idea.

A dial marked "low, medium, fast" was installed. (The medium speed was a little above the constant speed at which the engineers had previously set the belt.) After experimenting with the speeds, the girls settled on a definite pattern. For the first half hour of the day the dial was set at a point slightly above "medium." The next two-and-a-half hours were run at high speed. The half hour before lunch and the half hour after lunch were run at low. Then the speed was changed to high, and left there until the last forty-five minutes, which were worked at the medium setting.

The girls now reported that they were working at a comfortable pace; scarcely a hook went by empty; and rejects did not increase. It is not hard to surmise what happened to productivity. Two months before the learners' bonus was to end, production was 30 percent to 50 percent above the expected level. The girls were now collecting their base pay, learners' bonus, and regular bonus.

Thus, management was on the spot in the matter of pay relationships. The girls were earning more money than many skilled workers, and the latter knew it. Whyte reports:

". . . Without consultation, the superintendent revoked the learning bonus, and returned the painting operation to its original status: the hooks moved again at their constant, time-studied speed, production dropped again, and within a month all but two of the girls had quit. The foreman stayed on for several months, but feeling aggrieved, then left for another job."[4]

TAPPING THE POTENTIALS

There are a number of observations to be made about this case. One is that human beings are not comfortable always working at the same speed. (A handful of industrial engineers have, on their own, proposed varying speeds for machine paced work.) Another lesson is that basic changes should not be made in one part of an organization if management does not understand the changes and is not prepared to try them throughout the firm. Another problem is that of intergroup pay discrepancies.

But the central question here is: *Do we really tap the interest and capacity of work groups and hence improve productivity and morale unless we give workers some chance to have a say in their work*? Neither group nor individual bonuses do this automatically.

One of the deepest needs of psychologically healthy people is to be able to initiate action in some of the matters which are important to them. Rank-and-file workers who take part in decisions affecting their work nearly always change their attitudes favorably. Under such conditions, higher production and work standards are maintained, contrary to "old-line" management expectations.[5]

If we can generalize from the paint room case, we may conclude that when employees are allowed to take the initiative in a few minutes of direct concern to them, they can take production "through the ceiling." Could not the same principle apply with equal force to workers in the quality control, inventory, selling, and other areas? The possibilities of company-wide improvement seem great. Suppose, for instance, that in the foregoing case the other departments of the company had been given a comparable chance to initiate action—might not the company have captured a larger share of its market and increased its profits?

Some companies actually have used, on an organization-wide basis, a combination of group incentives and opportunities for employees to share in the task of thinking about their work:

• Such an approach is followed in principle by firms which use the Scanlon plan or some adaptation of it.

• In a plan devised by Allen Rucker of The Eddy-Rucker-Nickels Company, employee committees and meetings are a basic ingredient of the incentive operation.

• The Lincoln Electric Company does not use group bonuses, but does use a vigorous employee committee which has met with top management on all problems affecting work and workers since 1913.

• The Nunn-Bush Shoe Company has involved workers and union in some aspects of decision making, at the same time that it has given employees 52 paychecks a year based on labor's percentage share in value added by manufacture.

I could cite a number of other companies that have created similar successful combinations of group incentives and employee productivity improvement committees.

ELEMENTS OF COOPERATION

The concepts of participative and consultative management have frequently come under attack.[6] The validity of such challenges cannot be denied. Even in companies where executives sincerely want the values of participation, there are forces at work which push toward conventional (for example, highly authoritarian) leadership. Often a major force of this kind is the pre-existing relationship between company and union. Furthermore, many executives are incredulous and cynical in their attitudes toward the whole concept.

But a few companies *have* successfully employed these concepts, and their experience is a revealing one. It points up the vital importance of creating an appropriate philosophy and framework. Unless both a framework *and* a point of view prevail, "participation" tends to be one of the shortest-lived of management fads.

EMPLOYEE REACTION

Experience with Rucker and Scanlon plan companies, the behavior of the paint room girls, and records of other situations in which workers have responded well to group incentives and to the chance to initiate action regarding their work offer proof to the cynics that good results are obtained with such programs. There is testimony from many managements of conventionally run companies that *their* workers are apathetic and alienated. Researchers have substantiated this claim. They describe employees who regard their work only as a means to a paycheck. Also they often describe the work assignments of these workers, and the management controls which surround them, as conducive to indifference or alienation.

The president of a small company which has successfully installed and maintained a Rucker plan says that his employees were chiefly listless or anti-company before the plan installation, and that in the first few months after the program started many remained that way. Then, week by week, the change in the way people felt and acted became more noticeable. He told me:

> "I learned for the first time how much people can change when they have a reason to. A factory full of "don't care" employees is not inevitable. . . . The company and the union may make Rucker's plan fail. But if employees believe you're honest, *and you are*, you can stop worrying about *them*. Don't try to tell me that the main trouble isn't with us. Up till a few years ago I was reaping what I'd sowed, but I was blaming it on the other fellow."

This executive's experience may have made him overly optimistic, but interviews with top-management people in over 20 Rucker and Scanlon plan companies and with H. L. Nunn seem to bear him out. Every single employee does not "catch fire" as a result of these programs. Some employees dislike or ignore them. But the failures in using the plans seem to be management or union leadership failures. Employee response is good when leadership is good. Most employees not only respond to the well-run plan; they carry their apathetic colleagues along with them—or pressure the company to eliminate them, as in the California example described above.

HAMPERED BY HABIT

Management habits are so hard to break that most companies do not want to make the effort if they are "getting by" as is. Also, we have not cultivated much patience in matters involving worker-management cooperation. A few misunderstandings, delays, and instances of immature or hostile behavior on either side will lead the other to resort to the clichés with which each has castigated the other for so many years. Leaders, instead of trying again, triumphantly announce, "I told you it wouldn't work! Those so-and-so's (in management *or* working groups) can't be trusted."

Basic self-confidence on both sides of the fence is a prerequisite to cooperation. The less secure the leaders, the greater the problem of getting started on a cooperative relationship. Both management and leaders of organized labor are influenced by ways of thinking and repetitions of slogans about themselves and each other. They are often timid about what counterparts in labor or management will say of them if they try anything unfamiliar to less courageous colleagues. The gibes of conformists on both sides of the fence have sometimes frightened company presidents and union leaders into maintaining a wary stance, even after they have glimpsed a more productive relationship.

Many managers also fail to recognize the contributions which employees can make if given the opportunity. They are unaware of the barriers which they, their staff departments, and their foremen unconsciously set up to stall off workers' ideas, despite conventional suggestion systems and "open door" policies. According to one authority:

> "The worker has a highly detailed knowledge of the particular operations that are taking place around him. He knows from experience throughout the shift what causes bottlenecks and why. He can explain how raw materials differ from day to day.... He knows, too, where teamwork is falling down ... why the best methods are not being utilized.... On technical matters the worker often has ideas for improvement but he needs help to develop them. Where this help is readily available ... the worker can (avoid) the embarrassment of being told that his was a 'stupid idea.' "[7]

Unless management and workers—organized or not—undertake to create a built-in structure for listening to each other and working together, old habits of thought and attitudes of mutual doubt and fear are bound to continue. They do not disappear quickly or completely even under a structured program for cooperation. However, if in addition to a framework for product and method improvement, there is a group monetary incentive—departmental or company-wide—the drive to improve cooperation *and* performance is obviously enhanced. A few companies use structured improvement committees with time wages or piecework, but the records of their successes are not as well documented as in the cases which combine group incentives and a ladder of production committees.

THE SCANLON PLAN

I should like to turn now from general concepts and principles to some of the specific plans already mentioned. A logical place to begin is with the program named after the late Joseph Scanlon.

HOW IT WORKS

What actually happens when a company and its work force agree to adopt the Scanlon plan?

First of all they usually study the program at length. Then they set up an incentive plan which generally includes everyone in the company. In Scanlon plan companies, a formula is developed to measure and distribute gains made through resultant improvements in productivity. This formula is developed in different ways, depending on the nature of the company's work, labor cost experience, and other factors. A common method is to find a historically normal labor cost and then divide among covered employees the difference between the established "norm" and what is achieved under the plan.[8]

Once the relationship between total payroll and the sales value produced by it is established, a bonus pool is created for any month when labor costs are below the norm. To protect against deficit months, a reserve of 25 percent is set aside from the pool. If anything is left in this reserve at the end of the year, an extra payment is made. After the reserve has been taken out for a given month, the balance of the bonus is split, with 25 percent usually going to the company and the remaining 75 percent to employees. Take the following example:

> A plant finds that its labor cost is normally 40 percent of the sales value of production, plus or minus inventory change. If shipments plus inventory increase in a given month are $1,000,000 and labor costs are $370,000, there would then be a bonus pool of $30,000.

Since the company gets 25 percent of the pool, after reserves have been set aside, the ratio does not have to be adjusted for minor changes that would affect the norm. It *is* essential, however, that the norm be changed when price or wage changes, major purchases of labor- or time-saving machinery, or anything else materially affects the ratio of costs to the sales value of production. A "memorandum of understanding" lists the bases for ratio changes.

This concept of changes in the ratio alarms company and union leaders when there has been a history of union-management warfare over every issue involving pay. They cannot believe that realistic ratio changes can be made which will be regarded as fair by both sides. In Scanlon companies ratio changes *are* made, and the process of change becomes one of the elements of recognizing the mutual, though not identical, interests of workers and company.

There is no form of economic education in industry which compares in effectiveness with group incentives and group interaction based on facts about sales and costs. Because these matters come to be understood and are important to all, adjustments can be worked out.

COOPERATION STEPS

Companies with effective Scanlon installations point out that the money incentive, while essential, is not the heart of the plan. At Scanlon plan conferences held annually at the Massachusetts Institute of Technology, it is always observed that people sent to learn about the plan are much concerned about ratios and employee earnings. Firms using the plan are convinced that successful results depend on fundamental changes in concepts about working together.

We would do well to consider the procedure typically followed by companies adopting the Scanlon plan:

(1.) A basic structural step in cooperation is the elimination of the conventional suggestion system if there is one (many are already half-dead). In each department or other significant work group, employees elect by secret ballot a representative to meet with the supervisor to study better work methods. Meetings are held once or twice a month, and are attended not only by foremen and production committee members, but also by any other employees in the group who have suggestions about methods, materials, machines, scrap control, or other pertinent matters. Minutes are kept of each meeting.

(2.) If the suggestions are valid and do not involve other departments, significant money outlays, or other major changes outside the foreman's "area of freedom," they can be adopted as soon as perfected. If the foreman or another supervisor can show the employees that there are reasons why the idea will not work, it is either abandoned or reworked to make it usable.

(3.) If the idea seems good to employees, even though it is not reacted to favorably by the foreman, it can be referred to a screening committee. It must go to the screening committee if it requires interdepartmental action, or higher-level study or approval. The screening committee is composed of elected employee members and representatives of top management, usually the company president or executive vice president, the controller, and top production executives.

(4.) In this and the department committee there is no voting on suggestions. Top management has unqualified veto power on ideas. Worker representatives may act as advocates for suggestions, but in practice often are divided among themselves on the merits of a specific idea. Guests from department-level committees are often present to discuss ideas originating with them.

(5.) The screening committee also announces production and costs for the previous month, and the resulting bonus, if any. In addition, it studies ideas which come from its own membership, plus other problems of company-wide interest. What production and screening committees do and how they do it are a far cry from the operation of a conventional suggestion plan. An observer reports:

"Sometimes the workers throw the book at management; sometimes management points out where the shop has fallen down. Engineers argue against machine-tool operators; foremen attack the engineers for unrealistic blueprints."[9]

This sort of approach links incentives with technological change. It stands in marked contrast to the situation that exists, for example, in companies which combine suggestion systems and piecework—the effect being that the two are often directly opposed in employees' minds. If workers under piece rates submit suggestions for better work methods, industrial engineering departments usually restudy jobs. The result may be a new rate which makes it harder for employees to "make out." If a bright idea can be kept from the motion-and-time-study men, earnings will increase under existing piece rates, or former earnings will be maintained with less output of time and effort.

CHANGED ATTITUDES

A number of advantages usually result from the changed climate of a group program:

• The free and *continuous* opportunity for employees to initiate action in and of itself tends to create a production-centered climate. Arguments and conflicts of interest will take place as always, but the reason will be more because employees are *concerned* over their work than because they resent management or are out to "beat the company."

• Introduction of new methods and machines by management is regarded differently. One company executive says that resistance to change has disappeared within his firm.

• Because it is advantageous to do so, workers develop an interest in training new employees.

• Workers also tend to bear down on employees who are not responding to the program.

• Workers discipline themselves more. Hence in many companies with participative programs the foreman is freed almost completely from discipline problems. He can concentrate on better scheduling and other profitable activities.

• An observer can spend weeks in a Scanlon plan company without observing anything that suggests a "speed up." Employees do not look or act rushed, their work pace is comfortable, there are pauses for conversation but less time is wasted.

• Not only do employees show new interest in company success by doing more careful work, but they exert pressures on management to manage better.

If there is any trouble with the Scanlon plan, it may be that it is sometimes *too* successful. For example, after the program has been in operation for a while it may become startlingly clear that the piecework rates formerly used were extremely ineffective in motivating workers. Such a revelation is not calculated to please any supervisors who supported the piecework system. Again, the new program may lead to the discovery of waste in clerical departments, unrealistic activities in engineering, and absurdities in accounting practice—all of which can be corrected through the use of Scanlon plan principles, but which might be interpreted to reflect poorly on some managers' past performance.

Such danger lies in any major improvement, of course. I do not want to overestimate it, but only to note that, as always, tact and courage can do much to make the Scanlon machinery effective.

OTHER INCENTIVE PLANS

Two other group incentive programs deserve attention here. One of them is a widely used plan devised by Allen W. Rucker, a management consultant. The other was developed by a businessman, H. L. Nunn.

SHARE OF PRODUCTION

The Rucker plan is most often applied to hourly rated factory workers and to executives, but in some cases is developed to cover all employees in a company. It is based on sophisticated and extensive figure analysis. A historical relationship is established between total earnings (including fringe benefits) of hourly rated employees and the net production values created by the company. If major changes in products or processes occur, the plan is re-engineered.

Under this plan, company and workers share any increases in "value added by manufacture" which grow out of their joint efforts. This principle, of course, eliminates the cost of raw materials purchased and related costs such as supplies and power. For every 1 percent increase in production value the plan provides for an increase of 1 percent in total payroll credit for eligible workers. Thus an integrated incentive is provided for:

(1.) Reduction in material and supply costs.
(2.) Reduction in scrap and returns by customers.
(3.) Improvement in product quality.
(4.) Less labor cost for the same values, or the same cost for greater values.

Since the plan is based on realized production value income, the company's ability to increase sales volume and provide stable employment is increased, as is its ability to lower prices to meet competition.

Rucker has shown that, for the United States as a whole, factory workers' pay has been proportionate to production values for 50 years. The relationship has prevailed to within ± 1.663 percent. Labor's average share has been 39.395 percent; management's 60.605 percent. (For individual industries and companies similar stable relationships have been established.) Booms, depressions, wars, changes in political leadership in the nation, and the introduction of increasing amounts of labor- and time-saving machinery have scarcely affected the ratios. Labor *time*, says Rucker, has been cut about 70 percent since 1914, but wages have made up almost precisely the same percentage of value added by manufacture.

In installations of Rucker incentives, employee committees are used, although they are often set up somewhat differently from those used in Scanlon plans. In most companies a "share of production" committee is established, consisting of worker representatives from every major department, plus one third to one half as many shop supervisors. There are usually two co-chairmen, a top executive, and the current union president. If there is no union, an employee representative is co-chairman. Members may serve on the committee for as little as three months, with other members replacing them to bring in new ideas. In some companies worker representatives serve for a year.

Discussions with union and management personnel in Rucker plan companies show that in the most successful installations, employee committee members are as aggressive as in the Scanlon companies. However, they do not get to be this way automatically. Management must give them a free hand to criticize, suggest, and gather information if the program is to fully develop its potential.

LABOR AND MANAGEMENT

The Nunn-Bush Shoe Company plan started as a percentage-of-sales program. H. L. Nunn discovered that from 1926 through 1934 wages as a percentage of Nunn-Bush sales had varied within a narrow range—18.2 percent to 21.7 percent. He set 20 percent of sales as the ratio for a program involving 52 pay checks a year.

After learning of Rucker's work on value added to raw materials, Nunn felt that it was an economically sounder approach, but he did not persuade his employees and management to change to the new basis until sharp postwar increases in the price of leather got the original plan into trouble. Workers, after much discussion, voted in 1948 to switch to 36 percent of value added instead of 20 percent of sales. The percentage is reviewed and changed as conditions warrant.[10]

Long before the incentive plan was established in 1935, the company had developed an unusual relationship with its employees and an intramural union. The substance of the program, in addition to solicitation of employee ideas on production, is presented in the following statement, agreed to by company and workers in 1915:

"Management will forego all customary prerogatives of arbitrary discharge and discipline of members and will share the privilege of selecting new employees. Management will forego all arbitrary right to name conditions of employment and proposes to sit down with the elected representatives of this society [union] and come to mutual agreements on all these matters.

"From the members of this working force we will ask in return their solemn pledge to forego any action by force through power of strike or otherwise."[11]

Not only has this company never had a strike; it has never had to take a dispute to arbitration. A reading of the minutes of Nunn-Bush union meetings suggests a new concept of union-management cooperation. Here, in practice, is evidence of responsible industrial self-government.

CONDITIONS OF SUCCESS

From a technological point of view there seem to be few bars to greater use of programs that combine group incentives and structured opportunities for cooperation. The record shows that quite large companies and firms with complex production and marketing operations can use Scanlon or Rucker programs, or plans of their own devising. Such plans do, however, exact certain conditions from management and the union. Four in particular strike me as being very important.

(1.) *Management must be reasonably competent, and willing to become more so.* Competence, of course, involves, the ability to make decisions:

"Many organizations have developed the habit of postponing decisions wherever that is possible. Rather than decide the issue and risk being proved wrong, management may decide not to decide, to await further developments. But by the time these developments have occurred there is no decision left to make: there is only one alternative. This implicit type of decision making, more widespread than we might care to admit, is not consistent with the successful operation of the plan."[12]

(2.) *Management must be as honest as it is competent.* Petty attitudes and conscious or unconscious attempts to "pull just a few fast ones" will wreck a group program overnight. Nor do the moral lapses need to be major ones to destroy the possibility of success.

(3.) *Union leadership should also be above average in competence and integrity, for identical reasons.* Of course, much depends here on the attitude of the rank and file. Men with experience in interaction plans have observed that once company and workers truly commit themselves to making a plan work, the necessary leaders usually appear, in both groups, and assume responsibility.

(4.) *Ideally, firms should already have a management-training program which includes realistic consideration of problems of human relations.* As Chris Argyris has said, many such programs are concerned with "pseudo-human relations" techniques which usually do more harm than good.[13] And even if they are sound, they often have not included top executives!

There are several reasons why solid human relations training is needed. To quote from *The Scanlon Plan* again:

"[Decisions on production problems] must now be made after consultation with the employees. In many cases, such consultation shows up previous practices as ill-considered at best and just plain stupid at worst. That kind of dramatic exposition, often not put too diplomatically by the employee, may undermine the personal security of line management people. Initially, many of them try to suppress the efforts of the production committees, and only forceful and prompt action by top management makes the continuance of committee efforts possible. Others react with lengthy rationalization, explaining why none of the employees' suggestions can be carried out, or asserting that the ideas have been in their minds a long time, but that the employees would not cooperate in carrying them out."[14]

If supervisors and managers come to understand themselves and their own problems better, the difficulties just described will be lessened. Training also should include an attempt to help the managers see worker attitudes and problems more imaginatively. If the training has included a practical program in conference leadership and in helping groups arrive at decisions, supervisors will be better able to handle participative programs. Frustration, time wasting, and unproductive conflict will be reduced, although never eliminated completely.

Making Incentives Work

PRESSURES AND CONFLICTS

If a group incentive program really works, if it really stirs up company-wide interest in productivity, it should not be surprising that management finds itself receiving unaccustomed attention from the union. Union committees may bear down hard on management inefficiency. They may even be critical of entirely defensible company practices. It takes a strong patient management to work through this kind of situation. Indignation and anger are often spontaneous reactions. Executives would do well to recognize that group incentives can also make life more difficult at times for labor officials, too.

In some situations the union may develop an internal split. Prestige may gravitate to production committee and screening committee members at the expense of men holding other union jobs. Leadership in the union may become so involved in the plan that valid member grievances are neglected.

It is no surprise that maintaining union and program goals simultaneously creates conflicts for unions. Even in conventional situations the unions may be under great tension because of clashing interests within their own membership groups. The cause of internal peace may not be served by the addition of new problems and issues. However, I have encountered no union locals which wanted to drop the kind of plan discussed here.

MONETARY PAYOFFS

Peter Drucker has said that the major incentives to productivity and efficiency are social and moral rather than financial.[15] Certainly bonuses are not the most important thing about Scanlon- and Rucker-type plans, but their importance should not be underestimated.

PRODUCTIVITY INCREASES

Figures on productivity gains under the Scanlon plan are given by Elbridge S. Puckett in a report entitled "Productivity Achievements."[16] Some of his averages are listed in Table 11-1.

Table 11-1.   *Percentage Increases in Productivity*

Company	First-year Relative Efficiency (1)	Second-year Relative Efficiency (2)	Two-year Average Relative Efficiency (Unweighted) (3)
A	14.9%	10.9%	12.9%
B	21.9	12.7	17.3
C	16.7	13.2	15.0
D	36.7	29.3	33.0
E	28.9	49.4	39.2
F	32.9	42.9	37.9
G	38.7	25.1	31.9
H	14.1	16.5	15.3
I	12.9	23.2	18.1
J	6.8	13.7	10.3
Average (unweighted)	22.5%	23.7%	23.1%

Efficiency in each case is expressed as a percentage of efficiency in the base period. The average relative efficiency for the two-year period is unweighted. Puckett defends the unweighted average on the ground that it yields a more conservative result than would be developed by a weighted figure.

It will be seen that the poorest productivity gain in the first year was 6.8 percent, the best 38.7 percent. During the second year the range was 10.9 percent to 49.4 percent. Puckett notes that of the four firms which achieved gains of 30 percent or better, only one had had previous financial difficulties. This suggests that the company which is already relatively efficient and profitable may have the greatest capacity for improvement under a Scanlon program.

It is also interesting to see that the two largest firms in the group studied made gains equal to the average for all firms. The smallest of the ten plants had 30 employees, the largest 1,200. One company was nonunion, one had an independent union, and the rest were covered by locals of various international unions.

Three of the companies which attained the largest gains in productivity had a labor content of less than 35 percent of sales production value. The firm with the lowest labor content—under 20 percent—increased productivity as much as the ten-firm average. A job shop firm did as well as companies using mass production methods.

EMPLOYEE EARNINGS

In the firms studied by Puckett, bonuses in the two-year period averaged 17.4 percent of gross pay. In the plant with a productivity increase of 39.2 percent, the bonus averaged about 29.4 percent. (All firms split labor-cost savings 75 percent to participants and 25 percent to the company.)

In other companies which use programs of a similar type, excellent overall gains have been amassed. For instance:

A small tool company in Texas installed a "break-even point control bonus" which evolved from a suggestion made at an employee committee meeting. In 1948, plant volume was under $1 million; return on investment was 28 percent. In 1956, volume was above $2.5 million; income on investment, 177 percent.[17] Employees in 1957 were receiving 13.9 percent of gross sales, made after passing the break-even point or date—a sizable amount for distribution among some 135 employees.

Rucker plan companies report bonuses with ranges similar to those found in Scanlon plan companies (the bonuses being in addition to hourly rates competitive with other industries). During the recession of 1958, some of these firms dropped their programs (as did some Scanlon companies), but typical bonuses over the last eight years have been in the 17 percent to 20 percent range. In some companies much higher percentages have been maintained.

PROFIT SHARING

Many companies have used profit sharing as a group incentive. It is, of course, broader and looser than plans of the Scanlon and Rucker kind. Joseph Scanlon, however, installed profit sharing, plus production committees, in a few companies where he could not find a more specific accounting handle for the program. Any company with profit sharing can replace its conventional suggestion system with Scanlon-style production committees if it wishes. Pitney-Bowes is an example of a company combining profit sharing with a committee structure:

The company, which is nonunion, has four levels of committees. There are sectional, departmental, and divisional "councils," and a main council. Every two years employees elect deputies to represent them in these councils. The main council has a suggestion committee composed of both worker and management members. An exceptionally large number of suggestions per employee are submitted, and of these a large per cent are usable.

A few other companies combine profit sharing and employee-initiated action, but in most cases relationships between company and workers remain conventional. If the thesis is that participation, despite its imperfections, works better than nonparticipation, many profit-sharing companies may not be obtaining all the benefits which their programs could yield. They are not creating a "managerial" attitude among their workers.

SOME WEAKNESSES

Can profit sharing be a substitute for Scanlon- and Rucker-type programs? In my opinion it rarely can, unless a program like that of Pitney-Bowes is established.

For one thing, there are some weaknesses in profit sharing as an incentive. Profits may result from successful inventory speculations, auspicious patents, and a dozen other situations in which employees are not involved. Similarly, losses may be experienced when worker effort and ingenuity are at a maximum. If it becomes clear to employees in a bad year that nothing they can do will bring about a profit to the company, they may not be as aggressive in helping to reduce losses as they would be under a Scanlon or Rucker program where some bonus might be earned even in a bad year.

Also, the fact that most profit-sharing plans pay only once a year, or are taken as retirement compensation, tends to make the return seem remote to workers. Scanlon, Rucker, and similar programs usually pay off monthly. A few, with very uneven production, pay quarterly.

Notes

1. See William F. Whyte et al., *Money and Motivation*. New York: Harper & Brothers 1955, 39–49.
2. "The Other Side of Incentives," *Personnel*, January–February 1959, 32–41.
3. *Harvard Business Review*, January–February 1958, 111–119.
4. William F. Whyte, *op. cit.*, 90–96.
5. For a few examples of desirable outcomes in cases where workers have a hand in decisions involving their work assignments, see Chapters 8 and 9 of Norman R. F. Maier,

Principles of Human Relations. New York: Wiley, 1952; Lester Coch and John French, Jr., "Overcoming Resistance to Change," *Human Relations*, Vol. I, No. 4 (1948), 512–532; and F. J. Roethlisberger, *Management and Morale.* Cambridge: Harvard University Press, 1941, 14.

6. Robert N. McMurry, "The Case for Benevolent Autocracy," *Harvard Business Review* January–February 1958, 82–90.

7. Robert Saltonstall, *Human Relations in Administration.* New York: McGraw-Hill, 1959, 260.

8. See Chapters 3, 6, and 10 of *The Scanlon Plan*, edited by Fred Lesieur. Cambridge: The Technology Press; New York: Wiley, 1958.

9. *Ibid.*, 26.

10. H. L. Nunn, *The Whole Man Goes to Work.* New York: Harper & Brothers, 1953, Chapters 12 and 13.

11. *Ibid.*, 61.

12. Fred Lesieur, *op. cit.*, 62.

13. "The Organization: What Makes It Healthy?" *Harvard Business Review*, November–December 1958, 110.

14. Fred Lesieur, *op. cit.*, 61.

15. *The New Society.* New York: Harper & Brothers, 1949.

16. Fred Lesieur, *op. cit.*, 112–113.

17. Ruel McDaniel, "Profit Sharing for a Small Business," *American Business*, June 1957.

12

RICHARD BECKHARD

The Confrontation Meeting

*O*ne of the continuing problems facing the top management team of any organization in times of stress or major change is how to assess accurately the state of the organization's health. How are people reacting to the change? How committed are subordinate managers to the new conditions? Where are the most pressing organization problems?

In the period following a major change—such as that brought about by a change in leadership or organization structure, a merger, or the introduction of a new technology—there tends to be much confusion and an expenditure of dysfunctional energy that negatively affects both productivity and morale.

At such times, the top management group usually spends many hours together working on the business problems and finding ways of coping with the new conditions. Frequently, the process of working together under this pressure also has the effect of making the top team more cohesive.

Concurrently, these same managers tend to spend less and less time with their subordinates and with the rest of the organization. Communications decrease between the top and middle levels of management. People at the lower levels often complain that they are less in touch with what is going on than they were before the change. They feel left out. They report having less influence than before, being more unsure of their own decision-making authority, and feeling less sense of ownership in the organization. As a result of this, they tend to make fewer decisions, take fewer risks, and wait until the "smoke clears."

When this unrest comes to the attention of top management, the response is usually to take some action such as:
(1.) Having each member of the top team hold team meetings with his sub-

Reprinted from *Harvard Business Review*, 45, No. 2 (1967): 149–155. Used with permission. © 1967 by the President and Fellows of Harvard College; all rights reserved.

213

ordinates to communicate the state of affairs, and following this procedure down through the organization;
(2.) holding some general communication improvement meetings;
(3.) conducting an attitude survey to determine priority problems.

Any of these actions will probably be helpful, but each requires a considerable investment of time which is competitive with the time needed to work on the change problem itself.

ACTION PLANS

Recently I have experimented with an activity that allows a total management group, drawn from all levels of the organization, to take a quick reading on its own health, and—*within a matter of hours*—to set action plans for improving it. I call this a "confrontation meeting."

The activity is based on my previous experience with an action-oriented method of planned change in which information on problems and attitudes is collected and fed back to those who produced it, and steps are taken to start action plans for improvement of the condition.

Sometimes, following situations of organizational stress, the elapsed time in moving from identification of the problem to collaborative action planning must be extremely brief. The confrontation meeting can be carried out in $4\frac{1}{2}$ to 5 hours' working time, and it is designed to include the entire management of a large system in a joint action-planning program.

I have found this approach to be particularly practical in organization situations where there are large numbers in the management group and/or where it is difficult to take the entire group off the job for any length of time. The activity has been conducted several times with a one evening and one morning session—taking only $2\frac{1}{2}$ hours out of a regular working day.

The confrontation meeting discussed in this article has been used in a number of different organization situations. Experience shows that it is appropriate where:

• There is a need for the total management group to examine its own workings.

• Very limited time is available for the activity.

• Top management wishes to improve the conditions quickly.

• There is enough cohesion in the top team to ensure follow-up.

• There is real commitment to resolving the issues on the part of top management.

• The organization is experiencing, or has recently experienced, some major change.

In order to show how this technique can speed the process of getting the information and acting on it, let us first look at three actual company situations where this approach has been successfully applied. Then we will examine both the positive results and the possible problems that could occur through the use and misuse of this technique. Finally, after a brief summary there is an appendix for the reader interested in a more elaborate description of the phasing and scheduling of such a meeting.

CASE EXAMPLE A

The initial application of the confrontation meeting technique occurred in 1965 in a large food products company. Into this long-time family-owned and closely controlled company, there was introduced for the first time a non-family professional general manager. He had been promoted from the ranks of the group that had previously reported to the family-member general manager.

This change in the "management culture," which had been carefully and thoroughly prepared by the family executives, was carried out with a minimum number of problems. The new general manager and his operating heads spent many hours together and developed a quite open problem-solving climate and an effective, cohesive team. Day-to-day operations were left pretty much in the hands of their immediate subordinates, while the top group focused on planning.

A few months after the change, however, the general manager began getting some information that indicated all was not well further down in the organization. On investigation, he discovered that many middle-level managers were feeling isolated from what was going on. Many were unclear about the authority and functions of the "management committee" (his top team); some were finding it very difficult to see and consult with their bosses (his operating heads); others were not being informed of decisions made at his management committee meetings; still others were apprehensive that a new power elite was developing which in many ways was much worse than the former family managers.

In discussing this feedback information with his operating heads, the general manager found one or two who felt these issues required immediate management committee attention. But most of the members of the top team tended to minimize the information as "the usual griping," or "people needing too many decisions made for them," or "everybody always wanting to be in on everything."

The general manager then began searching for some way to
(1) bring the whole matter into the open;
(2) determine the magnitude and potency of the total problem;
(3) give his management committee and himself a true picture of the state of the organization's attitudes and concerns;
(4) collect information on employee needs, problems, and frustrations in some organized way so that corrective actions could be taken in priority order;
(5) get his management committee members in better tune with their subordinates' feelings and attitudes, and put some pressure on the team members for continued two-way communication within their own special areas;
(6) make clear to the total organization that he—the top manager—was personally concerned;
(7) set up mechanisms by which all members of the total management group could feel that their individual needs were noticed;

(8) provide additional mechanisms for supervisors to influence the whole organization.

The confrontation meeting was created to satisfy these objectives and to minimize the time in which a large number of people would have to be away from the job.

Some 70 managers, representing the total management group, were brought together for a confrontation meeting starting at 9:00 in the morning and ending at 4:30 in the afternoon. The specific "design" for the day, which is broken down into a more detailed description in the Appendix (page 220), had the following components:

(1.) Climate setting—establishing willingness to participate.
(2.) Information collecting—getting the attitudes and feelings out in the open.
(3.) Information sharing—making total information available to all.
(4.) Priority setting and group action planning—holding work-unit sessions to set priority actions and to make timetable commitments.
(5.) Organization action planning—getting commitment by top management to the working of these priorities.
(6.) Immediate follow-up by the top management committee—planning first actions and commitments.

During the day-long affair, the group identified some 80 problems that were of concern to people throughout the organization; they selected priorities from among them; they began working on these priority issues in functional work units, and each unit produced action recommendations with timetables and targets; and they got a commitment from top management of actions on priorities that would be attended to. The top management team met immediately after the confrontation meeting to pin down the action steps and commitments.

(In subsequent applications of this confrontation meeting approach, a seventh component—a progress review—has been added, since experience has shown that it is important to reconvene the total group four to six weeks later for a progress review both from the functional units and from the top management team.)

CASE EXAMPLE B

A small company which makes products for the military had been operating at a stable sales volume of $3 million to $4 million. The invention of a new process and the advent of the war in Vietnam suddenly produced an explosion of business. Volume rose to the level of $6 million within six months and promised to re-double within another year.

Top management was desperately trying to keep raw materials flowing through the line, get material processes, find people to hire, discover quicker ways of job training, and maintain quality under increased pressure.

There was constant interaction among the five members of the top management team. They were aware of the tension and fatigue that existed on the production line, but they were only vaguely aware of the unrest, fatigue, concern, and loneliness of the middle manager and foreman groups. However, enough signals *had* filtered up to the top team to cause concern and a decision that something needed to be done right away. But, because of the pressures of work, finding the time to tackle the problems was as difficult as the issues themselves.

The entire management group agreed to give up one night and one morning; the confrontation meeting was conducted according to the six component phases described earlier, with Phases 1, 2, and 3 being held in the evening and Phases 4, 5, and 6 taking place the following morning.

CASE EXAMPLE C

A management organization took over the operation of a hotel which was in a sorry state of affairs. Under previous absentee ownership, the property had been allowed to run down; individual departments were independent empires; many people in management positions were nonprofessional hotel people (that is, friends of the owners); and there was very low competence in the top management team.

The general manager saw as his priority missions the need to:
(1.) Stop the downhill trend.
(2.) Overcome a poor public image.
(3.) Clean up the property.
(4.) Weed out the low-potential (old friends) management.
(5.) Bring in professional managers in key spots.
(6.) Build a management team.
(7.) Build effective operating teams, with the members of the top management team as links.

He followed his plan with considerable success. In a period of one year year he had significantly cleaned up the property, improved the service, built a new dining room, produced an enviable food quality, and begun to build confidence in key buyers, such as convention managers. He had acquired and developed a very fine, professional, young management team that was both competent and highly motivated. This group had been working as a cohesive team on all the hotel's improvement goals; differences between them and their areas seemed to have been largely worked through.

At the level below the top group, the department and section heads, many of whom were also new, had been working under tremendous pressure for over a year to bring about improvements in the property and in the hotel's services. They felt very unappreciated by the top managers, who were described as "always being in meetings and unavailable," or "never rewarding us for good work," or "requiring approval on all decisions but we can't get to see them," or "developing a fine top management club but keeping the pressure on us and we're doing the work."

The problem finally was brought to the attention of the top managers by some of the department heads. Immediate action was indicated, and a confrontation meeting was decided on. It took place in two periods, an afternoon and the following morning. There was an immediate follow-up by the top management team in which many of the issues between departments and functions were identified as stemming back to the modus operandi of the top team. These issues were openly discussed and were worked through. Also in this application, a follow-up report and review session was scheduled for five weeks after the confrontation meeting.

POSITIVE RESULTS

The experience of the foregoing case examples, as well as that of other organizations in which the confrontation meeting technique has been applied, demonstrates that positive results—particularly, improved operation procedures and improved organization health—frequently occur.

OPERATIONAL ADVANTAGES

One of the outstanding plus factors is that procedures which have been confused are clarified. In addition, practices which have been nonexistent are initiated. Typical of these kinds of operational improvement, for example, are the reporting of financial information to operating units, the handling of the reservation system at a hotel, and the inspection procedures and responsibilities in a changing manufacturing process.

Another advantage is that task forces, and/or temporary systems, are set up as needed. These may be in the form of special teams to study the overlap in responsibilities between two departments and to write new statements and descriptions, or to work out a new system for handling order processing from sales to production planning, or to examine the kinds of information that should flow regularly from the management committee to middle management.

Still another improvement is in providing guidance to top management as to specific areas needing priority attention. For example, "the overtime policy set under other conditions is really impeding the achievement of organization requirements," or "the food in the employee's cafeteria is really creating morale problems," or "the lack of understanding of where the organization is going and what top management's goals are is producing apathy," or "what goes on in top management meetings does not get communicated to the middle managers."

ORGANIZATION HEALTH

In reviewing the experiences of companies where the confrontation meeting approach has been instituted, I have perceived a number of positive results in the area of organization health:

• A high degree of open communication between various departments and organization levels is achieved very quickly. Because people are assigned to functional units and produce data together, it is possible to express the real feeling of one level or group toward another, particularly if the middle echelon believes the top wants to hear it.

• The information collected is current, correct, and "checkable."

• A real dialogue can exist between the top management team and the rest of the management organization, which personalizes the top manager to the total group.

• Larger numbers of people get "ownership" of the problem, since everyone has some influence through his unit's guidance to the top management team; thus people feel they have made a real contribution. Even more, the requirement that each functional unit take personal responsibility for resolving some of the issues broadens the base of ownership.

• Collaborative goal setting at several levels is demonstrated and practiced. The mechanism provides requirements for joint goal setting within each functional unit and between top and middle managers. People report that this helps them to understand "management by objectives" more clearly than before.

• The top team can take corrective actions based on valid information. By making real commitments and establishing check or review points, there is a quick building of trust in management's intentions on the part of lower level managers.

• There tends to be an increase in trust and confidence both toward the top management team and toward colleagues. A frequently appearing agenda item is the "need for better understanding of the job problems of other departments," and the output of these meetings is often the commitment to some "mechanism for systematic interdepartmental communication." People also report a change in their stereotypes of people in other areas.

• This activity tends to be a "success experience" and thus increases total morale. The process itself, which requires interaction, contribution, and joint work on the problems and which rewards constructive criticism, tends to produce a high degree of enthusiasm and commitment. Because of this, the follow-up activities are crucial in ensuring continuation of this enthusiasm.

POTENTIAL PROBLEMS

The confrontation meeting technique produces, in a very short time, a great deal of commitment and desire for results on the part of a lot of people. Feelings tend to be more intense than in some other settings because of the concentration of time and manpower. As a result, problems can develop through misuse of the techniques.

If the top management team does not really use the information from its subordinates, or if there are great promises and little follow-up action, more harm can be caused to the organization's health than if the event were never held.

If the confrontation meeting is used as a manipulative device to give people the "feeling of participation," the act can boomerang. They will soon figure out management's intentions, and the reaction can be severe.

Another possible difficulty is that the functional units, full of enthusiasm at the meeting, set unrealistic or impractical goals and commitments. The behavior of the key man in each unit—usually a department manager or division head—is crucial in keeping suggestions in balance.

One more possible problem may appear when the functional units select a few priority issues to report out. While these issues may be the most *urgent*, they are not necessarily the most *important*. Mechanisms for working *all* of the information need to be developed within each functional unit. In one of the case examples cited earlier, the groups worked the few problems they identified very thoroughly and never touched the others. This necessitated a "replay" six months later.

IN SUMMARY

In periods of stress following major organization changes, there tends to be much confusion and energy expended that negatively affects productivity and organization health.

The top management team needs quick, efficient ways of sensing the state of the organization's attitudes and feelings in order to plan appropriate actions and to devote its energy to the most important problems.

The usual methods of attitude surveys, extended staff meetings, and so forth demand extensive time and require a delay between getting the information and acting on it.

A short micromechanism called a confrontation meeting can provide the total management group with:

- An accurate reading on the organization's health.
- The opportunity for work units to set priorities for movement.
- The opportunity for top management to make appropriate action decisions based on appropriate information from the organization.
- An increased involvement in the organization's goals.
- A real commitment to action on the part of subgroups.
- A basis for determining other mechanisms for communication between levels and groups, appropriate location of decisions, problem solving within subunits, as well as the machinery for upward influence.

APPENDIX

Here is a detailed description of the seven components which make up the specific "design" for the day-long confrontation meeting.

Phase 1. *Climate Setting* (Forty-five minutes to one hour): At the outset, the top manager needs to communicate to the total management group his goals for the meeting, and his concern for and interest in free discussion and issue facing. He also has to assure his people that there is no punishment for open confrontation.

It is also helpful to have some form of information session or lecture by the top manager or a consultant. Appropriate subjects might deal with the problems of communication, the need for understanding, the assumptions and the goals of the total organization, the concept of shared responsibility for the future of the organization, and the opportunity for and responsibility of influencing the organization.

Phase 2. Information Collecting (One hour): The total group is divided into small heterogeneous units of seven or eight people. If there is a top management team that has been holding sessions regularly, it meets as a separate unit. The rest of the participants are assigned to units with a "diagonal slice" of the organization used as a basis for composition—that is, no boss and subordinate are together, and each unit contains members from every functional area.

The assignment given to each of these units is along these lines:

> Think of yourself as an individual with needs and goals. Also think as a person concerned about the total organization. What are the obstacles, "demotivators," poor procedures or policies, unclear goals, or poor attitudes that exist today? What different conditions, if any, would make the organization more effective and make life in the organization better?

Each unit is instructed to select a reporter to present its results at a general information-collecting session to be held one hour later.

Phase 3. Information Sharing (One hour): Each reporter writes his unit's complete findings on newsprint, which is tacked up around the room.

The meeting leader suggests some categories under which all the data from all the sheets can be located. In other words, if there are 75 items, the likelihood is that these can be grouped into 6 or 7 major categories—say, by type of problem, such as "communications difficulties"; or by type of relationship, such as "problems with top management"; or by type of area involved, such as "problems in the mechanical department."

Then the meeting breaks, either for lunch or, if it happens to be an evening session, until the next morning.

During the break all the data sheets are duplicated for general distribution.

Phase 4. Priority Setting and Group Action Planning (One hour and fifteen minutes): The total group reconvenes for a 15-minute general session. With the meeting leader, they go through the raw data on the duplicated sheets and put category numbers by each piece of data.

People are now assigned to their functional, natural work units for a one-hour session. Manufacturing people at all levels go to one unit, everybody in sales to another, and so forth. These units are headed by a department manager or division head of that function. This means that some units may have as few as 3 people and some as many as 25. Each unit is charged to perform three specific tasks:

(1.) Discuss the problems and issues which affect its area. Decide on the priorities and early actions to which the group is prepared to commit itself. (They should be prepared to share this commitment with their colleagues at the general session.)

(2.) Identify the issues and/or problems to which the top management team should give its priority attention.

(3.) Decide how to communicate the results of the session to their subordinates.

Phase 5. Organization Action Planning (One to two hours): The total management group reconvenes in a general session, where:

(1.) Each functional unit reports its commitment and plans to the total group.

(2.) Each unit reports and lists the items that its members believe the management team should deal with first.
(3.) The top manager reacts to this list and makes commitments (through setting targets or assigning task forces or timetables, and so on) for action where required.
(4.) Each unit shares briefly its plans for communicating the results of the confrontation meeting to all subordinates.

Phase 6. Immediate Follow-up by Top Team (One to three hours): The top management team meets immediately after the confrontation meeting ends to plan first follow up actions, which should then be reported back to the total management group within a few days.

Phase 7. Progress Review (Two hours): Follow-up with total management group four to six weeks later.

13

FRED E. FIEDLER

Engineer the Job to Fit the Manager

What kind of leadership style does business need? Should company executives be decisive, directive, willing to give orders, and eager to assume responsibility? Should they be human relations-oriented, nondirective, willing to share leadership with the men in their group? Or should we perhaps start paying attention to the more important problem of defining under what conditions each of these leadership styles works best and what to do about it?

The success or failure of an organization depends on the quality of its management. How to get the best possible management is a question of vital importance; but it is perhaps even more important to ask how we can make better use of the management talent which *we already have*.

To get good business executives we have relied primarily on recruitment, selection, and training. It is time for businessmen to ask whether this is the only way or the best way for getting the best possible management. Fitting the man to the leadership job by selection and training has not been spectacularly successful. It is surely easier to change almost anything in the job situation than a man's personality and his leadership style. Why not try, then, to fit the leadership job to the man?

Executive jobs are surprisingly pliable, and the executive manpower pool is becoming increasingly small. The luxury of picking a "natural leader" from among a number of equally promising or equally qualified specialists is rapidly fading into the past. Business must learn how to utilize the available executive talent as effectively as it now utilizes physical plant and machine tools. Your financial expert, your top research scientist, or your production genius may be practically irreplaceable. Their jobs call for positions of leadership and responsi-

Reprinted from *Harvard Business Review*, 43, No. 5 (September/October, 1965): 115–122. Used with permission. © 1965 by the President and Fellows of Harvard College; all rights reserved.

bility. Replacements for these men can be neither recruited nor trained overnight, and they may not be willing to play second fiddle in their departments. If their leadership style does not fit the job, *we must learn how to engineer the job to fit their leadership style.*

In this article I shall describe some studies that illuminate this task of job engineering and adaptation. It will be seen that there are situations where the authoritarian, highly directive leader works best, and other situations where the egalitarian, more permissive, human relations-oriented leader works best; but almost always there are possibilities for changing the situation around somewhat to match the needs of the particular managers who happen to be available. The executive who appreciates these differences and possibilities has knowledge that can be valuable to him in running his organization.

To understand the problems that a new approach would involve, let us look first at some of the basic issues in organizational and group leadership.

STYLES OF LEADERSHIP

Leadership is a personal relationship in which one person directs, coordinates, and supervises others in the performance of a common task. This is especially so in "interacting groups," where men must work together cooperatively in achieving organizational goals.

In oversimplified terms, it can be said that the leader manages the group in either of two ways. He can:

• Tell people what to do and how to do it.

• Or share his leadership responsibilities with his group members and involve them in the planning and execution of the task.

There are, of course, all shades of leadership styles in between these two polar positions, but the basic issue is this: the work of motivating and coordinating group members has to be done either by brandishing the proverbial stick or by dangling the equally proverbial carrot. The former is the more orthodox job-centered, autocratic style. The latter is the more nondirective, group-centered procedure.

Research evidence exists to support both approaches to leadership. Which, then, should be judged more appropriate? On the face of it, the first style of leadership is best under some conditions, while the second works better under others. Accepting this proposition immediately opens two avenues of approach. Management can:

• Determine the specific situation in which the directive or the nondirective leadership style works best, and then select or train men so that their leadership style fits the particular job.

• Or determine the type of leadership style which is most natural for the man in the executive position, and then change the job to fit the man.

The first alternative has been discussed many times before; the second has not. We have never seriously considered whether it would be easier to fit the executive's job to the man.

NEEDED STYLE?

How might this be done? Some answers have been suggested by a research program on leadership effectiveness that I have directed under Office of Naval Research auspices since 1951.[1] This program has dealt with a wide variety of different groups, including basketball teams, surveying parties, various military combat crews, and men in open-hearth steel shops, as well as members of management and boards of directors. When possible, performance was measured in terms of objective criteria—for instance, percentage of games won by high school basketball teams; tap-to-tap time of open-hearth shops (roughly equivalent to the tonnage of steel output per unit of time); and company net income over a three-year period. Our measure of leadership style was based on a simple scale indicating the degree to which a man described, favorably or unfavorably, his least-preferred co-worker (LPC). This co-worker did not need to be someone he actually worked with at the time, but could be someone the respondent had known in the past. Whenever possible, the score was obtained before the leader was assigned to his group.

The study indicates that a person who describes his least-preferred coworker in a relatively favorable manner tends to be permissive, human relations-oriented, and considerate of the feelings of his men. But a person who describes his least-preferred co-worker in an unfavorable manner—who has what we have come to call a low LPC rating—tends to be a managing, task-controlling, and less concerned with the human relations aspects of the job. It also appears that the directive, managing, and controlling leaders tend to perform best in basketball and surveying teams, in open-hearth shops, and (provided the leader is accepted by his group) in military combat crews and company managements. On the other hand, the nondirective, permissive, and human relations-oriented leaders tend to perform best in decision- and policy-making teams and in groups that have a creative task—provided that the group likes the leader or the leader feels that the group is pleasant and free of tension.

CRITICAL DIMENSIONS

But in order to tell which style fits which situation, we need to categorize groups. Our research has shown that "it all depends" on the situation. After reviewing the results of all our work and the findings of other investigators, we have been able to isolate three major dimensions that seem to determine, to a large part, the kind of leadership style called for by different situations.

It is obviously a mistake to think that groups and teams are all alike and that each requires the same kind of leadership. We need some way of categorizing the group-task situation, or the job environment within which the leader has to operate. If leadership is indeed a process of influencing other people to work together effectively in a common task, then it surely matters how easy or difficult it is for the leader to exert his influence in a particular situation.

Leader–Member Relations. The factor that would seem most important in determining a man's leadership influence is the degree to which his group members trust and like him, and are willing to follow his guidance. The trusted and well-liked leader obviously does not require special rank or power in order to get things done. We can measure the leader–member relationship by the so-called sociometric nomination techniques that ask group members to name in their group the most influential person, or the man they would most like to have as a leader. It can also be measured by a group-atmosphere scale indicating the degree to which the leader feels accepted and comfortable in the group.

The Task Structure. The second important factor is the "task structure." By this term I mean the degree to which the task (a) is spelled out step by step for the group and, if so, the extent to which it can be done "by the numbers" or according to a detailed set of standard operating instructions, or (b) must be left nebulous and undefined. Vague and ambiguous or unstructured tasks make it difficult to exert leadership influence, because neither the leader nor his members know exactly what has to be done or how it is to be accomplished.

Why single out this aspect of the task rather than the innumerable other possible ways of describing it? Task groups are almost invariably components of a larger organization that assigns the task and has, therefore, a big stake in seeing it performed properly. However, the organization can control the quality of a group's performance only if the task is clearly spelled out and programmed or structured. When the task can be programmed or performed "by the numbers," the organization is able to back up the authority of the leader to the fullest; the man who fails to perform each step can be disciplined or fired. But in the case of ill-defined, vague, or unstructured tasks, the organization and the leader have very little control and direct power. By close supervision one can ensure, let us say, that a man will correctly operate a machine, but one cannot ensure that he will be creative.

It is therefore easier to be a leader in a structured task situation in which the work is spelled out than in an unstructured one which presents the group with a nebulous, poorly defined problem.

Position Power. Thirdly, there is the power of the leadership position, as distinct from any personal power the leader might have. Can he hire or fire and promote or demote? Is his appointment for life, or will it terminate at the pleasure of his group? It is obviously easier to be a leader when the position power is strong than when it is weak.

MODEL FOR ANALYSIS

When we now classify groups on the basis of these three dimensions, we get a classification system that can be represented as a cube; see Figure 13-1. As each group is high or low in each of the three dimensions, it will fall into one of the eight cells.

From examination of the cube, it seems clear that exerting leadership influence will be easier in a group in which the members like a powerful leader with a clearly defined job and where the job to be done is clearly laid out (Cell 1); it will be difficult in a group where a leader is disliked, has little power, and has a highly ambiguous job (Cell 8).

Engineer the Job to Fit the Manager 227

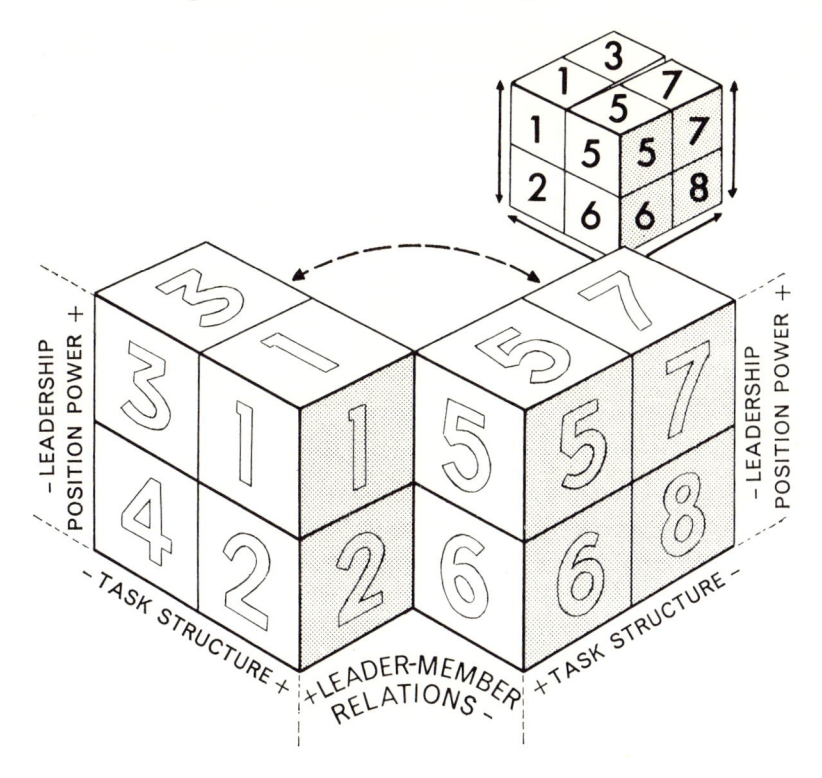

Figure 13-1. A Model for Classifying Group-Task Situations

In other words, it is easier to be the well-esteemed foreman of a construction crew working from a blueprint than it is to be the disliked chairman of a volunteer committee preparing a new policy.

I consider the leader–member relations the most important dimension, and the position-power dimension the least important, of the three. It is, for instance, quite possible for a man of low rank to lead a group of higher-ranking men in a structured task—as is done when enlisted men or junior officers conduct some standardized parts of the training programs for medical officers who enter the Army. But it is not so easy for a disrespected manager to lead a creative, policy-formulating session well, even if he is the senior executive present.

VARYING REQUIREMENTS

By first sorting the eight cells according to leader–member relations, then task structure, and finally leader position power, we can now arrange them in order according to the favorableness of the environment for the leader. This sorting leads to an eight-step scale, as in Figure 13-2. This figure portrays the results of a series of studies of groups performing well but (a) in different situations and conditions, and (b) with leaders using different leadership styles. In explanation:

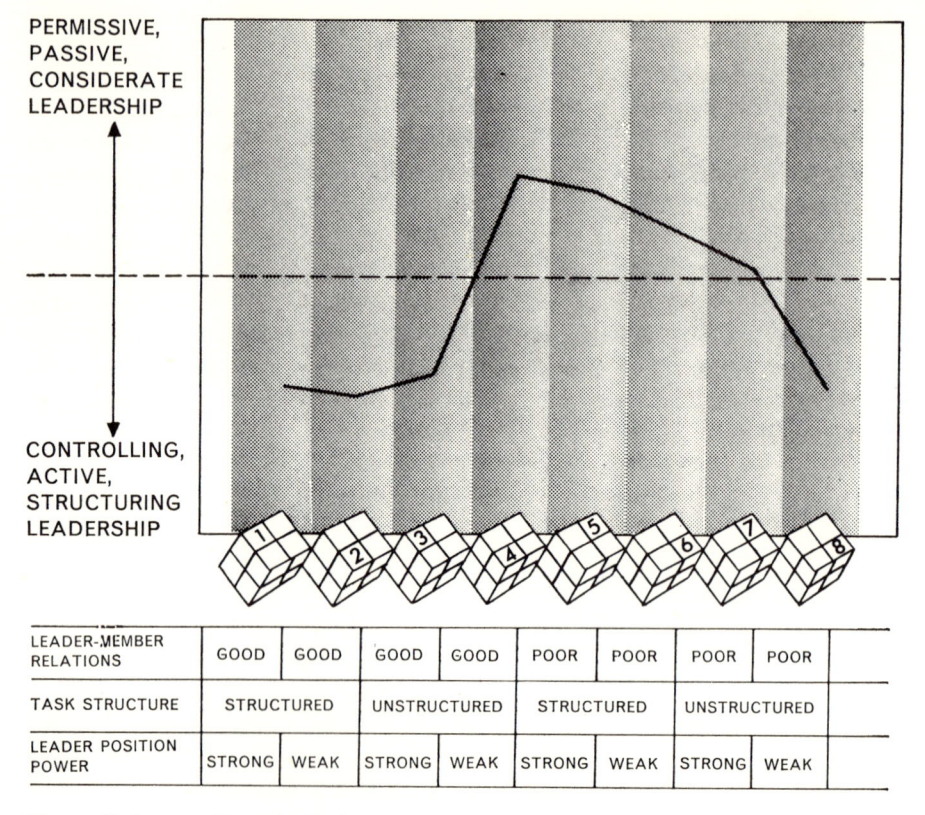

Figure 13-2. How the Style of Effective Leadership Varies With the Situation

The *horizontal* axis shows the range of situations that the groups worked in, as described by the classification scheme used in Figure 13-1.

The *vertical* axis indicates the leadership style which was best in a certain situation, as shown by the correlation coefficient between the leader's LPC and his group's performance.

A positive correlation (falling above the mid-line) shows that the permissive, nondirective, and human relations-oriented leaders performed best; a negative correlation (below the midline) shows that the task-controlling, managing leader performed best. For instance, leaders of effective groups in situation categories 1 and 2 had LPC-group performance correlations of $-.40$ to $-.80$, with the average between $-.50$ and $-.60$; whereas leaders of effective groups in situation categories 4 and 5 had LPC-group performance correlations of .20 to .80, with the average between .40 and .50.

Figure 13-2 shows that both the directive, managing, task-oriented leaders and the nondirective, human relations-oriented leaders are successful under some conditions. Which leadership style is the best depends on the favorableness of the particular situation for the leader. In very favorable or in very unfavorable situations for getting a task accomplished by group effort, the autocratic, task-controlling, managing leadership works best. In situations intermediate in difficulty, the nondirective, permissive leader is more successful.

This corresponds well with our everyday experience. For instance:

• Where the situation is very favorable, the group expects and wants the leader to give directions. We neither expect nor want the trusted airline pilot to turn to his crew and ask, "What do you think we ought to check before takeoff?"

• If the disliked chairman of a volunteer committee asks his group what to do, he may be told that everybody ought to go home.

• The well-liked chaiman of a planning group or research team must be nondirective and permissive in order to get full participation from his members. The directive, managing leader will tend to be more critical and to cut discussion short; hence he will not get the full benefit of the potential contributions by his group members.

The varying requirements of leadership styles are readily apparent in organizations experiencing dramatic changes in operating procedures. For example:

• The manager or supervisor of a routinely operating organization is expected to provide direction and supervision that the subordinates should follow. However, in a crisis the routine is no longer adequate, and the task becomes ambiguous and unstructured. The typical manager tends to respond in such instances by calling his principal assistants together for a conference. In other words, the effective leader changes his behavior from a directive to a permissive, nondirective style until the operation again reverts to routine conditions.

• In the case of a research planning group, the human relations-oriented and permissive leader provides a climate in which everybody is free to speak up, to suggest, and to criticize. Osborn's brainstorming method[2] in fact institutionalizes these procedures. However, after the research plan has been completed, the situation becomes highly structured. The director now prescribes the task in detail, and he specifies the means of accomplishing it. Woe betide the assistant who decides to be creative by changing the research instructions!

PRACTICAL TESTS

Remember that the ideas I have been describing emanate from studies of real-life situations; accordingly, as might be expected, they can be validated by organizational experience. Take, for instance, the dimension of leader–member relations described earlier. We have made three studies of situations in which the leader's position power was strong and the task relatively structured with clear-cut goals and standard operating procedures. In such groups as these the situation will be very favorable for the leader if he is accepted; it will be progressively unfavorable in proportion to how much a leader is disliked. What leadership styles succeed in these varying conditions? The studies confirm what our theory would lead us to expect:

• The first set of data come from a study of B-29 bomber crews in which the criterion was the accuracy of radar bombing. Six degrees of leader–member relations were identified, ranging from those in which the aircraft commander was the first choice of crew members and highly endorsed his radar observer and navigator (the key men in radar bombing), to those in which he was chosen by his crew but did not endorse his key men, and finally to crews in which the commander was rejected by his crew and rejected his key crew members. What leadership styles were effective? The results are plotted in Figure 13-3.

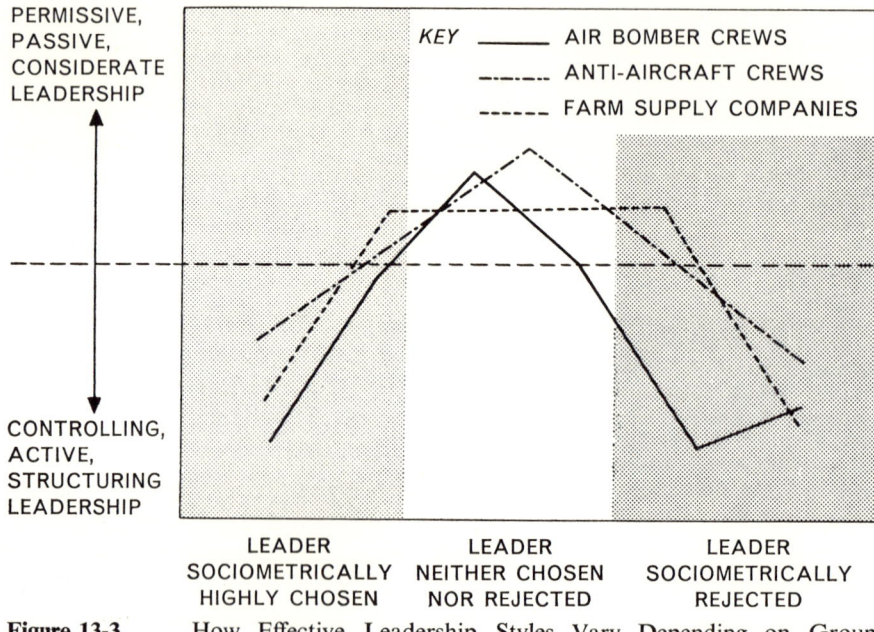

Figure 13-3. How Effective Leadership Styles Vary Depending on Group Acceptance

• A study of anti-aircraft crews compares the 10 most chosen crew commanders, the 10 most rejected ones, and 10 of intermediate popularity. The criterion is the identification and "acquisition" of unidentified aircraft by the crew. The results shown in Figure 13-3 are similar to those for bomber crew commanders.

• Figure 13-3 also summarizes data for 32 small-farm supply companies. These were member companies of the same distribution system, each with its own board of directors and its own management. The performance of these highly comparable companies was measured in terms of percentage of company net income over a three-year period. The first quarter of the line (going from left to right) depicts endorsement of the general manager by his board of directors and his staff of assistant managers; the second quarter, endorsement by his board but not his staff; the third quarter, endorsement by his staff but not his board; the fourth quarter, endorsement by neither.

As can be seen from the results of all three studies, the highly accepted and strongly rejected leaders perform best if they are controlling and managing,

Engineer the Job to Fit the Manager 231

while the leaders in the intermediate acceptance range, who are neither rejected nor accepted, perform best if they are permissive and nondirective.

Now let us look at some research on organizations in another country:

Recently in Belgium a study was made of groups of mixed language and cultural composition. Such teams, which are becoming increasingly frequent as international business and governmental activities multiply, obviously present a difficult situation for the leader. He must not only deal with men who do not fully comprehend one another's language and meanings, but also cope with the typical antipathies, suspicions, and antagonisms dividing individuals of different cultures and nationalities.

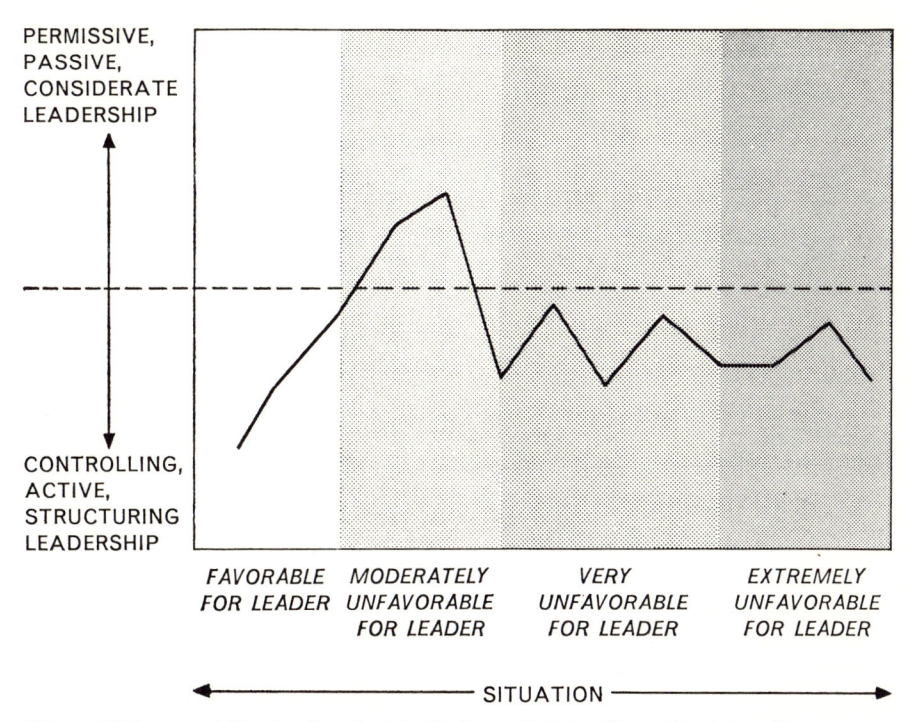

Figure 13-4. Effective Leadership Styles at Belgian Naval Training Center

At a Belgian naval training center we tested 96 three-man groups, half of which were homogeneous in composition (all Flemish or all Walloon) and half heterogeneous (the leader differing from his men). Half of each of these had powerful leader positions (petty officers), and half had recruit leaders. Each group performed three tasks: one unstructured task (writing a recruiting letter); and two parallel structured tasks (finding the shortest route for ships through 10 ports, and doing the same for 12 ports). After each task, leaders and group members described their reactions—including group-atmosphere ratings and the indication of leader–member relations.

The various task situations were then arranged in order, according to their favorableness for the leader. The most favorable situation was a homogeneous group, led by a well-liked and accepted petty offcer, which worked on the structured task of routing a ship. The situation would be espcially favorable toward the end of the experiment, after the leader had had time to get to know his members. The least favorable situation was that of an unpopular recruit leader of a heterogeneous group where the relatively unstructured task of writing a letter came up as soon as the group was formed.

There were six groups that fell into each of these situations or cells. A correlation was then computed for each set of six groups to determine which type of leadership style led to best team performance. The results, indicated in Figure 13-4, support the conclusions earlier described.

Of particular interest is the fact that the difficult heterogeneous groups generally required controlling, task-oriented leadership for good performance. This fits the descriptions of successful leader behavior obtained from executives who have worked in international business organizations.

CONCLUSION

Provided our findings continue to be supported in the future, what do these results and the theory mean for executive selection and training? What implications do they have for the management of large organizations?

SELECTION AND TRAINING

Business and industry are now trying to attract an increasingly large share of exceptionally intelligent and technically well-trained men. Many of these are specialists whose talents are in critically short supply. Can industry really afford to select only those men who have a certain style of leadership in addition to their technical qualifications? The answer is likely to be negative, at least in the near future.

This being the case, can we then train the men selected in one leadership style or the other? This approach is always offered as a solution, and it does have merit. But we must recognize that training people is at best difficult, costly, and time-consuming. It is certainly easier to place people in a situation compatible with their natural leadership style than to force them to adapt to the demands of the job.

As another alternative, should executives learn to recognize or diagnose group-task situations so that they can place their subordinates, managers, and department heads in the jobs best suited to their leadership styles? Even this procedure has serious disadvantages. The organization may not always happen to have the place that fits the bright young man. The experienced executive may not want to be moved, or it may not be possible to transfer him.

Should the organization try to "engineer" the job to fit the man? This alternative is potentially the most feasible for management. As has been shown already, the type of leadership called for depends on the favorableness of the situation. The favorableness, in turn, is a product of several factors. These include leader–member relations, the homogeneity of the group, and the position power and degree to which the task is structured, as well as other, more obvious factors such as the leader's knowledge of his group, his familiarity with the task, and so forth.

It is clear that management can change the characteristic favorableness of the leadership situation; it can do so in most cases more easily than it can transfer the subordinate leader from one job to another or train him in a different style of interacting with his members.

POSSIBILITIES OF CHANGE

Although this type of organizational engineering has not been done systematically up to now, we can choose from several good possibilities for getting the job done:

(1.) *We can change the leader's position power.* We can either give him subordinates of equal or nearly equal rank or we can give him men who are two or three ranks below him. We can either give him sole authority for the job or require that he consult with this group, or even obtain unanimous consent for all decisions. We can either punctiliously observe the channels of the organization to increase the leader's prestige or communicate directly with the men of his group as well as with him in person.

(2.) *We can change the task structure.* The tasks given to one leader may have to be clarified in detail, and he may have to be given precise operating instructions; another leader may have to be given more general problems that are only vaguely elucidated.

(3.) *We can change the leader–member relations.* The Belgian study, referred to earlier, demonstrates that changing the group composition changes the leader's relations with his men. We can increase or decrease the group's heterogeneity by introducing men with similar attitudes, beliefs, and backgrounds, or by bringing in men different in training, culture, and language.

The foregoing are, of course, only examples of what could be done. The important point is that we now have a model and a set of principles that permit predictions of leadership effectiveness in interacting groups and allow us to take a look at the factors affecting team performance. This approach goes beyond the traditional notions of selection and training. It focuses on the more fruitful possibility of organizational engineering as a means of using leadership potentials in the management ranks.

Notes

1. Conducted under Office of Naval Research contracts 170–106, N6-ori-07135 and NR 177–472, Nonr-1834 (36).
2. See Alex F. Osborn, *Applied Imagination.* New York: Charles Scribner's Sons, 1953.

ROBERT SOMMER

Small Group Ecology

Systematic study of spatial arrangements in face-to-face groups, or small group ecology as the field has been termed, is a comparatively recent development. Typically, the arrangement of people has been an incidental or background variable in psychological experimentation. The use of spatial arrangements as an independent variable in small group research can be traced to Steinzor (1950), who noted some unusual spatial effects while he was doing a study on other aspects of interaction. This pattern persists to the present, since at least half the published studies of small group arrangements involve the reanalysis of data collected for other purposes. Despite consistent and clear data, psychologists seem reluctant to make the arrangement of people a major independent variable. As Hall (1959) put it, "We treat space somewhat as we treat sex, it is there but we don't talk about it." Yet, enough studies, experimental as well as ex post facto, have accumulated to warrant some attempt to integrate the findings and indicate what directions further studies may profitably take.

This review focuses upon the arrangement of individuals in face-to-face groups. Studies of residential living units such as dormitories, housing developments, and communities are omitted. These phenomena require a different level of analysis (community or societal) than the relationship between individuals in face-to-face groups. The study of larger stable human aggregations has fallen to the fields of demography, human ecology, and geography. Because of space limitations, studies of crowding and density are excluded from consideration since these important topics deserve treatment in their own right. This study concentrates instead on two aspects of small group ecology—the way groups arrange themselves under various conditions, and the ways in which the resulting arrangements affect communication, productivity, and social relationships.

LEADERSHIP AND SPATIAL ARRANGEMENTS

Many of the concepts used in discussion of leadership, such as central figure, dominant position, upper echelon, and high status are based on spatial analogies. Studies of group dynamics and leadership have shown that concepts such as social distance, inner circle, and isolate have some geographic reference but there is no simple isomorphism between psychological and geographic concepts. While investigating discussion groups, Steinzor noticed a participant changing his seat in order to sit opposite another person with whom he had recently had a verbal altercation. In an ex post facto design using data already collected, Steinzor found that when one person stopped speaking, someone opposite rather than alongside was next to speak, an effect he attributed to the greater physical and expressive value a person has for those opposite him in a circle. Following this, Bass and Klubeck (1952) reanalyzed their discussion group data to determine if leadership ratings varied as a function of location in an inverted V or a parallel row arrangement. Although they found that persons occupying end positions attained higher status than people in middle seats, there were so many confounding factors, including a nonrandom selection of seats by people of different status levels, that their results were equivocal. Hearn (1957) reanalyzed small group data collected for other purposes and found that leadership style had a significant influence on what was termed the "Steinzor effect." With minimal leadership, members of a discussion group would direct more comments to people sitting opposite than people adjacent; when a strong leader was present, people directed more comments to adjacent seats than to people opposite; and when direction of the group was shared equally among the members, no spatial effect appeared. These results may be explained in terms of eye contact. Since it is impermissible to look directly at a dominant individual at close quarters, the individual restricts his gaze to his immediate neighbors when a strong leader is close by. Steinzor's expressive contact hypothesis has been further refined by Argyle and Dean (1965), who studied the connection between eye contact, distance, and affiliation. A one-way mirror was used to chart interaction between a naïve subject and a confederate who gazed continually at the subject. There was less eye contact and glances were shorter when the people were close together, and this effect was most pronounced for mixed-sex pairs. The authors believed that eye contact is a component of intimacy, which is governed by both approach and avoidance forces kept in a state of equilibrium during any given encounter. When this equilibrium is disturbed by increasing physical proximity or decreasing eye contact, there are compensatory changes along the other dimensions.

Communication flow as a function of spatial relationship was emphasized by Leavitt (1951), who continued the work of Bavelas (1950). Leavitt used groups of five subjects each who were seated at a table but separated from one another by vertical partitions. Channels of communication could be changed by manipulating slots in the partitions. Group leadership was closely correlated with a member's position in the communication net. Centrally located individuals enjoyed the task most and those in the peripheral positions enjoyed it least. Howells and Becker (1962) hypothesized that people who received greater numbers of messages would be more likely to be designated leaders than people who received fewer messages. They arranged groups of five subjects around small rectangular tables with three people on one side, two on the other. The results confirmed their predictions that more leaders than would be expected by chance would emerge from the two-man side of the table.

The studies described thus far have involved *relational* space, or the way people orient themselves towards one another. A second line of research has emphasized the cultural import of various fixed locations. In studies of leadership, the head chair at the table has a special significance. Sommer (1959) found that leaders in small discussion groups gravitated to the head position at rectangular tables. Strodtbeck and Hook (1961) reanalyzed data from experimental jury deliberations and found that people at end positions participated more and were rated as having greater influence on the decision process than people at the sides. It was also found that jurors from the managerial and professional classes selected the head chair more than did individuals of lower status. Hare and Bales (1963) did not work with leadership per se, but rather with dominance as measured by a paper-and-pencil personality test. Reanalyzing the data collected by Bales and his associates from five-man discussion groups, they found that subjects high on dominance tended to choose the central seats and do the most talking. Felipe (1966) used the semantic differential to assess dyadic seating arrangements along these dimensions: intimate-unacquainted, hostile-friendly, talkative-untalkative, and unequal-equal. The cultural influence of the head position was evident on the equality dimension—if one member of a pair was at the head of the table, this pair was rated significantly less equal than if members were both at ends of the table or only at the sides.

A weakness of all these studies is the limited range of cultures and populations sampled, almost all taking place in the United States. This would not be a serious limitation except that Hall indicated that leaders in other parts of the world use space differently. An equally serious problem concerns the confounding of location, status, and personality. All studies agreed that choice of seats is nonrandom with respect to status and personality. High status, dominant individuals in American culture gravitate to the head position, and people who occupy the head position participate more than people at the side positions (Strodtbeck and Hook, 1961), but there is no way to disentangle status from location in these studies. It is possible that occupancy of certain locations automatically raises an individual's status and/or dominance. On the other hand, it may be that dominant individuals choose these locations for reasons of tradition and would participate more wherever they sat, and thus their location has no essential connection with their participation. It may be that high status people tend to participate more *and* certain locations also increase participation, but the combination of the two results in greater participation than either by itself. The only way to disentangle these variables is to conduct experiments in which people are assigned randomly to various locations and their relative contributions noted. It must be recognized that these conditions are highly artificial in a society that typically allocates space according to status considerations. From the standpoint of designing experiments in natural settings, the policies of random assignments of location are not always adhered to in practice. In the prison camp studied by Grusky (1959), inmate leaders received the most desirable job assignments as well as the bottom bunks (which were status symbols in the dormitories) despite the official policy of random bed assignment. It is likely that the same pressures responsible for the connection between status and location operate against any assignment scheme in conflict with accepted spatial norms.

TASK AND LOCATION

The quest for effective spatial arrangements in working units such as relay assembly teams, seminars, and buzz groups has been a subject of considerable concern to applied psychologists. Textbooks of group dynamics recommend horseshoe or semicircular rather than straight-row arrangements for discussion groups and classrooms, rectangular tables have been criticized for fostering authoritarian leadership, and the improper location of individuals has been blamed for the failure of the working teams. Intuitively it would seem that the proper arrangement of people would increase production, smooth the flow of communication, and reduce the "friction of space," but the data are largely of the anecdotal variety. Perhaps more convincing data lie buried somewhere in applied psychology or human engineering journals and, if so, a valuable service could be rendered by bringing them to light.

Several recent studies have explored the connection between spatial arrangement and group taks. Sommer (1965) and Norum (1966) studied the arrangement of conversing, competing, coacting, and cooperating individuals. At a rectangular table, cooperating pairs sat side-by-side, conversing pairs sat corner-to-corner, and competing pairs sat across from one another, while coacting individuals sat in distant arrangements. In a separate study of cooperative and competitive working conditions using a like-sex decoy, the subjects sat opposite the decoy in the competitive condition and on the same side of the table in the cooperative condition.

The extent to which similar attitudes produce greater physical proximity remains in some dispute. Little, Ulehla, and Henderson (1965), using silhouette figures, found that pairs reputed to be Goldwater supporters were placed closer together than Goldwater-Johnson pairs, but the effect did not occur with Johnson-Johnson pairs. However, Elkin (1964), using actual discussion groups involving pro-pro, pro-anti, and anti-anti Medicare pairs of college students, found no differences in seating between concordant and discordant pairs. It is possible that the intensity of the discussion and the interest shown by each of the participants influences proximity more than attitude concordance or discordance.

Several psychiatrists and clinical psychologists have written speculative articles on the significance of various spatial arrangements in psychotherapy. Goodman (1959) made an intriguing comparison between the Freudian use of the couch, Sullivan's cross-the-table therapy, and the spatial freedom of the Gestalt therapists. Wilmer (1958), Winick and Holt (1961), and Horowitz (1965) all discussed seating position from the standpoint of nonverbal communication in group psychotherapy.

INDIVIDUAL DISTANCE

The term individual distance was first used by Burkhardt (1944) to refer to the spacing that animals maintain between themselves and others of the same species. Several studies have been directed toward the question of how close people come to one another and to physical objects. Hall (1959) developed a detailed schema for conversational distance under various conditions of social and psychological closeness which ranged from 3–6 inches for soft intimate whispers to 8–20 feet for talking across the room in a loud voice. It is also likely that noise, bustle, or threat brings people together. To measure conversational distance, Sommer (1961) sent pairs into a large lounge where they could sit either side-by-side or across from one another to discuss designated topics. On the basis of previous work, it was assumed that people would sit across from one another rather than side-by-side unless the distance across was too great. It was found that the upper limit for comfortable conversation *under these specified conditions* was approximately 5.5 feet between individuals. A subsequent study used four chairs instead of couches so that the distance side-by-side as well as the distance across could be varied. Again the 5.5-foot conversational distance prevailed. However, a cursory examination of conversational distance in private homes revealed a much greater conversational range than this, something like eight to ten feet between chairs.

Other investigators have used paper-and-pencil or projective tests to study individual distance. Kuethe (1962, 1964) instructed students to pin yellow felt figures (a woman, man, child, dog, rectangles of various sizes) on a blue felt background in various combinations. Kuethe found that the woman and the child were placed closer together than the man and the child, while the dog was typically placed closer to the man than the woman. In all conditions, the people were placed closer together than the rectangles. Little (1965) used line drawings of males and females to examine concepts of individual distance. It was found that the degree of prior acquaintance attributed to cardboard figures influenced the distance they were placed apart. A replication using silhouettes and another using live actresses who were posed by the subject in scenes involving different activities also showed that the distance apart which the figures were placed was a function of the closeness of the relationship between them.

Horowitz, Duff, and Stratton (1964) investigated individual distance among schizophrenic and nonschizophrenic mental patients. Each subject was instructed to walk over to either another person or a hatrack, and the distance between his goal and his stopping place was measured. It was found that both groups approached the hatrack closer than they approached a person. Each subject tended to have a characteristic individual distance which was shorter for inanimate objects than for people. McBride, King, and James (1965) did a similar study testing GSR to varying amounts of closeness between subject and male or female experimenters. It was considered that GSR effects would provide an indication of the level of arousal associated with the proximity of neighbors. The authors found that GSR was greatest (skin resistance was least) when the subject was approached frontally, while a side approach yielded a greater response than a rear approach. The response to experimenters of the same sex was less than to experimenters of the opposite sex. Being touched by an object produced less of a GSR than being touched by a person. Argyle and Dean (1965) invited the subjects to participate in a perceptual experiment in which they were to "stand as close as comfortable to see well" to a book, a plaster head, and a cutout life-sized photograph of the senior author with his eyes closed and another with his eyes open. Among other results, the subjects placed themselves closer to the eyes-closed photograph than the eyes-open photograph.

Systematic violation of individual distance was undertaken by Garfinkel (1964) and Felipe and Sommer (1966). Garfinkel reported that the violation of individual distance produced avoidance, bewilderment, and embarrassment, and that these effects were most pronounced among males. Felipe and Sommer systematically staged invasion sequences under natural conditions (people seated on benches and at library tables) and demonstrated observable flight reactions. Two recent studies have dealt with the relationship between individual distance and personality variables. Williams (1963) showed that introverts placed themselves further from other people than did extroverts. The same conclusion was reached by Leipold (1963), who noted the chair a person occupied vis-à-vis a seated decoy under anxiety and praise conditions. There was greater closeness under the praise than the anxiety conditions, and extroverts placed themselves closer to the decoy than introverts.

Sex differences in spacing have been found on a number of occasions, but the number of cultures sampled is limited. Several investigators (Elkin, 1964; Norum, 1966; Sommer, 1959) have found that females make more use of the side-by-side arrangement than do males. Side-by-side seating, which is generally considered to be the most intimate of all seating arrangements for people already acquainted, is comparatively rare among males if they are given the opportunity to sit across from one another. The idea that females can tolerate closer physical presence than males is underscored by observations of women holding hands or kissing one another, practices which are uncommon between males in this culture.

Campbell, Kruskal, and Wallace (1966) used seating arrangements of Negroes and whites as an index of attitude in three Chicago colleges. Clustering of Negroes and whites was found to be associated with differences in ethnic attitudes in the three schools. These authors and Strodtbeck and Hook (1951) attempted to develop appropriate statistical techniques for analyzing aggregation data. Tabulating the results of a single observation involving a large number of individuals whose behavior at times relates to one another and at times to aspects of the physical environment is no small achievement, but when one assembles the records of repeated observations of individuals, some observed many times and some just once, the difficulties multiply. It is fortunate that animal ecologists and zoologists have encountered these problems over the years and have developed useful methods for measuring aggregation, dispersion, home range, and social distance. McBride (1964) has developed computer programs to assess the degree of nonrandomness within an aggregation. Esser (1965), working on a closed research ward of a mental hospital with the available area divided into squares so that the location of each patient can be charted during the entire working day, has obtained detailed records of individual spatial behavior similar to those of the better tracking studies by animal biologists, but he has not yet reached the same level of precision in relating the individual patient's locations one to another. The problems in analyzing the interdependence between a large number of individuals with $n(n-1)$ dyadic relationships has led some investigators to use physical aspects of the environment such as walls, partitions, and chairs as coordinates for locating individuals. A new approach (Bechtel and Srivastava, 1966) is the development of the Hodometer, an electronic recording device placed on the floor of a building to measure use of given areas as well as pathways. A much cruder index of area usage was suggested by Webb, Campbell, Schwartz, and Sechrest (1966), who examined the wear on floortiles in front of different museum exhibits.

DISCUSSION

Knowledge of how groups arrange themselves can assist in fostering or discouraging group relationships. A library which is intended to be *sociofugal space* (Osmond, 1957), aimed at discouraging interaction, requires knowledge of how to arrange people to minimize unwanted contact. It may be possible to use the rank order of preferred arrangements by interacting groups as arrangements *to be avoided* in sociofugal space. On this basis, corner-to-corner seating would be less satisfactory than opposite or distant seating in a sociofugal setting. An Emily Post or Amy Vanderbilt may know these principles intuitively, and diplomatic protocol may codify them, but there is value in making them explicit and subjecting them to empirical test. To an increasingly greater extent we find ourselves being arranged by impersonal environments in lecture halls, airports, waiting rooms, and lobbies. Many aspects of the proximate environment, including furniture and room dividers, have been placed for ease of maintenance and efficient cleaning with little cognizance to their social functions. These principles will be of most help in institutional settings such as schools, hospitals, public buildings, and old folks' homes where the occupants have little control over their surroundings. The straight-row arrangement of most classrooms has been taken for granted for too long. The typical long narrow shape of a classroom resulted from a desire to get light across the room. The front of

Small Group Ecology

each room was determined by window location, since pupils had to be seated so that window light came over the left shoulder. However, new developments in lighting, acoustics, ventilation, and fireproofing have rendered invalid many of the arguments for the boxlike room with straight rows. In mental hospitals, the isolation of schizophrenic individuals can be furthered by sociofugal settings which minimize social contact, or reduced through sociopetal buildings aimed at reinforcing social behavior. The former approach is valid if one wants to provide an optimal environment in terms of the individual's present needs, the latter if society desires to shape the patient's social behavior to facilitate his return to society. It is mindless to design mental hospitals without taking cognizance of the connection between physical environment and social behavior. The study of small group ecology is important not only from the standpoint of developing an adequate theory of relationships that takes into account the context of social relationships, but also from the practical standpoint of designing and maintaining functional contexts in which human relationships can develop.

Several problems of method must be resolved before a relevant theory of group ecology can be developed. Having reviewed the studies themselves, problems in recording and some special characteristics of the settings in which the studies have taken place should be mentioned. The studies described have generally tabulated gross categories of behavior without any real specificity or precision. A person's location has been plotted as if this described his orientation, head angle, arm position, etc. Stated another way, the investigators whose work has been described here have relied almost exclusively on the eyeball technique of recording. Some, such as Esser and McBride, are moving into the electronic processing of observational data, but the improved precision is in data analysis rather than the integration of various facets of spatial behavior. Very little use has been made of photographic recordings. One would hardly undertake the study of comparative linguistics without a tape recorder, but only a handful of investigators whose work we have discussed have used still photographs, much less moving pictures. Twenty-five years ago, Efron (1941) hired a professional artist to sketch conversing groups. A few anthropologists, such as Birdwistell and Hall, are currently accumulating film libraries of interaction data. McBride found it necessary to photograph aggregations of fowl from small towers above the coops. It is difficult to get good photographs of the spatial arrangements of people from the horizontal plane, particularly if there are more than two individuals involved. Yet, it seems likely that the real breakthroughs in this field will occur when methods for monitoring angle of orientation, eye contact, and various other nonverbal cues are developed for use in standard interaction situations. The arguments for and against laboratory studies of group behavior which involve one-way mirrors, microphones, and hidden photographic equipment compared to field studies in playgrounds, schools, and city streets will not be reviewed here. However, a promising solution is the field-laboratory method used by Sherif (1954) in his camp studies where he employed a standard controlled situation, in the sense that relevant variables were specified in advance and introduced in specified ways by the experimenter but always under conditions that appeared natural and appropriate to the subjects. Another limiting element in the work to date is that almost all the studies have involved discussion groups around tables and chairs. We know little about the ecology of working groups (apart from sociometric data) or coacting individuals, particularly if they are standing or moving. Again, the technical problems of recording interaction patterns of moving individuals are much greater than if the individuals are seated in a classroom or around a conference table.

Along with this is a disproportionate number of environmental studies that have taken place under conditions of confinement, particularly in mental hospitals. At this time there are at least seven studies underway on the use of space by mental patients. As far as the writer knows, this exceeds the number of current studies of spatial behavior of non-hospitalized individuals. Mental hospital studies allow greater control and environmental manipulation than can be achieved outside a total institution, but they also confound the effects of schizophrenia and institutionalization as a social process over time with the effects of captivity and locked doors as spatial variables.

References

Argyle, M., and J. Dean. "Eye contact, Distance, and Affiliation," *Sociometry*, 28 (1965): 289–304.
Bass, B. M., and S. Klubeck. "Effects of Seating Arrangements on Leaderless Group Discussion," *Journal of Abnormal and Social Psychology*, 47 (1952): 724–727.
Bavelas, A. "Communication Processes in Task-Oriented Groups," *Journal of the Acoustical Society of America*, 22 (1950): 725–730.
Bechtel, R. B., and R. Srivastava. "Human Movement and Architectural Environment," *Milieu*, 2 (1966): 7–8.
Burckhardt, D. "Mowenbeobachtungen in Basel," *Ornithologische Beobachter*, 5 (1944): 49–76.
Campbell, D. T., W. H. Kruskal, and W. P. Wallace. "Seating Aggregation as an Index of Attitude," *Sociometry*, 29 (1966): 1–15.
Efron, D. *Gesture and Environment*. New York: Kings Crown Press, 1941.
Elkin, L. "The Behavioral Use of Space," unpublished Master's Thesis, University of Saskatchewan, 1964.
Esser, A., et al. "Territoriality of Patients on a Research Ward," in *Recent Advances in Biological Psychiatry*, Vol. 7. New York: Plenum Press, 1965.
Felipe, N. "Interpersonal Distance and Small Group Interaction," *Cornell Journal of Social Relations*, 1 (1966): 59–64.
Felipe, N. and R. Sommer. "Invasions of Personal Space," *Social Problems* (in press).
Garfinkel, H. "Studies of the Routine Grounds of Everyday Activities," *Social Problems*, 11 (1964): 225–250.
Goodman, P. "Meaning of Functionalism," *Journal of Architectural Education*, 14 (1959): 32–38.
Grusky, O. "Organization Goals and the Behavior of Informal Leaders," *American Journal of Sociology*, 65 (1959): 59–67.
Hall, E. T. *The Silent Language*. Garden City, N.Y.: Doubleday, 1959.
Hare, A. P., and R. F. Bales. "Seating Position and Small Group Interaction," *Sociometry*, 26 (1963): 480–486.
Hearn, G. "Leadership and the Spatial Factor in Small Groups," *Journal of Abnormal and Social Psychology*, 54 (1957): 269–272.
Horowitz, M. J. "Human Spatial Behavior," *American Journal of Psychotherapy*, 19 (1965): 20–28.

Horowitz, M. J., D. F. Duff, and L. O. Stratton. "Body-Buffer Zone," *Archives of General Psychiatry*, 11 (1964): 651–656.
Howells, L. T., and S. W. Becker. "Seating Arrangement and Leadership Emergence," *Journal of Abnormal and Social Psychology*, 64 (1962): 148–150.
Kuethe, J. L. "Social Schemas," *Journal of Abnormal and Social Psychology*, 64 (1962): 31–38.
Kuethe, J. L. "Pervasive Influence of Social Schemata," *Journal of Abnormal and Social Psychology*, 68 (1964): 248–254.
Leavitt, H. J. "Some Effects of Certain Communication Patterns in Group Performance," *Journal of Abnormal and Social Psychology*, 46 (1951): 38–50.
Leipold, W. D. "Psychological Distance in a Dyadic Interview," unpublished Doctoral Dissertation, University of North Dakota, 1963.
Little, K. B. "Personal Space," *Journal of Experimental Social Psychology*, 1 (1965): 237–247.
Little, K. B., J. Ulehla, and C. Henderson. "Value Homophily and Interaction Distance," unpublished manuscript, University of Denver, 1965.
McBride, G. *A General Theory of Social Organization and Behavior*. St. Lucia: University of Queensland Press, 1964.
McBride, G., M. G. King, and J. W. James. "Social Proximity Effects on GSR in Adult Humans," *Journal of Psychology*, 61 (1965): 153–157.
Norum, G. A. "Perceived Interpersonal Relationships and Spatial Arrangements," unpublished Master's Thesis, University of California, Davis, 1966.
Osmond, H. "Function as a Basis of Psychiatric Ward Design," *Mental Hospitals*, 8 (1957): 23–29.
Sherif, M. "Integrating Field Work and Laboratory in Small Group Research," *American Sociological Review*, 19 (1954): 759–771.
Sommer, R. "Studies in Personal Space," *Sociometry*, 22 (1959): 247–260.
Sommer, R. "Leadership and Group Geography," *Sociometry*, 24 (1961): 99–110.
Sommer, R. "Further Studies in Small Group Ecology," *Sociometry*, 28 (1965): 337–348.
Steinzor, B. "The Spatial Factor in Face-to-Face Discussion Groups," *Journal of Abronmal and Social Psychology*, 45 (1950): 552–555.
Strodtbeck, F. L., and L. H. Hook. "The Social Dimensions of a Twelve-Man Jury Table,' *Sociometry*, 24 (1961): 397–415.
Webb, E. J., D. T. Campbell, R. D. Schwartz, and L. Sechrest. *Unobtrusive Measures: Non-Reactive Research in the Social Sciences*. Chicago: Rand McNally, 1966.
Williams, J. L. "Personal Space and its Relation to Extroversion–Introversion," unpublished Master's Thesis, University of Alberta, 1963.
Wilmer, H. A. "Graphic Ways of Representing Some Aspects of a Therapeutic Community," in, *Symposium of Preventive and Social Psychiatry*. Washington, D. C.: United States Government Printing Office, 1958.
Winnick, C. and H. Holt. "Seating Position as Non-verbal Communication in Group Analysis," *Psychiatry*, 24 (1961): 171–182.

15

FRED I. STEELE[1]

Physical Settings and Organizational Development

*T*he last ten years have seen a revolution in the application of the behavioral sciences to organizational change. As we have become more experienced in the process of diagnosis and intervention in social systems, there has been a growing concern with the need for systematic and continuous organizational development (OD). Both academics and practitioners have described this process—see Davis, 1967; Bennis, 1966; Beckhard, 1969, Seashore and Bowers, 1963. Basically, the growing emphasis on organizational development has as its organizing focus the notion that the process of change in an organization—that is, of growth toward a more healthy system—should be a continuing one, and one that uses data from its own past and from accumulated knowledge in behavioral and management sciences. Another basic premise is that change activities in a system should be "systematic." That is, the impact of intervention or change activities should be thought through and include their likely effect on other parts of the system as well as on the specific group or process which is being changed.

The energy put into organizational development will grow larger as the rate of societal and environmental change increases, and as the need for constant renewal becomes more and more acute (Gardner, 1963). The times are loaded in this direction; there is going to be a greater need for trained change agents in organizations and for the use of temporary systems to complete necessary tasks (Bennis & Slater, 1968). These trends speak for continuing systematic organizational development efforts. In fact, an increasing number of personnel are becoming more concerned with OD, and other organizational roles having to do with change as a way of life for the system.

Written especially for this volume.

The organizational development efforts that have been most visible to date have focused on a selected number of variables, primarily concerned with the "social architecture" of the system such as team building activities, personal awareness and sensitivity, the values and norms of the organization as a system, intergroup relations and how they help or hinder the accomplishment of the primary task of the organization, and information flow. These efforts have also focused on technical skills, such as management information systems, new production processes, and new accounting or financial procedures.

OD AND THE PHYSICAL ENVIRONMENT

One frequently overlooked segment of organizations that vitally influences their health is the spatial arrangement of the system. In a sense, the source of the "social architecture" metaphor has been lost, and we have tended not to be aware of the impact that *physical life-space* may be having on the nature of life and of growth within a system. Such simple effects as the size of an office limiting the kinds of gatherings that can take place, or the proximity of two offices allowing their inhabitants to observe who is visiting the other, tend to come about more by default than from conscious problem solving about what kinds of interactions or moods could and should be promoted by the environment.[2]

The little work that has been done in this area focused more on what was traditionally called "human factors" engineering, that is, the impact of variables such as temperature, lighting, and machine placement on productivity and mood in factory workers. Environmental studies have not done much in the way of exploring environmental effects at different levels of the organization for different kinds of activities. It seems obvious that the study of broader environmental effects will complement both the OD trends and the socio-technical systems approach (Trist et al., 1963) of examining the alternative ways in which a system may structure itself and its technology in order to achieve its goals.

My aim is to sharpen the possibilities for using the physical setting as an important arena for organizational development, both in terms of changing the spaces to help effect changes in organizational functioning and in terms of using the spaces and issues around them as diagnostic of the state of the system. This article is intended to stimulate thinking and experimentation in using environmental forces in OD work, not to provide specific answers at this point about how things ought to be. We need to draw together the relevant theories and data from psychology, sociology, anthropology, and design and try new methods (while evaluating them) in order to build toward prescription.

I should add that I am focusing on the physical environment in this paper to highlight an overlooked dimension in organization change. This does not mean that I am claiming that the physical structure is the most important determinant of mood or behavior in an organization. In fact, indications are that the social architecture will be the dominant factor in most systems, with the physical setting reinforcing, diluting, or being irrelevant to the social system. In some cases, however, the impact of the physical setting can be to block the development of a useful social structure.

TRANSACTIONS WITH THE ENVIRONMENT

To help in the discussions that follow, it may be useful to briefly define what is meant by the effects of the environment. In general, these effects run the gamut from making it difficult or easy to interact face-to-face (our offices are 2500 feet apart or 10 feet apart; there is a wall with no opening between us, or a door or no wall at all) to influencing the mood of people who are in a particular place (all our walls are lime-green and the place "feels" like the early years of the Depression), to creating an interpersonal climate (when I am in your office, all your furniture is arranged so that it separates you and me, and I feel like an unwanted intruder who is looked on as somewhat unpredictable and dangerous).

From these kinds of effects, a rough category system can be evolved— one way of classifying the inputs that are received by a person (or group) from his (their) physical environment. The four basic inputs identified are the following:

Instrumental. The setting or space may have an effect on the performance of a task, on getting something done. It may help or hinder task performance or be irrelevant to it. A room whose location had as a feature a lot of street noise would be negatively loaded for important staff discussions where concentration and communication were important; a lounging area which made it easy for people to interact informally around research discussions would be positive, as would well-lighted areas for writing or reading, and so on.

Symbolic. The setting or space often serves as a communication mechanism —to tell others what we are like, what our status is; to send signals that say "come in" or "stay out" or "don't stay too long"; to communicate to other groups where territorial boundaries are located, and so on. This is an area that has been explored a good deal, particularly by the cultural anthropologist, E. T. Hall. Much of the lore around size of office, type of desk, furnishings, etc. as very specific signals of relative status in a given organization fits into this symbolic transaction. This is probably the most familiar organizational use of space. When spatial symbolic communication has been examined, the focus has generally been on the use of "formal" symbols, such as size of office or desk, that are part of a standard language that varies only slightly from system to system. The second kind of symbol, the "informal" one, such as a furniture arrangement which communicates the owner's desire for interpersonal distance, has received less conscious attention, both from researchers and from users.

Different parts of our own life space may vary in the degree to which they are useful in communicating what we want to say to ourselves and others. For example, we may have an office that was more influenced by others than by ourselves, and we tend to think of it as "not really me," simply a storage place that people should not use as data about what we are like. Other places we may see as centrally influenced by us and very representative of who we are.

Pleasure. Some inputs from the environment serve us mainly for pleasure or gratification in their own right, with no necessary connection to work or communication. Natural beauty, or a comfortable space, or attractive decorations all fit this category, as does any space that gives us a good feeling physiologically or emotionally. Elements of the environment may be positive, neutral, or negative on this dimension.

Growth. The fourth input is less familiar and less well-recognized than the other three. An environment may also be a force for growth, that is for learning about self, for stimulation to experimentation, and the like. It may also be neutral or negative, that is, stagnating rather than growth-producing. A space that demands that a person be aware of who he is and how he is using the space can be a positive force for growth. One that requires no consciousness to use it, such as a totally comfortable suburban house with all decisions made and no choices required, is likely to be a force toward non-growth, since the user is not called upon to think about why he prefers one thing over another, what this says about him as a person, or to deal with changes which open new ways of doing things. Carr and Lynch (1968) point out that cities may vary widely in terms of their quality on this dimension. Some stimulate responses and experimentation through variety and exciting resources that are visible, while others promote habitual behaviors and routines through a quality of sameness and/or low observability of the real workings of the system.

The assumption here is that any environmental feature, such as the arrangement of furniture in an office, can be a potential contributor to those who use it on any or all of the four dimensions. The arrangement may be high in instrumental value, neutral in symbolic, negative in pleasure, and slightly positive in growth. These values may also vary according to the people involved and the nature of the activities taking place there. As the composition of a group changes or the reasons for being there change, a place may become more instrumental, for instance. Probably the widest variation over time occurs in this dimension, and the least in pleasure. Symbolic and growth are likely to vary somewhat over time for specific people, as their relationships and their degree of awareness of the space around them change.

The primary use of these classifications in organizational development work to date is to train people to use them as a means for analyzing how they have made choices about space. In several instances of doing this, groups have discovered that their major layout choices, while originally overtly discussed in terms of instrumental value, were loaded almost entirely on the symbolic (i.e., status) dimension, and, in fact, were often negative in terms of usefulness for work. Making this choice process more visible has been a vehicle for more conscious problem-solving about what is trying to be done in a space and what factors contribute to this or block it. Among other effects, some groups have used the growth dimension more by shaping their spaces to make them more evocative and stimulating. This was a process that they valued before, but they were basically unaware of the unused potential of the environment to help it along.

SOME ISSUES AND GENERALIZATIONS

Having considered a more general approach to environmental transactions, the remainder of this article will discuss some more specific issues and tentative generalizations about environment effects and their connection with organizational development.

SPACE AS A DIAGNOSTIC TOOL

There are a number of ways in which a focus on physical settings and space can be useful in diagnosing the climate, structure, and major processes of an organization. One possibility is closely related to the symbolic transactions mentioned above. Hall has documented very nicely what he calls the "language" of space (1960), and it seems clear now that the ways in which people in a system use the space around them can tell us a great deal about the climate in that system: differentiations in power or status; what interactions are valued or encouraged; what kind of world it is for the people; and so forth. I have found rich data by just walking around an organization, trying to become aware of what the physical setting can tell about life there. Nothing can tell more quickly about the impersonality of an organization than seeing an area where there is very little individual influence on the space (decorations, markings, personal items, or whatever) by the people who actually work there. This can give a real "gut" sense of how little influence they may feel they have over the social system.

In a related vein, Colman (1968) indicates how different a patient's behavior can be in the foreign hospital setting (the doctor's turf) and in his home (his own turf). As consultants doing organizational diagnosis, it would be worth while to think about what individuals and groups define as foreign and home territories, and to observe behavior in each before concluding that we know how they feel about themselves and relate to the rest of the system.

Another major use of space for organizational diagnosis can come from looking at not just the physical *things* produced, but also at the social *processes* generated by the issues of how should space be structured, distributed, or organized. Conflicts over spatial arrangements often can be powerful generators of information about the state of the organization. Everyday experience demonstrates how much antagonism this can generate, especially at a moving time, and how strongly feelings can be expressed around the issue of new space or new facilities. We need to learn to use conflicts over space and relocation as data about the system and member relationships, not just as irritants to be extinguished as soon as possible. These are not irrelevant problems that just complicate the day, but real issues which signal what is going on for people in the social structure of the organization. People take a strong personal view on the use of space because: space is a central concrete representation of their place in the status and role systems of the organization, and therefore, is more important (e.g., "the territorial imperative") than many other issues; or they feel just as strongly about other processes in the organization, but these are less concrete and less observable, so it appears as though they feel more strongly about space.

In fact, they may be feeling disadvantaged by other organizational processes as well, but these do not provide an opportunity to take a concrete stand, as does the space issue.

These considerations also suggest that the period of a physical move is particularly rich for organization development activities, both because the choices made can have a major influence on how well the system uses its resources in the future, and because the data about where people see themselves in the system may be more visible during the moving phase than at other more stable times.

PHYSICAL AND SOCIAL EFFECTS

One generalization seems fairly self-evident: Both physical and social factors are intermingled in determining the climate in a given system. On the one hand, a change in the physical setting of a system may have little real impact on members' experiences in that system if social processes remain unchanged or work against improving the environment. For instance, a new small college recently built a very exciting physical structure to house itself—one that architects have acclaimed as being one of the most exciting educational buildings to be built in the last twenty years. When I met with some students and an architect to talk about the building, the students were generally negative about their experiences at the college and what was going on there. The architect then dismissed their views as an example of student insensitivity and lack of appreciation of fine architecture. With further questioning, however, it became clear that what was influencing them most in terms of their attitudes toward the school were their feelings about their place in the *social* architecture, not the physical. They were angry because they were subjected to almost one-hundred percent automated teaching activities (videotapes, audio-tape, and the like) and had no sense of being seen as individual human beings.

A similar case comes from the Ford Foundation building in New York, another highly acclaimed example of new architecture. The original notion in using glass interior walls and moveable curtains was to provide a large degree of choice for people about whether they wanted an open view or wanted a close private sense of personal space, and that this could be changed as they felt appropriate. That notion was fine, but rumor has it that a norm developed in the organization which stated, "anyone with nothing to hide will leave his drapes open." With the growth of this norm, any flexibility that was built into the architecture of the physical setting was overridden by the inflexibility of the social architecture. In fact, if people follow the norm, there is no more choice there than there was before, and the environment is no richer for having the potential of moveable drapes.

On the other hand, changing the social architecture of a system while maintaining the old physical setting may be just as futile. Several university professors have told me about their frustrating searches for classrooms that do *not* have all the chairs bolted down in rows facing the front—chairs to be occupied by eager receptacles who will soak in whatever is sent out from the fount at the front.

It is unlikely that a teacher who has some tentative feelings about experimenting (shifting his teacher–student relations from control toward joint exploration) will long maintain his excitement and energy, if he has to put it all into a search for a non-hierarchically structured room. Most classrooms are structured against a change in his teaching process.

As noted earlier, a reasonable but tentative generalization at this point is that while both physical and social forces are important in forming a person's life space, the social environment is probably predominant, but can be reinforced or cancelled by the physical environment. It also seems likely, however, that there are cases in which the physical setting is a major force in determining developments in a social system, and we should identify those instances as particularly relevant to physical OD work.

DESIGNING FOR CHANGE

The last example is by no means unique to school systems. Many organizations or groups could be described as having a high degree of *spatial viscosity*—as having relatively fixed physical structure or layouts which require a good deal of energy or resources to change. The more this is true, the more groups or relationships, once formed, will tend to resist change far past their usefulness. This can be quite costly to a system if its task organization requires temporary sytems (Bennis and Slater, 1968). For example, if the coming together and breaking up of temporary project teams working on particular problems is important, the physical layout should make it easy rather than difficult for team members to be located close to each other for the life of a project.

One task, then, of organization development is to reduce the spatial viscosity of the system, so that it can change its shape when a new configuration is more appropriate to mirror new important relationships. Spaces should be designed for change rather than for one particular set of activities. When an organization plans a new space, it should contract for a *process* for creation and change of spaces, rather than for just a building per se. In most cases the opposite happens: Many new multi-story buildings are being built by companies whose major thoughts about what happens on the inside are determined by relative status (symbolic) and the prevailing trends in interior decoration (pleasure—usually executives'). There is little or no serious consideration of what needs to take place in the space (instrumental) and how these needs change over time as tasks change (instrumental) and as people change (growth).

In this sense, a major goal of organizational development is to increase a system's ability to be an effective *problem-solver* about its own space (see Steele, 1969, for a discussion of this process), rather than be dependent on current "fads" in layout or design, such as it is good to have everything open, or it is good to have each person in his private place. I mistrust any simple rules about space, especially when they are proposed without knowing what it is the organization is trying to do, or what sub-groups in the organization are trying to do. For OD work, it is important to promote a conscious problem-solving process for structuring space around what is to be done, how people want to live, what individual styles are like, and so on. These choices depend upon the tasks, personal styles, values, and the rate of change in the organization—not on any single rule about what is good or bad as an arrangement. There are many individual and social forces which reduce spatial problem-solving (Steele, 1969), including habit, group norms, preferences for low control over one's life space, and low awareness of one's experiences. The goal of this problem-solving would be to have spatial decisions flow *from* definitions of organizational goals, structures, and values, in contrast to the usual backwards process of taking the *spaces* as given and shaping the organization to fit them.

For many people or systems, the level of spatial awareness is so low that the thought of taking responsibility for environment decisions just never occurs—whatever is, is assumed to have some logical basis for being that way. An extreme example occurred in an organization where the major determinant of the layout of secretaries' desks for the first six months after a move turned out to be where the moving men had gotten tired as they moved the desks into the new building. Everyone came in, assumed that the layout had behind it the reasoning of some "responsible" person, and took their places where they found their desks.

Use of the transactional dimensions described earlier is one mechanism for increasing this problem-solving. A consultant can help a system take a more conscious look at which dimensions it maximizes and minimizes with a given layout or process. It also happens that *within* a dimension a group may be gaining in one way and losing in a much larger (but less conspicuous) way. For instance, companies (and homeowners) often choose materials and set rules for use of space based on how easy it will be to *clean* it—an instrumental criterion.[3] What is seldom considered in that choice, however, is what may be lost in other instrumental areas, such as an antiseptic climate causing people to feel uncomfortable in the space, leading to their spending less extra time or unplanned moments there, resulting in fewer informal interactions which could produce new product ideas, leading to less vitality in the organization's choices of which tasks to pursue. It would pay a system to question its bank of long-held assumptions about what its spaces must be like and to examine the gains and costs of a clean wall.

PHYSICAL SPACE AND CURRENT VALUES IN OD

There is one particular issue about space and its relationship to organizational development that deserves particular attention here, since it is so potent in the process of change or blockage of change today. This is the extent to which spatial decisions are often controlled rigidly by the top of the organization—a process that is usually quite incongruent with the directions of change being fostered by an OD program.

A major system goal of OD as it is developing today is the creation of more effective working units (whether a system-wide organization or sub units of an organization), including the development of what Bennis (1966) has called the criteria of organizational health: reality centeredness, a sense of identity, and an ability to adapt and to solve problems in a way that keeps them solved. Towards these ends, one clear trend in OD has been the development of processes in the system which promote and allow more integration of individual and organizational goals, and more self control (or self motivation) on the part of the individual as a means of using the resources of the organization's members towards organizational health. This is closely akin to McGregor's discussion of Theory Y (that people can, in the right climate, willingly take on those kinds of responsibilities) as a set of assumptions about human beings (McGregor, 1960).

There is usually, however, an interesting blindness to the relationship of the physical environment to people's sense of self control and mastery over their own fate. There are many examples of organizations that say they are committed to movement toward Theory Y and organizational and individual development, while at the same time they continue to dictate from the top the kinds of physical settings in which each person will work. It is said that one major organization had its total headquarters decorated by a firm who had to get all final approval from the president of the organization. He, being in his eyes the holder of taste in the organization, made decisions about the decor for all the major offices in the system and he also instituted a rule that no changes could be made in this decor without his approval. This is a prime example of how a social and physical process can combine to produce a certain climate in an organization. One could struggle valiantly trying to spread responsibility for decision making in that organization, but as long as the rule about all control of the person's physical space being held by the president was in effect change would not occur because of the messages people read about the real power system in the organization. In the end, it would always be controlled from the top, visually represented by what people experienced in their life space each workday.

This suggests that one important way of using the physical environment in organizational development is to focus on the processes of *decision making* about space, rather than trying to pick some perfect solution about how all spaces ought to be structured. In this area, an OD consultant's greatest contribution will probably come from focusing on changing the ways in which spatial decisions are made, providing better information about the effects of space and engaging in activities which would increase people's awareness about the impact of the physical space upon them and their work group.

THE FUTURE AND ENVIRONMENTAL OD

The main theme here has been that spatial arrangements can stimulate and/or facilitate the processes of organization change, or they can work to suppress change if they are inappropriate or the decision process about space is incongruent with desired growth. The impact of space on behavior is increasingly being documented (see, for example, Hall, 1966; Sommer, 1967; 1969), and those interested in individual and organizational growth must become familiar with what is happening in this area in order to begin to make use of this untapped resource.

Coupled with the need to become familiar with present knowledge about environmental effects is the necessity for consultants, behavioral scientists, designers, and client systems to join in a commitment to greater experimentation with space and evaluation of results in on-going organizations. Until now, a majority of environmental studies have been done in schools or hospitals (they seem to be more open to the possibility that what they have is not necessarily better than what they might try; they also have relatively clear task definitions; see Srivastava and Good, 1968; and Architectural Research Lab, 1965), and this needs to be broadened to many other kinds of profit and non-profit institutions. In order for this experimentation to take place and useful feedback to be generated from it, a major effort is needed in defining specific independent and dependent variables and operational measures of them. If this does not occur, an understanding of the effects of a particular change in space will be lost in guess work or expectations held prior to the change, and the real effects on interaction patterns, mood, involvement, productivity, and self-awareness will be hidden.

From the viewpoint of the action-oriented consultant-researcher, the issues and processes discussed here suggest a number of concrete activities worth exploring. One is the rich potential for team building or other OD sessions that are held *in the group's own space*, not away at some neutral conference center. The non-neutrality of a group's territory is exactly what makes the issues more visible there, and this visibility should be used. The major problem to be solved in this process would be the buffering of the group from the usual outside inputs that would divert energy from self-analysis.

A second recommendation is to use *temporary moves* as an important resource rather than view them as a disruption. Many organizations make interim moves during a period of transition between inadequate old facilities and the creation of (soon to be inadequate) new facilities. These temporary moves could be used as experimental and training periods, testing out different groupings and looking at the impact of these differences on interaction, satisfaction, and production.

Talking about the temporary move and its impact is also one means for training organizational members to be more aware of the nature of spatial influences and how they can control them. Consultants should think of training and attitude change as a necessary process in helping a system to use and create better spaces.

Consultants should also work with client systems to increase the amount of conscious problem-solving that goes into the structuring of their space. This would include helping them look at all four spatial inputs (instrumental, symbolic, pleasure, and growth) rather than focusing on one or two, and would help them plan appropriately for change. In this way, the physical shape of the system will emerge from its central tasks and values and consequent activities, rather than vice-versa. This also serves as a concrete vehicle for inducing a system to be more explicit about its basic goals and values.

Notes

1. The author wishes to thank Clay Alderfer, Tim Hall, Saul Siegel and Chris Argyris for their helpful comments on an earlier draft of this paper.

2. Unless otherwise indicated, when the word "environment" is used, it refers to the physical settings in which the work of the organization takes place—not to the social climate, nor to the wider environment (such as the city or the natural setting) of the system as a whole.

3. The importance of cleanability as a criterion for elements in the environment probably stems partly from Puritanistic values ("next to Godliness"). At a more subtle level, as our environments become more finished and prepackaged, housewives particularly may focus on cleaning because they experience themselves as having very little ability to control or change their environment—cleaning may be all that they feel they can do to make a difference. Wade (1968) makes a similar point in reference to the need to manipulate litter if one can't influence anything else, and he suggests designing products which make a higher class of litter when discarded.

References

Architectural Research Laboratory, *Environmental Evaluations* [School Environments Research 2]. Ann Arbor: University of Michigan, 1965.

Beckhard, R. *Organization Development—Strategies and Models*. Reading, Massachusetts: Addison-Wesley, 1969.

Bennis, W. *Changing Organizations*. New York: McGraw-Hill, 1966.

Bennis, W., and P. Slater. *The Temporary Society*. New York: Harper and Row, 1968.

Carr, S., and K. Lynch. "Where Learning Happens," *Daedalus*, 97, No. 4 (1968): 1277–1291.

Colman, A. "Territoriality in Man: A Comparison of Behavior in Home and Hospital," *American Journal of Orthopsychiatry*, 38 (1968): 464–468.

Davis, S. "An Organic Problem-Solving Method of Organizational Change," *Journal of Applied Behavioral Science*, 3, No. 1 (1967), 3–21.

Gardner, J. *Self-Renewal*. New York: Harper, 1968.

Hall, E. "The Language of Space," *Landscape*, Fall, 1960, 41–45.

Hall, E. *The Hidden Dimension*. Garden City, New York: Doubleday, 1966.

McGregor, D. *The Human Side of Enterprise*. New York: McGraw-Hill, 1960.

Seashore, S., and D. Bowers. *Changing the Structure and Functioning of an Organization*, Ann Arbor: University of Michigan, SRC-ISR Research Monograph No. 33, 1963.

Sommer, R. "Classroom Ecology," *Journal of Applied Behavioral Science*, 3, No. 4 (1967): 489–503.

Sommer, R. *Personal Space: The Behavioral Basis of Design*. Englewood Cliffs, New Jersey: Prentice-Hall, 1969.

Steele, F. "The Impact of the Physical Setting on the Social Climate at Two Comparable Laboratory Sessions," *Human Relations Training News*, 12, No. 4 (1968): 1–3.

Steele, F. "Problem-Solving in the Spatial Environment." Paper presented at Environmental Design Research Association Conference, Chapel Hill, N. C., June 8–11, 1969.

Srivastava, R., and L. Good. "Patterns of Group Interaction in Three Architecturally Different Psychiatric Treatment Environments," Topeka, Kansas: Environmental Research Foundation, 1968.

Trist, E., G. Higgin, H. Murray, and A. Pollock. *Organizational Choice*. London: Tavistock, 1963.

Wade, J. "Disposal," *Industrial Design*, June, 1968.

White, R. "Motivation Reconsidered: The Concept of Competence," *Psychological Review*, 66 (1959): 297–334.

PART THREE

Data-Based Strategies of Social Intervention

*S*ocial systems and individuals often use data gathered from their environment in order to assess functional adequacy and to initiate behavior change. Sometimes the data are unsolicited. After touching a hot object, the experience of pain (data) causes people to withdraw. Industrial organizations examine absenteeism, turnover, and waste (data) as indicators of their functioning. Rioting and other forms of civil strife (data) sometimes provide governments with useful diagnostic data about the "state of the union." Although these data have the capacity to produce major social change, their use will not be considered a "social intervention," since the collection procedure lacks a *deliberate effort by a change agent to use data as a means of initiating and* *guiding change in a social system.* Our consideration will be limited to those interventions in which data are collected by a change agent, with the *intent* of using the data to produce change in a social system.

This limitation does not restrict the *kind* of data used by a change agent. It might include assessment of attitudes, perceptions, and behavior of system members; productivity and quality of work efforts; relationships among subgroups within the system; and changing economic and social conditions in the system's environment. Nor does the limitation restrict the procedures and design used for data collection. They might include interviews and observations, structured or unstructured surveys, as well as experimental or quasi-experimental research designs (Campbell and Stanley, 1963).

However, we have specifically excluded from our consideration data-based interventions which are inadvertent in the sense that they unintentionally introduce data into a social system (for example, Skinner's work with operant conditioning is beginning to have profound effects on school systems, though the relevant data were not published by Skinner with the intent of using them to produce change in school systems), and those interventions employing information, in the form of research knowledge, possessed by a consultant and used by him as he advises a social system.

Our major concern in this section will be with examining the procedures that two groups of change agents, called "affiliated" and "unaffiliated," have developed for coping with non-rational (psychological) factors that influence the success of data-based strategies for social intervention.

The Role of Non-rational Factors in the Success of Data-based Strategies of Social Intervention. Assume the improbable, if not the impossible: A group of researchers studying organization X developed procedures for data collection and analysis with such skill that they achieved pinpoint accuracy in the identification of X's problem, its causes, and its solution. Would the researchers bring about a successful change? Not necessarily. Comprehension of the data, acceptance of them as valid, and willingness to execute change in accordance with the implications of the data often depend less on skillfulness with research technology than on social and psychological factors which are affected by the change agent's strategy in collecting data and introducing them to the system.

Affiliated and Unaffiliated Change Agents. Change agents who are actually members of the system in which they are trying to produce change (for example, personnel research managers), and those who enter into a mutually agreed upon contractual relationship with the system will be referred to as "affiliated change agents." These persons can be internal or external to the system. In contrast, "unaffiliated change agents" are not members of the target system nor are they parties to any mutually agreed upon contractual arrangement with the system. Their role as change agents is often the result of their own unilateral decision or the prompting of third parties. It is common to find that unaffiliated change agents act because they are aggrieved by adverse conditions. Ralph Nader's (1965) exposé of unsafe conditions in automobiles and Selltiz's use here of survey

Introduction

feedback to end discriminatory restaurant practices are examples of data-based strategies for social intervention used by unaffiliated change agents.

Our first consideration will be with the assumptions, procedures, and principles used by affiliated change agents in their attempt to cope with the nonrational factors that determine "success" in the use of data-based strategies. Some of these same issues will then be examined for unaffiliated change agents.

AFFILIATED CHANGE AGENTS

In varying degrees, the data-based strategies for social intervention used by affiliated change agents reflect the influence of two principle aims, which are here called "initiatory" and "pragmatic."

The purpose of data, for strategies which emphasize *initiatory aims*, is to stimulate discussions and meetings in which system members can discuss their attitudes and feelings about organizational conditions. Typically, system members are provided with opportunities to consider the causes of a problem as well as alternative solutions. Strategies in which initiatory aims predominate do not necessarily assume that the data alone will accurately identify causes or solutions, but rather that they will provide a basis for discussions between the principal parties to a problem. The intervention is designed to initiate and maintain problem-solving discussions. The process used in collecting data, presenting them to a system, and formulating action steps is of primary interest and is a process that maximizes participation of system members.

Strategies in which *pragmatic aims* predominate are typified by attempts to maximize the data's precision in depicting environmental conditions, identifying the causes of a problem, and demonstrating the value of alternative solutions. The objective is to provide decision-makers with a rational, scientific basis for decision-making; a situation within which policy-makers are provided or confronted with unambiguous, objective data about the existence, cause, or solution of a problem. In contrast to the assumption of nonrationality implicit in initiatory aims, pragmatic aims assume the rationality of organizational decision-makers; that is, they will recognize and respond to reliable and valid data.

An example of this approach is presented in a discussion of experimental social innovation by Fairweather (1964). He suggests that the experimental group receiving the innovation ought to be compared to a group receiving the usual social practice, the control group. He says (p. 26):

> This is necessary because current social practice is the best social subsystem for the problem as far as society is concerned. Furthermore, it is desirable because current social practice is imbedded in the customs, mores, folkways, and other traditions which have been developed by a society, and it is possible that the current social practice is an excellent one. A society would not be willing to accept a different solution for the social problem *until* it had been clearly demonstrated to be superior to the current practice.

This statement assumes that decision-makers are rational by implying that they will accept the implications of scientifically valid data.

In considering the activities of unaffiliated change agents, the notion of maximizing the "political aims" of data-based interventions will be introduced. Before doing that, however, four data-based strategies commonly used by affiliated change agents should be summarized: diagnostic surveys, survey feedback, evaluation research, and action research. Initiatory aims predominate in survey feedback, and, in varying degrees, pragmatic aims predominate in the other three. These two different aims have a contrasting effect on a change agent's procedures for dealing with the non-rational factors that affect the success of data-based interventions.

The purpose of a summary of these four data-based strategies of social intervention is to highlight some of the assumptions and procedures that distinguish the strategies from one another; the summaries are not intended to teach technical details. To learn such fundamentals, readers are referred to Hyman (1955) for diagnostic surveys, Mann (in this text) and Miles *et al.* (in this text) for survey feedback; Suchman (1967) for evaluation research, and Jahoda *et al.* (1951) and Fairweather (1964) for action research.

(1.) *External and Internal Diagnostic Surveys.* Surveys are frequently used by social systems to determine a system's effect on its external environment and to detect changes in environmental conditions that might require adaptation by the system. Political opinion polls, survey studies of welfare needs within a community, and consumer research about future buying patterns are all example of diagnostic surveys. Ideally, the data are intended to provide information which will initiate and guide a social system's efforts to change. In these terms, successful use of diagnostic surveys depends on the *technical adequacy* of the data—the extent to which it accurately depicts environmental conditions. A primary, although often implicit assumption is that organizational decision-makers are rational as well as pragmatic and will respond to the "obvious" implication for change provided by the data. To the extent that data and their implications are ambiguous, there is an increased likelihood of dissension among system members about the causes of adverse environmental conditions and the need for remedial action. Even when diagnostic surveys appear to unambiguously identify a problem and its causes, system members may still disagree about desirable goals for change and means to achieve such goals.

A social system's internal conditions can also be assessed using diagnostic surveys. Manufacturing organizations often survey the attitudes and morale of employees in the hope of identifying grievances before they become crises. Still, this potentially useful barometer of adverse conditions often comes to no avail as management mistakenly assumes that administering the survey was enough and nothing more need be done. Thus, in the absence of specific instructions the data are easily filed and forgotten. The effects of such a procedure may be more harmful than useful. Some employees may be pleased that someone asked for their opinions; for others, however, the survey creates the expectation that management will respond to their opinions. Failure to satisfy such expectations can produce considerable dissatisfaction and distress.

(2.) *Survey Feedback.* To avoid those pitfalls a data-based intervention called

Introduction

survey feedback deliberately makes provision for system-wide discussion of data throughout the system by organizational families (Mann, in this text; Mann and Hoffman, 1969; Miles, *et al.*, in this text). An organizational family consists of a supervisor and all the subordinates reporting directly to him. If one envisages a chart of the organizational hierarchy, it becomes clear that these families overlap and that supervisors are generally members of two families. In one they are the supervisors; in the other, they are among the subordinates.

Beginning with the top family in the organizational structure, the feedback meetings descend through the hierarchy until all organizational families have been involved. During these meetings members are presented with data from their own family as well as with comparative data from other parts of the organization. Typically, the data include such matters as the actual and desired distribution of influence among different role groups, perceived and actual goals, communication adequacy, perceived norms, and perceived organizational problems. The meetings are intended to become problem-solving sessions in which groups attempt to use data as a vehicle which will enable them to discuss problems, determine causes, and agree upon solutions.

Mann identifies five characteristic conditions of survey feedback that enhance its efficiency as a strategy for changing social systems:

(1.) Participation of organization members in the *collection, interpretation*, and *analysis* of data develops a feeling of ownership in the proposed solutions.
(2.) Organizational families discuss data that are directly relevant to their functioning. They do not discuss abstract principle.
(3.) In time, the process of feedback provides members with immediate knowledge of success and failure of their action steps, which acts to further motivate their efforts.
(4.) Group norms develop to support individual efforts.
(5.) By beginning the process at the top of the organizational hierarchy it receives legitimacy throughout the system.

(3.) *Evaluation Research.* Sponsors of social change projects frequently demand proof of a project's effectiveness. Evaluation research is a set of scientific procedures for collecting and analyzing data which make it possible to prove rather than assert the worth of some project (Suchman, 1967). The procedures that are used vary from relatively unsophisticated experimental designs, employing pre- and post-questionnaire measures (Riecken, 1952; Hyman and Wright, 1956), to complex experimental designs which provide for the manipulation of environmental conditions and the inclusion of control groups (Fairweather, 1964).

The primary objective in evaluation research is to demonstrate the extent to which a specific program of training or action alters a criterion variable in some desired direction. There is relatively less concern with accurately and unequivocally identifying the factors causing change in the criterion variable. Presumably, knowing whether such change has occurred influences decisions about continuing the program or changing its format. It should be recognized, however, that demonstrating failure for a program does not always provide the clues necessary for designing success. One may be left knowing what has failed, rather than what will succeed. This difficulty can be compounded when members of the social system are in conflict about the criteria for success and failure—one man's success may become another's failure.

Action Research. In contrast to evaluation research, this strategy attempts to go beyond a determination of whether or not an action program has succeeded; it attempts to identify the causal factors in success or failure. To determine the "why" of success rather than simply demonstrating its occurrence ordinarily entails complex research designs (see Campbell and Stanley, 1963, for an excellent discussion of research design) and a clear formulation of the research problem, including specific and systematic hypotheses of causal determinants of success. A fine example of this process is provided by Jahoda *et al.* (1951) in their discussion of the formulation and execution of the Deutsch and Collins (1951) study on interracial housing.

Consider the Coch and French (1948) study with the Harwood Corporation as an example. The Harwood Corporation underwent frequent changes in production methods. When these changes occurred the groups involved usually showed increased turnover, reduced efficiency, and hostility toward management. To study ways of improving the process of change, Coch and French created different work groups. For the *control group*, the job changes occurred in the usual way (introduced by management decision), and the work group had no opportunity to influence the process. Another work group, the *partial participation group*, had an opportunity to influence the way the changes took place through a group of representatives who were selected by the entire work group. The representatives met with management to plan the details of the change and learn the new method. Subsequently, they trained their co-workers in the new work procedures. Finally, *total participation groups* were created in which every one, not merely the representatives of the group, could influence the decisions.

The results of this experiment were encouraging. Prior to the change, all three groups were producing about 60 units per hour. After the change, the control group's production dropped to 50 units and did not recover. The group became hostile toward management and filed a number of grievances. Moreover, some seventeen percent of the group quit. The behavior of the partial and total participation groups, however, provided a very different picture. After the change, production for these groups dropped but recovered rapidly. The total participation group soon exceeded their pre-change rate of production and had no resignations in the first forty days following the change. On a subsequent occasion, members of the original control group were permitted full participation in decision-making about an additional changeover. Once again, production immediately fell, but rapidly recovered to a point exceeding pre-change rates.

This study has several components which are characteristic of action research programs. First, the research problem was formulated in order to determine which social and psychological processes were influencing the ease of technological change. In this case, the researchers were testing the notion that the opportunity to participate in decision-making changes group standards

Introduction

and creates self-induced motivation forces toward group goals. Second, the research was conducted in a field setting, the Harwood Corporation, rather than a laboratory. Third, the research had action objectives, namely the improvement of the process of technological change. Finally, as is true of many action research programs, the research was conducted in cooperation with one or more sub-units of the organization, in this case the management group.

In the final section here, we will examine the activities of unaffiliated change agents. Before doing that, however, the consequences of emphasizing "initiatory" as opposed to "pragmatic" aims will be discussed in terms of several procedural problems common to all data-based strategies. The problems include formulation of the intervention objective, data collection procedures and designs, presentation and interpretation of data, action steps, and dissemination of findings.

FORMULATING THE INTERVENTION OBJECTIVE

Whether data-based interventions emphasize initiatory or pragmatic aims depends on three conditions: (1) the predisposition and skill of the change agent, (2) the definition of the problem, and (3) the existence of an action program.

The Predisposition and Skill of the Change Agent. Without belaboring the obvious, it is reasonable to assert that the background of change agents is heterogeneous. Their individual histories create biases which are reflected in their adherence to initiatory or pragmatic aims. Those change agents with a scientific bias tend to prefer evaluation and action research since these strategies employ the key tools of science, especially the controlled experiment. By using research procedures developed in the behavioral sciences they hope to collect data which, by itself, can provide valid answers which will be accepted and employed by policy-makers.

Other change agents assume that successful solutions to organizational problems depend equally as much on attitudes, feelings, and commitment of system members (elements which tend to be more a consequence of the process used in data feedback) as on the technical precision of data. The agents prefer survey feedback with its emphasis on system-wide, group problem-solving and decision making—procedures that they assume will elicit positive attitudes, feelings, and commitment about solutions to organizational problems.

The Definition of the Problem. The strategies that emphasize pragmatic aims require a relatively sharp definition of a system's problem. Evaluation and action research cannot be conducted unless the action program under investigation specifies the variable it is trying to alter—prejudice toward blacks, recidivism in prisons, or adherence to religious tenets. Diagnostic surveys also require a designated target, such as consumer patterns in the purchase of soap or opinions about exploring the moon. Survey feedback does not necessarily require rigorous specification of a problem. The survey is primarily investigatory, although questions may be included because of hunches derived from research findings, previous experience, and comments from system members.

The Existence of an Action Program. In most instances, the purpose of emphasizing initiatory aims is to develop an action program. Survey feedback is an intervention that precedes an action program. To the extent that diagnostic surveys lead policy-makers to a course of action, they also reflect initiatory aims. Evaluation and action research, however, occur concurrently with the execution of an action program. The purpose of these two strategies is to provide data which will guide policy decisions about continuing and/or remodeling existing action programs.

To summarize, initiatory aims in data-based strategies tend to be accompanied by a relatively diffuse problem identification and an intent to develop action programs whereas pragmatic aims tend to be accompanied by a relatively rigorous definition of the problem and a concurrent action program.

DATA-COLLECTION PROCEDURES AND DESIGNS

In survey feedback and other strategies emphasizing initiatory aims, precision of data is relatively less important than is the *process* of data collection and analysis. Commonly, the techniques seek to involve system members in designing the survey and collecting data (see Miles *et al.*, in this text). Through their participation, the survey's relevance is insured and there is an increased likelihood that they will be committeed to the data collection and the feedback processes as well as to subsequent action steps. Moreover, by providing for feedback of the data and problem-solving discussions in overlapping organizational families, there is additional pressure for maintaining the relevance of data and furthering commitment of system members.

To create conditions favorable to the success of data-based interventions, strategies emphasizing initiatory aims rely heavily on the Lewinian distinction between *own* and *induced* motivational forces. Presumably, own motivational forces develop when persons have an opportunity to influence decisions that affect their activities. By having the opportunity to influence a decision, they have an investment in its successful completion. This investment reduces the need for close surveillance and continuous social influence. Behavior which is a consequence of induced motivation, however, fails to develop a sense of personal responsibility and requires relatively more surveillance and influence if the behavior is to be maintained (Lippitt and White, 1943).

Adherence to these principles has encouraged affiliated change agents to endorse collaboration with the client system as a principle procedure for achieving success with data-based intervention. They recognize, however, that own motivational force is only one of the benefits that accrue as a consequence of collaboration. For example, Jahoda *et al.* (1951) suggest that system members who participate with change agents in the design and execution of a data-based intervention act as public relations people for the intervention, and develop an audience for its findings. In addition, those who collaborate with the change agent may gain skills in the intervention technology being used and thereby become a useful resource to the system. This same group may also become the nucleus for an active organizational change effort.

Although strategies that emphasize pragmatic aims may use similar collaborative procedures, there is an additional, and more influential emphasis on collecting valid and reliable data (Fairweather, 1967; Jahoda *et al.*, 1951; Suchman, 1967).

Often, participation of system members must be limited because of the demands of experimental research. There is a danger that participation of system members in formulating research questions, designing interventions, and examining data before completion of an action program may lead to results which reflect their knowledge of the study and its findings, not the independent variable—the action program. At other times, collaboration is neglected because change agents assume that system members will respond to carefully collected data with a researcher's dispassion, objectivity, and reliance on experimental logic. Although this may be true in some instances, in others acceptance of the data and its implications depends upon nonrational factors such as those that have already been discussed. For example, Beveridge (1950) relates one tragic case from medical research that demonstrates the role nonscientific factors can play in the rejection of research findings. He tells the story of the famed physician Semmelweis who discovered that washing hands before examining patients reduced the incidence of mortality from puerperal fever from twelve percent to almost one percent. His findings were accepted and used in some hospitals, but they were rejected in many others. Beveridge suggests that, in part, the rejection was because the findings implicitly incriminated physicians. It might be added that Semmelweis lost his appointment in the very hospital where he made his discovery.

PRESENTATION AND INTERPRETATION OF THE DATA AND ACTION STEPS

As must already be evident, in the case of survey feedback, the procedures used for presentation and interpretation of the data to the system are paramount. Commitment of system members to the process and relevancy of the data is established by feedback of the data to organizational families. Group members have responsibility for interpreting the data; they have responsibility for scheduling meetings, and they have responsibility for formulating and implementing decisions.

Great reliance is placed on problem-solving discussions in which work groups commit themselves to a course of action. Even if data fail to accurately or comprehensively describe a problem, the discussion, which may be attended by consultants, provides a forum in which the principals to a problem can share attitudes and feelings. In fact, a change agent will often make a deliberate effort to elicit such sharing behavior. Hence, the discussions, not the data, are the necessary condition for selecting one course of action over another.

Interventions that emphasize pragmatic aims assume that proof about the value of choosing a course of action can be found in the data. Consequently, the data must be interpreted correctly. This often means that experts interpret the data and present their views in the form of interim and final reports. Interim reports are useful in aiding in the digestion of masses of data and in providing inputs to aid decision-making prior to the final report.

It should *not* be assumed that such reports have little or no value in initiating discussion; they do. Often they enable members of a social system to focus the concerns around identifiable issues, and weigh proposed concrete solutions. Nevertheless, the data are regarded as research evidence that can be used to unambiguously support or refute certain assumptions; they are not numerical Rorschachs subject to interpretation by system members.

DISSEMINATION OF FINDINGS

Data-based interventions, like survey feedback in which initiatory aims predominate, produce data that have value limited to the system for which they were collected. Except where they might be used for comparative purposes (such as showing personnel of one school system the data from another school system), there is ordinarily no attempt to disseminate the findings. Interventions which have more pragmatic aims, however, provide data which support general statements about cause and effect: "Given condition X, children who experience teaching method A will read with fewer errors than those who experience teaching method B." Such propositions can be generalized to situations other than the one in which the study was conducted. Hence, myriad techniques have been developed for dissemination of such data—dissemination by social scientists acting as consultants to other social systems (Zetterberg, 1962); dissemination through literature; conferences; and the development of an enlightened elite (Snow, 1961).

In summary, four technologies commonly used by affiliated change agents have been discussed—diagnostic surveys, survey feedback, evaluative research, and action research. It was suggested that, more than the others, survey feedback illustrates an emphasis on the initiatory aims of data-feedback strategies—that is, the primary objective is to collect and present data in order to initiate problem-solving discussions among system members. In varying degrees, the other technologies illustrate an emphasis on pragmatic aims, on the use of scientific procedures in order to collect data which will provide policy-makers with a rational, scientific basis for decision-making and problem-solving.

By emphasizing one or the other of these two different aims, data-based strategies differ in the procedures they have developed for data collection and design, presentation and interpretation of the data, formulation of action steps, and dissemination of findings. The primary difference is in the manner and extent of collaboration with system members, with those strategies which emphasize initiatory aims requiring more collaboration than those which emphasize pragmatic aims.

THE CASE OF THE UNAFFILIATED CHANGE AGENT

Persons and groups who control change in social systems are not always well-disposed toward making needed changes. Sometimes they are disinterested and even opposed to any alteration of the status quo. Data-based strategies are not

Introduction

limited for use in situations where the system implicity endorses change by contracting itself to internal or external change agents. Unaffiliated change agents—those who are not contracted to the system—can also use data-based strategies of social intervention. Consequently, these strategies (as well as strategies of confrontation and nonviolence) can be directed against social systems in which change is restricted because it is controlled by persons with vested interests in the status quo. Not being part of a system frees the unaffiliated change agent to formulate questions that might otherwise be forbidden.

The unaffiliated change agent's problems are obvious. Target system resources are not at his disposal (including money, private records, and, in some instances, personnel) and during the early periods of his work, he may be unable to secure commitment of policy makers to data collection efforts or to using data to evaluate alternative courses of action.

TECHNOLOGY

The technology available to unaffiliated change agents includes experimental research, observation and survey (questionnaire) techniques including the use of data from public records. The use of experimental research to influence social policy is demonstrated by work of psychologists who have investigated the effects of segregation (e.g., Clark and Clark, 1952); such research was cited by the Supreme Court in its 1954 decision on segregated but equal educational facilities. Experimental medical research also has provided evidence for a link between cigarette smoking and cancer and has led to an increasing number of Federal government rulings about cigarette advertising.

Use of observational and survey data is demonstrated by the influence of individual testimonies before congressional committees, public opinion polls, and more informal presentations using mass media. Consider, for example, the legislative consequences of Upton Sinclair's novel, *The Jungle*, which dealt with unsanitary conditions in the Chicago stockyards. Ralph Nader's *Unsafe at Any Speed* is an excellent example of the use of public records by an unaffiliated change agent. Another example was the hospital study reported by the *New York Post* (Feb. 20, 1969) which found 1200 people per year are electrocuted by medical equipment in the course of their diagnosis or treatment.

TARGET GROUPS

It is not accidental that in these examples the change agents used their data to influence the judgments of legislators, the judiciary, and aggrieved populations. The immediate target of their efforts was not the person or persons controlling change within the social system they hoped to eventually change. Instead data were used to mobilize legislators, courts, and an aggrieved population to use their influence in changing a designated social system.

Presumably, if the immediate target is the judiciary (or, in some instances, the legislature), then the primary aim is pragmatic—that is, to provide these groups with data that are maximally valid and reliable. This assumes that these groups are impartial and objective in evaluating the data, that their interest is in determining the "truth," and that they will respond favorably to the unbiased precision of scientific procedures.

On occasion, legislators have been known to have a vested interest in achieving some outcome. Their motivations are not always unbiased. Under these circumstances the problem is not to persuade (although persuasion may be an objective, if a sympathetic legislator needs proof to convince others of the value of his position); the primary aim is to provide a rallying point, a standard which will cause this sympathetic group to cohere and be moved to action. Data can be used in similar fashion with an aggrieved population. By providing groups with data that demonstrate they are being financially exploited, socially deprived, or endangered by unsafe automobiles, hospitals, or unclean air, it is sometimes possible to unite public sentiment. Until data are introduced, aggrieved groups may experience the adverse effect of undesirable conditions, but intensity of feeling and readiness to act may require that a problem and/or its solution first be put into focus.

Using data to mobilize sympathetic legislators and aggrieved populations does not ordinarily require the same order of scientific precision that is required in trying to persuade (presumably) impartial and objective courts or legislative assemblies. Instead, the data must *sharply define* an adverse condition in a way that is *consonant* with the experiences and feelings of legislators or aggrieved populations. Hence, unaffiliated change agents sometimes employ data-based strategies that have political, rather than initiatory or pragmatic aims. Their objective is to use data to create an influential constituency which will seek to effect changes in a designated social system.

To act as a rallying point, data must be (1) *unambiguous*—they must clearly identify a problem; (2) *dramatic*—they must arouse interest by their relevance to the concerns of the target groups; and (3) *comprehensible*—they must be understood by target groups. In addition, data also have to be *credible*, but their credibility may or may not be based on scientific precision. Credibility, and therefore acceptance of data, may be determined by qualities of the change agent. Two common qualities of the change agent that are known to effect acceptance of persuasive communications are the communicator's prestige and objectivity (Hovland *et al.*, 1953). For these reasons, it is common to find data attributed to prestigious sources or to independent research agencies, or endorsed by scientists, ministers, and other groups whose motivations are not easily impugned.

In presenting data to the target group that they intend to mobilize, unaffiliated change agents sometimes use a mode of communication not ordinarily used by affiliated change agents—public or mass media. In fact, mass media—newspapers and television news agencies—may take the role of unaffiliated change agents. Newspaper and television exposés on crime, poverty, waste of natural resources, and air pollution are all examples of the mass media acting as an unaffiliated change agent.

To summarize: in attempting to emphasize political aims, an unaffiliated change agent provides legislators or aggrieved populations with data that are easily understood, vivid, and consonant with their own experience of adverse conditions. In presenting these data, the change agent's objective is to mobilize a constituency influential enough to cause change in the social system that is assumed to be responsible for the adverse conditions.

It is clear that unlike affiliated change agents, the unaffiliated seek little or no collaboration with a social system, regardless of whether they are formulating the procedures for data collection, presenting and interpreting data, or designing action steps. Although there are costs to this lack of collaboration, the alienation of the unaffiliated agents from the system provides them with the freedom to ask questions and examine alternatives that agents within the system would never consider. Nevertheless, their noncooperative (though *not* necessarily uncooperative or competitive) stance does not have to lead to change strategies which are extra-legal or illegal in nature, as do strategies of confrontation and nonviolence. Rather, data-based strategies used by unaffiliated change agents are an attempt to engage in rational (albeit sometimes emotionally tinged) persuasion by using objective, scientifically sound data, or an attempt at political influence by mobilizing a sympathetic constituency.

OVERVIEW

The six papers that have been included in this part can be distinguished along three dimensions: (1) the procedures used for data collection and feedback; (2) the relationship of a change agent to the target system—affiliated or unaffiliated; (3) the kind of social system that is the target of a change effort. In the following paragraphs, these three dimensions will be used as a framework for briefly summarizing the readings in this section.

One of the early steps in a data-based intervention is to decide what variables will be measured. One asks: what variables make a difference in the functioning of a social system? The first paper in this part, "The Use of Socio-Economic Research in Developing a Strategy of Change for Rural Communities," by Adams and Havens, provides a useful discussion of a number of social and economic variables that may influence a change agent's definition of a problem, formulation of a solution, and methods for producing change. Their discussion of these socio-economic variables uses language that is appropriate for changing communities. Readers should not be constrained by the language, however; rather they should recognize the generalizability of the views represented in this paper. All social systems have historical patterns of change, relationships with other social systems, educational and other orienting procedures, and decision-making processes. These and other variables must be considered in any effort at changing social systems, regardless of the intervention procedures that may be used.

Survey feedback as one form of data-based social intervention is the concern of three papers in this section. The Beckhard paper, "Helping a Group with Planned Change: A Case Study," describes the use of informal interviews by a change agent as a procedure for generating data for feedback. Both Mann, and Miles *et al.* discuss the use of survey questionnaires, an apparently more objective means of data collection, as a method of producing data for feedback. In all three of these papers, the change agent is affiliated with the system. In contrast, Selltiz in her paper, "The Use of Survey Methods in a Citizen's Campaign Against Discrimination," describes one use of survey data by an unaffiliated change agent. Moreover, in the change effort described by Selltiz, the goal—reduction of racial discrimination in restaurants—was well focussed. In the efforts described in the other three papers, the goals were initially less well defined and became defined only after consideration of the data by members of the system.

Fairweather, in his paper "Methods for Experimental Social Innovation," also describes an intervention procedure which can be used by affiliated and unaffiliated change agents. Fairweather's procedure is to conduct controlled social experiments in which different solutions to critical social problems are experimentally compared for their efficacy in producing a desired result. Hence, the procedures for data collection are more rigorous than ones used in the other approaches and call for sophistication in experimental design and statistical analysis.

One final word: These papers place their discussions of data-based interventions in different social contexts, including industrial organizations (Beckhard and Mann), communities (Adams and Havens, and Selltiz), and hospitals (Fairweather). It is important to keep in mind, however, that these techniques for social intervention are not limited to these few social contexts. To assess the applicability of an intervention technique, one must combine one's knowledge of a social situation with his understanding of the technique.

References

Campbell, Donald T., and Julian C. Stanley. *Experimental and Quasi-Experimental Designs for Research*. Chicago: Rand McNally and Co., 1963.

Clark, K. B., and M. K. Clark. "Racial Identification and Preference in Negro Pre-School Children," in E. E. Maccoby, T. M. Newcomb, and E. L. Hartley (eds.). *Readings in Social Psychology*. New York: Holt, Rinehart and Winston, 1947, 602–611.

Coch, L., and J. R. P. French. "Overcoming Resistance to Change," *Human Relations*, 1 (1948): 512–532.

Deutsch, M., and M. E. Collins. *Interracial Housing: A Psychological Evaluation of a Social Experiment*. Minneapolis: University of Minnesota Press, 1951.

Fairweather, George (ed.). *Social Psychology in Treating Mental Illness: An Experimental Approach*. New York: Wiley, 1964.

Hovland, E. I., I. L. Janis, and H. H. Kelley. *Communication and Persuasion*. New Haven: Yale University Press, 1953.

Hyman, H. *Survey Design and Analysis*. Glencoe, Illinois: The Free Press, 1955.

Hyman, H. H., C. R. Wright and K. H. Terence. *Application of Methods of Evaluation: Four Studies of the Encampment for Citizenship*. Berkeley, California: University of California Press, 1962.

Lippith, R., and R. K. White. "The 'social climate' of children's groups," in R. G. Barker, J. S. Kounin, and H. F. Wright (eds.). *Child Behavior and Development*. New York: McGraw Hill, 1943, 485–508.

Introduction

Mann, F. C., and F. R. Hoffman. *Automation and the Worker: A Study of Social Change in Power Plants.* New York: Holt, Rinehart and Winston, 1960.

Mann, F. C. "Studying and Creating Change: A Means to Understanding Social Organization," in C. M. Arensberg *et al.* (eds.). *Research in Industrial Human Relations.* New York: Harper, 1957.

Miles, M. B., H. A. Hornstein, P. H. Calder, D. M. Callahan, and R. S. Schiavo. "Data Feedback: A Rationale," presented at American Sociological Meetings, August 28, 1966.

Nader, R. *Unsafe at Any Speed: The Designed-In Dangers of the American Automobile,* New York: Grossman, 1965.

Riecken, H. W. "Some Problems of Consensus Development," *Rural Sociology,* 17 (1952): 245–252.

Selltiz, C. "The Use of Survey Methods in a Citizens Campaign Against Discrimination," *Human Organization,* 14, No. 3 (1955): 19–25.

Selltiz, C., M. Jahoda, M. Deutsch, and D. Cook. *Research Methods in Social Relations.* New York: Holt, Rinehart and Winston, 1951.

Sinclair, Upton, *The Jungle.* New York: Doubleday, 1906.

Snow, C. P. *Science and Government.* Cambridge, Massachusetts: Harvard University Press, 1961.

Strauss, G. "The Set-Up Man: A Case Study in Organization Change," *Human Organization,* 13 (1954): 17–25.

Suchman, E. *Evaluative Research: Principles and Practice in Public Service and Social Action Programs.* New York: Russell Sage Foundation, 1967.

Zetterberg, H. *Social Theory and Social Practice.* New York: Bedminister Press, 1962.

16

D. W. ADAMS AND A. E. HAVENS

The Use of Socio-Economic Research in Developing a Strategy of Change for Rural Communities: A Colombian Example[*]

*t*he purpose of this paper is to discuss the use of socio-economic research in development programs that are aimed at directly effecting change at the local level. It will suggest a role for socio-economic research in less developed countries and present a research model which points out some of the types of data needed to construct a workable strategy of change.

The paper will argue that the role of the researcher in these areas includes the following functions: (1) to isolate a meaningful unit of analysis; (2) to assemble and classify necessary data; (3) to identify relevant problem areas, given the framework of society's goals; (4) to formulate alternative solutions for problems; (5) to present criteria for selecting a problem, as well as its solutions; and (6) to formulate a workable strategy for the action-takers to effect the selected change. Moreover, it is argued that in many cases data must be assembled on a wide range of variables in order to construct a workable strategy of change.

THE ROLE OF RESEARCH IN LESS DEVELOPED COUNTRIES

In many of the more developed countries, where resources for socio-economic research are relatively abundant, researchers are often able to concentrate on so-called "basic" or "applied" research. That is, some researchers focus on establishing relationships between certain variables and constructing appropriate theories, while others concentrate on applying data and theories to specific problem areas. It is often the case that individuals other than the researchers draw on these findings, plus their own broad knowledge of the existing situations which surround a problem, to construct informally a method for solving a given problem.

In rural areas of less developed countries, much of the social science research has been carried out in a similar manner, although conditions are strikingly different. In some cases, for example, researchers feel they need to conduct broad "basic" studies in order to formulate an idea of existing conditions.[1] Many research projects terminate with a mass of data which may or may not assist in problem-solving. On the other hand, some research activities are very narrow in nature and are aimed at justifying a predetermined course of action. In the first case, the decision-maker often finds that he does not have enough background to integrate the basic studies into his analysis of the problem. In the second case, the decision-maker finds that the results of past research activities do not materially assist him in solving similar problems which occur later.

Because in less developed countries research resources are extremely scarce and time to solve pressing social problems is limited, it becomes imperative for research techniques to lead to satisfactory solutions of problems, as well as forming a useful residual of hypotheses, theories, and models which will make the solution of future problems less taxing. The role, therefore, of the social science researcher in a less developed country is often substantially broader than he might realize. He must be prepared to carefully define a functional unit of analysis which will serve for studies that are typically interdisciplinary. He must be capable of assembling a broad range of data, in order to describe the population being analyzed. This includes using research techniques which are the most functional, given the restraints of budget, general background information available, personnel, and time.[2] He must be ready to define carefully the problems on which he is focusing his research. He must also be prepared to relate his data to the problems identified and to propose plausible alternative solutions. Furthermore, he must be ready to present criteria for selecting both a problem and a method of solution. Next, the researcher must, although he typically has not done so, be able to suggest a strategy for introducing or stimulating the selected change.

As used here, a strategy of change can only be constructed after the researcher has completed all of the above-mentioned steps. Thereupon, he can order the problems observed during the analysis, postulate a series of plausible solutions for each of the problems, and then assign weights to both the problems and methods of solution. By the use of these weights, and by working within the various restraints which apply to the specific situation, he can then select both the problem and the method of solution. Finally, the researcher should formulate, from his data, the alternative methods of introducing the change. This includes some statement of the probability of success of the various alternatives, the limitations of these alternatives, and something about the penalties which might result if the proposed change fails.

A MODEL FOR CONSTRUCTING A STRATEGY OF CHANGE

The logical starting point in formulating a strategy of change is to define a functional unit of analysis. In traditional areas the community[3] may offer advantages as a focal point for socio-economic studies. First of all, the community frequently approaches self-sufficiency and also contains a majority of the important social institutions within its confines. Furthermore, it is often isolated from outside communications.[4] Any effective change, therefore, must be generated within these types of communities, rather than stemming from general outside activities. Such a community can be illustrated by Contadero, Narino.[5]

In a community like Contadero, information on a broad range of social variables is needed to define problems, suggest solutions, and help formulate methods for introducing change. The general types of information which were gathered in the study of Contadero included descriptions of (1) the physical conditions found in the community; (2) the cultural patterns which were superimposed upon the local social system; (3) the historical patterns of diffusion and change; (4) the community's articulation with other systems of government; (5) the economic make-up of the community; (6) the human resources available; (7) the family structure; (8) the educational system; (9) the ecclesiastical system; and (10) the decision-making processes of the behavioral units.

PHYSICAL CONDITIONS

A community's physical environment places important limitations on the types of economic activities that may be pursued. Factors such as rainfall, altitude, terrain, quality of soil, and seasonal variations dictate, to a certain degree, the enterprises which can be undertaken there.

Contadero, for example, varies in altitude from 6,500 to 9,800 feet. The community center and the majority of the population are located at an altitude of 8,000 feet. The climate is generally cool to cold, with temperatures ranging from zero to 18 degrees centigrade. Rainfall is fairly well distributed throughout the year, but is usually more concentrated during the March-May and October-December periods. The threats of frosts and the presence of lower quality soils force owners of land at higher altitudes to emphasize pastures in their farm operations. At lower altitudes most of the land is double-cropped. The topography of the area is rolling to very steep. The soils are rather acidic, but respond well to lime and commercial fertilizer applications.

CULTURAL PATTERNS

Similarly, a knowledge of cultural patterns is of utmost importance for the development of programs of change. Distinguishing these cultural factors can lead to an understanding of why members may be likely to reject change introduced at the community level. The patterns which encompass the existing social structure provide blueprints for the type of social behavior which is present in the community. If certain innovations are introduced, it is possible that they will be perceived as threats to the existing social order, in that they may create hardships for certain members of the society. Changes may also run counter to established ways of doing things, attitudes, and prejudices.[6]

The cultural patterns and physical conditions largely dictate the type of economic organization found in the community. Among other things, cultural patterns affect the rhythm of work, the way the labor supply is mobilized, the incentive system for labor, the method of land transference, and the general organization of the family. Information on these patterns not only helps in deciding on what change to introduce, but provides clues as to the best method to employ in introducing the change.

A starting point for collecting data on cultural patterns is a historical analysis of the community. Contadero, for example, was originally an Indian reservation. For more than two centuries there has been a merging of Spanish and indigenous cultures, brought about by a dominant group which controlled the means of authority and which could, therefore, specify the roles to be performed. This domination is so complete that today all members of the community speak only Spanish and are members of the Catholic Church. Only a few of the original customs are retained, such as native health remedies, eating habits, forms of dress, and methods of crop cultivation.

The Indian reservations, according to law, were governed by a locally elected council, called a *Cabildo*, which was in turn responsible to the representative of the colonial or national government in the region. Emphasis was placed on group, rather than on individual pursuits within the subordinate, indigenous group. The dominate group, however, was more concerned with its individual, self-oriented, pursuits. The *Cabildo* was responsible for granting rights to exploit plots of land and for the general organization of the community. A form of communal activity which still exists is called *minga*, and refers to the exchange of labor between members of the reservation for harvesting and planting crops.

When the Indian reservation was disbanded in 1941 and land titles were given to private owners, no one individual controlled a large quantity of land. The land was more or less evenly distributed into small holdings. Social differentiation was based upon being an Indian or a white, but these distinctions were not biologically based and today are completely confused. The two positions of legitimate authority which remained in the community were, and still are, those of the parish priest and the mayor. Without any significant social differentiation, and lacking any one group which controlled the means of authority in recent years, the community developed into a homogeneous unit, with the family being the major collectivity.

Contadero, then, is a community in which individual decisions are largely based upon values which represent traditional patterns and are reinforced by the "hard cake of custom," and where the family strives to maintain itself by means of direct exploitation of fragmented plots of land which are equally inherited by the family offspring.

HISTORICAL PATTERNS OF DIFFUSION AND CHANGE

It is important to study past patterns of diffusion and change, in order to have some idea of what types of alterations have taken place in the community, to present some clues as to how these changes were introduced, and to help determine why some changes took place and others did not. A knowledge of the historical patterns of diffusion and change can also be valuable in helping to focus the field study. In the study of Contadero, it was convenient to classify the historical changes into two groups: the broad social changes which have occurred since the Spanish Conquest, and the changes recently experienced in customs and production practices.

Unlike some parts of Colombia, Contadero *has not* experienced drastic social changes that might have disrupted existing structural forms.[7] Since this has not occurred in Contadero, and since the family has been able to maintain the social order, the changes that have taken place in the social structure have been gradual.[8] Recent changes in the community include the use of some modern health facilities, such as the local dentist, the health clinic, and manufactured drugs. Most of these changes have taken place since 1956, and the major source of information has been by word-of-mouth communication.

A number of changes have also occurred recently in agricultural production practices. Several new varieties of barley and wheat have been introduced and adopted by most producers in the past eight years. The use of commercial credit, insecticides for potatoes, commercial fertilizers, lime, and small portable mechanical threshers are also fairly recent changes. Some of these practices were introduced by the agricultural development bank. Producers often heard of an improved production practice through market-middlemen, who in turn had purchased grains or potatoes in other areas where these practices had already been adopted. After some individuals in the area had tried the new technique, a number of people received information about the practice by direct contact with these early adopters. The newly informed farm operators then contacted the local agricultural development bank and were able to purchase the new technique. In some cases, the bank encouraged the adoption of these practices by granting credit only when these practices were used.

With this brief review of the patterns of diffusion and change in Contadero, we can note that recent alterations in agricultural production practices have been undertaken after the producers were informed that better practices existed, by sources upon which they could rely, after some local application and success, and finally through the efforts of the agricultural bank. It can also be noted that people placed more credibility on word-of-mouth sources of information than on other types of communication. Moreover, it was apparent that local opinion leaders were of little importance. These patterns were reinforced by the holders of legitimate authority within the community, so we now turn to a consideration of these authority figures.

THE ECCLESIASTICAL STRUCTURE

Knowledge of the ecclesiastical structure is often essential for forming a strategy of change for a rural community. In most traditional societies, a church is the central figure of authority, particularly where Catholicism is predominant.

The ecclesiastical structure in Contadero is entirely made up of the Catholic Church. The major historical function of the Church there was to convert and train the Indians in Catholicism and to teach them Spanish. The Church is still closely associated with the educational system, influencing the formation of the curriculum, providing teacher training, and giving adult education by means of radio schools. The major formal source of information for the members of Contadero is the weekly newspaper, *El Campesino*, which is published by a Catholic organization (Jesuits).

Much has been said about the role of the local parish priest in Latin America. In many areas, he legitimizes as well as introduces change. In Contadero, the parish priests (the community is divided in two parishes) are not active agents for change. Nevertheless, they are important legitimizers.[9] Therefore, the Church, as an authority structure, exerts control over the local people and, as such, is an important variable to consider in changing programs.

THE FAMILY STRUCTURE

The family performs two all-important functions: (1) it transmits the values and goals of the community to offspring; and (2) it serves as an economic unit by providing food and shelter for itself. Most changes which are introduced will be evaluated by the family in terms of these two functions. In order to be accepted, a change must not run entirely counter to the established patterns of behavior present in the culture, and it must not threaten the family's ability to perform its economic function of providing for its maintenance.

In Contadero, the family structure is one of transition between extended and nuclear. Many family units have developed which are entirely nuclear. In most of these cases, however, the father of either the husband or wife, or of both, resides nearby and is looked to as a major source of information for decisions. The behavior patterns present during the *resguardo* days of the community are, therefore, changing, but have not completely disintegrated. In the *resguardo*, the *gobernador* was almost always one of the elders of the community and was considered by many as the sage. This respect for age is still present in the family structure.

The division of labor within the family is well established by cultural pattern. Domestic duties are delegated to the wife and older daughters, while day-to-day farm duties are carried out by the husband and his older sons. All of the family's labor resources are utilized during the planting and harvesting periods.

Changes to be introduced in Contadero, given the type of family organization present, must be somewhat in accord with the established patterns of behaviour within the family structure. A change which varies the economic relationships within the family could have a serious impact upon the authority structure currently present in the community. If children become economically independent from the family, it is quite likely that they would be less willing to accept the oldest male family member as a key determiner of their actions.[10]

It is, therefore, likely that any change to be introduced will be more widely accepted if it is tailored to fit these culturally defined behavior patterns of the family.

POLITICAL STRUCTURE OF THE COMMUNITY

A final factor which embodies legitimate authority for the community members is the political structure. Almost every community has some formal or informal means of governing itself, and although it may be largely self-sufficient, it must have some extra-community ties with broader forms of government. It is, therefore, often vital to identify how local group decisions are made, to describe the formal as well as informal rules by which the community lives, and to assess what capabilities the various local political institutions have with respect to a strategy of change.

In Contadero the local unit of government is the *municipio*.[11] The *alcalde*, who is in charge of the *municipio*, is appointed by the *departmento*[12] governor, who in turn is appointed by the popularly elected president of the republic. The *alcalde* is recognized as a legitimate authority figure by the community members, probably as a carry-over from the reservation days, but his sphere of influence in agricultural production decisions is negligible. He is assisted in making decisions by a locally elected town council. As has been true throughout the country since development of the *Frente Nacional* in 1958, the membership in the council is divided equally between the liberals and conservatives, despite the fact that less than one percent of the population is liberal.

For practical purposes, it is difficult to separate the group decisions made by the Church and those made by the *municipio* officials in Contadero. It is almost always the local priest who makes the announcements and enlists popular support for any group project. Furthermore, he is often closely consulted by the *alcalde* and town council on significant matters.

One of the more important ties which Contadero has with broader forms of government is through its participation in the *departmento* tax revenues on liquor and tobacco, but this amounts to only five to ten percent of the *municipio's* operating budget.[13] The largest source of revenue, fifty to sixty percent of the budget, is derived from a tax on the declared value of the registered land. The bulk of the expenditures are for salaries, a few public works, and office building repair.

A Strategy of Change for Rural Communities

Aside from the agricultural development bank and the national police, individuals in Contadero have very little contact with, or knowledge of, the national government. In fact, less than 15 percent of the farm operators in Contadero knew who their representative was to the national congress. In general, the residents of Contadero identify themselves only slightly with outside governmental activities. The building of a new health center and some of the school buildings, the appointment of the *alcalde*, and the small contribution made to the *municipio*'s budget by the *departamento* are the principal outside relationships.

This description of the community's political structure and its articulation with broader forms of government shows several important factors. The first is the extremely weak identification which the members of the community of Contadero have with any form of authority outside of the Church and family. The second is the general debility of all the political institutions relating to Contadero with respect to effecting some type of change. The third is the importance of the Church in group and individual decisions.

Now that the major cultural patterns and authority structures of the community have been described in general terms, we turn our attention to the economic organization of the community.

THE ECONOMIC STRUCTURE OF THE COMMUNITY

Even in the most traditional communities, economic factors play an important part in programs of change. Among other things, these factors include: (1) the types of production within the community; (2) the organization of the producing units; (3) the manner in which the rights to land resource use are distributed; (4) the method in which labor and capital resources are applied; (5) the make-up of the families' occupational structures; and (6) how the local marketing system functions. Since it is often true that a large percentage of the total output in traditional communities is derived directly from agricultural production, the analysis will often focus on the farm units found in the area.

Farm Organization. In spite of the presence of several small flour mills and a substantial amount of handicrafts in the homes, over three-quarters of the goods and services produced in Contadero stem directly from agricultural production.

Farms in Contadero are typically small, highly fragmented, and oriented toward production for home consumption. Usually, one-quarter of the area in each unit is devoted to native corn, interplanted with several varieties of beans and squash. About the same proportion of land is devoted to barley and wheat and a similar amount in potatoes and other vegetables. The remaining one-quarter of the land is devoted to pastures. The livestock enterprises often include one or two dairy cows plus replacements, a few sheep, several pigs, one or two draft animals, a few chickens, and some guinea pigs for home consumption. Wheat, barley, and potatoes are almost always double-cropped. Corn and beans, on the other hand, take up a full crop year.

Farm units range in size from less than one hectare to over 80 hectares.

The modal size is three to four hectares. Almost all units include more than one parcel of land, the average being about four. Oxen plus hand labor are the means of cultivation.

Generally, operators use a set rotation of corn-potatoes-cereals-corn in their various lots. Commercial fertilizers are applied in limited quantities to potatoes, but are only rarely applied directly to cereals, corn, or pastures. Limestone is occasionally applied,[14] and potatoes are regularly sprayed with insecticides.

Land Tenure. Land tenure arrangements have significant implications for the kinds of enterprises which will be undertaken on the farm, the types of investments that will be made, the flexibility which is present in the farm operation, and the manner in which production decisions are made and carried out.

Although most of the land in Contadero is owned in fee simple by local residents, it is common to find complex sets of tenure arrangements involved in the actual operation of the land. For example, just 20 percent of the farm units in Contadero included only land which was "purely" owner-operated.[15] Production decisions are often shared in these units through a method of sharecropping called *medias*. Under this arrangement, the land owner supplies one-half the seed and one-half the fertilizer (if used). The sharecropper furnishes all of the labor and the balance of the production inputs. This arrangement is especially prominent between the older individuals or single women who own land and younger individuals who take the land as "croppers." A number of special arrangements for the use of land are also common between relatives. Production decisions are, therefore, often shared between at least two individuals, Few of the tenure contracts are written, and the length of time is only occasionally for more than one year. Nothing exists in these contracts which would encourage sharecroppers to make any long-run land improvements.

Capital and Labor Resources. As is true for land, capital resources are extremely limited in Contadero. Almost all of the institutional credit is provided by the agricultural development bank, but this amounted to only a little over ten dollars per capita in 1964. Interest rates for loans from this bank are very reasonable, but loans by private individuals often carry rates of three to five percent per month. Most of the smaller farmers do not or cannot obtain credit from the bank. They typically rely on private sources of credit to meet unexpected needs. Private capital outside of investments in land and livestock is practically nonexistent. Most people, when faced with a sudden cash outlay, sell livestock or land to cover the cost.

Labor resources, in contrast to capital, are overabundant in Contadero. Farm labor wages are only 20 to 30 cents per day, about one-quarter the national average. In spite of a large out-migration of young individuals, sufficient numbers of able-bodied workers are still available to meet peak harvesting and planting needs.

Occupational Structures. Partly because people have substantial amounts of free time outside of agricultural production, almost all farm families have sources of income from some other employment in the community. This means that decisions as well as time are shared between several activities and that farm operators' reactions to change can be substantially different than in a case where agricultural production is the only source of income.

Most of the families in Contadero derive a part of their real income directly from agricultural production. But a substantial part of the cash income is obtained from other sources. Almost all of the farm operators and their mature sons, for instance, work part-time as day laborers on other farms during planting and harvesting periods. Moreover, practically all of the women spend their spare time spinning and weaving wool. Other men gather firewood for sale, hire out with their oxen for custom farm work, or spend time buying and selling various commodities. In a number of cases, small stores located in the family home furnish additional income.

Marketing Systems. Another reason for the diversified occupational structures in Contadero is the uncertain marketing conditions which face the individual farm operators. These conditions shape a number of farm production decisions. Except for the largest farm operators and the more important merchants, almost all marketing activities in Contadero are centered in the local village. The production in excess of family requirements is sold to local middlemen, assembled into larger lots, and trucked to outside market areas.

Items for local consumption are brought in by various merchants, including rice, salt, crude sugar, and coffee for home consumption. Fertilizer, limestone, sacks, cereal seed, and insecticides are the main purchases for production purposes. Seven small shops in the village retail these commodities throughout the week, but a large proportion of the sales are made on the Sunday market day in the open plaza. Many families are largely self-sufficient, but almost all buy some commodities each week and appear to understand the fundamental elements of the money marketing system.

Almost no farm storage capacity is present, and practically all of the crops are sold immediately upon harvesting. Wide fluctuations in the prices of potatoes, beans, and corn often occur as a partial result of this. It is not uncommon, for example, for prices of these products to drop 25 to 50 percent during the harvesting season. Year-to-year variations in prices are also common. For instance, in January 1963 farmers received as low as 60 cents per 100 pounds of potatoes in Contadero, yet in May 1964 the farm price was over six dollars per hundred. Prices for barley, wheat, and animal products tend to be more stable.

HUMAN RESOURCES

Attention must also be directed towards the human resources available in the community. Such considerations as the number of inhabitants relative to other resources, age-sex distribution, health, and education are important elements to study in this respect. In addition, it is necessary to understand the process of migration in and out of the community, in order to ascertain how the relationships between human and other resources have been changing.

As could be expected, there are somewhat more females than males in Contadero. Young men often leave the area for military service and later find occupations in other parts of the country. It is often true, moreover, that the individuals with the most education find opportunities outside of the community. Heavy out-migration in the past 20 to 30 years has apparently kept total population more or less stable in Contadero and has had a substantial impact on the educational level-age-sex distribution.

In many traditional communities, the health characteristics of the population could be an important factor to take into account in developing a strategy of change. Although infant mortality rates are quite high (1.1 per 100 live births) and dental conditions very poor, the average level of health in Contadero is somewhat better than in warmer climates of Colombia (where infant mortality rates are about 2 per 100 live births). In this case, health would probably not be a seriously limiting factor for most programs of change.

THE EDUCATIONAL SYSTEM

Closely associated with a study of the human resources is an analysis of the educational factor. This includes not only a study of the level of formal education but also an analysis of the ability of the educational system to participate in a strategy of change.

Total learning experience, and thus "real education," is difficult to measure, but the level of formal education is often a useful indication of a person's learning experience. In Contadero formal education is critically lacking. Of the twelve primary schools in the community, only three offer more than three years of study. No school offers more than five years of formal education. Not many students attend past the second or third year, and few can functionally read or write. Some educational facilities are available throughout the community, but almost one-quarter of the eligible children are not enrolled in school. Heavy school drop-out rates often reduce enrollment by one-half during a school year. Sickness, lack of family interest, and labor requirements on family farms during harvesting and planting seasons are prime factors here. Only four of the twelve teachers in the community have more than ten years of formal schooling.

The low over-all level of education in the community poses restraints on the methods which can be used to introduce change. In brief, the educational system does not serve as a means of upward mobility for the residents, since it does not prepare them for occupations other than those encountered in the local area. It does not give the young members of the community new ways of perceiving their situation and therefore perpetuates the *status quo*. Furthermore, the general debility of the educational system seriously limits its utility as an agent to help introduce or reinforce any selected change.

DECISION-MAKING PROCESSES

During the process of constructing a strategy of change, the investigator must be able to identify the critical decision-making units which might relate to the strategy. The key units may be different from study to study, but it is likely that they will include the farm operators, the town council, the educational system, the Church, local leaders, and various governmental agencies. Since the selection of the key decision-making unit is dependent upon both the change selected and characteristics of the units themselves, it is likely that no definite selection can be made until most of the field research is completed. It is therefore necessary to assemble information on several of the decision-making units which might be involved in the strategy.

In Contadero the decision-making units were initially grouped as follows: (1) those which might introduce the change to the community; (2) those which might carry out the change; and (3) those that might reinforce the change. After the study was almost completed, the appropriate change selected, and the method of introduction chosen, the key decision-making units were identified. On the basis of the evidence available, it appeared that some outside agent would have to introduce the selected change, that farm operators would be making the critical decisions with regard to the implementation of the change, and that the agricultural development bank would be a key unit in reinforcing and furthering the change.[16] Of these three, it was decided that the decisions made by the farm operators would be the most critical *vis-a-vis* the success of the strategy.

Farm operators in Contadero can be classified into two general groups with respect to farm production decisions. The first group includes operators of the small units where home consumption requirements guide production decisions. Larger units are typically oriented toward market conditions and profit maximization. The criteria used for making production decisions on smaller farms, on the other hand, are distinctly different and were analyzed separately.

Small farm operators in Contadero make most of their production decisions on the basis of minimizing the risk and uncertainty involved. The small margin of family operations above the survival level, the extreme variability in some marketing conditions, the lack of cash reserves, and the high subjective value of land as a source of wealth combine to make a cash loss almost intolerable for farmers in this group.[17] The abundance of family labor and the limited range of alternatives available for that labor are also important factors in farm operators' decision-making criteria.

Based upon the previous discussions, we may now turn to the part in the research role which is concerned with the identification of the problem and the selection of the method of solution.

PROBLEM IDENTIFICATION AND SOLUTION SELECTION

With the above-mentioned data, the next step in constructing a strategy of change is to identify the relevant problems, given society's goals.[18] This includes listing the problems which are possible to solve, given the resource restraints, as well as assigning some types of values to the solution of these problems.[19] Next, criteria must be established for selecting a specific problem for solution and for determining the method of solution. One criterion, for example, might be the maximization of expected social returns from a given unit of input.

In Contadero, several relevant problems can be identified. Focusing just on agricultural production, for example, we can note that crop yields are substantially lower than could be expected with the use of improved techniques. Potato production is less than one-third that which can be obtained with improved seed, lime applications, and economic levels of fertilizing and spraying. Likewise, corn yields are only about one-third to one-half that which could be expected with the use of improved seed.

Based on the resources which were available for introducing a change and the social value of solving the problem, it was decided that increasing the yield of corn would be the problem selected in this case. A number of possible solutions could be suggested to resolve this problem. Irrigation, proper fertilization, improved seed, farm specialization in corn production, liming, and the use of insecticides were a few of the more apparent solutions.

Irrigation was rejected because of the physical characteristics of the area, the lack of any institution which could administer the irrigation project, and the high investment costs of installing irrigation. Likewise, farm specialization in corn was discounted, because it would run sharply counter to the traditional farm organization, force farm operators to incur substantial risks and uncertainties, and make poor utilization of the available family labor. Encouraging the application of lime was also rejected, because the requirements for supplementary educational material to show why lime was necessary would likely be beyond the capabilities of the change agent. Encouraging additional fertilizer application would require expanded use of credit, which is already in short supply. Furthermore, detailed agro-economic data was not available on how much fertilizer could profitably be used in this area. The introduction of the use of insecticides on corn was viewed favorably, since it would be very similar to the practice, already widespread, of spraying potatoes. It was thought, however, that a new improved corn variety[20] could be introduced more easily and could be expected to show a larger increase in production. Further considerations which led to the selection of a new corn variety as the means of solution were: (1) a new corn variety would be a logical step for farm operators to take after they have already successfully adopted new wheat and barley varieties; (2) a new corn variety would be compatible with established cultural patterns; (3) no major changes in established farming practices would be required for adoption; (4) relatively little damage would be done if the change did not succeed;[21] (5) the change could be reinforced and continued with relatively little effort on the part of the change agent; (6) the new change was easy to communicate by word of mouth, since it involved no complex ideas; and (7) as long as taste requirements were fulfilled, no family objections would be likely.[22]

METHOD OF CHANGE INTRODUCTION AND CONTINUANCE

After the problem has been carefully defined and one of the alternative solutions selected, the method of introducing the change must be chosen. This includes deciding which agent is to introduce the change, what unit is going to receive the stimulation, the timing of introduction, and finally, the technique with which the change is passed between the change agent and the unit to be stimulated. After these steps have been considered, it is necessary to give some attention to the ways the change can be reinforced and continued.

The study of Contadero revealed that there were only two agencies remotely capable of carrying out the introduction of the improved corn seed. One was the Church, through the local priest, and the other was the local agricultural development bank. For several reasons, already mentioned, neither agency was thought to be ideal for this purpose. But it appeared that both could be used to reinforce and continue the change, once it was introduced.

A number of possible techniques for introducing new corn seed in Contadero could be suggested. Among the more plausible were: (1) free distribution or sale of seed in the local plaza; (2) sale through the agricultural development bank or local merchants; (3) free distribution of some sample seed to local opinion leaders; and (4) some sort of random-sample distribution of free seed.

Each of these techniques of introduction could be accompanied and reinforced by various types of communication. Public announcements by the priest, for example, would be one way to inform people of what the change was. Public posters, notices in the Church paper, public meetings, written instruction, or word-of-mouth communication were all plausible alternatives.

In this particular case, it was decided that timing of the introduction would be especially critical. If the seed were introduced sometime after the traditional corn planting period of October and November, there was a substantial chance that the seed might be eaten, lose some of its germination power, or be destroyed by rodents before planting time. It was therefore decided that introducing the seed about one month before the planting time would be the best possible timing.

Finally, it was decided that an outside change agent should introduce the corn seed during the latter part of September to the 130 farmers who were interviewed in getting basic information for the study. About one pound of improved seed would be given to each producer. Verbal information at the time of distribution, an article in the Church paper, and an annoucement by the local priest were considered sufficient communication reinforcement. Lastly, sufficient time would be spent with the local priest and the head of the agriculture development bank so that they would understand the advantages of the improved seed over the native varieties. Furthermore, attempts would be made to encourage the development bank to start carrying the improved corn seed for the next planting.

A final step in the analysis would include returning to the area a year later to observe the results. This would involve rechecking the original strategy's effects against desired outcomes and evaluating why the program might not have turned out as expected.

SUMMARY AND CONCLUSIONS

The present paper has attempted to illustrate how researchers in less developed countries can construct strategies for economic and social changes at the local level. It was argued that this process cannot be carried out successfully until the role of the researcher is clearly understood. It is our contention that the role often includes not only data gathering and analysis, but also problem identification and concrete suggestions of methods for solving the problem, i.e., constructing a complete strategy of change. We further contend that this research is often interdisciplinary by nature and requires the analysis of a broad range of variables before the obstacles and facilities for change can be identified.

Although the data required to formulate a successful strategy of change will likely vary from place to place, it is hoped that the general approach herein outlined can serve as a guide for developing research programs in a number of different areas.

Notes

* The present study is based upon research conducted by the authors for the Land Tenure Center at The University of Wisconsin under a contract with the United States Agency for International Development. The views expressed herein are those of the authors and do not necessarily reflect those of the above-mentioned entities.

1. This is not surprising, since most research workers are foreigners, foreign-trained nationals with little local experience, or nationals who lack knowledge of conditions in the rural parts of their respective countries.

2. For a treatment of problems encountered in field work in developing countries, see A. Eugene Havens, "Methodological Problems Encountered in Sociological Survey Research in Colombia," *America Latina*, XIV (May 1964).

3. We are using "community" broadly, so that one "community" may contain several village centers. See T. Lynn Smith, "The Role of the Village in American Rural Society," *Rural Sociology*, V (1942): 10–21.

4. As a general rule, the more developed an area is, in terms of market economies, commercial farm production, transportation, education, and communications, the more limited is the use of the community as a focal point for this type of research.

5. Located in Colombia not far from the Ecuadorian border and the subject of one of a number of community studies conducted by the Land Tenure Center in Colombia during the past two years.

6. See Walter R. Goldschmidt, "The Interrelations between Cultural Factors and the Acquisitions of New Technical Skills," in Bert F. Hoselitz (ed.). *The Progress of Underdeveloped Areas*. Chicago: University of Chicago Press, 1952, 139.

7. The region in which Contadero is located was one of the few areas in Colombia which has not been wracked by violence since 1948.

8. See Bert F. Hoselitz, *Sociological Aspects of Economic Growth*. Glencoe, Illinois: Free Press, 1960, 46, for a discussion of what happens when traditional patterns of family organization break up.

9. This is why research teams should make the parish priest one of their first contacts, so that he can inform the local people of the purpose of the research activities.

10. See Ruth Anshen, *The Family: Its Function and Destiny*. New York: Harpers, 1959, 488–523.

11. A *municipio* resembles an organization somewhat between a township and a county in the United States.

12. In most respects, a *departamento* serves the same functions as a state in the United States.

13. In 1963, the *municipio's* annual budget amounted to a little over one dollar per capita.

14. Even though limestone is generally applied to soils to change the pH, most farm operators in Contadero thought it was applied to kill flies and other insects.

A Strategy of Change for Rural Communities 285

15. See Dale W. Adams *et al.*, *Public Law 480 and Colombia's Economic Development.* Medellin: Facultad de Agronomia, 1964, 179, for an example of similar farm tenure characteristics in another area not far from Contadero.

16. Given the structure and functioning of the community, which has been previously described, these selections were reached by elimination.

17. Essentially, what we are suggesting here is that, almost regardless of the promised pay-off, farmers will not gamble if a cash loss is involved which would encumber his land.

18. These goals may or may not be consistent, and they may be wholly or partially competitive or complementary.

19. In some cases, this may include assigning negative values to not solving the problems.

20. An improved variety rather than a hybrid was selected, because farmers were not accustomed to purchasing corn seed each year. Fortunately, in Colombia, a number of suitable corn varieties are available, through the joint research efforts of the Rockefeller Foundation and the Ministry of Agriculture.

21. That is to say, the change is divisible, so that small trials could be made. This would also help reduce the degree of uncertainty for the decision-taker.

22. Since the decision to grow corn in Contadero is basically to fulfill family needs, the taste requirement is extremely important. The corn must be suitable for eating on the cob while it is green and also provide a tasty flour.

17

RICHARD BECKHARD

Helping a Group With Planned Change: A Case Study

*t*his article reports an attempt by a consultant to assist a client system in an industrial setting to diagnose management communications and to plan systematically a change in relationships among the key executives, the department heads, and their different departments. The events to be described took place over a period of about a year, and indicate the trend toward a change which took place and is taking place in this particular management group.

THE CLIENT SYSTEM

The Vernon Company is a small company of about 200 employees. They manufacture chemical products which go into household cleaners. The president of the company has held his office for ten years. He believes strongly in the importance of effective human relations and in keeping up-to-date with modern management theory and practices. The vice-president of sales has been with the company for fifteen years and is largely responsible for its tremendous growth since World War II. Two other department heads make up the executive committee: a vice-president in charge of production, research, and engineering, and a controller.

Reporting to these four men are eleven department heads. With the exception of two regional sales managers, the entire group works together in a small headquarters office and members are in daily contact with each other. Because it is a small organization strong "family feeling" has developed. They have

Reprinted from the *Journal of Social Issues*, 15, No. 2 (1959): 13–19. Used with permission. ©1959 The Society for the Psychological Study of Social Issues.

developed a high degree of awareness of each other and of each other's way of work.

THE STATUS OF SOME OF THE RELATIONSHIPS PRIOR TO THE CHANGE EFFORT

Since the change goal was an improvement of various relationships in the work situation, it will be useful to look briefly at some relationships that existed at the beginning of the change effort.

The president and the sales vice-president, who are very different people with differing backgrounds, had tremendous difficulty in communicating with each other. There was considerable competition between the two men in executive meetings and a tendency to reject each other's ideas.

The vice-president of production and research had, when he moved into the position, made one of his subordinates director of the laboratory. This man, who is an excellent research man, proved to be an inadequate administrator. The laboratory was not producing new ideas, or new applications of existing products, fast enough to meet the sales department's needs and requirements.

The regional sales managers felt that the home office sales people were overdemanding in their requirements and lacked understanding of field problems. There was open conflict between one of these men and the vice-president of sales.

The following is illustrative of relationship problems that existed. As an outgrowth of a permissive management policy, each supervisor freely interpreted office procedures in a way he deemed functional to his department. For example, if one supervisor wanted to give his secretary an afternoon off because she had worked overtime the previous week, he had freedom to do this. Discipline was fairly lax in terms of morning arrival time. Coffee breaks were overextended. A few supervisors who were enforcing the policies literally were both frustrated and unhappy with the other supervisors who tended not to enforce them and were even more unhappy with a system which allowed this flexibility.

It should be remembered that the specific illustrations of difficulties did not reflect low morale or an inefficient operation. On the contrary, the management group was quite cohesive and highly committed to the organization's goals. This very cohesiveness caused what might be minor irritations in another setting to become items of high importance, since they were seen as threats to the cohesiveness of the group.

ASSUMPTIONS UNDERLYING THE CONSULTANT'S STRATEGY

Following is a more or less chronological account from the first contact by the client system to the point of replanning. Before describing the step by step process, it might be helpful to the reader to understand the assumptions which the consultant brought to the relationship.

The first assumption was that there are several developmental phases in a client-consultant relationship which more or less follow in sequence and are repeated. One way of thinking about the phases is that there are two parallel and simultaneous agenda on which the client and the client system must work: the work on the problem, and the work on the relationship.

A further set of assumptions underlying the change agent's strategy was that this type of change problem was essentially a learning problem and that for the persons involved in the client system to change in their behavior toward each other and for relationships therefore to improve, *it was essential that the individuals in the system learn some new diagnostic skills, some new behaviors and some better ways of getting information about the effects of their own behavior on other members of the system.* The aim of the consultant then was to help set up conditions which would optimize learning. These conditions would include establishing a training climate, interpersonal exposure, some personal feedback, and some opportunities for individuals to experiment with new behaviors.

A third assumption was that a *major function of the consultant was to help the client collect appropriate and correct information about feelings in the situation and then to help create a training or learning situation in which those concerned could, in a supportive climate, look at this information and work jointly on ways of dealing with it.*

STEP 1: INITIAL CONTACT BY CLIENT SYSTEM

The president of the organization knew the consultant from other affiliations and initiated the request for help. He saw the problem as one of improving communication between himself and the sales vice-president since both needed to find ways of listening to each other better and solving problems together with less emotionality. He also felt that the executive committee was overdependent on him and that it was not taking the initiative which he would like to see it take in acting as a leadership group. He had some questions about the effectiveness of a junior management board which he had set up and to which all of the members of the management group belonged, exclusive of the executive committee. This board acted in an advisory capacity to the executive group. It was seen by the president as a way of getting more participation from the junior executives and more feeling of involvement in the management of the company.

STEP 2: DEFINING THE PROBLEM AND ESTABLISHING THE RELATIONSHIP

The president felt that there was a need for some formal training of the management group on communications, improving meetings, and leadership skills. He felt initially that what was needed was some sort of training program, perhaps a series of monthly management conferences, or some weekend workshops for the top management group.

As the president discussed his problem, it became clear to the consultant that it was necessary to collect much additional data before planning any activity. The consultant team proposed a fact-finding step to ascertain how the various members of the client system saw the "work world" and where they saw difficulties in communication, relationships, and problem-solving. The president agreed to this fact-finding step. Members of the consulting team held individual interviews and collected attitude and perception data at four levels in the organization: the president, the vice-president, the department heads, and a sample of supervisors reporting to the department heads. These data were tabulated and classified into four categories: decision-making, authority, communications, and meetings.

After the data were put together in crude form, the consultant met with the president and "fed back" the information to him, using quotes from the interviews. The president then convened a meeting of his executive committee. The consultant fed back the same data to them without editorial comment. The president then held a discussion with his vice-presidents on the implications of the data. Subsequent meetings were held with all the department heads by area.

The consultant made no attempt to interpret the data except in terms of clarification and suggested no action at this time.

STEP 3: PLANNING FIRST ACTION STEP

After the data had been fed back to all concerned, the consultant met again with the president and the executive committee to re-diagnose the problem and to make specific plans for the first action step. It was decided to convene a three-day weekend meeting of the executive group and the junior management group at an isolated location removed from the work setting. At this time the data collected in the interviews would be fed back again in an organized form as the basis for setting up problems on which the group could work during the conference.

A meeting plan was developed using the data as a basis. Some appropriate theory was developed which, it was hoped, would help the client group to understand some of the reasons for concerns they expressed as well as pointing out to them some possible ways of dealing with them.

The general plan for the three-day conference included three types of activities: (1) presentations of organization behavior and communications theory; (2) problem-solving sessions dealing with relationship problems that existed within the group; and (3) demonstration-helping sessions in which the total group worked on some back-home operational problem.

To indicate how the plan actually worked, we will describe the activities of the first day.

The conference opened with a presentation of charts containing a summary of the material which the participants had produced. The consultant asked the group to analyze and discuss the meaning of the various items on the board. This discussion took most of the morning of the first day. At the end of the morning, one of the consultants presented a lecturette on some ways of looking at organizations. He included some organization behavior theory that would help the group to see the relationships among structure, functions, and roles.

In the afternoon, the consultants, who by then had created a fairly high degree of dependency on the part of the participants, changed roles and suggested that they would act as resources if needed but that the task for the afternoon was to identify some of the problems mentioned in the data and begin to work on them. The group accepted the task and very quickly identified one relationship problem that had been part of the original data: the problem of the director of research in his relationships with his laboratory people, the vice-president, the president, and the other departments. This provided a common "case" for the group.

For example, it became apparent that the vice-president of research and engineering had been over-protecting the research director, and was doing the same thing in the meeting. This behavior was called to the vice-president's attention by a number of members of the group who used the vice-president's presentation of the research director's problem as an illustration. This "feedback" came as quite a shock to the research vice-president but he was able to absorb it and use it in his subsequent behavior.

The three days were spent in a series of such problem-solving sessions interspersed with theory presentations. On the second evening, the entire group served as consultants on a particular program which the sales department was contemplating and one on which they wished help from other departments. This was a fairly dramatic session with the whole group bringing its resources to bear on a corporate problem which directly affected only one department but which had consequences for all of them.

One assumption underlying the conference design was that unless whatever learnings came out during the conference could be made consciously transferable to the back-home situation, the group would not be getting maximum value from the conference. Accordingly, the third morning was spent meeting in vertical "family groups."

In the latter half of the morning, the groups came together and reported those items on which they wanted help from other departments. The group then discussed further steps in the development of its own working together. Several action steps were taken. (1) Each area planned to have weekly staff meetings of its whole group for the next few months. (2) It was agreed that four to six months later there should be another quick sampling of how things were going through a series of group interviews, and a brief conference with the total group. (3) It was felt that for a period of a couple of years the group should meet as a total group at least once a year and perhaps twice. (4) The junior management group was to study its own functions and report back in the Fall.

STEP 4: ASSESSMENT OF EFFECTS

It had been agreed that there would be no further contact between the client system and the consultant until people had had a chance to apply some of the findings of the conference to their work settings. The consultant team did predict, on the basis of the conference itself, that some of the following relationship changes might be observable.

Helping a Group With Planned Change

(1.) The president and the sales vice-president, who had had considerable interaction during the meeting and who had given each other quite a bit of feedback, might be able to listen a little more effectively to each other.
(2.) The overcontrolling behavior of the vice-president of production and research might be eased.
(3.) A somewhat more realistic self-image might be developed on the part of the junior management group.
(4.) Communications between heads of areas and the people reporting to them might be improved.

It was agreed that these predictions would be checked with subsequent data.

STEP 5: REPLANNING AND REESTABLISHING THE RELATIONSHIP

Approximately four months after the first conference the client group again contacted the consultant team and said that they were ready to explore next steps. A number of changes had been noticed in terms of relationships. Some specific problems of the first conference had been dealt with to everyone's satisfaction. Some problems, particularly the relationship between junior and senior management, showed little change. People were ready to review their progress and see "where we go from here."

The consultant felt that it would again be desirable to collect information on perceptions and feelings from various parts of the system and that it would also be important to have the maximum amount of participation on the part of the members of the management group in the further planning of their work toward this general change and improvement. He therefore arranged a two-day meeting in which he met with the total training group in two subgroups for a group interview. In addition he held individual interviews with a number of the key people.

At these two meetings, the groups identified those items on which some progress had been made and also identified the key concerns which had emerged during the intervening few months.

The following day, the total group met with the consultant. The consultant put in agenda form the various issues which had been identified the previous day in the interview groups. The group tackled the problems, taking some action where action was indicated. Some of the specific actions of that day were:

(1.) Revising of the job descriptions for the junior group, redefining their responsibilities and the boundaries of their authority.
(2.) Setting up a study of the wage and salary program.
(3.) Establishing new communications procedures between the junior and senior management group.
(4.) Deciding to meet as a total group every three months without a consultant for a one-day management conference.
(5.) Planning to have a consultant meet periodically with the executive committee

and be available during those visits to meet with any individual of the total group who wished to talk with him.

The reader will note here a marked change in the relationship between the client system and the consultant. The client is moving toward a more independent status. He recognizes the consultant's possible contribution but wishes to be able to move forward without this help wherever he can. At the same time he does not want to cut off the help.

There were several rather marked differences in the tone and activities between this conference and the first one. The reader will note that in the first conference the general theme was diagnosing the relationships between the parts of the system and trying to find some way of giving and accepting feedback. The giving and accepting of feedback had been developed as a group standard. The theme of the second conference was learning to solve problems better. Out of this second meeting came joint planning and establishment of procedures for implementing the planning. Now the group could be more self-determining. It selected its own procedural development with the three monthly conferences. It identified the need for maintaining the group as a group. And it also defined a different role for the consultant.

SUMMARY

A few comments relative to the assumptions made prior to consultation in this particular case may be useful in thinking about the consulting process.

(1.) It is necessary to establish a relationship with the several parts of the system before any effective problem-solving can be started.
(2.) It is important to establish a climate and procedures for feed-back both between the helper and the client system and among the parts of the client system if effective change is to take place.
(3.) The consultant must continuously assess the readiness and the capacity of the client system to change.
(4.) Because a change situation of this kind is primarily a learning situation, it is incumbent on the consultant to create a series of conditions in which the client system can learn.
(5.) The consultant must be critical of his own motivations in terms of types of material presented or help offered. He must be sure that the material is designed to meet both perceived and real client needs, not only the consultant's perception of client needs.
(6.) The consultant should be aware at all times that in a healthy change relationship the client should always be able to reject the ideas, the help, and the relationship.
(7.) It is desirable to create conditions where the consultants can withdraw, at least temporarily, so that the group can become independent and can grow.
(8.) It is equally important after an initial change effort that some procedural planning be done for reestablishing the relationship, evaluating the interim action, and evaluating the consultant's role.

(9.) It is desirable for the consultant to be prepared to accept and help develop new role relationships as the client system gets stronger so that it can move from a dependent relationship to a more independent and finally an interdependent state.

18

FLOYD C. MANN*

Studying and Creating Change: A Means to Understanding Social Organization

Social organizations are functioning entities with interdependent structures and processes. They are not fixed, static structures, but rather continuously moving patterns of relationships in a much larger field of social activity. To understand what their essential elements and dimensions are, what it is that gives an organization its unity, it is necessary to study and create social change within organizational settings.

Relatively little is known about organizational change. Social scientists stress the study of the dynamic in social systems, but few[1] accept the risks involved to gain the knowledge and skills needed to create and measure changes in functioning organizations. This is not surprising, for research within large-scale organizations is at such an early stage that the social scientist knows little about how (1) to gain access to these research sites; (2) to initiate and sustain organizational change; and (3) to measure such changes. We have only begun the systematic codification of the working knowledge and skills necessary for the researcher to get into, and maintain himself within, the social science laboratories of functioning organizations.[2] Systematic, quantitative measurement of change processes in complex organizational settings is in its infancy. Longitudinal studies are rare—social scientists seldom attempt to obtain more than a single "before" and "after" measurement and are often content to try and decipher findings from *ex post facto* study designs. The actual steps and skills necessary to initiate and sustain changes within an organization are not only relatively unknown, but there is even some suspicion that knowledge of social action and an ability to engineer change are not appropriate for the social scientist.

Reprinted from *Research in Industrial Human Relations*, Industrial Research Association, Publication No. 17 (1957). Used with permission.

While social scientists are not spending any sizable proportion of their time in learning how to change interpersonal and intergroup relations in functioning organizations, a wide variety of practitioners are. These include at the one extreme the consultants or the "operators" who take over organizations which are failing and rebuild them, and at the other extreme, the "human relations" trainers. Most of these men know very little theoretically about processes of organizational, attitudinal, and behavioral change, but they do know a great deal intuitively about the problems of changing people in an organization. This is especially true of the training men.

This suggests that there should and can be a closer working relationship between those concerned with actually *changing* organizational structure and processes and those researchers concerned with *understanding* organizational change. Social scientists have not begun to take advantage of their opportunities for learning about organizations from those in the "practicing professions"—those who are *doing*.[3] Observations and systematic measurements around the practitioner's efforts to alter systems of relationships in organizations can provide the researcher with valuable insights into the dynamics of organization. Gaps in knowledge become excruciatingly apparent; new sources of data and problems for research emerge. In turn, social scientists can contribute to practitioners by helping them assess what effect their actions as change agents have. Most practitioners—and especially those trainers who are concerned with changing the human relations skills of supervisors—have very little systematic, and no quantitative, evidence on the success of their efforts to create changes in individuals or organizations. It seems clear that there is a broad basis for cooperation here. Systematic studies of the work of those attempting to change the way things are done in an organization may contribute to our understanding of social organizations. And developments in measurement and the procedures used by researchers to understand organizations better may contribute to the working knowledge of trainers and others in the "practicing professions."

In this chapter we will focus on the description and evaluation of several different types of procedures designed to change interpersonal and intergroup relations in complex organizations. We will first look at two human relations training programs whose effects have been systematically and quantitatively studied. Then we will describe briefly the development and evaluation of a change procedure with which we are experimenting to increase the understanding, acceptance, and utilization of survey research findings. At the close of the chapter these two specific types of procedures for creating change in organizational settings are contrasted as a first step in identifying facets of change processes which merit greater experimentation and in providing insights into the structure and functioning of organizations.

CHANGING INTERPERSONAL RELATIONS THROUGH TRAINING SUPERVISORS

Recurrent opportunities for social scientists to study a change process within an organizational setting are provided by human relations training programs for supervisors. As change procedures, these programs are formal, rational, purposeful efforts to alter institutional behavior. In contrast to the day-to-day attempts of management to bring about change, they are bounded in time and organizational space, and are thus easily studied intensively.

Management by the late forties began to be convinced that training might be useful for their supervisors, and there has since been a wholesale adoption of human relations training programs. While there was and still is a remarkable range in the content, methods, and settings of these programs, nearly all of them have centered around improving supervisory skills in dealing with people—either as individuals or in face-to-face groups. They are freqeuntly directed at teaching the supervisor how to work with an employee as an individual, occasionally at working with employees as members of a small group, but only rarely at understanding and working within the complex social system of the large corporation or factory. Another way of saying this is that the courses have drawn heavily from psychology, to a lesser extent from social psychology, and usually not at all from sociology.

There are no commonly agreed-upon ways by which these programs can be described. The following headings are, however, useful: objectives, content, methods, setting, training leader, and training unit. For example, the objectives of these programs are usually very general and quite ambitious: "to assist supervisors in developing the skills, knowledge, and attitudes needed to carry out their supervisory responsibilities," or "to improve morale, increase production, and reduce turnover." Their contents usually include human nature, personality, motivation, attitudes, and leadership, and other information about relevant psychological principles and research findings may also be included. More often than not the methods of training are some variant of the "lecture-discussion method." The settings are frequently in a classroom away from the job. The trainers are generally staff men whom the trainee did not know before the training; the trainees, first-line supervisors or foremen meeting with other suprvisors from other parts of the organization.

Few systematic, quantitative studies have been made to investigate the effectiveness of these programs.[4] This is not to say that there has been no interest in evaluation. Any review of the literature will indicate many such attempts and many testimonials about the relative advantages of different procedures of training. Mahler and Monroe[5] reported a number of "evaluative studies" after reviewing the literature and conducting a survey of 150 companies known to have training programs. While these studies almost without fail acclaim the many benefits of such training, few of them meet more than a fraction of the requirements necessary for a rigorous test of the basic underlying assumptions.

What are these assumptions? In general, they are that training supervisors in human relations will result in changes in the supervisors' attitudes and philosophy, that these changes will be reflected in their behavior toward employees on the job, that this changed behavior will be seen by the employees, and that they will in turn become more satisfied with their work situation, then more highly motivated, and, ultimately, more productive workers.

While there is a good deal of evidence that human relations training programs do meet part of these assumptions—for example, they do appear to change the verbal veneer of supervisors—there are few scientifically rigorous, quantitative studies which have demonstrated that these changes in what supervisors *know* affect their attitudes and behavior as seen or experienced by their subordinates. Few studies show that human relations training of supervisors is related to changes in the attitudes or productivity of employees under those supervisors.

It is not possible to make a complete review of these studies here. A review of the findings from several recent, major evaluative studies will, however, provide a good deal of evidence concerning the effectiveness of certain types of training programs. The findings will certainly emphasize the need for more systematic, quantitative research to assess the most effective combinations of content, methods, settings, training units, and trainers.

THE CANTER–TYLER STUDIES

In 1949, Canter[6] developed a human relations training course for first-line supervisors in the home offices of a large insurance company. The three objectives of the course were: (1) "to establish facts and principles concerning psychological aspects of behavior and group functioning to enable supervisors to become more competent in their knowledge and understanding of human behavior; (2) to increase supervisors' capacities for observing human behavior; and (3) to present personality adjustment concepts to aid in integration of achievements made in the first two objectives." This training was designed to provide a foundation of information on which to build later through additional practice and "technique" training. Specific content was primarily psychological: human nature, personality, motivation, attitudes, leadership, and group structure. Method was lecture-discussion. The training occurred in the conference rooms of the company; Canter himself was the trainer. The trainees were eighteen supervisors whose superiors had participated in a preliminary run for executives. The course was presented in ten two-hour weekly sessions.

To determine the influence of this training, Canter employed a battery of paper-and-pencil questionnaires and tests which were given before and after training to two groups of supervisors: an experimental group of eighteen from one department who received the training, and a control group of eighteen from two other departments who did not receive training. The two groups were similar in type of work performed, age (about thirty), education (thirteen years), and proportion of men and women. While the control group had more years of service with the company (7.5 and 4.6, respectively) and higher mean scores on a mental alertness test, the statistical technique used in the final analysis did not require prematched individuals or groups.

Six tests, yielding a total of twelve separate scores, were used: (1) General Psychological Facts and Principles; (2) "How Supervise"; (3) General Logical

Reasoning: (4) Social Judgment Test; (5) Supervisory Questionnaire; and (6) Test for Ability to Estimate Group Opinion. The major findings were that the trained supervisors obtained mean scores on all tests better than would have been predicted on the basis of the performance of the untrained group alone. For five out of the twelve measures, the differences were statistically significant at the five percent level; for two other measures, differences were significant at the ten percent level. Other important conclusions were that trained supervisors became more similar in abilities measured by the tests and more accurate in estimating the opinions of employees in their departments, but not their sections. It was also found that those holding highest scores initially gained the most on all measures except the Test of Ability to Estimate Group Opinion, where the opposite result was obtained.

While Canter assumed in his design that cognitive training—that is, an ability to understand human relations concepts and principles—would have to precede any behavioral training in supervisory skills, practices, and attitudes, Tyler[7] designed a companion study to measure any changes in employee morale which might be attributed to this training. Her morale surveys indicated improvement in employee morale scores for *both* the experimental and control departments. Morale improved by an average of 11 points per section (range 2-25 points) in five of seven sections in the experimental group, and decreased slightly in two others. "In the control groups, morale increased in eight of the nine sections by an average of 14 points (range 5-32 points). The decrease in the other section was seven points. The only category which showed a somewhat consistent change among sections was 'supervision' on which scores for over half of the sections decreased." After warning the reader of the possible effect of the before-test experience, she notes: "Undoubtedly, the difference in change in morale between the control and the experimental groups is not large enough to be significant" (page 47). Canter, however, points out that in Tyler's study "morale was quite high initially, which might account for the lack of any improvement in the experimental department over the control."

The strength of the Canter–Tyler studies is that they used both *before* and *after* measures for experimental and control groups. Canter's use of multiple criteria against which to evaluate the various sub-goals of the training program is also noteworthy. The use of Tyler's perceptual and employee morale measures in conjunction with Canter's attitudinal and cognitive measures permits an evaluation of the course's effectiveness at two levels: the supervisors' intent, and his on-the-job performance. The findings from this combination of studies make it obvious that classroom learning does not guarantee the translation of such learning into job performance. It should be remembered, however, that Canter did not set out to change supervisors' skills and practices, but only their understanding of human relations concepts and ideas.

FLEISHMAN–HARRIS STUDIES

Working with the education and training staff of a large company manufacturing trucks and farm machinery, Fleishman[8] developed a study design and a battery of research instruments for measuring the continuing effectiveness of leadership training. The general objectives of this training[9] were to change understanding, attitudes, habits, and skills of foremen by giving them solid foundation in four basic areas of industrial knowledge. These areas were personal development, human relations, economics, and company operations. The method was primarily lecture-discussion. The training staff included full-time instructors, former supervisors, and part-time university faculty. The training was given to foremen who were taken from a wide variety of operations and plants and sent to a central school in Chicago for two weeks of eight-hours-a-day intensive development.

To determine the effects of this course on foremen from one motor-truck plant who had taken this training, Fleishman employed an *ex post facto* design with four groups of about thirty each. One group had not received the training; the other three had, 2-10, 11-19, and 20-29 months earlier. The groups were alike on a number of background characteristics: age (early forties), education (eleven years), length of service (sixteen years), supervisory experience (seven years), size of work group (about twenty-eight), and supervisory experience with present work group (six years). Seven paper-and-pencil questionnaires were used to obtain opinion, expectation, and perceptual data about leadership practices from the trainees, their superiors, and their subordinates. This battery gave Fleishman an opportunity to investigate the differences between supervisory beliefs as reported by the foreman himself and supervisory practices as reported by his employees, and to explore the interaction of training effects with the supervisor's "leadership climate." Each questionnaire contained two independent leadership dimensions which had been identified by factor analysis: "consideration"—the extent to which the supervisor was considerate of the feelings of employees; and "initiating structure"—the extent to which the supervisor defined or facilitated group interactions toward goal attainment.

The results obtained by giving attitude questionnaires to foremen on the first and last days of their training in Chicago provide evidence of how the topics stressed in this leadership training affected these two dimensions. The results obtained from these before and after measures showed a significant increase in "consideration" (.05 level) and an even more marked decrease in "initiating structure" (.01 level). The on-the-job effects of the training, however, appeared to be "minimal." "The training did not produce any kind of permanent change in either the attitudes or behavior of the trained foremen." The employees under the most recently trained foremen actually saw them as *less* considerate than the employees under the untrained foremen saw their superiors. This statistically significant finding was supported by other trends toward more structuring and less consideration by those foremen who had the training. Thus, while the human relations approach was stressed in the course and understood at least well enough to be registered as an opinion change on a paper-and-pencil questionnaire, it was not evident in what trained foremen said they did, or what their employees saw them doing in the actual work situation.

The most important variable found to affect leadership was the climate within which the foreman worked. In fact, the kind of superior under whom the foreman operated seemed "more related to the attitudes and behavior of the foremen in the plant than did the fact that they had or had not received the leadership training."

These results, showing that the training was not meeting its objective of making foremen more human-relations oriented in the plant, left two alternatives open: redesign the course, or initiate an intensive criterion study relating supervisory behavior to group effectiveness. The latter alternative was chosen, and Harris[10] designed a study in the same plant to investigate: (1) the relationship between these two dimensions of leadership behavior and various measures of work efficiency; and (2) the effects of a training course planned as a brief refresher for the central school training in Chicago. It is the findings from this second objective in which we are primarily interested here.

The course, lasting one week, was given at a small nearby college. The effects were evaluated by field experimental design with before and after measures for experimental and control groups. Two groups of thirty-one foremen were established through matching on a number of variables, including length of time since attending the central school (almost three years), scores on before measures (including leadership climate), and other personal factors. One group was given the training. Questionnaires, similar to Fleishman's, were used to obtain information from employees and foremen about the foremen's attitudes and behavior.

Harris used several different methods of analyzing his findings. His most rigorous method indicated there were no statistically significant differences in the foremen's own leadership attitudes or the workers' descriptions of their foremen's behavior—before and after this additional refresher course. The only significant difference he found was a decrease in the degree to which the foremen in the *control* group showed structuring in their leadership behavior as described by their employees. Building on Fleishman's gradual decreases in structuring and increases in consideration the longer the foreman is back on the job, Harris suggests this finding might be interpreted to mean that the refresher course may have "tended to retard a general decrease in structuring."

Harris and Fleishman[11] in analyzing the data from both of their studies in the same plant have uncovered one finding which tends to qualify the general, completely negative conclusion of their findings regarding the effectiveness of this training. This finding concerns the stability of leadership patterns of individual foremen who did not have the training in contrast to those foremen who had the training. They find there is *less* stability in the pre-post measures for the foremen who had the training than for those foremen who did not have training. This suggests that the course had markedly different effects on different foremen, and that "large individual shifts in scores occur in both directions." They conclude that their research findings show no significant changes in *group* means among trained foremen and that future research should be directed toward investigating personal and situational variables which interact with the effects of training.

At best, these two studies suggest that this type of training had little or no general effect on the behavior of foremen in the plant. At worst, they suggest that the unanticipated consequences of separating foremen from their work groups and making them keenly aware of their role in management more than offset the anticipated consequences of making the foremen more considerate of employees as human beings. Fleishman's finding that *leadership climate* appeared to be a better predictor than *training* of foremen's plant attitudes and behavior underscores the importance of considering the constellation of expectation patterns in which the trainee is embedded. Training which does not take the trainee's regular social environment into account will probably have little chance of modifying behaviour. It may very well be that human relations training—as a procedure for initiating social change—is most successful when it is designed to *remold the whole system of role relationships of the supervisor*.[12]

The findings from these four studies suggest that trainers, researchers, and others interested in social change need to rethink what forces are necessary to create and sustain changes in the orientation and behaviors of people in complex systems of relationships. There is a good deal of evidence that management and trainees are enthusiastic about these training courses in general. Management's enthusiasm may be an index of whether the training will continue, but it does not indicate whether training is achieving changes in behavior. And while trainee satisfaction and acceptance may be important as an antecedent to learning, these factors do not indicate whether the training will produce attitudinal and, more significantly, on-the-job behavioral changes.

It should be stressed that the criterion which has been used here for measuring the effects of human relations training is not easily met. There is ample quantitative evidence in the preceding studies that supervisors' information about, and verbal understanding of, human relations principles can be increased. There is much less evidence that these courses have an effect on the trainee's on-the-job behavior as seen by those working under him. And the hard fact remains that there are no quantitative studies which indicate that these courses in leadership affect workers' job satisfactions or motivations.

FEEDBACK: CHANGING PATTERNS OF RELATIONSHIPS BETWEEN SUPERIORS AND SUBORDINATES BY USING SURVEY FINDINGS

Long-range interest in the actual varying of significant variables in organizations has necessitated that members of the Human Relations Program of the Institute for Social Research, University of Michigan, not only study existing programs for training and changing people in organizations, but that we *develop* new techniques for changing relationships, and that we learn how to *measure* the effects of such changes within organizations. As a result, we have invested a good deal of professional effort in exploring the effectiveness of different procedures for changing attitudes, perceptions, and relationships among individuals in complex hierarchies without changing the personnel of the units. The latter is an important qualification, for we have found that the changes in subordinates' perceptions and attitudes which follow a change in supervisory personnel are frequently of a much larger order than those generated by training or other procedures for changing the attitudes or behavior of incumbents.

EXPLORATORY AND DEVELOPMENTAL PHASE

One procedure which we developed and subsequently found to be effective in changing perceptions and relationships within organizations has been called "feedback." This change process evolved over a period of years as we[13] tried to learn how to report findings from human relations research into organizations so that they would be understood and used in day-to-day operations. Work began on this process in 1948 following a company-wide study of employee and management attitudes and opinions. Over a period of two years, three different sets of data were fed back: (1) information on the attitudes and perceptions of 8000 nonsupervisory employees toward their work, promotion opportunities, supervision, fellow employees, etc.; (2) first- and second-line supervisor's feelings about the various aspects of their jobs and supervisory beliefs; and (3) information from intermediate and top levels of management about their supervisory philosophies, roles in policy formation, problems of organizational integration, etc. We had, several aims in this exploratory phase: (1) to develop through first-hand experience an understanding of the problems of producing change; (2) to improve relationships; (3) to identify factors which affected the extent of the change; and (4) to develop working hypotheses for later, more directed research.

The process which finally appeared to maximize the acceptance and utilization of survey and research findings can be described structurally as an interlocking chain of conferences. It began with a report of the major findings of the survey to the president and his senior officers, and then progressed slowly down through the hierarchical levels along functional lines to where supervisors and their employees were discussing the data. These meetings were structured in terms of organizational "families"[14] or units—each superior and his immediate subordinates considering the survey data together. The data presented to each group were those pertaining to their own group or for those subunits for which members of the organizational unit were responsible.

Members of each group were asked to help interpret the data and then decide what further analyses of the data should be made to aid them in formulating plans for constructive administrative actions. They also planned the introduction of the findings to the next level. The meetings were typically led by the line officer responsible for the coordination of the subunits at a particular level. Usually, a member of the Survey Research Center and the company's personnel staff assisted the line officer in preparing for these meetings, but attended the meetings only as resource people who could be called upon for information about the feasibility of additional analyses.

These meetings took place in the office of the line supervisor whose organizational unit was meeting, or in the department's own small conference room. All of the survey findings relative to each group were given to the leader and the members of his organizational unit; they decided what to consider first, how fast to work through each topic, and when they had gone as far as they could and needed to involve the next echelon in the process.

This feedback change procedure was developed in an organization where a great amount of effort had already been invested in the training of management and supervisors. During the war the company had participated in the various J-programs sponsored by the War Manpower Commission, and more important, during the several years we were experimentally developing the feedback process, Dr. Norman R. F. Maier was working with all levels of management to improve their understanding of human relations and supervision.[15] The supervisors with whom we were working to increase their understanding of their own organizational units therefore had a great deal of training in the application of psychological principles to management.

Our observations of the feedback procedure as it developed suggested that it was a powerful process for creating and supporting changes within an organization.[16] However, there was no quantitative proof of this, for our work up to this point had been exploratory and developmental.

A FIELD EXPERIMENT IN ACCOUNTING DEPARTMENTS

In 1950, when eight accounting departments in this same company asked for a second attitude and opinion survey of their seventy-eight supervisors and eight hundred employees, we[17] had an opportunity to initiate the steps necessary to measure the effects of this organizational change process. The questionnaires used in this resurvey were similar to those used in 1948 and provided the basis for a new cycle of feedback conferences. The general plan for the handling of these new resurvey data was to let everyone in the departments—employees and department heads—see the over-all findings for eight accounting departments combined as soon as they were available, and then to work intensively on their use in *some* departments, but not in others until there had been a third survey.

While our objective was to test the effectiveness of the basic pattern of feedback developed during the preceding two years, we encouraged department heads and their supervisors to develop their own variations for reporting data to their units and maximizing their use in the solution of problems. After the all-department meetings had been concluded, the chief executive of the accounting departments held a meeting with each department head in the experimental group. At this meeting, the findings for the department head's unit were thoroughly reviewed. The findings included comparisons of (1) changes in employee attitudes from 1948 to 1950, (2) attitudes in that department with those in all other departments combined, and (3) employees' perceptions of supervisory behavior with supervisory statements about their behavior. Department heads were encouraged to go ahead with feedback meetings as soon as they felt ready, tentative next steps were discussed, and assistance from the researchers and the company personnel staffs was assured. Four departments launched feedback activities which were similar to each other in purpose but somewhat different in method. The programs varied in duration (13–33 weeks), in intensity (9–65 meetings), and in the extent to which nonsupervisory employees were involved in the process. During the eighteen months that these differences were unfolding, nothing was done in two of the remaining four departments after the first all-departments meetings. This was done so they might be available as "controls." Changes in key personnel eliminated the remaining two departments from any experimental design.

A third survey of attitudes was conducted in these departments in 1952 after the natural variations in the feedback programs had run their courses. In 1950 and 1952 surveys were then used as "before" and "after" measurements, the four departmental programs as "experimental variations," with the two inactive departments as "controls."

Our findings indicate that more significant positive changes occurred in employee attitudes and perceptions in the four experimental departments than in the two control departments. This was based on two measures of change: (1) a comparison of answers to sixty-one identical questions which were asked in 1950 and 1952, and (2) of a comparison of answers to seventeen "perceived change" questions in which employees had an opportunity to indicate what types of changes had occurred since the 1950 survey. In the experimental group, a fourth of the sixty-one items showed relative mean positive changes, significant at the .05 level or better; the change for another 57 per cent of the items was also positive in direction, but not statistically significant. Major positive changes occurred in the experimental groups in how employees felt about (1) the kind of work they do (job interest, importance, and level of responsibility); (2) their supervisor (his ability to handle people, give recognition, direct their work, and represent them in handling complaints); (3) their progress in the company; and (4) their group's ability to get the job done. The seventeen perceived-change items were designed specifically to measure changes in the areas where we expected the greatest shift in perceptions. Fifteen of these showed that a significantly higher proportion of employees in the experimental than in the control departments felt that change had occurred. More employees in the experimental departments saw changes in (1) how well the supervisors in their department got along together; (2) how often their supervisors held meetings; (3) how effective these meetings were; (4) how much their supervisor understood the way employees looked at and felt about things, etc. These indicate the extent to which the feedback's effectiveness lay in increasing understanding and communication as well as changing supervisory behavior.

Comparisons of the changes among the four experimental departments showed that the three departments which had the two feedback sessions with their employees all showed positive change relative to the control departments. The change which occurred in the fourth was directionally positive, but it was not significantly different from the control departments. In general, the greatest change occurred where the survey results were discussed in both the departmental organizational units *and* the first-line organizational units. The greater the involvement of all members of the organization through their organizational families—the department heads, the first-line supervisors, *and* the employees—the greater the change.

IMPLICATIONS OF THESE FINDINGS

The basic elements of this feedback process described above are not new. They involve (1) the orderly collection of information about the functioning of a system, and (2) the reporting of this information into the system for (3) its use in making further adjustments.

Work by Hall[18] and others who have had considerable practical experience with the use of information about a system for creating change show a similarity in both action steps and basic approach. This suggests there are certain psychological and sociological facts which must be taken into consideration in attempting to change the attitudes and behavior of an *individual* or a *group of individuals* in an *organizational setting*.

(1.) Attitudes and behavior of an individual are functions of both basic personality and social role. *Change processes need to be concerned with altering both the forces within an individual and the forces in the organizational situation surrounding the individual.*

(2.) Organizations, as systems of hierarchically ordered, interlocking roles with rights and privileges, reciprocal expectations, and shared frames of reference, contain tremendous forces for stability or change in the behavior of individuals or subgroups. Change processes need to be designed to harness these forces for creating and supporting change. *As forces already in existence, they must first be made pliable, then altered or shifted, and finally made stable again to support the change.*

(3.) Essentially, unilateral power and authority structures underlie the hierarchical ordering of organizational roles. *Expectations of the superior are therefore more important forces for creating change in an individual than the expectations of his subordinates.* Also, those with a direct authority relationship—line superiors—have more influence than those without direct authority—staff trainers.

(4.) The attitudes, beliefs, and values of an individual are more firmly grounded in the groups which have continuing psychological meaning to him than in those where he has only temporary membership. The supervisor's role of interlocking the activities of two organizational units requires that he have continuing membership in two groups: (a) the organizational unit directed by his superior in which he is a subordinate along with this immediate peers; and (b) the organizational unit for which he is responsible. *Change processes designed to work with individual supervisors off the job in temporarily created training groups contain less force for initiating and reinforcing change than those which work with an individual in situ.*

(5.) Information about the functioning of a system may introduce a need for change. This is especially true when the new data are seen as objective and at variance with common perceptions and expectations. Change processes organized around objective, new social facts about one's own organizational situation have more force for change than those organized around general principles about human behavior. *The more meaningful and relevant the material, the greater the likelihood of change.*

(6.) Involvement and participation in the planning, collection, analysis, and interpretation of information initiate powerful forces for change. Own facts are better understood, more emotionally acceptable, and more likely to be utilized than those of some "outside expert." *Participation in analysis and interpretation helps by-pass those resistances which arise from proceeding too rapidly or too slowly.*

(7.) Objective information on direction and magnitude of change—knowledge of results—facilitates further improvement. *Change processes which furnish adequate knowledge on progress and specify criteria against which to measure improvement are apt to be more successful in creating and maintaining change than those which do not.*

COMPARISON OF "CLASSROOM" HUMAN RELATIONS TRAINING AND ORGANIZATIONAL FEEDBACK

This is only a partial listing of the points with which a scientifically based technology of social change in organizational settings will have to be concerned. Our conceptualization and the identification of the relevant individual and organizational variables and their interrelationship is at a primitive stage. The systematic quantitative investigation of the effectiveness of different change procedures has scarcely begun. Even at this early date, however, a comparison between the structure and process of feedback and "classroom" human relations training as two different types of change procedures may be a useful exercise. It may help identify variables or facets of change processes which merit greater experimentation and investigation both by the practitioners and by those researchers interested in organizational change. By a "classroom" human relations program we mean a training which would consist of a series of classroom-like meetings in which supervisors from many different points of the organization meet to listen to a presentation of psychological principles which a trainer from the personnel department thinks they ought to know about and be ready to use on the job after a brief discussion following the training. This kind of training experience differs from the feedback process in a number of respects. These differences are stated to keep the comparisons reasonably brief and to sharpen the contrasts.

(1.) What are the objectives?

"Classroom" Training—Improve supervisor-subordinate relations through changing the supervisors' understanding of human behavior, attitudes, and skills.

Organizational Feedback—Improve organizational functioning through changing understanding, attitudes, and behavior among all members of the organization.

(2.) What is the setting in which change is being attempted?

"Classroom" Training—Trainees are taken off the job and out of the network of interpersonal relationships in which they normally function for training in an "encapsulated"[19] classroom-like situation.

Organizational Feedback—Change is attempted as a regular part of the day's work in established organizational relationships.

(3.) What is the informational content?

"Classroom" Training—General psychological principles of human behavior, case materials, or data from outside the training group and often the organization, only occasionally using problems from the group's own experience.

Organizational Feedback—Objective quantitative information about attitudes, beliefs, and expectations of the trainees themselves, or the subordinates in their own organization.

(4.) What is the method?

"Classroom" Training—Lectures, presentations, films, skits, and occasionally role-playing followed by discussion on how to apply what has been learned back on the job.

Organizational Feedback—The progressive introduction of new information about the problems within the groups for which the trainees are responsible. Group discussions of the meaning and action implications of the findings, followed by group decisions on next steps for changing or handling the situation.

(5.) Who are the trainees?

"Classroom" Training—First-line supervisors and foremen whose superiors may have, but more often have not, had the course.

Organizational Feedback—Everyone in the organization from the top down[20]—the president, top management, intermediate and first-line supervision, *and* employees.

(6.) What is the training unit?

"Classroom" Training—An aggregate or collection of individual supervisors from different departments throughout the organization. A functional conglomerate without continuing psychological meaning for the individuals. Frequently seen as a "group" simply because the individuals are in close spatial proximity to one another.

Organizational Feedback—An organizational unit whose members have an organizational function to perform and whose members (a superior and his immediate subordinates) have continuing psychological meaning perceptually and behaviorally to one another as a team or family.

(7.) Who is the change agent?

"Classroom" Training—An outsider—an expert, a staff man—who has no direct, continuing authority or power over the trainee and few recurrent opportunities to reinforce the training.

Organizational Feedback—The organizational unit's line supervisor, who is given some help through pre- and post-meeting coaching by the expert outsider.

(8.) How is the pace or rate of change set?

"Classroom" Training—The trainer sets the pace, attempting to gear the training to average trainee's ability to comprehend and assimilate the material.

Organizational Feedback—The members of the group move from one topic to another as they are ready for the next step.

(9.) How long does the change process continue?

"Classroom" Training—A fixed number of days or weeks, seldom less than 16 or more than 80 hours.

Organizational Feedback—No fixed length of time, the change procedure usually continues over a period of months—6 to 24 months.

(10.) How much tension is there?

"Classroom" Training—Usually relatively little, most trainees feel they already know a good deal about human behavior and how others feel.

Organizational Feedback—Frequently considerable, as objective information and particularly the differences between supervisory beliefs and practices come into a focus so sharp that complacency is shattered and the security about what is social reality is shaken.

(11.) What assumptions are made about attitudes and how they are changed?[21]

"*Classroom*" *Training*—The primary assumption is that the trainee does not know certain facts, that his previous organization of relevant information will be altered when he understands the new facts. Attitudes are seen as a function of the range of information available to the trainee; they are changed by altering cognitive structure.

Organizational Feedback—Here the assumptions are that the trainee already has satisfying ways of seeing things and relating to others, that attitudes and behavior can be changed only by altering their motivational bases. Norms of psychologically relevant groups are seen as more important determinants of attitudes than cognitive processes. (12.) How is effectiveness of the change measured?

"*Classroom*" *Training*—Usually by informal comments of trainees, occasionally by interviews or questionnaires with the trainees after the training.

Organizational Feedback—By changes in employees' perception of their supervisor's behavior.

The differences drawn between these two types of procedures for creating change in an organizational setting may not be as marked as presented here. Human relations training programs do vary tremendously from company to company and from time to time. There is no single pattern. Since we know little about the frequency of different species of human relations training programs, the specific mix of content, method, setting, etc., which we used as the basis of our contrast may no longer be found in organizations. Our comparison aimed to emphasize the extent to which various characteristics of change processes vary on the basic dimension of *motivation for change*.

Different contents, different methods, different settings, different training units, and different change agents contain different motivational impacts for change. What constitutes the most effective combination for changing behavior in organizations is not known. Few practitioners have really done any bold experimenting; almost none have combined measurement and experimenting to search for the most significant dimensions and variables in change processes. This is an area in which there is a great need for social experimentation and social invention.

In the social sciences, as in the physical sciences, invention plays a crucial role. Inventions in social technology—skills and processes for creating change—and innovations in measurement both contribute speedily to progress in understanding social phenomena. The responsibility of experimenting with different methods of measuring change and with new procedures for investigating the interrelationship of functioning organizational processes rests heavily with the students of social organization. The rate at which knowledge about organization is developed will probably be closely correlated to the rate at which we try new approaches to the study of problems in this area.

Notes

* Drs. Rensis Likert, Daniel Katz, Robert Kahn, and Norman R. F. Maier have made especially helpful suggestions concerning the organization and presentation of this material. They can, of course, in no way be held responsible for the shortcomings which remain.

1. For an account of a conspicuous exception to this, see N. C. Morse and E. Reimer, "The

Experimental Manipulation of a Major Organizational Variable," in *Journal of Abnormal and Social Psychology* (1956).

2. F. Mann and R. Lippitt (eds.), "Social Relations Skills in Field Research," *Journal of Social Issues*, 8, No. 3 (1952).

3. Donald Young, "Sociology and the Practicing Professions," *American Sociological Review*, 20 (December 1955): 641–648.

4. A nonquantitative, but extraordinarily thorough and insightful study of foreman training was made by A. Zalenznik, *Foreman Training in a Growing Enterprise*. Boston: Graudate School of Business Administration, Harvard University, 1951.

5. W. R. Mahler and W. H. Monroe, *How Industry Determines the Need for and Effectiveness of Training*, Personnel Research Section Report 929. Washington: Department of the Army, 1952.

6. R. R. Canter, "A Human Relations Training Program," *Journal of Applied Psychology*, 35 (February 1951): 38–45.

7. B. B. Tyler, "A Study of Factors Contributing to Employee Morale," Master's thesis, Ohio State University, 1949.

8. Edwin A. Fleishman, "Leadership Climate, Human Relations Training, and Supervisory Behavior," *Personnel Psychology*, 6 (Summer 1953): 205–222.

9. Charles L. Walker, Jr., "Education and Training at International Harvester," *Harvard Business Review*, 27 (September 1949): 542–558.

10. E. F. Harris, "Measuring Industrial Leadership and Its Implications for Training Supervisors," Doctoral thesis, Ohio State University, 1952.

11. E. F. Harris and E. A. Fleishman, "Human Relations Training and the Stability of Leadership Patterns," *Journal of Applied Psychology*, 39 (February 1955): 20–25.

12. For a full account of these two studies combined, see E. A. Fleishman, E. F. Harris, and H. E. Buntt, *Leadership and Supervision in Industry*. Columbus: Personnel Research Board, Ohio State University, 1955.

13. A number of people contributed to the design of this feedback process during its developmental phase. They included Sylvester Leahy, Blair Swartz, Robert Schwab, and John Sparling from the Detroit Edison Company, and Rensis Likert, Daniel Katz, Everett Reimer, Frances Fielder, and Theodore Hariton from the Survey Research Center.

14. F. Mann and J. Dent, "The Supervisor: Member of Two Organizational Families," *Harvard Business Review*, 32 (November-December 1954): 103–112.

15. For a thorough description of this training see N. R. F. Maier, *Principles of Human Relations*. New York: Wiley, 1952.

16. F. Mann and R. Likert, "The Need for Research on Communicating Research Results," *Human Organization*, 11 (Winter 1952): 15–19.

17. F. Mann and H. Baumgartel, *Survey Feedback Experiment: An Evaluation of a Program for the Utilization of Survey Findings*, Survey Research Center, University of Michigan.

18. Milton Hall, "Supervising People—Closing the Gap Between What We Think and What We Do," *Advanced Management*, 12 (September 1947): 129–135.

19. M. Haire, "Some Problems of Industrial Training." *Journal of Social Issues*, 4, No. 3 (1948): 41–47.

20. N. R. F. Maier, "A Human Relations Program for Supervision," *Industrial and Labor Relations Review*, 1 (April 1948): 443–464.

21. I. Sarnoff and D. Katz, "The Motivational Bases of Attitude Change," *Journal of Abnormal and Social Psychology*, 49 (January 1954): 115–124.

19

M. B. MILES, H. A. HORNSTEIN, P. H. CALDER, D. M. CALLAHAN, AND R. STEVEN SCHIAVO

Data Feedback: A Rationale

*S*urvey feedback has three operationally verifiable components: First *data* are presented; second, *meetings* of various family groups occur; third, in the course of these meetings, staff and eventually clients begin to *analyse the process* of their interaction. Some of these analyses refer to "here and now" interactions occurring just as the data are discussed and analyzed; others are more historically-oriented, involving analysis of events and processes occurring during the immediate past in the organization.

DATA

In survey feedback the client system examines data about itself. Psychotherapy and the laboratory method of human relations training (Schein and Bennis, 1965) are analogous in this respect. But they differ from survey feedback in two ways. First, in psychotherapy and human relations training the process of feeding back *subjective* data is mediated by the therapist and/or other group members, respectively; in survey feedback, however, the process is mediated by *objective* data which group members have planned, collected, analyzed, and interpreted. Second, in therapy and training the analysis of data occurs mostly at the intrapersonal, interpersonal or group level; survey feedback usually focusses more centrally on the role, inter-group, and organizational levels.

Presenting the data may have any combination of the following three effects. The data may *corroborate* the client's feelings ("Yes, that is just how things are."); or the data may have a *disconfirming* effect if they contradict beliefs ("I never would have expected that people could see things that way.") In addition, the data have *inquiry-encouraging* effects; clients begin to wonder why people responded as they did, what the underlying causes were, and how they might be

Data Feedback: A Rationale

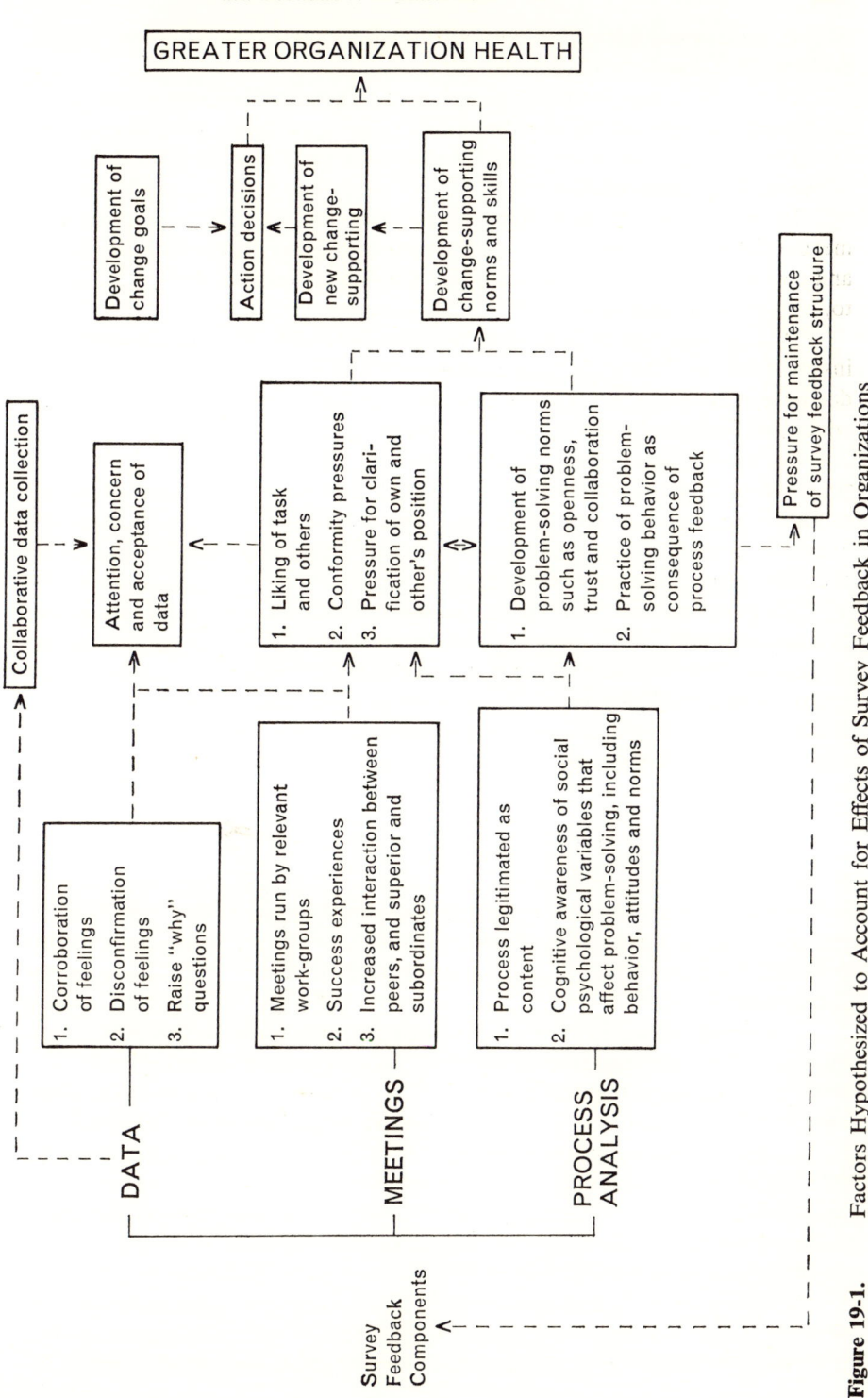

Figure 19-1. Factors Hypothesized to Account for Effects of Survey Feedback in Organizations

altered. Also, examination of the data usually leads to discussion of related problems not directly dealt with by the data.

Two or more people or role groups may, of course, have simultaneous and conflicting reactions to the same set of data. These reactions are in themselves useful for interpreting the data; making such reaction differences salient is part of the staff's process analysis task.

To the extent that these three effects occur, the data become increasingly meaningful for the clients. They see the data as reflecting their work-day needs and concerns, and not as abstract, irrelevant sets of statistics. Hence, attention to, concern with, and acceptance of data increases.

Their involvement with the data is intensified still further because of earlier involvement in data collection activities, which enabled them to influence decisions concerning the kinds of data to be collected. Consequently, the data which are finally collected are as much theirs as they are the staff's.

One further note regarding acceptance of the data: Neff (1965) suggests that the meaningfulness of the data may be increased if one produces work-efficiency or other basic output data from the various sub-units. When such data are available, feelings about what conditions lead to success and failure can be checked against these objective criteria.

The point we have been making is that the data corroborate or disconfirm feelings and raise "why" questions. These effects tend to encourage acceptance of the data. This is more likely to be true when the client group has collaborated in data collection. This acceptance, however, is also affected by events that occur during the course of survey feedback meetings. And it is to this second component of survey feedback meetings, that we now turn.

MEETINGS

We assume that insofar as meetings result in successful experiences with work on problems, the data and the meetings themselves will be increasingly attractive to the participants. Conversely, if the meetings lead to failure experiences and frustration, we can expect the data and the meetings to be less attractive to the participants.

We further assume that regardless of how much work is actually accomplished at these meetings, the group members are more likely to evaluate their work positively when they feel that they are responsible for the work done at the meeting. Survey feedback insures the group's responsibility for meetings by having the meetings organized around the existing work structures, and by having each family work-group conduct its own meeting. Thus, the client group becomes its own change agent. Group members have responsibility for interpreting the data; they have responsibility for conducting and scheduling meetings; and they have responsibility for making and implementing action decisions.

All this requires increasing interaction within family work-groups composed of peers as well as superiors and subordinates. This increased interaction, which is probably fundamental to the success of survey feedback has three effects which are of interest here: (1) increased liking among the parties who interact; (2) increased pressure for clarifying one's position on relevant issues; and (3) increased pressure for conformity to group norms.

The increased liking for others, we believe, stems basically from the increased interaction in a positively-valued setting (Riecken and Homans, 1954). The positive sentiments are probably also a consequence of the novelty of the situation, the opportunity of working on lingering problems, and the success that one experiences in working on these problems.

As the data are presented and work on problems begins, staff interventions, as well as the group's own efforts, make the need for individual reactions to data increasingly apparent. That is, as problem-solving efforts begin, if the group has developed a data-using, process-analytic orientation, they will feel hampered to the extent that members of the work-group are seen as withholding their feelings. In addition, the increased visibility of *all* members of the family work-group will increase pressures to clarify one's own position.

Finally, as individual views on issues become clearer, it becomes increasingly difficult to hold a minority position. When this heightened visibility is combined with the pressures toward conformity which ordinarily accompany the formation of norms, uniformity in viewpoints increases.

Such uniformity is useful in some respects, for example, when it encourages a common view of the urgency of a problem, the nature of the immediate goal in front of the group, and so on. It can also tend to impoverish solution-generation, and eliminate creative conflict. The major corrective to such consequences of conformity-pressure lies in efforts to help the group become steadily and reflexively aware of their existing norms, and to alter them when they prove barriers to productive work. Such efforts are part of the third component of survey feedback—process analysis.

PROCESS ANALYSIS

As groups work, they develop implicit and explicit normative notions of right and wrong, as well as characteristic ways of goal-setting, problem-solving, and decision-making. These social-psychological variables affect the group's work; but, all too often, groups focus on the official content of their work, and do not explicitly or publicly attend to these aspects of their life together. As a result, process problems which arise are frequently unresolved, and problem-solving on crucial issues is adversely affected.

In the beginning, staff members are the primary source for process analysis. They make comments on such things as interpersonal interactions, norms, and problem-solving procedures. Attention to these phenomena by staff (who are perceived as externally-based authorities) legitimates this area of work. Consequently, other members of the group begin to think reflexively, and to comment on the group's process and the behavior of others explicitly, from time to time.

As the group's process is focused upon and diagnosed, we suggest that two things occur. First, members of the group (and, perhaps, the whole group) inhibit old behaviors and attempt to practice new behaviors in response to the feedback they are receiving about their current behavior. The second consequence is that the group develops norms (including the second-order process-analytic norm itself) which facilitate productive work by enabling direct expression of feeling, and self-corrective behavior when group problem-solving is effective.*

Two sets of norms are most critical. One set, which is in operation as soon as the group accepts process feedback as legitimate, facilitates the *communication of information*. These can be thought of as norms centering around openness and trust. The implicit assumption is that open, two-way channels of communication facilitate the amount and accuracy of information which, in turn, improves problem-solving. The second set of norms, those which reward *collaborative activity*, affects not only communication (particularly by opening two-way channels) but also determination of goals, group cohesiveness, and group pressures for conformity.

Up to this point, we have suggested that the three primary components of survey feedback (namely, data, meetings, and process-analysis), lead to attention to, and acceptance of, the data; liking of the family work-group and its activities, clarification of own and other's position, practice of new behaviors; and development of norms which support open, collaborative problem-solving. To the extent that these effects do occur, we can expect group members to see their work in the survey feedback meetings as both pleasant and productive. Hence, there will be some pressure for the maintenance of survey feedback as an organizational structure.

So far, effects have been limited to the family work-group immediately at hand. If these effects are strong, we hypothesize that developmental, organization-changing effects will follow. Working with the data, for example, leads groups to develop *new change goals* whenever they perceive problems to exist. These change goals, in combination with the newly-developed *change-supporting norms and problem-solving skills* will lead to increasingly effective work on problems. This work may take the form of *action decisions* about solutions to resolve the problems, or the design of new, change-oriented, problem-solving structures. Thus, survey feedback not only tends to perpetuate itself as a method of planned organizational change, but also gives birth to other adaptive structural changes as well.

Note

* Process analysis is, of course, the central feature of the human relations training group or T-group (Bradford, Benne, and Gibb, 1964); more and more it has also been applied to intact family work groups, with or without survey data available (Clark, 1966).

References

Bradford, L. P., K. D. Benne, and J. R. Gibb. *T-Group Theory and Laboratory Method.* New York: Wiley, 1964.

Clark, J. V. "Task Group Therapy." Los Angeles: Institute of Industrial Relations, University of California, 1966. Mimeographed.

Neff, F. W. "Survey Research: A Tool for Problem Diagnosis and Improvement in Organizations." in A. W. Gouldner and S. M. Miller (eds.). *Applied Sociology.* New York: The Free Press, 1966, 23–38.

Riecken, H. W., and G. Homans. "Psychological Aspects of Social Structure." In G. Lindzey (ed.). *Handbook of Social Psychology.* Vol. 2. Reading, Massachusetts: Addison-Wesley Publishing Company, Inc., 1954, 768–832.

Schein, E. H., and W. G. Bennis. *Personal and Organizational Change through Group Methods: The Laboratory Approach.* New York: Wiley, 1965.

20

CLAIRE SELLTIZ

*The Use of Survey Methods in a Citizens Campaign Against Discrimination**

*I*n 1950 a group of citizens of New York City, working with limited and unpaid professional assistance, organized and carried out a campaign to reduce discrimination in restaurants in an area around the United Nations building. The event is of interest to social science because the group evaluated its success by a systematic comparison of restaurant practices before and after the campaign. While a number of communities have undertaken "self-surveys" of discriminatory practices, this is the only case known to the writer in which the results of the undertaking have been objectively measured.

The project was carried out by the Committee on Civil Rights in East Manhattan. The Committee was organized in the spring of 1949, "to compare public practices now existing in East Manhattan and those principles upon which our democracy was founded." The Committee is composed of representatives of 23 affiliated organizations, plus a few individual members-at-large. About half of the member groups represent specific minorities or have as their primary concern the reduction of discrimination and prejudice. The others represent broad community interests; they include such groups as branches of the American Association of University Women, of Americans for Democratic Action, of the Welfare and Health Council of New York City, and the Uptown Chamber of Commerce.

Both the organizational representatives and the members-at-large are more or less ordinary citizens. Although above average in education and in concern

Reprinted from *Human Organization*, 14, No. 3 (1955): 19–25. With permission of the Society for Applied Anthropology.

with problems of civil rights, they are not especially prominent in the community. They include, for example, housewives, school teachers, a public relations consultant, an editor, a photographer, a salesman, a biochemist, a group worker, a personnel director, an attorney, and a few persons working professionally in the field of intergroup relations. In addition to these "ordinary citizens," CCREM enlisted a number of prominent persons as sponsors and several social scientists as technical consultants.

In selecting its first project, CCREM recognized two criteria: the importance to the life of minority group members of practices in the area, and feasibility of investigating them.

Employment and housing were considered more important than public accommodations in their effects on the lives of minority group members, but they presented serious problems by way of gathering accurate information. Committee members were generally skeptical of the trustworthiness of information from interviews with persons responsible for policy and practices. Nor were they more favorably inclined to basing their conclusions on information from people opposed to discrimination and presumably in a position to know the facts. They wanted to come out with findings which could not be successfully challenged. Thus, they wanted to test practices—specifically, by determining whether majority group and minority group members, matched in all other relevant respects, would be treated alike in a given situation.

The fields of housing and employment seemed too formidable for such testing by the as yet inexperienced Committee. Public accommodations seemed to be much easier to tackle by this approach. The Committee recognized that this field is less crucial than others in its bearing on the lives of minority group members, but nevertheless it seemed sufficiently important to merit investigation. It was, therefore, decided that the Committee's first survey would deal with the practices of eating places—with the further simplification of limiting the study to one minority group, Negroes.

To reduce the scope of the project still further, the Committee decided to cover only the eastern half of midtown Manhattan, with its high concentration of restaurants. At the time, it seemed likely that a similar group would investigate the practices of eating places in west midtown. An area of about 150 square blocks was selected—from Fifth Avenue to the East River, and from Thirty-fourth Street to Fifty-ninth Street. This neighborhood was especially interesting because it includes the site of the United Nations building, with its personnel from many lands.

PREPARING FOR THE INITIAL SURVEY
DEVELOPMENT OF THE MEASURING INSTRUMENT

In the course of the discussions which led to the selection of eating places as the subject of the first survey, it had been decided that two teams—one consisting of two Negroes, the other of two white persons—would go to each restaurant, ostensibly as ordinary diners. Starting from the assumption that democratic practice requires the giving of equal service to all persons regardless of race, discrimination was defined as any inequality between the treatment accorded the two teams, unless there seemed reason to believe that the difference in treatment was due to some factor other than the difference in race.

The measuring instrument, then, must be such as to provide accurate comparison of the treatment given the two teams. It took the form of a questionnaire report to be filled out separately by each team after they had left the restaurant. Emphasis was placed on objective information which could easily be subjected to statistical analysis rather than on subjective or narrative reports.

The first step in preparing the questionnaire was to list the possible ways in which discrimination might be shown. The most obvious, of course, would be refusal to serve the Negro team. In view of the New York State Civil Rights Law, such refusal might be expressed deviously rather than forthrightly, by claiming, for instance, that reservations were necessary, or by simply keeping the Negroes waiting indefinitely. Short of refusal to serve the minority team, the following possible milder forms of discrimination were listed:

(1.) Evidence of confusion at the appearance of the Negro team or of hesitation about admitting them, such as a hasty conference between headwaiter and waiter, shifting of waiters, etc.
(2.) Directing the Negro team to a table in an undesirable location: one which would be considered poor by most customers, regardless of race (tables near the kitchen, near a lavatory, etc.); or one which placed the Negroes out of view of other diners (tables in a back corner, on a balcony, in a separate room, etc.).
(3.) Poor service: markedly slower than that given other customers; markedly faster than that given other customers, in an apparent attempt to get the Negroes out of the restaurant as quickly as possible; rudeness by restaurant employees; statements that items of food ordered were not available when in fact they were.
(4.) Inferior food: excessive amounts of salt or other spices added to the food served the Negro team; decayed food; etc,
(5.) Overcharges.

Questions were framed to get the information necessary to judge whether or not each form of discrimination had been practiced. Wherever possible, the questions called for short factual answers: "When did you enter the restaurant?" "Where were you seated?" "Did you pick your own table, or were you assigned by a restaurant employee?" "Was the table assigned to you located in any of the following places . . . ?" A few questions called for evaluations or subjective impressions; for example, "Did you feel you were being hurried as compared with other persons served by the same waiter?" Such questions were followed by attempts to get the evidence on which such judgments were based: "What made you feel that way?" or "State your reasons" or "Please describe."

In order to make possible an analysis of characteristics of restaurants which might be related to discrimination, the questionnaire called for information on the following points: price of dinner, nationality of cuisine, location of restaurant, number of employees, race of employees, extent of occupancy at the time of the test.

PILOT SURVEY OF LUNCHEONETTES

At about the time the questionnaire was being put into final form, two students from the New York School of Social Work of Columbia University volunteered to conduct a pilot survey. Luncheonettes and drug stores serving food were selected for this pilot study, which took place in the period May 8–29, 1950. The procedures and findings have been reported fully by the two students who took responsibility for this part of the survey;[1] only a brief summary will be given here. Forty-nine of the 227 luncheonettes and drug stores in the area (that is, approximately one-fifth of the total number) were tested. No discrimination of any kind was found in any of the places tested; in every case the treatment given the Negro team was substantially the same as that given the majority team.

This pilot test indicated the need for only minor revisions in the testing instructions and report form. However, it revealed serious organizational and administrative problems—in recruiting testers, making assignments, filling out and returning report forms, supervising progress, etc.—and led to much more careful planning of these aspects in the survey of restaurants proper.

SELECTING THE SAMPLE OF RESTAURANTS TO BE TESTED

Since no complete list of restaurants was available, a complete enumeration was made during the winter and spring of 1950 by volunteers who walked through every block in the area, recording each eating place—its name, address, price range, and any other relevant information which could be secured. The enumeration produced a list of 771 eating places within the area—including restaurants proper, luncheonettes, drug stores, cafeterias, bars and grills, cocktail lounges and night clubs

In view of the findings of the pilot study, the 227 luncheonettes and drug stores were removed from the list. As the Committee proceeded in its deliberations, its originally ambitious plans were gradually whittled down by realistic considerations. It was finally decided that limitations of personnel and funds made it impossible to test an adequate sample of the remaining 544 eating places; some categories would have to be omitted from the survey. Cafeterias were dropped on the ground that their practices were probably quite similar to those of luncheonettes, in which no discrimination had been found. It was decided also to omit bars and grills, cocktail lounges, and night clubs, on the grounds that these were not primarily eating places and that they presented special problems in testing.

Hence, the survey concentrated on restaurants proper, of which there were 364 listed in the area, ranging in price of an average meal from 75¢ to $10.00. It was decided to stratify on the basis of price, the variable most suspected of being relevant to the likelihood of discrimination.

The cards on which the data about each restaurant had been entered were arranged in order of the estimated price of an average meal. At the beginning of the week scheduled for testing, teams were available for 47 tests. It was decided to reduce the population about which statements were to be made, rather than to reduce the accuracy of the findings, by using less than a 25 percent sample. This was done by narrowing the price range to be covered, focusing on restaurants in the middle of the range. The median card was selected as the first case in the sample; the other cases were selected by taking, alternately, every fourth card above and every fourth card below the median. As additional teams were set up during the week, the sample was expanded. The final sample consisted of 62 restaurants, constituting 25 percent of the 248 restaurants with average prices from $1.30 to $3.75.

RECRUITING AND TRAINING THE TESTERS

The volunteers who carried out the tests were recruited from the member organizations of CCREM, from other interested organizations, and from among friends of Committee members. There were 153 testers in all: 68 Negroes and 85 white persons, from 25 different organizations. All the testers were of pleasing appearance, quiet in manner, well but not ostentatiously dressed. All the minority group members were judged to be recognizably Negro; persons so light-skinned that they were not likely to be identified as Negroes by restaurant personnel were asked not to participate.

In both the minority and the control groups, there were twice as many women as men. More than 80 percent of each group were between the ages of 21 and 45. The testers were distinctly above average in education and socio-economic status. The great majority (90 per cent of the control testers and 76 percent of the Negro testers) had attended college. Only one (a member of the control group) had not attended high school. Of the minority group, 34 percent were engaged in professional or semiprofessional work, 25 percent had clerical or sales jobs, and 16 percent were students. Of the control group, 49 percent were engaged in professional or semiprofessional work, 21 percent had clerical or sales jobs, and 14 percent were housewives.

An intensive training session was held the evening before testing began. The training instructions had four main themes: an injunction that all testers approach the situation open-mindedly, without preconceptions that they would either find or not find discrimination; the need for all teams to follow the same standardized procedures, so that the results would be comparable; the importance of remaining passive regardless of the treatment given the minority team, in order not to affect the practices of the restaurant and thus invalidate the test results; and the necessity for careful but unobtrusive noting of details of time, location, etc.

THE INITIAL SURVEY

The testing took place on six nights during the period June 16–23, 1950, omitting

Saturday and Sunday. All tests were conducted during the dinner hour, with teams entering the restaurants between 6:30 and 7:30 p.m.

The basic procedure was very simple: a Negro team and a white team went to each restaurant, and the treatment given the two teams was compared. The white team had two functions: first, to serve as a control against which the treatment given the Negro team could be measured; second, to observe, insofar as they could, the treatment given to the Negro team.

As far as possible, the two teams were matched except in skin color. If the Negro team consisted of two men, the white team going to the same restaurant consisted of two men; similarly, both teams might consist of two women, or of a man and a woman. With few exceptions, both teams were of about the same age. Since the entire group of testers was quite homogeneous in socio-economic level, in dress, and in general social behavior, no special effort was made to match teams on such factors as these.

The two teams assigned to a given restaurant separated before reaching the vicinity of the restaurant they were to test. The minority team entered the restaurant first so that there could be no question as to which team was entitled to be seated first and no possibility that the white team might be given a more desirable table simply because they had arrived first. The minority team was followed closely—less that a minute later—by the control team. All testers had been given general instructions as to the type of meal to order, to eliminate possible differences in time needed to prepare food or possible differences in treatment related to the prices of the meals ordered within a given restaurant.

Each team left the restaurant as soon as its two members had finished eating, still without giving any indication of acquaintance with the other team, and returned to the Committee's headquarters. There the two members of each team jointly filled out the team's report form, without discussing their experiences with the opposite team or indeed with any one else until the form had been completed. The questionnaire was checked for completeness and clarity by a member of the Committee. Then the two teams who had tested a given restaurant came together, and a member of the Committee compared the two reports, asking for details on any points which were not clear or where the reports differed. At this time, most disagreements between the teams (and there were very few) were resolved by discussion; in the two or three cases where there was genuine disagreement as to what had happened or why it had happened, the supervisor wrote a detailed report of the versions given by each team. Final judgment as to whether the two teams had in fact been given approximately equal treatment was left to a committee of eight coders.

DESCRIPTION OF THE RESTAURANTS TESTED

As stated earlier, 62 restaurants were tested, constituting 25 percent of all the restaurants within the geographic area and price range previously described. The sample was checked against the enumeration in terms of price and location and was found to be representative, except for a slight under-representation of one corner of the area.

Of the 62 restaurants tested, 39 served American food and 23 specialized in foreign dishes (11 French, 8 Italian, 2 French-Italian, one German, one Swedish). At the time the teams entered, 42 percent of the restaurants were less than half full, 21 percent were about half full, 21 percent were about three-quarters full, 11 percent were about full but with no people waiting, and five percent had people waiting for tables. About one-third had less than five waiters or other visible service staff, another third had from five to nine, and another third had 10 or more. About three-fourths of the restaurants had a headwaiter or hostess. Only nine of the 62 had any non-white employees who were visible, that is, waiters, bus boys, etc.

DECIDING WHETHER DISCRIMINATION HAD OCCURRED

As has been stated, the questionnaire, the training of testers, and the testing procedures were all designed to secure objective information and to minimize the effects of possible bias on the part of the testers. The judgment as to whether the treatment reported actually showed inequality, and hence discrimination, was left to eight members of the Committee who served as coders. Preliminary classification was done by coders working in pairs; finally the whole group of coders, acting as a committee, reviewed all the tests and made the final decisions as to whether or not there had been clear inequality of treatment.

The decisions of the coders as to whether the minority team had received discriminatory treatment in a given restaurant were based on their judgment as to whether the facts reported indicated clearly that the minority team was treated less well than the control team and that the inferior treatment could not reasonably be considered accidental. In reaching their decisions, the coders took into account such factors as whether discriminatory treatment was manifested in more than one way (thus lessening the likelihood that any given action might have been accidental), whether both teams reported the treatment as unequal, etc. The final decision rested on the convincingness of the evidence reported. Whenever there was reasonable ground for believing that inferior treatment given the minority group might have been accidental, the case was not considered one of discrimination even if both teams reported that the minority was given less good treatment.

FINDINGS

In no restaurant was the minority team refused service, nor was there any attempt to avoid serving them by such devices as saying that reservations were needed or by making them wait indefinitely without being given a table. However in 26 restaurants (42 percent of those tested; $Op = 6.3$) the minority team was given treatment so clearly inferior to that given the control team as to be considered discriminatory. In no case was the control team treated less well than the minority team.

Types of Discriminatory Treatment. Unequal treatment was of two general types: assignment of the Negro team to a table in an undesirable location, and giving poorer service to the Negro team than to the control team. Table 20-1

Table 20-1. Types of Discriminatory Treatment, Initial Survey

Discriminatory Treatment	Number of Restaurants
Less desirable location only	5
Poorer service or rudeness only	9
Both less desirable location and poorer service	12
	26

shows the number of restaurants in which each of these types of discriminatory treatment was encountered.

In about 70 percent of the restaurants, the testers were assigned to tables by a headwaiter or other restaurant employee. In these restaurants where tables were assigned, there was a marked tendency to give the minority team a less desirable table than the control team. The control teams were given undesirable tables in nine of the 62 restaurants tested, whereas the minority teams were given undesirable tables in 28 of the 62 restaurants. In each case, in addition to rating the desirability of the table given each team, the testers rated the comparative desirability of the two tables. In only one case was the control team reported as having a less desirable table than the minority team. In 17 restaurants the minority teams were given clearly less desirable tables than the controls even though other tables were available.

In no case did the control team report being treated rudely, being made to wait out of turn for a table, receiving unduly slow service, or other evidence of reluctance to serve them. In contrast, there were 21 cases in which the minority team was given such clearly inferior service that the restaurants were classified as discriminatory. In 19 of these cases, the minority team was treated rudely by one or more restaurant employees; in seven of these 19, they were also made to wait considerably longer for service than diners at nearby tables. In three restaurants the minority team was hurried to the point of inconvenience although nearby diners were not hurried.

Characteristics of Discriminatory Restaurants. The only observed characteristic in which the restaurants which discriminated differed significantly from those which did not discriminate was price.[2] As shown in Table 20-2, discrimination was encountered in one-seventh of the restaurants in the $1.30–$1.99

Table 20-2. Frequency of Incidents of Discrimination in Restaurants in Various Price Ranges—Initial Survey

Price of Average Meal	Number Tested	Number With Incidents	Percent of Incidents to Number Tested
$1.30–1.99	21	3	14
$2.00–2.99	26 ⎱ $41	15 ⎱ $23	58 ⎱ $56
$3.00–3.99*	15 ⎰	8 ⎰	53 ⎰

* The prices actually paid differed slightly from the estimates based on the enumeration. This is why the upper price limit here is higher than that reported in the selection of the sample.

price range, and in slightly more than half of those where the average price of the meal was between $2.00 and $3.99.

When price was held constant, no significant differences in frequency of discrimination were found between American and foreign restaurants, between restaurants with and without headwaiters, nor among the geographic sections of the survey area. There was no relation between the size of the visible staff and the occurrence of discrimination, nor between the occupancy of the restaurant and the occurrence of discrimination.

THE ACTION PROGRAM

The next question was: What steps should be taken to reduce—or, hopefully, eliminate—discriminatory practices? CCREM enunciated two principles: that its approach would be "educational" and persuasive rather than militant, and that it would attempt to enlist broad community support for a change in practices. There was no assumption that this approach would necessarily be the most effective one under all circumstances, but it seemed promising, and it seemed the one most appropriate for a group representing such a range of organizations as CCREM's affiliates.

ACTIVITIES DIRECTED TOWARD THE RESTAURANT FIELD

The Committee turned its attention first toward the organizations of persons with responsibility for policies and practices in restaurants; associations of restaurant owners and unions of restaurant employees. There were nine such organizations operating in the area at the time: seven management associations, and two union groups (one of which was a Joint Board representing 12 hotel and restaurant unions). Representatives of CCREM held one or more conversations with the officers of each of these organizations. Within four months after the first contact, all of the groups had signed pledges of equal treatment to all patrons both in seating and in service.

The next step was to send a letter to the owner or manager of each of the 364 restaurants in the area, informing him of the survey findings and of the organizational pledges, and enclosing an individual pledge for his signature. This letter was followed by three others during the next year. A total of 127 pledges were signed and returned, representing approximately one-third of the restaurants in the area. Eleven of the owners added notes expressing their sympathy with the campaign and offering to help.

A more direct personal approach seemed called for in the case of restaurants which had been found to discriminate. A fundamental policy of the Committee was that no individual restaurant would be named in any public discussion of the survey findings, since the sample had been selected randomly and was assumed to be representative of all restaurants in the area. This did not, however, rule out the possibility of individual conferences with the managers of restaurants where discrimination had been encountered.

The Committee planned to talk individually with the managers of each of the restaurants in which discrimination had been found. This program was not completed, largely because of lack of personnel; most of the Committee members have full-time jobs and are not able to visit restaurants at the odd day-time hours when restaurateurs are free. The interviews which were carried out, however, were of considerable interest and showed a wide range of reactions. At one extreme was the manager of a small relatively inexpensive hotel restaurant. She seemed completely cooperative, expressed surprise at the Committee's report of the treatment received in her restaurant, and volunteered to issue instructions to her employees that all patrons were to be treated alike. At the other extreme was the owner of a small "exclusive" French restaurant in the upper price bracket, who denied that discrimination had occurred in his restaurant and was generally hostile toward the Committee members. There were two conversations with this owner, and two follow-up tests of his restaurant; the final one showed no discrimination.

ACTIVITIES DIRECTED TOWARD THE COMMUNITY

The decision to adopt a persuasive approach toward the restaurant industry had entailed a decision not to publicize the survey findings until some progress could be reported—or until the Committee was satisfied that no progress was going to be achieved through persuasion. The Committee's first press release was issued immediately after the signing of pledges by all the restaurant unions and management associations; it reported not only the survey findings but the restaurant industry's pledge to eliminate discrimination. This story was carried in three major New York City newspapers and in two Negro papers with national circulation; it led to mention of the survey or personal appearances of CCREM members on five broadcasts over four radio stations. Later, 10,000 copies of a popular pamphlet about the survey and the follow-up action program, entitled "Have You Heard What's Cooking?", were distributed.

CCREM's conception of its work with the community, however, focused on direct appeals to individuals in organizations rather than on broadside appeals through the mass media. The first step along these lines was a meeting, in April 1951, of those who had participated in the initial test, to inform them of the success in securing pledges from the restaurant organizations and to discuss further plans. This was followed by reports and sociodramatic presentations at meetings of 10 groups affiliated with CCREM or interested in its work.

THE FINAL SURVEY

A re-test was carried out in the spring of 1952 to determine what changes, if any, had taken place in the almost two years since the initial test.

SELECTING THE SAMPLE

The major question in planning the re-survey was whether to re-test the same restaurants used in the first audit or to select another representative sample of restaurants in the area. Re-testing the old sample had great research advantages because of the greater confidence that any changes found would not reflect chance sampling variations, and because of the possibility of detailed analysis of the characteristics of restaurants which had changed their practices. On the other hand, taking a new sample was attractive for a number of practical reasons. Information about a new sample, when added to that from the original audit, would give data about the practices of a larger total number of restaurants; this was particularly important if subsequent action was to be taken with regard to those which discriminated. Further, testing a new sample would increase the number of restaurants which had at least once had the experience of serving Negro customers. And, incidentally, the members of the Committee would find a new batch of restaurants more interesting.

Resources were not great enough to allow for re-testing the entire old sample and a sufficiently large new sample to give reliable results, so a compromise was adopted. It was decided to re-test all the restaurants which had been found discriminatory in the first survey and half of those which had been found non-discriminatory, and to test a new sample of 50 restaurants. In the analysis, the non-discriminatory restaurants would be weighted so that they would account for their proper proportion of an original sample.

No sampling procedure was needed, of course, to identify the old discriminatory restaurants; all 26 of them were to be tested. The cards of the 36 which had not discriminated in 1950 were arranged in order of price, and every other one selected. One of these turned out to have gone out of business, leaving 17 to be tested. The enumeration cards which has been prepared in the winter and spring of 1950 were used as the basis for selection of the new sample. After the cards for the 62 restaurants in the original sample and those of a few which were known to have gone out of business were removed, there were 175 cards within the price range covered by the initial survey. From these cards, arranged in order of price, a sample of 50 restaurants was selected by taking every fifth card, then every tenth one of the remaining cards.

PROCEDURES

The tests were carried out at the dinner hour during the period of March 21 to April 1, 1952, omitting Saturday and Sunday. Training, testing, reporting and coding procedures were essentially the same as in the first audit, except for minor changes designed to insure greater clarity in the reports.

In this second audit there were 272 testers: 130 minority group members, 142 in the control group. They came from about 40 different organizations. Although only 37 of the 272 had taken part in the initial survey, as a group they were very similar to the 1950 testers in age, sex, education, and occupation.

DESCRIPTION OF THE RESTAURANTS TESTED

A total of 93 restaurants were tested. The old sample, of course, remained the same in such characteristics as geographical location, nationality of food, size of staff, and character of staff. The new sample differed slightly in some of these characteristics.

The geographic distribution of the restaurants tested again differed slightly from that of the total population of restaurants within the area. Again about two-thirds of the restaurants tested served American food, one-third specialized in foreign dishes, mostly French or Italian. Again, about one-third of the restaurants had less than five waiters or other visible staff, one-third had from five to nine, and one-third had 10 or more. Approximately 80 percent had a headwaiter or hostess. Again, only a very few restaurants had any visible non-white employees.

As might be expected, prices had risen; whereas the prices paid per meal in the first test had ranged from $1.30 to $3.99, they now ranged from $1.37 to $4.77. Since the percentage increases were fairly consistent, it was possible to set up new categories which included approximately the same proportions of restaurants as those in the first survey. The two sets of categories are shown in Table 20-3.

Table 20-3. *Price Categories, 1950 and 1952*

Category	1950	1952
"Lower priced"	$1.30–1.99	$1.37–2.27
"Medium priced"	$2.00–2.99	$2.28–3.37
"Higher priced"	$3.00–3.99	$3.38–4.77

Although no relation between the occurrence of discrimination and the fullness or emptiness of the restaurant had been found in the first survey, the hypothesis had been offered that restaurant business might be worse (or better) in 1952 than it had been in 1950, and that this might account for any difference found in the prevalence of discrimination. The extent of occupancy during the two audits, however, was found to be almost identical.

In summary, the second sample was similar in all major aspects to the one originally tested, both being fairly representative of all restaurants in the given price range within the geographical area bounded by Fifth Avenue, the East River, 34th Street and 59th Street.

FINDINGS

As in 1950, in no restaurant was the minority team refused service. More important, there was a marked reduction in the number of restaurants where the minority team encountered discriminatory treatment. In only 16 percent of the restaurants was the minority team given treatment clearly inferior to that of the control team.[3] This figure (16 percent) was the same both for the restaurants which were being re-tested and for the new sample. The difference between this proportion and that found in the first survey—42 percent—is significant at the one-percent level.

Types of Discriminatory Treatment. Again the two major types of discrimination encountered centered around location of tables and quality of service. Table 20-4 shows the frequency of occurrence of these two types of treatment.

Characteristics of Discriminatory Restaurants. The initial survey had shown markedly greater incidence of discrimination among the restaurants in the middle and upper part of the price range tested than among those in the lower part of the price range. Table 20-5 shows the percentages of restaurants in each price range which discriminated in 1950 and in 1952.

Table 20-4.* *Types of Discriminatory Treatment, Final Survey*

	Number of Restaurants
Less desirable location only	6
Poorer service or rudeness only	2
Both less desirable location and poorer service	7
	15

* This table, as well as all subsequent discussion which deals only with the discriminatory restaurants, is based on the 15 restaurants in which discrimination occurred; in view of the small number of cases, the two formerly non-discriminatory restaurants which now showed discrimination have not been weighted.

Table 20-5. *Frequency of Incidents of Discrimination in Restaurants in Various Price Ranges—Initial and Final Surveys*

Price Range	1950 Percentage Which Discriminated	1952 (total sample, weighted) Percentage Which Discriminated
Lower	14	14
Middle	58	17
Upper	53	15

Obviously there was no decrease in the proportion of lower-priced restaurants which discriminated; however, the original low frequency of discrimination in this price range left relatively little room for improvement. The drop in discrimination for both the middle- and upper-priced restaurants is significant at the one-percent level.

The small number of restaurants in which discrimination occurred during the re-test makes it impossible to carry out any statistical analysis of characteristics related to discrimination. Factors such as nationality of cooking, presence of head waiter, size of staff, geographical location, and occupancy were inspected, but no trends sufficient to establish significance in such a small number of cases appeared.

COMMENT

The drop in discrimination between the first and second surveys provides interesting evidence of the ease and speed with which discriminatory practices can be changed under favorable conditions. There is no assumption that the work of CCREM was exclusively responsible for the marked reduction of discrimination in Manhattan restaurants. The period between the two tests was marked by a general liberalizing of practices with regard to minority groups in many areas of living. Moreover, just before the second survey there had been a change in New York State law, providing for more effective enforcement of the law forbidding discrimination in public accommodations which had long been in existence. Although the new law had not yet gone into effect at the time of the re-survey, it is possible that the news of its passage may have affected restaurant practices. It remains to be seen whether a program of objective fact-finding, followed by educational and persuasive action directed toward the persons responsible for policy and practices in the area and an attempt to enlist community support for the change in practices, can be effective in areas where discrimination is more strongly supported by economic considerations and personal prejudice.

Notes

* The project reported here was carried out by a group of citizens, all volunteers. Limitations of space make it impossible to give credit to all those who participated. Among the lay participants, however, special mention should be made of Mr. Snowden T. Herrick and Mrs. Edna A. Merson, who served as chairmen of the Committee. A number of social scientists served as technical consultants: Drs. Kenneth B. Clark, Dan Dodson, Samuel H. Flowerman, Herbert Hyman, Patricia Kendall, Sophia M. Robison and the author. Miss Selltiz is currently a Research Associate at the Research Center for Human Relations at New York University.

1. Phyllis Landa and Gerard Littman, "A Pilot Study to Test Discriminatory Practices against Ethnic Minority Groups in Public Eating Accommodations: An Audit to Determine the Degree of Discrimination Practiced against Negroes in Luncheonettes." Unpublished thesis, New York School of Social Work of Columbia University, 1950.

2. Where the number of cases and the lowest expected theoretical frequencies were sufficiently large, probabilities were calculated by Chi-square. Where the number of cases or the theoretical frequencies were too low to justify the use of Chi-square, probabilities were calculated by Fisher's exact test for fourfold tables and multiplied by two to make them comparable to a two-tailed test such as Chi-square. The difference in the frequency of discrimination between restaurants in the $1.30 to $1.99 price range and those in the $2.00 to $3.99 range, as shown in Table 20-2, is significant beyond the one percent level ($p = .003$). With regard to all of the other characteristics considered, as described in the following paragraph, the statistical tests indicated that the obtained differences in frequency of discrimination between restaurants in different categories might be expected to occur by chance more than eight times in 100 (p's ranged from .09 to .07).

3. In one case the reporting was not sufficiently clear to permit a decision as to whether there had been discrimination. This case was dropped from the analysis. The present figure is based on the 92 cases which could be coded, with the non-discriminatory cases from the original sample weighted (doubled) to account for their proper proportion.

21

GEORGE W. FAIRWEATHER

Experimental Social Innovation Defined

The history of science reveals that experimental methodology proceeds from crude observations and measurement toward more precise observations and accurate measuring instruments. Each science gradually develops its own theory and methods as scientists become more knowledgeable about its subject matter and the particular problems which differentiate it from other sciences. Because experimental methods for social innovation are evolving step-by-step from successive attempts at problem solution, they are comprised of some old and some new methods. The general attributes of social innovative experiments may be described as follows:

(1.) Definition—defining a significant social problem.
(2.) Naturalism—making naturalistic field observations to describe the social parameters of the problem in its actual community setting.
(3.) Innovation—creating different solutions in the form of innovated social subsystems.
(4.) Comparison—designing an experiment to compare the efficacy of the different subsystems in solving the social problem.
(5.) Context—implanting the innovated subsystems in the appropriate social settings so that they can be evaluated in their natural habitat.
(6.) Evaluation—continuing the operation of the subsystems for several months or even years to allow adequate outcome and process evaluations to be made.
(7.) Responsibility—assumption of responsibility by the researchers for the lives and welfare of participants in the subsystems.
(8.) Cross-disciplinary—using a multidisciplinary approach with the social problem determining the subject matter—economic, political, sociological, and the like.

Reprinted with permission from *Methods for Experimental Social Innovation* New York: Wiley, 1967, Chapter 2.

Research methods of investigating social problems are, of course, not new to the social sciences. These methods have been developed by the pioneering efforts of individuals interested in the social issues of their society. Collectively, their work contains some, but not all, of the methods for social innovative experiments. It is therefore necessary to review some common research methods so that the similarities and differences between them and experimental methods for social innovation can be clarified. Because the contributions are so numerous, it is also useful for clarity to categorize approaches to the investigation of social problems into six commonly used methodologies. A summary of these six categories of methodology is presented in Table 21-1.

Table 21-1. *Characteristics of Methods for Social Problem Solution*

Methods	Significant Social Problem	Naturalistic Observations	Innovates Subsystems	Designs Experiment	Implants Subsystem	Longitudinal	Responsible for Participants	Multi-disciplinary
Descriptive-theoretical	X							X
Survey	X	(X)		(X)				X
Laboratory	X			X		(X)		(X)
Participant-observer	X	X		(X)		X	(X)	X
Service	X	X	X		X	X	X	X
Experimental	X	X	X	X	X	X	X	X

X Present
(X) Sometimes present

First, there are the *descriptive-theoretical* discussions of important social problems. These publications serve as the basis for the formulation of hypotheses and they generate interest which can result in social innovative experiments. These are to be distinguished from more general theoretical works such as those presented in the recently published *Social Change* (Etzioni and Etzioni, 1964) which approaches such problems mainly from the perspective of sociological theory and is not necessarily restricted to specific social problems or by empirically-gathered data. Descriptive-theoretical treatises, in contrast, summarize empirical facts to illustrate theoretical positions about selected problems. Often problem solutions are proposed. No new empirical evidence is presented. Their impact upon the subsequent course of social change is frequently great since quite often these summaries and deductions from them arouse interest in the selected social problems. Most often the writings define and describe social problems by synthesizing current knowledge. Myrdal's (1944) provocative work about the social and economic position of the American Negro, as presented in *An American Dilemma*, is one example of such a descriptive theoretical discourse.

Another contemporary social problem, the effects upon people of mental hospitals and other total institutions, is summarized and discussed by the sociologist Goffman (1962) in his book, *Asylums*. Galbraith (1958), an economist, identifies and discusses the social problems that accrue to a society possessing extraordinary wealth in his work, *The Affluent Society*. And Harrington (1962) presents the problems created by poverty in such a society. These four selected works illustrate descriptive-theoretical writings that are concerned with particular social problems. They analyze and describe specific social problems. Descriptive-theoretical formulations have two of the eight attributes of experimental methods for social innovation. They define a significant social problem and use a multidisciplinary approach. They do not require naturalistic field observations, designing experiments, creating new social subsystems, implanting them in their natural social setting, or assuming responsibility for the lives and welfare of the participants.

A second category of methods used in exploring social problems is the *survey*. Surveys are most frequently utilized to define clearly the variables operative in social problems. Demographic studies such as the census, public opinion polls, and attitude questionnaires about consumer products are all examples. In the arena of social problems, *The Academic Market Place* (Caplow and McGee, 1958) presents a survey concerning the mores and folkways of the academic institution. Other outstanding illustrations of the survey technique as applied to the social problems of mental illness and of drug addition are Hollingshead and Redlich's (1958) *Social Class and Mental Illness* and Chein's (1963) *The Road to H*. The survey gives information which makes the parameters of the social problem more definitive. The survey method, like the descriptive-theoretical method, has two of the eight attributes of experimental methods for social innovation—problem definition and a multidisciplinary approach. They survey does not require naturalistic observations, longitudinal study, designing experiments, creating new social subsystems, implanting them in society, or assuming responsibility for the lives and welfare of the participants.

A third category of research methods for social problems are those used in *laboratory* settings. Here, important social problems are explored by artifically creating various conditions for learning or performing. Studies with biracial work groups (Katz and Benjamin, 1960) and teams (Katz and Cohen, 1962), under artificially created and controlled conditions, are excellent examples of this method. Experiments with democratic, laissez-faire, and authoritarian social climates are classic examples of this method (Lewin, Lippit, and White, 1939; Lippit, 1939). Laboratory research has two of the eight experimental social change attributes. The laboratory method defines a significant social problem and designs experiments to explore selected aspects of it. It does not require observations in the real-life setting, innovating new social subsystems, implanting them in appropriate social institutions, nor are they, necessarily, longitudinal in time or multidisciplinary in subject matter.

A fourth category of methods utilizes the *participant-observer*. An example can be found in the research done by Stanton and Schwartz (1954) as presented in *The Mental Hospital* and Caudill (1958) in *The Psychiatric Hospital as a Small Society*. Such researchers gather data by the formal methods of interviews, testing and questionnaires as well as the informal methods of taking notes in situations such as lunch hours, spontaneous or arranged meetings, and so forth. Other examples of such research are to be found in the Sherif and Sherif (1964) publication, *Reference Groups*, and in Whyte's (1955) book, *Street Corner Society: The Social Structure of an Italian Slum*. The participant-observer method allows for direct experience and observation while the processes are in action. This is its chief characteristic. Studies using participant observation usually have four of the eight characteristics of experimental methods for social innovations. They define a significant social problem, make naturalistic observations, use a multidisciplinary approach, and are longitudinal in time. They do not create new social subsystems, implant them in appropriate social settings, or experimentally compare them; nor do the researchers, necessarily, take the responsibility for the lives and welfare of those members participating in the observed social situations.

A fifth method establishes new social subsystems by providing *services* for its members. The Synanon House for drug addicts, as described by Yablonsky (1964), is an example of one service program. Alcoholics Anonymous (1955) and sheltered workshops (Olshansky, 1960) are examples of others. In the field of treating mental illness, Maxwell Jones' (1953) *The Therapeutic Community* is a classic representative work. It describes the establishment of a new social subsystem in a mental hospital.

This method meets seven of the eight requirements for experimental social innovation. It defines a significant social problem and, hence, does not design experiments to compare these created solutions.

Experimental methods for social innovation combine features of these five methods as well as introducing some of their own. Some examples of experimental social innovation can be found in Madge's book *The Tools of Social Science* (1953, pp. 254–289). It can be most clearly understood in the context of a recent experimental study completed in a mental hospital. Here, the significant social problem was the effect of usual hospital treatment upon the recidivism and low discharge rate of chronic mental patients (Fairweather, 1964). This problem had been documented in previous studies (Fairweather and Simon, 1963; Fairweather et al., 1960). Naturalistic observations were made on mental hospital wards which are the natural social action units of a mental hospital. A new social organization (subsystem) for an entire ward was innovated and implanted on a selected ward while a second experimental ward in the same hospital utilized the traditional treatment subsystem (the existing social practice). An experiment was designed to compare both the outcome and processes of these two social organizations (subsystems). Evaluations were made over several months' time. The research staff was held responsible by the hospital management for the welfare of all the patients participating in both programs. The staff was multidisciplinary, representing social work, psychology, psychiatry, nursing, and sociology. All staff members participated in planning and carrying out the program. Instruments to measure administrative, social psychological, and sociological processes were created and used, as were many different measures of outcome. This study has all the aforementioned attributes of a social innovation experiment. The reader will find a detailed account of all its experimental procedures in *Social Psychology in Treating Mental Illness: An Experimental Approach* (Fairweather, 1964). (Phases of experimental social innovation are outlined in Table 21.2.)

Table 21-2. *Phases of Experimental Social Innovation*

Phases	Method
Planning	Choosing the problem
	Obtaining the administrative commitments
	Forming the research team
	Making the subsystems comparable
	Defining the population and obtaining the sample
	Identifying the variables of the subsystems
	Measuring the variables
	Selecting the comparative, relationship and process methods
	Stating the experimental hypotheses
	Creating the plan for the experiment
Action	Initiating the subsystems' operations
	Collecting the data
	Keeping the experimental conditions constant
	Following the experimental design
	Scoring the research data
	Closing the subsystems
Evaluation	Scoring the remainder of the data
	Preparing the computer sheets
	Analyzing the data
Dissemination	Making inferences from the experimental data
	Preparing the publication of the experiment
	Providing consultants who can establish the successful research programs as service programs
	Planning the next experiment

A social subsystem may be defined as the social organization within which an individual lives. A man may be a father, lawyer, country club member, and churchgoer. Each of these statuses prescribes his rights and obligations as well as his particular role behaviors. The interrelationships among these several statuses and roles define the subsystem within which he lives. As another example, individuals in total institutions have status relationships with all other individuals living in the institution—other inmates and staff alike—and this complex of statuses defines their social subsystem. Institutions are also often linked with the general society. An individual may be a member of the junior class in a high school, a basketball player, a member of certain clubs, and hold a part-time job. The institution—the school, in this case—is intimately linked with the general community, and all these statuses define the social organization (subsystem) within which this adolescent lives. Or a mental patient may live with his relatives and return to the mental hospital daily for treatment while at the same time working in the community. It is this set of status relationships and roles which describes the mental patient's social subsystem. All persons in a society live within a circumscribed subsystem. *A subsystem is the total social environment that is generated for any person by his statuses in the different social institutions of which he is a member.*

The development and comparison of *model* social subsystems that clearly define the status relationships between the subsystem and society, usually with small representative samples, is the task of the social innovative experimentalist. Such researches are controlled longitudinal studies carried out in the naturalistic social setting. Variables important in these settings are controlled either by equating the various subsystems for them or through statistical manipulation. For example, a simple comparison for exploring two different subsystems to integrate prisoners into the society could be established. To do this, the researcher might create the following two subsystems: (1) the usual subsystem of prison, parole, and seeking employment in the community, compared with (2) prison, attending designated schools in the community, and placement in employment upon completion of educational programs.

There are many unique characteristics of the methods for experimental social innovation. Foremost among them is one of the design characteristics of each innovative experiment. *The control subsystem is always defined as the usual social practice for the social problem.* This is necessary because current social practice is the best social subsystem for the problem as far as society is concerned. Furthermore, it is desirable because any current social practice is imbedded in the customs, mores, folkways, and other traditions which have been developed by a society, and it is therefore possible that the current social practice is an excellent one. A society would not be willing to accept a different solution for the social problem *until* it has been clearly demonstrated to be superior to the current practice. For this reason, it would be foolhardy for the researcher to recommend changes in working social subsystems until he has sufficient empirical evidence to warrant such advice.

It also must not be overlooked that in order to be allowed the opportunity to do research in social innovation, many subgroups within a society need to approve such research. It is highly improbable that realistically-oriented lay people would be willing to set aside social traditions without a great deal of evidence indicating that the new methods are better. An attempt to change the educational system can be used as an example. Teachers, school boards, taxpayers, parents, and state and federal authorities who grant money to the educational institutions must all be shown that any changes are warranted. Therefore it is in the best interest of a society to require that experimental practices demonstrate a greater beneficial effect than current practices before social changes are made. Of course, once a new ongoing social subsystem is established as the basic comparative social practice it can be compared with several other subsystems, some quite deviant.

Another unique characteristic of experimental methods for social innovation is the need for agreements among affected members of society. For example, researches which involve institutions, such as prisons, schools, and industries, require commitments from the administrators of the involved institutions. They must be willing to allow the establishment of various subsystems and to support them for the duration of the research program. Furthermore, the research staff itself will initially be comprised of members of various academic disciplines. The research endeavor therefore requires clear delineation of all roles and a commitment to the research program by the members of the research team as well as the participating social institutions. All these agreements must be made prior to the onset of the research project.

Experiments involving social innovation may also be differentiated from other researches because they are primarily empirical in nature. Most theoretical models in the social sciences are specific to a given subject matter such as psychology, sociology, and economics. Since the subject matter for social problem comes from all disciplines, there are few, if any, appropriate theoretical models. Therefore it is probable that theoretical models will necessarily follow the empirical findings of such experiments. Indeed, it is possible that this sequence of events represents the historical development of theories in all the sciences.

Not only does experimental social innovation have unique characteristics concerning its social organization, but it also requires new approaches to measurement and analyses. Few instruments are available to measure dynamic social processes that involve economic, psychological, biological, and sociological variables. The investigator is often faced with the task of creating new instruments, determining their reliability, and attempting to establish their units of measure. This is exceedingly difficult when social processes are continuously changing. In addition, the longitudinal nature of the research program may require the creation of new instruments during the course of the research project. Nonetheless, measurement can be achieved and measuring devices created to meet changing conditions.

Of paramount importance, however, is the selection of an appropriate outcome criterion which is socially acceptable and meaningful for those who are acquainted with the problem. For example, in the previous prison model, where different subsystems for re-entry of the prisoner into society were mentioned, a combined criterion of days out of prison, employment, and personal satisfaction might be an appropriate outcome criterion. This is based upon the knowledge of a high recidivism rate, unemployment, and dissatisfaction with a lowly status, particularly among those criminals who have had several incarcerations (State of California, 1956, pp. 90-94). Of course, many other types of measurement will be necessary in order to describe fully the social processes and the perceptions of the individuals involved. The relationship of these measures to the criterion can be ascertained through the appropriate associative techniques. Nevertheless, it is essential that the basic criterion be a socially useful one. *Such a criterion should represent the consensus of members of the social institutions that have been charged by society with the responsibility for solving the problem.*

It is also important to note here that the usually accepted sampling, design, and statistical procedures are frequently inappropriate for investigation and analysis of social problems. In sampling, for example, the continuous input and output of individuals participating in dynamic social processes often require a combination of random and stratified sampling techniques, the combination varying at different moments in time. The data may be "nonparametric" or "parametric," simple or complex, and therefore any one study may require the use of many different statistical techniques. Current techniques frequently need to be modified, and new ones that are appropriate for the problem must be developed.

Another characteristic of social innovative experiments which, although not unique to them, is exceedingly important and frequently minimized in other social science researches, is that of field observations in the naturalistic social setting. The investigator must have observed in the natural setting the phenomenon upon which he wishes to experiment. Illustratively, a great deal of research has been published on treating mental illness without the researcher having spent much time in mental institutions where the chronic psychotic lives. Such researchers frequently emphasize one aspect of chronic mental illness to the exclusion of others. The same could be said for the social problems of the ghetto, the prison, and other such social sub-systems.

Finally, it is of great importance that the results of these longitudinal studies dealing with socially significant problems be published in journals or books to which the public has access. This is particularly important because each research represents a great investment in both time and money and the expense is most frequently borne by the public. It is also important that the information is available to legislative and administrative officials.

Since existing experimental methods for social innovation are in an embryonic stage, their eventual status is, of course, unknown. Although the methodology is borrowed from the humanities and the sciences, it appears that the methods for social innovation to date are following a developmental pattern most similar to that which transpired in the field of agronomy. In this regard, the chemistry laboratory provides the chemical research that creates different fertilizers and agriculture itself presents the agronomist with hybrid seeds and farming methods. The agricultural field researcher, who has a working knowledge of both agriculture and chemistry, is charged as an agronomist with the responsibility of bringing together his knowledge of chemistry and agriculture in designing and carrying out controlled experiments under field conditions which will evaluate the effect of the experimental variables—fertilizers, seeds, and the rest—upon crop yield. Usually such experiments compare several different variables. They are carried out on plots of land where soil, water, and other natural variables are equivalent. This historical development occurred because agricultural experts were aware that in order to make accurate *recommendations* to farmers about planting and fertilizing their crops, researchers must experiment with agricultural products in their natural setting.

While the agronomist's role was being established, he faced many new problems which are now being shared by experimentalists concerned with social change. He found, for example, a great difference between his responsibilities when making recommendations to farmers about crop yield compared with his conducting chemical experiments in the laboratory. Furthermore, he was held responsible by the farmers and other members of society for his recommendations. This had the effect of making him cautious about excessive experimental claims, for he received direct feedback from affected farmers when his recommendations were inaccurate. He also found resistance to change in agricultural practices. For, on many occasions, even though replicated experiments showed the advantage of particular fertilizers, farmers who had a tradition of not using them sometimes refused to accept the experimental findings. He also found resistance from affected social organizations. For example, when his research results affected the economic position of the dairy industry, as was the case when oleomargarine was discovered, the anger of the affected industry was borne by him. Thus the agricultural researcher found that society held him responsible for his findings and, in addition, that his research affected social institutions. To the extent that favored cultural traditions were threatened, he received a hostile response. At the present time, the social innovative experimentalist is entering an era where he is experiencing many of the phenomena previously experienced by the agronomist. First, he has discovered, as the agronomist did, that social variables must be evaluated under equivalent field conditions. Second, when the results of his experiments are utilized by appropriate societal agencies, the researcher is held responsible for the participants and the results. And finally, even when the results of experiments are highly significant, the forces of cultural lag often oppose their implementation.

Although there exists this developmental analogy between experimental agriculture and social innovation, the subject matter of these fields is quite different and requires a different experimental methodology. Social subsystems have more variables and they are continuously operative; they are dynamic and not static. Agronomists design the experiment, control important variables, supervise the growth of the experimental plants, measure their yield, analyze the data, and make inferences from the experiments. At this point the process has temporarily stopped. This is not true of social phenomena. Such variables as age of the culture, population increases, differing fads, new mores, and economic conditions affect each situation and can change rapidly with time. These variables may very well have different effects at the end of the experiment than they do at the beginning. Consider, for example, the use of employment as a criterion in a longitudinal research when economic conditions are changing rapidly; or consider the meaning of hospitalization for mental illness in peace or in war. In addition to these time changes, the importance of any given variable, whether it is economic, psychological, sociological, or whatever, changes with the situation as well as with time. To take but one example, formal authoritarian status relationships are of great importance in a medical institution, but of far less importance in agricultural work camps.

Table 21-1 shows that social innovative experiments most closely resemble service programs. It is therefore important to understand clearly their differences. Psychiatrists, psychologists, social workers, criminologists, economists, and political scientists are involved daily in programs to meet the needs of society.

In this capacity they are considered experts and frequently bear the label of consultant, psychotherapist, human relations specialist, to name a few. They meet human problems in their daily work as professional persons. One thinks here of the criminologist who works in a prison conducting group meetings where criminals explore their personal problems and make future plans; one thinks also of the school consultant, the industrial consultant to management, the human relations expert, the private practitioner, and others. These experts are not usually researchers and their duties involve establishing or carrying out existing programs. The generic label used to define these statuses is *service personnel* because they are giving programmed service to the public. In this regard, service and research personnel are similar.

But in spite of the similarities resulting from the public responsibility shared equally by service and research personnel in conducting such programs, there are pronounced differences in other aspects of their social statuses. Even at a time when both are involved in programs designed to promote the welfare of individuals and society, service personnel are usually utilizing the accepted practices of their particular professions which are based upon historical tradition. On the other hand, researchers are attempting to evaluate these same practices and to create new ones. For this reason service personnel, who are the bearers of the culture, and researchers, who are attempting to evaluate that culture, may be in conflict.

It is apparent that researchers must entertain the hypothesis that any service program may or may not be beneficial to the problem population. The researcher adopts this position until comparative empirical evidence indicates which service programs are in fact the most beneficial. This is a simple matter of logic and need not serve as the basis for conflict between service and research personnel. The goal of each is the same. Moreover, research evaluating service programs shows what needs to be changed and should be considered an indispensable part of service. Indeed, research provides a logical basis for social change in the whole of society and may be one effective way of instituting progressive and orderly social change by establishing a procedure through which society can adjust to changing social conditions. It also highlights the responsibility of researchers interested in social problems to investigate impartially any social practice that may be helpful to the individual. Not only should he compare traditional practices but he should also propose and evaluate new programs that have, to the full extent of his knowledge, an opportunity to advance the humanitarian values of his society, for, unlike the traditional image of science, social innovative research is not value free.

In this regard, research activities that might have detrimental effects—for example, inflicting painful injuries on people merely to discover the effects of such painful injuries, or jury tampering, which might destroy the judicial process itself—are, in view of these humane principles, logically unacceptable as investigatable problems. As far as service programs are concerned, the researcher denies no one aid. Until the relative merits of different programs are experimentally established, the beneficial or deleterious effects produced by different treatments are unknown. There is no other logical way to evaluate their effects. The aim of research in service programs is to provide new and better treatment than currently exists. One can readily generalize the personnel conflict mentioned above in the field of mental health to similar situations in education, programs for the socially disadvantaged, and rehabilitation programs for prisoners, delinquents, and other marginal persons.

It is precisely because of service personnel's lack of experimentally-validated knowledge that social innovative research must be carried out. The humanitarian approach to social problems *is* a research approach since its end goal is to separate those programs which provide the highest probability of solving social problems from those that are deleterious or not helpful. Social subsystems, whether designed for rehabilitation, education, aid to the socially disadvantaged, or whatever, can and should be subject to such experimentation. But such researches require a full-time commitment to and interest in solutions for such critical social problems.

Methods for experimental social innovation are not independent of the experimenter himself and cannot be fully understood without describing the personal characteristics needed by such a researcher. Of paramount importance is his interest in and dedication to the solution of social problems. He receives rewards from values that are different from those of either the practitioner or the academician. In contrast to the practitioner, he does not claim any "expert" knowledge except his competence as a researcher. His approach to social problems is one aimed at solving them through experimentation. Although the very act of choosing problems indicates that he is biased, as are all researchers in this manner, he is aware of this and, therefore, he makes every attempt to provide an equal opportunity for the success of every experimental program so that his results may be unbiased. He is not content with current social practices. His role is also markedly different from the academic social scientist. He must be satisfied with fewer publications since each single study may take months or even years. He is an astute observer who attempts to describe the variables important in real-life situations without regard to method or discipline. There is no place for disciplinary chauvinism in his role. He must be willing to bear the label of an "applied" contrasted with a "basic" researcher—a comparison that is a shibboleth with prestige connotations. Whereas the academician or consultant may enter and leave the field of social action without taking responsibility for the participating people, the social innovative experimenter cannot. His full-time position and commitment to experimental social innovation require that he, in common with the practitioner, be responsible for the lives and welfare of individuals participating in the subsystems being compared. Whether his research is carried out in an institution, the community, or both, his comparative evaluations have a humanitarian aspect consistent with the mores of his society and he chooses for evaluation those programs which have a potential of advancing the general welfare. He is always a skeptic but never a cynic. Along with all researchers, his attitude is best described in the phrase, "I don't know, but I do know how to study the problem."

References

Alcoholics Anonymous: The Story of How Thousands of Men and Women Have Recovered from Alcoholism. (Rev. ed.) New York: Alcoholics Anonymous, 1955.

California, State of, Dept. of Corrections. *California Prisoners*, 1961, 1962 *and* 1963. Sacramento, Calif.: Dept. of Corrections, Research Div., 1965.

Caplow, T., and R. J. McGee. *The Academic Marketplace.* New York: Basic Books, 1958.

Caudill, W. A. *The Psychiatric Hospital as a Small Society.* Cambridge, Massachusetts: Harvard University Press, 1958.

Chein, I., D. L. Gerard, R. S. Lee, and Eva Rosenfeld. *The Road to H.* New York: Basic Books, 1963.

Etzioni, A., and Eva Etzioni, *Social Change.* New York: Basic Books, 1964.

Fairweather, G. W. (ed.) *Social Psychology in Treating Mental Illness: An Experimental Approach.* New York: Wiley, 1964.

Fairweather, G. W., and R. Simon. "A Further Follow-up Comparison of Psychotherapeutic Programs." *Journal of Consulting Psychology*, 27 (1963): 186.

Fairweather, G. W., R. Simon, Mildred E. Gebhard, E. Weingarten, J. L. Holland, R. Sanders, G. B. Stone, and G. E. Reahl. "Relative Effectiveness of Psychotherapeutic Programs: A Multicriteria Comparison of Four Programs for Three Different Patient Groups." *Psychological Monographs*, 74, No. 5 (1960).

Galbraith, J. K. *The Affluent Society.* Boston, Massachussetts: Houghton Mifflin Co., 1958.

Goffman, E. *Asylums* (*Essays on the Social Situation of Mental Patients and Other Inmates*). Chicago: Aldine, 1962.

Harrington, M. *The Other America: Poverty in the United States.* New York: Macmillan, 1962.

Hollingshead, A. B., and F. C. Redlich. *Social Class and Mental Illness: A Community Study.* New York: Wiley, 1958.

Jones, M. *The Therapeutic Community: A New Treatment Method in Psychiatry.* New York: Basic Books, 1953.

Katz, I., and Benjamin L. "Effects of White Authoritarianism in Biracial Work Groups. *Journal of Abnormal and Social Psychology*, 61 (1960): 448–456.

Katz, I., and M. Cohen. "The Effects of Training Negroes upon Cooperative Problem Solving in Biracial Teams." *Journal of Abnormal and Social Psychology*, 64 (1962): 319–325.

Lewin, K., R. Lippitt, and R. White. "Patterns of Aggressive Behavior in Experimentally Created 'social climate.' " *Journal of Social Psychology*, 10 (1939): 271–299.

Lippitt, R. "Field Theory and Experiment in Social Psychology: Autocratic and Democratic Group Atmospheres." *American Journal of Sociology*, 45 (1939): 26–49.

Madge, J. *The Tools of Social Science.* London, England: Longmans, Green, and Co., 1953.

Myrdal, G. *An American Dilemma.* New York: Harper and Row, 1944.

Olshansky, S. "The Transitional Sheltered Workshop: A Survey." *Journal of Social Issues*, 16 (1960): 33–39.

Sherif, M., and Carolyn W. Sherif. *Reference Groups.* New York: Harper and Row, 1964.

Stanton, A. H., and M. S. Schwartz. *The Mental Hospital.* New York: Basic Books, 1954.

Whyte, W. F. *Street Corner Society: The Social Structure of an Italian Slum.* (2nd ed.) Chicago: University of Chicago Press, 1955.

Yablonsky, L. *The Tunnel Back.* New York: Macmillan, 1964.

PART FOUR

Organization Development: Cultural Change as a Strategy of Social Intervention

*O*rganization Development (OD) focuses on changing social norms and values as a primary mediator of social change. The process of OD can be defined as *the creation of a culture which institutionalizes the use of various social technologies to regulate the diagnosis and change of interpersonal, group, and intergroup behaviors, especially those behaviors related to organizational decision-making, communication, and planning.* In its technology, OD encompasses aspects of both the individual-oriented and techno-structural approaches described in other sections of this book. But it differs from these two approaches in several important ways.

The techno-structural approach to social intervention, for example, attempts to alter a social system by changing formal organizational structure or technical and environmental features of the system. As such, the intervention is a temporary *project*, although it may have far-reaching effects. It accomplishes a limited goal without providing the skill and facility for handling subsequent individual and organizational problems. In contrast, by creating a culture which institutionalizes the use of various social technologies, OD creates a *permanent change* in a social system. The major objective of this cultural change is to provide a basis for continuing planned change efforts.

Individual-oriented interventions focus on changing some aspects of individuals in an effort to create system change. Although training may lead to individual change (Bunker and Knowles, 1967; Crawford, 1962; Dunnette 1969; Rubin, 1967; Schein and Bennis, 1965), and in some instances, small group change (Hall and Williams, 1966; 1970), there is very little evidence that training individuals has impact on an organization*, particularly in the areas of behavior and attitude change (Campbell and Dunnett, 1968). These findings are discussed by Schein (1965). In commenting about a classical study on the effects of human relations training by Fleishman (1953), Schein says (p. 38):

The effects of training were intimately related to the culture, or climate, of the departments from which the men came. These climates had as much of an effect on the trainee as did the training. Consequently, the training was effective, in terms of its own goal, only in those departments in which the climate from the outset supported the training goals.

The approach here will be to define this relatively new strategy of cultural change called OD. To do this, it will first be necessary to understand some of the history of the development or evolvement of this point of view as well as to compare the more traditional descriptions or models of organizations with the one proposed in an OD model. After this comparison we will describe the sequential process of cultural change as it is usually mounted in an OD effort, and discuss some of the typical interventions of social technology used in the various change efforts.

HISTORICAL ROOTS OF OD

The most appropriate point to begin is 1924. At that time, several researchers from Harvard began a study of worker performance at the Hawthorne Works of the Western Electric Company (Homans, 1950; Roethlisberger and Dickson, 1964). Initially, these investigators were concerned with the differential effects of varying particular working conditions such as the amount of ventilation and illumination. To their surprise, they found that the rate of production increased regardless of whether they increased, decreased, or held constant the intensity of light or the degree of ventilation. These findings led the experimenters to study other variables, such as modifying the length of rest breaks, working days and working weeks. After a number of years of work, the researchers continued to find that almost any variable they manipulated *seemed* to cause an increase in

Introduction

production. In continuation of the same research problem, Roethlisberger and Dickson (1964) decided to study one of these experimental groups rather intensively and concluded that these unusual results could be explained by the effects of informal social factors, i.e., the cohesive social organization of the experimental work group, which resulted partly from the novelty of being studied. This group developed its own standards of work behavior which were endorsed by the group members. Any deviance from the group standard was met with strong pressure to conform. Those members who did not meet group production standards were either pressured to conform or helped in some way to keep up. Conversely, those members whose production exceeded the group standard were quickly brought into line. These findings demonstrate the profound role that group norms and standards play in regulating individual behavior.

Lewin (1958), Bennett (1955), and Pelz (1958) conducted a series of studies which demonstrated the effectiveness of using groups to facilitate individual change. They created conditions whereby the basic attitudes and habits of house wives were changed so that they purchased and prepared certain kinds of unpopular foods, e.g., kidneys and beef hearts. On the basis of these findings, Lewin concluded (p. 210): "As long as group standards are unchanged, the individual will resist changes more strongly the further he is expected to depart from group standards. If the group standard itself is changed, the resistance which is due to the relation between individual and group standard is eliminated."

In carrying this notion further, psychologists (Bowers, 1964; Likert, 1961; Tannenbaum and Kahn, 1957, 1958; Bachman, Smith, and Slesinger, 1966; Hornstein, Callahan, Benedict and Fisch, 1968) have demonstrated that work performance and satisfaction is greater when employees perceive themselves as influencing the formulation of work group standards. One of the most definitive studies in this area was conducted by Coch and French (1948).† This study and the others that we have discussed suggest that individual and group behavior in organizations and organizational change are primarily regulated by group norms (organizational culture). The changing of group norms and values is the initial focus of OD efforts.

TOWARD A DEFINITION OF OD

The early stages of any new field are likely to produce multiple and sometimes contradictory definitions of terms. OD is no exception.‡

Blake and Mouton (1968a) define their particular approach to OD as "achieving an ideal of corporate excellence to strive toward and to perfecting a sound system of management which can convert striving into execution."

Bennis (1966) refers to OD (although he never actually uses the term) as planned organizational change. This process of planned change centers around a change agent who, in collaboration with the client system, attempts to apply valid knowledge from the behavioral sciences to the client's problems.

According to Lippitt (1969), OD "is the strengthening of those human processes in organizations which improve the functioning of the organic system so as to achieve its objectives."

Beckhard's (1969) definition is probably closest to the one used in this chapter. OD is "a planned organization-wide effort, managed from the top, to increase organization effectiveness and health through planned interventions in the organization's 'processes', using behavioral science knowledge."

Although there are differences in these definitions, some commonalities emerge: OD is described as a continuing process rather than a discrete event. It involves deliberate change efforts, and uses behavioral science technology. The definition employed in this chapter encompasses these aspects by describing OD as a process of *cultural change* that attempts to *institutionalize* the use of various social technologies which are designed to *regulate* subsequent cultural and technological change. The major components of this definition are considered below.

CULTURAL CHANGE

Arensberg and Niehoff (1964, p. 15) have provided a clear and useful definition of "culture": "Culture is the sum total of what human beings learn in common with other members of the group to which they belong." Organizational culture may be defined similarly. It is a set of learned and shared assumptions about norms (rules) which regulate member behavior. These norms are learned informally "through the grapevine" or formally through orientation classes and handbooks which teach new employees about the culture.

Cultural change is continuous and inevitable. It arises from such factors as new technology and competition between social systems. But there is a paradox or contradiction: Even though cultural change is inevitable, there is a conservative or resistant force within the culture to preserve itself. Resistance to cultural change is as constant and as inevitable as cultural change itself. According to Arensberg and Niehoff (1964, pp. 56–57), cultures have "a built-in drive toward continuity . . . each wishes to see its own culture perpetuated. In fact, the drive for technological and economic change itself is viewed by them mainly as a device by which they may survive in a competitive world and yet preserve their own way of life." These statements also apply to organizational cultures.

CURRENT ORGANIZATIONAL CULTURE

According to Katz and Kahn (1966), the culture of an organization is reflected in its (1) system of norms and values, (2) history of internal and external struggles, (3) types of people attracted, (4) work processes and physical layout, (5) modes of communication, and (6) exercise of authority. Using these six factors as a "cultural" framework for describing organizations, Table IV-1 presents three views of the current prevailing culture of organizations in comparison with the desired organizational culture that should result from an OD effort. Argyris (1964, 1962, 1957) and Bennis (1966) use the term "pyramid" in describing the structure of current organizational life, which they label *formal organizations* and *bureaucracies*, respectively. Massie (1965) has outlined the

Introduction 347

characteristics of the *classical* theory of organizational management. These three descriptions and their underlying assumptions about people and behavior are quite similar to one another and are also similar to McGregor's (1960) Theory X. Beckhard's (1969) notions of the organizational culture which should result from an OD effort are in marked contrast to these three descriptions, as can be seen in the table.

Although Katz and Kahn (1966) do not contrast the bureaucratic organization of today with an organization practicing OD, they speak to this contrast in their assertion that (on p. 469): "Perhaps the greatest organizational dilemma of our type of bureaucratic structure is the conflict between the democratic expectations of people and their actual share in decision-making." They further suggest changes which they believe would help to alleviate this conflict. These suggestions are consistent with the cultural changes surrounding an OD effort. Their suggested changes are:

(1.) Most organizations can profitably move toward some decentralization of decision-making in substructures.
(2.) Democratic forms can be introduced by shifting the source of authority from the officials to the members rather than by consultation of leaders with followers.
(3.) Distinctions between classes of citizenship can be eliminated.
(4.) The Likert principle of overlapping organizational families can improve communication.
(5.) Feedback from organizational functioning can include systematic communication from organizational members.
(6.) Closed circuits of information which make captive their own initiators can be opened up through operational research.
(7.) Role enlargement is often possible within existing structures and, with automation, may be a significant trend of the future. Such enlargement increases the sense of participation of members.
(8.) Group responsibility for a set of tasks can insure greater psychological involvement of individuals in organizations.
(9.) More explicit recognition is needed of the nature of bureaucratic systems. They are by nature open systems and the tendency to act as if they were closed, rigid structures makes people their servants rather than their masters.

These suggestions by Katz and Kahn reflect the same norms and values that are evidenced by Beckhard's objectives for OD, Bennis' (1966) notions for changing organizations, Blake and Mouton's (1968a) Grid approach, Lippitt's (1969) renewing organization, and Argyris' (1964) ideal organization where the individual's need for self-actualization is integrated with the organization's goals and objectives.

Assuming the desirability of the OD culture, the problem is to "move" the organization from its adherence to a traditional culture to the new culture.

THE INSTITUTIONALIZATION OF THE NEW CULTURE

The institutionalization process is conceptualized as having at least three com-

Table IV-1. Comparison of Contemporary Organizational Cultures with Culture of Organization Involved in OD

Factors Reflecting Culture of an Organization	Formal Organizations (Argyris)	Descriptions of Cultures of Contemporary Organizations Bureaucracies (Bennis)	Classical Organizations (Massie)	Culture of Organization Involved in OD (Beckhard)
1. Norms and Values	Individuality is repressed and no value placed on self actualization.	Interpersonal relationships are impersonal and conformity is rewarded.	Activities of group are viewed on an objective and impersonal basis; Highest value placed on productivity; People do not value the freedom of determining their own approaches to problems.	Individuality is stressed through norm of utilizing human resources to the maximum; Feelings expressed as well as logic; collaborative efforts rewarded with less emphasis on competitition; High value on democratic process of working and interacting.
2. History of Internal and External Struggles (A) CLASSICAL CONFLICT	The organization's demands and the individual's need to self-actualize usually differ considerably.	Interpersonal and organizational, since it is common in a bureaucracy to have bosses without technical competence and subordinates with it.	Between boss and subordinate since supervision is required to get work done.	No conflict; conflict among human beings is inevitable.
(B) STYLE OF CONFLICT RESOLUTION	To submerge individual needs, since organizational demands come first.	To ignore it, since the boss will eventually retire or be "promoted."	Varies, but is in the hands of the boss; he handles it in any way he sees fit, typically autocratically.	To bring it into the open and work to manage it creatively.
3. Types of People Organization Attracts	Logical thinkers; highly rational persons who suppress their feelings.	Conditioned "organization men"; persons who desire order, structure and stability in their lives.	Rational persons who do not like to work but if they have to, they prefer (a) the security of a definite task, (b) to be directed, and (c) money as their primary incentive.	Persons with strong need for self-actualization.

4. Work Processes and Physical Layout	Logical, systematic, i.e., according to scientific management principles.	Clear-cut patterns of work established and predicted; simple tasks are stressed because they are easier to master and lead to higher productivity.	Form of organizational structure follows function; self-renewing, viable system which organizes in a variety of ways depending on tasks.
5. Modes of Communication	Conforms to what organizational charts and manuals prescribe.	Restricted to limits of the specific job and hierarchical channels, otherwise members will tend to trespass on the domains of others.	Freedom of communication upward, downward, and laterally with emphasis on openness and candor.
6. Exercise of Authority	Authority-obedience principle	Authority has its source at the top of a hierarchy and is delegated down; coordination will not be achieved unless it is planned and directed from above; members in a cooperative endeavor are unable to work out the relationships of their positions without detailed guidance from their superiors.	Authority is a function of knowledge and competence as well as role; decision-making is on the basis of information source rather than organizational role.

Follows well-defined system based on rights and duties of employees.

Follows well-defined hierarchy of authoritative positions.

Division of labor based on functional specialization.

ponents: (1) Entry—initiating cultural change; (2) Normative support—taking steps to protect the nascent culture through social change; and (3) Structural support—altering the organization structure with the placement of internal OD personnel to help regulate subsequent cultural and technological change. These components, particularly the second and third, may occur simultaneously or in sequence.

The Entry Problem—Initiating the Change. A guiding principle for most practitioners in initiating change is Lewin's emphasis on the distinction between own and induced motivational forces. These are forces which emanate from within a person (own motivation) or from the surrounding environment. This distinction was useful in explaining the results of the classic research by Lewin and his associates on the effects of different leadership styles on the "climate" or "atmosphere" of group life (Lewin, Lippitt, and White, 1939; Lippitt and White, 1958). With autocratic leadership (induced force regulating behavior), group members tended to develop little of their own motivation with respect to group activities and followed the leader's directions only when he was present. In his absence group members worked very little and generally wasted time. With democratic leadership, group members worked productively whether or not a person of authority was present. In this latter case, a norm of productive work quickly developed and was followed by all group members. When group members are relatively free to decide their *own* direction and to set their *own* norms rather than have standards imposed on them, they behave responsibly and productively.

Some years later, Coch and French (1948) demonstrated that when workers participated in setting their work goals, instead of being coerced toward new goals, they developed group norms which allowed for higher production. Likert's (1961) theory of organization is based on the same principle, i.e., self- and group-motivated work leads to greater adherence to work goals than work motivation which is arbitrarily induced by someone in authority.

In this section the primary question can be formulated as follows: How are members of a classical organizational culture going to experience a felt need for change so that they will participate in planning and conducting a change effort? At least three techniques for initiating cultural change which involve the participation of the total system and provide for self-motivation can be identified:

(1) Steps toward cultural change may be stimulated when *dissonant information* is introduced in the system. This technique can be related to Festinger's (1957) theory of cognitive dissonance which proposes that when an individual experiences information which contradicts his own belief system, values or opinions, he will be motivated to reduce this dissonance.

Contrasting the actual state of affairs with what people believe exists or would ideally like is a technique for creating dissonance. The assumption is that when a group perceives a difference between present conditions and preferable alternatives, the group will be motivated to work toward those alternatives. Procedures for determining the present situation usually involve data collection. Procedures for data collection range from individual interviews (Beckhard,

1969; Shepard, 1965) to organization-wide attitude or morale surveys (Mann, 1957). Once the data are collected, they are then "fed back" to individuals in the system. These data help to disconfirm beliefs about social conditions or they help to increase the salience of adverse conditions. For more detail about this methodology, see the section on data feedback.

Another dissonance-producing technique is to conduct a demonstration project. This may range from a two-hour "OD Clinic" to a long-range effort with a sub-unit of the organization. For example, Lake and Beckhard (in this section) began their work with a unit relatively low in the organizational hierarchy. The success of this group provided other units with information about how things "might be." These other units later asked the "experimental" unit for assistance in solving some of their own problems.

(2) Steps toward cultural change may occur when it can be demonstrated that an OD approach will meet a *felt need*. Beckhard (1969) lists some ten "felt needs" that have initiated OD efforts. These have been expressed as the need for change in (1) managerial strategy, (2) structure and roles, (3) intergroup collaboration, (4) the communication system (to become more open), (5) motivation of the work force, (6) organization climate to be more consistent with both individual needs and the changing needs of the environment, (7) cultural norms (toward trust, openness, collaboration), (8) future planning, (9) handling the problems of merger, and (10) adapting to a new environment. Although a part of this strategy may be to create an awareness of a need for change, the *critical* aspect is to demonstrate that OD can respond effectively to the need.

Arensburg and Niehoff (1964) in their approach to planned change stress that the effort must begin where the client feels the greatest need and not where the change agent sees the greatest need. They add that a change agent should delay creating the felt need he deems critical until after he (change agent) has gained some measure of confidence from his client.

This suggests that in attempting to create a felt need for change, the change agent should select those issues which are closest to the client's own felt needs for change.

(3) Steps toward cultural change can be initiated with a direct change in the interpersonal skills, the attitudes, and, particularly, the values of *key persons* in the organization. This technique is educative in nature. Blake and Mouton (1968a) rely on this strategy in Phase I of Grid Organization Development which consists of a five-day seminar on the Managerial Grid—a model for conceptualizing various strategies of managerial style. Argyris also relies on this approach in applying his model of interpersonal competence (1965a, 1965b) which typically requires an early period of human relations training for key organizational members. Organizational change via the laboratory method of human relations training with primary emphasis on changes in attitudes, values, and interpersonal skill, is explained extensively by Bradford, Gibb, and Benne (1964); by Schein and Bennis (1965); and in the section of this book which covers the individual-oriented strategy for change.

Laboratory training alone has little explicit impact on the organization (Campbell and Dunnette, 1968; Dunnette and Campbell, 1968). As an initial step to gain entry followed by planned changes in the organization's culture which support the learnings from the laboratory, it can, however, be a useful part of an OD effort (see, for example, Chapter 7 in Beckhard's (1969) book and the selection by Lake and Beckhard in this section).

Normative Support for the Change. At the next stage of the change effort, the emphasis is on spreading the effect of initial cultural changes of the entry process throughout the organization. This not only legitimizes early changes but also strengthens the changes by providing social support. Mann (1957) insures this effect by planning for all relevant persons to be involved in the data feedback and problem-solving phase of his survey-feedback method of organization change. Similarly, Blake and Mouton (1968a) expect all levels of management to become involved in their Grid OD effort and Beckhard (1969) stresses that OD involves the "total system" with their effort being *managed from the top.* If top management is seen as (1) having knowledge of the OD efforts, (2) being committed to the goals of the efforts, and (3) actively supporting the methods used in achieving the goals, there is a greater guarantee of maintaining the normative change. A widespread use of team development, including the "top" team if possible, is an effective way to establish some of the norms of the new culture. Blake and Mouton (1968a) incorporate this procedure as Phase 2 of their Grid OD approach.

Structural Support for the Change. One way to insure that an organization continues to be self-critical and self-renewing—to use Lippitt's (1969) and Gardner's (1965) terms—is to develop "guardians" of the new culture. These protectors, as well as facilitators, of the new culture are a group of people whose primary job is to (1) collect information on the "state of the organizational members," (2) feed back the information to relevant organizational members, (3) provide help in diagnosing the causes of problems, (4) assist in the planning and implementing of change, and (5) provide technical assistance in training and development. These people occupy a role in which the primary responsibility is to help regulate social change as "a way of organizational life."

Hence, the third phase in the institutionalization of change technology is to establish a role in the organization which helps to *regulate* the process of OD. Initially, this role is typically fulfilled by an outside consultant to the organization. Frequently, he attempts to work in conjunction with some person (or persons) inside the organization. If the internal person is not trained in OD technology, the external consultant will usually encourage the internal person(s) and other key individuals in the organization to develop their own resources in this area. One of the external consultant's primary objectives is to reduce the organization's dependency and "to work himself out of a job" by having organizational members fulfill his role functions.**

Not all approaches to OD advocate the development of internal OD specialists. Blake and Mouton (1968a; 1968b), for example, in their Grid OD model do not provide for internal OD specialists, although they do arrange for someone either from a staff or line position to serve as an internal coordinator for the Grid OD program. As the term coordinator implies, his function is more limited than the ones discussed by Beckhard (1969) and Bennis (1966) and Burke and Schmidt (in this section). In Grid OD, the coordinator sees that the questionnaires and other instruments for intervention are on hand. He also helps groups to analyze and interpret data they have generated, but he rarely acts as a consultant. The fundamental "intervenors" in Grid OD are the paper and pencil "instrument" (the questionnaire) and the overall planned sequence of events.

OD specialists, on the other hand, are persons who are skilled in such areas as organization diagnosis, consultation, and laboratory training, and they are highly competent interpersonally. These lists of professional skills begin to suggest the type of technology that is required for OD. It is to this technology that we will now turn our attention.

THE TECHNOLOGY OF OD

There are at least two categories of OD technology which roughly correspond to the phases of an OD effort—a period of *diagnosis* followed by one of *intervention*. It is misleading to consider these activities as rigidly sequential, however, since the process of diagnosis is itself an intervention.

ORGANIZATION DIAGNOSIS

The diagnostic phase of OD can be described further as a three-step process: (1) gathering system-wide information, (2) identifying problem areas, and (3) determining the causes of the problems which have been identified.

Data Gathering. Collecting information about the "state of the system" is appropriate for analysis and possible action. These data may include (1) people's reactions to recent changes in the organization, *e.g.*, installation of a computer system; (2) the general state of employee morale; (3) individuals' perceptions of current organizational problems or problems existing between subparts of the organization; (4) management's opinion about needed organizational changes; or (5) specific matters such as subordinates' feelings about and attitudes toward their boss.

The procedure for collecting these data may involve any one or a combination of several methods. For example, interviews may be held with individuals or small groups by external or internal OD specialists (Argyris, 1962; Beckhard, 1969; Shepard, 1965). Or one of several different group sessions may be conducted: (1) confrontation meetings (Beckhard, 1967—included in this volume); (2) intergroup competition/collaborations (Blake, Shepard, and Mouton, 1964); (3) problem-solving conferences (Burke and Ellis, 1969); or (4) "deep sensing" sessions (Lewis, 1969). A rather comprehensive approach to the collection of data is Mann's (1967) survey feedback technique. With these special techniques, data gathering, diagnosis, problem-solving, and plans for action steps are all conducted within one block of time as brief as a few hours or as long as several days.

Identifying the Problem and Diagnosing its Causes. Whatever diagnostic technique OD specialists use, the underlying principle which is widely shared is that organization members must participate in the diagnostic process. One model that is used for thinking about the causes of social problems is Lewin's Force Field Analysis (Lewin, 1947; Coch and French, 1948; Jenkins, 1949; McGregor, 1944).

Relying on their knowledge of contemporary organizational life, some OD specialists such as Argyris (1965a, 1965b) and Blake and Mouton (1968b) have identified several basic causes of problems that are common to many organizations. Argyris subsumes these causes under the label of "interpersonal competence" and Blake and Mouton label them "managerial style." Argyris has developed a model of interpersonal competence (1962) and a system for categorizing interpersonal behavior (1965a; 1965b). By observing social interaction in an organization and recording his observations according to a certain classification scheme, Argyris assesses the level of interpersonal competence and reports that contemporary organizations are dominated by such values as rationality, intellectual clarity, and the suppression of feelings. These values create an imbalance between the level of interpersonal competence and that of intellective, rational competence. This imbalance is identified as a central cause of many organizational problems (Argyris, 1962).

Collecting data from managers in 198 different companies throughout the world, Blake and Mouton (1968a) have evidence which suggests that the major barrier to organizational effectiveness (or "corporate excellence," to use their terminology) is communication. They contend that communication problems are symptomatic of a deeper and more significant cause. The basic cause of organizational ineffectiveness is (as they say on p. 5) "to be found in the character of supervision. . . . Managers are not really managing behavior in most corporations today. They may be driving it, criticizing it, monitoring it, tolerating it, accepting it, or buying it. Only rarely are they really leading it." Their learning model, the Managerial Grid (Blake and Mouton, 1964), facilitates the development of this skill by helping the manager diagnose his managerial problems and by providing him with an objective for a more effective style of managerial behavior.

Other examples of what consultants believe are central problem areas in organizations include: socio-technical problems (Trist, 1960), employee motivation (Herzberg, 1966), and the depersonalization that exists in many organizations (Bennis, 1966; Shepard, 1965).

OD INTERVENTIONS: A SOCIAL TECHNOLOGY

After completing the diagnosis, there is a need to develop a strategy for dealing with a problem or problems. Space limitations do not permit a detailed discussion of OD intervention technology. Instead, a summary of the major characteristics of various interventions will be presented. The interventions are usually, but not always, experience-based, and require collaborative participation of the client group in most phases of the change effort.

Techno-Structural Interventions. These interventions are discussed at length in the techno-structural section of this text. The approach involves environmental, technological, or structural change, including reformulating the organization chart, planning for the arrangement of office space, and operations research interventions such as modifying some aspect of work flow in a manufacturing division or redesigning the technological details of a person's job.

Team-Development. Organizations can be viewed as consisting of overlapping teams, sometimes called "family groups." These groups may be a permanent part of an organization, *e.g.*, a manager and his key subordinates or a cross-departmental team which has the mission of coordinating the two departments' functions, or they may be *ad hoc*, such as committees, task forces, or project teams.

Hence, team development has been a major tool in OD intervention technology (Argyris, 1962; Blake and Mouton, 1968a; Crockett, 1970; McGregor, 1967). It frequently consists of a two or three day off-site meeting at which team members consider a reorganization of their department (or any other subsystem in the organization) and work to develop new relationships that will facilitate the reorganization. The work is ordinarily concerned with changes in individuals' authority and responsibility and a different allocation of work functions.

Team development may also include sessions in which team members reflect on their interpersonal relationships. This type of team development often occurs in response to internal conflict or when members are confused about their relationships with a team leader.

Skill training may also be a part of team development. This development may include training in group decision-making, problem-solving or conflict resolution (Burke and Ellis, 1969; Harvey and Boettger, 1970; Kepner and Tregoe, 1965).

Data Feedback Intervention. A brief discussion of these techniques was covered in the earlier section on data gathering. For a more comprehensive discussion of these interventions, see Part Three, "Data-Based Strategies of Social Intervention."

Action-Research Interventions. In its original formulation by Lewin—as interpreted by Chein, Cook, and Harding (1948)—action research is undertaken to solve an existing problem. One of the best examples of this approach is illustrated by Coch and French (1948) (reported earlier). A number of issues in the use of action research are discussed in the section on data feedback.

Intergroup Interventions. Intergroup problem-solving sessions or intergroup laboratories have been used as a procedure for alleviating dysfunctional conflict and promoting collaboration (Blake, Mouton, and Sloma, 1965).

A general design for one of these interventions follows this sequence of events: Competing groups (*e.g.*, sales and production, manufacturing and maintenance, or union and management) are separated and each is asked to generate a list of terms which they think accurately describes themselves as a group. Then they develop a second list of descriptive terms or phrases which they believe depicts the *other* group. Finally, each group develops a speculative list of terms which they believe the other group is saying about them. After completing the set of three lists, the groups come together to share one another's perceptions and predictions. This two-way communication accomplishes two things: (1) Distorted and stereotyped perceptions, misunderstandings, and misconceptions between the two groups are identified and examined; and (2) issues and problem areas are listed and ranked according to importance. This listing and ranking may be done in separate groups first and then synthesized, or competing groups may work together. At this point, the groups reorganize themselves into task forces, consisting of members from all competing groups, to propose alternative solutions to the problems and generate action steps for implementing the more feasible solutions.

Although different behavioral scientists vary the procedure described above (cf. Beckhard, 1969; Blake, Shepard, and Mouton, 1964), this type of design is typical.

Training Interventions. Training is an intervention which is frequently used in OD. It is usually most effective when it is planned as a response to some diagnosed need in the organization.

Many different training approaches such as skill training, management development, laboratory (or experienced-based) training, and on-the-job training, are used in organizations today. Although certain kinds of skill training, *e.g.*, Kepner-Tregoe training in decision making or learning "management by objectives," are utilized in OD, laboratory training is probably relied on more than other methods.

A training laboratory is a process of education in human interaction. This process is one in which participants in small groups of 8–12 persons examine their own behavior as they relate with others and explore new (and quite possibly more effective) ways of interacting. Thus, the training process is labeled a *laboratory* since the participants examine present modes of behavior and experiment with new ones. Although participants interact under their own initiative and control in a relatively unstructured situation, a skilled professional in behavioral science is also present who provides the group with new knowledge, consultation, and, at times, guidance for activities.

Following the principles of Lewinian theory and practice, the training laboratory is based on the assumption that *skills in human interaction* (a major objective of the laboratory programs) can be learned most effectively when the learner (participant) is centrally involved in providing the learning experience.§

Other Interventions. There are many other interventions that OD specialists may use. The collaborative approach to setting organizational goals, referred to as "management by objectives," has been employed in efforts to change organizations (Drucker, 1964). Herzberg's (Herzberg, 1968; Paul, Robertson and Herzberg, 1969) procedures for enriching jobs is often a useful strategy in OD, especially when motivational factors have been identified as problems. When there has been serious friction between labor and management, the

Scanlon Plan has proved to be an effective intervention for change (Lesieur, 1958).

The basic rationale in choosing a technique for an OD intervention is that it is one which will (1) respond to some felt need for change, (2) facilitate change in the organization's culture, and (3) involve the client group itself in planning and implementing the change.

SUMMARY

Organization development is a process of planned cultural change. The emphasis in OD initially is on some form of diagnosis followed by an intervention which responds to the need as diagnosed. OD does not attempt to impose some pre-planned package on the organization as a way of solving problems. What the process does involve is the development of new norms of member behavior which "state" that it is not only permissible to examine continually the *way* people in the organization relate and work with one another, but this kind of activity is just as important as "making a profit" or "rendering a service."

As a strategy for social change, the OD change agent helps create conditions in the organization whereby its members can assume the responsibility and authority for solving the problems that directly affect them. The conditions created by the change agent are those labeled as the "social technology of OD." The technology discussed in this chapter is quite new especially with respect to accumulated experience with the various methods. Undoubtedly these methods will be refined and others added in the next decade.

OVERVIEW

The purpose for including the articles which follow in this part was to provide (1) further clarification of this relatively new strategy for social change, (2) different perspectives on the strategy by considering some varying approaches, and (3) illustrations of OD in action. Although different viewpoints are discussed, all of the articles do fit within the general framework of OD as defined here earlier.

Bennis, in his discussion of "Changing Organizations," establishes a societal setting for OD. He develops reasons for why OD is quite timely today, at least in the United States. In his discussion of organizations of the future, Bennis paints a picture of the organization of some 25 to 50 years hence. As the reader will note, his organization of the future is consistent with the goals and objectives of OD.

The Burke and Schmidt article helps to clarify OD, a fairly new strategy for organizational change, by comparing it with a more traditional strategy for change, management development. Burke and Schmidt show how the two strategies differ, and they provide a rationale for how the two should be related.

Buchanan provides further clarification of OD by examining several actual cases and by determining the issues and elements of strategy they have in common. He divides the cases into two categories: Those he considers successful, and those that were not. The two issues Buchanan associates with success are whether linkage was established (1) between the target system and the larger system, and (2) among the various parts within the target system. For Buchanan, then, the major avenue for OD success is the spreading of the normative change throughout the total organization.

Grid organization development is also a process of cultural change, but the social technology used is more structured and "programmed" than the approaches discussed by the other authors. Blake and Mouton, the creators of Grid OD, present the underlying rationale for this particular strategy and then compare Grid OD with what they label as the "T-Group-consultant" approach. This latter approach, while not limited to the T-Group as its major intervention, is represented by most, if not all, the other authors in this OD section.

Lake and Beckhard describe an actual OD case, explain the research methodology used to evaluate the change effort, and discuss the results. This paper represents one of the few cases of OD that has been systematically studied and reported.

Notes

* Some possible exceptions include studies by Argyris (1962); Blake, Mouton, Barnes and Greiner (1964); and White (1967), although Dunnette and Campbell (1968) raise doubts about these. Another exception is the selection in this part by Lake and Beckhard.

† This study is described in some detail in the part on data feedback.

‡ For example, see a recent compilation of papers edited by Walter R. Mahler entitled, "What is Organization Development?" This series of papers has been published by the OD Division of the American Society for Training and Development.

** With the growth of OD, this role of being a "change agent" or an "OD practitioner or specialist" is becoming more common. Some organizations have created departments of OD and members of these departments have the explicit role of being a change agent. Other organizations have combined this change function with some of the more traditional organizational functions such as personnel, training, industrial relations, or manpower development. According to Beckhard (1969) the major advantage of having an OD department is that it brings together a group of specialists who are skilled and knowledgeable in applied behavioral science. There is, however, a serious limitation of an internal OD department. Such a department tends to locate the speciality away from and, therefore, disconnected from other "people" areas of the organization such as personnel and industrial relations.

§ The training laboratory has been explained and discussed in a variety of sources. Some of the more thorough sources are Bradford, Gibb, and Benne (1964), Schein and Bennis (1965), Batchelder and Hardy (1968), and the quarterly issues of the *Journal of Applied Behavioral Science*.

References

Arensberg, C. M. and A. H. Niehoff. *Introducing Social Change: A Manual for Americans Overseas*. Chicago: Aldine, 1964.

Argyris, C. "Explorations in Interpersonal Competence—I," *Journal of Applied Behavioral Science*, 1 (1965a): 58–83.

Introduction

Argyris, C. "Explorations in Interpersonal Competence—II," *Journal of Applied Behavioral Science*, 1 (1965b): 255–269.
Argyris, C. *Integrating the Individual and the Organization*. New York: Wiley, 1964.
Argyris, C. *Interpersonal Competence and Organizational Effectiveness*. Homewood, Illinois: Dorsey Press, 1962.
Argyris, C. *Personality and Organization: The Conflict Between System and the Individual*. New York: Harper and Row, 1957.
Bachman, J., C. Smith, and J. Slesinger. "Control, Performance and Satisfaction: An analysis of Structural and Individual Effects," *Journal of Personality and Social Psychology*, 4 (1966): 127–136.
Batchelder, R. L. and J. M. Hardy. *Using Sensitivity Training and the Laboratory Method*. New York: Association Press, 1968.
Beckhard, R. *Organization Development—Strategies and Models*. Cambridge, Massachusetts: Addison–Wesley, 1969.
Beckhard, R. "The Confrontation Meeting," *Harvard Business Review*, 45, No. 2 (1967): 149–155.
Bennett, Edith B. "Discussion, Decision, Commitment, and Consensus in Group Decisions," *Human Relations*, 7 (1955): 251–274.
Bennis, W. G. *Changing Organizations*. New York: McGraw-Hill, 1966.
Blake, R. R. and J. S. Mouton. *The Managerial Grid*. Houston: Gulf Publishing, 1964.
Blake, R. R. and J. S. Mouton. *Corporate Excellence Through Grid Organization Development*. Houston: Gulf Publishing, 1968 (a).
Blake, R. R. and J. S. Mouton. *Corporate Excellence Diagnosis*. Houston: Gulf Publishing, 1968 (b).
Blake, R. R., J. S. Mouton, L. B. Barnes, and L. E. Greiner. "Breakthrough in Organizational Development," *Harvard Business Review*, 42 (1964): 133–155.
Blake, R. R., J. S. Mouton, and R. Sloma. "The Union-Management Intergroup Laboratory" *Journal of Applied Behavioral Science*, 1 (1965): 25–57.
Blake, R. R., H. A. Shepard, and J. S. Mouton. *Managing Intergroup Conflict in Industry*. Houston: Gulf Publishing, 1964.
Bowers, D. "Organizational Control in an Insurance Company," *Sociometry*, 27 (1964): 230–244.
Bradford, L. P., J. R. Gibb, and K. D. Benne (eds.). *T-Group Theory and Laboratory Method*. New York: Wiley, 1964.
Bunker, D. R., and E. S. Knowles. "Comparison of Behavioral Changes Resulting from Human Relations Training Laboratories of Different Lengths," *Journal of Applied Behavioral Science*, 3 (1967): 505–524.
Burke, W. W., and B. R. Ellis. "Designing a Work Conference on Change and Problem Solving," *Adult Leadership*, 17 (1969): 410–412, 435–437.
Campbell, J. P., and M. D. Dunnette. "Effectiveness of T-Group Experiences in Managerial Training and Development," *Psychological Bulletin*, 70 (1968): 73–104.
Chein, I., S. Cook and J. Harding. "The Field of Action Research," *American Psychologist*, 3 (1948): 43–50.
Coch, L., and J. R. P. French, Jr. "Overcoming Resistance to Change," *Human Relations*, 4 (1948): 512–533.
Crawford, M. P. "Concepts of Training," in R. M. Gagne (ed.). *Psychological Principles in System Development*. New York: Holt, 1962, Chapter 9.
Crockett, W. J. "Team Building—One Approach to Organizational Development," *Journal of Applied Behavioral Science*, 6 (1970).
Drucker, P. *Managing for Results*. New York: Harper and Row, 1964.
Dunnette, M. D. "People Feeling: Joy, More Joy, and the 'Slough of Despond,'" *Journal of Applied Behavioral Science*, 5 (1969): 25–44.
Dunnette, M. D., and J. P. Campbell. "Laboratory Education: Impact on People and Organizations," *Industrial Relations*, 8 (1968): 1–45.
Festinger, L. *Theory of Cognitive Dissonance*. Evanston, Illinois: Row, Peterson, 1957.
Fleishman, E. A. "Leadership Climate, Human Relations Training, and Supervisory Behavior," *Personnel Psychology*, 6 (1953): 205–222.
Gardner, J. W. "How to Prevent Organizational Dry Rot," *Harper's*, October, 1965.
Hall, J. and M. S. Williams. "Group Dynamics and Improved Decision Making," *Journal of Applied Behavioral Science*, 6 (1970).

Hall, J. and M. S. Williams. "A Comparison of Decision-Making Performances in Established and ad hoc groups," *Journal of Personality and Social Psychology*. 3 (1966): 214–222.
Harvey, J. B., and C. R. Boettger. "Improving Communication in Managerial Work Groups," *Journal of Applied Behavioral Science*, 6, (1970).
Herzberg, F. "One More Time: How Do You Motivate Employees?" *Harvard Business Review*, 46 (1968): 53–62.
Homans, G. C. *The Human Group*. New York: Harcourt, Brace, 1950.
Hornstein, H. A., D. M. Callahan, E. Fisch, and B. A. Benedict. "Influence and Satisfaction in Organizations: A Replication," *Sociology of Education*, 41 (1968), 380–389.
Jenkins, D. H. "Social Engineering in Educational Change: An Outline of Method," *Progressive Education*, 26 (1949): 193–197.
Katz, P., and R. L. Kahn. *The Social Psychology of Organizations*. New York: Wiley, 1966.
Kepner, C. H., and B. B. Tregoe. *The Rational Manager*. New York: McGraw-Hill, 1965.
Lesieur, F. G. *The Scanlon Plan*. Cambridge: Technology Press of MIT and Wiley, 1958.
Lewin, K. "Group Decision and Social Change." in E. E. Maccoby, T. M. Newcomb, and E. L. Hartley (eds.). *Readings in Social Psychology*. New York: Holt, 1958, 197–211.
Lewin, K. "Frontiers in Group Dynamics: Concept, Method, and Reality in Social Science, Social Equilibria and Social Change," *Human Relations*, 1 (1947): 5–41.
Lewin, K. "Action Research and Minority Problems," *Journal of Social Issues*, 2 (1946): 34–46.
Lewin, K., R. Lippett, and R. K. White. "Patterns of Aggressive Behavior in Experimentally Created 'Social Climates,'" *Journal of Social Psychology*, 10 (1939): 271–299.
Lewis, J. W. "Deep Sensing: A Diagnostic Intervention for Organizations." Unpublished manuscript, Case-Western Reserve University, 1969.
Likert, R. *New Patterns of Management*. New York: McGraw-Hill, 1961.
Lippitt, G. L. *Organization Renewal*. New York: Appleton-Century-Crofts, 1969.
Lippitt, R., and R. K. White. "An Experimental Study of Leadership and Group Life." in E. E. Maccoby, T. M. Newcomb, and E. L. Hartley, (eds.). *Readings in Social Psychology*. New York: Holt, 1958, 496–511.
McGregor, D. *The Professional Manager*. New York: McGraw-Hill, 1967.
McGregor, D. *The Human Side of Enterprise*. New York: McGraw-Hill, 1960.
McGregor, D. "Conditions of Effective Leadership in the Industrial Organization," *Journal of Consulting Psychology*, 8 (1944), 55–63.
Mann, F. C. "Studying and Creating Change: A Means to Understanding Social Organization," in C. M. Arensburg et al. (eds.). *Research in Industrial Human Relations*. New York: Harper, 1957.
Massie, J. L. "Management Theory," in J. G. March (ed.). *Handbook of Organizations*. Chicago: Rand McNally, 1965.
Paul, W. J., K. B. Robertson, and F. Herzberg. "Job Enrichment Pays Off," *Harvard Business Review*, 47 (1969), 61–78.
Pelz, Edith B. "Some factors in 'group decision,'" in E. E. Maccoby, T. M. Newcomb, and E. L. Hartley (eds.). *Readings in Social Psychology*. New York: Holt, 1958, 212–219.
Roethlisberger, F. J., and W. J. Dickson. *Management and the Worker*. Cambridge, Massachusetts: Harvard University Press, 1964.
Rubin, I., "Increasing Self-Acceptance: A Means of Reducing Prejudice," *Journal of Personality and Social Psychology*, 5 (1967), 233–238.
Schein, E. H. *Organizational Psychology*. Englewood Cliffs, N.J.: Prentice-Hall, 1965.
Schein, E. H. and W. G. Bennis. *Personal and Organizational Change Through Group Methods: The Laboratory Approach*. New York: Wiley, 1965.
Shepard, H. A. "Changing Interpersonal and Intergroup Relationships in Organizations," in J. G. March (ed.). *Handbook of Organizations*, Chicago: Rand McNally, 1965.
Tannenbaum, A. S., and R. L. Kahn. *Participation in Union Locals*. Evanston, Illinois: Row Peterson, 1958.
Tannenbaum, A. S., and R. L. Kahn. "Organizational Control Structure: A General Descriptive Technique as Applied to Four Local Unions," *Human Relations*, 10 (1957), 127–140.
Trist, E. L. *Socio-Technical Systems*. London: Tavistock, 1960.
White, S. T. "*Evaluation of an Analytic Trouble-Shooting Program:* A Preliminary Report." Research memo, Kepner-Tregoe and Associates, July 28, 1967.
Yarrow, M. R., J. D. Campbell, and L. J. Yarrow. "Acquisition of New Norms: A Study of Racial Desegregation," *Journal of Social Issues*, 14 (1958), 8–28.

22

WARREN G. BENNIS

Changing Organizations

THE IDEA OF CHANGE

*n*ot far from where the new Government Center is going up, in downtown Boston, a foreign visitor walked up to an American sailor and asked why the ships of his country were built to last for only a short time. According to the foreign tourist, "The sailor answered without hesitation that the art of navigation is making such rapid progress that the finest ship would become obsolete if it lasted beyond a few years. In these words, which fell accidentally from an uneducated man, I began to recognize the general and systematic idea upon which your great people direct all their concerns."

The foreign visitor was that shrewd observer of American morals and manners, Alexis de Tocqueville, and the year was 1835. He would not recognize Scollay Square today. But he caught the central theme of our country—its preoccupation, its *obsession* with change. One thing, however, *is* new since de Tocqueville's time: the prevalence of newness, the changing scale and scope of change itself, so that, as Oppenheimer said, ". . . the world alters as we walk in it, so that the years of man's life measure not some small growth or rearrangement or moderation of what was learned in childhood, but a great upheaval."

Numbers have a magic all their own, and it is instructive to review some of the most relevant ones. In 1789, when George Washington was inaugurated, American society comprised fewer than 4 million persons, of whom 750,000 were Negroes. Few persons lived in cities; New York, then the capital, had a population of 33,000. In all, 200,000 individuals lived in what were then defined as "urban areas"—places with more than 2,500 inhabitants. In the past ten years, Los Angeles has grown by 2,375,000, almost enough to people present-day Boston. In July, 1964, the population of the United States was about 192 million. The U.S. Census Bureau estimates that the population in 1975 will be

Reproduced by special permission from *The Journal of Applied Behavioral Science*, Vol. 2, No. 3 (1966): 247–263, published by the NTL Institute for Applied Behavioral Science.

between 226 and 235 million and that in 1980 it will be between 246 and 260 million. World population was over 3 billion in 1964. If fertility remains at present levels until 1975 and then begins to decline, the population of the world will reach 4 billion in 1977, 5 billion by about 1990.

In 1960, when President Kennedy was elected, more than half of all Americans alive were over 33 years of age and had received their formative experiences during the Great Depression, or earlier. By 1970, only ten years later, more than half of all Americans alive were under 25 and born after World War II. In one short decade the mid-age of the United States will have dropped by a full eight years—the sharpest such age drop recorded in history.

Observe the changes taking place in education. Thirty years ago only one out of every eight Americans at work had been to high school. Today four out of five attend high school. Thirty years ago 4 percent or less of the population attended college. Now the figure is around 35 percent, in cities about 50 percent.

Consider one more example of social change. We are all aware of the momentum of the Scientific Revolution, whose magnitude and accelerating rate—to say nothing of its consequences—are truly staggering. By 1980 science will cut even a wider path, for in that year the government alone will spend close to $35 billion on research and development: $10 billion on arms and arms control, $7 billion on basic research, and $18 billion on vast civilian welfare programs and new technology

"Everything nailed down is coming loose," an historian said recently, and it does seem that no exaggeration, no hyperbole, no outrage can realistically appraise the extent and pace of modernization. Exaggerations come true in only a year or two. Nothing will remain in the next ten years—or there will be twice as much of it.

And it is to our credit that the pseudo-horror stories and futuristic fantasies about *accelerations* of the rate of change (the rate of obsolescence, scientific and technological unemployment) and the number of "vanishing" stories (the vanishing salesman, the vanishing host, the vanishing adolescent, the vanishing village)—it is to our credit that these phenomenal changes have failed to deter our compulsive desire to invent, to overthrow, to upset inherited patterns and comfort in the security of the future.

No more facts and numbers are needed to make the point. We can *feel* it on the job, in the school, in the neighborhood, in our professions, in our everyday lives. Lyndon Johnson said recently, "We want change. We want progress. We want it both at home and abroad—and we aim to get it!" I think he's got it.

CHANGING ORGANIZATIONS

How will these accelerating changes in our society influence human organizations?

Let me begin by describing the dominant form of human organization employed throughout the industrial world. It is a unique and extremely durable social arrangement called "bureaucracy," a social invention perfected during the Industrial Revolution to organize and direct the activities of the business firm. It is today the prevailing and supreme type of organization wherever people direct concerted effort toward the achievement of some goal. This holds for university systems, for hospitals, for large voluntary organizations, for governmental organizations.

Corsica, according to Gibbon, is much easier to deplore than to describe. The same holds true for bureaucracy. Basically, bureaucracy is a social invention which relies exclusively on the power to influence through rules, reason, and the law. Max Weber, the German sociologist who developed the theory of bureaucracy around the turn of the century, once described bureaucracy as a social machine: "Bureaucracy," he wrote, "is like a modern judge who is a vending machine into which the pleadings are inserted together with the fee and which then disgorges the judgment together with its reasons mechanically derived from the code."

The bureaucratic "machine model" Weber outlined was developed as a reaction against the personal subjugation, nepotism, cruelty, and capricious and subjective judgments which passed for managerial practices in the early days of the Industrial Revolution. The true hope for man, it was thought, lay in his ability to rationalize, to calculate, to use his head as well as his hands and heart. Bureaucracy emerged out of the need for more predictability, order, and precision. It was an organization ideally suited to the values of Victorian Empire.

Most students of organizations would say that the anatomy of bureaucracy consists of the following "organs": a division of labor based on functional specialization, a well-defined hierarchy of authority, a system of procedures and rules for dealing with all contingencies relating to work activities, impersonality of interpersonal relations, and promotion and selection based on technical competence. It is the pyramidal arrangement we see on most organizational charts.

Allow me to leap-frog to the conclusion of my paper now. It is my premise that the bureaucratic form of organization is out of joint with contemporary realities; that new shapes, patterns, and models are emerging which promise drastic changes in the conduct of the corporation and of managerial practices in general. In the next 25 to 50 years we should witness, and participate in, the end of bureaucracy as we know it and the rise of new social systems better suited to twentieth-century demands of industrialization.

REASONS FOR ORGANIZATIONAL CHANGE

I see two main reasons for these changes in organizational life. One has been implied earlier in terms of changes taking place in society, most commonly referred to as the population and knowledge explosions. The other is more subtle and muted—perhaps less significant, but for me profoundly exciting. I have no easy name for it, nor is it easy to define. It has to do with man's historical quest for self-awareness, for using reason to achieve and stretch his potentialities and possibilities. I think that this deliberate self-analysis has spread to large and more complex social systems, to organizations. I think there has been a dramatic upsurge of this spirit of inquiry over the past two decades. At new depths and over a wider range of affairs, organizations are opening their operations up to self-inquiry and analysis. This really involves two parallel shifts in values and outlooks, between the men who make history and the men who make knowledge. One change is the scientist's realization of his affinity with men of affairs, and the other is the latter's receptivity and new-found respect for men of knowledge. I am calling this new development *organizational revitalization*. It is a complex social process which involves a deliberate and self-conscious examination of organizational behavior and a collaborative relationship between managers and scientists to improve performance.

This new form of collaboration may be taken for granted by many members of the Sloan School of Management. For myself, I have basked under the light of Professor Douglas McGregor's foresight and have simply come to regard reciprocity between the academician and the manager as inevitable and natural. But I can assure you that this development is unprecedented, that never before in history, in any society, has man, in his organizational context, so willingly searched, scrutinized, examined, inspected, or contemplated—for meaning, for purpose, for improvement.

I think this shift in outlook has taken a good deal of courage from both partners in this encounter. The manager has had to shake off old prejudice about "eggheads" and long-hair intellectuals. More important, he has had to make himself and his organization vulnerable and receptive to external sources and to new, unexpected, even unwanted information—which all of you know is not such an easy thing to do. The academician has had to shed some of his natural hesitancies. Scholarly conservatism is admirable, I think, except to hide behind, and for a long time caution has been a defense against reality.

It might be useful to dwell on the role of academic man and his growing involvement with social action, using the field of management education as a case in point. Until recently, the field of business was disregarded by large portions of the American public, and it was unknown to or snubbed by the academic establishment. Management education and research were at best regarded there with dark suspicion, as if contact with the world of reality—particularly monetary reality—was equivalent to a dreadful form of pollution. In fact, academic man has historically taken one of two stances toward The Establishment, *any* Establishment—that of rebellious critic or of withdrawn snob. The former (the rebel) can be "bought," but only in paperback books under such titles as: *The Power Elite, The Lonely Crowd, The Organization Man, The Hidden Persuaders, The Tyranny of Testing, Mass Leisure, The Exurbanites, The Death and Life of Great American Cities, The American Way of Death, Compulsory Mis-Education, The Status Seekers, Growing Up Absurd, The Paper Economy, Silent Spring, The Child Worshippers, The Affluent Society, The Depleted Society*. On the basis of these titles and reports of their brisk sales, I am thinking of writing one called *Masochism in Modern America*, practically a guaranteed success.

The withdrawn stance can be observed in some of our American universities but less so these days. It is still the prevailing attitude in many European universities. There, the university seems intent to preserve the monastic ethos of its medieval origins, offering a false but lulling security to its inmates and sapping curriculum of virility and relevance. Max Beerbohm's whimsical and idyllic fantasy of Oxford, *Zuleika Dobson*, dramatizes this: "It is this mild, miasmal air, not less than the grey beauty and the gravity of the buildings that has helped Oxford to produce, and foster, eternally, her peculiar race of artist-scholars, scholar-artists. . . . The buildings and their traditions keep astir in his mind whatsoever is gracious; the climate enfolding and enfeebling him, lulling him, keeps him careless of the sharp, harsh exigent realities of the outer world. These realities may be seen by him. . . . But they cannot fire him. Oxford is too damp for that."

"Adorable dreamer," said Matthew Arnold, in his valedictory to Oxford, "whose heart has been so romantic! who has given thyself so prodigally, given thyself to sides and to heroes not mine, only never to the Philistine! . . . what teacher could ever so save us from that bondage to which we are all prone . . . the bondage of what binds us all, the narrow, the mundane, the merely practical."

The intellectual and the manager have only recently come out of hiding and recognized the enormous possibilities of joint ventures. Remember that the idea of the professional school is new; this is true even in the case of the venerable threesome—law, medicine, and engineering—to say nothing of such recent upstarts as business and public administration. It is as new as the institutionalization of science, and even today, this change is not greeted with unmixed joy. Colin Clark, the economist, writing in a recent *Encounter*, referred to the "dreadful suggestion that Oxford ought to have a business school."

It is probably true that we in the United States have had a more pragmatic attitude toward knowledge than anyone else. Many observers have been impressed with the disdain European intellectuals seem to show for practical matters. Even in Russia, where one would least expect it, there is little interest in the "merely useful." Harrison Salisbury, the *New York Times*'s Soviet expert, was struck during his recent travels by the almost total absence of liaison between research and practical application. He saw only one great agricultural experimental station on the American model. In that case, professors were working in the fields. They told Salisbury, "People call us Americans."

There may not be many American professors working in the fields, but they can be found, when not waiting in airports, almost everywhere else: in factories, in government, in less advanced countries, more recently in backward areas of our own country, in mental hospitals, in the State Department, in educational systems, and in practically all the institutional crevices Ph.D. recipients can worm their way into. They are advising, counseling, researching, recruiting, interpreting, developing, consulting, training, and working for the widest variety of client imaginable. This is not to say that the deep ambivalence which some Americans hold toward the intellectual has disappeared, but it does indicate that academic man has become more committed to action, in greater numbers, with more diligence, and with higher aspirations than at any other time in history.

Indeed, Fritz Machlup, the economist, has coined a new economic category called the "knowledge industry," which, he claims, accounts for 29 percent of the gross national product. And Clark Kerr, the President of the University of California, said not too long ago, "What the railroads did for the second half of the last century and the automobile did for the first half of this century may be done for the second half of this century by the knowledge industry: that is, to serve as the focal point of national growth. And the university is at the center of the knowledge process."

CHANGES IN MANAGERIAL PHILOSOPHY

Now let us turn to the main theme and put the foregoing remarks about the reciprocity between action and knowledge into the perspective of changing organizations. Consider some of the relatively recent research and theory concerning the human side of enterprise which have made such a solid impact on management thinking and particularly upon the moral imperatives which guide managerial action. I shall be deliberately sweeping in summarizing these changes as much to hide my surprise as to cover a lot of ground quickly. (I can be personal about this. I remember observing Professor McGregor's class some seven years ago, when he first presented his new theories, and I remember the sharp antagonism his Theory X and Theory Y analysis then provoked. Today, I believe most of you would take these ideas as generally self-evident.)

It seems to me that we have seen over the past decade a fundamental change in the basic philosophy which underlies managerial behavior, reflected most of all in the following three areas:

(1.) A new concept of *man*, based on increased knowledge of his complex and shifting needs, which replaces the over-simplified, innocent push-button idea of man.

(2.) A new concept of *power*, based on collaboration and reason, which replaces a model of power based on coercion and fear.

(3.) A new concept of *organizational values*, based on humanistic-democratic ideals, which replaces the depersonalized mechanistic value system of bureaucracy.

Please do not misunderstand. The last thing I want to do is overstate the case. I do not mean that these transformations of man, power, and organizational values are fully accepted or even understood, to say nothing of implemented, in day-to-day affairs. These changes may be light-years away from actual adoption. I do mean that they have gained wide intellectual acceptance in enlightened management quarters, that they have caused a tremendous amount of rethinking and search behavior on the part of many organizations, and that they have been used as a basis for policy formulation by many large-scale organizations.

I have tried to summarize all the changes affecting organizations, resulting both from the behavioral sciences and from trends in our society, in the table of human problems confronting contemporary organizations (Table 22-1).

Changing Organizations

Table 22-1. *Human Problems Confronting Contemporary Organizations*

	Problem	Bureaucratic Solutions	New Twentieth-Century Conditions
INTEGRATION	The problem of how to integrate individual needs and management goals	No solution because of no problem. Individual vastly oversimplified, regarded as passive instrument or disregarded.	Emergence of human sciences and understanding of man's complexity. Rising aspirations. Humanistic-democratic ethos.
SOCIAL INFLUENCE	The problem of the distribution of power and sources of power and authority	An explicit reliance on legal-rational power but an implicit usage of coercive power. In any case, a confused, ambiguous, shifting complex of competence, coercion, and legal code.	Separation of management from ownership. Rise of trade unions and general education. Negative and unintended effects of authoritarian rule.
COLLABORATION	The problem of managing and resolving conflicts	The "rule of hierarchy" to resolve conflicts between ranks and the "rule of coordination" to resolve conflict between horizontal groups. "Loyalty."	Specialization and professionalization and increased need for interdependence. Leadership too complex for one-man rule or omniscience.
ADAPTATION	The problem of responding appropriately to changes induced by the environment of the firm	Environment stable, simple, and predictable; tasks routine. Adapting to change occurs in haphazard and adventitious ways. Unanticipated consequences abound.	External environment of firm more "turbulent," less predictable. Unprecedented rate of technological change.
REVITALIZATION	The problem of growth and decay	?	Rapid changes in technologies, tasks, manpower, norms and values of society, and goals of enterprise and society all make constant attention to the processes of the firm and revision imperative.

These problems (or predicaments) emerge basically from twentieth-century changes, primarily the growth of science and education, the separation of power from property and the correlated emergence of the professional manager, and other kinds of changes which I will get to in a minute. The bureaucratic mechanism, so capable of coordinating men and power in a stable society of routine tasks, cannot cope with contemporary realities. The chart shows five major categories, which I visualize as the core tasks confronting the manager in coordinating the human side of enterprise:

(1.) The problem of integration grows out of our "consensual society," where personal attachments play a great part, where the individual is appreciated, in which there is concern for his well-being—not just in a veterinary-hygiene sense but as a moral, integrated personality.

(2.) The problem of social influence is essentially the problem of power, and leadership studies and practices reveal not only an ethical component but an *effectiveness* component: people tend to work more efficiently and with more commitment when they have a part in determining their own fates and have a stake in problem solving.

(3.) The problem of collaboration grows out of the same social processes of conflict, stereotyping, and centrifugal forces which inhere in and divide nations and communities. They also employ the same furtive, often fruitless, always crippling mechanisms of conflict resolution: avoidance or suppression, annihilation of the weaker party by the stronger, sterile compromises, and unstable collusions and coalitions. Particularly as organizations become more complex they fragment and divide, building tribal patterns and symbolic codes which often work to exclude others (secrets and noxious jargon, for example) and on occasion to exploit differences for inward (and always, fragile) harmony. Some large organizations, in fact, can be understood only through an analysis of their cabals, cliques, and satellites, their tactics resembling a sophisticated form of guerrilla warfare; and a venture into adjacent spheres of interest is taken under cover of darkness and fear of ambush.

(The university is a wondrous place for these highly advanced battle techniques, far overshadowing their business conterparts in subterfuge and sabotage. Quite often a university becomes a loose collection of competing departments, schools, and institutes, largely noncommunicating because of the multiplicity of specialist jargons and interests and held together, as Robert Hutchins once said, chiefly by a central heating system, or as Clark Kerr amended, by questions of what to do about the parking problem.)[2]

(4.) The real *coup de grace* to bureaucracy has come as much from our turbulent environment as from its incorrect assumptions about human behavior. The pyramidal structure of bureaucracy, where power was concentrated at the top—perhaps by one person or a group who had the knowledge and resources to control the entire enterprise—seemed perfect to "run a railroad." And undoubtedly, for tasks like building railroads, for the routinized tasks of the nineteenth and early twentieth centuries, bureaucracy was and is an eminently suitable social arrangement.

Nowadays, due primarily to the growth of science, technology, and research and development activities, the organizational environment of the firm is rapidly changing. Today it is a turbulent environment, not a placid and predictable one, and there is a deepening interdependence among the economic and other facets of society. This means that economic organizations are increasingly enmeshed in legislation and public policy. Put more simply, it means that the government will be in about everything, more of

Changing Organizations

the time. It may also mean, and this is radical, that maximizing cooperation, rather than competition between firms—particularly if their fates are correlated—may become a strong possibility.

(5.) Finally, there is the problem of revitalization. Alfred North Whitehead sets it neatly before us: "The art of free society consists first in the maintenance of the symbolic code, and secondly, in the fearlessness of revision. . . . Those societies which cannot combine reverence to their symbols with freedom of revision must ultimately decay." Organizations, as well as societies, must be concerned with those social conditions that engender buoyancy, resilience, and fearlessness of revision. Growth and decay emerge as the penultimate problem where the environment of contemporary society is turbulent and uncertain.

FORECAST OF ORGANIZATIONS OF THE FUTURE

A forecast falls somewhere between a prediction and a prophecy. It lacks the divine guidance of the latter and the empirical foundation of the former. On thin empirical ice, I want to set forth some of the conditions that will dictate organization life in the next 25 to 50 years.

THE ENVIRONMENT

Those factors already mentioned will continue in force and increase. Rapid technological change and diversification will lead to interpenetration of the government—its legal and economic policies—with business. Partnerships between business and government will be typical. And because of the immensity and expense of the projects, there will be fewer identical units competing for the same buyers and sellers. The three main features of the environment will be interdependence rather than competition, turbulence rather than steadiness, and large-scale rather than small-scale enterprises.

POPULATION CHARACTERISTICS

The most distinctive characteristic of our society is, and will become even more so, its education. Peter Drucker calls us the "educated society," and for good reason: within 15 years, two-thirds of our population living in metropolitan areas will have attended college. Adult education is growing even faster. It is now almost routine for the experienced physician, engineer, and executive to go back to school for advanced training every two or three years. Some 50 universities, in addition to a dozen large corporations, offer advanced management courses to successful men in the middle and upper ranks of business. Before World War II, only two such programs existed, both new and struggling to get students.

All of this education is not just "nice" but necessary. For as W. Willard Wirtz, the Secretary of Labor, recently pointed out computers can do the work of most high school graduates—and they can do it cheaper and more effectively.

Fifty years ago education used to be regarded as "nonwork," and intellectuals on the payroll (and many staff workers) were considered "overhead." Today, the survival of the firm depends, more than ever before, on the proper exploitation of brain power.

One other characteristic of the population which will aid our understanding of organizations of the future is increasing job mobility. The lowered cost and growing ease of transportation, coupled with the real needs of a dynamic environment, will change drastically the idea of "owning" a job—or "having roots," for that matter. Participants will be shifted from job to job and even employer to employer with little concern for roots and homestead.

WORK VALUES

The increased level of education and mobility will change the values we hold about work. People will be more intellectually committed to their jobs and will probably require more involvement, participation, and autonomy in their work.

Also, people will tend to be more "other-directed," taking cues for their norms and values more from their immediate environment than from tradition. We will tend to rely more heavily on temporarily social arrangements, on our immediate and constantly changing colleagues. We will tend to be more concerned and involved with relationships than with relatives.

TASKS AND GOALS

The tasks of the firm will be more technical, complicated, and unprogrammed. They will rely more on intellect than muscle. And they will be too complicated for one person to comprehend, to say nothing of control. Essentially, they will call for the collaboration of specialists in a project or team form of organization.

There will be a complication of goals. Business will increasingly concern itself with its adaptive or innovative-creative capacity. In addition, meta-goals—that is, supra-goals which shape and provide the foundation for the goal structure—will have to be articulated and developed. For example, one meta-goal might be a system for detecting new and changing goals; another could be a system for deciding priorities among goals.

Finally, there will be more conflict and contradiction among diverse standards of organizational effectiveness, just as in hospitals and universities today there is conflict between teaching and research. The reason for this is the increased number of professionals involved, who tend to identify more with the goals of their profession than with those of their immediate employer. University professors can be used as a case in point. More and more of their income comes from outside sources, such as foundations which grant them money and industries for whom they consult. They tend not to be good "company men" because they divide their loyalty between their professional values and organizational goals.

STRUCTURE

The social structure of organizations of the future will have some unique characteristics. The key word will be "temporary"; there will be adaptive, rapidly changing *temporary systems*. These will be problem-oriented "task forces" composed of groups of relative strangers who represent a diverse set of professional skills. The groups will be arranged on an organic rather than a mechanical model; they will evolve in response to a problem rather than to programmed role expectations. The "executive" thus will become a coordinator or "linking pin" among various task forces. He must be a man who can speak the diverse languages of research, with skills to relay information and to mediate between groups. People will be differentiated not vertically according to rank and status but flexibly and functionally, according to skill and professional training.

Adaptive, problem-solving, temporary systems of diverse specialists, linked together by coordinating and task-evaluating specialists in an organic flux—this is the organizational form that will gradually replace bureaucracy as we know it. As no catchy phrase comes to mind, I call this an organic-adaptive structure.

MOTIVATION

The organic-adaptive structure should increase motivation, and thereby effectiveness, since it will enhance satisfactions intrinsic to the task. There is a harmony between the educated individual's need for meaningful, satisfactory, and creative tasks and a flexible organizational structure.

There will, however, also be reduced commitment to work groups, for these groups, as I have already mentioned, will be transient and changing. While skills in human interaction will become more important, due to the growing needs for collaboration in complex tasks, there will be a concomitant reduction in group cohesiveness. My prediction is that in the organic-adaptive system people will have to learn to develop quick and intense relationships on the job and learn to bear the loss of more enduring work relationships. Because of the added ambiguity of roles, more time will have to be spent on the continual research for the appropriate organizational mix.

In general, I do not agree with those who emphasize a new utopianism in which leisure, not work, will become the emotional-creative sphere of life. Jobs should become more rather than less involving; man is a problem-solving animal, and the tasks of the future guarantee a full agenda of problems. In addition, the adaptive process itself may become captivating to many.

At the same time, I think that the future I describe is not necessarily a "happy" one. Coping with rapid change, living in temporary work systems, developing meaningful relations and then breaking them—all augur social strains and psychological tensions. Teaching how to live with ambiguity, to identify with the adaptive process, to make a virtue out of contingency, and to be self directing will be the task of education, the goal of maturity, and the achievement of the successful manager. To be a wife in this era will be to undertake the profession of providing stability and continuity.

In these new organizations, participants will be called on to use their minds more than at any other time in history. Fantasy, imagination, and creativity will be legitimate in ways that today seem strange. Social structures will no longer be instruments of psychic repression but will increasingly promote play and freedom on behalf of curiosity and thought.

Bureaucracy was a monumental discovery for harnessing the muscle power of the Industrial Revolution. In today's world, it is a lifeless crutch that is no longer useful. For we now require structures of freedom to permit the expression of play and imagination and to exploit the new pleasure of work.

One final word: While I forecast the structure and value coordinates for organizations of the future and contend that they are inevitable, this should not bar any of us from giving the inevitable a little push here and there. And while the French moralist may be right that there are no delightful marriages, just good ones, it is possible that if managers and scientists continue to get their heads together in organizational revitalization, they *might* develop delightful organizations—just possibly.

I started with a quote from de Tocqueville and I think it would be fitting to end with one: "I am tempted to believe that what we call necessary institutions are often no more than institutions to which we have grown accustomed. In matters of social constitution, the field of possibilities is much more extensive than men living in their various societies are ready to imagine."

Notes

1. Bennis, W. G. "Changing Organizations." Paper read at Alfred P. Sloan School of Management, Massachusetts Institute of Technology, Cambridge, October, 1965. The initial Douglas Murray McGregor Memorial Lecture, the first of a series of lectures to be given at M.I.T. to honor the memory of a great pioneer in the study of organizational behavior, this material appears in expanded form in a book by the same title by W. G. Bennis, New York: McGraw-Hill, 1966.

2. For this quote, as well as for other major influences, I want to thank Professor Kenneth D. Benne.

23

W. WARNER BURKE AND WARREN H. SCHMIDT

Primary Target for Change: The Manager or the Organization?

*t*his article's purpose is to present a way of comparing two basic approaches to the improvement of managerial effectiveness within an organization—management development: the educational development of *individual* managers, and organization development (OD): the development of the organizational units. During the past twenty years, the concept of "management development" has received wide acceptance. Management development involves a variety of activities, such things as training, counseling, job rotation, coaching, sabbatical leaves, and career planning. In this article we are discussing management development primarily as an educational and training endeavor. Organization development is a concept of recent origin—but has already received significant interest and attention. Underlying both approaches is the assumption that the most effective manager or specialist is a learning person— one who is capable of continually improving his insight, knowledge and skill.

A COMPARISON OF MANAGEMENT DEVELOPMENT AND OD

The concept and scope of OD can be more sharply defined by comparing it with the more traditional forms of management development along several critical dimensions:
(1.) Typical goals.
(2.) Reasons for and difficulties in initiating management development or OD.
(3.) Strategies and interventions for producing change.
(4.) Time frame.

Written especially for this volume.

Table 23-1. *A Comparison of Management Development and Organization Development*

Category/Dimension	Management Development	Organization Development
Typical Goals	Teach manager new skills Expand manager's conceptual understanding Upgrade and/or update manager's present knowledge and skills	Facilitate problem-solving on the job Plan and implement changes more systematically Increase sense of "ownership" of organization objectives throughout work force Create conditions where conflict is managed, rather than handled indirectly Create conditions so that decisions are made on the basis of competence rather than organizational role
Reasons for Initiating Management Development or OD	Something wrong with the manager Managers do not know company policy or philosophy Managers do not have a needed skill	Something wrong with the system Problems with a recent merger Present organization structure and roles within it are not efficient Competition hurting more than helping Managers do not understand company policy or philosophy
Difficulties in Initiating Management Development or OD	Individual resistance and feelings of threat Making training relevant	High risk Support from many persons, especially top management, is needed Strong need for long-term commitment to change efforts
Strategies and Interventions for Producing Change	Send manager to some educational program Job rotation of managers Courses and/or conferences Specialized training "packages" Reading books and/or articles	Treatment is usually on the job; learning while problem-solving and solving problems while learning Team building Techno-structural intervention Action research Certain training programs Survey feedback Intergroup interfaces for problem-solving
Time Frame	Short, intense	Prolonged
Staff Requirements	Teacher/Trainer Program manager Designer of training programs	Diagnostician Catalyst/Facilitator Consultant/Helper Knowledge and skill in planned change Experience in laboratory training
Common Problems and Criticisms	Lack of continuity, follow-up, reinforcement on the job to transfer of learning Usually middle managers only Dependence on experts Lip service given but little transfer Difficult to make training relevant to manager's everyday problems	May become "another program" Top management must be perceived as supportive Requires considerable risk taking on the part of management

(5.) Staff requirements.
(6.) Common problems and criticisms.

Each of these dimensions will now be discussed in order to identify the ways management development and OD are alike and different. A summary of these comparisons is presented in Table 23-1.

TYPICAL GOALS

Although management development and OD are concerned with such issues as communication, motivation, and coordination, the goals of these two strategies are stated quite differently. For example, one large American corporation's management development program has as its objectives the following:

(1.) To transmit the philosophy and values of the company as expressed through a review of the organization's principles, policies and practices.
(2.) To provide practice in those management skills which will improve organizational performance and cooperation.
(3.) To increase ability to plan, coordinate, measure and control the efforts of company units.
(4.) To improve skills in problem analysis and decision making.
(5.) To develop a greater awareness of the company's functional and divisional organizations and their inter-relationships.

These objectives cover the areas that most management development programs stress—knowledge, skill, and attitudes—and, as can be seen, the emphasis is on the individual manager.

When the *organization* "goes to school," however, the goals are likely to be stated as follows:[1]

(1.) To create an open, problem-solving climate throughout the organization.
(2.) To supplement authority associated with role or status with authority of knowledge and competence.
(3.) To locate decision-making and problem-solving responsibilities as close to the information sources as possible.
(4.) To build trust among individuals and groups throughout the organization.
(5.) To make competition more relevant to work goals and to maximize collaborative efforts.
(6.) To develop a reward system which supports achievement of the organization's mission as well as individual efforts toward personal development and achievement.
(7.) To have organizational objectives "owned" by the entire work force.
(8.) To help managers to manage according to relevant needs and objectives rather than according to "past practices."
(9.) To increase self-control and self-direction for people within the organization.
(10.) To develop a process for continuing organizational self-renewal.

From these two examples of goals, it can be seen that the emphasis in management development is different from that of OD. Management development strives toward developing managers who will be able to contribute more to the organization, and OD attempts to create conditions in which the manager can make these contributions. Even though this latter statement points out an obvious difference of emphasis, it also states that the two areas of development have objectives which dovetail. Furthermore, both are attempts at improving the management of an organization and, at times, both may concentrate on changing the managerial strategy in the organization. These two sets of goals are not incompatible, but complementary.

REASONS FOR AND DIFFICULTIES IN INITIATING MANAGEMENT DEVELOPMENT OR OD

A common reason for beginning a program in management development is that top management or a personnel department has determined that some inadequacy exists or improvement is needed for individual managers. For example, new supervisors may need to learn something about "handling people." Or, staff personnel who have moved to a line position may know very little about the basic principles of management. Or, managers may lack some particular skill—interviewing, developing budgets, and so forth. Such inadequacies may suggest training programs for the individuals to increase their competence in their managerial positions.

Participating in a training program, by definition, provides the opportunity for individual as well as organizational change. Whenever this type of change interrupts a manager's routine, he may respond with resistance. When a superior or someone from personnel suggests to a manager that he might like to attend a conference or take a course, it is not uncommon for him to feel threatened, wondering whether he is doing a poor job. (Why else would he be "asked" to go to some program?)

Often resistance can be reduced if the potential participant is involved in deciding which programs to attend. As one approach toward involvement, some personnel departments spend considerable time interviewing a cross section of managers to determine which kinds of training programs should be planned.

The reasons for starting OD are more varied than those for management development. Some typical reasons for initiating OD are as follows:

(1.) Lack of cooperation between two departments or divisions—manufacturing and sales, or finance and research, or production and maintenance.
(2.) Ambiguous lines of responsibility and authority as a result of a merger.
(3.) Perennial labor-management disputes.
(4.) Dull and ineffective staff meetings.
(5.) A project team or task force which needs some work on their internal interpersonal relationships.

Even though a definite need for some OD effort may be called for, getting started may prove difficult. To decide on OD is to agree to a process which not only requires total system involvement, but commitment to a long-term renewal effort as well. Although OD may involve projects which have a beginning and an ending, OD is not a one-shot, *ad hoc* program geared toward accomplishing a single task. It is an all-out effort toward more effective organizational functioning which involves all members. As such, the risk is greater than it is for management development.

STRATEGIES AND INTERVENTIONS FOR PRODUCING CHANGE

In recent years, we have witnessed a rapid increase in the kinds of activities that can be used in management development or OD. Some can be used in both management development and OD; others are primarily suited to either management development or OD.

Typical activities in management development include:
(1.) In-company workshops and special conferences.
(2.) Specialized training, often outside the organization, *e.g.*, skill training such as public speaking.
(3.) Correspondence courses.
(4.) University programs.
(5.) The sabbatical (some organizations recently have been granting a sabbatical year during which a person either teaches at some college or university, conducts a pet research project, writes, or does some combination of all these).

Change strategies in management development, then, involve having the manager participate in one of these educational activities. Efforts are made to free him from job pressures for a specified period of time, allowing him to concentrate solely on up-grading his knowledge and skills. Another common strategy is job rotation—giving the rising manager a chance to get the feel of various aspects of the organizational system.

In OD efforts, interventions for change also take a variety of forms. Typically the strategy is to deal with problems *on the job*. There is a deliberate attempt to learn while in the process of solving problems and to solve problems while in the process of learning. A case example of this process is given here:

Case Example: Misunderstood Memos*

Recently, a vice president in a large U. S. corporation was having trouble with his division managers occasionally responding inappropriately to his memos. The vice president had the choice of (a) sending his subordinates to a communications course, (b) attending a communications course himself, (c) both (a) and (b), (d) trying to live with the problem, or (e) working on the problem directly. He chose the last alternative. An external OD consultant and an internal consultant from the Employee Relations Division worked on the problem with the vice president in a team development session. They designed a work session to be held from 9:00 a.m. to lunch on a regular work day in the staff meeting room. Before the meeting, several memos from the vice president to the division managers were selected and prepared on a glass slide which could then be shown on a screen via a projector. With the vice president and consultants present, all division managers considered several of the memos according to a certain

* From a paper by J. B. Harvey and C. R. Boettger to be published in a future issue of the *Journal of Applied Behavioral Science.*

procedure. After reading the memo on the screen, they were asked three questions: (1) What do you think the message says? (2) What priority would you give to the message: (a) HIGH, take care of the matter immediately, (b) MEDIUM, take care of the matter relatively soon, or (c) LOW, take care of it when I can get to it. (3) What action would you take?

After everyone responded to the three questions by writing their answers, each manager was asked to read his response to the total group. Considerable differences occurred among the managers. Later, the vice president explained what he meant the memo to say, what priority he desired, and what action he wanted. As might be expected, a number of misunderstandings were corrected and learning resulted, both learning on the vice president's part, as well as the division managers'.

An interesting side effect resulted later in time; the vice president's memos decreased in number by 40 percent. Also, after a year of collecting relevant data, a considerable monetary saving amounting to approximately twenty thousand dollars was realized as a result of changes in communications procedures.

In organization development, the underlying strategy is to plan and develop a process which will bring about change in the organization's culture. A fundamental change effort in OD, then, is to change group norms. For example, if a group norm is such that competitive behavior on the part of individuals is expected and implicitly rewarded, but the organization's effort is hurt as a result, then an OD strategy is to develop an intervention which will help the group to change this competitive norm to one that is more collaborative— provided individuals will be rewarded appropriately for this change in behavior.

Referring again to the case example, a norm concerning interpersonal communication was changed as a result of this particular team development session. Prior to the session, there was an implicit norm between the subordinates and the vice president that few of the subordinates after receiving a memo from the vice president communicated with him directly to question or seek clarification of the memo even when the message might have been ambiguous. During the months following the team development session, the vice-president's memos decreased in number. Further exploration (by interviews) as to why showed that more communication between the vice president and his subordinates was now being conducted via the telephone and in face-to-face dialogue. Thus, the norm of one-way communication was modified such that a norm of two-way communication began to develop.

This case represents not only the kinds of results that are possible from team development sessions like this one, it illustrates one type of OD intervention as well. Representative of the range of interventions in the OD arena are the following:

(1.) Team building (or team development) which may include off-site meetings of a training or problem-solving nature as well as long-range planning.

(2.) Techno-structural, such as a confrontation meeting[2] or a change in the organization chart.

(3.) Action research.[3]

(4.) Specific training programs, such as laboratory training[4] or specific skill training like the programs in decision making and problem solving by Kepner-Tregoe, etc.

(5.) Survey feedback[5].
(6.) Intergroup or inter-departmental interfaces for training and/or problem solving.[6]

To summarize, the strategy for change in management development is to improve the individual manager's knowledge and skill and, in some cases, to modify his attitudes. Typical interventions are those of an educational nature represented by courses, conferences, seminars, and the like.

The strategy for change in OD is to develop a process which will help the organization to diagnose its problems, plan ways to solve them, and implement these plans. Stated somewhat differently, the strategy is to change the organization's culture from one of dealing with problems "as we have always done" to a culture that takes full advantage of the human resources the organization has available, and allows for a process to develop which will insure that the organization can plan and implement needed change at all levels rather than having to adjust to change that is already in process.

TIME FRAME

Due to the nature of management development, the time frame, with respect to the manager's degree of involvement, is relatively brief. The longest time span would probably be a university master's or doctoral program which covers anywhere from twelve to thirty-six months. The shortest might be a one- or two-hour session where managers hear a speaker.

OD has a beginning, but, ideally, there is no end since the process of OD is a continuing one. There is a time frame, however, regarding the use of outside consultants. At the outset an organization's use of consultants is usually quite heavy with a tapering off as progress is made. After a time, external OD consultants work themselves out of a job by helping to develop personnel within the organization who can perform many of the services that they provide early in the relationship. Subsequently, an organization may want periodically to retain the external consultant's services to check matters and to receive help on special concerns or projects.

STAFF REQUIREMENTS

The critical factors affecting the success of any program in management development are the design and implementation of the learning experience. It is essential that the training staff have not only considerable skill in planning and conducting a training session, but they should have a workng understanding of the dynamics of human learning as well. Managers of programs in management development may have these abilities and knowledge themselves, they may hire skilled staff, they may engage outside instructors, or they may combine all of these possibilities in their training efforts.

Thus, an important and, perhaps, the critical, capability which management development staff must possess is that of skill and knowledge in the educational process.[7] This is not the only capability required, however. Today, persons in management development are being called on for such things as career development, that is, helping managers to plan their careers more systematically, and for managerial counseling, that is, helping managers to deal with some of the problems they face in supervising subordinates. In fact, the management development function in many organizations is expanding to such an extent that the staff is beginning to work in the broader area of organization development. Let us now consider the staff requirements for this organizational function.

At least five general areas of competence should be represented on an OD staff:

The Ability to Diagnose Accurately Problems of an Organizational Nature—such as appropriateness of various organizational structures for different tasks. To be an effective diagnostician in this area requires a thorough understanding of the consequences of different structures like a pyramidal structure, the matrix principle of organization, decentralization, team management, temporary systems, etc. The OD practitioner should also be competent in diagnosing human problems within the organization, especially in the areas of small group behavior, interpersonal relationships and intergroup competitiveness.

The Ability to Function as Facilitator and/or Catalyst Within the Organization. This ability reflects itself in interventions which are appropriate, timely, and facilitating. Interventions may take the form of suggesting to a manager how he might design his next staff meeting or helping to plan the strategy for a major change in the reward system.

Facilitation is also pertinent for team building where an OD practitioner helps the team: (1) to diagnose its blocks to more effective work, (2) in working on their interpersonal relationships, (3) to make long-range plans or to set goals, and other related activities.

There are, of course, other catalytic and facilitating functions which the OD practitioner can and should implement. These examples are not exhaustive, they are intended to provide only a general idea of the various activities.

Understanding and Skill in the Consultative Process. A substantial portion of an OD practitioner's activity is to give help to other people. Being able to render help effectively to others is not easy. The successful OD consultant should (1) be able to work in such a way that he is as non-threatening and non-judgmental toward the client as possible, (2) focus on a joint exploration of the problem area with his client, and (3) be able to assess his client's readiness and capacity for change.

An Understanding of the Dynamics and Realities of Planned Change. Bennis[8] has pointed out that "adaptability to change becomes increasingly the most important single determinant of survival." Although at this point Bennis was talking about American life, in general, he later stresses that this ability to adapt to change is just as critical and relevant for organizations, in particular. If Bennis is correct in this proclamation, and we believe that he is, it behooves modern organizations to develop resources which will enable them to respond to change not only by adapting, but also learn by *planning* needed change before the onset of crises. The most effective way to adapt to change is to plan for it. It is a matter of learning to control change and not being controlled by it. The organization can facilitate this adaptability-to-change process by having access to people who are not only knowledgeable in the literature of planned change,[9] but, also, know how to apply this knowledge. The OD practitioner, or organizational change agent, plays a key role in this planning and adapting process. He is the educator and the facilitator in the planning of change.

The OD practitioner is not an advocate of change for the sake of change. He helps the manager in the organization to diagnose the problems he faces to see if change is needed. If change is needed, he helps the manager and relevant others plan for the changes in such a way that the least amount of resistance will develop. He continues to help the manager during the changing period, to identify and diagnose the causes of resistance and to plan ways of working with the resistance, whether it be to try to overcome the resistance or to accept it and not push for change if it makes sense not to do so. It could be that what a manager may learn in the process is that change in a certain area is really not called for after all.

Skill and Knowledge in Applied Behavioral Science, in General, and Reasonable Competence in Experienced-based Learning or Laboratory Training, in Particular. Since OD is a process of applying behavioral science knowledge, it is important that the OD practitioner have some theoretical background and research knowledge about behavioral science. Being competent in the particular area of experienced-based learning is highly relevant because many of the interventions a practitioner makes in OD are based on principles derived from laboratory training. Interventions in OD commonly serve a dual purpose: (1) They help a person or group solve a problem, and (2) they illustrate a procedure which a person or group can learn to solve problems more efficiently in the future.

The OD practitioner will find that improving his skill and knowledge in experienced-based learning will help him to have a better understanding of his own strengths and limitations, so that he can more effectively use himself as an instrument of change.

In summarizing this section on the five general areas of competence for an OD practitioner, it can be seen from the space devoted to each that effective work in OD requires a wider range of skill and knowledge than is required for the practitioner in management development. This is not to say that one activity is more important than the other. What we mean is that the field of OD is complex and diversified, and it is difficult for any one person to be highly competent in all of its aspects.

COMMON PROBLEMS AND CRITICISMS

As with most training programs, the major problem in management development is transferring learning to the job situation. In training programs, it is always difficult to create conditions similar to those faced on the job. In more technical areas this is often easier than in areas of human behavior. Most training programs teach general principles rather than specifics—making transfer difficult for many participating managers.

Even if the program does include elements of learning that are easily transferable, there is also the problem of follow-up and reinforcement. All too often a manager will attend a program, learn something new about management, return to his job and never try to apply it. Or, if he tries to put into practice what he has learned, he is frequently faced with questioning and lack of support from his superior and/or subordinates.

Other problems in management development include: a heavy dependence on a small number of outside "experts" with no expertise being developed within the organization; lip service given to management development with little, if any, actual support from top management (often this is manifest by abandonment of training when financial conditions worsen); and the restricted participation in management development programs: the majority of attendees are from middle management. Little attention is paid to the development of first line supervisors or top management. Some organizations still assume that when a person has reached a certain position, he no longer requires any development as a manager. (Fortunately, the number of such organizations is shrinking.)

One other criticism of management development programs is that planners rarely incorporate in their design plans for continuity of the program elements. Many programs represent a smorgasbord of content sessions. On one day of a program, Professor X from Ivy U. speaks on Subject A. The remainder of the day is spent on Case B, which has nothing to do with Professor X's Subject A, and so it goes throughout the week or the two weeks. Seldom do these programs have a central theme.

There are just as many, if not more, problems in OD as in management development. Currently, OD faces the problem of being seen as "just another program," or "only a passing fad." In fact, in some organizations with which we are familiar, OD is really nothing more than a new name for sensitivity training or management development. As with any new area of professional activity, OD (less than 10 years old as an approach to organizational change) suffers the growing pains of being perceived as something temporary.

One pitfall is that top management may give lip service "support" only, without fully understanding the consequences of an OD process. Support for change efforts from managers at all levels in the organization is critical to the success of OD and it is best if all relevant levels of management are involved in any change process.

Related to this support issue is the matter of risk taking. OD typically involves change of one kind or the other, and managers must take some risks if they are to be involved in the process. For example, when two departments in an organization are having difficulty with one another, the conflict is often handled by bucking the problem "upstairs" for some superior to resolve or the two department heads get together to negotiate and reach some compromise. In OD, an interdepartmental conflict, which concerns many persons in both departments and not the department heads only, is frequently managed by arranging "interface problem-solving sessions." These are sessions which involve as many of the persons who are relevant to the conflict as possible.

Briefly, the two departmental groups gather to: explain to one another their view of the conflict; describe to the other group what they *think* their (other group's) view of the problem is; and work together in small groups (with the groups being composed of individuals from both departments) to develop ways in which the conflict can be managed and resolved. More managerial risk is involved when conflict is handled in this manner. Responsibility and authority for managing the conflict is not exclusively in the hands of the two department heads nor is the conflict exclusively up to them to resolve. The advantage of sharing the responsibility and authority for managing the conflict is that with the greater involvement of departmental personnel participating together in confronting the problems, the commitment to implementing plans for resolving the conflict will be considerably greater than it would be if only the superiors dealt with the problems.

SUMMARY AND CONCLUSIONS

We began this paper by asking some questions. We would like to conclude by again posing questions and responding to them.

For the organization which desires maximum effectiveness in its functioning and output, which will help most, management development or OD? If our bias regarding this question has not been apparent in the paper thus far, let us now make it clear. We do not believe that this question can be answered with an either/or response. The effective organization must have both management development and OD. In an attempt to clarify differences and issues, we have chosen the method of comparing management development and OD. While we have found this has been useful, the method should not dictate the message. We contend that management development and OD are not incompatible processes in an organization. The two are not only compatible, but complementary. Our view is that management development is an arm of OD; it is, in practice, a slice of the OD pie. But each slice of the pie is different. While one slice is management development, another is techno-structural interventions, and another is survey feedback, etc.

To be more specific about our belief in the complementarity of management development and OD: The first step in any OD process is data gathering and diagnosis, the second step is intervention. (Technically speaking, the distinction may not be so clear. When a person enters a system to gather data, an intervention is being made in the process.) Suppose that in the diagnostic phase we find the following problem. "We have to make a significant number of decisions in groups, and our managers and staff people seem to know very little about group decision making." An appropriate intervention in this case might be that of calling on our management development staff to develop a training program in group decision making.

Although the Grid approach to OD[10] also combines management development and OD in a complementary manner, Blake and Mouton's bias with respect to this combination is somewhat different. Their approach to OD is a highly educative and sequential one. The beginning phase is that of management development, especially in the area of developing, and, possibly, changing one's managerial style. Their diagnosis assumes that managerial styles in the organization should be considered initially. Other phases in Grid OD, such as teamwork development and intergroup development, follow, but management development is first on the list.

How does one decide whether his organization needs OD? A manager may be able to answer this question by reflecting on his responses to some more specific questions. Do people in his organization feel that they are doing meaningful work and their abilities are being fully utilized? Are meetings of committees, task forces, staffs, and other groups productive, interesting, and considered a good use of one's time? Do young persons who have recently graduated from college or obtained an MBA tend to stay with the organization? Does the competition that may exist between organizational departments lead to higher efficiency for the overall organization? There are other questions which could be raised. If a manager's answers to these questions tend to be "no," then we can conclude that OD would be valuable for his organization. This is not to say that OD is a cure for all organizational ills. When an organization is deeply immersed in OD, problems continue to arise and crises may develop. What OD does provide is a *process* for handling these problems that lead to maximum use of human resources, the learning of procedures for diagnosing causes of problems and innovative ways of dealing with them, and a greater integration of individual needs with organizational goals.

Notes

1. Taken from "What Is OD?" in NTL Institute *News and Reports*, 2, No. 3 (June, 1968).
2. This type of intervention is explained in an article by Richard Beckhard, "The Confrontation Meeting," *Harvard Business Review*, Vol. 45, No. 2 March–April (1967): 149–155.
3. A fairly formal discussion of this technique may be found in the following article: Chein, I., S. Cook, and J. Harding, "The Field of Action Research," *American Psychologist* Vol. 3 (1948): 43–50. Succinctly, action research is "research" undertaken to solve a problem for a client. At the simplest level, it involves the gathering of data from the client, feeding it back for understanding and ownership, and then helping the client to take action in order to solve the problems identified in the initial data collection phase.
4. A discussion of the relationship between laboratory training and organization change may be found in Chapter 10, "Principles and Strategies in the Use of Laboratory Training for Improving Social Systems," in Schein, E. H. and W. G. Bennis. *Personal and Organizational Change Through Group Methods: The Laboratory Approach*. New York: Wiley, 1965.
5. An explanation of this type of intervention may be found in a chapter by Miles, M. B., H. A. Hornstein, P. H. Calder, D. M. Callahan, and R. S. Schiavo, entitled, "Data Feedback and Organization Change," in Bennis, W. G., and R. Chin (eds.). *The Planning of Change*, published by Holt, Rinehart & Winston, 1968. See also: Mann, F. C. "Studying and Creating Change: A Means to Understanding Social Organization," in C. M. Arensberg *et al.* (eds.). *Research in Industrial Human Relations*. New York: Harper, 1957.
6. Pertinent references for this type of activity are as follows: Blake, R. R., H. A. Shepard, and J. S. Mouton, *Managing Intergroup Conflict in Industry*. Houston, Texas: Gulf Publishing Co., 1964; Blake, R. R., J. S. Mouton, and R. L. Sloma, "The Union-Management Intergroup Laboratory," *Journal of Applied Behavioral Science*, 1, No. 1: (1965), 25–47; Shepard, H. S.,

"Changing Interpersonal and Intergroup Relationships in Organizations," in J. March (ed.). *Handbook of Organizations.* Chicago: Rand McNally and Co., 1967.

7. A description of trainer characteristics may be found in the article, Lippett, G. L. and L. E. This, "Is Training a Profession?" *Journal of the American Society of Training Directors,* 14, No. 2 (1960).

8. Bennis, W. G. *Changing Organizations.* New York: McGraw Hill, 1966, 19.

9. Two of the most important books in this area are R. Lippitt, J. Watson, and B. Westley, *The Dynamics of Planned Change.* New York: Harcourt, Brace and World, 1958; and Bennis, W. G., K. Benne, and R. Chin, *The Planning of Change* (rev. ed.). New York: Holt, Rinehart and Winston, 1964.

10. Blake, R. R. and J. S. Mouton, *Corporate Excellence Through Grid Organization Development.* Houston: Gulf Publishing Co., 1968.

24

PAUL C. BUCHANAN

Crucial Issues in Organizational Development

INTRODUCTION

*O*rganization development has become an important area of concern to behavioral scientists as well as to executives in educational, industrial, and other kinds of organizations, and several strategies of development have been formulated and applied. In this article I examine several cases of organization development in order to determine if there are any common and critical issues discernible among the different strategies applied in a selected group of cases.

METHOD OF STUDY

As a basis for attempting to identify crucial issues in organization development (OD), I first located as many studies[1] as I could which met the concept of OD as outlined in my paper "The Concept of Organization Development, or Self-Renewal, as a Form of Planned Change" (Buchanan, 1967), and provided sufficient information to indicate the outcome of the undertaking. These two criteria are interrelated, in that to be a program of OD rather than organization improvement there needs to be indication that planned improvement continued after the OD project itself was terminated. There must be indication that a "take off" point has been passed and the organization continues to improve under its own initiative and with its own resources. On this basis it is necessary to "track" a program over an extended period of time. Thus, in this study

Reprinted by permission from *Change in School Systems*, G. Watson (ed.), Washington: NEA, 1967, 51–67.

several cases have been excluded which, on the basis of short-range data, were imaginative and promising.[2] Other studies similar to OD in objective but focusing on communities[3] have been excluded since I believe it would unduly complicate the task of identifying differences between successful and unsuccessful cases to introduce too great a variety in the kind of system which was the focus of development effort. However, there will be occasion to refer to some of these cases in analyzing crucial issues later on in this paper. The same is true regarding the growing body of information on the development of nations—it seems to me there is much to be gained from analysis of case studies of organization, community and national development.

Cases of OD to which I had access at the time I undertook this study and which I considered to be "successful" were Guest (1962), Blake and Mouton as described by Greiner (1965), Jaques (1951), Beckhard (1966), Shepard and Buchanan's work with a refinery (Buchanan, 1964a), Dennis (1964), and Zand, Miles, and Lytle (1964). Cases which I considered to be "unsuccessful" were Argyris (1962), Buchanan and Brunstetter (1959), and Buchanan (1964b).

An explanation is in order regarding the classification of cases. In one— that reported by Argyris—the change effort in many ways attained the objectives toward which it was directed, since changes occurring in the interrelations among the top management group were identifiable several months after the major "interventions." I list it as a failure, however, since the changes in the relationships among the top group did not spread to their relations with other members of the organization and apparently did not result in further improvements. Two cases (Buchanan and Brunstetter, 1959, and Buchanan, 1964b) achieved initial success, one for a period of about two years and the other for about six months, in that the changes spread throughout the unit which was the focus of the effort and involved more and more dimensions of the operations of the units; however, both became failures later, for reasons which are examined below.

Having selected the cases, I tried to identify the strategy, or main action steps, in each. This is not easy and is bound to be only roughly accurate since some of the cases are not reported in much detail. These strategies are presented in the following section of this paper.

Next, on the basis of a study of these cases, and after examining analyses which have been made of the process of planned change (Argyris, 1960; Bennis and others, 1961; Schein and Bennis, 1965; Sofer, 1962), I attempted to identify issues or elements of strategy which the process involves. Most relevant in this regard is the work by Lippitt, Watson and Westley, *The Dynamics of Planned Change*, from which I have borrowed heavily. A summary of issues from these sources, augmented by my own experiences, is given in the second section below.

Finally, from comparison of the successful and the unsuccessful cases, and by looking at similarities and differences among the successful cases, I attempted to identify which of these issues were "crucial"—*which made a difference*—in the process of organization development. Again, this is a difficult process, since many of the questions one would like to ask are not answerable from the case descriptions.

STRATEGIES OF ORGANIZATION DEVELOPMENT

In this section an attempt is made to outline the major steps in the different strategies reported in the cases selected for study.

"SOCIO-ANALYTIC CONSULTATION" (JAQUES)

In describing his approach, Jaques (1964) says it ". . . requires that an individual or individuals in an organization with a problem concerning the working of the organization should seek the help of an analyst in sorting out the nature of the problem." Once this help is sought the steps appear to be as follows:

(1.) The relationship between the consultant and the client system is worked out, written down, and made known to all members of the organization.
(2.) At the request of the individuals, the consultant discusses with them, individually or in small groups, problems raised by the members. He "listens for the principles and concepts behind the words."
(3.) The consultant formulates a report consisting of information obtained from members of a work group ("command team") and of his analysis of this information.
(4.) The consultant presents his report at meetings of the work group.
(5.) He regularly attends the periodic meetings of the work group during which his role again is to listen for principles and concepts behind the words, and to help members identify and work through issues they are avoiding, anxieties which influence their problem-solving abilities, and so on.
(6.) This leads to the formulation of projects undertaken by special task forces or command groups, in which, if the members request it, the consultant participates in the role indicated previously—listening for principles, identifying and helping the group work through issues being avoided, and so forth.

In Glacier Metals, where Jaques did this work, he was available on a full-time basis for four years, during which major changes were made in the functioning of the company. Projects included change in the appeals procedures of the company, modification of the executive system, working out a new method for measuring performance, modification of the pay system, changes in company policy, and others. One of the consequences was the development within the company of ability to "continue socio-analytic consultation under its own steam," and subsequently Jaques has been used only on a part-time basis.

SURVEY-FEEDBACK-TRAINING-PROBLEM SOLVING

Two of the cases (Dennis, 1964, and Buchanan, 1964a) involved strategies which were basically similar yet included some variations which will be identified:

(1.) Survey of all members of management to determine what the members considered to be problems in working effectively. This was done by interviews.

(2.) Formulation of the survey data into a conceptual scheme considered appropriate by the consultants.
(3.) Report-back and analysis of the findings in a series of meetings of the top management group and the consultants.
(4.) Laboratory training for all members of management. In one case this was a conventional one-week laboratory (Dennis, 1964); in the other it was a modified laboratory, with the training groups assigned responsibility for studying the survey report, formulating issues requiring further work, and exploring means of increasing teamwork in the plant (Buchanan, 1964a).
(5.) Systematic problem solving. In one case (Dennis, 1964) this was done by utilizing a modified form of the Scanlon Plan (Lesieur, 1958). In the other, task groups were formed around issues formulated at the laboratory sessions, the project being coordinated by a committee representing each of the training groups. At the end of a year, groups composed of members of management who worked on the same product met for two days off the job to again identify problems and develop actions plans. These plans were systematically discussed with the top management group and then carried through with assistance as needed from top management.

CYCLICAL SURVEY-FEEDBACK-PROBLEM-SOLVING-TEAM TRAINING

Beckhard used an approach similar to that outlined above, but sufficiently different to be described separately:
(1.) Interviews with the top management team.
(2.) Formulation of the data into a conceptual scheme considered appropriate by the consultant.
(3.) Series of three-day meetings of top management, with the task being carefully controlled so the group first understood the data, then set priorities for action, then determined the group or person responsible for action, and then worked on those which were within the action responsibility of the managers who participated in the meeting.
(4.) Steps (1) through (3) followed by successively lower levels of managers with the top manager joining each group toward the end of each group's meeting to hear and consider issues requiring attention at his level.
(5.) Introduction of theory and some skill-practice in the problem-solving meetings.
(6.) Laboratory training conducted for middle levels of management, and technical training for those entering jobs for which they needed additional skills.
(7.) Intergroup problem-solving sessions held by groups where the need was indicated.
(8.) Teams formed to open new plants (hotels) received team training.

A variation of Beckhard's approach was used by Zand, Miles, and Lytle: Instead of gathering information in advance, consultants and members of management met for three days away from the job, the middle and upper level managers meeting one week and the first-line supervisors meeting the following. With both groups some time was spent in training regarding the problem-solving process, but the major activity was to identify and plan action regarding on-the-job problems. A unique aspect of the design was that the consultants carefully separated the group's work in the various stages of problem solving: diagnosis of difficulties was completed before effort was made to formulate problems; agreement among the participants regarding the statement of problems was reached before attempts were made to formulate possible solutions; and so on. A second unique aspect was that several of the higher level managers participated in the last day of the meeting of the first-line supervisors and thus provided a means of integrating the plans of the two groups. The third phase of the program involved task groups carrying out, on the job, plans made in the previous phases, with guidance and support from a steering committee formed from both groups. The effectiveness of this approach as OD, or self-renewal, is indicated by the fact that the task troups completed their work; then the total group of managers met again (without a consultant), they formulated additional action plans, and they were continuing their developmental efforts at the time the case report was prepared (two years after the first off-the-job meeting was held).

SURVEY-FEEDBACK-TEAM TRAINING

Argyris proceeded as follows:
(1.) He interviewed and observed members of the top management group to determine the extent to which their values as reflected in their job behavior conformed to a predicted set of values.
(2.) He fed the results back to the group in a meeting away from the job. On the basis of their interpretation of these findings, the group decided improvement was called for.
(3.) The managers as a team participated in a T-group.
(4.) The group analyzed its own manner of working by having part of the team conduct problem-solving meetings while being observed by the other members and by consultants, the analysis being used to determine the extent to which they were applying what they had decided from their T-group experience to be desirable.

"MANAGERIAL GRID ORGANIZATION DEVELOPMENT"

Although Blake and Mouton (1964) described their program as consisting of six phases, the case description (Greiner, 1965) that I am using in this paper involved some important additional steps. To keep the record straight, I will star the steps mentioned by Blake and Mouton.
(1.) The consultant spent approximately two weeks in the target system, getting a "feel" for it and its problems.
(2.) The top management group in the plant and a group in headquarters to whom they reported met for three days to explore and improve each group's perceptions of the other and to improve their ability to work effectively with one another.

(3.) The top manager and a few members of the plant participated in a public managerial grid laboratory.
(4.) A pilot managerial grid laboratory was conducted within the plant for managers from all levels and departments of the plant.
(5.) *All members of management in the plant participated in a managerial grid laboratory.
(6.) *Family groups, beginning with the top, met to improve their working relations and their effectiveness as teams. (This was done in only a few of the teams in the case reported by Greiner.)
(7.) *Meetings were held of members of groups which had working inter-relationships, the purpose and procedure being similar to Step (2) above. (In the case described by Greiner such meetings were held only by top plant and headquarters management.)
(8.) *Organizational improvement goals were worked out. Beginning in the grid laboratories and in the team development meetings, conditions requiring change were formulated in systematic terms. In this phase, action goals were formulated on a personal, team, and organization-wide basis, and "unresolved problems preventing attainment of organization competence" were identified and plans for solving them were worked out.
(9.) *Plans for attaining established goals were carried out. This was done in part by use of "task paragraph discussions" which followed a procedure designed to facilitate effective problem solving (Blake and Mouton, 1964, 277).
(10.) *Stabilization. This step involved "establishing a sound relationship between goals and actions previously set in motion and current activities." Greiner presents little information regarding what, if anything, was done in this phase of the program.

CHANGE CONDUCTED BY A NEW MANAGER (GUEST)

Unlike all the other cases in this study, Guest (1962) describes one in which there was no consultant, the change being planned and effected by the new plant manager. The steps taken were as follows:
(1.) Higher management changed its actions in relation to the plant manager. How this came about is not made clear in the case description, although Guest speculates that a new corporate officer urged the division manager to allow the plant manager latitude in "running his own show."
(2.) The new plant manager communicated (by action and words) his philosophy and approach to all members of plant management.
(3.) The plant manager held informal meetings to find out the problems of the plant as seen by all levels of the management group.
(4.) The manager initiated regular problem-solving meetings with his high-level subordinates. Steps (2), (3), and (4) resulted in a new pattern of interaction between superiors and subordinates, and among peers, which spread to all levels of the management group.
(5.) Many managers were transferred laterally within the plant.

(6.) Plans were put into effect as changes were agreed upon in staff meetings. These consisted of changes both in the plant's technical system and in procedures. In this phase the manager "played an increasingly important role in gaining divisional support of such changes."

(7.) Long-range plans, based upon consensus of the management group, were formulated and carried out.

As can be noted from even these brief summaries of strategies, the cases utilized a variety of types and mixtures of "inputs" (interventions) while still having the similarities mentioned in my earlier paper (Buchanan, 1967). The next section lists some dimensions on which these comparisons can be made.

ISSUES IN ORGANIZATION DEVELOPMENT

The following are issues which appear to be potentially important as a consultant attempts to help an organization develop its effectiveness:[4]

(1.) Clarify or develop the client's motivation to change.

(2.) Assess the change agent's potential helpfulness:
 a. Relevance of his resources, interests, and competence to the client's need.
 b. His job security in relation to the client system.
 c. Relations among members of the change-agent team.
 d. Compatibility of his different objectives (to help the client, to conduct research, to get promoted within the company, and so on).
 e. Time he has available.

(3.) Establish effective relations between the change agent and the client system.
 a. Role of each in planning and conducting the program.
 b. Expectations of each regarding the amount and kind of effort required of each in the change program.
 c. Restrictions (if any) upon the kinds of changes which are allowable.
 d. Who the client is—whom the change agent's relations are with.
 e. Expectations regarding the role(s), or kind(s) of help, the change agent is to provide.

(4.) Clarify or diagnose the client system's problems.
 a. Concepts in terms of which diagnosis is to be made.
 b. How information is to be obtained, and from whom.
 c. Use of data in diagnosis.
 d. Develop diagnostic skills of members of the system.
 e. Determine the boundaries of the client system.

(5.) Establish instrumental objectives for change. (How should we operate?)

(6.) Formulate plans for change.
 a. Link to other persons, issues, and/or parts within the internal system.
 b. Link to other persons, parts, and/or issues in the external system.
 c. Develop time schedule and build time expectations.
 d. Develop procedures and/or structures for carrying out plans.
 e. Provide for anticipatory testing of plans.
 f. Develop competence of these involved in taking actions.

g. Develop motivation for carrying out plans.
(7.) Carry out plans for change.
   a. Maintain support and understanding from the larger system.
   b. Obtain feedback on consequences of early action steps.
   c. Coordinate efforts of different people and groups involved.
(8.) Generalize and stabilize changes.
   a. Assess the effects of the change upon the total system.
   b. Look for "regression."
   c. Facilitate spread to other parts of target system and to adjacent interdependent systems.
(9.) Institutionalize planned development or self-renewal.
   a. Develop problem-sensing and problem-solving skills and mechanisms in all components of the system.
   b. Develop reward systems which facilitate innovation.
   c. Establish a change-agent role in the system.

We are now in a position to determine which, if any, of these issues are "crucial" by returning to an examination of the ten actual cases outlined in the previous section.

CRUCIAL ISSUES IN ORGANIZATION DEVELOPMENT

Comparing the successful and the unsuccessful cases, the issue which appears to be most conspicuous is that of *linkage between the target system and the larger system* (Issue 6b). In two of the three unsuccessful cases, changes were initiated and progress was being made, only to come to a halt because of action by management above the top man in the target system. While the change agents in these cases recognized the importance of linkage with higher management, steps taken to accomplish such linkage were not effective. The difficulty[5] in one case was partly due to disagreement among members of the change-agent team regarding the approach to be followed (Issue 2c), and in part to the way the change agents related to the company president (Issue 3a). The program in question was initiated by the head of a department in a large company, and he requested help from both an inside and an outside consultant. The consultants were in agreement that the program plan of the department should be fully understood by corporate managers, and a two-day conference to accomplish this was worked out by the outside consultant and the president. The consultants jointly planned the two-day conference, but under the tensions which arose regarding the corporate officers' reactions to the meeting, the consultant who had the central role in the conference changed the plan, creating tension and role ambiguity between the consultants. This reduced the quality of the meeting, and at the end of the first day the president postponed the second day of the conference—which was never held. The department decided to go ahead with its program, with the support of a vice president, and it proved to be highly effective. Then the vice president left the company, leaving the change program in the target department going full swing but with no effective links between it and an uninterested and rather hostile corporate management. Shortly after the vice president left, a higher official called the top managers of the focal department into his office, and said, in effect, "You do the technical work and leave the management to me."

In the other case, work was being done to effect the linkage, but the meeting where this was intended to be accomplished was not effective, apparently due to Issue 3b, expectations by the top man regarding what was required of him, and to the lack of competence (Issue 2a) and/or job security (Issue 2b) of the change agent. Thus, when the changes being made in the norms, reward system and methods of decision making in the department required accommodating changes in the practices and values of higher management, such changes were not possible. Furthermore, higher management replaced the three key people in the target department with managers who were unfamiliar and unsympathetic with the change program and the development effort was discontinued.

In the third unsuccessful case (Argyris, 1962), there is no indication that the issue of linkage upward arose. Perhaps this was due in part to the fact that a high-level manager (division president) initiated and was a participant in the program, and in part because the kinds of changes which resulted did not require accommodating changes in other parts of the company.

In contrast to two of the unsuccessful cases, there is indication of effective linkage with the external system in two of the successful ones. Both Greiner (1965) and Guest (1962), in describing the cases, emphasize the importance of this issue. In three other cases the top manager of the organization was included in the target system (Jaques, 1951; Dennis, 1964; and Beckhard, 1966). In another case (Zand, Miles, and Lytle, 1964) linkage was not given much attention, and this almost led to termination of the program: A higher level manager heard of the meetings the first-line supervisors were holding, and he called the head of the target unit, wanting to know about the "unionization of foremen." The head of the focal unit was able to explain the program to the higher manager's satisfaction. In the seventh case (Buchanan, 1964a) the plant which was the target system was sufficiently autonomous so that relations with higher levels didn't become a problem during the four years of the program. There was a change of manager during this time, but the new one had participated in a training laboratory and was enthusiastic about the program which was going on when he took over. Yet the top managers in the plant took "linking" steps which are worth noting. At the third of a series of off-the-job meetings during which they were formulating long-range plans, the plant managers asked two key managers from headquarters to meet with them. They were thus enabled to integrate plant plans with headquarters' plans.

A case described by Schein and Bennis (1965, 255) adds further support of the importance of linkage to the larger systems (Issue 6b). Laboratory training was undertaken with lower levels of management, only to be abruptly terminated when the top manager learned about what was going on.[6] Linkage has also been highlighted as a factor in effective community development (see Lasswell,

1962, 122). Additional support of the importance of this issue, and an interesting way of trying to attain it, are reported by Whyte and Hamilton (1965): One consultant worked with lower managers and employees, the other with the general manager.[7] As the one working with lower levels encountered difficulties resulting from the behavior of the general manager, he talked with the other consultant, who brought up the issues in his next meeting with the general manager. But the method seemed to be only partially successful; while the general manager approved of changes requested at lower levels, and he encouraged the development effort, he seemed not to become involved. In sharp contrast is the method of linking used by Blake (see Greiner, 1965). Sensing that the plant managers and their superiors in headquarters disagreed over important issues, he proposed a three-day meeting of the two groups to explore their perceptions of each other. The openness, mutual understanding, and role clarification which resulted from the meeting seemed to be an important factor in the magnitude and depth of change which was subsequently accomplished in the plant. In contrast to the Whyte-Hamilton case, the linkage was made not via the consultant as intermediary but through direct changes in the relations between the plant and headquarters managers.

Another issue suggested by comparison of the successful and unsuccessful cases is *linkage with other persons, issues, and/or parts within the target system* (Issue 6a). The case described by Argyris indicates success in effecting the change which that program attempted: members of the top management group who were involved in the program seemed to have become more authentic and open in their dealings with each other. However, the evidence seems rather clear that this change did not lead to changes in their dealings with their subordinates, nor was there a spread of the program to other units of the organization or to other dimensions of the unit's operation.

In all the successful cases linkage with several levels of people within the target system was established either as part of the change-induction plan (Blake, 1964; Buchanan, 1964a; Dennis, 1964; Zand, Miles, and Lytle, 1964), or by steps taken early in the program which led to such action (Beckhard, 1966; Jaques, 1951; Guest, 1962). It seems that such linkage was either in the form of *working on operating problems* which involved units or groups beyond the original focal unit (for example, in one case work on the issue of cost reduction led to involving the union in the development program), or linkage was in the form of involving large numbers and levels of organizational members at the problem-identification phase of the program.

Support for the centrality of Issue 6a also comes from the field of community development. In describing their work in Peru, Holmberg and Dobyns state that "the project has selected values and institutions to change which would then foster more change by the (members of the community) themselves" (Holmberg and Dobyns, 1962, 107).

Now what can be learned from *differences among the successful cases*?

One thing which stands out is the variety of ways in which the different programs coped with many issues listed in the previous section:

(1.) One difference among the successful cases was the *kind* of model introduced by the change agents, both as a basis for diagnosis (Issue 4a) and for determining how the members thought they should try to operate their organization (Issue 5). There appear to be three types of models used in the seven cases: *cognitive, process,* and *procedural.* While most of the cases involve more than one, it appears that Blake and Mouton make primary use of the cognitive one, in the form of the managerial grid: through assigned readings, tests on the readings, and demonstration exercises, managers are taught the distinctions among five managerial styles and some consequences of the use of each. Jaques used primarily a process model: he focused on how members related to each other and on the fact, for example, that the way they felt about exercising authority influenced their effectiveness. Zand, Miles, and Lytle used primarily a procedural model: they guided the managers through a carefully controlled series of steps in identifying, diagnosing and planning action regarding problems in the operation of the target system. (Guest's manager used a procedural model while Beckhard, Buchanan, and Dennis used mixtures of process and procedural models.)

(2.) The cases also varied greatly in the *manner* in which models for formulating goals were introduced into the organization. In the case of Blake and Mouton it was done primarily by an extensive training program. At the other extreme, Guest introduced the model by the example set by the change agent—the top manager: in his first meeting with his management group he described how he intended to operate; then he set about illustrating it, with the result that the procedure spread to all levels of the organization. It appears that Jaques introduced a model partly by demonstrating it (see Bennis, 1963, for an analysis of Jaques' method) and partly by helping members identify "spontaneously emerging solutions to problems" by "listening for the principles and concepts behind the words" (Jaques, 1964) and holding them up for examination and comparison with current practices. Beckhard, and Zand, Miles, and Lytle (although in somewhat different ways) also demonstrated use of a problem-solving procedure.

What strikes me as of special significance is that each of these different approaches resulted in the introduction of a model which was incorporated into the practices of the organization—it became institutionalized. It is my impression, although I cannot prove it from these cases, that successful introduction of a new and viable model, relating to a fundamental aspect of the organization's operation, was one of the single most important contributions of the change agent in the successful cases.

In light of the differences in (1) the kind of model used and (2) the way it was introduced, it appears that a change agent should be wary of believing that he alone helds the key to utopian organizations.

(3.) In one case the change agent was the top manager in the target system (Guest), in two they were "internal" consultants from headquarters working with a plant (Buchanan, Dennis), while in the rest they were "outside" consultants. Apparently the location of the change agent was not, in itself, a crucial factor. This is consistent with the fact that the "catalysts" in General Electric's Program of Business Effectiveness, which appears to be successful in accomplishing organization development, also are "internal" consultants. However, it seems likely that the location of the change agent is closely related to several other issues: role of the change agent in planning (Issue 3a), the change agent's motivation (Issue 2d), who his "client" is (Issue 3d), and his job security (Issue 2b).

(4.) While all of the successful cases involved all levels of management in the target system, they differed in the time at which additional levels were involved. In Beckhard's case the main program began with the top management group; then as issues were identified and progress made, the same or similar activities were undertaken at successively lower levels (activity at the higher levels being continued). In three cases (Jaques; Blake; and Zand, Miles, and Lytle) all levels of management—and in Jaques' case some non-managers—were involved during the early stages of the program. In the case described by Guest there was some activity involving all levels of management. At an early meeting of all management personnel the change agent announced his intention, and he immediately began obtaining information and ideas from a sample at all levels; yet the major work was done at the top of the target unit. While it is difficult to draw generalizations from Guest's case, since the change agent was the manager, this case suggests that we hold open the issue of whether the change agent is needed at all levels, or whether if significant changes on a central issue are made at the top, they will spread throughout the subordinate organization.

Finally, we need to look at what can be learned from the *similarities in the successful cases*.

(1.) As has been indicated, in all seven cases the top manager of the target system was actively involved in the project. It appears that this is important, although this was not an issue which differentiated the successes from the failures. Determining the boundaries of the target system (Issue 4e) is probably of more importance, since this helps define who is the "top person in the system."

(2.) In all cases the change agent introduced a model for collecting data and for diagnosing the system's needs (Issue 4a), which could be considered by the members of the system in establishing goals for improvements (Issue 5).

(3.) Although the models differed, and were introduced into the system in different ways, all concerned the problem-solving process of the organization.

(4.) All of the models resulted in changes in the power structure of the target system, such changes being in the *kind* of power or influence used (away from authority and toward increased use of information), in the *distribution* of influence among the members of management (proportionately greater influence by people at lower levels), and in the total *amount* of influence exerted, or in the "size of the influence pie" (after the development program, the target systems appeared to have more self-control, and their operation appeared to be less determined by chance or by forces outside the system).

(5.) The models used also emphasized the development of norms and of skills which facilitated a shift from relationships based on negotiation or bargaining toward relationships based on problem solving or collaboration.

Obviously the cases varied in the extent of change in the above respects; yet because of the crude measurements used in assessing the cases, it is difficult to determine which resulted in the most change and, therefore, which strategy of development was most effective.

(6.) In all cases the change agent came from outside the target organization and was new to the target system. Since this was also the situation in the three unsuccessful cases, it is difficult to assess the implications.

CONCLUSIONS AND IMPLICATIONS

Of approximately 33 issues which there was some reason to believe are important in organization development, three have been identified as being of particular centrality in this study of ten cases. These issues are:

(1.) Introducing a new model of operation which the members of an organization can consider as a basis for formulating improvement goals regarding a dimension or operation which is central to the performance of the organization (Issue 5).

(2.) Sequencing objectives and action steps in such a way that linkage is established between the initial point of change and other persons, parts, and dimensions of operation *internal* to the target system (Issue 6a).

(3.) Sequencing objectives and action steps in such a way that linkage is established between the initial point of change and other persons, parts, and dimensions of the *external* system with which the target system has important interdependency (Issue 6b).

Why did so few issues emerge as crucial?

One possibility is that the cases studied all represent a similar approach to organization development—what Leavitt calls the "people approaches" and what Bennis refers to as "change agents working on organizational dynamics" (Bennis, 1963, 140). It is to be expected that the more the similarity of approach, the less any differences are highlighted, and thus the greater the difficulty in discerning crucial or significant differences.

Perhaps of greater importance is the fact that the differences in the outcomes of what I have called the successful and unsuccessful cases were not as pronounced as my discussion of them has implied. Probably cases that are "really" failures do not get reported, and so we do not have access to cases required for a thorough study of the effectiveness of change strategies and of issues which are crucial to the process.

A third, and in my judgment the most important, possible explanation for the emergence of so few crucial issues is that information required to determine the importance of each of the 33 issues listed earlier in this paper was not included in the case reports. The reports vary considerably in what is reported, and the reasons for the inclusions and omissions are not clear. It may be that the reporter is including what he considers most important either in the particular case or in cases in general; he may be reporting either what he is willing to reveal about his own work or what the organization concerned will permit him to print. At any rate, it appears to me that if organization development is to advance as an application of behavioral science, and if we are to practice our own beliefs it is important to engage in systematic self-study. This can be done only if we document our work in such a form that it can be studied by ourselves and our associates. And this, it seems to me, requires that we agree upon a format, or at least upon some key issues to be covered in reports. I hope that the list of issues presented in the middle section of this paper is a fruitful beginning of such a format.

Notes

1. One will note that all of these cases involve what Leavitt (1964) refers to as the "People Approaches" to change. One reason for this is that the "People Approaches," more than others, emphasize *development* or *self-renewal*.

2. Examples: Sofer's work with a small company, the research unit in a hospital, and a department of a technical college (Sofer, 1962); Morton and Weight's work at Aerojet (Morton and Weight); the work of General Electric's Business Effectiveness Staff; and Whyte and Hamilton's work with a hotel (Whyte and Hamilton, 1965).

3. Examples: Klein's work with a community in New England (in Schein and Bennis, 1965); Holmberg's work with a community in Peru (Holmberg, 1965).

4. In addition to the sources mentioned earlier, I have also benefited from comparing issues in my preliminary list with observations made about the change process by people familiar with the Vicos Project of Community Development in Peru. (See Holmberg, 1965; Holmberg and Dobyns, 1962; and Lasswell, 1962.)

5. The information upon which these observations are made is not in the case reports, but was available to me from direct sources.

6. Schein and Bennis interpret this failure as due to introducing a set of values in a component of an organization where the prevailing value system is too greatly different from that being introduced. I believe the linkage issue is a better way of formulating the difficulty, since the cases described by Guest and by Greiner indicate that a change program can be effective even when the new values are distinctly different from those currently prevalent in the system. However, the analysis by Schein and Bennis regarding "crucial issues" in the use of laboratory training is very relevant to our subject. (See Schein and Bennis, 1956, Chapter 10.)

7. Fantani and Weinstein (1966) report a similar approach to linkage in their work with a school system.

References

Argyris, Chris. "Organizational Development: An Inquiry into the Esso Approach." Unpublished monograph, July 1960.

Argyris, Chris. *Interpersonal Competence and Organizational Effectiveness*. Homewood, Illinois: Richard D. Irwin, 1962.

Beckhard, Richard. "An Organization Improvement Program in a Decentralized Organization," *Journal of Applied Behavioral Science* 2 (January–March 1966): 3–25.

Bennis, W. G., K. D. Benne, and R. Chin. *The Planning of Change*. New York: Holt, 1961.

Bennis, W. G. "A New Role for the Behavioral Sciences: Effecting Organizational Change," *Administrative Science Quarterly* 8 (September 1963): 125–65.

Blake, Robert R., and Jane S. Mouton. *The Managerial Grid*. Houston: Gulf Publishing Co., 1964.

Buchanan, Paul C. *Organization Development Following Major Retrenchment*, 1964 (a). Mimeograph.
Buchanan, Paul C. "Innovative Organizations—A Study in Organization Development," *Applying Behavioral Science Research in Industry*. Monograph No. 23. New York: Industrial Relations Counselors, 1964 (b).
Buchanan, Paul C. "The Concept of Organization Development, or Self-Renewal, as a Form of Planned Change," in Goodwin Watson (ed.). *Concepts for Social Change*. Washington, D.C.: Cooperative Project for Educational Development, National Training Laboratories, National Education Association, 1967, 1–9.
Buchanan, Paul C., and Phillip H. Brunstetter. "A Research Approach to Management Development." Parts I and II, *American Society of Training Directors Journal* (January–February 1959).
Dennis, Jamie, *A Modified Scanlon Plan as Part of an Organization Development Program*. 1964. Mimeograph.
Fantini, Mario D., and Gerald Weinstein. "Strategies for Initiating Change in Large Bureaucratic School Systems," in Arthur B. Shostak (ed.). *Sociology in Action*. Homewood, Illinois: Dorsey Press, 1966.
Greiner, Larry E. *Organization Change and Development*. Doctor's thesis. Cambridge, Massachusetts: Graduate School of Business Administration, Harvard University, 1965.
Guest, Robert H. *Organizational Change: A Study in Leadership*. Homewood, Illinois: Richard D. Irwin, 1962.
Holmberg, Allan R. "The Changing Values and Institutions of Vicos in the Context of National Development," *American Behavioral Scientst* 8 (March 1965): 3–8.
Holmberg, Allan R., and H. F. Dobyns. "The Process of Accelerating Community Change," *Human Organization* 21 (Summer 1962): 107–109.
Jaques, Elliott. *The Changing Culture of a Factory*. London: Tavistock Publications, 1951.
Jaques, Elliott. "Social-Analysis and the Glacier Project." *Human Relations* 17 (November 1964): 361–375.
Lasswell, H. D. "Integrating Communities into More Inclusive Systems," *Human Organization* 21 (Summer 1962): 116–24.
Leavitt, H. J. "Applied Organization Change in Industry: Structural, Technical and Human Approaches" in Cooper, W. W., H. J. Leavitt, and M. W. Shelly, II (eds.). *New Perspectives in Organization Research*. New York: John Wiley and Sons, 1964, Chapter 4.
Lesieur, F. G. (ed.). *The Scanlon Plan*. New York: John Wiley and Sons, 1958.
Lippitt, Ronald, J. Watson and B. Westley. *The Dynamics of Planned Change*. New York: Harcourt, Brace and Co., 1958.
Morton, R. B. and A. R. Weight. "A Critical Incidents Evaluation of an Organizational Training Laboratory," *California Management Review*. (In press.)
Schein, Edgar H., and Warren G. Bennis. *Personal and Organizational Change Through Group Methods: The Laboratory Approach*. New York: John Wiley and Sons, 1965.
Sofer, Cyril. *The Organization from Within*. Chicago: Quadrangle Books, 1962.
Whyte, William F., and E. L. Hamilton. *Action Research for Management*. Homewood, Illinois: Richard D. Irwin, 1965.
Zand, Dale E., Matthew B. Miles, and William O. Lytle. *Organizational Improvement Through Use of a Temporary Problem-Solving System*. 1964. Mimeograph.

25

ROBERT R. BLAKE AND JANE SRYGLEY MOUTON

Grid OD: A Systems Approach to Corporate Excellence*

The purpose of organization development is to achieve an excellent corporation. "Excellence" means the corporation is truly well managed and utilizes members most fully toward its productive aims.

Corporations are complex organisms of society.[1] Through their activities, efforts are made to satisfy man's goals and aspirations. Operating an organization effectively to achieve corporate purpose of profit through the soundest utilization of human capacities is recognized as one of society's major problems. It is also one of society's great opportunities. Few organizations have as yet realized excellence. Most miss it by a wide margin. The Grid approach to organization development is a way to achieve excellence by changing a corporation from what it *is* to what it *should be*.

History provides many examples of ways managers have tried to improve organization effectiveness. Beginning with the industrial revolution, continuing with the emergence of scientific management, and up to today's application of sophisticated computer-based systems and simulation techniques, men have sought to control the operational variables thwarting success. On the dynamic side, the subject of human motivation has found fascination throughout recorded history but with more systematic learning on this subject in the last fifty years than in the preceding 5,000.

Until recently, however, these two areas of human exploration have not been brought together effectively. In fact, much of what has been developed down these two paths has produced conflict and often appears mutually exclusive.

*Reprinted by permission of the authors from a report given at the McGregor Conference (see note).

Grid OD is an integrated approach which brings these two great areas of human achievement into a coherent whole.

CONCEPTS OF CHANGE

The roots of Grid OD lie in four major concepts of change. These powerful ideas that are present in today's society already have had a great influence on the course of human affairs. They are discovery, education, correction, and prevention. *Discovery* is the first concept—that through the application of scientific methods, basic processes of nature can be brought under human control. *Education* is based on the idea that knowledge and skill can be transmitted, acquired, and used to upgrade organization competence. *Correction* is one way of using knowledge to rectify or eliminate conditions that are barriers to effectiveness. *Prevention* is based on the concept that through the use of knowledge and skill, barriers which reduce effectiveness can be anticipated and avoided so that correction is unnecessary. Grid OD is not restricted to the use of any one of these concepts. It utilizes all in a planned manner in the achievement of corporate excellence.

CORPORATE EXCELLENCE

What is meant by "corporate excellence"? Is there a giant yardstick to measure each corporation to determine whether or not it is "excellent"? Are there criteria to apply to the large and small, to the single product, the integrated company, and the conglomerate?

An excellent corporation is able to achieve and sustain an outstandingly high return on investment over long periods of time.[2] Its managers have learned how to identify and create new opportunities for growth while meeting present responsibilities even in the face of stiffening competition and rising costs. The excellent corporation strives to increase the organizational competence of its managers to manage and its employees to produce. There is upgrading in the sophistication of technological aspects of marketing, production, and research and development. The concept of synergy is understood and exploited. Excellence involves the enrichment of the capacities of members of the corporation for using facts and data as the basis for thinking and analyzing and for finding quick and valid solutions to the inevitable parade of problems of operational life. The aim in an excellent corporation is to insure that its members apply their unbounded energies in a self-committed and enthusiastic way to contribute to reaching difficult but challenging corporate objectives.

BARRIERS TO CORPORATE EXCELLENCE

Many executives agree that top priority should be assigned to attaining corporate excellence. Yet they also acknowledge that their corporations have not come close to achieving it. Why has progress not been far more rapid in closing the gap? Only through a valid answer to this question is it likely that barriers to business effectiveness can be eliminated and excellence achieved. Rather than speculating about the answer to this question, what are the barriers to business effectiveness as identified by *managers*? These are shown in Table 25-1.

The foremost barrier to corporate excellence is communication; the next most widespread is planning. This is true whether the company being described operates in the United States, Great Britain, Japan, or elsewhere.[3] While other problem areas vary in importance and reveal interesting differences between countries, none approach these two as such significant barriers to corporate effectiveness.

Table 25-1. *Communication and Planning Are the Two Foremost Barriers to Corporate Excellence*

Barriers to Effectiveness	Percent of Companies in Which This Is Identified as One of Seven Key Barriers		
	UNITED STATES	GREAT BRITAIN	JAPAN
1. Communication	74.24	63.63	84.84
2. Planning	62.12	63.63	65.15
3. Morale	45.45	45.45	46.96
4. Coordination	45.45	22.72	31.81
5. Critique	42.42	28.78	33.33
6. Commitment	39.39	45.45	21.21
7. Control	33.33	28.78	35.29
8. Profit consciousness	31.81	36.36	31.81
9. Creativity	25.75	45.45	48.48
10. Getting results	21.21	30.30	45.45

Managers from 198 companies, 66 each in the United States, Great Britain, and Japan representing a wide variety of businesses provided these data. Corporations from the three countries were matched with one another by nature of the business and corporate size. Managers were matched by responsibility and level in the firms. They identified corporate areas regarded as the most significant barriers to be overcome in achieving excellence in their own corporations. While barriers beyond the first two vary in importance, the first two are the same regardless of country, company, or characteristics of the managers reporting.

Communication. What is meant when communication is identified as the number one problem? Here are illustrations of what managers say:

"People work in their little niches as though they had blinders on. They don't talk with one another enough to see what needs to be connected."

"If you really want to know what's going on in the company, ask your wife. Even better than that, the elevator men operate the real message center. It comes through them faster than it goes down the pipeline."

"Management thinks we are union baboons and are trying to steal the front gate."

"The union doesn't understand we have to make money to stay in business. They think the old man is Simon Legree with dollar signs etched on the gold buttons of his blazer."

"When the boss asks me what I think, I tell him what he wants to hear."

Are these problems of communication? Indeed they are. Achieving understanding and overcoming misunderstandings are widespread and pervasive difficulties of modern corporate life. But from another point of view, they are *not* communication problems. They are symptoms of far deeper and more significant causes. The likelihood is that the effort to communicate could be doubled by spreading the word—out, up, down, and sideways—with the result of a multiplication of misunderstanding rather than an increase in understanding. If communication is not the obstacle, what is it?

As interpreted in the frame of reference of Grid OD, the underlying causes of communication difficulties are to be found in the character of executive leadership, management, and supervision. Effective management includes sound relationships between boss and subordinates, within work teams, and between divisions of the corporation. When these are carried out within a work-oriented culture which provides clear objectives that arouse commitment, close cooperation to achieve high standards, and quick response, it is unlikely that problems of communication arise or keep recurring. The solution to the problem of communication, then, is for men to manage by achieving production and excellence through sound utilization of people.

Use of behavior theory as a basis for integrating people into the productive and profit objectives of a firm is essential in mobilizing human resources. Managers are not really managing behavior in most corporations today. They may be driving it, criticizing it, monitoring it, tolerating it, accepting it, or buying it. Many are going along with mediocrity, not because they like it but because they cannot see how to motivate others to thorough, problem-solving excellence.

Behavior theory has demonstrated its usefulness for solving problems of communication. An objective of Grid OD is to use behavior theory. The Grid is a strong foundation for solving communication problems by providing for sound interaction in the pursuit of organization goals.[4] Use of behavior theory to achieve results in an excellent corporation can no longer be regarded as a luxury. It is an urgent necessity. As we see, it is a key to the untapped reservoir of human energy which must be utilized if a corporation is to increase its operational effectiveness.

Planning. The second most widespread barrier to business effectiveness, as reported in over sixty percent of companies in the United States, Great Britain, and Japan, is planning. "Planning" means designing and implementing programs of operational effort which insure that anticipated results will be achieved. What do managers mean when they say planning is their number two problem? Here is what they say:

"How in the devil can you plan around here? You can't plan crises. It's all I can do to put out the fires, the big ones, that is."

"What do you mean, a plan? We don't have plans. All we have is pressure for results."

"Everything is planned, down to the smallest detail. We plan to the point where flexibility is completely sacrificed. People have learned—don't challenge it, just do it. As a result, we turn out great reports, but profitability is on a declining slope."

As communication is seen as a symptom rather than the real problem, planning also is seen as a symptom of a deeper difficulty. Both reflect barriers to effectiveness rather than causing ineffectiveness. Just working harder at planning or being more precise about it or taking more variables into consideration is no more likely to solve the planning problem than working diligently at spreading the word is likely to solve the problem of communication. The deeper cause of planning difficulties is an absence of business strategy or the use of a strategy which is based upon faulty business logic.

There are several elements of business logic which are important to achieving corporate excellence. One is having clearly financial objectives, preferably expressed in terms of return on investment, including minimum and optimal rates and amounts of return on investment. An ideal strategy contains clear-cut descriptions of the nature of the business or businesses that a company has committed itself to pursuing. The markets it intends to penetrate are well defined and analyzed, not only for present customer potential but also for future prospects. A business strategy provides specifications for how the organization structure should be arranged for the soundest integration of effort. It contains a statement of twenty-five to thirty major policies which systematically express logical foundations that serve as guidelines for decision and action. Finally, development requirements are identified that make specific the basis for increasing or sustaining corporate growth.

Conditions for sound planning have been created when these properties of an ideal business strategy have been clearly thought out and concisely expressed and when they are understood throughout the organization. Corporate members know where the company is headed. Planning provides the maps showing the routes for getting there. This kind of fundamental solution to planning problems can come about when those who lead the firm have designed and implemented an ideal strategic model for corporate operations. An objective of Grid OD is to solve problems of planning by implementing a strategic corporate model based on business logic.

Neither communication nor planning exist in isolation. Each contributes either to exaggerate or to reduce difficulties in the other. Effectiveness in work relationships contributes directly to strengthening the organization's capacity to design an ideal strategic model and to implement plans for achieving it. An ideal strategic model contributes directly to the reduction of problems of communication. The effect is not additive. It is synergistic; that is, members work together in a cooperative way so that the total effect is greater than the sum of the separate parts acting independently. Many if not all of the remaining problems shown in Table 25-1 appear to be consequences of difficulties stemming from faulty behavior theory or business logic. Effective corporate members operating under sound corporate strategy may gain the strength essential for achieving a truly excellent corporation.

Barriers to corporate excellence are not difficult to identify. Doing something about them is another matter. The changes required are fundamental. Managers must perfect their ways of managing. The corporation has to perfect its strategies of doing business. Viewed from this perspective, it is mandatory upon any approach to organization development that it deal with the total system, not solely with subsystems or pieces of subsystems.

CHANGING THE CORPORATE CULTURE

Since the objective of Grid OD is to move the total corporation from one plane of effectiveness to a higher plane, where is the point of access? The fundamental concept is that of corporate *culture*. For change in the corporation to occur the culture of the corporation must be changed. This calls for a strategy of development which assists an organization to free itself from its web of conventional thoughts and attitudes, of outmoded traditions, precedents, and past practices. For many corporations, culturally ingrained influences include poor teamwork, inappropriate use of authority, destructive intergroup relations, and lack of direction or sense of corporate purpose. Others result from faulty business logic and the handling of specific business problems on the basis of trial and error, hunch and intuition, or dogma and edict. Corporate members recognize that such characteristics of culture bring about a variety of problems, which they label problems of communication and problems of planning. Through experiments in Grid OD, it has come to be seen that the way to achieve excellence is not to treat these symptoms but to change and correct the corporate culture itself where the causes of the symptoms reside. Solving corporate problems by changing the culture calls for an entirely different approach from treating symptoms. The approach must inevitably be educational. It requires that the members of the organization learn basic concepts for increasing effectiveness, acquire skills in their application, and develop that intense degree of motivation which spurs striving and propels the change from what *is* to what *should be*.

In an educational approach to cultural change, many dimensions of organization behavior and performance respond to methods of discovery, education, correction, and prevention. Knowledge rooted in several disciplines, including business logic and management science and in the behavioral sciences of psychology, sociology, cultural anthropology, institutional economics, and political science, must be acquired and applied to the conduct of the business. Then existing problems can be identified and in the light of new knowledge, ways found for solving them. Grid OD provides a framework of concepts and methods of application calculated to bring about such changes.

THE PYRAMID THEORY OF CORPORATE EXCELLENCE

The culture of a corporation can be described through use of a pyramid as an analytical model. This is shown in Figure 25-1. Phases of Grid OD are described in Table 25-2.

At the pinnacle of the pyramid, the significant components of corporate culture essential for full organization competence come together as the point of excellence. Each of the four sides represents a body of knowledge, understanding, technology, and skills which are seen to be essential and utilized throughout the corporation. Starting at the front and moving counterclockwise around the pyramid, Side 1 represents knowledge of behavioral science; Side 2, the skills and instrumentation to implement it; Side 3 identifies fundamental precepts of

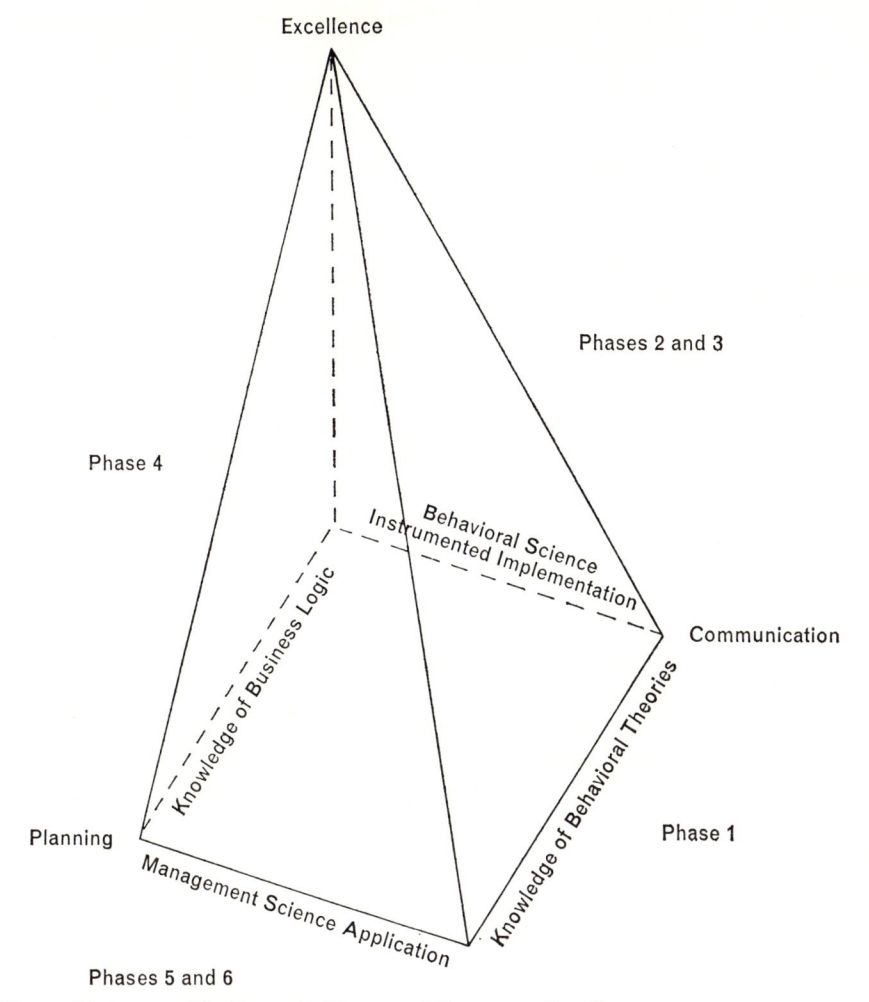

Figure 25-1. The Pyramid Theory of Corporate Excellence

business logic; and the skills of applying management science to operations are represented by Side 4.

THE BEHAVIORAL SYSTEM OF A CORPORATION

As members of an organization pursue business objectives, they must and do interact with one another. The quality of interaction shapes the organization's behavioral system. When communication is clear and unobstructed and problem solving is approached in the light of the firm's objectives, one kind of culture unfolds. When communication is closed, hidden, defensive, and circumspect and when problem solving is approached in the light of personal gain or vested interests, another kind of culture prevails. Still a third kind of culture is present when interactions are tentative, political, or opportunistic, when organization

Table 25-2. *How the Six Phases of Grid Organization Development Contribute to Corporate Excellence*

Communication	Planning
PHASE 1: GRID SEMINAR Organization members learn theories of behavior on a one-by-one basis.	**PHASE 4: DEVELOPING AN IDEAL STRATEGIC MODEL** Executive leaders specify in terms of business logic the intellectual foundations of the firm.
PHASE 2: TEAMWORK DEVELOPMENT Work teams apply Grid theories to increase their effectiveness.	**PHASE 5: PLANNING AND IMPLEMENTATION** For each definable business segment, planning teams use management science and technology to design and the line organization to change its operations by implementing the operational specifications for each business segment.
PHASE 3: INTERGROUP DEVELOPMENT Organized units that must cooperate to achieve results apply Grid theories to increase effectiveness with which they coordinate effort.	**PHASE 6: SYSTEMATIC CRITIQUE** The total effort is evaluated in order to review and consolidate progress made and to plan next steps of development.

members are prepared to go part way, or salute the tenets of bureaucracy. Corporate excellence is most likely to be achieved when:

(1.) A culture is created within which organization members are motivated to become involved in corporate problems and committed to solving them.
(2.) Teamwork characterized by a genuine sense of participation produces synergistic results.
(3.) Conflicts are brought out into the open for analysis and resolution.
(4.) Solutions that fall short of soundness are rejected for ones that actually solve problems.

The behavioral culture is most likely to be improved if the underlying thinking and attitudes which influence the actions of corporate members are changed.

Side 1. In the Grid approach to organization development, bringing about a sound behavioral culture requires two steps. The first is learning theories of the Grid which is Phase 1. This provides organization members a basis for thinking and analysis, and for defining and evaluating production-people problems. It supplies an intellectual, emotional, and motivational foundation from which planning for change becomes possible. The second part is implementation, which is Phases 2 and 3. All three phases involve use of behavioral science instruments which are based on Grid theories for examination of the aspects of the behavioral culture of an organization.[5] Both steps are indispensable. Learning theory without going forward to apply it is little more than an intellectual exercise. Trying to change the behavioral culture without using theory is likely to be little more than trial and error action.

In Phase 1, the firm's members participate in one-week Grid Seminars conducted by line manager-instructors on a diagonal slice basis. The learning is conceptual and systematic on the one hand, involving study and investigation of principles of behavior that apply in the general case. On the other hand, it is specific and concrete since each corporate member is able to evaluate the quality and character of his own thinking, emotions, and motivation in the light of the principles acquired.

Typical findings regarding the kinds of changes in intellectual, emotional, and motivational outlooks associated with Grid Seminar participation are:
(1.) Increased clarity of approaches for solving production-people dilemmas.
(2.) More open listening and more candid speaking.
(3.) Greater understanding of how to use critique.
(4.) Reduction in self-deception.
(5.) Improved understanding of intergroup dynamics. These findings are based on data gathered from over a thousand managers from a variety of companies in the United States, Great Britain, and Japan.

As a result of attending a Grid Seminar, managers change their conception of how they handle conflict. Essentially, managers see their approaches to conflict as less 9, 9 and more 9, 1 after a Grid Seminar than before. Thus, managers' self-perceptions of their own theories of managing conflict tend to reflect more of a win-lose, fighting type of strategy as opposed to one which relies more on reason and collaborative strategies.

In summary, managers from different countries, that is, United States, Great Britain, and Japan, all tend to agree after attending a Grid Seminar that 9, 9 is the soundest theory for operating a corporation and that they do not see 9, 9 management theory practiced in their own organizations.

Side 2. Side 2 of the pyramid represents implementation. Instruments are used throughout to apply the behavioral concepts and principles learned in the Grid Seminar to the problem-solving operations of the firm. This is accomplished through Phases 2 and 3 of Grid OD. Phase 2, Teamwork Development, involves all the teams in the organization, starting at the top and proceeding downward.[6] By comparing how the team actually works with what would constitute sound teamwork, members of each team are able to study, evaluate, and change their sometimes hidden and quasi-silent culture—the team-based traditions, precedents, and past practices.

The objective of Phase 2 is to create conditions under which each of the natural units of the organization can evaluate its culture and design strategies for changing it to achieve excellence of performance. With respect to evaluation, data show that when team members agree on the properties of an ideal team culture, they are more self-critical of their actual team culture. Thinking through what constitutes ideal specifications as a preliminary to evaluating the present situation and as a prelude to setting objectives for future performance is a general strategy for bringing about change which is used throughout the various phases of Grid OD.

With respect to change in team culture, data gathered before and after Phase 2 show that as a result of Teamwork Development teams:
(1.) Become more objective in evaluating their performance.

(2.) Develop a culture which helps to insure that those traditions which have a positive impact on team performance will be carried into the future.
(3.) Communicate internally more openly.
(4.) Develop higher standards of excellence.
(5.) By setting objectives become more motivated for achievement.
(4.) Increase their teamwork skills.
(7.) Critique their work more frequently in solving problems.

The other major point of application, Intergroup Development as Phase 3, is another level of subsystems that interact in the corporation, namely intergroup relations.[7] It involves an examination of the behavioral cultures of units of the corporation that must coordinate efforts and cooperate to achieve corporate objectives. The Grid is used to evaluate what the quality of the interaction *is* as contrasted to what it *should be* to be truly sound. Plans for change, when implemented among interacting groups where cooperation and coordination are essential, result in the possibility of strong and effective intergroup behavior culture.

Data collected from work done in Phase 3 have shown that (1) relationships between headquarters and field have changed from that of disrespect to that of confidence; (2) international cleavages rooted in cultural differences have been bridged; and (3) union-management relationships have been significantly improved.

As a result of an examination of the behavioral theories that underlie the communication problems existing within work teams and between work teams in Phases 2 and 3, the behavior culture of the firm is strengthened and in such a manner as to increase the likelihood that effective communication can and will take place.[8]

THE BUSINESS CULTURE OF A CORPORATION

One of the major barriers to corporate excellence is that a corporation develops its own culture of business precepts, assumptions, and beliefs, just as it develops its own behavior culture. To the extent that its business precepts are out of line with business logic, limitations are present which impede excellence.

Side 3. Without undue risk, no corporation can take for granted that it has at its core sound and rigorous business logic. Yet it follows that if corporate success is to be achieved, the logic of the business must be in line with the tenets of success in a free enterprise society. Side 3 of the pyramid represents the contribution to corporate excellence possible from sound business logic.

The Phase 4 activity involves evaluating present business thinking against the thinking that would be required under sound free enterprise business logic as the basis for integrating operational effort. With the completion of Phase 4, the leadership of the company has reached committed agreements about its short and long term financial objectives, the nature of the business, its markets, what would constitute sound structure and policy and development requirements for strong and sustained growth. Characteristic changes in key executives' thinking as a result of designing an ideal strategic model are typical outcomes of Phase 4 activities. With an explicit statement of the logic it intends to pursue, the organization is prepared to move on to the next phase.

Side 4. The applications of management science and technology in the firm are represented by Side 4 of the pyramid. In Phase 5, members throughout the organization use management science techniques not only to evaluate the operation of the existing business but also to specify necessary changes in operations to meet the requirements of business logic identified in the Phase 4 ideal strategic model. A wide range of management science techniques is called into use, from computer simulation of alternative operational models to systematic study of plant layout and design, and manufacturing and marketing methods.

But nothing is static. Businesses change. The tendency toward backsliding is always present and even in the strongest behavioural and business cultures, standards of excellence will be eroded. No corporate system is a closed one, operating according to static properties. An equilibrium achieved by one phase or a sequence of phases of development can by no means be presumed to be even quasi-stationary. Influences that shift the level and the inevitable changes that result are as likely to be retrogressive as progressive. Phase 6, which is also part of the fourth side of the pyramid, provides for continual corporate self-examination insuring that new actions brought about during the earlier phases do not become precedents, no longer suited to emerging requirements. It insures that practices initiated in response to be one set of circumstances do not become today's sacred cows, no longer valid but blindly accepted. Phase 6 involves the use of techniques of critique which have been employed throughout the first five phases of Grid OD.

SUMMARY

The pinnacle of corporate excellence is supported on each side and reached through a corporate culture of behavioral theory, behavioral science instrumented implementation, business logic, and management science and technology. Any approach which concentrates upon only one or two of the sides of the pyramid and disregards the others is unlikely to result in a corporation which can achieve and sustain excellence within the demands and challenges of a free enterprise society. Based upon a decade of experimentation in its application, it is our conclusion that Grid OD is a practical, workable, and realistic way to attain corporate excellence.

ISSUES OF ORGANIZATION DEVELOPMENT

The model of Grid OD presented above has evolved through field experiments and applications in large and small companies in many countries, in government agencies, hospitals, universities and school systems. These Grid OD projects have afforded opportunities for both systematic experimentation, where conditions of application have been deliberately altered according to plan, and "natural" experimentation, where, because of local circumstances, conditions have varied sometimes in a negative way from what appeared at the time to be the soundest course of action.[9] Under these circumstances, some projects have been of greater success; some have been of lesser success. Thus, the variations afforded have made it possible to critique and generalize as to stronger and weaker strategies of inducing development.

Organization development as a profession may be forwarded by making basic premises on which it rests as clear as possible. In order to do this, a comparison between Grid OD and the T-group-consultant method of organization change is provided here. Identifying similarities and differences between Grid OD and the T-group-consultant approach is a complex task. To the best of our knowledge, no description of the T-group-consultant approach reflecting explicit agreement among consultants is available as yet.[10] T-group consultants vary among themselves over a wide assortment of tactics and assumptions. Some common elements in basic strategy can be specified, however. Before the two approaches are compared what appear to be key underlying properties of the T-group-consultant approach are outlined briefly:

(1.) An educational phase involving an unstructured group learning experience with a trainer present, usually an applied behavioral expert. The language for describing this basic learning group varies and includes T-group, development group, basic encounter group or sensitivity training. The aims are described in a wide variety of specific ways, but increased personal and social understanding are a significant objective.

(2.) More than one member of the organization must engage in this kind of learning, though not necessarily simultaneously.

(3.) To foster organization change, consultant followup is desirable.

Within these communalities, there is considerable diversity in approach, and it is for this reason that comparison becomes complex and objectivity of comparison more difficult.

The T-group-consultant approach to organization change is continuing to unfold according to its own traditions. Recent emphasis within the laboratory training movement, involving the structured intergroup design, the use of instrumentation, and the programmatic phase concept, for example, suggests that the T-group-consultant methodology is beginning to shift in the direction of Grid OD methodology.[11]ABer, the basic premises of these two approaches are sharply divergent from one another at many points.

INCLUSIVENESS OF CORPORATE SYSTEMS

Behavioral culture, business logic, and management science and technology constitute three major systems of the corporation. Each in turn is the topic of development in Grid OD. While they can be separated for study and improvement, in the final analysis, they are interdependent.

By contrast, the T-group-consultant approach concentrates on behavioral aspects, sometimes individual, sometimes interpersonal and group. Systematic examination of the organization culture within which individual, interpersonal and group aspects of behavior are embedded is not provided for, although sometimes acknowledged to be important. Similarly, business logic and the operational skills of problem solving reflected in the use of management science and technology are not dealt with in a deliberate way.[12]

An approach to organization development which does not explicitly concentrate developmental effort on all of these three major systems is a limited and partial one unlikely to lead to corporate excellence in the fuller meaning of that word.[13] Behavioral consultants concerned with development and change have almost wholly disregarded the internal logic of the business system. Their operating assumption appears to have been that "good relationships" are the necessary and sufficient conditions for bringing about improvement. Thus, if relationships are sound, difficulties of business logic and operational problem solving skills will be rectified without programmatic effort. Management science specialists on the other hand have made the same error but in the reverse direction, presuming that embedded precepts, assumptions, and beliefs about business will automatically be corrected if only business analysis techniques are known and utilized by a few members of the firm or by an operations research group.[14] When this outlook is compounded by a disregard of the barriers to effectiveness that are embedded in the behavioral culture of the firm, the result is almost certain to be severely limited.

INCLUSIVENESS OF CORPORATE MEMBERSHIP

Grid OD is designed to permit everyone in the company to be engaged in development action. The premise is that every member of the company is a "culture carrier" and a problem solver.

The T-group-consultant approach commonly deals with segments of the corporation such as middle management, a key executive group or pockets of interest.[15]

To the degree that those who carry the culture or who are employed to solve company problems are not included in the development effort, limitations are likely to be present in the extent of developmental achievement possible. Furthermore, inclusion of some and exclusion of others has repeatedly been observed to produce cleavages which may reduce rather than increase effectiveness.

THE ROLE OF SYSTEMATIC FORMULATION

It is not taken for granted in Grid OD that any of the three major systems of the corporation necessarily is functioning well. Through systematic study, diagnosis, evaluation and change, each of the major systems can be maintained at or brought to a plane essential for effectiveness. By this kind of an orderly approach across the three major systems it becomes possible to identify those already sound and therefore not needing development and those in most need of correction.

The T-group-consultant approach, for the most part, is one that ordinarily deals with behavioral issues as they are presented or as they come to be recognized. In this sense, the T-group-consultant approach is not programmatic but takes its character and direction from the immediate situation in an inductive way. Beyond that, it is a collaborative approach between the consultant and the client organization which results in the definition of goals to be set and problems to be worked on.[16]

The restriction of an eclectic approach is related to the points made in the earlier section which described management's identification of communication and planning as major barriers to corporate excellence. The thesis was presented that such problems are symptomatic of underlying causes rather than being the sources of difficulty. An eclectic approach, tending to deal with problems as presented, may be justified as a point of departure in a new or emerging situation. Progress in scientific endeavors and application is tied directly to the ability to shift rapidly from eclectic and trial and error approaches to systematic ones.

PRIMACY OF INSTRUMENTATION

The Grid OD approach relies heavily on instrumentation throughout its phases rather than upon the interventions of consultants, with the values underlying the approach made explicit in the written materials themselves. Where consultation is introduced, it is supplemental rather than primary. Through the use of learning and application instruments, the Grid OD approach is internally administered by line managers which means that those who are responsible for results are, in fact, responsible for the change effort. To the degree that the developmental approach is theory-based, programmatic and instrumented, to that degree, it is not only self-administering, but also self-catalyzing and self-correcting. The contributions that otherwise would be made by a consultant are unneeded to the extent that corporate members presently have or develop skills in participant-observation. Strengthening of such skills is provided for in the initial phases.

The T-group-consultant approach relies almost exclusively on the consultant as a catalyst in learning and development situations. This means that the values of the external or internal change agent are likely to be significantly influencing the development effort. To the degree that the change agent's values are not made explicit, or are at variance with those in the organization, the use of the T-group-consultant approach may be based more upon faith than upon factual understanding.

The use of learning and application instruments, as contrasted with a consultant-based approach, is a significant issue of organization development. The task of designing an instrument for studying and understanding behavioral or business concepts places on the designer the necessity for clarity of his own knowledge and understanding of the theories, concepts, and logic involved in the appropriate design for study and evaluation of the concept. The continuous effort to achieve such clarity can lead to an unending process of concept correction, strengthening, and expansion. A criticism of the theory-based instrumented approach is that it *can* be mechanical and blur the dilemmas and dynamic realities of organization life. Whether one *is* mechanical or dynamic hinges upon whether the issues dealt with are vital and whether the learning raises cognitive, emotional, and motivational aspects of behavior to a threshold where they can be treated insightfully.

An advantage of the consultant approach is that he may be able to see and through his interventions bring examination to bear on obstacles to effectiveness that are extremely difficult for participant-observers to identify and deal with. The disadvantage is that there is likely to be the side effects of dependency-hostility in the consultant's relationships within the organization. To the degree that an organization values the contribution of a consultant, there is the likelihood that those benefiting from it feel not only affection for him because of his helpfulness but dependence upon him for further assistance. Thus, a consultant may become a semi-permanent member of an organization without really belonging to it. Such dependency, unless well worked through, often evokes counter-dependent hostilities and resistances. In this connection, the number of applied behavioral consultants who have joined firms and moved on to other firms or back to university environments since 1955 should not be ignored. The problem may be more real than illusory.

DEGREE OF STRUCTURE

Grid OD and the T-group-consultant approaches are in agreement as to the significance of action-based learning about emotions and motivation. Both appear to be at variance with approaches where the effort is limited to the learning of concepts or to the examination of questionnaire or survey data.[17] However, the exploration of emotional and motivational factors takes place under learning situations with different degrees of structure in the two approaches.

Grid OD, throughout its phases, is both programmatic and structured. The activities are planned, pretested and subjected to continuous revision and rapid focusing of key developmental problems, but also to reducing confusion, floundering, and frustration. The approach is based on the premise that human beings are structure-seeking. The issue is not the rejection of structure to gain egalitarianism but rather the development and use of structure and hierarchy for sound, problem-solving relationships.

Learning situations under the T-group-consultant approaches are unstructured in the sense that the experiences that are studied are not predetermined. The idea is that when participants are confronted with an unstructured situation, they acquire an understanding of how the conventional structures of thoughts, assumptions, and procedures under which they live influence and may limit their effectiveness. T-group-consultants might agree that in the absence of structure, an unfreezing process becomes possible which is a condition for genuine learning. Some would further agree that without the aid of the unfreezing that unstructuredness produces, significant learning about personal effectiveness is unlikely to result.

Findings to date, at least as they relate to the development of organization competence among managers, suggest that unstructured situations seem to produce similar kinds of behavioral learnings as those resulting from structured ones. Thus, a reexamination of the use of unstructured learning situations as a condition of change may be indicated. A trend among some T-group-consultants may be emerging that emphasizes project learning, organization diagnostic sessions, and so on, which suggests that there may be a movement underway in the direction of increasing the structuredness of change situations. Another indication of concern about unstructured learning is apparent in the already mentioned recent efforts sponsored by NTL that seem to be leading toward structure and instrumentation.

Another point of comparison is general strategy of change. In the Grid OD approach, repeated use is made throughout all phases of creating an ideal model toward which development is oriented. The gap created by the discrepancy between the actual situation confronting an individual or a corporation motivates effort to change. In this respect, "evaluative" feedback may be of key significance, that is, *what is* is not as good in comparison with what would be ideal. In the T-group-consultant approach, a common point of coherence appears to be in the tactical approach of creating a climate of support and trust in which current behavior can be accepted and new or different behavior tried out. A key here is in the significance of ruling out evaluative feedback in favor of non-evaluative feedback. In the latter approach, emphasis is placed primarily upon psychological success, while the Grid OD approach acknowledges that becoming more dissatisfied with the current situation may be a pre-condition to change.

Each of the issues presented is an important one relating to an overall definition of conditions for effective organization development. While our preferences for solving each of the theoretical issues are clearly evident in the strategies of Grid OD, it is not to be expected that others will find these views synonymous with their own. Still it is important to attempt to describe alternatives precisely and definitely. Only through clarity as to the strength and limitations of each of the several alternatives is it possible to make sound and fundamental progress in learning how to develop the effectiveness of a corporation.

SUMMARY AND CONCLUSIONS

Grid OD as a systems approach to organization development, which is aimed at the removal of barriers to corporate excellence that arise in communication and planning, has been described. Three major systems are involved.

One is the behavioral system which creates a culture of attitudes, expectations, obligations, and responsibilities within which management, supervision and operations take place. The key to changing the behavioral culture is in corporate members' learning and utilizing the Grid framework as a conceptual model for identifying, analyzing, and planning solutions to those behavioral problems that are barriers to their effectiveness. In the first three phases significant attention is applied to the faulty management of conflict in interpersonal, team and intergroup relationships. The objective is to confront and resolve human and operational problems in a 9, 9 way rather than managing them through suppression, withdrawal, smoothing or compromise.

The second system involves business logic. The undergirding of business thinking in many companies today is replete with precepts, assumptions, and values which have evolved through history and which cannot be accepted at face value as squaring with the financial realities essential for survival, profit, and growth. Only when systems of business logic have been identified, studied, evaluated and corrected to bring them into line with the requirements of rigorous thinking does a firm have a valid basis for sustaining its operations.

Operational and technological skills constitute a third system of corporate performance. Outmoded, over-simplified, narrow gauge methods of analysis, calculation, and evaluation are insufficient as a foundation for business decisions in a technologically sophisticated world. The era in which hunch, intuition and hip pocket solutions could be relied upon is rapidly drawing to a close. The techniques of management science now widely available provide powerful strategies of business analysis and decision making. Only when the operational and technological systems of a business organization employ these methods throughout is it able to support operational efforts capable of survival, profit, and growth.

Key theoretical issues in organization development were examined by contrasting two different strategies. Evaluative comments were introduced to specify the advantages and limitations of the Grid OD approach and the T-group-consultant approach in order to aid in the clarification of basic premises on which organization development rests.[18] Indeed, it may be appropriate to challenge the use of the concept *organization development* in some of its current applications. Many uses of the term have nothing to do with the development of organizations. They sometimes refer to the development of the individual manager or the development of isolated managerial teams or to aiding in the solution of a specific behavioral problem confronting the firm. The minimum conditions for the use of the term "organization development" might very well be that the approach encompass strengthening basic systems of the organization and that those who are its cultural carriers be actively involved in developmental endeavors designed to increase their organizational competence. Any approach that falls short of these two aspects hardly merits inclusion under the description organization development.

The stakes involved in effective OD are of the highest order. The tempo of society seems ever to accelerate, particularly on the material side. Effectively managing the behavioral, cultural, conceptual, and analytical aspects of society has lagged. Until this decade, the gap between material opportunities and human actualities has continued to widen. Organization development is generally considered as perhaps the major hope of closing this gap. The spread of mass education, mass communication, and rapid travel has created understanding of and expectations for sophistication in the management of organization affairs. It has also created an ever greater awareness of and concern about the existence of this gap between what is and what can be. Organizations, as the organisms of society, are comprised of members who are ready and eager to engage in the study, investigation, and solution of human and organization problems which constitute barriers to excellence. A theory-based insight approach that integrates mental, emotional, and motivational aspects of human reaction into a meaningful and rewarding career experience provides one answer to a problem of great social urgency.

Notes

* Prepared for the McGregor Conference, MIT, October 12–14, 1967. For a fuller treatment, see Robert R. Blake and Jane Srygley Mouton, *Corporate Excellence Through Grid Organization Development: A Systems Approach*. Houston, Texas: Gulf Publishing Company, 1968

1. Other significant social organisms of society are government agencies, educational institutions, hospitals, and so on. They have barriers to excellence that parallel those of the corporation. The content of this paper applies to them as well as to corporations except that, because they are not operated for profit, they have objectives that must be formulated in different terms.

2. As used throughout this paper, "return on investment" conveys the concept of return on assets employed including outside financing. This concept of return on investment is one index of the effectiveness with which a corporation employs the assets available to it. The way in which this measurement is applied must be defined concretely to fit the requirement of a particular corporation. Service corporations and nonindustrial organizations, such as government organizations, do not have such an index but often do have or can develop quantitative indexes that are equally useful for measuring organization achievement.

3. Data from these three countries are used for comparison purposes. Data available from companies in other countries including Europe, Australia, the Middle East, and North and South America yield generally comparable findings. The research and field reports summarized here represent studies conducted in connection with Grid OD activities.

4. The first publication of Grid theory is in Blake, R. R. and J. S. Mouton, *The Managerial Grid: Problems and Possibilities of Improving Production Through the Participation of People*. Austin, Texas: The University of Texas, 1961, 1–303; which also introduces the language and concepts of organization development. The most comprehensive treatment is presented in Blake, R. R. and J. S. Mouton, *The Managerial Grid*. Houston, Texas: Gulf Publishing, 1964.

5. The concept of instrumentation contains three aspects: (1) a theory on which the instrument is formulated, (2) application of the instrument to measure an organizational episode, and (3) scoring and interpretation of the findings by the person who completed the instrument under conditions permitting him to generalize his findings. This concept of instrumentation was first introduced in Mouton, J. S., & R. R. Blake, University Training in Human Relations Skills. National Training Laboratories, Selected Readings, Series Three, *Human Forces in Teaching and Learning*, 1961, 88–96. The current tendency to refer to instrumentation to include any rating scales, questionnaires, or other measuring devices, obscures these through subtle but important attributes of a learning instrument.

6. Bidwell, A. C., J. J. Farrel, and R. R. Blake, "Team Job Training—A New Strategy for Industry," *Journal of the American Society of Training Directors*, 15 (1961): 3–23. Also: Blake, R. R., J. S. Mouton, and M. G. Blansfield, "How Executive Team Training Can Help You and Your Organization," *Journal of the American Society of Training Directors*, 16 (1962): 3–11.

These articles present early versions of team training from which the present methods of Teamwork Development emerged.

7. Early applications of the intergroup development design to training and industrial situations include: Blake, R. R. "Psychology and the Crisis of Statesmanship," *The American Psychologist*, 14 (1959): 87–94; R. R. Blake and J. S. Mouton, "The Story Behind Intergroup Conflict," *Petroleum Refiner*, 39 (1960): 181–185; R. R. Blake and J. S. Mouton, "Why Problem-solving Between Groups Sometimes Fails," *Petroleum Refiner* 39 (1960): 269–273; R. R. Blake and J. S. Mouton, "Union-Management Relations: From Conflict to Collaboration," *Personnel*, 38 (1961): 38–51; R. R. Blake and J. S. Mouton, "Headquarters-field Team Training for Organizational Improvement," *Journal of the American Society of Training Directors*, 16 (1962): 3–11; R. R. Blake, and J. S. Mouton, "The Intergroup Dynamics of Win-Lose Conflict and Problem-Solving Collaboration in Union-management Relations," in M. Sherif (ed.). *Intergroup Relations and Leadership*. New York: Wiley, 1962. An extended treatment is available in: R. R. Blake, H. A. Shepard, and J. S. Mouton, *Managing Intergroup Conflict in Industry*, Houston: Gulf Publishing, 1964.

8. The origin of our work embracing the organization development concept as contrasted with management development or T-group approaches, can be traced to: R. R. Blake and

J. S. Mouton, "Human Relations Problem Areas in Work," *Group Psychotherapy*, 9 (1956): 253-264.

9. Representative articles depicting Grid OD applications include: R. R. Blake, J. S. Mouton, L. B. Barnes, and L. E. Greiner, "Breakthrough in Organization Development," *Harvard Business Review* (November-December, 1964): 133-155: B. F. White, "A Line Manager Looks at Team Training," *Training Directors Journal*, 18 (1964): A. Marsh, "The Managerial Grid," *Industrial Welfare*, 47 (1965): 256-259; B. Portis "Management Training for Organization Development," *The Business Quarterly*, 39 (1965): 44-54; W. Robertson, "The Managerial Grid in Action," *Monetary Times*, 5 (1965): 39-45; E. A. Clasen "Blake in the Corporate Bloodstream," *Proceedings: NAWGA's 1966 Mid-Year Executive Conference*, (September, 1966): 37-39; G. Foster, "The Managerial Grid in Action at Ward's," *Stores*, 48 (1966): 42-44; J. McAllister, "The Pursuit of Excellence, *Sales Management*, 97 (1966): 81-98; B. F. White, "A Higher Dimension for Management Development," prepared at the Request of the Presidential Task Force on Career Advancement, November, 1966; G. R. Simmonds, "Organization Development: A Key to Future Growth, *Personnel Administration*, 30 (1967): 19-24; A. D. McCormick, "Management Development at British-American Tobacco," *Management Today* (June, 1967): 126-128.

10. Edited volumes which provide an indication of the degree of congruence and of the diversity among T-group consultants include: E. H. Schein and W. G. Bennis, *Personal and Organizational Change Through Group Methods: The Laboratory Approach*. New York: Wiley, 1967; L. P. Bradford, J. R. Gibb, and K. D. Benne: *T-Group Theory and Laboratory Method*. New York: Wiley, 1964.

11. See *NTL Institute for Applied Behavioral Science*, Center for Organization Studies, Washington, D. C., 1967-1968, for representative laboratory training programs. Typical consultant approaches which provide an example of convergence toward the Grid OD approach of programmatic effort using the first three phases, with a T-group as the educational phase, are to be found in: A. Winn, "Social Change in Industry: From Insight to Implementation," *The Journal of Applied Behavioral Science*, 2 (1966): 170-184; S. A. Davis, "An Organic Problem-Solving Method of Organization Change," *The Journal of Applied Behavioral Science*, 3 (1967): 3-21.

12. Indeed Bennis depicts the T-group-consultant approach and operations research as being in many ways opposite but essentially equivalent methods of inducing change rather than complementary. W. G. Bennis. *Changing Organizations*. New York: McGraw-Hill, 1966, 85-94.

13. Likert describes a systems approach, but the systems he depicts are four systems of managerial behavior rather than corporate systems. In the terminology of this paper, these would be alternative ways of managing roughly analogous with alternative theories of the Grid. He does not deal explicitly with the corporate systems of business logic or operational systems utilizing management science and technology per se. R. Likert, *The Human Organization*. New York: McGraw-Hill, 1967.

14. H. I. Ansoff. *Corporate Strategy*. New York: McGraw-Hill, 1965; M. Bowers. *The Will to Manage*. New York: McGraw-Hill, 1966; G. Nadler, *Work Design*. Homewood, Illinois: Irwin, 1963.

15. C. Argyris, *Interpersonal Competence and Organizational Effectiveness*. Homewood, Illinois: Irwin-Dorsey, 1962; A. Winn, *op. cit.*; S. A. Davis, *op. cit.*; J. P. Jones, "People—The Independent Variable," in Haire, M. (ed.). *Organization Theory in Industrial Practice*. New York: Wiley, 1962, 48-55; Marrow, A. J. "Managerial Revolution in the State Department," *Personnel* (November-December, 1966).

16. R. Beckhard, "The Confrontation Meeting," *Harvard Business Review*, 45, No. 2 (1967): 149-155.

17. D. Katz and R. Kahn. *The Social Psychology of Organizations*. New York: Wiley, 1966, 416-425.

18. Three recent examples reflect failure to grasp the implications of differences regarded here as important between Grid OD and the T-group-consultant approach. C. M. Hampden-Turner, in "An Existential 'Learning Theory' and the Integration of T-Group Research," *The Journal of Applied Behavioral Science*, 2 (1966): 367-386, used research on the theory based, structured, instrumented, trainerless Grid Seminar as published by R. R. Blake, J. S. Mouton, L. B. Barnes, and L. E. Greiner, "Breakthrough in Organization Development," *Harvard Business Review* (November-December, 1964): 133-155, in support of a theory he presents which purports to explain learning which presumably takes place in the unstructured,

theoryless, trainer-directed T-group. Similarly Winn (*op. cit.*) describes incompany T-group laboratories and, while presenting no data to evaluate the outcomes of his T-group-centered approach, refers to the same Blake, Mouton, Barnes, and Greiner study as "an excellent and elaborate evaluation of laboratory training" (p. 176). The contradiction can further be seen in *Explorations*, Human Relations Training and Research, 2 (1967). In "A Bibliography of Research since 1960" Eric S. Knowles makes no reference to the Blake, Mouton, Barnes, and Greiner article. This kind of disregard of differences within the applied behavioral science community suggests either that genuine differences are not recognized or that they are ignored. The analogy in some respects is akin to using research on the outcome of client-centered therapy as the basis for evaluating the therapeutic outcomes of psychoanalysis.

26

RICHARD BECKHARD AND DALE G. LAKE

Short- and Long-Range Effects of a Team Development Effort

*O*f the many-planned, behavioral-science-based improvement efforts in organizations, very few include any measurement of change. The measures that are available usually entail collecting data during or immediately after the "intervention" or program.

This article describes an attempt to create a team approach to management during a period of change from mechanized bookkeeping to electronic data-processing in a large investment and commercial bank.[1] During the course of this effort, a period of one year, "hard" and "soft" measures of changes were collected. Four years later, a similar set of measures was again collected, in a follow-up study. In essence, the follow-up study indicated that a large number of changes and improvements, reported at the end of the first year, continued over the succeeding three years.

An examination of the environment within which the change effort took place will precede a brief description of the effort. Next, an examination will be made of the findings of changes in the group undergoing the change effort, and the group's performance will be compared to two "control" groups or divisions engaged in similar work in the organization. Finally, there will be a summary of the follow-up study four years later and, again, a presentation of performance comparisons with the control groups.

BACKGROUND

Historically, the bank was managed in a benevolent, autocratic mode—low

Written especially for this volume.

pay, good benefits, supervision of varied quality (with very direct supervision at the lower levels) and a class society with very limited communications.

The upper-level management of the organization felt that upgrading the quality of supervision at middle management levels would increase productivity, and introducing more modern systems would meet the changing demands. These efforts to introduce new methods were not working well due to a high degree of resistance among "old line" managers at all levels, but particularly in middle management.

The training management, on the other hand, believed there was need for a major change in the whole atmosphere of the organization—particularly in middle levels of supervision—if any significant improvement was to occur. The turnover rate was extremely high, and in the preceding few years, the recruitment effort had slipped. The bank was able to recruit good men from the better colleges, but recently had been losing them, at an alarming rate, after only the first few years. High-potential young men did not see the bank as an exciting place to work. There had also been an increasing number of resignations of effective middle managers.

The training people felt that if real improvement was to occur, an essential first condition was for the upper-level management to look at its own attitudes, style and managerial behavior. They felt there would have to be a change in the attitudes and values at the "top" if anything significant were to occur in the "middle."

Over a period of two years a number of strategies, directed toward changing the attitudes of the upper-level management, had been considered or tried by the change agents in the training department. First, there were discussions about initiating the planned changes with the upper-level managers. The response had been, "As we've told you, the problem is not with us; we know we've got difficulties in the organization or we wouldn't be after you to fix them. The problem is with the middle management—go and work with them."

The second strategy considered was to initiate an attitude survey, on the assumption that the data would make clear to the upper-level management that what was needed was change on their part. After discussing this strategy with outside consultants, the training people recognized that such a report might simply increase resistance and defensiveness.

A third strategy was to hold a meeting of the upper-level management with their counterparts in other organizations that had engaged in some successful planned-organizational improvement programs. Descriptions and favorable results of these efforts impressed the management of the bank and led the change agents to try a fourth strategy.

The fourth strategy was to expose the upper-level management, in a non-threatening way, to some current thinking about organizational values, motivation, and effectiveness. Luncheons were arranged with leading thinkers in the field. The management's response to this effort was that these were interesting meetings and very informative, but the inputs were somewhat theoretical and not particularly applicable to the bank's situation.

Eighteen months after these attempts, a fifth strategy was suggested—A pilot project to see if significant difference could be made in the climate, operating effectiveness, and productivity of a small segment of the organization through a planned "intervention." This was to be a basis for considering larger efforts. Top management agreed to support this experiment and the total change effort began.

INTERVENTION STRATEGY

In the securities division of the organization there were two groups whose work was heavily interdependent—Mortgage Production and Methods. Relationships and work effectiveness were not satisfactory in these groups. The task of the methods specialists was to try to help Mortgage Production upgrade its work methods. As a part of a bank-wide plan, much of the work currently handled through mechanized bookkeeping was going to be computerized. The Methods group had the specific task of getting the computer installed and operating in the Mortgage Production.

It was decided to engage in a one-year project with a team composed of the management of these two groups. The stated purposes were improving their operational effectiveness as a problem-solving unit and facilitating the introduction of the computer into Mortgage Production.

The team engaged in the pilot project was composed of nine managers from the Mortgage and three from the Methods group. We will call this group the "experimental team." The steps taken with the experimental team included preparatory work for everyone on the team before the first of three off-site meetings with the group.

As part of this preparation, each of the members of the team went to a sensitivity training laboratory. After this, the team met with the consultant for half a day. The consultant described the goals and the possible outcomes of the project, and asked each member of the experimental group to submit an anonymous letter to him listing the obstacles to more effective operation of this team, of the environment around this team, and of the total bank. Then the consultant organized the information from the letters as a basis for initial analysis with the team. During the first weekend conference, the consultant began the meeting by reporting back a summary of the information from the letters. The group then discussed the list of problems, set priorities and began to work on them. These problems included such items as:

(1.) Style of the group's supervisor.
(2.) Relationships between a supervisor and his section heads.
(3.) Relationships between operations groups and methods specialists.
(4.) The status (perceived as being low) of this group compared to other groups in the bank.
(5.) Relationships between this group and bank management.

As a result of individual exposure to the sensitivity training, a large number of real problems, and the *fact* of the meeting, there was a high commitment among members to confront the problems and to try to improve the state of affairs. Discussions were frank, open, and sometimes painful.

By the end of the weekend the group had decided:
(1.) To continue meeting monthly at the bank (without a consultant).
(2.) To create three task forces to work on some internal problems.
(3.) To have the supervisor of mortgage operations call a meeting of his two counterparts to establish an on-going interdepartmental communications mechanism.
(4.) To contact the central personnel department for some help in rectifying poor personnel practices and procedures.

Six months later, a second weekend conference was held with the consultant attending; in the interim, the team had met monthly and carried out most of their action plans. This conference with the consultant was planned by the team and included an agenda of priority problems that they believed required more time than was available in their monthly meetings. They worked on these problems and set action plans to be carried out during the following six months. In order to reduce the number of monthly meetings, a steering committee of three people was authorized to appoint task forces of "resources" from the group to work on specific problems.

The total group met again six months later with the consultant to review the year's work and to assess future needs. They decided that there was no further need for meetings for a year because work was being handled through the appropriate task forces. They also decided that there was a need for the group to meet as a whole with the administrative group "uptown," to develop ways of increasing collaboration and communication between the two organizations.

EVALUATING THE CHANGE EFFORT

The original evaluation design created by Matthew B. Miles of Teachers College, Columbia University, had a number of unique features. First, after an initial meeting in which Miles agreed to do the evaluation, there was no further communication between the change agent, Beckhard, and Miles. This arrangement was designed in order to negate any bias or inadvertent confirmation of expectancies which might result if the change agent and evaluator were in close communication. Secondly, Miles consistently employed multiple measurement techniques in order to increase confidence in the results. The following components were used:

First, the members of the management team were interviewed, before and after the training, to collect data on operations and problems of the team as perceived by its members. Prior to the first off-site meeting team members indicated that they preferred *not* to be interviewed as part of the study; hence, no "pre-intervention" interviews were held. A year later, however, they were very open to participating in the research (this itself may be regarded as an outcome of the project), and each team member was interviewed. These "post-intervention" interviews focused upon the nature of the changes which had taken place.

A second feature of the design involved interviews with managers from other parts of the bank who had occasion to give or to receive work from the experimental group. These interviews provided an indication of how the other groups who formed the immediate environment of the management team reacted to its effectiveness. In addition, the head of the securities division, intermediate manager above the team, was interviewed (before and after the intervention) about his perceptions of the team and its work.

In a third component of the study, team members' subordinates, primarily clerical-level personnel, were surveyed using a questionnaire which asked for their attitudes toward work, their morale and the perceived effectiveness of their sections, how much they interacted with others on the job, and their perceptions of the leadership behavior of their own section head. This instrument was administered before and after activity to subordinates of the experimental team and in two control divisions.

A fourth part of the study involved the scrutiny of data already being collected by the firm as a regular part of operations. These data consisted of: turnover, absenteeism, and productivity.

Many questions were left unanswered by the original design: How durable are the results of team training? What happens to the team when the outside consultant has withdrawn? Are the original experimental team members able to disseminate team management practices to their subordinates? Can a successful team development effort in one part of the organization be disseminated to higher levels of management throughout the bank?

Because such questions were left unanswered the consultant, the personnel manager, and another researcher decided to repeat some of the measurement procedures of the original design. Four years after the team training activity, data were recollected through interviews with the team managers, questionnaires to their subordinates, and productivity measures.

Leavitt, in a 1965 study, noted that four major variables may interact to effect organizational change processes. The variables are called Task, People, Technology, and Structure. For Leavitt, the People, Technology, and Structural variables can also become change strategies, and each one developing its own cadre of specialists who utilize them to improve organizational Task performance. The data in this study show, quite conclusively, how interdependent each of the three change strategies are for an organizational development effort. These data demonstrate a team development effort (the People approach), altered work-flow procedures (the Structural approach), to make the transition from mechanized bookkeeping to electronic data processing (the Technological approach) smoother and more efficient.

DATA RESULTS

In the individual interviews with team members there was almost unanimous agreement that prior to team development there had been cumbersome decision-making, divisional protectiveness, lack of promotional opportunity, and poor communication. One team member describes these conditions:

> There used to be a need to protect your own division; whenever a new job came up the first impulse was to reply with some stock answer such as, "We don't have the equipment or men to handle that type of job." "It would increase our overall load too much," etc.

When asked to indicate what changes occurred during the year of team training, managers were quick to say that they could recall no instances of events, activities, or procedures which had changed for the worse. Positive changes included:

(1.) Improved communication, for example, staff being more directly aware of new information needed by the line.
(2.) More flexible structural arrangements were created by adding another division head to the management team.
(3.) A personnel man was added.
(4.) New promotion policies came into effect.
(5.) There was enhanced self-direction and ability of the team to accept responsibility for coping with turnover, training, absenteeism and orientation.
(6.) There was increased motivation to produce which was related to reduction of perceived unreasonable pressures from the uptown division of the bank.

Table 26-1.   *Amount and Sources of Change***

RESPONDENT	NO. OF CHANGES	Source I Sr. Officers	Source II Team	Source III Self & Subs.
1	24	25%	70%	5
2	22	33	65	—
3	22	15	85	—
4	20	10	90	—
5	19	—	80	10*
6	17	25	75	—
7	17	20	80	—
8	17	20	70	10
9	17	—	75	—*
10	14	—	80	15*
11	13	—	90	5*
12	12	—	95	—*
13	11	5	95	—
14	11	15	80	5
15	10	—	90	5*
	246			
	16.4			

* In arriving at this distribution a change was tabulated only when it was described and an example was given. For instance, a respondent says, "We have now better cooperation between our division. Now, we don't approach problems looking for a scapegoat. Our team has become a tool for solving problems." In scoring the interview schedule this is tabulated as one change.

** All change sources could not be identified.

(7.) There was more capacity to accept and deal with the technological changes in the organization such as the switch to Electronic Data Processing.

The number and source of the changes described by the fifteen team managers are displayed in Table 26-1.

PRODUCTION

After the intervention, the managers reported that they felt personally more productive because they were able to control their own work flow. For instance, four of those interviewed reported that prior to the team training, whenever an important new job came along, they were advised by their supervisor, "You had better do this job yourself rather than trust it to one of your clerks." Thus, much of their time was spent doing work that their subordinates were competent to do. Following team development, three of the four respondents reported positively. A sample:

> I have more time for planning now; procedural write-ups used to lag behind schedule, now they are ahead of time. I have more time because my assistants do much more. I do more administrative work now and am less involved in immediate problems of operations.

Data from subordinates of the team members demonstrate impact on perceptions which have been shown to be related to changes in productivity. In the questionnaire, subordinates were asked to indicate how closely their superior (one of the team members) watched their work. In comparing subordinates of team members to subordinates from the control division, we find that team members' subordinates indicated they were watched less closely. Also, positive differences were found on the following items between subordinates of team members and control.

(1.) He has reasonable expectations about amount of work.
(2.) He explains reasoning behind changes in methods.

However, it must be concluded that results from subordinates are not as clear as the manager's own attitude shifts, or other data on productivity to be discussed subsequently.

Four managers immediately above the management positions of the persons involved in team training also were interviewed. They also perceived differences in productivity of the team managers. One felt that the improved ability to cope with pressure resulted from better cooperation between Mortgage Production and Mechanized Books (two divisions that were represented in the team). Another mentioned that he had not had to intervene at all during the team development year on behalf of his subordinates in order to obtain needed services. Previously, this was a common occurrence. All four noticed an increased tendency for Mortgage Production to take a more universal view of problems than they had before. One manager reported, "They no longer try to pin blame on someone. They try to do what is best for all."

Finally, before turning to the actual data on productivity, it should be noted that all of the above *perceptions* were reported to researchers prior to the existence of actual data on productivity.

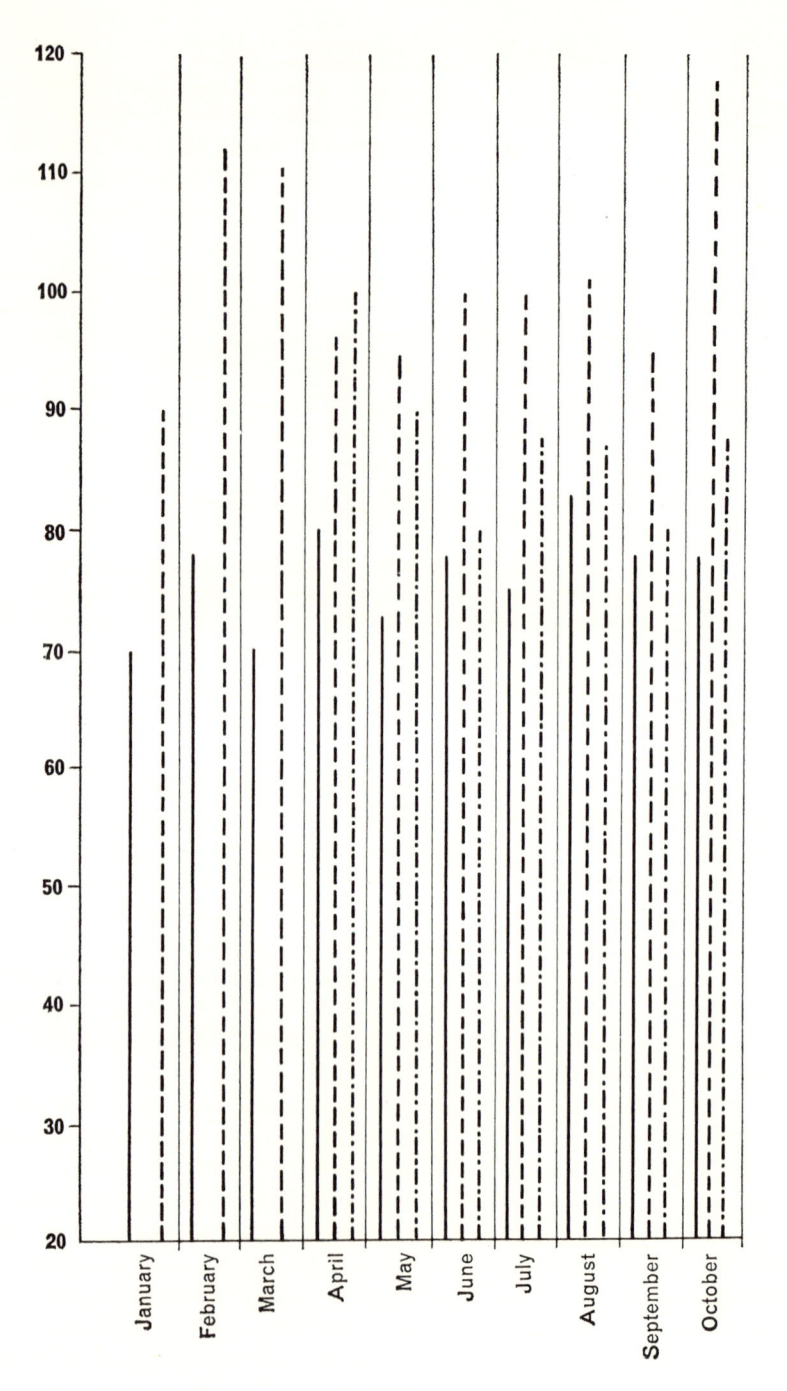

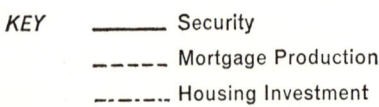

Figure 26-1. Performance Measurement

Independently of the other research activities, the work measurement division of the bank was routinely collecting productivity data on the experimental division (Mortgage Production and two comparable divisions, Sequential Security, and Housing Investment). The results are described in Figure 26-1.

The work measurement staff noted that in comparing the three divisions the following should be pointed out:

(1.) The Sequential Security work-load is fairly consistent and its effectiveness depends on the number of people in the section over which management has no control. Overall the productivity is constant for the year.

(2.) Housing Investment work-load varied during this period yet the hours applied to measure work remained constant indicating no effort to increase the effectiveness. On a yearly basis the effectiveness of this division is decreasing.

(3.) Mortgage Production demonstrated an increase in effectiveness which probably can be traced to the organization improvement program. The officers became more aware of the needs for establishment of control over the work flow, which resulted in greater productivity.

TURNOVER–ABSENTEEISM

There are additional data on absenteeism and turnover which support and influence the data just reported on productivity. Although the ultimate success of the management team training program could quite justifiably be judged by whether routine measurements of variables such as productivity, turnover, or absenteeism showed improvement, certain assumptions are involved in such a decision. These include (1) that the variables involved are meaningful ones as shown on *a priori* or empirical bases; (2) that the measures made are valid ones; (3) that the variables are subject to control by management during the one year period of the study; (4) that other concomitant variables, such as morale, attitudes toward work, and perceptions of leadership do not show a net decrease "at the expense" of changes found in these areas (the "short-run," "long-run" problems).

In Table 26-2, comparisons show that while Mortgage Production turnover was considerably higher than that in the two control departments and the bank as a whole in 1963, the rate was reduced sharply by the end of 1964, bringing it nearly into line with the bank-wide rate. Meanwhile, turnover (both Measures) was increasing in Sequential Security and in Housing Investment and Advisory Operation (total Measure) and indeed in the bank as a whole. The relative percentage increase or decrease over the 1963 base shows this quite clearly. In general, then, Mortgage Production was bucking a bank-wide trend toward increased turnover. It may be argued, of course, that turnover reduction is easier when higher rates of turnover are present. This should probably be considered in assessing these differences.

As of the end of the third quarter of 1963 (beginning of the effort), Mortgage Production had more days lost per individual, and a higher percentage of absenteeism than the control divisions. However, by the end of 1964 (end of

Table 26-2. *Turnover Statistics*

	12/31/63 CONTROLLABLE RATE	12/31/63 TOTAL T/O RATE	9/30/64 CONTROLLABLE RATE	9/30/64 TOTAL T/O RATE	1963–1964 IMPROVEMENT Controllable (percent)	1963–1964 IMPROVEMENT Total (percent)
Mortgage Production Housing Investment and Advisory Operation	33.83	39.80	29.05	31.96	14.1	19.6
Sequential Security	19.11	22.59	15.55	23.84	18.6	−5.5
	16.13	20.34	26.72	33.18	−65.8	−62.5
Total Bank	21.35	26.30	25.36	29.70	−18.8	−13.2

(Data supplied December 22, 1964)

Table 26-3. Illness Absenteeism

		9/30/63 TOTAL					9/30/64 TOTAL				1963-64 IMPROVEMENT (PERCENT)	
	N	Days Available	Days Absent	Average Days Absent*	Percent Absent**	N	Days Available	Days Absent	Average Days Absent**	Percent Absent**	In Average Days Absent	In Percent Absent
Merger Production	101	6,363	146	1.45	2.29	99	6,534	107	1.08	1.64	25.5	28.3
Housing Investment and Advisory Operation	114	7,182	138	1.21	1.92	130	8,580	203	1.56	2.36	28.9	—22.9
Sequential Security	139	8,757	182	1.31	2.08	145	9,570	188	1.30	1.96	0.8	5.8

* This ratio represents the average days lost per individual, and is arrived at by dividing the total days absent by the number of individuals in the department.
** This percentage of absenteeism is arrived at by dividing the number of days absent by the number of available work days in the quarter.

planned intervention), this picture showed a striking difference: Mortgage Production was lowest in days lost, and in percentage of absenteeism. The relative change (1963–1964 differences expressed as a percentage increase or decrease over the 1963 base) show this quite sharply: Mortgage Production showed clear improvement, while Sequential Security stayed fairly steady and Housing Investment and Advisory Operation dropped.

Having examined the "hard" data of productivity, turnover, and absenteeism, it is now important to look at those changes which preceded and helped to cause these results.

COMMUNICATION

Interviews of the team managers revealed that hostility, fear, distrust, and a lack of openness distorted the flow of communication prior to the team development effort. For instance, one division manager reported,

> Whenever I used to receive a request for work, I first really had to decide whether my division should really be doing this job or whether we were just being a scapegoat for the division requesting the work. It hurts your business when you question whether a request is valid or not.

Team training led to an appreciation of how difficult communication is and of what can be done to improve it. This is revealed in the following comments from team members,

> Our personal relations with the methods division have really improved. The actual amount of information being passed back and forth is fantastic. So our study of communications problems in the team has helped immensely.

The top manager in the experimental team commented,

> I actually see fewer people now than before the team was begun, but I know they are more free to come to see me now.
> I now go out of my way to explain the background of my decision; before I took it for granted that they would know.
> At the same time there is more likelihood of their accepting a directive at face value now, which I guess indicates that they trust me more.

Others expressed increased feelings of being able to influence others and be influenced themselves,

> Now we go to the other division staff directly and get their views, which speeds up our work-flow. There was a time when I felt no one else knew my work well enough to help.
> It used to be that the only time you heard from above around here was when you were getting hell. Now, he seeks me out on work and personnel decisions and when I make a request for a salary increase it takes, or I know why.

Feedback on work performance, especially deficient work performance, was an important area for improving communications.

> When I first started with my unit heads I had difficulty being critical of them. I had to work myself up into a state of anger before I could really tell them that they had done a poor job. The result was that they usually thought that I was mad at them and

Effects of a Team Development Effort

not their work. In the team I learned that when someone else criticized me they didn't do it to punish—they did it to be helpful. Now, I have learned to criticize my subordinates without getting angry which helps them to correct their mistakes and improve their own work. In the long run this has helped me because their own performances are interdependent with my own.

Furthermore, the team managers indicated that there was much more sharing of each other's special resources across the divisions involved and there was, generally, wider participation in decision-making.

Decisions used to be made in the central office; I gave all supervisors back their responsibility to make decisions. Now, all they do is appraise me of the decision unless it's a policy decision.

Now, when I make a decision the first thing I do is consider who will be involved in carrying out the decision and I call them in for a discussion of the decision.

Now I can go to any division within the department for help in making a work decision. Previously, there might have been a working problem you couldn't discuss with another supervisor.

It used to be that meetings were taboo; now they are considered advantageous.

Those immediately above the managers involved were also encouraged by the team to work on improving communication. As one vice-president stated,

Mortgage Production feels that communication could be better. I must go along with them. We don't forewarn them fast enough. We see that now.

In comparing subordinates of the experimental team with those in a comparison or control division, it was found that experimental group employees had more contact with peers in their own sections in both years than control group employees; control group people had more contact than experimental with people outside their sections. Although there was not much change in these items in either group, the general tendency was toward more increase in contact with those outside the sections in the experimental group than in the control group. This observation supports data from the independently-conducted higher management interviews. They reported improvement in the Mortgage Production team communication with them.

Turning now to amount of interaction with one's own section head, we find (Table 26-4) that in both 1963 and 1964, employees in the control group conferred more frequently with their section heads than did employees in the

Table 26-4. *Frequency with which Employees Confer with Section Head, by Year and by Experimental and Control Groups*

	Experimental Group 1963 %	1964 %	Differences (Points)	Control Group 1963 %	1964 %	Differences (Points)
Frequency of Content						
More than once a day	23	24	1	40	34	−6
About once a day	14	15	1	18	10	−8
A few times a week	30	35	5	18	22	4
Once a week or less	32	26	−6	24	33	9
N equals	(90)	(105)		(147)	(164)	
No answer	—	—		(3)	(1)	

experimental group. But between 1963 and 1964, the percent of control group employees who spoke to their section heads a few times a week or more moved from 76 percent to 66 percent, a net drop of 10 percentage points. At the same time, in the experimental group, the percent in this category increased from 67 percent to 74 percent, 7 percentage points. The frequency of "once a week or less" shows it decreases for experimental group section heads for the control group. Thus, it seems clear that experimental group section heads were perceived as increasing their contact with employees, while perceived contact with control group section heads decreased. The reader is reminded that not only did experimental group contact improve, but employees also felt their work was less pressured and less closely supervised; this suggests that the contact was more egalitarian.

Supporting evidence for increased upward contact in the experimental group and decreased contact for control group is shown in Table 26-5. The

Table 26-5. *Employees' Preferred Change in Frequency of Conferring with Section Head, by Experimental and Control Group, 1963 and 1964*

	EXPERIMENTAL GROUP			CONTROL GROUP		
	1963 %	1964 %	Differences (Points)	1963 %	1964 %	Differences (Points)
Employees' Preferences						
Should confer more	20	16	−4	16	23	7
Should confer same as now	77	83	−2	83	75	−8
Should confer less	3	1	−2	1	2	1
N equals	(90)	(105)		(148)	(164)	
No answer	—	—		(4)	(3)	

percent of control group employees who feel that they should confer with their section heads more frequently increased between 1963 and 1964 from 16 percent to 23 percent, while during this period the percent of experimental group employees who felt the same way decreased from 20 percent to 16 percent. Thus not only has contact increased, but actual and ideal contact were getting closer together in the experimental group and farther apart among controls.

Even a cautious interpretation of the data from subordinates of the team managers shows a perception of increased upward influence because these subordinates' ratings improved markedly on such items as: "His evaluation carries weight in getting promotions, he would go to bat for me and he wants me to come to him with work complaints." (As compared with their pre-scores and with the control division post scores on these same items.)

STRUCTURAL-TECHNOLOGICAL

The following work-flow arrangements were described by the team, subsequent to their participation in the development effort:

Electronic Data Processing was installed and used to replace certain mechanical bookkeeping procedures.

Parts of two divisions were combined so that any given account could be handled from beginning to end by a single working unit.

Promotion policies were enlarged and several team members were promoted during the year. For instance, one manager reports, "we created three subgroups within my unit; each unit has a supervisor; this permits more advancement within the unit and pushes responsibility for training down the line."

"Linking-pin" positions were created of people who knew what the demands in two different divisions were. These new positions help to facilitate the progress of accounts through complex operations involving their divisions.

The team also assumed the additional function of long-range planning and goal setting. During its first year after the planned improvement effort was initiated, it focused effort on reorganization, personnel orientation and training, developing operational effectiveness and expanding the team concept.

Plans were made to change the image that was implicit in their title "production." That title seemed to connote the assembly line of an industrial plant. They desired an image that was congruent with their own, which suggested that the work requires creativity and intellectual skill.

In the area of personnel and training, the team planned to develop closer ties with the staff service personnel division in order to facilitate the flow of information, including opportunities to test their understanding of feedback and to share their responses to feedback. The team planned to create additional opportunities for promotion within the division, as well as providing more extensive orientation to the goals of the bank for new employees, and reviewing turnover, salary administration, absenteeism, hiring and firing.

Operationally, the team hoped to develop better communication with its sister divisions, the Administration and Investment branches, and also planned to make changeover to electronic data processing as smooth and as effective as possible. It planned to develop ways of confronting operating problems as a team whenever two or more divisions were involved. They expected this to increase the efficient use of funds. Also, they hoped to provide for their efficient functioning by making provisions for agenda development, sub-committee work, and the development of procedures for formalizing its own policies.

Finally, the team wanted to initiate the team concept of management development throughout the bank (keeping in mind the value of mixing levels of supervision in any particular team), to increase its self-development and push this downward to subordinates, and to develop the norm whereby each senior person has trained someone who could replace him upon very short notice.

STABILITY OF THE CHANGE EFFORT

The change efforts since 1964 are as far-reaching as those reported above: two other related groups in the trust division have begun similar programs of team development and from all three groups (these two and the original team) a permanent management team for coordination purposes was formed. A similar team was developed at the section manager level (the next lower managerial level).

New communications mechanisms link the organization, including closed circuit television for weekly joint conferences (the divisions "live" at different locations in the same city). The original group and one of the others held a joint meeting to resolve a number of relationship problems which had emerged from the two individual team development programs. These two groups then met with representatives of the third group to resolve additional relationships and procedural problems. New relationships were established between this entire division and the corporate staff of the bank, particularly with the personnel department.

One year after the end of the experiment, the top thirty managers in the organization went to a four-day workshop. They examined their own functioning and its effects on the total bank effort. Outputs of that top management meeting included a change in the recruitment structure, the development of a management trainee position, some changes in the reward system for young men and the appointment of task forces to examine the entire reward system. Bankwide management training and development efforts were started. Today there is a consulting group of several applied behavioral scientists working with various units in the bank, and off-site team development meetings of operating units are a regular part of the operating method.

A description of the stability of this project in team management is not complete without collecting data after any "halo" effects have had a chance to wear off. For this reason, in 1968, four years after the original intervention, one of the authors, Lake, and the project manager of the first research effort, with the assistance of the director of personnel, conducted follow-up interviews with the team managers, collected data from subordinates, and data on turnover absenteeism, and productivity, experimental and control divisions.

Before reviewing these additional data some *caveats* are in order. First, although it would have been possible to compute exact statistical tests of differences between subordinates' sources on a questionnaire in 1963, 1964, and 1968, and to present the data according to "significant" differences, a closer examination suggested this to be an inappropriate practice. The items requesting subordinates' perceptions of the team managers are most clearly interpreted if they are separated by managers and taken from only those subordinates who filled out the questionnaire on all three occasions. Such a procedure seemed inappropriate since we were interested in impact on the overall department not in differences between managers. Presenting aggregate data should actually work against "hoped for" directions because differences will tend to balance out.

Second, comparison with the original control group is certainly inappropriate as it has undergone personnel changes since 1964 as well. Finally, in a strictly technical sense, the 1968 results cannot be described as *caused* by the original team training. Instead, we relied upon the managers to describe the state of the department in 1968 and make any associations they thought appropriate to the original team training.

LONG-TERM RESULTS

An early goal of the team was to improve the promotion policies within the

Effects of a Team Development Effort

department. Managers reported that the very first promotions occurred during the team training year, in 1964. Since then, thirteen of the original sixteen team members have been promoted, some more than once. Two members of the team hold top positions in the department and although they could not be promoted, they were advanced in rank. The sixteenth member of the team left the bank.

Team management today means something quite different from its original conception in 1963. The original team, a heterogeneous group representing a cross-section of local divisions, seldom meets more than once or twice a year. Now, teams are *not* composed of members from different divisions but are homogeneous. For instance, each manager interviewed reported that he was a member of at least three different working teams within his division, but frequently served as a liaison for his team with teams in other divisions.

Another development of the team concept has been to create inter-departmental teams (at all levels of management) to work on specific interface problems. When the problems are resolved, the teams are dissolved. These inter-departmental teams usually use an outside consultant initially, but subsequent work is supported by specially trained personnel staff from within the bank.

In general, the managers report that teams are much more problem-oriented.

Table 26-6. *Subordinates' Perception of Team Managers in 1968 (N equals 130)*

	\multicolumn{5}{c}{RESPONSE DESCRIBES MY SUPERIOR...}
	Extremely well	Very well	Moderately well	Not very well	Not at all well
25. He has reasonable expectations about the amount of work I should do.	40%	32%	19%	5%	4%
26. He isn't interested in helping me get ahead in the company.	11	8	12	21	48
28. He wants me to come to him if I have a complaint about my work.	49	27	11	6	7
30. He doesn't want to give a new employee as much help as he needs to learn.	10	7	17	25	41
32. He treats me as a person rather than just someone to get a job done.	40	32	12	9	7
34. When I have a new job to do, he explains it carefully in detail.	39	21	20	10	10
36. His evaluation of how his employees do their jobs carries a lot of weight in getting them promotions or salary increases.	36	36	19	3	6
39. If I had an idea of how to change things for the better, he would not want to hear about it.	9	9	9	20	53

438   *Organization Development*

They are also more short-lived. One manager described what appears to be the norm of the department, "People believe in getting together when they have problems around here now, and that *is* different."

All managers report that they have tried to push the team concept downwards. If this were so, one who would expect that their subordinates would see them as egalitarian, open to influence, and able to influence others. The data in Table 26-6 from subordinates support these predictions. It shows quite clearly that subordinates perceive that they are able to influence their supervisors and that supervisors are also able to influence upward (Item 36).

Table 26-7.   *Turnover Statistics*

	CONTROLLABLE RATE			TOTAL RATE		
	12/63	12/64	12/68	12/63	9/64	12/68
Mortgage Production (Experimental)	33.83	19.05	38.79	39.80	31.96	40.61
Housing investment and Advisory Operations	19.11	15.55	36.08	22.59	23.84	38.66
Sequential Securities (Operations)	16.13	26.72	54.86	20.34	33.18	54.86
Total Bank	21.35	25.36	45.90	26.30	29.79	51.04

Most of the managers interviewed expressed concern regarding the current state of turnover. As one manager stated, "It is remarkable that we are able to maintain any people within the department because of our being invaded by the brokers on 'The Street'; they buy off our system analysts as fast as we can train them." Their concern is appropriate because turnover has increased since 1964. (See Table 26-7.) However, it should be noted that Mortgage Production is *well below* the total bank turnover rate. (Even though the Mortgage Production rate is somewhat inflated because of the increased demand for systems analysts throughout the industry.)

Productivity has remained high. Work measurement statistics shown in Table 26-8 continue to show outstanding performance by Mortgage Production.

A number of the managers interviewed thought that absenteeism would increase during the last year because the entire area of the country had been hit

Table 26-8.   *Productivity Index* 12/31/68

	Standard Productivity Index*
Mortgage Production	94.5%**
Housing Investment and Adv. Oper.	71.8%
Sequential Security	85.2%
Install. Loan Collections	87.3%

* As of first quarter 3/31/69.
** Note that the index has been revised so that it is not possible to go over 100% as it was in 1964.

Table 26-9. *Illness Absenteeism Compared for Three Measurement Periods*

	9/30/63 AVERAGE DAYS ABSENT	N	9/30/64 AVERAGE DAYS ABSENT	N	12/31/68 AVERAGE DAYS ABSENT	N
Mortgage Production	1.45	101	1.08	99	2.57	183
Housing Investment and Advisory Operations	1.21	114	1.56	130	2.47	124
Sequential Security	1.31	139	1.30	145	3.09	102

with debilitating viruses. Again their perceptions were accurate as seen in Table 26-9 (also see Table 26-3).

Finally, in the 1968 interviews, all managers reported that it was no longer necessary to send persons to sensitivity training prior to doing effective work in teams. The reasons were not entirely clear, although it seems evident that the entire department was characterized as being more open, more willing to take the risks, more authentic and more able to engage in interpersonal confrontations. It would seem that the values learned in sensitivity training have become the department norms.

CONCLUSION

This report describes team management development as a strategy for coping with overly centralized decision-making and changes in the external environment which require changing the internal environment. It illustrates how a specific pilot intervention, such as team development, can be a way of spreading an organizational development effort to all of management within the organization. This effort is eased by good documentation that is made public.

This team effort development became a vehicle for facilitating: (1) changes in work-flow arrangements such as combining persons from more than one division in order to provide continuity for the processing of major accounts; (2) the efforts to improve productivity and at the same time reduce turnover and absenteeism, and (3) the introduction of electronic data processing.

In addition the team development activities resulted directly in more flexible decision-making, increases in influence below and above the team, an enhanced sense of self-direction for the managers involved, and concern for the entire bank's problems.

Note

1. The research was conducted by Matthew B. Miles, Teachers College, Columbia.

PART FIVE

Violence and Coercion as Strategies of Social Intervention

*t*he intent of this part is to examine the use of violence as a planned strategy of social intervention. It may seem strange that the authors have chosen to include a section on violence, since the primary focus in this volume has been on more "appropriate" and "legitimate" approaches to change. To many change agents, violence is *not* an alternative strategy to be considered when faced with a social intervention problem; such a position, as well as the position of those who advocate violent social change, will be examined in this introduction and the papers that are included in this section. Let us begin with a brief definition of violence and some comments on the problem of definition. Next, factors that influence the use of violence as a social intervention strategy will be reviewed, including personality dynamics, social structural variables, ideological conditions and social–psychological variables. Finally, some of the consequences of violent social intervention will be examined, particularly the effects on the participants in the change effort, as well as on third parties and the social system as a whole. Throughout the analysis, examples of situations, strategies, and tactics will be drawn primarily from three contemporary theatres of violent social intervention—ghetto riots, university confrontations, and guerilla warfare. It should be realized that these contemporary settings do not always reflect the use of violence as a *planned* social intervention; this represents a divergence from other approaches in this volume. But the three situations do provide a useful study of the factors regulating the causes and effects of violence, a study which ultimately may be helpful to the architects of violent social change.

There are several strict limitations on the scope of material covered. The first is historical: While it is apparent that violent strategies of change are as old as mankind, it is obviously not possible to review the history of mankind for examples or incidents. This chapter thus focuses on *contemporary* theories, strategies, and tactics for change through violent methods. A second limitation is on the *scope* of violent tactics that are related to social change: While violence frequently leads to social change, it also leads to counterviolence, or attempts to block social change by violent means. Thus social change could be either a serendipitous side effect of a conflict or part of a planned effort; it either can be specifically designed to include violence or can accidentally lead to violence. This part will restrict its analysis to those change attempts in which violent methods are a deliberate ingredient in the formulation and execution of a social intervention. In addition, the consideration of violence in this section will be as an independent or causal variable in the change process (or as a mediating variable), rather than as a dependent variable or outcome of a change strategy.

One final issue must be clarified, particularly for the behavioral scientists. The clearest statements of the role of violence in social intervention are found in political and philosophical theory. In reviewing this theory, it is often difficult to separate assumptions about change from political ideology and dogma, or to extract strategy and tactics out of exhortation and propaganda. In this introduction, an attempt has been made to do just that: to clarify the social–psychological assumptions underlying the strategies and tactics of political and philosophical figures who do not always think of themselves as "change agents," as the term has been used in this volume. It is also probable that the political beliefs and value systems of the authors of this book, as social scientists, will influence the writing and review of these approaches more dramatically than other introductions of this volume.

The need to draw heavily on political science and philosophy for theoretical and empirical resources on violence reflects behavioral science's neglect of this area. Bienen (1968), in a recent compilation of violent strategies for social change, suggests that this obvious neglect might be explained by the interaction of the problem and the lives of social scientists. "Perhaps there is something in the theoretical and methodological perspectives of social scientists (including historians) which prevents them from exploring group violence and its consequences for social change beyond their limiting concern for precision and rigor." Several other explanations for this blindness may be offered:

(1.) By assuming that violence is socially destructive in all situations, some social scientists tend to focus on strategies to repress, convert, or eliminate violence as an intervention strategy. Recent studies by Coser (1956, 1967) and Deutsch (1969) approach this problem more objectively by examining both the functions and dysfunctions of violence and conflict.

(2.) Often, the study of violence is limited because it is an illegitimate tactic for social intervention, or, conversely, what is perceived as legitimate social change is also perceived as a legitimate area of scientific study. For example, many would support Bienen's (1968) view that violence is legitimate when used by elites to overthrow totalitarian governments. Yet there is minimal work on the role of violence in the building of certain organizations (for example, radical movements), in the use of organizations (particularly political institutions) for instituting violence and in the socio-therapeutic and group-development effects of violence (Simmel, 1955; Fanon, 1966; Coser, 1967). Normative decisions that prejudge violence as illegitimate and pathological have at least two major consequences: They preclude the recognition of the functional consequences of violence and the consideration of violence as an intentional, planned element of a change strategy.

(3.) The current techniques of social science may not facilitate the study of violence. Eckstein (1964) argues that reliance on experimental designs, control groups, and rigorously quantitative methods does not facilitate the study of mass social phenomena. Since topics of research are often determined by the apparent ease of their "researchability," the absence of appropriate research methods may deem a phenomenon "unstudyable."

This discussion should not necessarily lead to the conclusion that violence as a strategy for social change is advisable, workable, or effective in all situations; clearly that is not true. But there *are* instances in which violence may be seen as necessary, appropriate, and functional in both its direct and indirect consequences. It is the purpose of this part to systematically explore some of the causes and effects of violence in planned social interventions.

HOW IS VIOLENCE DEFINED?

Many of the elements needed for a complete definition of violence are contained in the previous discussion. Probably the most critical characteristic of these elements is their evaluative quality. For example, consider Wolin's (1960) definition of violence: "Force exerted with unnecessary intensity, unpredictability, or unusual destructiveness." Graham and Gurr (1969) observe that words like "force", "protest" and "legitimacy" are differentially used to define violence, depending on who performs the violence and whether it is endorsed by observers.

For our purposes, the definition of violence used by Graham and Gurr will suffice: " 'Violence' is narrowly defined as behavior designed to inflict physical injury to people or damage to property." It is presumed to be an element in the more general category of force, "the actual or threatened use of violence to compel others to do what they might not otherwise do." The authors note that both of these differ from "protest"—"the expression of dissatisfaction with other people's actions" in either peaceful or violent form.

This definition of violence effectively avoids the problems in Wolin's definition and others, since it omits any evaluative terminology. The definition does not, however, help to solve a second major problem, that of developing guidelines to distinguish between violence and nonviolence. Two elements in Graham and Gurr's definitions cloud this distinction:

(1.) Most theorists of *nonviolence* define certain types of nonviolent action as force: The actions can compel others to do what they might not otherwise do. Under these conditions violent behavior is neither observed *nor* intended. Therefore, Graham and Gurr's definition of force does not mesh with the use of nonviolent force to induce compliance. Their definition could be improved by defining force as synonymous with coercion, and indicating that coercive pressures can be either violent or nonviolent.

(2) These definitions of violence do not establish guidelines for identifying conditions of "psychological violence." This problem is also raised in the next part of this book, "Nonviolence as a Strategy for Social Intervention." Under what conditions do strikes, or boycotts, or fasts (all forms of nonviolent action) become psychological violence? It is not difficult to think of situations in which the dramatic success of these tactics leads to considerable suffering for both actor and target groups. The question is: Are these strategies now violent?

Many authors have avoided the problems of formulating a definition of violence by developing typologies of violent action. Bienen (1968), for example, discusses violence and social change by highlighting major areas of concentration—ghetto violence, internal war, revolution, and totalitarianism. Other typologies are also available, particularly in Johnson (1964) and Conant (this volume).

THE CAUSES OF VIOLENCE

Many theories of violence are not valid or internally consistent; others are not supported by available case data or merely attempt to explain violence after it happens. We will examine these theories only briefly; the variations, modifications, and alterations on them have become far too numerous to consider here. In order to help the reader, the theories have been categorized into four major blocks: (1) intraindividual influences—biological ones, as well as those related to personality and socialization; (2) social-structural influences—the effects of economic and political elements in the social structure that lead to violence; (3) cultural influences—particularly social class; and (4) social-psychological influences—the effects of power, deviance, and the dynamics of interpersonal or intergroup conflict.

Introduction

INTRAINDIVIDUAL AND PERSONALITY INFLUENCES

While biological, personality, and socialization theories of aggressive behavior have received much attention in current psychology, they are given minimal attention in this chapter. The prime reason is that these theories are only peripherally helpful to the change agent intending to design a violent intervention. Unless the agent wants to train and socialize violent behavior over a lifetime, these theories will not necessarily be helpful to him.

Biological Theories. There has been a recent renewal of interest in man's innate aggressiveness. The source of this aggressiveness is traced to man's heritage in the animal kingdom. Like that of his lower-order ancestors, man's aggression is based on instinctual tendencies to survive, and to protect himself and his territory. Proponents of this approach include Lorenz (1966), Ardrey (1961, 1966), Morris (1968) and Storr (1968).

Although the instinct theories are helpful in understanding aggression, numerous authors have taken these theorists to task for gross oversimplification of such behavior, for overgeneralization from studies of lower order animals, for inadequacies and contradictions in their theories, and for denial of the role of learning. Adequate critiques can be found in works by Berkowitz (this volume; 1969), and Montagu (1968).

Psychanalytic Theories. One of the instincts postulated in Freudian theory was the one labeled *Thanatos*. According to Freud, "The aim of all life is death," or an instinctual drive to return to the earth from which man was created (Hall and Lindsey, 1968). Although the death instinct is not commonly accepted among modern psychoanalysts, the concept of innate aggression still prevails. Critiques of Freudian theory can be found in Berkowitz (1962), and in Deutsch and Krauss (1965).

The Authoritarian Personality. Aggressive behavior is a primary component of this personality type (Adorno, Frenkel-Brunswik, Levinson and Sanford, 1950). Among the general characteristics of the "high-F" person (a general antidemocratic disposition expressed by a high score on the Fascism scale) is a strong tendency to condemn, reject, and punish others who violate conventional values, a tendency to be submissive and uncritical of authority figures, and a disposition to use power and cynicism liberally.

The theory of the authoritarian personality has undergone tremendous revision, qualification, and modification by critics (Christie and Jahoda, 1954) and theoreticians working on similar approaches (Rokeach, 1960; Eysenck, 1954; Harvey and Schroeder, 1963). While these later theorists have accounted for the behavior of a much larger number of aggressive, intolerant individuals, their work is still an inadequate explanation of the widespread use of violence.

Child-Rearing Practices. There are a variety of popular theories that attempt to explain violent persons in terms of certain patterns of child rearing (for excellent reviews, see Bandura and Walters, 1963; Becker, 1964; Keniston, 1968; Zigler and Child, 1969). A primary problem with these studies is that they report contradictory evidence in detailing the factors that breed violent children. The critical dimensions appear to be parental permissiveness vs. ridigity in disciplining the child's aggressiveness, conditional vs. unconditional love for the child, and level of parental status consciousness. Glazer and Moynihan (1963) also suggest that the absence of a father figure in many ghetto homes may contribute to the level of violence. However, the studies do not agree on those dimensions which consistently lead to violent behavior.

Frustration–Aggression Theory. This classic approach has been continually invoked to explain recent outbreaks of violence. Its prime tenet is that goal-directed behavior which is frustrated will lead to aggression in order to vent the inhibited energy. It is particularly popular as an explanation of how constraining social conditions breed frustration among social groups and lead to violence in an attempt to remove those conditions.

Since Dollard, Doob, Miller, Mowrer, and Sears (1939) articulated the original theory, there have been many refinements and modifications (Berkowitz, 1962; Zigler and Child, 1969). Briefly summarized, the theoretical revisions suggest: (1) Frustration does not necessarily lead to aggression in all instances. It may lead to regression, fantasy, or reaction formation. Berkowitz (1962) proposed that frustration leads to anger, which *may* lead to aggression, contingent upon situational stimuli that authorize the expression of a violent response. (2) All aggression does not necessarily arise from frustration. Patterns of frustration leading to aggression are strongly modifiable by socialization and learning.

Since we cannot be sure when social conditions are so objectionable that they will lead to frustration, or what social circumstances will permit frustration to be vented as aggression, the model maintains low predictive power. A clear amplification of some of these social-structural factors is presented by Gurr (1967) in the next part.

Social Learning Theory. There has been some imposingly strong research suggesting that the frequency of aggressive behavior is enhanced by the imitation of aggressive social models. Following Miller and Dollard's (1941) pioneering work, the most convincing research in this area has been done by Bandura and Walters (1963), particularly when their findings are applied to the causes of violence (Walters, 1966). There are particularly knotty problems with this theory in predicting which model will be selected from many available alternatives, when imitation will take place, and which behaviors will be modeled. For a review of the most recent work, see Zigler and Child (1969).

Recent research on the social learning of aggression, particularly when mediated through film or cartoon models, has contributed to the current furor over violence in television and the motion pictures. Studies by Bandura, Ross, and Ross (1963); and Lovaas (1961), among others, indicate that children will reliably imitate violence that they observe through the media. Many who endorse this research have argued that the implications are clear for both Saturday morning cartoon festivals and news coverage of the Vietnam War, ghetto riots, or campus demonstrations.

Their arguments are only partially convincing. Many children and adults observe violence, but do not act violently. It is essential to identify the conditions that determine when the observation of life or symbolic aggressive models will

Introduction

lead to aggressive behavior. For our purposes, it is reasonable to speculate that frustrated persons who are seeking redress may be influenced to use violent social intervention. The probability of use will be strongly encouraged by the observation of the successful use of violent interventions by others and the endorsement of violent intervention by esteemed authorities and other third parties.

THE FUNCTIONS OF VIOLENCE AND CONFLICT

For many years, violence was treated as pathological by social scientists. Few realized that conflict and violence have functional consequences, both for social change and for the groups themselves. One of the first to discuss the functions of conflict was Simmel (1955); his arguments have been clarified and elaborated by Coser (1956, 1967), Fanon (1966) and by Deutsch (1968).

Coser summarizes a variety of arguments that delineate the functional consequences of violent social conflict. First, violent conflict permits internal dissension and dissatisfaction to rise to the surface, and enables a group to restructure itself or deal with dissatisfactions. Second, it provides for the emergence of new norms of appropriate behavior, by symptomatically indicating inadequacies in the current system and warning of needed social change. Third, it provides a means of ascertaining the strength of the current power structure, by estimating the degree of internal dissent within a system. Fourth, it has the effect of creating bonds between loosely structured groups, thus unifying previously dissident or unrelated elements. Fifth, it may work to strengthen the boundaries between groups, to help them distinguish themselves from others or from the environment. Finally, it works as a stimulant to reduce stagnation, and to increase interest and curiosity toward an issue. This "novelty" effect underlies many of the strategies using nonviolence as well.

This analysis has been updated to explain internal violence, particularly ghetto riots (Coser, 1967). Violence serves as a mechanism for the *reduction* of conflict between groups in the social structure, particularly when one group is not being heard in its appeals for social change. To initiate and sustain violence requires a tremendous mobilization of hate, frustration, disappointment, and despair with the current social and political structures. Coser predicts that it will occur *only* when conditions are at a "last resort" stage. Hopefully, before this occurs, those in power will recognize the intensity of feelings that lead to violence, and will turn their attention to the violent group's needs. Thus, violence has a social function of alerting society to the fact that a serious malaise exists, and that it needs attention and treatment.

Two major issues are raised by Coser's analysis. First, interventionists who may be considering the use of violence should be aware of the functions of violence. Specific strategies that include violence may be designed to elicit some of the consequences that Coser suggests—exposing dissent, ascertaining the power of the current authorities, or unifying groups against a common enemy. While there are strategies *other than* violence that also elicit these consequences violence should *not* necessarily be ruled out as an undesirable choice. Particular tactics that interventionists can use to promote the functional consequences will be reviewed later here.

The second issue is related to Coser's recent analysis of internal riots: What are the social-structural conditions that lead a group to use violence in order to express its frustrations and despair? We will now focus on some of these.

SOCIAL-STRUCTURAL VARIABLES THAT LEAD TO VIOLENCE

Although there is disagreement over which aspects of social structure are the most important variables (for example, economic vs. political), theorists representing the social-structural viewpoint tend to agree that violence is a response to inequalities along these lines that create a felt need for change.

Economic theories of revolution and violent social change assume that the major dissatisfactions in social conditions are financially based; political revolution, they argue, is a response to economic problems (Fanon, 1966; McLeish, 1969). Most of these theories were written with an orientation to *absolute* economic deprivation, determined by some arbitrary standards of income level and position in the social structure. The more sophisticated version of this thinking is the concept of *relative deprivation* (de Tocqueville, 1945), applied to contemporary social conditions by Shannon (1967) and Fanon (1966). Their view is that violence is not due to actually *being* in a state of deprivation, but *perceiving* oneself to be deprived. It does not matter whether the general economic level of the lower classes in America has risen dramatically in recent years, nor whether the economic level of the lower class is above that of any other nation in the world. The *critical variable* is the *perception* of one's own status *vis-a-vis* others in the status hierarchy. In this regard, Bienen (1968) notes:

If one chooses to focus on "conditions," it follows that massive attacks on the economic and social order are called for. If one emphasizes perceptions of conditions and introduces the concept of relative deprivation—a deprivation relative to where you are, where others are, where you think you ought to be—one must be aware of the possibility of more violence through betterment of conditions and a heightening of feelings of deprivation.

One of the clearest statements of the relationship between relative deprivation and violent change is the work of Gurr (1967). It is also an *empirical* study of the issues, a unique event in this area of scholarship. The basic proposition of the study is as follows:

The occurrence of civil violence presupposes the existence of relative deprivation among substantial numbers of individuals in a society; concomitantly, the more severe the relative deprivation, the greater the likelihood and magnitude of civil violence.

Gurr uses frustration-aggression theory as the motivational basis for violence, and relative deprivation as the primary motivating force. Awareness of deprivation leads to feelings of frustration, which arouse anger. If the situational

Introduction

cues permit anger to be overtly expressed, aggression will occur as a manifestation of the anger and lead to drive reduction. "Magnitude of civil violence" refers to the proportion of the population involved; "severity of relative deprivation" is defined by the degree of discrepancy between the social status that an aggrieved group occupies and the one that they feel they should occupy. Severity is determined by two sets of variables: instigating variables, which determine the intensity of anger as a result of the perceived discrepancy; and mediating variables, which determine the magnitude and frequency of civil violence as a result of this anger.

Four instigating variables are said to affect the intensity of anger. Two of them are based on people's *value expectations* of society and its functioning: the aggrieved group's commitment to the social goals from which they are being deprived access; and the perceived illegitimacy of the deprivation. The other two are based on people's *perceptions* of current society and its capabilities to satisfy these needs and values: the degree of deprivation (the magnitude of difference between values desired and values currently attainable); and the number of instances that the group has been blocked from valued or desired goals.

Anger is not equivalent to civil violence. Whether it becomes civil violence is determined by two groups of variables—social control variables and social facilitation variables. Social control variables "denote the social system's capacity for suppressing, displacing, and providing alternatives for violent behavior as a response to anger." Social facilitation variables are defined as "a set of cultural, ideological, organizational and structural factors that contribute to the potential for violence." Three propositions relevant to the *social control* variables are stated:

(1.) There is a curvilinear relationship between the likelihood and magnitude of civil violence and the amount of retribution or punishment expected for a violent outbreak. The greatest likelihood and magnitude of violence can be expected when retribution is at a moderate level.

(2.) "Inhibition of civil violence by fear of external retribution tends in the short run to increase the strength of anger, but in the long run to reduce it."

(3.) "The likelihood and magnitude of civil violence tend to vary inversely with the availability of institutional mechanisms that permit the expression of nonviolent hostility."

Gurr derives these predictions from previous testing of the frustration-aggression theory in laboratory and field settings, in laboratory studies of aggression, and the systematic examination of social opportunities for the mechanisms of nonviolent, alternative political action.

There are two social-facilitation variables that affect the course of civil violence. First are the *social-commonality* factors that encourage and permit the expression of violent responses to anger, for example the imitation of social heroes as aggressive models, violence in the theatre and television, and the willingness of the government to use violence in war and repression. Second are *group-characteristic* factors that legitimize aggression, for example, membership in a highly cohesive group, or in one with a strong basis of common deprivation; characteristics of the group, particularly size or environment, that guarantee anonymity and hence introduce a possible protection from retribution or assuming responsibility for damage done; and availability of a focal person or focal event to mobilize and catalyze the violent action—a coordination function that serves to unite the effort around a single act and prevent random action.

Gurr examined the validity of these propositions in an extensive study of 119 political states with population of over one million. His findings are hard to summarize because of the numerous interrelationships between the instigating, mediating, and dependent variables. Briefly, they suggest that *instigating variables* that breed intense anger (value expectations and perceptions) were more successful in predicting riots and rebellions than were the *system characteristics* (social control and social facilitation variables). On the other hand, *system characteristics*, particularly retribution, predicted organized internal war more successfully. Relative deprivation was a powerful predictor of the intensity of anger (although not the only predictor), and was more reliable in predicting anger than absolute deprivation. Finally, the power of the country to carry out retribution for civil violence was a strong inhibitor of civil violence:

> The measures of the social control variables . . . contribute nearly half the explanatory capacity of the theory. The most striking finding is the curvilinear relationship between one measure of retribution—military personnel per 10,000 adults—and levels of civil strife. High levels of deterrence, consistently applied, tend to inhibit civil violence. Inconsistently applied deterrence and increase in deterrence capacity as a response to strife, however, are more often associated with increased than with reduced strife. Very low levels of deterrence tend to be accompanied by low levels of strife . . .

The causal connections for these effects are not clear, particularly since Gurr fails to consider the effect of previous historical incidents of civil violence in the country. Nevertheless, his findings demonstrate the strong impact of relative deprivation and the curvilinear relationship between deterrence and violence.

Gurr's study provides a potential interventionist with a number of approaches that could be used to induce violent social change; there are three major strategic steps. First, the interventionist must *increase* the perception of relative deprivation among the potentially violent group. This would be done by minimizing the group's perceptions of the rewards and benefits to be obtained at its current social position, while enhancing the perceived discrepancy between the group and other segments of society. The perceived discrepancy would then lead to feelings of frustration and anger. Second, in order to maximize the *intensity* of anger (using the four instigating variables that Gurr has suggested), the interventionist should argue that (1) the social goals are indeed desirable (*e.g.*, the benefits of economic and social well-being); (2) the deprivation is illegitimate (*e.g.*, highlight instances of social discrimination); (3) the deprivation is severe (*i.e.*, highlight the discrepancies between the group and its desired state, while minimizing the similarities); and (4) the deprivation continually occurs. Finally, the interventionist must emphasize the social facilitation variables and minimize the social control variables that translate anger into civil violence.

Emphasizing the social facilitation variables includes (1) providing examples that the society is violent in other spheres (so well summarized by Rap Brown's classic "Violence is as American as cherry pie!"), (2) enhancing racial, communal or environmental in-group ties by emphasizing shared states of deprivation and pointing out harassment by outgroups, and (3) providing critical incidents that will trigger violence at optimal points in time (although critical incidents are often defined *ex post facto*). Minimizing the effects of the social control variables is more difficult, but there are two primary approaches that must be used: (1) create conditions which will evoke either no retribution or an overreaction, and (2) create conditions that cut off the availability of mechanisms that discharge anger nonviolently. The first has often been easy to do in civil violence, since police have traditionally overreacted to ghetto and campus violence, and thus helped the violent interventionists. The second may involve creating community incidents that introduce curfew, prevent mass gatherings, close recreational facilities, etc.

There are other theories that have considered economic conditions as important factors in determining violent behavior; however, the economic deprivation is symbolic of deeper conditions of political and social disenfranchisement. One currently important viewpoint focuses on the role of "white racism" (Carmichael and Hamilton, 1967; National Advisory Commission on Civil Disorders, 1968). This view suggests that the primary precipitants of riots are not the physical ghetto environment or incidents of police brutality, *per se*. Ghettos and police brutality are symbolic of the political and economic effects of a white-controlled society that prevents participation by blacks, exploits them, and refuses to share power and decision-making processes in the governance of the black community. Economic and political black power is seen as the solution to ghetto problems. It is reasoned that political and economic control by blacks increases the effectiveness of communication, problem-solving and decision-making in ghetto communities; it permits blacks to control the environmental conditions that affect their lives.

If an interventionist took this "symbolic violence" idea seriously, there are several tactics that he might employ to create symbolic significance in a social environment, and elicit a violent response. The critical elements in this strategy would be to emphasize the unpleasantness of the current social environment, and to link the cause and source of this unpleasantness to already-hated objects, persons or groups. The interventionist then might suggest that destruction of the symbol will eliminate the unpleasantness and its causes, dramatically alter the chosen persons or groups who have caused the problem, and perhaps move the social system closer to the idealized environment.

There are some social environments where this linkage may be appropriate; however, there may be other environments where there is no logical connection between the symbol and the causes of the symbolic conditions. Regardless of the existence of this logical linkage, the threat of violence to destroy the symbol may itself lead to change. For example, if interventionists in the ghetto environment linked ghetto conditions to movie theaters, threats to destroy movie theaters might motivate theater owners and urban officials to apply pressures and initiate desired changes. By using hate symbols to begin a movement one may ultimately gain enough leverage to create desired system changes.

A second theory that discusses the symbolic significance of economic conditions is proposed by Janowitz (1969). He has labeled ghetto violence "commodity" riots, in that the forces of violence are expressed in looting, burning, and destruction of white-owned businesses. Both Janowitz and Fanon argue that commodity riots take place because the participants are too afraid to express their hostility against the real causes of deplorable ghetto conditions—in this case, white society. Fear of repression, and retaliation by white society (epitomized in the police and National Guard) redirects the violent action towards one's self, as a form of social masochism. Since the ghetto is a representation of the evils of white society, it is destroyed as a symbol of underlying black desire to destroy the white social establishment. Moreover, looting and burning symbolize a destruction of private property; black ownership of private property is minimal, and blacks are well aware of the undying dedication to property rights in white society (Quarantelli and Dynes, 1968). Interventionists must decide whether destruction of ghetto property and environments is functional for the community (*e.g.*, if new buildings in the ghetto would provide better housing or services than those which are destroyed), or, should attempts be made to focus the hostility more directly against white control and dominance.

A word should be said about *political* conditions which lead to violence. The theoretical work in this area is primarily concerned with the distribution of political power, and posits the lack of power to influence policy as the ultimate source of violence (Nieburg, 1969). Rustin (1967) also argues that ghetto violence is a response to the lack of power and social identity felt by Negroes. Ghetto residents destroy their own living environment as a symbol of that powerlessness; this acts as a temporary solution in a long-range program of increased economic reform and political unification with other poor people (Third World Movement) to gain power. George Peabody has prepared an excellent review of power-building strategies for this volume, describing some of his work with Saul Alinsky. These strategies may be adapted by interventionists to increase the economic and political power in a low-power group.

Other revolutionary theories which focus on changes in the *political* (rather than economic) structure are found in the writings of Mao (1960), Lenin (Osanka, 1962), Machiavelli (1966) and Arendt (1963). Their view is that the revolution is primarily sparked by ideological and political issues, not economic conditions. Revolution is the central element to initiate major changes in the political structure. Organized plans of attack (often guerrilla warfare) are encouraged over spontaneous riots or outbursts of anger and hostility. The basic intention is to promote the ideology and to enhance the power of the dissident group, particularly in the overthrow of totalitarian regimes (Bienen, 1968).

The structural theories have had a major impact on current explanations of violence. Perhaps this is true because they are endorsed by liberal academic theoreticians, who are predisposed to advocate changes in the social structure, particularly when these changes remedy social, economic, and political inequalities. But many of the theories are generally inadequate on two major fronts. First, the economic theories lend the impression that violence is a spontaneous outburst when conditions become intolerable. Examination of history tells us that is only true under certain conditions, and that violence can be planned and organized as well. Second, their relative deprivation hypothesis fails to establish guidelines for defining the critical mass of frustration. A number of other questions remain unanswered. How do participants decide when conditions are ripe for violent outbreaks? How do leaders develop? How are tactics chosen? All of these issues must be resolved if violence is to be effectively used as a strategy of social intervention.

INTER-CLASS THEORIES OF VIOLENCE

Theories of class conflict are based on the assumption that ties to one's own cultural or class group lead to an emphasis on (1) the cultural similarities within groups, (2) the cultural differences between groups, and (3) a concentrated effort by the actor to change the social structure and conquer his cultural oppressors. Dahrendorf (1959) has developed a theory of class conflict, based on two major variables: intensity and violence. Intensity relates to the importance of the issues and degree of involvement for the participants; violence relates to the degree of militancy and physical injury inflicted by the participants on one another. Two relationships are proposed: First, the more *intense* the conflict is, the more *radical* will be the change in social structure—that is, the more complete will be the change in values. Secondly, the more *violent* the conflict, the more *sudden* will be the change in the social structure—that is, the shorter will be the time for the change to be effected. These two dimensions operate independently —thus, it should be possible to classify changes which are radical but gradual, or sudden but conservative.

Dahrendorf offers several predictions concerning the nature of the social structure, the resultant levels of violence and intensity, and their concomitant effects on structural change. He predicts that conflict *intensity* will *decrease* between classes as: the classes are more sociologically organized, power is decentralized among the major institutions (*e.g.*, church leaders are not also government leaders), institutions face different problems and are not focused on the same areas of conflict, the reward–punishment power of various authorities is also decentralized, and mobility is possible between social classes. Conflict *violence* will *decrease* between classes as: the classes are more sociologically organized, relative deprivation takes precedence over absolute deprivation, and class conflict is effectively controlled and managed.

Generally, the model lacks specificity, and is therefore hard for an interventionist to use. It is also not supported (other than anecdotally) by confirming data. One exception is the work of Kroes (1966). Studying the Hungarian revolution, Kroes demonstrated support for *all* of the propositions except the one relating relative deprivation and social conditions. Kroes modifies the propositions such that degree of violence is related to absolute deprivation, while degree of intensity is related to relative deprivation. This modification beings Dahrendorf's model closer to the theories previously discussed.

SOCIAL PSYCHOLOGICAL VARIABLES THAT LEAD TO VIOLENCE

This final section on the causes of violence will point out some of the interpersonal and intergroup variables that are involved in violent social change. These theories are concerned primarily with the phenomena of deviance, strategic deterrence, power, crowd behavior, and intergroup conflict.

DEVIANCE THEORY

"A spirit of national masochism prevails [in America], encouraged by an effete corps of impudent snobs who characterize themselves as intellectuals."
Vice President Spiro T. Agnew,
"The New York Times," October 29, 1969

The Vice President has aptly characterized the prime tenet of the deviance, or "riffraff" theory of violent social change. The theory holds that Communists, outside agitators, criminals and anti-American conspirators are responsible for inspiring, initiating, and executing violent social change in the ghettoes and the campuses. For example, Nieburg (1969) articulates three common assumptions of the deviance theory in ghetto violence: that only 2 to 3% of the black community participated in any contemporary riot in the last ten years, that the rioters primarily represented the uneducated, criminal, unemployed, and teenager elements, and that the overwhelming majority of the ghetto were opposed to the riots.

Data have provided little support for this theory. Nieburg (1968) cites evidence that disproves all three assumptions; Keniston (1968) and others have consistently disproven the same assumptions in the campus confrontation arena. Yet the continued popularity of the theory may suggest that it is a conscious or unconscious attempt to counteract advocates of social change by publicly discrediting them. Name-calling of this type (*e.g.* McCarthyism) has often been used to malign those with different political views.

PATTERNS OF EXTERNAL CONTROL

According to Grimshaw (1962), racial violence in the United States occurs as a *response* to a reaction from the white establishment when a minority group challenges the establishment's norms, social customs, or practices. Challenges to white supremacy in the South (rape of white women, slurs toward whites, and demands of equality in transportation and public accommodations), and in the North (*de facto* school segregation, discrimination in housing and employment) lead to repression by the white establishment, and counterviolence by the Negro. Grimshaw predicts that the "eruption or non-eruption of internal violence is determined by the character of external forces of constraint and control, especially the police forces" (Grimshaw, 1962). In this perspective, the police are *not* seen as neutral but as representatives of the establishment. It does not matter what the level of social tension is—when the controls grow weak, violence will erupt. Nitish De, in an article following this chapter, points out that political forces which inhibit police action are directly responsible for the increased level of violent confrontation between Indian industrial workers and management.

Wallace Lambert, cited by Grimshaw, articulates patterns of social control in order to develop a testable model. Lambert predicted that an overwhelming command of physical police force decreases the likelihood of violence. If that power is absent, social control can still be maintained if (1) the police can be mobilized quickly, (2) criticism of the government can be suppressed, (3) police violence is used to suppress insurrection, (4) control principles are uniformly applied, and (5) there is strict and harsh punishment after the insurrection to prevent future outbreaks. Frequency of the use of police or deterrent power decreases its effectiveness. Finally, systematic increments in force by the police to control riots are much more effective than the initial onslaught of superior force.

These are the clear "law-and-order" arguments to justify both the police suppression of dissent and the suppression of violence with counterviolence. They are based on the strategy of deterrence, frequently discussed by Kahn (1969) and Snyder (1961), and commonly applied to contemporary situations. While interventionists may have little direct control over police action, they can focus on three tactics: (1) maintain dissent and criticism of the government, (2) use all possible legal tactics to minimize punishment and elicit police over-reaction, and (3) create as many incidents as possible to reduce the effectiveness of the deterrence.

Research in deterrence is both incomplete and contradictory. Analysis of current foreign policy has consistently advocated deterrence as a necessary strategy for modern America, as symbolized by early involvement in the Vietnam conflict and recent decisions to develop an ABM system. Gurr (1967), reported earlier, proposed a curvilinear relationship between violence and deterrence: Civil violence is low with consistently high or consistently low levels of deterrence; violence increases as the deterrence is applied at moderate levels of intensity or applied inconsistently. In contrast laboratory studies that have explored the impact of deterrent strategies (Solomon, 1960; Lave, 1965; Deutsch, Epstein, Canavan, and Gumpert, 1967) indicate that high levels of deterrence lead to an *increased* level of aggressiveness and competition. The popularity of deterrence as a strategy may have evolved because other strategies have not been thoroughly explored. In addition, much of the support for deterrence evolves from mathematical and game-theoretic models, which are essentially barren of the intergroup and interpersonal elements inherent in social encounters. Many of these arguments which are reviewed by Sherif (1966) demand intensive study in laboratory and field research settings.

POWER

The problem of power, particularly in political terms, was discussed earlier. Several social psychologists have also been interested in power, particularly the ways in which persons who are low in power can increase their relative influence and status. Deutsch (1969) indicates that low power groups can use strategies of harassment, civil disobedience, and noncooperation, but also exhibit behaviors that symbolize a willingness to engage in cooperative relationships. Gamson (1968) conceptualizes the challenges to power relations in terms of two groups: (1) authorities, who make the binding decisions in a social system; and (2) low power potential partisans, who are significantly affected by those decisions and attempt to influence the decision-making process. The underlying relationship between the two groups is mediated by the partisan's attitude of trust toward the authorities: the authorities' ability to rule is contingent upon the level of trust of those who support him. The greater the distrust, the more discontent there will be among the potential partisans, and this will lead to increased influence attempts to change or replace the authorities.

Other discussions of the problem of power and status may be found in Thibaut and Kelley (1959) and Flacks (1969). Thibaut and Kelley define power as the ability of one party to affect the outcomes of a second party; they examine this relationship in terms of behavior control (party A's behavior strongly influences party B's behavior) and fate control (party A influences party B, regardless of B's behavior). Flacks focuses upon the perceived legitimacy of the existing authority, and views much of the current unrest among students as a challenge to the legitimacy of parental, university, and government authority systems.

GOAL ATTAINMENT

Several authors have proposed that conflict and violence arise when two groups have incompatible goals. Deutsch (1962) proposes a theory of cooperation and competition that involves two groups with promotively interdependent (cooperative) or contriently interdependent (competitive) goals. These analyses and others (e.g., Bernard, 1957) are helpful, but do not easily help us to predict the occurrence of violence as the result of goal conflict. Deutsch (1965, 1969), in summarizing his own work, suggests several variables which might be integral to the conditions that lead to violence: inadequate or misleading communication, interpersonal perception that minimizes similarities and enhances differences, suspicious and hostile attitudes, and a win–lose orientation to achieving the desired goal.

CROWD BEHAVIOR

Several authors have described and analysed the behavior of individuals in collective masses. A number of variables are of interest to them: structural features (shape and boundaries, use of physical space, orientation to a focal point, and size), composition (the nature of the individuals in the crowd), and information flow (usually through rumor and distortion). Gustav LeBon (1921) proposed three basic mechanisms of crowd behavior: (1) the anonymity of the individual in the crowd, concomitant with a loss of individual responsibility for action; (2) emotional contagion; and (3) heightened suggestibility to perform destructive behaviors. Presumably this last element encourages violence in crowds that may not occur through individual acts.

LeBon's theory has come under heavy criticism from more recent theorists (for an excellent review, see Milgram and Toch, 1969). A number of criticisms are directed at his florid, unscientific writing style, but others have more scholarly relevance. One major argument is that crowds which become violent are composed of an overrepresentation of antisocial individuals, many of whom seek the anonymity of crowd environments to release violent behavior. Although it is true that crowds have been violent, Milgram and Toch state that it is not possible to estimate whether they have been more violent than other groupings. ". . . the question is not whether violence is ever found in crowds, but rather, whether it is disproportionately represented in crowds, as opposed to individual violence, on the one hand, and institutional violence, on the other."

In summary, it is easy to be overwhelmed by the number of causes that have been identified as leading to violence. The magnitude of the problem becomes greater when one recognizes that each two- or three-paragraph summary in this chapter represents volumes and lifetimes of work. There is a current need for some elaborate synthesis, expansion and testing of the propositions reported here. This requires interdisciplinary work, and a commitment to long-range projects by many social scientists.

The remainder of this section is devoted to an elaborate typology of violence in societies, developed by Chalmers Johnson (1964). Following that, we shall return to consider the impact of violence on participants and observers in the conflict arena.

Johnson (1964) postulates that we can examine internal warfare and revolution on four basic dimensions: the identity of the revolutionaries, the target group of the violent change effort, the goals or ideologies of the revolutionary group, and the nature of the revolutionary action as spontaneous or planned.

In identifying the revolutionaries, Johnson specifies a preference for the identification of *social groupings* rather than individuals. He feels that the attempts to psychologically classify, understand, or systematically describe the life styles and behavior of revolutionaries are inadequate because they do not deal with the characteristics of the social structure. It is impossible for single individuals, or even a small group of them, to change a social structure if the structure is not ready to change. Moreover, by concentrating on the social structure as being in a "necessary state of readiness" for revolutionary change, it should be possible to demonstrate that catalytic individuals are *not* necessary to initiate the change effort. It is *not* helpful, according to Johnson, to draw inferences about the social system from the behavior of particular critical individuals or because "some revolutionaries are lunatics, that (therefore) revolution is social lunacy."

Johnson's typology identifies six types of revolutionary action: jacqueries, millenarian rebellions, anarchistic rebellions, jacobian communist revolutions, conspiratorial *coups d'etat* and militarized mass insurrections. These are assessed in terms of the four specified criteria—target, actors, goals and ideology, and spontaneity. *Targets* represent the group to be changed or replaced by the insurrection, either the structure of the community (democracy, monarchy, dictatorship, etc.) or the community itself (basic ties, tribal affiliations, or feelings of national consciousness). *Actors* are those who lead the revolution, usually the ones who have suffered the brunt of injustices. *Ideologies* are the proposals of plans or new systems that the revolutionaries seek to introduce. Finally, *spontaneity* refers to the extent of major planning before the violence takes place—military take-overs are usually systematically and openly planned, whereas *coups d'etat* are more impulsive. The complete typology is presented in Table V-1.

Current events render the militarized mass insurrection as one of the more interesting aspects of this typology: How can a revolutionary group, directed by an elite and sufficiently armed, overthrow an established government or regime that is itself protected by the country's professional army? Five basic elements determine the relative success or failure of this type of effort:

(1) Need for *mass support* of a guerrilla effort. Writers on guerrilla warfare have repeatedly emphasized this factor as a basic element in the success of any revolutionary effort (Mao, 1960; Guevara, 1961; Debray, 1967; and Lenin, 1962). Although these theorists differ in their assumptions about the populace and their endorsement of techniques for mobilizing the populace, Mao, Debray, and Guevara see the masses as apathetic, disinterested and lacking in political consciousness. An "elite" or "vanguard" is necessary to alert the masses to the social problems that must be solved and establish leadership that will control the flow and direction of change until the masses become politically aware. Moreover there is disagreement about *how long* the elite vanguard can proceed before it requires mass support. Johnson argues that mass support must be available initially; Guevara, Mao, and Lenin feel that measurable steps can be taken by independent guerrilla movements (even an overthrow of the established army) before mass support is required.

If Guevara, Mao, and Lenin are correct, guerrilla movements can operate independently of, or prior to, a felt need by the masses for change in existing social conditions. Change agentry which succeeds in bringing about a change before there is a "felt need" in the social system is far more advanced and subtle than current change strategies in other organizational climates which presuppose "felt need." Unfortunately, the data from change efforts through guerrilla warfare are so ephemeral that any coherent evaluation of this tactic is impossible.

(2) *Need for organization of the mass population* to support the new ideology and the guerrilla army. This goal is pursued through *education* and *indoctrination* to teach the new ideology and to enlist support of the new leadership; or *purges*, *deportation*, and *assassinations* of the "uneducable," *i.e.* those who will not support the movement. For example, Mao specifies that many of the

Table V-1

	What Is the Target?	Who Are the Revolutionaries?	What Is the Ideology?	Spontaneous/Planned
Jacqueries	The government, in order to restore the status quo ante on some specific set of conditions.	Mass revolutions—peasants with peasant leaders	Government has been betrayed and we need to restore the previous "good conditions" that existed before; old order is restored.	Spontaneous
Millenarian rebellions	Widespread system dysfunctions, whose sources are obscure and vague; there is a felt need for widespread radical change.	Elitist-leading-masses (usually messiahs, prophets)—arise only because the dysfunctions are so obscure that change can only seem to come out of the eventual millennium.	The new system will leave the "faithful" elite in control of a better world. We must change the community/society to create a paradise-on-earth (the millennium).	Spontaneous
Anarchistic rebellions	The government (usually)—to restore an *idealized* status-quo-ante.	Either elites or peasants. They perceive that they do not support government changes, that the changes are themselves dysfunctions, and that their own goals have not been satisfied by the changes. Times-make-the-man approach to leadership.	A response to social conditions, in which the government has already instituted changes to relieve certain dysfunctions. We must restore an idealized status-quo-ante, and reverse changes that are leading to false nationalism.	Spontaneous—but needs a powerful accelerator, like a direct attack by the distressed, failure of the army to support the changing status quo, etc.
Jacobian communistic rebellions	Alter the community—(like the French Revolution).	Elitist-leading-masses; everyone feels the dysfunctions; accelerators in one group increase the dysfunction felt by others and continue the chain reaction.	Establish a more enlightened society. Social reorganization, develop new nationalism and community.	Spontaneous; it never achieves the new community, hence it leads to a greater awareness of dysfunctions and generates subsequent revolutions.
Conspiratorial coups	Perceived dysfunctions by a small group; it does not spread to the macro-system level unless the system *is* dysfunctional.	Elitist-small brotherhoods with grievances that may or may not reflect objective dissatisfaction of society—it is "microdysfunctionality."	Seize power in the name of the masses without masses' consent; endorse disciplined brotherhood.	Calculated; does not include masses.
Militarized mass insurrections	The old regime/government.	Elitist leading masses—militarized, conspiratorial staffs mobilizing the masses.	Replacement of the old regime with a new regime—"nationalistic"—typically guerilla warfare.	Calculated.

upper class will be unwilling to give up their property, support the new social system, and submit to indoctrination. The remedy is a brief "reign of terror" to eliminate counterrevolutionaries and cleanse the society of its bad elements. (Whether one views this process as a "cleansing of the social system" or a "reign of terror" obviously depends on political position and time-perspective.)

Another element in organizing the masses is the maintenance of mass support of the guerrilla army through a decentralized government in territorial areas or communities. These facilities supply shelter, food, military supplies, and training programs for the immediately surrounding area.

(3) *Need to build a large revolutionary army.* Can success in revolution be obtained by a peasant uprising or a small body of ardent insurrectionists? Again, there is disagreement. Johnson and Debray argue that mass uprisings of peasants by themselves will not bring long-standing change; a trained revolutionary army must be assembled to sustain the revolution. Mao, on the other hand, feels that peasant uprisings (particularly in rural areas) are sufficient to cleanse the state of undesirable elements; armies are only needed to protect against domestic and foreign "common enemies." The disagreement here may be more apparant than real, since any national paronoia will lead to a large, "permanent" army (*e.g.* the Maoist Red Guard). At any rate, such armies are trained by the elitist military group, discipline is stressed above all other virtues, and a strong relationship is maintained to the peasantry in rural and urban areas. These ties to the mass population are used effectively to train citizens to spy, to collect data about undesirable citizens, and to provide food and shelter for roving guerrilla bands.

There is considerably less disagreement over the last two factors that affect the success or failure of militarized mass insurrections: perfection of military tactics, particularly guerrilla warfare (Debray, 1967; Oppenheimer, 1969), and commitment to a long-term protracted effort that will build the guerrilla base and wear down the opposition. Most strategists agree that these are necessary and integral elements to the success of planned change through violent means.

VIOLENCE AND THE DYNAMICS OF INTERGROUP CONFLICT

The final section here considers the effects of violence and conflict on the parties involved: the *actor* (or violent group), the *target* (recipient of the violence), and *third parties* who witness the violence. With respect to the actor and target, we will first look at the effects of conflict on the perceptions and feelings of one's own group and the other group. The feelings that a group has about itself will be known as "in-group" phenomena, and the feelings that a group has about the other group will be known as "out-group" phenomena.

Before discussing the effects of violence on each of these groups, it is appropriate to briefly review the basic paradigm of the intergroup conflict model. The most noted theorist allied with this research is Muzafer Sherif (1961, 1966, 1969); his often-reported study of boys in a summer camp has been replicated in many different settings. Sherif found that (1) it was possible to create distinct groups among boys who did not know one another, and to study the formation of these groups; (2) it was possible to study the behavior of the groups when they were brought together under conditions of competition and conflict with one another; and (3) it was possible to introduce activities which reduced the conflict and increased the cooperative behavior among the groups.

The first phase of the intergroup model is the development of separate groupings, or in-groups. These groups may form around an issue or an ideology, (as in a political campaign), a set of similar characteristics (racial or religious), similar goals and interests (gangs or clubs), or conditions of mutual fate (captives or prisoners). When an out-group threatens an in-group, normative pressures increase to maintain loyalty to the in-group, suppress internal dissent, and develop strong feelings of solidarity and cohesiveness. In time, the social distance between the groups increases, while the distance within groups decreases. Frequent stereotyping occurs, with derogatory images applied to the out-group and glorified images to the in-group. Invectives and slurs toward the out-group increase, and a self-fulfilling prophecy of competitiveness enhances the distance between the groups. This may eventually lead to violence, manifested in aggression toward members of the out-group and in-group violence to suppress internal dissent or obliterate factionalism and struggles for power.

THE EFFECTS OF VIOLENCE AND CONFLICT ON THE IN-GROUP

From Sherif's analysis, and from the earlier contributions of Coser, violence appears to have functional consequences for the in-group. Solidarity and cohesiveness are strengthened; bridges are built to unite previously existing factions; member similarities are created as a basis for identification with the group, to protect it from outside threat and coercion. Group grievances are aired, dissatisfactions are expressed with the existing conditions, and there is direct expression of frustration and hostility against social inequities and injustices.

The presence of an out-group has a dramatic effect on the strengthening of in-group ties. In-group cohesiveness is strengthened by the presence of an external enemy. A concomitant effect will be internal pressures to present a unified expression of ideology and sentiment. To quote from Coser:

> Groups engaged in continued struggle with the outside tend to be intolerant within. They are unlikely to tolerate more than limited departures from the group unity. Such groups tend to assume a sect-like character: they select membership in terms of special characteristics and so tend to be limited in size, and they lay claim to the total personal involvement of their members. Their social cohesion depends upon total sharing of all aspects of group life and is reinforced by the assertion of group unity against the dissenter. The only way they can solve the problem of dissent is through the dissenter's voluntary or forced withdrawal.

Since the increase of intergroup conflict will reliably produce effects within the in-group, as research by Sherif (1961) and Blake, Shephard and Mouton

(1964) and others will confirm, it has become a useful tool for those interested in building in-group solidarity. Revolutionary leaders, ghetto organizers, campus militants and other interventionists apparently search for enemies in order to provoke conflict and unify in-group bonds. In recent disorders, the police have often served the role of an out-group. For example, the Newark riot of 1967 was linked to the catalytic agent of a Negro cab driver being arrested on a traffic charge. The surrounding community perceived the arrest as the use of unnecessary police force, but the history of relations with the police had long been simmering below the surface of outright rebellion (National Advisory Commission on Civil Disorders, 1968). The police have been a relevant out-group in campus demonstrations as well. At Columbia, Harvard, Berkeley, San Francisco State, and other places, dramatically diverse groups were unified in their opposition to police action against the demonstrators. Coalition student groups worked effectively as long as the police were present, but dissolved into internal chaos when the threat was removed.

While these effects on the in-group continually occur, it must not be concluded that the effects are functional in all cases. One of the consequences of strong pressures toward cohesiveness is to present a singular, united front to the enemy. Expressions of within-group dissent are thereby suppressed or stifled. Recent pressures in American society to minimize dissent over the Vietnam war have only enraged the dissenters, not silenced them, since they do not share a perception of the Vietcong or the North Vietnamese as an enemy or threat. A second dysfunctional consequence may also occur. The pressures toward unanimity in an in-group seldom lead to consensual decision-making to determine the group's ideological position. Differences of opinion are often distorted or suppressed as people are coerced and power is centralized in the hands of a few. As a result, there is low commitment to the position by those who did not participate in its development, and a high possibility of defection for these members. Finally, the group dissolves into disaffection and factionalism as soon as the external enemy is removed.

THE EFFECTS OF VIOLENCE AND CONFLICT ON THE OUT-GROUP

Although every out-group is an in-group to itself, there is a special case we would like to consider: when an out-group is the target, rather than the initiator, of a violent action. Current events lead us to consider the case where the target is an established regime, authority or administration, whose power and authority have been challenged by dissidents. Their behaviors are familiar, and some have already been discussed.

First, the patterns of external control and the forces of deterrence are likely to be clarified, redefined and strengthened. In situations of guerrilla warfare, this may mean increasing the strength of the regular army and suspending certain civil liberties (for example, prohibiting crowds to gather, searching homes for weapons and enemy, establishing curfews). Similar conditions have existed in the urban ghettos following riot conditions. In the university environment, the patterns of deterrence are more sophisticated and articulate, but still exist. "Guidelines for dissent" are established, liberal use of student suspension is employed, court injunctions are secured if necessary, and due process for dissenters is often ignored in order to insure effective, immediate action by the administration. It is interesting to note that several university administrators have persuaded their own faculty to wilfully limit faculty action in times of crisis. In the name of "all deliberate speed," faculties have voted to turn over the power to administrators for action in times of confrontation. These resolutions may well become the "Gulf of Tonkin Resolutions" for university environments.

Second, out-groups often experience a strong need to maintain both face and decorum. This may reflect itself in a hard bargaining position *vis-a-vis* the dissidents, as well as a strict adherence to traditional rules of behavior. The two can be integrally tied together. For example, an administration may be embarrassed to yield a previously maintained position on an issue, but may be even more loath to do so when the tactics of social change are perceived as reprehensible as the change itself.

Finally, it is possible to examine the mutual perceptions that each group has of the other group. One effect of intergroup conflict is that the groups develop stereotypes of one another; these stereotypes inhibit effective communication, decreasing trust, collaboration and effective decision-making. In dissident vs. established authority conflicts, the stereotypes have been relatively recurrent. The dissidents tend to question the legitimacy and power of the established authority, suggesting an overly centralized regime and unrepresentative control. The established group usually subscribes to the riffraff theory (or more sophisticated variations), and also invokes arguments of legitimacy and representativeness. Once this process has begun, mediation by third parties or dramatic disconfirmation of the stereotypic images is often necessary to improve communication.

EFFECT OF VIOLENCE AND CONFLICT ON THIRD PARTIES

In many ways, the impact of third parties is similar to their role in nonviolent confrontations. In the section on nonviolent strategies of social intervention, it is proposed that third parties could have three major effects: They may (1) support either group and lend weight to that group's position in the change process; (2) communicate to groups (particularly the established authority) that they were made to look foolish by the dissidents (such communication is likely to increase the rigidity and competitiveness of the embarrassed group); (3) be used as impartial agents to arrange and monitor the process of conflict resolution, which may involve meeting with each side, arranging joint bargaining sessions, proposing possible solutions, and enforcing solutions once they have been arranged.

In some instances, a third party might reduce intergroup conflict by acting as a common enemy to both groups. Sherif (1966) has classified defeat of a common enemy as one type of superordinate goal; these are goals which are unobtainable by one group but achievable if both groups work together. Thus, students and administration may agree to settle their differences in order to avoid repressive control by trustees or state legislatures, which neither party desires.

SUMMARY

We have reviewed the more popular theories that link violence and social change, and have suggested action strategies and tactics that interventionists might use to take advantage of the essence of these theories in order to facilitate violent social change. It may seem to many readers that we have overstressed the functions of violence and conflict, while ignoring the dysfunctional consequences. We have also neglected the myriad of complex factors that dictate the appropriateness of violent social change, as opposed to other tactical approaches. These issues are left for future scholars of intervention theory and change.

However, we do feel that it is appropriate to indicate one preference in the selection of strategy and tactics: The potential interventionists should choose an approach that maximizes the potential for mutually beneficial relationships between the actor and target in future interactions. Perhaps this is best stated in the following segment from Morton Deutsch's "Productive and Destructive Conflict":

> The question, I repeat, is not how to eliminate or prevent conflict, but rather how to make it productive, or minimally, how to prevent it from being destructive. There are inherent ambiguities in this question because of the ambiguity of such value-laden terms as "destructive" and "productive." One may well ask can not a conflict be productive for the victor and destructive for the vanquished? And isn't it possible for a conflict to be productive in relation to certain values but destructive in relation to others? However, my concern is with conflict situations where it is possible for there to be an outcome of mutual satisfaction and mutual net gain for the participants and I am interested in the conditions which lead to this mutually positive outcome rather than either to an outcome of mutual dissatisfaction and loss or to an outcome in which one party gains while the other party loses.

OVERVIEW

The articles that are reproduced following this chapter represent a variety of theory, research, and personal experience in factors related to violent social change. The first two articles examine the general area of spontaneous violence, although much of the material is relevant to more systematically planned violent intervention. Leonard Berkowitz, in "The Study of Urban Violence; Some Implications of Laboratory Studies of Frustration and Aggression," reviews the basic tenets of the frustration and aggression theory, and responds to some of the major arguments proposed by ethnological–biological theorists of aggression. He then relates these concepts to urban riots, disorders, and other incidents of violence. James Conant, in "Rioting, Insurrection and Civil Disobedience," discusses riots in systematic detail, particularly the preconditions that lead to riots, and the characteristic phases of riot progression. Conant also reviews civil disobedience and insurrection forms of protest, and discusses the justification of these tactics in modern American society.

Introduction 465

The next two articles examine the process of confrontation as a strategy of change. Irving Howe's "The Politics of Confrontation" discusses the "theory" of confrontation politics, and the factors that affect the legitimacy of using this strategy. Nitish De presents data on the use of confrontation politics in Indian industrial environments. His "Gherao as a Technique of Social Intervention" represents an entirely different perspective on the use of this tactic.

The third set of articles relate to planned social revolution as a change strategy. The theoretical article is by Zbigniew Brzezinski, "Revolution and Counterrevolution (But Not Necessarily About Columbia!)," and discusses the preconditions, evolution and critical incidents in revolutionary situations. It was published soon after the student confrontation at Columbia University in 1968, and there are many parallels between the circumstances described by Brzezinski and the actual events in university confrontations. The other article on revolution is by Jerry Rubin, "What the Revolution Is All About." Rubin presents a personal statement of the American environmental conditions that initiated his revolutionary behavior.

The last two articles represent other important elements in the process of violence and social change. In "Bang," by William Goring, the author discusses the history and philosophy of the anarchist movement in recent times. Goring contrasts the movement to revolution and other forms of violent social change, and underlines the general tactics of the anarchist movement.

In the final article, "Power, Alinsky, and Other Thoughts," George Peabody does not limit his conceptualization of power to the use of violence; he takes a pragmatic view of the role of power and its integral function in social change strategy. Peabody reports on his work with Saul Alinsky in community organizing, and describes in detail the necessary elements in building a community organization to effect change.

References

Adorno, T. W., Else Frenkel-Brunswik, Daniel J. Levinson, and Robert N. Sanford. *The Authoritarian Personality*. New York: Harper and Row, 1950.
Ardrey, Robert. *African Genesis*. New York: Atheneum, 1961.
Ardrey, Robert. *The Territorial Imperative*. New York: Atheneum, 1966.
Arendt, Hannah. *On Revolution*. New York: Viking Press, 1963.
Bandura, Albert, Dorothea Ross and Sheila A. Ross. "Imitation of Film-Mediated Aggressive Models," *Journal of Abnormal and Social Psychology*, 66 (1963): 3–11.
Bandura, Albert, and Richard H. Walters. *Social Learning and Personality Development*. New York: Holt, Rinehart and Winston, 1963.
Becker, W. C. "Consequences of Different Kinds of Parental Discipline," in M. L. Hoffman and L. W. Hoffman (eds.). *Review of Child Development Research*. New York: Russell Sage Foundation, 1964, 159–208.
Berkowitz, Leonard. *Aggression: A Social Psychological Analysis*. New York: McGraw-Hill, 1962.
Berkowitz, Leonard. "The Concept of Aggressive Drive," in L. Berkowitz (ed.). *Advances in Experimental Social Psychology*, vol. II. New York: Academic Press, 1965.
Berkowitz, Leonard. "The Study of Urban Violence: Some Implications of Laboratory

Studies of Frustration and Aggression," *American Behavioral Scientist*, 11 (4) (1968): 14–17.
Berkowitz, Leonard. "Simple Views of Aggression: An Essay Review," *American Scientist*, 57 (1969): 372–383.
Bernard, Jessie. "Parties and Issues in Conflict," *Journal of Conflict Resolution*, 1 (1957): 111–121.
Bienen, Henry. *Violence and Social Change*. Chicago: The University of Chicago Press, 1968.
Blake, R. R., and Jane Mouton. "The Intergroup Dynamics of Win-Lose Conflict and Problem-Solving Collaboration in Union-Management Relations," in M. Sherif (ed.). *Intergroup Relations and Leadership*. New York: John Wiley, 1962.
Blake, R. R., H. A. Shepard, and J. Mouton. *Managing Intergroup Conflict in Industry*. Texas: Gulf Publishing Company, 1964.
Carmichael, Stokely, and Charles Hamilton. *Black Power*. New York: Random House, 1967.
Carr, E. H. *Studies in Revolution*. New York: Grosset and Dunlap, 1964.
Christie, Richard, and Marie Jahoda (eds.). *Studies in the Scope and Method of the "Authoritarian Personality."* New York: The Free Press, 1954.
Coser, Lewis. *The Functions of Social Conflict*. New York: The Free Press, 1956.
Coser, Lewis. *Continuities in the Study of Social Conflict*. New York: The Free Press, 1967.
Dahrendrof, R. *Class and Class Conflict in Industrial Society*. California: Stanford University Press, 1959.
Debray, Regis. *Revolution in the Revolution*. New York: Grove Press, 1967.
Deutsch, Morton. "Cooperation and Trust: Some Theoretical Notes," *Nebraska Symposium on Motivation* (1962): 275–320.
Deutsch, Morton. "Conflict and Its Resolution," paper presented to the American Psychological Association, September 5, 1965.
Deutsch, Morton. "Conflicts: Productive and Destructive," *Journal of Social Issues*, 25 (1969): 7–40.
Deutsch, Morton, Y. Epstein, D. Canavan, and P. Gumpert. "Strategies of Inducing Cooperation: An Experimental Study," *Journal of Conflict Resolution*, 11 (1967): 345–360.
Deutsch, Morton and Robert Krauss. *Theories in Social Psychology*. New York: Basic Books, 1965.
Dollard, John, L. W. Doob, N. E. Miller, O. H. Mowrer, and R. R. Sears. *Frustration and Aggression*. New Haven: Yale University Press, 1939.
Eckstein, Harry, (ed.). *Internal War*. New York: Macmillan, 1964.
Eysenck, H. J. *The Psychology of Politics*. London: Routledge and Kegan Paul, 1954.
Fanon, Frantz. *The Wretched of the Earth*. New York: Grove Press, 1966.
Flacks, Richard. "Protest or Conform: Some Social Psychological Perspectives on Legitimacy," *Journal of Applied Behavioral Science*, 5 (1969): 127–150.
Gamson, William A. *Power and Discontent*. Homewood, Illinois: The Dorsey Press, 1968.
Glazier, Nathan, and Daniel Moynihan. *Beyond the Melting Pot*. Cambridge, Massachusetts: M.I.T. Press, 1963.
Graham, Hugh Davis, and Ted R. Gurr. *The History of Violence in America*. New York: Bantam Books, 1969.
Grimshaw, Allen. "Factors Contributing to Colour Violence in the United States and Britain," *Race*, 3 (1962).
Guevara, Che. *On Guerrilla Warfare*. H. C. Peterson (ed.). New York: Fredrick A. Praeger, 1961.
Gurr, Ted. *The Conditions of Civil Violence: First Tests of a Causal Model*. New Jersey: Center for International Studies, Monograph #28, 1967.
Hall, Calvin S., and Gardner Lindzey. "The Relevance of Freudian Psychology and Related Viewpoints for the Social Sciences," in Gardner Lindzey, and Elliot Aronson (eds.). *The Handbook of Social Psychology*, Vol. 1. Reading, Massachusetts: Addison-Wesley Publishing Company, 1968.
Harvey, O. J., and Harold M. Schroeder. "Cognitive Aspects of Self and Motivation," in O. J. Harvey, (ed.). *Motivation and Social Interaction*. New York: The Ronald Press, 1963.
Janowitz, Morris. "Patterns of Collective Racial Violence," in Hugh Davis Graham and Ted Gurr, (eds.). *The History of Violence In America*. New York: Bantam Books, 1969.
Johnson, Chalmers. *Revolution and the Social System*. California: Hoover Institution Studies No. 3, Stanford University, 1964.
Kahn, Herman. *On Thermonuclear War*. New York: The Free Press, 1969.

Keniston, Kenneth. *The Young Radicals*. New York: Harcourt, Brace and World, 1968.
Kroes, Robert. "Revolution and Scientific Knowledge, 1966," as cited in Henry Bienen *Violence and Social Change*. Chicago: The University of Chicago Press, 1968.
Lave, L. B. "Factors Affecting Cooperation in the Prisoners Dilemma Game," *Behavioral Science*, 10 (1965): 26–38.
Le Bon, Gustav. *The Crowd*. New York: MacMillan, 1921.
Lenin, V. "Partisan Warfare," in Franklin Mark Osanka (ed.). *Modern Guerrilla Warfare*. Glencoe, Illinois: The Free Press, 1962.
Lorenz, Conrad. *On Aggression*. London: Methuen, 1966.
Lovaas, O. I. "Effect of Exposure to Symbolic Aggression on Aggressive Behavior," *Child Development*, 32 (1961), 37–44.
Machiavelli, Niccolo. *The Prince and Selected Discourses*. Daniel Donno (tr.). New York: Bantam Books, 1966.
Mao Tse-Tung. *On the Protracted War*. Peking: Foreign Languages Press, 1960.
McLeish, John. *The Theory of Social Change*. New York: Schoeken Books, 1969.
Milgram, Stanley, and Hans Toch. "Collective Behavior: Crowds and Social Movements," in Garner Lindzey and Elliot Aronson (eds.). *Handbook of Social Psychology*. New York: Addison-Wesley Publishing Company, 1969.
Miller, Neal E., and John Dollard. *Social Learning and Imitation*. New Haven: Yale University Press, 1941.
Montagu, Ashley. *Man and Aggression*. London: Oxford University Press, 1968.
Morris, Desmond. *The Naked Ape: A Zoologist's Study of the Human Animal*. New York: McGraw-Hill, 1968.
Nieburg, H. L. *Political Violence: The Behavioral Process*. New York: St. Martin's Press, 1969.
Oppenheimer, Martin. *The Urban Guerrilla*. Chicago: Quadrangle Books, 1969.
Quarantelli, E. L., and Russell Dynes. "Looting in Civil Disorders: An Index of Social Change," *American Behavioral Scientist*, 11 (1968): (4), 7–10.
Report of the National Advisory Commission on Civil Disorders. New York: Bantam Books, 1968.
Rokeach, Milton. *The Open and Closed Mind*. New York: Basic Books, 1960.
Rustin, Bayard. "A Way Out of the Exploding Ghetto," *New York Times Magazine*, August 13, 1967.
Shannon, William V. "Negro Violence vs. the American Dream," *The New York Times*, July 27, 1967.
Sherif, Muzafer. *In Common Predicament*. Boston: Houghton Mifflin, 1966.
Sherif, Muzafer, O. J. Harvey, B. J. White, W. R. Hood, and Carolyn W. Sherif. *Intergroup Conflict and Cooperation: The Robbers Cave Experiment*. Oklahoma: University of Oklahoma Book Exchange, 1961.
Sherif, Muzafer, and Caroline W. Sherif. *Social Psychology*. New York: Harper and Row, 1969
Simmel, Georg. *Conflict and The Web of Group Affiliations*. New York: The Free Press, 1955.
Snyder, Glenn. *Deterrence and Defense*. New Jersey: Princeton University Press, 1961.
Solomon, Leonard. "The Influence of Some Types of Power Relationships and Game Strategies on the Development of Interpersonal Trust," *Journal of Abnormal and Social Psychology*, 61 (1960): 223–230.
Storr, Antony. *Human Aggression*. New York: Atheneum, 1968.
Thibaut, John, and Harold H. Kelley, *The Social Psychology of Groups*. New York: Wiley, 1959.
de Tocqueville, Alexis. *Democracy in America*. Translated by Henry Reeve. New York: Oxford University Press, 1947.
Walters, Richard H. "Implications of Laboratory Studies on Aggression for the Control and Regulation of Violence," *Annals of the American Academy of Political Science*, 364 (1966): 60–72.
Wolin, Sheldon. *Politics and Vision*. Boston: Little Brown and Company, 1960.
Zigler, Edward, and Irvin L. Child. "Socialization," in Gardner Lindzey and Elliot Aronson (eds.). *The Handbook of Social Psychology*. New York: Addison-Wesley Publishing Company, 1969.

LEONARD BERKOWITZ

The Study of Urban Violence: Some Implications of Laboratory Studies of Frustration and Aggression

The frustration-aggression hypothesis is the easiest and by far the most popular explanation of social violence—whether political turmoil, the hot summers of riot and disorder, or robberies and juvenile delinquency. We are all familiar with this formulation, and there is no need to spell out once again the great number of economic, social, and psychological frustrations that have been indicted as the source of aggression and domestic instability. Espoused in the social world primarily by political and economic liberals, this notion contends that the cause of civil tranquility is best served by eliminating barriers to the satisfaction of human needs and wants. Indeed, in the version that has attracted the greatest attention, the one spelled out by Dollard and his colleagues at Yale in 1939, it is argued that "aggression is always the result of frustration."[1]

The widespread acceptance of the frustration-aggression hypothesis, however, has not kept this formula safe from criticism. Since we are here concerned with the roots of violence, it is important to look closely at the relationship

"The Study of Urban Violence: Some Implications of Laboratory Studies of Frustration and Aggression" by Leonard Berkowitz is reprinted from *Riots and Rebellion: Civil Violence in the Urban Community* (1968), pages 39–49, edited by Louis H. Masotti and Don R. Bowen, by permission of the Publisher, Sage Publications, Inc.

between frustration and aggression and consider the objections that have been raised. These criticisms have different, sometimes radically divergent, implications for social policy decisions. Before beginning this discussion, two points should be made clear. One, I believe in the essential validity of the frustration-aggression hypothesis, although I would modify it somewhat and severely restrict its scope. Two, with the Yale psychologists I prefer to define a "frustration" as the blocking of ongoing, goal-directed activity, rather than as the emotional reaction to this blocking.

One type of criticism is today most clearly associated with the ideas and writings of the eminent ethnologist, Konrad Lorenz. Throughout much of his long and productive professional career Lorenz has emphasized that the behavior of organisms—humans as well as lower animals, fish, and birds—is largely endogenously motivated; the mainsprings of action presumably arise from within. Behavior, he says, results from the spontaneous accumulation of some excitation or substance in neural centers. The external stimulus that seems to produce the action theoretically only "unlocks" inhibitory processes, thereby "releasing" the response. The behavior is essentially not a reaction to this external stimulus, but is supposedly actually impelled by the internal force, drive, or something, and is only let loose by the stimulus. If a sufficient amount of the internal excitation or substance accumulates before the organism can encounter a releasing stimulus, the response will go off by itself. In his latest book, *On Aggression*, Lorenz interprets aggressive behavior in just this manner. "It is the spontaneity of the [aggressive] instinct," he maintains, "that makes it so dangerous"[2] (p. 50). The behavior "can 'explode' without demonstrable external stimulation" merely because the internal accumulating *something* had not been discharged through earlier aggression. He strongly believes that "present-day civilized man suffers from insufficient discharge of his aggressive drive . . ." (p. 243). Lorenz's position, then, is that frustrations are, at best, an unimportant source of aggression.

We will not here go into a detailed discussion of the logical and empirical status of the Lorenzian account of behavior. I should note, however, that a number of biologists and comparative psychologists have severely criticized his analysis of animal behavior. Among other things, they object to his vague and imprecise concepts, and his excessive tendency to reason by crude analogies. Moreover, since Lorenz's ideas have attracted considerable popular attention, both in his own writings and in *The Territorial Imperative* by Robert Ardrey, we should look at the evidence he presents for his interpretation of human behavior. Thus, as one example, he says his views are supported by the failures of "an American method of education" to produce less aggressive children, even though the youngsters have been supposedly "spared all disappointments and indulged in every way" (*On Aggression*, p. 50). Since excessively indulged children probably expect to be gratified most of the time, so that the inevitable occasional frustrations they encounter are actually relatively strong thwartings for them, Lorenz's observation must leave the frustration-aggression hypothesis unscathed. His anthropological documentation is equally crude. A psychiatrist is quoted who supposedly "proved" that the Ute Indians have an unusually high neurosis rate because they are not permitted to discharge the strong aggressive drive bred in them during their warlike past (p. 244). Nothing is said about their current economic and social frustrations. Again, we are told of a psychoanalyst who "showed" that the survival of some Bornean tribes is in jeopardy because they can no longer engage in head-hunting (p. 261). In this regard, the anthropologist Edmund Leach has commented that Lorenz's anthropology is "way off," and reports that these Bornean tribes are actually having a rapid growth in population.

Another citation also illustrates one of Lorenz's major cures for aggressive behavior. He tells us (p. 55) that quarrels and fights often tear apart polar expeditions or other isolated groups of men. These people, Lorenz explains, had experienced an unfortunate damming up of aggression because their isolation had kept them from discharging their aggressive drive in attacks on "strangers or people outside their own circle of friends" (p. 55). In such circumstances, according to Lorenz, "the man of perception finds an outlet by creeping out of the barracks (tent, igloo) and smashing a not too expensive object with as resounding a crash as the occasion merits" (p. 56). According to this formulation, then, one of the best ways to prevent people from fighting is to provide them with "safe" or innocuous ways of venting their aggressive urge. Efforts to minimize their frustrations would presumably be wasted or at least relatively ineffective.

I must strongly disagree with Lorenz's proposed remedy for conflict. Informal observations as well as carefully controlled laboratory experiments indicate that attacks upon supposedly safe targets do not lessen, and can even increase, the likelihood of later aggression. We know, for example, that some persons have a strong inclination to be prejudiced against almost everyone who is different from them. For these prejudiced personalities, the expression of hostility against some groups of outsiders does not make them any friendlier toward other persons. Angry people may perhaps feel better when they can attack some scapegoat, but this does not necessarily mean their aggressive tendencies have been lessened. The pogroms incited by the Czar's secret police were no more successful in preventing the Russian Revolution than were the Russo-Japanese and Russo-Germanic wars. Attacks on minority groups and foreigners did not drain away the hostility toward the frustrating central government. Aggression can stimulate further aggression, at least until physical exhaustion, fear, or guilt inhibits further violence. Rather than providing a calming effect, the destruction, burning, and looting that take place during the initial stages of a riot seem to provoke still more violence. Further, several recent laboratory studies have demonstrated that giving children an opportunity to play aggressive games does not decrease the attacks they later will make upon some peer, and has a good chance of heightening the strength of these subsequent attacks.[3]

These misgivings, it should be clear, are not based on objections to the notion of innate determinants of aggression. Some criticisms of the frustration-aggression hypothesis have argued against the assumption of a "built-in" relationship between frustration and aggression, but there is today a much greater recognition of the role of constitutional determinants in human behavior. However, we probably should not think of these innate factors as constantly active instinctive drives. Contemporary biological research suggests these innate determinants could be likened to a "built-in wiring diagram" instead of a goading force. The "wiring" or neural connections makes it easy for certain actions to occur, but only in response to particular stimuli.[4] The innate factors are linkages between stimuli and responses—and an appropriate stimulus must be present if the behavior is to be elicited. Frustrations, in other words, may inherently increase the likelihood of aggressive reactions. Man might well have a constitutional predisposition to become aggressive after being thwarted. Clearly, however, other factors—such as fear of punishment or learning to respond in non-aggressive ways to frustrations—could prevent this potential from being realized.

It is somewhat easier to accept this interpretation of the frustration-aggression hypothesis, if we do not look at frustration as an emotionally neutral event. Indeed, an increasing body of animal and human research suggests that the consequences of a severe thwarting can be decidedly similar to those produced by punishment and pain. In the language of the experimental psychologists, the frustration is an aversive stimulus, and aversive stimuli are very reliable sources of aggressive behavior. But setting aside the specific emotional quality of the frustration, more and more animal and human experimentation has provided us with valuable insights into the frustration-aggression relationship.

This relationship, first of all, is very widespread among the various forms of life; pigeons have been found to become aggressive following a thwarting much as human children and adults do. In a recent experiment by Azrin, Hutchinson, and Hake,[5] for example, pigeons were taught to peck at a key by providing them with food every time they carried out such an action. Then after the key-pressing response was well established, the investigators suddenly stopped giving the bird food for his behavior. If there was no other animal present in the experimental chamber at the time, the pigeon exhibited only a flurry of action. When another pigeon was nearby, however, this burst of responding did not take place and the thwarted bird instead attacked the other pigeon. The frustration led to aggression, but only when a suitable target was present. This last qualification dealing with the nature of the available target is very important.

Before getting to this matter of the stimulus qualities of the target, another aspect of frustrations should be made explicit. Some opponents of the frustration-aggression hypothesis have assumed a person is frustrated whenever he has been deprived of the ordinary goals of social life for a long period of time. This assumption is not compatible with the definition of "frustration" I put forth at the beginning of this paper or with the results of recent experimentation. Contrary to traditional motivational thinking and the motivational concepts of Freud and Lorenz, many psychologists now insist that deprivations alone are inadequate to account for most motivated behavior. According to this newer theorizing, much greater weight must be given to anticipations of the goal than merely to the duration or magnitude of deprivation per se. The stimulation arising from these anticipations—from anticipatory goal responses—is now held to be a major determinant of the vigor and persistence of goal-seeking activity. As one psychologist (Mowrer) put it, we cannot fully account for goal-striving unless we give some attention to "hope." Whether a person's goal is food, a sexual object, or a color TV set, his goal-seeking is most intense when he is thinking of the goal and anticipating the satisfactions the food, sexual object, or TV set will bring. But similarly, his frustration is most severe when the anticipated satisfactions are not achieved.[6]

The politico-social counterpart of this theoretical formulation is obvious; the phrase "revolution of rising expectations" refers to just this conception of frustration. Poverty-stricken groups who had never dreamed of having automobiles, washing machines, or new homes are not frustrated merely because they had been deprived of these things; they are frustrated only after they had begun to hope. If they had dared to think they might get these objects and had anticipated their satisfactions, the inability to fulfill their anticipations is a frustration. Privations in themselves are much less likely to breed violence than is the dashing of hopes.

James Davies has employed this type of reasoning in his theory of revolutions.[7] The American, French, and Russian Revolutions did not arise because these people were subjected to prolonged, severe hardships, Davies suggests. In each of these revolutions, and others as well, the established order was overthrown when a sudden, sharp socioeconomic *decline* abruptly thwarted the hopes and expectations that had begun to develop in the course of gradually improving conditions. Some data recently reported by Feierabend and Feierabend[8] can also be understood in these terms. They applied the frustration-aggression hypothesis to the study of political instability in a very impressive cross-national investigation. Among other things, they observed that rapid change in modernization within a society (as indicated by changes in such measures as the percentage of people having a primary education and the per capita consumption of calories) was associated with a relatively great increase in political instability (p. 265). It could be that the rapid socioeconomic improvements produce more hopes and expectations than can be fulfilled. Hope outstrips reality, even though conditions are rapidly improving for the society as a whole, and many of the people in the society are frustrated. Some such process, of course, may be occurring in the case of our present Negro revolution.

Let me now return to the problem of the stimulus qualities of the target of aggression. Recall that in the experiment with the frustrated pigeons the thwarted birds did not display their characteristic aggressive behavior unless another pigeon was nearby. The presence of an appropriate stimulus object was evidently necessary to evoke aggression from the aroused animals. Essentially similar findings have been obtained in experiments in which painful electric shocks were administered to rats.[9] Here too the aroused animals only attacked certain targets; the shocked rats did not attack a doll placed in the experimental chamber, whether the doll was moving or stationary. Nor did they attack a recently deceased rat lying motionless in the cage. If the dead animal was moved, however, attacks were made. Comparable results have been obtained when electrical stimulation was applied to the hypothalamus of cats.[10] Objects having certain sizes or shapes were attacked, while other kinds of objects were left alone.

This tendency for aroused animals to attack only particular targets can perhaps be explained by means of Lorenz's concept of the releasing stimulus. The particular live and/or moving target "releases" the animal's aggressive response. But note that the action is not the product of some gradually accumulating excitation or instinctive aggressive drive. The pigeon, rat, or cat, we might say, was first emotionally aroused (by the frustration, pain, or hypothalamic stimulation) and the appropriate stimulus object then released or evoked the action.

Similar processes operate at the human level. A good many (but not all) aggressive acts are impulsive in nature. Strong emotional arousal creates a predisposition to aggression, and the impulsive violent behavior occurs when an appropriate aggressive stimulus is encountered. Several experiments carried out in our Wisconsin laboratory have tried to demonstrate just this. Simply put, our basic hypothesis is that external stimuli associated with aggression will elicit relatively strong attacks from people who, for one reason or another, are ready to act aggressively. A prime example of such an aggressive stimulus, of course, is a weapon. One of our experiments has shown that angered college students who were given an opportunity to attack their tormentor exhibited much more intense aggression (in the form of electric shocks to their frustrator) when a rifle and pistol were nearby than when a neutral object was present or when there were no irrelevant objects near them.[11] The sight of the weapons evidently drew stronger attacks from the subjects than otherwise would have occurred in the absence of these aggressive objects. Several other experiments, including studies of children playing with aggressive toys, have yielded findings consistent with this analysis.[12] In these investigations, the aggressive objects (guns) acquired their aggressive stimulus properties through the use to which they were put. These stimulus properties can also come about by having the object associated with aggression. Thus, in several of our experiments, people whose name associated them with violent films shown to our subjects later were attacked more strongly by the subjects than were other target-persons who did not have this name-mediated connection with the observed aggression.[13]

These findings are obviously relevant to contemporary America. They of course argue for gun-control legislation, but also have implications for the riots that have torn through our cities this past summer. Some of our political leaders seem to be looking for single causes, whether this is a firebrand extremist such as Stokely Carmichael or a history of severe social and economic frustrations. Each of these factors might well have contributed to this summer's rioting; the American Negroes' frustrations undoubtedly were very important. Nevertheless, a complete understanding of the violence, and especially the contagious spread from one city to another, requires consideration of a multiplicity of causes, all operating together. Some of these causes are motivational; rebellious Negroes may have sought revenge, or they may have wanted to assert their masculinity. Much more simply, a good deal of activity during these riots involved the looting of desirable goods and appliances. Not all of the violence was this purposive, however. Some of it arose through the automatic operation of aggressive stimuli in a highly emotional atmosphere.

This impulsive mob violence was clearly not part of a calculated war against the whites. Where a deliberate anti-white campaign would have dictated attacks upon whites in all-white bastions, it was often Negro property that was destroyed. Moreover, aggressive stimuli had an important role. A lifetime of cruel frustrations built up a readiness for aggression, but this readiness had to be activated and inhibitions had to be lowered in order to produce the impulsive behavior. Different types of aggressive stimuli contributed to the aggressive actions. Some of these stimuli originated in the news reports, photographs, and films from other cities; research in a number of laboratories throughout this country and Canada indicates that observed aggression can stimulate aggressive behavior. This media-stimulated aggression may not always be immediately apparent. Some aggressive responses may operate only internally, in the form of clenched fists and violent ideas, but they can increase the probability and strength of later open aggression. The news stories probably also lower restraints against this open violence. A person who is in doubt as to whether destruction and looting are safe and/or proper behavior might have his doubts resolved; if other people do this sort of thing, maybe it isn't so bad. Maybe it is a good way to act and not so dangerous after all. And again the likelihood of aggression is heightened.

Then a precipitating event occurs in the Negro ghetto. The instigating stimulus could be an attack by whites against Negroes—a report of police brutality against some Negro—or it might be the sight of aggressive objects such as weapons, or even police. Police probably can function as stimuli automatically eliciting aggression from angry Negroes. They are the "head thumpers," the all-too-often hostile enforcers of laws arbitrarily imposed upon Negroes by an alien world. Mayor Cavanagh of Detroit has testified to this aggression-evoking effect. Answering criticism of the delay in sending in police reinforcements at the first sign of rioting, he said experience in various cities around the country indicates the presence of police can inflame angry mobs and actually increase violence (*Meet the Press*, July 30, 1967). Of course the events in Milwaukee the week after Mayor Cavanagh spoke suggest that an army of police and National Guardsmen swiftly applied can restrain and then weaken mob violence fairly effectively. This rapid, all-blanketing police action obviously produces strong inhibitions, allowing time for the emotions inflamed by the precipitating event to cool down. Emptying the streets also removes aggression-eliciting stimuli; there is no one around to see other people looting and burning. But unless this extremely expensive complete inhibition can be achieved quickly, city officials might be advised to employ other law-enforcement techniques. Too weak a display of police force might be worse than none at all. One possibility is to have Negroes from outside the regular police department attempt to disperse the highly charged crowds. There are disadvantages, of course. The use of such an extra-police organization might be interpreted as a weakening of the community authority or a sign of the breakdown of the duly constituted forces of law and order. But there is also at least one very real advantage. The amateur law enforcers do not have a strong association with aggression and arbitrary frustration, and thus are less likely to draw out aggressive reactions from the emotionally charged people.

There are no easy solutions to the violence in our cities' streets. The causes are complex and poorly understood, and the possible remedies challenge our intelligence, cherished beliefs, and pocketbooks. I am convinced, however, that the roots of this violence are not to be found in any instinctive aggressive drive, and that there is no easy cure in the provision of so-called "safe" aggressive outlets. The answers can only be found in careful, systematic research free of the shopworn, oversimplified analogies of the past.

Notes

1. John Dollard *et al. Frustration and Aggression.* New Haven: Yale Univ. Press, 1939, 3.
2. Konrad Lorenz. *On Aggression.* New York: Harcourt Brace and World, 1966.
3. For example, S. K. Mallick and B. R. McCandless, "A Study of Catharsis of Aggression," *Journal of Personal and Social Psychology*, 4 (1966): 591–596.
4. See L. Berkowitz, "The Concept of Aggressive Drive," in L. Berkowitz (ed.). *Advances in Experimental Social Psychology*, Vol. II. New York: Academic Press, 1965.
5. N. H. Azrin, R. R. Hutchinson, and D. F. Hake, "Extinction-Induced Aggression," *Journal of Experimental and Analytical Behavior*, 9 (1966): 191–204.
6. See Berkowitz, *op. cit.*, for a further discussion, and also L. Berkowitz (ed.). *Roots of Aggression: A Re-examination of the Frustration-Aggression Hypothesis.* New York: Atherton Press, 1968.
7. J. C. Davies, "Toward a Theory of Revolution," *American Sociological Review*, 27 (1962): 5–19.
8. I. K. Feierabend and R. L. Feierabend, "Aggressive Behaviors Within Polities, 1948–1962: A Cross-National Study," *Journal of Conflict Resolution*, 10 (1966): 249–271.
9. R. E. Ulrich and N. H. Azrin, "Reflexive Fighting in Response to Aversive Stimulation," *Journal of Experimental and Analytical Behavior*, 5 (1962): 511–520.
10. P. K. Levison and J. P. Flynn, "The Objects Attacked by Cats During Stimulation of the Hypothalamus," *Animal Behavior*, 13, (1965): 217–220.
11. L. Berkowitz and A. Le Page, "Weapons as Aggression-Eliciting Stimuli," *Journal of Personal and Social Psychology*, 7 (1967): 202–207.
12. *E.g.*, Mallick and McCandless, *op. cit.*
13. See Berkowitz, note 4, *op. cit.* for a summary of some of this research.

28

RALPH W. CONANT

Rioting, Insurrection and Civil Disobedience

  *R*ioting is a spontaneous outburst of group violence characterized by excitement mixed with rage. The outburst is usually directed against alleged perpetrators of injustice or gross misusers of political power. The typical rioter has no premeditated purpose, plan or direction, although systematic looting, arson and attack on persons may occur once the riot is underway. Also, criminals and conspirators may expand their routine activities in the wake of the riot chaos. While it is quite clear that riots are unpremeditated outbursts, they are not as a rule *senseless* outbursts. The rage behind riots is a shared rage growing out of specific rage-inducing experiences. In the United States, the rage felt by Negroes (increasingly manifested in ghetto riots) is based on centuries of oppression, and in latter times on discriminatory practices that frustrate equal opportunity to social, economic and political goals. While all riots stem from conflicts in society similar to those that inspire civil disobedience, they ordinarily do not develop directly from specific acts of civil disobedience. Yet repeated failures of civil disobedience to achieve sought-after goals can and often do result in frustrations that provide fertile ground for the violent outbursts we call riots.

  The factors universally associated with the occurrence and course of any riot are preconditions, riot phases, and social control. The discussion here is drawn from a review of the literature of collective behavior as well as on studies currently underway at the Lemberg Center for the Study of Violence at Brandeis University.

THE PRECONDITIONS OF RIOT

VALUE CONFLICTS

All riots stem from intense conflicts within the value systems that stabilize the

Reprinted from *The American Scholar*, Vol. 37, No. 3, Summer, 1968. Copyright © 1968 by the United Chapters of Phi Beta Kappa. By permission of the publishers.

social and political processes of a nation. The ghetto riot is a concrete case of a group attempt to restructure value conflicts and clarify social relationships in a short time by deviant methods.

There are two classes of value conflicts, each of which gives rise to a different kind of struggle. The first calls for normative readjustment in which the dominant values of a society are being inequitably applied. In this case, the aggrieved groups protest, and if protest fails to attain readjustment, they riot.

The anti-draft rioter at the time of the Civil War was protesting the plight of the common man who could not, like his wealthier compatriots, buy his way out of the draft. American egalitarian values were not being applied across the board. The readjustment came only after the intensity of the riots stimulated public concern to force a change.

The contemporary ghetto riots grow out of the failure of the civil rights movement to achieve normative readjustment for black people through nonviolent protest. This failure has produced lines of cleavage which, if intensified, will result in the second type of value conflict, namely, value readjustment.

In this case, the dominant values of the society are brought under severe pressure for change. The social movement that organizes the activities of an aggrieved sector of the population, having given up hope for benefiting from the going value system, sets up a new configuration of values. The movement becomes revolutionary. When Americans gave up hope of benefiting from the English institutions of the monarchy and the colonial system, they set up their own egalitarian value system and staged a revolution.

Now, Black Power and Black Nationalist leaders are beginning to move in the direction of value readjustment. They are talking about organizing their people on the basis of separatist and collectivist values and they are moving away from the melting pot, individualistic values of our country, which are not working for them.

THE HOSTILE BELIEF SYSTEM

An aggrieved population erupts into violence on the basis of a preexisting hostile belief. During the anti-Catholic riots in the early part of the nineteenth century, the rioters really believed that the Pope, in Rome, was trying to take over the country. The anti-Negro rioters in Chicago and East St. Louis (and even in Detroit in 1943) really believed that Negroes were trying to appropriate their jobs and rape their women and kill their men.

Today, many rioters in black ghettos really believe in the malevolence of white society, its duplicity, and its basic commitment to oppressing Negroes. An important component of the hostile belief system is that the expected behavior of the identified adversary is seen as *extraordinary*—that is, beyond the pale of accepted norms. In the black ghettos, people are convinced, for example, that the police will behave toward them with extraordinary verbal incivility and physical brutality, far beyond any incivility and brutality displayed towards whites in similar circumstances.

The hostile belief system is connected, on the one hand, with the value conflict, and, on the other, with the incident that precipitates a riot. It embodies the value conflict, giving it form, substance and energy. It sets the stage for the precipitating incident which then becomes a concrete illustration of the beliefs. A police officer shooting and killing a young black suspected car thief (as in San Francisco in September, 1966), or beating and bloodying a black taxi driver (as in Newark in July, 1967), confirms and dramatizes the expectations incorporated into the hostile beliefs and triggers the uprising.

Hostile beliefs bear varying relations to "reality." Their systemization means that in some aspects they are incorrect exaggerations; in others, very close to the truth. In the 1830's, the Catholic Church wanted more power and influence locally, but it did not, consciously, want to take over the country. Today, large numbers of white people want to keep Negroes where they are by allowing them to advance only gradually. But they do not, at least consciously, want to oppress them.

RELATIVE DEPRIVATION

An important and almost universal causal factor in riots is a perception of real or imagined deprivation in relation to other groups in the society. As James R. Hundley has put it, the aggrieved see a gap between the conditions in which they find themselves and what could be achieved given a set of opportunities. Ghetto residents in the United States use middle-class white suburban living as a comparative point, and they feel acutely deprived. The areas of relative deprivation for the black American are pervasively economic, political and social.

OBSTACLES TO CHANGE

Another universal causal factor behind riots is the lack of effective channels for bringing about change. Stanley Lieberson and Arnold Silverman, in their study of riots in United States cities between 1910 and 1961, note a correlation between cities in which riots have occurred and cities that elect officials at large rather than from wards. In this situation, Negroes are not likely to have adequate representation, if any. The result is that they feel deprived of a local political voice and are in fact deprived of a potential channel through which to air grievances. An aggrieved population with no access to grievance channels is bound to resort to rioting if one or more of their grievances become dramatized in a precipitating incident.

HOPE OF REWARD

While riot participants do not ordinarily think much in advance about the possible outcome of a riot, still those who participate harbor hopes, however vague, that extreme and violent behavior may bring about desired changes. Certainly the contagion effect had a significant role in the crescendo of ghetto riots in the United States during 1967. Part of the spirit was that things could not be made much worse by rioting, and riots might achieve unexpected concessions from influential whites. Any hard-pressed people are riot-prone and the more so if they see others like themselves making gains from rioting. What happens is spontaneous, but hope raises the combustion potential.

COMMUNICATION

Ease of communication among potential rioters is less a *precondition* of riot than a necessary condition to the spread of riot, once started. Riots tend to occur in cities during warm weather when people are likely to be congregated in the streets and disengaged from normal daily activities.

THE PHASES OF A RIOT

A riot is a dynamic process which goes through different stages of development. If the preconditions described above exist, if a value conflict intensifies, hostile beliefs flourish, an incident that exemplifies the hostile beliefs occurs, communications are inadequate and rumor inflames feelings of resentment to a fever pitch, the process will get started. How far it will go depends upon a further process of interaction between the local authorities and an aroused community.

There are four stages within the riot process. Not all local civil disturbances go through all four stages; in fact, the majority do not reach stage three. It is still not certain at what point in the process it is appropriate to use the word "riot" to describe the event. In fact more information is needed about the process and better reporting of the phase structure itself.

PHASE 1. THE PRECIPITATING INCIDENT

All riots begin with a precipitating event, which is usually a gesture, act or event by the adversary that is seen by the aggrieved community as concrete evidence of the injustice or relative deprivation that is the substance of the hostility and rage felt by the aggrieved. The incident is inflammatory because it is typical of the adversary's behavior toward the aggrieved and responsible for the conditions suffered by the aggrieved. The incident is also taken as an excuse for striking back with "justified" violence in behavior akin to rage. The event may be distorted by rumor and made to seem more inflammatory than it actually is. In communities where the level of grievances is high, a seemingly minor incident may set off a riot; conversely, when the grievance level is low, a more dramatic event may be required to touch off the trouble.

A significant aspect of the precipitating event, besides its inflammatory nature is the fact that it draws together a large number of people. Hundley explains that some come out of curiosity; others because they have heard rumors about the precipitating event; still others because they happen to be in the vicinity. Some of the converging crowd are instigators or agitators who are attempting to get a riot started; others come to exploit the situation and use the crowd as a cover for deviant activities. Local officials, church and civic leaders come because they see it as their duty to try to control the violent outburst.

PHASE 2. CONFRONTATION

Following the instigating incident, the local population swarms to the scene. A process of "keynoting" begins to take place. Potential riot promoters begin to articulate the rage accumulating in the crowd and they vie with each other in suggesting violent courses of action. Others, frequently recognized ghetto leaders, suggest that the crowd disband to let tempers cool and to allow time for a more considered course of action. Law enforcement officers appear and try to disrupt the "keynoting" process by ordering and forcing the crowd to disperse. More often than not, their behavior, which will be discussed below, serves to elevate one or another hostile "keynoter" to a position of dominance, thus flipping the riot process into the next phase.

The outcome of Phase 2 is clearly of crucial importance. The temper of the crowd may dissipate spontaneously, or escalate explosively. The response of civil authorities at this point is also crucial. If representatives of local authority appear, listen to complaints and suggest some responsive method for dealing with them, the agitation tends to subside; a "let's wait and see" attitude takes over. If they fail to show up and are represented only by the police, the level of agitation tends to rise.

How the news media handle Phase 2 has a critical effect on the course of the riot. During the "sensationalizing" era of a few years ago in the United States, almost any street confrontation was likely to be reported as a "riot." In the current policy of "restraint," a street confrontation may not be reported at all. Neither policy is appropriate. A policy of "adequate communication" is needed. The grievances stemming from the precipitating incident and agitating the crowd should be identified. The response of local authorities should be described. The adversary relations and their possible resolutions, violent or nonviolent, should be laid out insofar as possible.

PHASE 3. ROMAN HOLIDAY

If hostile "keynoting" reaches a sufficient crescendo in urban ghetto riots, a quantum jump in the riot process occurs and the threshold of Phase 3 is crossed. Usually the crowd leaves the scene of the street confrontation and reassembles elsewhere. Older persons drop out for the time being and young people take over the action. They display an angry intoxication indistinguishable from glee. They hurl rocks and bricks and bottles at white-owned stores and at cars containing whites or police, wildly cheering every "hit." They taunt law-enforcement personnel, risk capture, and generally act out routine scenarios featuring the sortie, the ambush and the escape—the classic triad of violent action that they have seen whites go through endlessly on TV. They set the stage for looting, but are usually too involved in "the chase" and are too excited for systematic plunder. That action comes later in Phase 3, when first younger, then older, adults, caught up on the Roman Holiday, and angered by tales of police brutality toward the kids, join in the spirit of righting ancient wrongs.

Phase 3 has a game structure. It is like a sport somehow gone astray but still subject to correction. Partly this openness derives from the "King-for-a-

Day" carnival climate. Partly it is based on the intense ambivalence of black people toward the white system and its symbolic representatives, its hated stores and their beloved contents, its despised police and their admired weaponry, its unregenerate bigots and its exemplary civil rights advocates, now increasingly under suspicion. Because of the ambivalence, action and motive are unstable. Middle-class or upwardly mobile Negroes become militants overnight. Youths on the rampage one day put on white hats and armbands to "cool the neighborhood" the next. It is because of the ambivalence felt by Negroes, not only toward whites but toward violence itself, that so few Phase 3 disturbances pass over into phase 4.

PHASE 4. SIEGE

If a city's value conflict continues to be expressed by admonishment from local authorities and violent suppression of the Roman Holiday behavior in the ghetto, the riot process will be kicked over into Phase 4. The adversary relations between ghetto dwellers and local and City Hall whites reach such a degree of polarization that no direct communications of any kind can be established. Communications, such as they are, consist of symbolic, warlike acts. State and federal military assistance is summoned for even more violent repression. A curfew is declared. The ghetto is subjected to a state of siege. Citizens can no longer move freely into and out of their neighborhoods. Forces within the ghetto, now increasingly composed of adults, throw fire bombs at white-owned establishments, and disrupt fire fighting. Snipers attack invading paramilitary forces. The siege runs its course, like a Greek tragedy, until both sides tire of this fruitless and devastating way of solving a conflict.

SOCIAL CONTROL

Studies of past and present riots show that the collective hostility of a community breaks out as a result of inattention to the value conflict (the long-range causes) and as a result of failures in social control (immediate causation). These failures are of two sorts: under-control and over-control. In the condition of under-control, law-enforcement personnel are insufficiently active. Although the condition may be brought about in various ways, the effect is always the same. The dissident group, noting the weakness of the authorities, seizes the opportunity to express its hostility. The inactivity of the police functions as an invitation to act out long-suppressed feelings, free of the social consequences of illegal behavior.

In some communities, as in the 1967 Detroit riot, under-control during early Phase 3 produces an efflorescence of looting and is then suddenly replaced with over-control. In other communities, over-control is instituted early, during Phase 2. Local and state police are rushed to the scene of the confrontation and begin to manhandle everyone in sight. Since the action is out of proportion to the event, it generates an intense reaction. If over-control is sufficiently repressive, as in the 1967 Milwaukee riot, where a 24-hour curfew was ordered early in

Phase 3 and the National Guard summoned, the disturbances are quieted. In Milwaukee, the ghetto was placed under a state of siege as the Roman Holiday was beginning to take hold in the community. No "catharsis" occurred and there was no improvement in ghetto-City Hall communications. The consequences of such premature repression cannot yet be discerned. Short of the use of overwhelming force, over-control usually leads to increased violence. The black people in the ghetto see the police as violent and strike back with increasing intensity. Studies being conducted currently at the Lemberg Center show that in the majority of instances, police violence toward ghetto residents precedes and supersedes ghetto violence.

An adequate law-enforcement response requires an effective police presence when illegal activities, such as looting, take place. Arrests can and should be made, without cruelty. It is not necessary that all offenders be caught and arrested to show that authorities intend to maintain order. Crowds can be broken up or contained through a variety of techniques not based on clubbing or shooting. The avoidance of both under- and over-control is a matter of police training for riot control. This was the deliberate pattern of police response in several cities (notably Pittsburgh) to the riots following the assassination of Martin Luther King in April.

Commenting on the interaction between a riot crowd and social control agencies, Hundley observes (1) that the presence of police tends to create an event, provide a focal point and draw people together for easy rumor transmittal; (2) that the result of too few police is uncontrolled deviant behavior; (3) that a legitimate police activity (from the standpoint of riot participants) will not escalate the incident, but even if the original police activity *is* seen as legitimate, policemen observed being rude, unfair or brutal at the scene may touch off a riot; (4) success of a police withdrawal *during* a riot depends upon officials contacting the legitimate leaders of the community and allowing them to exert social control; (5) when officials do not know the community leaders (or no effective ones are available), their withdrawal simply allows the instigators and exploiters to create or continue the riot; (6) the presence of police who do *not* exert control promotes the emergence of norms that encourage deviant activity.

Hundley adds these further observations on social control factors: (1) the sooner help comes from outside control agencies, the sooner the riot stops, although we think a riot can be stopped too soon, before catharsis or settlement of grievances can occur. Hundley's next point, however, takes this matter into account: (2) the sooner the larger community seeks out real ghetto leaders *and satisfies their grievances,* the sooner the riot stops. (3) The sooner the audience ceases watching the riot activity, the sooner the riot disappears. (4) The greater degree of "normalcy" maintained in the community during the riot, the more likely it is that the riot will remain small or cease.

CIVIL INSURRECTION

When community grievances go unresolved for long periods of time and efforts at communication and/or negotiation seem unproductive or hopeless, despair in the aggrieved community may impel established, aspiring or self-appointed leaders to organize acts of rebellion against civil authorities. Such acts constitute insurrection and differ from riots in that the latter are largely spontaneous and unpremeditated. The exceptions are riots that are instigated by insurrectionists.

Although insurrection is deliberate rebellion, the aim of the insurrectionist, unlike that of the revolutionary, is to put down persons in power, to force abandonment of obnoxious policies or adoption of desirable ones. The insurrectionist is not out to overthrow the system. (The organizers of the Boston Tea Party were insurrectionists, they were not yet revolutionaries.) Like the civil disobedient (or the rioter), the insurrectionist will settle for some specific adjustment in the system, such as a change in political leadership, increased representation in the system, repeal of an objectionable law, or abandonment of an inequitable policy. The revolutionary has lost hope for any effective participation in the existing system (as had the American revolutionaries by 1776) and presses for a total overthrow.[1]

Civil insurrection is in effect a stage of *civil protest* that develops from the same set of conditions that inspire acts of civil disobedience or riot. Riots do not turn into insurrection, although insurrectionists are often encouraged by riots to employ organized violence as a means to attain sought-after goals. The participants in acts of civil disobedience and riots are obviously seen by insurrectionists as potential participants in organized acts of violent protest. Indeed, the disobedients and the rioters may themselves be converted to insurrection tactics, not by existing insurrectionists, but by disillusionment and frustration in the other courses of action.

Civil disobedience and insurrection, both of which are deliberate acts, characteristically involve relatively few of the aggrieved population, because it is hard to get ordinary people to participate in planned disobedience of the law (and run the risk of punishment) or premeditated acts of violence (and run the double risk of physical harm and punishment). Also the various social control mechanisms, aside from the law-enforcement agencies, tend to keep most people from willful, premeditated violence and disobedience. Riots, on the other hand, may involve large numbers of people, many of whom are usually law-abiding, not because a riot is any more acceptable than insurrection or civil disobedience, but because these are irresistible elements of contagious emotion rooted in commonly shared and commonly repressed feelings of frustration and rage. These feelings of frustration and rage are linked to and grow out of hostile beliefs about the adversary, and in the early stages of a riot are inflamed by some incident that seems to be an example of the adversary's typical behavior. The incident becomes an excuse for an angry, concerted outburst, which can spread very rapidly in the aggrieved community and rationalize otherwise unacceptable acts. Law-abiding citizens who participate in a riot are not so easy to organize for insurrection. Persons who can be recruited for organized acts of violent protest are more likely to be those who have already become involved in some form of criminal activity as an individual, private (perhaps unconscious) protest against a hostile society. It may also be easier to organize insurrection in a community with an established tradition of either rioting or insurgency.

THE JUSTIFICATION OF CIVIL PROTEST

There is substantial agreement among legal and political thinkers that nonviolent challenges to the policies and laws of civil authority are an indispensable mechanism of corrective change in a democratic society. Insofar as possible, procedures for challenge which may involve open and deliberate disobedience should be built into the laws and policies of the system, for such procedures give the system a quality of resilience and flexibility, the capacity to absorb constructive attack from within.

As George Lakay has pointed out, one great strength of democratic institutions is that they build a degree of conflict into the decision-making structure just so that conflicts can be resolved publicly and without violence. Adequately designed democratic institutions deliberately reflect shifting views and power relations of interest groups and the normal workings of compromise and settlement, and equilibrium is usually maintained. Civil disobedience, and other forms of civil protest, are resorted to when political adversaries exhaust means of compromise in the political arena. Then the less powerful of the adversaries is forced to carry his challenge into a legal procedure or to the public in a show of protest.

Agreement on a policy of deliberate tolerance of peaceful challenge does not imply automatic agreement on what conditions *justify* challenges that involve disobedience. Moreover, agreement on a policy of tolerance toward nonviolent civil disobedience bears no necessary relationship at all to the question of the justification of civil protest involving violence, as riots and insurrection always do.

Nonviolent civil disobedience is justified under the following circumstances:

(1.) When an oppressed group is deprived of lawful channels for remedying its condition; conversely, a resort to civil disobedience is never politically legitimate where methods of due process in both the legal and political systems are available as remedies.

(2.) As a means of resisting or refusing to participate in an obvious and intolerable evil perpetrated by civil authorities (for example, a policy of genocide or enslavement).

(3.) When government takes or condones actions that are inconsistent with values on which the society and the political system are built, and thus violates the basic assumptions on which the regime's legitimacy rests.

(4.) When it is certain that the law or policy in question violates the constitution of the regime and, therefore, would be ruled unconstitutional by proper authority if challenged.

(5.) When a change in law or policy is demanded by social or economic need in the community and the normal procedures of law and politics are inadequate, obstructed or held captive by antilegal forces.

(6.) When the actions of government have become so obnoxious to one's own personal ethics (value system) that one would feel hypocritical in submitting to a law that enforces these actions: for example, the Fugitive Slave Law.

It seems to me that a citizen is justified in originating or participating in an act of civil disobedience under any of these circumstances, and, as Herbert Kelman has argued, that an act of civil disobedience in such circumstances should be generally regarded as *obligatory* in terms of the highest principles of citizenship. This does not mean that acts of civil disobedience should be ignored by civil authorities; on the contrary, aside from the damage such a policy would do to effectiveness of the act of civil disobedience, it must be considered the obligation of the regime to punish a law breaker *so long as the violated law is in force*. As William Buckley has argued, it is the individual's right to refuse to go along with his community, but the community, not the individual, must specify the consequences. For the regime to act otherwise would be to concede the right of personal veto over every act of government. At the same time, a conscientious challenge to civil authority (with full expectation of punishment) aimed at repairing a serious flaw in the system of justice is a step every citizen should know how *to decide* to take.

WHEN IS CIVIL PROTEST INVOLVING VIOLENCE JUSTIFIED?

Americans like to think of themselves as a peace-loving people, yet violence is and always has been an important and sometimes indispensable instrument of social, economic and political change in our national history. We do not need to be reminded of the role it has played in United States foreign policy and in domestic relations.

The fact is that Americans are *both* peace-loving and willing to resort to violence when other avenues of goal achievement seem closed or ineffective. In our national history violence was the ultimate instrument in our conquest of the lands on the North American continent that now comprise the nation. Violence freed the American colonists from British rule and later insured freedom of the seas (1812–1815). Violence abolished slavery, established the bargaining rights of labor, twice put down threatening tyrannies in Europe and once in the Asian Pacific. In the present day, violence is the unintended instrument of black citizens to break through oppressive discrimination in housing, employment, education and political rights.

Americans have always taken the position that violence could be justified *as an instrument of last resort* in the achievement of critical national goals or in the face of external threat.

While it is true that we have always felt most comfortable about government-sponsored violence and especially violence in response to an external threat, we have often rationalized *post factum* the use of violence by aggrieved segments of the population *when the cause was regarded as a just one in terms of our deeply held egalitarian values*. The anti-draft riots during the Civil War are one example; labor strife that finally led to legitimizing workers' bargaining rights is another. Two or three generations from now, the ghetto riots (and even the spasmodic insurrection that is bound to follow) will be seen as having contributed to the perfection of our system of egalitarian values. Thus, I conclude that violence in the cause of hewing to our most cherished goals of freedom, justice and equal opportunity for all our citizens is and will remain as indispensable a corrective ingredient in our system as peaceful acts of civil disobedience. The sole qualification is that all other avenues of legitimate and peaceful change first be substantially closed, exhausted or ineffective.

When an aggrieved segment of the population finds it necessary to resist, riot, or commit deliberate acts of insurrection, the government must respond firmly to enforce the law, to protect people and property from the consequences of violence, but it must, with equal energy and dedication, seek out the causes of the outbursts and move speedily to rectify any injustices that are found at the root of the trouble.

Note

1. In the dictionary, insurgency is a condition of revolt against recognized government that does not reach the proportions of an organized revolutionary government and is not recognized as belligerency. This definition squares with my own as outlined above. An important distinction between insurrection (which I am using synonymously with insurgency) and revolution is the existence of a revolutionary government which is installed when the existing government is brought down.

IRVING HOWE

From *The Politics of Confrontation*

a new term has entered the American language—"confrontation politics," the equivalent in public life of Russian roulette in private life. Some who play this new political game are authentic desperadoes, mostly young Negro militants; others are white middle-class students acting—or acting out—a fantasy-wish of revolution.

For the black desperadoes, "confrontation politics" can bring large risks: prison, violence, death, For the white students, the risks until recently were small; but now, after the ghastliness of Chicago and the growing popular obsession with "law and order," they will surely increase. For the country as a whole the problem is perplexing. At a time of social disorder, when gross injustices continue to plague us, there arise combative minorities charged with moral idealism and apocalyptic emotion, which have developed tactics of protest going beyond the usual democratic methods, yet short of the usual insurrectionary ones.

Like many other New Left notions, "confrontation politics" has not been well articulated as a theory. It is a kind of politics that grows up through improvisation, and it has been improvised as a way of getting around the sense of futility which has usually beset American radicalism. It has been choreographed as an out-of-doors explosion, a sort of real-life theater.

The purpose is to prod and incite a dormant, insensitive society into recognizing its moral failures. No longer committed, as were the Marxists, to the idea that the proletariat would be the crucial lever for the transformation of history, the young semi-anarchists who practice "confrontation" see themselves as a minority probably doomed to remain one for a long time. They have no expec-

Condensed from "The New Confrontation Politics is a Dangerous Game" by Irving Howe, *The New York Times Magazine*, October 20, 1968. © 1968 by The New York Times Company. Reprinted by permission.

tation of creating new electoral majorities and small expectation of persuading large numbers of people; for they see the mass of Americans as brainwashed by "the media" (the very media which give them vast amounts of publicity). Their politics is a politics of desperation: at best, moral shock, and at worst, nihilist irritation. They assign to themselves the task of sacrifice and assault, as a self-chosen vanguard which must destroy the complacency of "corporate liberalism." One aim of confrontation politics is the "polarization" of society. In plain English, this means that by constant assault the activists hope to drive a segment of the liberals into radicalism; thereupon the "mushy middle" of the country will be broken up, and we can then look forward to an apocalypse, with two extremes hardened and ready for a final conflict.

When they invoke this vision the confrontations are drawing upon political emotions that have been very powerful in the twentieth century—emotions concerning "the seizure of power," a political Second Coming. Having shared these emotions and still being susceptible to them, I can appreciate their force. But I must nevertheless ask what, in the present circumstances, would be the likely outcome of such a "polarization" in the United States?

Were anything of the sort to happen, millions of ordinary Americans—for whom student protest-drugs-hippiedom-Negro rioting forms a stream of detested association—would also be activated. Lower-class white ethnic groups would be stirred up. *Lumpen* elements would be emboldened. Both respectable and marginal classes would turn to demogogues promising order in the streets.

Despite its talk about "the power elite" and the idiotic notion it sometimes proposes that we live under "liberal fascism," the New Left clings to an excessively optimistic view of American society. Its spokesmen have neither memory nor awareness of what fascism—the real thing, *fascist* fascism—would be like. They fail to recognize that there are sleeping dogs it would be just as well to let lie. And they are shockingly indifferent to the likelihood that the first victim of a new reaction in America would be the universities in which they now find shelter.

Only in terms of a theory of "polarization" can one explain the peculiar intensity with which New Left students kept trying to break up the meetings of Hubert Humphrey, while virtually ignoring those of Richard Nixon. (I am against breaking up anyone's meetings.) They were acting on the premise that liberalism is their main enemy, and some of them have even said that they would find attractive an alliance between far left and far right.

Such notions tacitly continue the old Stalinist tradition of "the worse, the better," and "*Nach Hitler, uns.*" Yet all of recent history enforces the lesson that misery cannot be the seed-bed of progress or chaos of freedom. Polarization helps, not the left, but the right; not those with grievances, but those with guns.

In any case, is the prospect of "polarization" an attractive one? How many of us would like to face a choice between an America symbolized by George Wallace and an America symbolized by Tom Hayden? Morally, because he is against racism, Hayden is superior, but politically neither has much respect for democracy. I for one would fear for my safety almost as much with one as with the other. Wallace might have me pistol-whipped as a Communist, and Hayden have me sent to a labor camp as a Social Democrat. Hayden would be more accurate politically, but what sort of consolation would that be?

For a while confrontation politics seems to work. Caught off balance, the enemy panics. College administrators aren't sure how to cope with students who seize buildings. But in time, for better or worse, they are going to figure out a way of dealing with this problem.

There is some truth in the claim—it constitutes a damning criticism of our society—that provocative demonstrations spilling over into violence have a way of gaining attention, certainly from TV, which programmatic and disciplined protest does not. But it is a truth easily overstated. The ghetto riots in Detroit and Watts have not brought notable improvements to their communities; they have not led to those increased federal appropriations which are the only serious way of starting to clear the slums. At best they have enabled these communities, at enormous cost to themselves, to gain a slightly larger share of the funds already available. And as the California election of Ronald Reagan showed, the violence helped set off an electoral trend which can only signify a tight-fisted and mean-spirited policy toward the blacks.

Concerning this matter, let me quote from a discussion between Bayard Rustin, the Negro leader, and myself in the November (1968) issue of *Dissent:*

Howe: I keep encountering the argument in regard to riots: "We know in principle it's not a good thing. But when you have a society that is not susceptible to pressure or moral appeals, the only way you can get them to pay attention is through raising hell."
Rustin: There are two tragedies here. One is that to some extent they're right. You don't get concessions until there's been trouble . . . The second tragedy is that although we receive minor concessions from the establishment, once the rioting reaches a certain point there will be repression against the entire Negro community.
Howe: Raising the ante indefinitely isn't going to work . . .
Rustin: Right. To repress one-tenth of the population will require an assault on the civil liberties of everyone. And in such an atmosphere, no genuine progress in the redistribution of wealth can take place . . . There's another factor. Sooner or later the unity of the Negroes, small as it is, in making demands on the whole society will be splintered, because the Negro community gets into a debate, are you or are you not for violence, instead of uniting around a fight for political and economic objectives.

The advocates of "confrontation" seem undisturbed by the fact that they are setting precedents which could lead to a major crisis for democracy.

If it is permissible for opponents of the war to burn government records, why may not neo-Fascists do the same thing a few years later? If it is permissible for left-wing students to seize buildings in behalf of virtuous ends, why may not their action become a precedent for doing the same thing in behalf of detestable ends? At the very least, such problems must be discussed.

Some will say that violence and illegality are already rampant in the society, and that they are merely responding to its official use. This has a measure of truth. But I would reply that democratic procedures, incomplete as they may still be, have been established only after decades of struggle, and that it would be feckless to dismiss them as mere sham. Those of us who see the need for radical change have the most interest in preserving democracy.

A few years ago Staughton Lynd wrote about an anti-war demonstration in Washington:

> It was unbearably moving to watch the sea of banners move out . . . toward the Capitol . . . Still more poignant was the perception that as the crowd moved toward the seat of government . . . our forward movement was irresistibly strong . . . nothing could have stopped that crowd from taking possession of its government. Perhaps next time we should keep going, occupying for a time the rooms from which orders issue . . . (*Liberation*, June-July 1965)

One must ask Staughton Lynd: under whose mandate were the marchers to occupy the government? And if they did "perhaps next time" arrogate to themselves the privilege of a *coup d'etat*, even a symbolic one lasting five minutes, how will they keep other crowds, other causes—equally sincere, equally "moving"—from doing the same "perhaps the time after next?"

The policies of confrontation bears an inherent drift toward anti-democratic elitism. Electoral processes are declared irrelevant, majorities mere formalities. Once such notions are indulged, the choice is either to sink back into apathy with pot or to plunge into a desperate elitism which dismisses the people as boobs and assigns the "tasks of history" to a self-appointed vanguard. And in the current atmosphere, it isn't hard to drift from elitism to talk of violence. Mostly, so far, it is talk.

But there are troubling signs. This past summer the office of Stanford University's president was set afire, an event that followed in time a season of student sit-ins. I see no reason to connect these two, and would never have dreamed of doing so had I not read the following in a New Left paper, the *Midpeninsula Observer* (July 15, 1968).

> . . . most leftists in this area seem to feel that the fire was politically motivated, and a split of opinion has developed with regard to the tactical efficacy of the act. Some believe that the fire was an effective attack on state power and that it was a logical extension of the leftist activity that has been going on at and around Stanford. Others think that the fire itself was a mistake . . . since it is not clearly connected with a political movement and since most of the people who might be educated by such an act are gone for the summer.

Significant here is not the speculation that the fire was politically motivated —a speculation I refuse to accept—but the argument offered by those leftists opposed to setting fires. They seem to have a seasonal theory of the revolutionary uses of arson. In the winter, apparently, when more people can be "educated" by such an act, these critics would find arson more acceptable. The whole thing, I must say, reminds one of Dostoevsky's *The Possessed*—as also of George Orwell's caustic remark that a certain kind of infantile leftism is "playing with fire on the part of people who don't even know that fire is hot."

Or here, to cite another instance, is a report by Robert Maynard in the *Washington Post* (August 25, 1968) about a feud between SNCC and Black Panthers. At a meeting between leaders of the two groups, writes Maynard, there was a sharp dispute which "resulted in Panthers drawing guns on James Forman," the SNCC leader. Another SNCC leader, Julius Lester, is quoted by Maynard as having written:

> The shoot-out was averted, fortunately, but there was no doubt . . . that whatever merger or alliance may have existed was finished.

As a sign of the fraternal spirit induced by Black Power this isn't much more convincing than the civil war in Nigeria. No doubt, much of this gun-drawing is a kind of play-acting; but play-acting can lead to acting.

Nor is the rhetoric of violence likely to diminish soon. The New Left will continue to talk blithely about revolution, but the police will do most of the shooting. Might it not therefore be in order to plead with the young confrontationists that if the ethic of democracy seems to them hollow or irrelevant, they at least think in terms of common prudence? And perhaps that they take off an hour to read Lenin's *Left-Wing Communism: An Infantile Disorder* in which the great revolutionist explains why compromise and even retreat is sometimes necessary?

One defense sometimes offered for confrontation politics is that, effective or not, it provides a dramatic way of releasing emotions. Of all the arguments, this seems to me the least tolerable. It means that on behalf of self-indulgence, one is ready to bring down on oneself *and others* the forces of repression, of which the first victims would surely be the Negroes about whom the New Left declares itself so deeply concerned. This is a form of middle-class frivolity; a politics of the kindergarten. About such carryings-on (Yippies' trippies) I would cite a remarkable statement recently made by the English writer David Caute, himself a New Left sympathizer, after his return from Czechoslovakia:

> These observations reveal to me a certain perversity in my own attitude. Nostalgia for student riots, clashes with the police, and totally exposed thighs suggests a false romanticism, an irritable desire to inflict on an ostensibly sane society a form of chaos which, as a way of life, is superficial and nihilistic. The manner in which the young Czechs are conducting themselves is really a model of civic control and enlightenment, whereas we have become alcoholic on sensation and violence. (*New Statesman*, June 21, 1968.)

Far more serious are those who advance the view that as a matter of conscience and regardless of consequences, they must break a given law. If a man finds the Vietnam war a moral crime and says he cannot serve in the army even though the result be his imprisonment, then I think he merits respect and often admiration. He is ready to accept punishment for his behavior, ready to pay the price of his convictions. His violation of the law is undertaken in behalf of a higher principle and out of respect for law in general. He hopes to stir the conscience of society or failing that, to live according to his own. Such a version of civil disobedience, Spiro Agnew notwithstanding, is a legitimate act when seriously undertaken in a democratic society.

What is not legitimate is to use tactics that look like civil disobedience but are meant to further "revolutionary" ends (for example, blocking draft boards), since these can only lead to displays of impotence and are likely to harm those who genuinely care about civil disobedience. Nor is it legitimate to resort to civil disobedience, or a tactic easily confused with it, every Monday and Thursday morning. Acts of conscience violating the law can be taken seriously only if they are concerned with the most fundamental moral issues. And there is also, I think, an obligation to obey many laws one dislikes, in order to preserve the possibility for peacefully changing them.

This is a bad moment in American politics. The Vietnam war is a scandal and a disaster, social obligations pile up shamefully in the cities. Radical measures are needed. The exploited cannot remain silent. Militant protest is therefore needed. Yet we must try to make certain that the methods we use to fight against injustice should not give the opponents of liberty the occasion for destroying both the struggle for justice and the procedures of liberty. That would be to invite disaster through a celebration of mindlessness.

30

NITISH R. DÊ

Gherao *as a Technique for Social Intervention*

INTRODUCTION

*t*his article will describe a contemporary Indian phenomenon, *gherao*. The phenomenon is a collective militant movement that has primarily occurred in the industrial environments of an eastern seaboard state, West Bengal and a southwestern state, Kerala. Both states are currently in the midst of a political transition from the right to the left.

How is *gherao* defined? *Gherao* has been described by a State High Court Justice as follows:

"*Gherao* is a comparatively new form of demonstration which is being resorted to by labourers in this country. Generally, it assumes the form of keeping the management or the managerial staff of industrial and other establishments in wrongful confinement, thus depriving them of their personal and other liberties. Occasionally, it assumes the form of physical surrounding of such establishments, thus shutting off access of the management thereto, thereby depriving them of their right to property. The last mentioned form may be described as encirclement in depth, so deep that the encircling persons over-run the establishments themselves and shut out the management. Once commenced, *gheraos* tend to degenerate into further criminal activities, for example, wrongful restraint, trespass, mischief, annoyance, intimidation and worse. The object of both the forms of *gherao* is to coerce the management and make them concede to the demands of labour."[1]

SOME CHARACTERISTICS OF THE *GHERAO* MOVEMENT

The first task is to highlight some of the significant characteristics of this new form of working class militancy, and the impact of the movement on the social system.

Written especially for this volume.

The "encirclement" movement is coercive in nature and violates the sanctity of the right to property; it is therefore *ultra vires* the Indian legal system. In 1967, when the movement first occurred, the Courts of Law emphatically denounced *gherao*. They made it clear that the police, as custodians of law and order, should intervene to neutralise the movement and bring the offenders to justice. However, when the movement reappeared in 1969, the police continued to remain inactive. The judiciary took a further step and indicted the police for contempt of court authority. The police seem to have accepted this adverse verdict stoically.

One consequence of the union-management confrontation through *gherao*, therefore, has been a rupture between the Judiciary and the Executive (the police agency). But the problem is more complicated than this simple explanation. In the Indian federal system, with its parliamentary form of government, the administrative machinery is directly subordinate to the political forces that dominate the state legislature. In early 1967, the centrist and left political parties rose to power in West Bengal. Later that year, the United Front Government was deposed, but it was returned to power by the electorate in early 1969. The communist and allied parties are the dominant partners in these coalition governments. These leftist parties voted to make the executive branch of law enforcement depend upon the authority of the ministers. Thus, the legal authority of the police was rendered subservient to the political authority of the ministers. One effect of this leftist action was to neutralise the coercive power of the police against the working class members that were practicing *gherao*. Since the legal structure of Indian society would not ban the militant tactics, the parties inconvenienced by *gherao* took shelter in the Courts of Law. The judicial machinery took full responsibility for terminating the overt conflict generated by *gherao*. Of the 1131 cases examined in March–October, 1967, 38 percent were resolved by the judiciary, while 12 percent of the cases were settled by the police.

Despite the primacy of the judiciary as the restorer of social "stability" in industrial relations, there remains a hiatus between social legality and social reality. In September 1967, the highest judicial tribunal in the state sentenced *gherao* as an illegal activity; only ten isolated instances of *gherao* occurred in October 1967. Apparently, the judicial pronouncement had effectively curbed the use of this militant weapon by the working class. But *gherao* reemerged *tout de suite* with the reestablishment of the leftist government in early 1969. This time, the "encirclement" movement was used as a quick-action tactic to harass the managerial class, but it was short-lived because the courts would ultimately intervene.

Despite the wide publicity *gherao* has received in the Indian and international press, and the sense of terror it has created in the hearts of the industrial elite, only 10 percent of Indian industrial establishments were affected by *gheraos* in 1967.[2] This study also shows that the white collar clerical employees (who are highly politicised and actively unionised) did not participate in the movement, nor did the employees in organizations that have had a history of successful collective bargaining. Those organizations plagued by *gherao* have had distributive bargaining relationships with the workers, characterized by mutual distrust, competition and a win-lose atmosphere.

There are other characteristics of organizations that have had a high frequency and duration of *gherao*. For example, employers often have not observed their legal obligations towards the employees. Even those organizations which were legally correct were so rule-ridden that employees were treated as human machinery. The author's case studies indicate that managerial insensitivity of a company's human environment is positively correlated with the intensity of *gherao*.

The *gherao* movement, despite its political overtones, is primarily concerned with the rights and privileges of the industrial employees. The issues of the conflict fall into two distinct categories: action motivated by a desire to maintain the existing financial benefits; and rights and action motivated by a desire to improve upon the existing rights and benefits. Table 30-1 illustrates the percentage of cases in each of these categories.

Table 30-1. Gherao *as Maintenance Action/Action for Improvement in Engineering Industries**

1 Size of industries	2 No. of Cases Analysed	3 Cases Dealing With Action for Improvement	4 Percentage $\frac{\text{Col. 3}}{\text{Col. 2}}$	5 Cases Dealing With Maintenance	6 Percentage $\frac{\text{Col. 5}}{\text{Col. 2}}$
Large and medium engineering:	214	131	61	83	39
Small engineering:	236	72	31	164	69

* Dê, Nitish R., and Suresh Srivastva. "Gheraos in West Bengal—II," *Economic and Political Weekly*. Bombay, November 26, 1967.

In large- and medium-size engineering enterprises, the struggle to secure improvement in benefits and privileges encountered almost as much resistance as the struggle for preserving the employment conditions in small enterprises. In the former, the employer could successfully withstand the assault by recourse to legal protection; in the latter the employer suspended business operations either temporarily or permanently.

Despite the climate for political support of the movement, *gherao* cases did not bring about uniform success in securing the immediate objectives. In Table 30-2, this point is illustrated from the engineering industries.

In a number of cases, *gherao* began peacefully, but rapidly took a violent, coercive turn resulting in physical torture and assault on managerial employees. In other cases, the initial phase began with strongly aggressive behavior. Coercion usually took the form of deprivation, particularly in the denial of access to food, drink, and toilet facilities. In other instances, supervisory personnel (whose role in organizational decision-making was limited or peripheral), were subjected to acts of humiliation or torture.

In some cases, worker violence and hostility was inflamed by the employers' over-reaction to a peaceful *gherao*. In many other instances, destructive behavior was the result of a long, painful history of management's callousness and inequity. Finally, some *gherao* have become violent due to the sadistic involvement of participants who are in need of therapeutic help.

Table 30-2.   *Futility Rate of* Gherao *in Engineering Industries**

1 Size of industry	2 No. of Cases Analysed	3 No. of Cases Where Immediate Fulfilment of Demands Was Frustrated	4 Futility Rate Col. 3 / Col. 2 (percent)
Large and medium engineering:	187	105	56
Small engineering:	230	135	59

In addition to focussing attention on the state of pathology in industrial relations, *gherao* has highlighted the existence of a constant flux in interunion relations. In 1967, enterprise-level *gheraos* were sought to integrate workers emotionally and physically into the leftist ideology; to a degree this was achieved. In 1969, however, the objective seems to have shifted; this time the aim was to create a differentiation between leftist groups. The left political parties in the Leftist United Front have sought to use *gherao* to establish their respective superiority and hegemony over the left-oriented working class. In this sense, *gherao* possesses the characteristics of both competition and conflict. It is object-centered as well as opponent-centered.[3]

A TECHNIQUE FOR SOCIAL INTERVENTION?

Although the trend was visible in 1967, it is evident from the resurgence of *gherao* in 1969 that this new technique need not necessarily remain confined to the industrial scene. Educational institutions, research organizations and medical hospitals have undergone the experience; even the courts of law have not enjoyed immunity. Faced with this reality, it seems appropriate to question the role of the new technique in the current Indian social ferment. What is the meaning of this mode of confrontation between the people and the authority? Where will this social conflict lead to? In other words, in the event that *gherao* is looked upon as a tool for social intervention, what kind of change will be ushered in by this intervention technique?

First, *gherao* stands as a verdict by the working class on the failure of the industrial relations system over a period of two decades. The legalistic framework created to resolve industrial conflict has been assessed by the working class as a major impediment to the fulfilment of their goals and expectations. The significance of the *gherao* movement is that it symbolizes the challenge to the legitimacy of the bureaucrats and the politicians in power. *Gherao* has seriously questioned the human relationships implicit in a bureaucratic fabric, in which impersonality and dehumanization are inescapable facts. But it has gone a step further and challenged the "sham" constitutionalism, attitudes, and values of the ruling elite.

Second, and more directly, the "island" existence of the managerial class, their distance (measured in terms of the insensitivity and lack of concern for the working class) and lack of interpersonal competence in resolving human problems have been questioned by the *gherao* movement. Rephrasing Leon Festinger, we may speak of "input outrage" and "output outrage."[4] *Gherao*, an instance of overt output outrage, has sought to unmask the hidden input outrage of the industrial elite. This input outrage is epitomized by attitudes of apathy and even hostility to the working people's interests and expectations, and results in the elite's inability or unwillingness to become involved in resolving workers' problems.

This is not simply a question of the material gains for the working class. A feeling has been generated that the industrial elite is bereft of any feeling of empathy with the workers: their poverty, sorrows, toils and tribulations, human indignity and the hollowness of their existence convey no meaning to the elite. Alienation of the managerial and industrial elite is so deep and pervasive that the reality of working class existence is unreal to them. There is no emotional awareness of the world of the workers, even though there is high degree of working class and managerial interdependence in the production system.

Gherao is accordingly a forced compliance method to make the industrial elite experience the kind of life that the working class lead. One trade union leader expressed the following feelings:

The physical and mental torture that we may have occasionally inflicted on the managers is not simply a form of punishment. We also want them to feel our agonies and our mood of desperation born out of the feeling that, other than monetary reward, *work* has no meaning for us.

Third, the *gherao* movement has provided a "blood-and-sweat" program of apprenticeship for grass-root-level trade union leaders. This program has two basic aspects. On the one hand, the local leaders—the employees of an enterprise—have moved through this movement, from a state of "adolescence" to a state of "adulthood" in their relationship with the national leaders—professional politicians who have taken the reins over a multitude of trade unions in a region. By confronting the managerial elite, the locals have confronted their elders and mentors—the nationals. The movement is, in some sense, an assault on the trade union oligarchy. Here is a dramatic example from a 1969 incident.

In one enterprise, long known for its strained industrial relations history, a *gherao* was organised. The managers including the general manager were collected together and compelled to stand for a long stretch of time under the scorching sun. The general manager, a heart patient, fainted but no immediate medical help was made available.

The incident gained wide publicity. The local trade union leader was hauled up before the Party boss who sought to censure him. The "local" leader responded this way:

"For twenty years your method has failed. We have always been dragged to a

Tribunal where long delay in decision-making has been a matter of routine. So, now let us have our method."

The ascendancy of the locals has been possible because of their closeness to the members, their ability to establish rapport with them and their ability to provide a common, shared experience in confronting the authority figure directly. This last aspect is the second major objective of the apprenticeship program. In a society with a long history of social inequality and other conventions, the concepts of superiority and inferiority are social reality. The industrial elites are superior, and the symbols of superiority are their rank and status, authority, educational levels, attire, residence, etc. The working class is inferior, and the symbols are their misery, lowly status, meagre income, poor housing and undernourished children. There has been a history of submission to this harsh reality as if it were inevitable. There has also been an acceptance that the superiority of the industrial elite is not merely a functional superiority on the job, but a total superiority as human specimens.

The *gherao* movement has sought to alter this tradition by challenging the elite's legitimacy of authority. The local leaders have shaken the roots of the unassailable upper class. The managerial elite has not only been challenged, but the confrontation process has proved to the working people that elite power can be symbolically equalised; it is now possible to level with the upper stratum, and the awareness of their own strength has made it realizable.

What is the significance of the *gherao* movement for the future? What is the future of the industrial relations system? What kinds of change can we predict from the *gherao* experience? To pinpoint the issue, these questions can be restated in the language of Lewis A. Coser:[5] Does the *gherao* movement envisage a change *within* the social system or a change *of* the social system?

The weight of evidence does not currently clarify the answers to these issues. The current visible impact of the movement is to secure economic gains. The ostensible demands are either to preserve the current economic status of the workers or to augment the economic gains. The threat to security of employment and the attempt to thwart this threat by resorting to *gherao* can also be conceived in economic terms. The cases of enterprise-level *gheraos* confirm this. Each enterprise subjected to *gherao* has been pressured to yield financial gains for the workers. Viewed in this light, the movement does not possess an organic character nor does it enjoy a universality of purpose raising it above the level of narrow economic calculus.

Thus the *gherao* movement is an aggregate of incidents and not a planned movement having noneconomic objectives. The purpose of the conflict is to secure more favorable terms of trade within the existing relations of production. There is no disposition toward initiating change of the social system. What the working class has sought to achieve in the Western democracies, through the legal instrument of collective bargaining, is what the working people in West Bengal are seeking to gain through this conflict-ridden instrument known as *gherao*.

A different picture is portrayed if one searches for the less obvious aspects of the movement. In August–September, 1969, two of the most organized, export-oriented, and traditional industries—jute textiles and tea estates—were paralysed by total strikes. Between .1 and .2 million workers in each of these industries succeeded within two weeks in securing substantial economic gains, unprecedented in their history. What is most significant, however, is that there was strong consensus on goals, unity of purpose and direction of strategy among the major trade union federations incorporating hundreds of enterprise-level trade unions. Earlier it was mentioned that the 1969-style *gherao* has accentuated interunion rivalry. While this is true, the spirit of *gherao* has generated a feeling of confidence and eloquence among the working class. Despite the differences in political shades of the leftist parties, the workers could ask their leaders for a redress of their long-standing grievances. Even as the *gherao* cases are unrelated incidents of struggle against specific employers, the spirit fostered by these instances is one of liberation, and fusion of the working class.

Where will this spirit lead to? Admittedly, the response must be speculative. It is conceivable that the spirit of unionization sparked by *gherao* will lead the working class and their local leaders to business unionism, as it is known in the West. The *gherao* movement has put management on the defensive. But it has also forced management to realise that the existence and functioning of the trade union is inevitable; its role will be to provide, in Mancur Olson's phrase, "collective goods and services" to its members.[6] In other words, the impact of Western industrial culture may lead the leftist trade unions to constantly seek to improve the economic status of the working class.

There is also the possibility that the awareness of collective strength, born out of the *gherao* movement, may lead the working class to involvement in the political process of decision-making in the enterprise. The history of unions in India shows that the trade union has been concerned with organizing members with a view to securing *what* from the management—more this or more that. But the newly found strength may also elevate the interest of the members to the *how* of this process. An interest in the personnel function as well as the production function implies a substantive interest in worker participation in the decision-making. Antonio Gramsci, a stalwart of the communist movement in Italy, visualised this kind of extended role for the working class in the capitalist system.[7]

There seems to be an additional motivational factor for the political role of the unions. One way of looking upon an active human organization is to view it as a socio-technical system. In India, whether it is industry or education, the technology is undergoing a process of dynamic change. There is also a readiness to accept the changing technological system, but there is no concomitant built-in change process in the social system. On the contrary, the weight of custom and tradition has created a change-resistant managerial cosmology. To take two examples, the working population and the student community (who are close to technology and are concerned with its utilisation) are caught in a dissociative pull between the productive technology and the obsolescent social system. The resultant tension may motivate the working population to surmount the conservatism of the current social system. In this context, it seems appropriate that the *gherao* movement has the potential to provide the necessary strength and urge to shake up the stability of the social system.

This crucial issue—whether the working class will take to business unionism or to the dynamic role of changing the power-balance in industry and other organized human activities—has a particular significance in India. An analysis of the social realities of the Indian society will reveal that the poor have paid a terrible price for the peaceful change that has been the history of India.[8] The modern Indian bureaucracy has failed to spearhead the social change process, just as the Indian *bourgeoisie* have failed to produce innovative change process. The performance of the Indian *kulaks* in pushing through a major social change program is equally disappointing.

Thus we are left with the residual social clusters—the industrial working class and the poor peasantry. Should Fanon's thesis be accepted, that the "pampered and sheltered" working class can be "bought off," then the *gherao* movement has no change-inducing property. Fanon says that:

"The peasants alone are revolutionary, for they have nothing to lose and everything to gain. The starving peasant, outside the class system, is the first among the exploited to discover that only violence pays."[9]

While it is beyond our scope to assess the revolutionary potency of the poor peasants, we need not altogether rule out the doubt expressed by Fanon about the working class. On the other hand, the Fanon thesis that violence pays and that it has a catalytic effect on the progress of society does not have the unqualified support of history. The trade union movement in the United States provides an example. The railroad strike of 1877 is the beginning of a forty-year history of violence-ridden industrial strife.[10] Yet the collective anger has resulted in a bureaucratic mould of business unionism (which proves the case of Fanon). It has not led to political action, or a major role in the decision-making process, thereby facilitating the change of the social system (as visualized by Gramsci).

The one significant factor that distinguishes the actors of the *gherao* movement is the nature of their cosmology. They are change-prone, anti-*status quo* oriented, and believe that history is a product of *processes* which are fashioned, by human actors. The dismal poverty of the millions is a constant reminder to them that their social intervention technique might betray "the misery of decay" but must, nonetheless, ensure "the zest of new life."[11] It is the author's hypothesis that the change-prone working people, students and low status employees do carry an optimistic image of the future, just as the high-status, power based and conservative elements in society carry a pessimistic image of the future. What Fred Polak and Kenneth Boulding have said may very well fit the picture we have drawn.

"Polak's major point is that in the dynamics of a society, the principal factor is not so much the particular content of the image of the future as its quality of optimism or pessimism. A society which has a negative or pessimistic image of the future is likely to be disorganized and its image of the future is all too likely to be fulfilled. On the other hand, the society which has an optimistic image of the future . . . will be well-organized and will go forward into some future. . . ."[12]

Notes

1. Banerjee, B., "Jay Engineering Works Ltd. Versus State of West Bengal," *Indian Law Reports.* (Calcutta Series), Vol. II, West Bengal Government Press, Calcutta, 1967.
2. De, Nitish R., and Suresh Srivastva. *Reflections on Industrial Conflict.* Unpublished manuscript. Calcutta: Indian Institute of Management, 1967.
3. Fink, Clinton F. "Some Conceptual Difficulties in the Theory of Social Conflict," *The Journal of Conflict Resolution*, XII (1968): 412–460.
4. Festinger, Leon, "Violent Man—A Seven-way Conversation," *Psychology Today* (June 1969).
5. Coser, Lewis A., *Continuities in the Study of Social Conflict.* New York: Free Press, 1967.
6. Olson, Mancur, *The Logic of Collective Action.* New York: Schocken Books, 1968.
7. Cammett, J. C., *Antonio Gramsci and the Origins of Italian Communism.* Stanford: Stanford University Press, 1967.
8. Moore, Barrington, Jr. *Social Origins of Dictatorship and Democracy.* Boston: Beacon Press, 1966.
9. Fanon, Frantz, *The Wretched of the Earth.* New York: Grove Press, 1968.
10. Bell, Daniel, *The End of Ideology.* Glencoe, Illinois: The Free Press, 1960.
11. Whitehead, A. N., *Adventures of Ideas.* London: Penguin Books, 1942.
12. Boulding, Kenneth E., "The Place of the Image in the Dynamics of Society," in G. K. Sollschan and W. Hirsch (eds.). *Explorations in Social Change.* Boston: Houghton-Mifflin, 1964.

ZBIGNIEW BRZEZINSKI

Revolution and Counterrevolution (But Not Necessarily About Columbia!)

a revolutionary situation typically arises when values of a society are undergoing a profound change. The crisis in values in its turn is linked to profound socioeconomic changes, both accelerating them and reacting to them. For example, the transition from an agrarian to an industrial society produced very basic changes in outlook, both on the part of the elites ruling the changing societies and also of the social forces transformed by the changes and produced by them. Similarly, it can be argued that today in America the industrial era is coming to an end and America is becoming a technetronic society, that is a society in which technology, especially electronic communications and computers, is prompting basic social changes. See "The American Transition," *The New Republic*, December 23, 1967. This automatically produces a profound shift in the prevailing values.

The crisis of values has several political consequences of relevance to revolutionary processes. First of all, it prompts ambivalent concessions by the authorities in power. The authorities do not fully comprehend the nature of the changes they are facing, but they are no longer sufficiently certain of their values to react in an assertive fashion—concessionism thus becomes the prevailing pattern of their behavior. Secondly, increasingly self-assertive revolutionary forces begin an intensive search for appealing issues. The purpose is to further radicalize and revolutionize the masses and to mobilize them against the *status quo*. Thirdly, limited claims begin to be translated into more fundamental

Reprinted by permission of *The New Republic*, © 1968, Harrison-Blaine of New Jersey, Inc.

claims. Expedient escalationism of demands is typically a revolutionary tactic, designed deliberately to aggravate the situation and to compensate for initial revolutionary weakness.

A revolutionary situation is thus a combination of objective and subjective forces. Revolutions do not come by themselves, they have to be made. On the other hand, unless a ripe revolutionary situation exists, revolutionary efforts can be abortive. Abortive efforts can contribute to the creation of a revolutionary situation, but a truly revolutionary situation arises only when a society is ill at ease with itself and when established values, legitimacy and authority are beginning to be seriously questioned.

In that setting, confrontations, the test of will and power, begin to be more and more frequent. Revolutionary forces engage in repeated probes to test the reactions of established authorities, while searching for appealing issues around which to rally. The initial phase of the revolutionary process thus involves a protracted game of hide-and-seek. The authorities try as skillfully as they can to avoid a head-on confrontation: they concede in a limited fashion while trying to avoid confronting fundamental issues. The revolutionary leaders, by their probes, seek to identify weak spots and to provoke a head-on, direct clash.

The critical phase occurs when a weak spot has been identified, appealing issues articulated, and the probe becomes a confrontation. At this stage the purpose of revolutionary activity is to legitimize violence. If the initial act of violence is suppressed quickly by established authorities, the chances are that the revolutionary act itself will gain social opprobrium; society generally tends to be conservative, even in a situation of crisis of values. Thus a revolutionary act is likely to be condemned by most, provided it is rapidly suppressed. If the revolutionary act endures, then automatically it gains legitimacy with the passage of time. Enduring violence thus becomes a symbol of the authorities' disintegration and collapse, and it prompts in turn further escalation of support for the revolutionary act.

Simply by enduring defiantly, the initial act of revolutionary self-assertion becomes legitimized and it contributes to further escalation of support as latent social grievances surface and are maximized. In every society latent grievances exist and a social crisis brings them to the forefront. Moreover, equally important is the manufacturing of grievances and demands to express unconscious resentment of authority. Most individuals and groups to some extent resent authority; a defiantly enduring revolutionary situation brings out this unconscious resentment and prompts the manufacturing of grievances and demands which are designed to define an anti-authority posture.

An important role in this revolutionary process is played by legitimist reformers and intellectuals. Intellectuals by their very nature are unwilling to pick sides, since they are better at identifying gray than siding with black and white. In a revolutionary situation, they are particularly concerned with not being stamped as counterrevolutionary conservatives. They are thus desirous of proving their reformist convictions, even at the cost of compromising their posture as reformers and becoming more closely identified with revolutionaries.

Moreover, many intellectuals tend to be frustrated power-seekers, and a revolutionary situation creates a ready-made opportunity for the exercise of vicarious statesmanship.

In a revolutionary situation, their desire for power yet their inability to side with one or the other side prompts intellectuals to adopt a third posture, namely that of interposing themselves between the revolutionary and anti-revolutionary forces. In doing so, they often place their intellect in service of emotions rather than using emotions in the service of intellect. Many are highly excitable; their political weakness and lack of organization inclines them increasingly in a revolutionary situation, to rely on demagogy. At the same time, accustomed generally to dealing with established authorities, they are more experienced in coping with the authorities than with the revolutionary forces. Thus, in the process of interposing themselves, they are inclined to apply most of their pressure against the established authority, with which they have many links, than equally against established authorities and the revolutionary forces on behalf of reformist appeals. In effect, irrespective of their subjective interests, the legitimist reformers and intellectuals in a revolutionary situation objectively become the tools of the revolutionary forces, thus contributing to further aggravation of the revolutionary situation and radicalizing the overall condition.

When faced with a revolutionary situation, the established authorities typically commit several errors. *First of all*, because they are status quo oriented, they display an incapacity for immediate effective response. Their traditional legalism works against them. Faced with a revolutionary situation, instead of striking immediately and effectively, they tend to procrastinate, seeking refuge in legalistic responses. *Second*, in so doing, they tend to opt for negotiating with the new interposing element, thus obscuring the clear-cut confrontation. An early confrontation would work to the advantage of the authorities, since mass support begins to shift to the revolutionaries only after the situation has been radicalized. *Third*, while negotiating with the interposing element, they tend to dribble out concessions rather than to make them in one dramatic swoop, thereby gaining broad support. *Fourth*, when finally force is employed, the authorities rarely think ahead to post-use-of-force consequences, concentrating instead on the application of force to the specific challenge at hand. They thus neglect the important consideration that the use of force must be designed not only to eliminate the surface revolutionary challenge, but to make certain that the revolutionary forces cannot later rally again under the same leadership. If that leadership cannot be physically liquidated, it can at least be expelled from the country (or area) in which the revolution is taking place. Emigrants rarely can maintain themselves as effective revolutionaries. The denial of the opportunity for the revolutionary leadership to re-rally should be an important ingredient of the strategy of force, even if it is belatedly used. *Fifth*, in the application of force, a sharp distinction should be made between the direct challenge and the masses which the challenge has tended to bring out. Thus, in the event of violence in a specific setting, the first objective of force ought to be the clearing of the area of those not directly committed and not involved in the revolutionary process. Only after the direct revolutionary participants have been fully isolated should force be directed directly against their strongholds. Moreover, if isolated for a period of time, the revolutionaries themselves may be more inclined to bargain. Finally, established authorities often fail to follow up effective violence with immediate reforms. Such reforms ought to be designed to absorb the energies of the more moderate revolutionaries, who can then claim that though their revolution had failed, their objectives were achieved. This is very important in attracting the more moderate elements to the side of the authorities.

For every revolution that succeeds, at least ten fail. It is not always a matter of abortive revolutionary situations. Frequently, the revolutionary leaders are themselves guilty of certain errors, typically tactical ones. Under the pressure of dramatic events, they tend to make more and more excessive demands, designed to radicalize and politicize specific grievances. In so doing, they often outrun their supporters and end up losing mass support. Moreover, they often engage in wrong symbolization, focusing on personalities rather than on basic issues. Such personal symbolization does not have staying power over the long haul, and it gives the other side the option to change or to keep the personalities involved, depending on the other side's judgment of the utility of one or the other tactic. Secondly, revolutionary leaders frequently overdo their reliance on emotionalizing appeals. For example, the condemnation of violence by revolutionaries is too transparent to be long effective. If sincerely meant, it stamps the revolutionaries as naïve, for violence necessarily accompanies a revolutionary process; if used as a tactic to mobilize support, it tends to backfire after a while because it eventually becomes evident that the revolutionaries themselves court violence in the hope of further radicalizing the situation. Finally, there is a tendency, and this is very important, of the revolutionaries to overestimate the revolutionary dynamic that they have set in motion. Revolutionaries tend to operate in a fishbowl atmosphere and to assume that their context and their appeals have universal validity. They thus underestimate the non-revolutionary context of their own specific revolution. The French revolutionaries expected their revolution to sweep all over Europe; so did the Bolshevik revolutionaries. In most cases, this does not happen, and the revolutionaries, because they lose touch with reality, increasingly become separated from the reformers on whose support they desperately depend for their long-range success.

In that setting, the task of the reformers is to isolate both the revolutionaries and the reactionaries as extremists. This is a terribly difficult task, for in a revolutionary situation there is very little room for reformers. Accordingly, they must formulate tangible and attainable reforms, together with highly concrete action programs for their attainment. It is only through positive involvement that the reformers can begin to gain broader support. Moreover, they must not participate in activities designed to keep the pot boiling, for this, if successful, will benefit the extremist revolutionaries; if it fails, it benefits the reactionaries. Accordingly, if the revolutionary process is itself in motion, the reformers must decide whom to trust more. If they trust the promises of the authorities, they have little choice but to side with them until the revolution is crushed; if they do not trust them, they must side with the revolutionaries and eventually let the revolution consume them. In any case, they should not mislead themselves into thinking that by staying in the middle, they will impose a middle solution.

A crucial consideration in judging the validity and significance of the revolutionary process is to determine whether it is historically relevant. Some revolutions, by relating themselves to the future, clearly were. This was the case with the French Revolution, with the 1848 Spring of Nations, and the Bolshevik Revolution. They all were part of, as well as having ushered in, new historical eras. But very frequently revolutions are the last spasm of the past, and thus not really revolutions but counterrevolutions, operating in the name of revolutions. A revolution which really either is non-programmatic and has no content, or involves content which is based on the past but provides no guidance for the future, is essentially counter-revolutionary.

Indeed, most revolutionary outbreaks are of this character—they respond to the past, not to the future, and ultimately they fail. Examples are provided by the Luddites and the Chartists in England, who reflected the traumas of an agrarian society entering the Industrial Era; their response was spasmodic and irrelevant to the future. Peasant uprisings, whatever the merit of specific grievances, essentially fail for they do not provide a meaningful program for the future. Anarchist revolutions fall into this category. More recently, the National Socialists, the Fascists, and now the Red Guards in China are essentially counter-revolutionary: they do not provide meaningful programs and leadership for the coming age on the basis of an integrative analysis which makes meaningful the new era. Rather, they reflect concern that the past may be fading and a belated attempt to impose the values of the past on the present and on the future.

If it can be said that America today is ceasing to be an industrial society and is becoming a technetronic society, then it is important to decide whether some—though not all—of the crises and violence of today really add up to a meaningful revolution, or whether at least some manifestations are not counter-revolutionary in their essence. A revolution which has historically valid content for the future and which provides an integrated program for the future is historically relevant. In that sense, the civil rights revolution is a true and a positive revolution. Similarly, the important function of Marxism was that it made meaningful the revolutionary activities of communists by providing them with a sense of historical relevance and a pertinent program.

No such broad integrative ideology exists today in the United States, a country which confronts a future which no other society has yet experienced. On the contrary, it is revealing here to note that some of the recent upheavals have been led by people who increasingly will have no role to play in the new technetronic society. Their reaction reflects both a conscious and, even more important, an unconscious realization that they are themselves becoming historically obsolete. The movements they lead are more reminiscent of the Red Guards or the Nazis, than of the Bolsheviks or the French revolutionaries. Thus, rather than representing a true revolution, some recent outbursts are in fact a counterrevolution. Its violence and revolutionary slogans are merely— and sadly—the death rattle of the historical irrelevants.

JERRY RUBIN

What the Revolution Is All About, or We Are All Vietcong and We Are Everywhere

The revolutionary, apocalyptic spirit expressed by members of the "New Left" is unique in the history of American protest action. America has always been a land of protest: the Boston Tea Party, the Abolitionist movement, the Draft Riots of the Civil War, the Suffragette movement and the continuing protest against the war in Vietnam. In all these cases, the aims of the protesters were specific and limited. The modern youth protest is unlimited in its ambitions. In place of specific demands it pits its new life style, described by its proponents as "free, emotional and ecstatic," against the orderly, constrained, moralistic life style of so-called middle class America.

i support everything which puts people into motion, which creates disruption and controversy, which creates chaos and rebirth.

Adlai Stevenson made me a radical in 1952 by picking up my hopes for change. The system crushed those hopes.

Eugene McCarthy is training the future street disrupters of tomorrow in the futility of party politics.

What The Revolution Is All About by Jerry Rubin, Copyright ©, 1969 by Jerry Rubin. Reprinted by permission of Brandt and Brandt.

The revolution is taking place everywhere.

The stable middle class home is falling apart.

The church cannot attract its own children.

The schools are becoming centers of rebellion, and the streets are theaters of political action.

I approve of letters to the editor, peace candidates and peace referendums, peaceful marches, symbolic sit-ins, disruptive sit-ins, disruptive street demonstration and sabotage.

That is guerrilla war in America: everyone doing his own thing, a symphony of varied styles, rebellion for every member of the family, each to his own alienation.

The respectable middle-class debates LBJ while we try to pull down his pants.

A good question: can America be changed through "peaceful transition?"

can the beast be tamed within her own rules and laws? within the electoral system, within law and order, within police permits and regulations, within the boundaries of middle class America?

can a society which makes distinctions between rich and poor, white and black, employers and employees, landlands and tenants, teachers and students, reform itself? Is it interested in reform, or is it just interested in eliminating nuisances?

what's needed is a new generation of nuisances, a new generation of people who are freaky, crazy, irrational, sexy, angry, irreligious, childish, and mad.

people who burn draft cards

people who burn dollar bills

people who burn MA and doctoral degrees

people who say: "To hell with your goals"

people who lure the youth with music, pot and lsd

people who proudly carry Vietcong flags

people who re-define reality, who re-define the norm

people who wear funny costumes

people who see property as theft

people who say "f—"* on television

people who break with the status-role-title-consumer game

people who have nothing material to lose but their bodies

The war in Vietnam will be stopped by the United States when the embarrassment of carrying on the war becomes greater than the embarrassment of admitting defeat.

A lot of things embarrass America, a lot of things embarrass a country so dependent on image:

Youth alienation, campus demonstrations and disruptions, peace candidates, underground railroads of draft dodgers to Canada, trips to banned countries, thousands of people giving the middle finger to the Pentagon over national television—

* Word deleted by Brandt and Brandt.

We can end this war—we've got America on the run. We've combined youth, music, sex, drugs, and rebellion with treason—and that's a combination hard to beat....

What breaks through apathy and complacency are confrontations and action, the creation of new situations which previous mental pictures do not explain, polarizations which define people into rapidly new situations.

The struggle against the war is freeing American youth from authority hang-ups and teaching us democracy through action.

Every draft card burning is a body blow to Mother America because its impact sweeps throughout the elementary schools with the message: baby, something's happening, and your teacher don't know what it is, and the draft is not sacred or from heaven or from Washington and Jefferson, it is up to you.

The movement is a school and its teachers are the Fugs/Dylan/Beatles/Ginsberg/mass media hippies/students fighting cops in Berkeley/blood on draft records/sit-ins/jail.

Repression turns demonstration/protests into wars; actors into heroes; masses of individuals into a community; repression eliminates the bystander, the neutral observer, the theorist; it forces everyone to pick a side.

A movement cannot grow without repression.

The left needs an attack from the center and right.

Life is theater and we are the guerrillas attacking the shrines of authority, from the priest, to the holy dollar, to the two-party system, zapping people's minds and putting them through changes in actions in which everyone is emotionally involved.

The street is the stage.

You are the star of the show and everything you were once taught is up for grabs.

the economy is rich; overproduction is the problem; now everyone can dig life, and we know it.

we want a communal world where the imagination runs supreme, and where human institutions respond to human needs. Feeling and emotion will be unsuppressed. Everyone will be free. People will go to museums to look at dollar bills. There will be no nations, only rich communities and rich cultures.

This generational movement cuts across class and race lines. It is a war between historical generations, and the future belongs to us because America is defending institutions like ownership and nation—and these institutions no longer respond to needs.

We did not build CBS, the Democratic Party or the Catholic Church and we want no place in them.

Vietnam is a case of the past trying to suppress the future.

The American economy has rendered white middle class youth and black working class youth useless, because we are not needed to make the economy run. Uselessness breeds revolution. The only exciting and meaningful thing to do in America today is to disrupt her institutions and build new ones.

subvert! that's the task of every young person. Spread ideas that undercut the consistent world of America and then top it off by burning her symbols—from draft cards to flags to dollar bills.

We must alienate middle class America. We must get middle class America all whipped up emotionally.

America suffers from a great cancer: it's called APATHY.

moral persuasion may work on the guilt feelings of the American middle classer; it may even win his mind or vote; but how are you going to get him off his ass?

alienating people is a necessary process in getting them to move.

Mr. America: The War is at home!

It is not on Huntley-Brinkley; it is right outside your window; wait, now it is inside your living room, in your child's head.

Disruption of American society is going to become about as frequent as Yankee planes over Vietnam.

Persuasion will follow the disruption.

Crisis will replace the coffeebreak.

When we were simply marching, and petitioning, and making moral pleas to the government to end the war, the good hard commonsense soul of America knew we were only kids, that we were not serious.

Americans know how hard it is to move City Hall.

"Ah, c'mon off it, you ain't going to end the war that way," was the truck driver's likely response to vigils, marches, peace candidates, and peace literature.

Instinctively, the American knew more about his government than did the anti-war movement.

He knew that it was way up there, made up of good-for-nothing politicians, hard to reach, and then reachable only through the language of power and violence.

When the movement moved into the streets, and began to act in the dialect of power, when the movement got tough, we broke away all those barriers preventing us from reaching the average guy. America understands Stokely Carmichael and America understands peace demonstrators fighting in the streets, and that's why we are much more dangerous than a hundred Martin Luther Kings.

Scenario One:

The time: spring 1968   The place: New York City

The city is thrown into a psychological paralysis by the plans of 50,000 peace demonstrators to close down Manhattan by disrupting the 50 most crowded traffic thoroughfares at peak working hours.

Scenario Two:

The time: late August, 1968   The place: Chicago

Chicago is in panic. The American Youth Festival (Youth International Party) has brought 500,000 young people to Chicago to camp out, smoke pot, dance to wild music, burn draft cards, and roar like wild bands through the streets, forcing the President to bring troops back from Vietnam in order to keep order in the city while he is renominated under the protection of tear gas and bayonets.

Scenario Three:

The time: sometime in the future   The place: America

The government sends more troops to the spreading fires of guerrilla war throughout Laos, Thailand and Vietnam, while strikes and guerrilla action continue to mount in India, Indonesia, the Congo and Brazil.

At home, Chicago, Watts, Oakland and Harlem are burning, and the people there have poured into the streets taking the goods they claim are rightfully theirs and broadcasting that all white businesses and buildings now belong to the black community.

Law and order seem to have completely broken down.

One hundred colleges have been hit by student strikes, and hundreds of thousands of young white people are jamming the downtown areas of many big cities, paralyzing traffic.

Some young white and black teenagers broke into the studios of the major TV networks and are now broadcasting to the nation. They are demanding the withdrawal of all American troops from around the world, the immediate distribution of food and clothing free, the immediate conversion of all areas of the economy to serve people's needs free, and the replacement of the police by a peoples' militia.

The authority of the government of the United States is in grave danger.

WILLIAM GORING*

Bang: An Anarchist Approach to Social Intervention

*a*narchism, though normally regarded as a political philosophy, is perhaps better described as an attitude or set of values. Every culture or doctrine known contains some elements of an incipient anarchist theory. Thus, throughout history there has been a conflict between those who seek authority and those who seek freedom, but both groups have sprung from the same sources. The theology that produced the Roman Catholic hierarchy also produced the Brethren of the Free Spirit; the economic philosophy that produced Barry Goldwater also produced Murray Rothbard; the tsarist tyranny that caused a Lenin also caused a Kropotkin. The anarchist can be socialist or capitalist, collectivist or individualist, mystic or materialist. In other words, there is no such thing as *the* anarchist movement, *the* anarchist ideology, or *the* anarchist strategy.

Certain elements are common to most anarchist theories. Freedom is held to be the greatest good. The state is held to be an outgrowth of conquest or protection racketeering, and serves as an instrument of exploitation and suppression. Therefore, the so-called "revolutionary state" is not the proper tool to rectify injustice. The task of the anarchist is to destroy or replace present authoritarian structures without simply exchanging the old elite for a new.

One other element is crucial. Anarchism must be *lived*. The anarchist is not a liberal or Marxist hoping to seize the state machinery and use it to implement his goals. He intends to supplant it with a totally new system and set of values. Having put himself outside the state and its "protection," he must create new institutions and a new culture. Unfortunately, some think that a new life style is the end point. Correctly seeing that the movement, while fighting for freedom

Written especially for this volume.

achieves a certain degree of freedom within itself, they decide that the free community has been achieved. ("The revolution is over and we won," as one group recently announced.) They simply drop out—into retreatism or nomadism or utopian communities.

What they fail to see is that the establishment is powerful enough to accommodate a few largely irrelevant eccentrics. Should they threaten to become more, they can be coopted (for example, some Black cultural nationalists) or crushed (for example the Anabaptists and numerous hippy communes). The movement does approximate a free community, to be sure; and to struggle effectively for freedom one must learn to live as a free man, but the word "struggle" is not used idly. Living the hip life is insufficient tactically; there is a dichotomy between just living a new life style and nurturing it. The movement must have an overall offensive strategy to gain converts and ultimately prevail, and it must have a defensive strategy because the ruling class fought to get where they are and are unlikely to give up without a fight.

Violence has been a very minor part of the anarchist arsenal although it has been employed from time to time—as working-class, syndicalist violence, common to any militant union movement but in this case with the ultimate goal of the general strike, or as insurrectionary violence. Anarchist insurrectionism has seldom been important except in the Ukraine where a 20,000 man peasant army established communes and fought off both the Reds and Whites from 1918 to 1922. In this article we shall deal with propaganda of the deed and with illegalism—two forms of violent anarchist strategy which, though minimal in importance and shunned by nearly all anarchists, are unfortunately identified in the popular press and in the popular mind with anarchism.

A decade after the fall of the Commune, France was under the near total control of a powerful, exploitative, vulgar *bourgeoisie*; every attempt of the workers' movement to assert itself was brutally suppressed.

During this same period Russian and Italian revolutionists were resorting more and more to tyrannicide as a tactic. By 1881, under their influence, a large number of anarchists, Kropotkin included, had become interested in propaganda by the deed, that is, the use of sabotage and assassination in the early stages of a struggle. A few French anarchist journals began to carry articles on chemistry, and began to advocate the use of explosives (the first journal to do so was the creation of the police and one of their provocateurs); but actual acts of violence were rare.

Little by little the idea picked up steam, aided by the heavy-handedness of the authorities who treated each instance of anarchist or proletarian violence with such brutality as to invite reprisals. Finally this chain of events, accentuated by a long series of exposures of corruption that effectively discredited the government, led to a period of terror that lasted for two years.

The key man in sparking off the "heroic period" of 1892–1894 was a laborer named François-Claudius Ravachol. An early illegalist, Ravachol had tried his hand at theft, counterfeiting, and other minor crimes. In 1891 he entered the big time with a series of rather brutal murders and robberies. Infuriated by the imprisonment of some anarchist workingmen whose only crime had been shooting back when attacked by police, he began to stage *attentats*. (This word, meaning outrages, was used by the French press to distinguish anarchist violence from governmental violence, which was OK). After blowing up the houses of two of the magistrates involved, he was captured, tried, and executed. Initially the anarchists were leary of Ravachol, suspecting him of being a madman or even a provocateur. However, before long his obvious courage, intelligence, and defiant demeanour convinced them that, however misguided, he was a comrade.

Even before his trial was over, the Restaurant Véry, where he was captured after a waiter tipped off the police, was blown up, providing the movement with a number of jokes about *Vérification*. After his death he was elevated from the rank of suspected spy to a symbol of defiance, a martyred saint, and, in the words of one admirer, "*le Renovateur du Sacrifice Essentiel.*" To the French language he contributed a dance—*La Ravachole*, an explosive—*ravacholine*, and a verb—*ravacholiser*, "to blow up."

Despite his courage and ferocity, Ravachol was a scrupulous and idealistic man who sincerely believed that the violence he committed would someday help to bring about a world of peace and brotherhood.

Only one other terrorist, Emile Henry, surpassed Ravachol in violence. He was atypical in that he was a well educated man, not a poor laborer. He was also completely ruthless and cold-blooded. Other terrorists approached their work as executioners, not as killers pure and simple. They bombed *bourgeois* institutions —the stock exchange, the parliament, or symbols of bourgeois decadence— expensive dance halls, and so forth; but when they attacked individuals, it was in reprisal. Henry, however, shunned the passionate human approach of the working-class revolutionary for the purely dispassionate, logical approach of the ivory tower intellectual. He declared war on the *bourgeoisie* itself. His first *attentat* killed five police; but his second horrified the entire movement, including the literary dilettantes who from their own towers often showed a rather bloodthirsty detachment. (As one poet had remarked, "What do the victims matter if the gesture is beautiful?") Henry threw a bomb into a cafe filled with diners, wounding twenty and killing one.

After his capture he continued to show a cold, implacable logic but no sign of remorse. Since all *bourgeois* ultimately profited from exploitation, there were no innocent parties. And as for non-*bourgeois* patrons of the cafe, "It is necessary to hit the bourgeois, but also those who are satisfied with the present order, those 300 franc a month employees who applaud the government's actions . . . that pretentious and silly mass . . ."[1] Stressing the cultural as well as the political aspects of the struggle, he declared that, "I have carried in this fight a profound hatred, accentuated each day by the revolting spectacle of this society where everything is low, everything is suspicious, everything is ugly, where everything is an obstacle to the pouring out of human passions, to the generous propensities of the heart, to the free flight of thought."[2]

Convicted, he remained an intellectual fanatic to the end. "In this pitiless war that we have declared on the *bourgeoisie*, we ask no pity. We give death; we know how to undergo it. Thus, I await your verdict with indifference."[3]

Most of the terrorists shared certain outlooks and beliefs, even the psychopathic Henry who, because of his education, was articulate about them. To begin with, the enemy had three faces: Property, Authority, and Religion. Property was theft, being taken from the wealth produced by labor. This robbery and exploitation was sanctified by the institutional church and enforced by the state.

As to the value and validity of individual actions, there was a widespread feeling in the 1880's that the Revolution would not come as a clash of two great armies, but as a series of small skirmishes, so that individuals and small groups had a definite role. Unlike Russia where assassinations were always determined by a central committee of social revolutionaries, all the French *attentats* were the actions of individuals or tiny groups of individuals.

Violence served both moral and educational ends. First of all, it punished rulers for their actions. Fallen comrades, strikers, the oppressed—all could be avenged. Furthermore, the dramatic nature of the *attentat* would scare hell out of the ruling elite. Realizing that they could never again feel safe, they would become demoralized. In their fear and desperation they would show even more clearly their true nature, thus angering and radicalizing the populace. ("There will be one more anarchist in prison but one hundred more in the street. And our example will be followed."—Léveillé.) The proletariat would realize its own strength and the extreme vulnerability of the *bourgeoisie* at the same time that it perceived that it was the anarchists who fully backed the workers' cause. What was needed were acts that would "arouse the mass, jolt it with a violent whiplash, and show it the vulnerable side of the *Bourgeoisie*, all a-tremble even at the moment that the Revolutionary walks to the scaffold."[4]

There was also a strong element of martyrdom for some terrorists. The average bombthrower or assassin was wretchedly poor, uneducated or semieducated, and desperate. The revolution would come someday but it might not be for a long time. Their own actions could at best speed the process a little. In the meantime, faced with a future of poverty, oppression, and frustration, they chose instead a wild, libidinal outburst—a violent assertion of their own individuality. They would end quickly, violently, and with glory—fighting or under the guillotine. Some, sentenced to prison, died leading prison revolts. At least, however, they had hit back and their deeds and their deaths served as example and inspiration for their comrades who would someday establish a society in which violence and coercion played no part.

The assassination of President Carnot in 1894 marked the end of the "heroic period." The government had armed itself with harsh new legislation to crush the terrorists, but it was too late. The movement had changed its form. A few newspapers were closed and one mass trial of militants was held; most were released except for one small group of illegalist bandits. The small circles of propagandists, having assessed their past tactics and found them wanting, had disbanded and entered the unions to build an anarcho-syndicalist labor movement. The future, save for a few *attentats* and outbursts of illegalism, was devoted more to building the new than to destroying the old.

"When society refuses you the right to existence, you must take it and not hold out your hand—that is cowardice." Duval[5]

As early as 1886 the anarchists had found themselves confronted with the question of illegalism. A burglar named Clément Duval maintained at his trial that he was guilty not of robbery, but of restitution. A tiny segment of anarchist opinion had held that since *bourgeois* property was the result of theft and exploitation, there was no moral wrong in taking it back for one's personal needs and for the support of the movement. As with Ravachol a few years later, initial suspicion changed to sympathy as the anarchists studied Duval's speeches and actions. Nonetheless, though it found some practitioners (for example, Pini, who on being sentenced in 1887 cried out, "Long live Anarchy! Down with the thieves!"),[6] illegalism and *la reprise individuelle* played no important role until the turn of the century.

From 1900 to 1905 Marius Jacob ran one of the most unique "criminal" organizations in history. A bit of a dandy and the prototype of the gentleman burglar so dear to fiction, Jacob was an extreme individualist who rejected all laws and moral codes except his own. His gang of about forty burglars carried out hundreds of successful operations, conscientiously devoting ten percent of the take to anarchist propaganda. Jacob would rob no one who did anything useful, only "social parasites"—Church prelates, nobles, judges, military officers, and so forth. Once while burgling a naval officer's house, he discovered that Viaud, the officer, was also Pierre Loti, the writer, and left emptyhanded. He did the same another time when, on reading some business papers in the desk, he discovered that his victim was nearly bankrupt. Finally captured, he took the blame for all his gang's crimes and any others the cops had lying around. He turned his trial into a farce, making jokes, insulting court officials, and preaching anarchism. He displayed an excellent memory during cross-examination, reminding a priest that he had neglected to list the dirty pictures among the stolen items, and explaining to a rich housewife after hearing the prices she had payed for her valuables that she had already been robbed. Sentenced to a penal colony, he devoted his years there—until his pardon in his old age—to repeated escape attempts.

As to theft itself, Jacob was against it. "I also would like to live in a society where theft would be banned. I only approve and have only made use of theft as a means of revolt appropriate in combatting the most iniquitous of all thefts: individual property.

"To destroy an effect you must first of all destroy its cause. If there is theft, it is only because there is abundance on one hand and scarcity on the other; because everything belongs to only a few. The struggle shall not disappear ... until everything belongs to everyone."[7]

During the period of Jacob's operations, two new intellectual currents altered the nature of illegalism. One was the revival of interest in Max Stirner. Stirner was a Young Hegelian whose views, expressed in 1844 in his major work, *The Ego and His Own*, had shifted to an anarchistic individualism of such vehemence as to make Nietzsche or Ayn Rand pale by comparison. Only the individual consciousness, the Ego, has any validity and such validity applied only to the owner of that Ego. Since each Ego should have a totally subjective and self-interested view of all existence and all other Egos, all moral codes, laws, religions, and even society itself were meaningless myths imposed on the Ego from outside. The only society possible is a temporary pact between or among individuals, to last only so long as it remained beneficial to all parties.

The second new influence was a sort of scientific determinism. Too poor for schooling, some young anarchists seized upon science as a new faith. "Live in accordance with reason and science."[8] What seemed to follow the laws of logic and scientific method *had* to be true. Was alcohol and bad food debilitating? They became teetotalers, food faddists and physical culturalists; women, obviously, should not play a subservient role. The political aspects of this determinism were more harmful. Most of these workers had been through the syndicalist movement. They were aware that "leaders" and "spokesmen" always sell out. They were annoyed that so many workers could be bought off by small concessions. They knew that revolution in the standard sense was both societal and reformist and often likely to develop into a new "revolutionary state." So, instead of remaining to radicalize the anarcho-syndicalists, they felt that their "rigorous dialectic" compelled them to turn their back on the working class—those "sheep." In the words of Victor Serge (in those days known as *Le Rétif* before he became a Bolshevik), "We ... came, by force of revolutionary spirit (*révolutionnarisme*) to have no more need of the revolution."[9]

Then there was Albert, better known as *Libertad*. His real name was unknown. He arrived in Paris in 1902 and established himself immediately in the movement. A cripple, he was a skilled streetfighter, lying on his back and using his crutches to full effect. He established a series of weekly discussions and a newspaper, *L'Anarchie*, to which many illegalists and their opponents contributed. "His doctrine, which became ours, was this: 'Don't wait for the revolution. Those who promise revolution are tricksters like the rest. Make your revolution yourself. Be free men, live in comradeship.'"[10] And so they did. But though these new illegalists rejected strikes and mass movements, though many of them despised the workers, and though their devotion to their own pockets sometimes overruled their devotion to the cause, they were still anarchists. Their actions had to be examples, a showcase of a better way of life for the workers.

The finest flowering of this ideology was the Bonnot Gang, *la Bande Tragique*. In 1911 and 1912 Victor Bonnot and his friends set an example as they fought across France leaving a long trail of robberies and shootouts behind them. As much as their violence horrified people, their guts and audacity won them grudging admiration. They defied and mocked the police in letters to the press, defended their tactics in the largely hostile anarchist press, offered to turn themselves in if the rewards were raised any higher. They knew, of course, that their case was hopeless, and one after another they were killed or captured. One of the last was Bonnot who held off a rifle club, the Paris police, three National Guard companies, and a number of infantrymen long enough to write a statement of principles and a confession taking all blame on himself and maintaining the innocence of his comrades. Then he shot himself.

Despite the courage and idealism of these comrades, their tactics were wrong. In setting themselves up as judges and executioners the terrorists forsook anarchism's humanism and respect for human life and sovereignty and created, not the basis of a free society, but the basis of an aristocratic, authoritarian proto-state. The illegalists were, despite their defiance of society, essentially co-opted into a *bourgeois* emphasis on the accumulation of capital as an end in itself—even Marius Jacob. Some illegalists were not even radicals so much as hoods seeking a rationalization for their actions—the so-called *deviation apache*.

The necessity of total secrecy isolated the terrorists from the masses (the illegalists by their actions alienated themselves even more), thus leaving themselves unable to properly explain their positions and having little chance of concealment or of popular support. Having thus eliminated both aspects of a true revolutionary dynamic—namely, overall offensive and defensive strategies—they were as doomed to irrelevancy and failure as any retreatist hermit or utopian colonist.

Living the free life, development of new cultures and life styles, and exemplary actions can be an important part of an offensive strategy; but there is also a need for mechanisms of transition—institutions capable of implementing the new society so that it doesn't fall apart, for example cooperatives, soviets, syndicates, workers' committees. If the revolution is not total, old-guard forces and institutions will retain enough strength to be a menace. The individualists failed to see that technical skills, instruments of coordination and communication, and so forth would be necessary. And so, they failed. In Catalonia, by contrast the movement had a powerful union structure, technicians, defense squads, communications systems, everything. Thus, without interfering with their new life styles the Catalonians also built a total new civilization which was able to take over and run an industrial society until it was crushed by overwhelming outside force.

Similarly, the French individualists failed to consider psychological and educational factors. An anarchist movement also needs schools and teachers to teach the uneducated and to help those whose ability to think for themselves, to harness their own potentialities, and to control their own destinies has been harmed by the brainwashing that normally passes for education.

The terrorists failed to see that the real center of *bourgeois* power did not lie in individuals or symbols or even in buildings, but in powerful institutions against which only other strong institutions—revolutionary unions, federations of unions and agrarian communes, guerilla armies—could prevail. Failing to see the real source of power is a common and often tragically wasteful mistake of revolutionaries (for instance, the Irish patriots in 1916 who died holding government buildings in Dublin when the power was in London.)

Few *revolutionary* anarchists would deny the efficacy of any form of syndicalist violence, up to and including the general strike and seizure of capitalist and governmental holdings. Individual violence, however, is another matter, but as long as we have pointed out its faults, let us look at its beneficial aspects.

Even illegalism, if it has been properly handled and the funds do go to the movement, is hardly reprehensible and has in the past been carried out by groups as conservative as the Bolsheviks without sullying the movement's "good name" (Stalin's bank job in Tiflis). A better example for our purpose would be the selfless pistoleros who helped finance the Spanish anarchist movement in the days when its very existence was outlawed.

At times, a carefully planned operation against a hated symbol (for example, the statue of Nelson in Trafalgar Square that was bombed a year or two ago by Irish revolutionaries) can be worth the risks involved when the cause needs a psychic shot in the arm.

Basically, however, propaganda of the deed is of value primarily for short-term reformist ends. Reprisals against individuals do not change the system but they may make it more liveable—anything from beating a scab to the violent campaigns of the Spanish pistoleros and the Molly Maguires in the Pennsylvania coalfields. Even the French terrorists probably made the police a bit more judicious in their clampdowns on propagandists. More than once concessions have been scared out of rulers. It is doubtful that anarchism could have gotten so far in Catalonia had the police not been all too often afraid to enter working class neighborhoods. The mistake the French terrorists made was in thinking that propaganda by the deed could be the principal cause agent of the revolution.

In the final analysis the state is institutionalized violence. Created out of violence by strong men, it has been sophisticated and "routinized" by bureaucrats, but the common denominator of all states is power—that is, potential violence. The state is more than an instrument of a class, as nineteenth century revolutionaries and some more modern ones, who should know better, have all believed; it is a sovereign, self-perpetuating body which strives to centralize all the violence and power of society within itself. Any source of violence outside the state but within its boundaries weakens it. The movement must have a capacity for violence, but must not use it blindly like our Parisian comrades. We must use it pragmatically, weighing needs and consequences, but when needed, *it must be used.*

For obvious reasons the propagandists of the deed and the illegalists have left relatively little literature other than a few short polemical articles, explosives manuals, etc. The best source for their beliefs is their confessions and statements made after their arrests. Fortunately Jean Maitron reprints large portions of this material in two of his books: the excellent and very thorough *L'Histoire du Mouvement Anarchiste en France, 1880–1914*, and the collection of statements *Ravachol et les Anarchistes*. Guilbert Guilleminault and André Mahé have good but romanticized accounts of anarchist exploits in their history, *L'Épopée de la Révolte*. Some good material can be found in a special issue (January, 1937) of *Le Crapouillot*, particularly in the articles; "*Le Terrorisme Anarchiste*" by Alexandre Croix, and "*La Pensée Anarchiste*" by Victor Serge. In English there is little of note. For a general view I would recommend the chapter on France in George Woodcock's *Anarchism* (Meridian). There is one as yet unpublished but very good analytical view of the internal life of the Stirnerite milieu after the turn of the century, in Richard Greeman's *Victor Serge: The Making of a Novelist, 1890–1928*. (Ph.D. dissertation at Columbia University.)

Notes

* Bill Goring is a Columbia College graduate, a stevedore, and a member of the Industrial Workers of the World (I.W.W.). The views expressed in this paper do not necessarily represent Columbia College, stevedores, or the I.W.W.
 1. Guilleminault and Mahé, p. 121.
 2. Maitron, *Ravachol*, p. 105.
 3. *Ibid.*, p. 112.
 4. Maitron, *L'Histoire*, p. 221. Henry is the speaker.
 5. *Ibid.*, p. 169.
 6. *Ibid.*, p. 171.
 7. Maitron, *Ravachol*, p. 24.
 8. Serge, in *Le Crapouillot*.
 9. *Ibid.*, p. 6.

34

GEORGE L. PEABODY

Power, Alinsky, and Other Thoughts

*I*n the Spring of 1969 black students at Cornell University legally armed themselves with shotguns and rifles. University policies changed.

In the Fall of 1969 the United States threatened to cut off tourism to Mexico. Marijuana crops were destroyed.

These were two effective actions because they produced intended results. They demonstrate that power is simply the ability to act effectively.

I shall deal here with a working description of power and its solid basis—self-interest. Then I shall show how men organize for power. Finally, I shall provide guidelines for the strategic and tactical use of power.

PRACTICALLY SPEAKING

The measure of power is results, regardless of the force of the applied effort. In the above examples, force was only threatened, not applied, but the strength of the power is clear.

Consider other examples: A manager sends a directive and people jump. A lady raises an eyebrow and men flock. Minimal efforts but effective results. That is power. However, a boxer may smash only air with a wild punch. Half a million American soldiers fight for years in a country the size of Montana. Much effort; no results. That is impotence. Any social effort that fails to get results is not power. It is only effort. Power is as power does.

"Power is the ability to give rewards and punishments *as seen by* the persons receiving them."[1] While no shots were fired at Cornell and no United States tourism was cut off from Mexico, both the University and the Mexican government *believed* they were confronted by overwhelming forces to which they had to accede.

Written especially for this volume.

If A is the agent(s) exerting power and P is the person(s) upon whom power is exerted, then P's perception of A's strength is more important than A's actual strength. Of course A's power is related to his objective strength, but the two are not identical as they are in physics. *Social* power is in the eyes of the beholder.

Early in the power game, Gideon routed a large army of Midianites (a host, to be exact) with three hundred noisy men. At night they gave the illusion of being a host themselves (Book of Judges, Chapter 7). Illusion has been the name of the game ever since, except that now we have technicians paid to project images into the minds of voters, consumers and enemies. If A is to have power, then his first task is to make P perceive him as one able to reward or punish.

Men organize for power. All individuals have power; everyone can do some things effectively by themselves, but in the power world individuals have the weight of social dust. Whatever the purposes (to govern, make money, pray, administer, have a party, make war, teach), the reason for the organizing effort is to act more effectively. In union is the strength to give substantial rewards and punishments.

Organization may mean a network of friends or a loosely-tructured movement or a disciplined outfit. The type of organization depends on the amount of power needed—the more muscle required, the more solid must be the organizational skeleton.

In the first Federalist Paper, Alexander Hamilton wrote, "The vigor of government is essential to the security of liberty." Calling for the acceptance of the new Constitution, he proposed to discuss "The utility of the Union to your political prosperity and the insufficiency of the present Confederation to preserve that Union." Hamilton was calling for "a more perfect union" in order to constitute power on a more solid basis. With organization, then, there is significant power to act.

SELF-INTEREST

Politicians assume that what makes a man move is his own self-interest. If P sees A as strong enough to reward or punish his self-interest, then A has power. Therefore, a keen understanding of self-interest is a practical necessity.

We live in a culture where self-interest is not openly valued. People with "higher" motivations feel uneasy about their own self-interests, or don't wish to recognize such "base" motivations in others. Quite simply, working with self-interest produces results, regardless of how noble or base the motives. Power is what works and that is our only concern for the moment.

A change agent who wishes to be effective cannot afford to be confused about his *own* self-interests. Most people feel naked if they reveal their true motivations. Understandably, they design wonderful morals and rationalizations to clothe this reality. As Mark Twain wrote, "Humanity lives a life of uninterrupted self deception." But at the critical moments, when power confronts power, there is the deepest kind of personal confrontation. Your allies have to know exactly "where you are at." "Are you with us or not?" If they don't know and you can't tell them, they will be justifiably afraid to move with you. Adlai Stevenson once said, "The important thing is not to believe your own propaganda." When recognizing one's own interests, it is vitally important to be unprincipled. And when Harry Truman said, "I can't be moral on my country's time," he was saying quite succinctly that national interests cannot be entrusted to a moralizing man.

Only the solidly-supported people and institutions can afford to believe their own rhetoric (for example, the very rich, some monks and the fellows of academies and foundations). The protected state of their self-interests enables them to live in outer space. Mark Twain described an ethical man as a Christian who holds four aces. If you've got them you can afford to be "ethical"; the rest of us must live more functionally.

Nor can an effective change agent afford to be confused about the self-interests of *others*. We already know that illusion is the first rule of the game. It is essential to distinguish self-interest from propaganda, naked power from its disguises, four aces from bluffing, Gideon's army from the noise. Political survival depends on it. "What is prestige?" John Kennedy once asked. "Is it the shadow of power or the substance of power? We are going to work on the substance of power."[2]

There is no reason to believe the propaganda of the antipoverty program, for instance. Is anyone still naive enough to think that it was enacted in the spirit of the American myth of "maximum feasible participation" of its citizens, or because poverty is a tragic condition? The punitive welfare program already attests to the general public perception of the "lazy" poor. Antipoverty programs exist because ghetto residents see the affluence around them and are beginning to demand a share of it. The fact that the programs have been poorly funded and disastrously administered suggests that more powerful interests might be affected if the programs were to succeed.

President Kennedy knew that the fairness, if not the favoritism, of the reporters had helped to elect him, but he was not fooled. He also knew that most of the editors and publishers had been out to defeat him. "Always remember," he once told Sorensen, "that their interests and ours ultimately conflict."[3]

BUILDING AN ORGANIZATION—A CHANGE MODEL

Whatever your role—company manager, self-styled Castro, college dean, missionary or society hostess—if you need more power to act, your aim must be to build (or change) an appropriate organization to provide it for you. The change processes you must consider are defined by the change needs of any human system.

I will describe Saul Alinsky's[4] model for building a community organization, with a few alterations in his terminology. The model contains most of the change phases that are also described by Lippitt, Watson and Westley in *Planned Change*.[5] Moreover, the core of Alinsky's model (Entry, Data collection, Goal-setting, and Organizing) corresponds exactly to the four model concerns in group development identified by Jack and Lorraine Gibb (Acceptance, Data flow, Goal Formation and Social Control).[6] These parallels are no coincidence; the study of power requires the keenest observation of social dynamics. Whether or not he read any of these behavioral scientists, Alinsky made similar observations years ago, and applied them to his own imaginative manner. Let us look at his model:

A CHANGE TEAM IS ORGANIZED

A few people coalesce over several similar self-interests. These interests are no vague, do-good concerns; the problem is clear to them, they own it and feel keenly about it. Alinsky stresses that no change can occur until people are hurting.

They analyze the self-interests of persons and groups in the social system to determine who can significantly reward or punish their efforts—a power analysis.

They decide that the anticipated results will be worth the organizing effort.

THEY MOVE INTO THE LARGER ORGANIZATION OR COMMUNITY TO COALESCE POWER

Two tasks become apparent:

Entry. "Entry" really means developing credibility, or getting a licence to operate. The power given with this trust is essential for further activity. Even elected leaders have limited credibility, and it is their task to obtain further authorization. It is a subtle testing process. Has A been checked out by the local leaders? Has he been introduced by the right people? What is *his* self-interest? Can he be depended upon to understand and work competently for our interests? Has he proved himself at critical times? Can he be trusted to mean what he says?

John Kennedy made instant entry into Germany when he resolved these questions in a single dramatic sentence "Ich bin ein Berliner!" Usually, it takes more time for the people to understand and believe. You work and you wait, knowing that nothing can happen until you are authorized. The doors are opening when you begin to see signs of confidence and acceptance. Or else you don't. If public opinion crystallizes against you, the closed doors are locked. Lyndon Johnson lost his license because a "credibility gap" forced him to abdicate. His successor has had similar difficulties. A newspaper columnist put it this way: "It (Vietnam war) has robbed the average citizen of a precious heritage: his feeling of trust in his government. We are lied to by the Pentagon, the CIA, the Army and—most shameful—by the President."[7] The media are so instantaneous today that the effective lie is far more difficult to execute than it was in Lincoln's day, for example. Credibility and entry today require the most simple truth-telling, or else much more skillful mendacity than is being practiced.

Data Collection. Two kinds of information are particularly needed: (1) What are the self-interests of the people? Go to them directly. No one knows their interests as well as they do.

(2) Who are the natural leaders in the system? These are the people to work with. "If you know who these are," says Alinsky, "you have the telephone number of the community." When I was working with an organizer among the "Untouchables," along the Malabar coast in southwest India, we would create situations requiring leadership; then we would see who moved. We would stop to care for a sick man, lying in the road, and call out for water, a place to shelter him or strong hands to move him. In the gathering crowd, a few townspeople responded. We ran a similar test the next week, and selected those who had responded both times.

A friend of mine opened a store-front pool room as a base for organizing people in a Connecticut town. For several weeks, he noticed that only a few young men were coming in to play pool and talk with him; after a while, others drifted in. When he asked them why they came, he was told that he had been checked out and approved by the earlier fellows. By accident, he had found his local leaders, and had also made entry.

GOAL-SETTING AND ORGANIZING

The power of self-interest is harnessed when it is translated into common goals. Alinsky's experience in community organization has shown that as people come together to unify their efforts for power, they tend to see that their self-interests are related to those of their colleagues. "I need your help with my housing problem and you need my help with your school problem, so let's make a deal. I'll support you if you support me." After this negotiation is completed, the dynamics for collaboration begin. People being to learn that "my" world needs other people and communities—this is at the heart of organizing. There will be a variety of interests requiring several goals; together they make up the program (or platform).

Alinsky specifies three criteria for working goals:

(1.) They must be highly *specific*: people won't work for "justice" but they will work to prevent a highway from being built through their community.

(2.) They must be *realizable*: there should be reasonable hope of success, however small. A limited goal gives the opportunity for visible success, and success is needed by most people in order to feel their strength. The gained confidence will enable them to take more vigorous steps next time.

(3.) They must be *immediate*: people get excited when they feel they can do something effective immediately. Hope releases energy, and this is power if it is used right away.

ESTABLISH A TIGHT-KNIT ORGANIZATION THAT CAN STAND UP UNDER PRESSURE

A movement without any organization can lose its shape and become impotent under pressure from other power groups. Therefore, its structure and discipline should enable it to make its own independent decisions and to sustain efforts toward its goals. In Alinsky's model, this process culminates in an organizing convention, where representatives of the community groups meet to elect officers and establish a legal constitution and by-laws for the community organization.

One final note about organizations: One of the pervading myths about power is that 51 percent of the people are required to effect change. Nothing could be further from the truth. A survey of several organized groups (that is, Unions and Churches) revealed that 4 percent of the membership was giving the direction;[8] 96 percent of the people were politically passive, either neutral or apathetic. As long as the general mass of the people is not against a small organization, it appears that the organization has a license to operate in that community. According to Alinsky, when the mass is generally *in favor* of the organization, then a well-disciplined core of as little as one to 2 percent has that power. "History is made and saved by creative minorities" (Arnold Toynbee).

You may remember the Old Testament story in which the Lord told Abraham that he would not destroy Sodom if there were as many as fifty righteous men in the city. After further negotiations with Abraham, he reduced the number to ten. That is a very small minority. Since even ten could not be produced, the city was destroyed. In that case, the minority necessary for urban renewal was just too small.

THREE ACTION STRATEGIES: COLLABORATION—FIGHT—NEGOTIATION

Strategy is the policy selected for exerting power for one's interests. Tactics are the maneuvers made to effect the strategy.

Action begins when one man moves out to confront another. He can collaborate with him to build power, fight to take the other's power, or negotiate for a desirable exchange of power. When power groups do business, they have the same three choices. A city politician described these three power strategies as "Personal, Clout and Chits." How is the proper strategy selected? The test is: If one party satisfies his self-interest, will the other be able to satisfy his? Let us consider this further.

PERSONAL

The currency is trust and the action is collaboration. If two men belong to the same political party, same athletic team or same business, they both can win if their groups win. It may even be that one can win only if the other wins also. Their self-interests converge; collaboration is appropriate.

Putting together a program which reflects the various self-interests of a community is a highly collaborative process. As people learn that they can meet their own needs better by helping each other, they are ready to move together.

CLOUT

The currency is force and the action is coercion. If two parties are political opponents campaigning for the same office, or tenants and landlords concerned about rent levels or two business concerns producing the same product, both cannot win. Their interests conflict. To the degree that one wins, the other loses. Fighting is appropriate, provided at least one party estimates the cost of the fight to be worth it. Otherwise, negotiation is in order.

It is naive to assume, as many do, that power is used only in fight strategies. Power is used just as much, if less dramatically, in negotiation and collaboration. But it is equally naive to assume that fighting is avoidable or unproductive. When fight conditions exist, it is dangerous to collaborate and useless to negotiate.

Alinsky, who has helped thousands to collaborate, says that "Change means movement and movement means friction and friction means heat and heat means conflict.... You just can't get the rocket off the ground discreetly and quietly.... Disengagement from conflict is disengagement from the world, and that is death, not peace." Senator Fulbright has said the same thing, perhaps more elegantly: "It is our expectation that these proceedings may generate controversy. If they do, it will not be because we value controversy for its own sake, but rather because we accept it as a condition of intelligent decision making."[9]

CHITS

The currency is obligation and the action is exchange. It is appropriate to consider negotiating when the parties have conflicting interests, but *both* respect the other's power enough to reject fight strategies as too costly. By entering into negotiations, both sides admit that they have power, and that they are willing to compromise their interests in an exchange of value for value. The important thing to remember is that the powerful and the powerless cannot negotiate. If both should come to the same bargaining table, the latter is simply a beggar.

Informal negotiating goes on every day. When I do you a favor, this gives me a chit of obligation which I can cash in for a favor from you. A press officer in New York City spends most of his time doing favors for the key people in his work. When a story breaks he will need help fast and won't have time to go about negotiating for it; he simply cashes in his chits.

FIGHT TACTICS

As we have seen, the appropriate strategy is determined by the relative self-interests and power of the groups involved. When the strategy has been selected, action is required to make that strategy effective. The action steps (or tactics) are always tailored to the immediate situation, but they should be carefully designed along certain guidelines.

The following guidelines are for designing fight tactics. They were developed by Saul Alinsky (a master tactician), during his experience in mass-based community organizations. Showing a keen perception of human behavior, these guides are also helpful in designing tactics for negotiation and collaboration, although these two strategies will not be stressed here.

"START FROM WHERE YOU ARE AND USE WHAT YOU'VE GOT"[10]

Obviously one can't do anything else, but many people still find it difficult to take the world as it is and not as they would like it to be. When I was consulting with a national organization in East Africa, my clients were incapable of planning a vigorous strategy because they saw themselves as poor. They had only £50,000 sterling and saw nothing else that they had as usable resources. They would not start from where they were. Once they realized how rich they were in land and people, they made splendid plans.

When Gandhi was fighting the British for control of India, he was confronted by a well-disciplined imperial army.[11] What did Gandhi have?—millions of illiterate, demoralized, undernourished fellow countrymen. All over India they just sat around apathetically. There was no chance of mobilizing and training this rabble to do battle. Gandhi didn't try. What else did he have? At the time, the imperial power was knit together by the railway network, which provided necessary communications and transport. Gandhi designed a tactic to employ his fellow Indians, simply by asking them to do their natural sitting-around—on the railroad tracks. They ultimately disrupted communication and transport as effectively as any well-trained army. Gandhi had something else which he needed to make this tactic possible—a certain decency of the British in their unwillingness to shoot the rail-sitters. This was critical; without this "support" the tactic could have been a disaster.

Surely Gandhi, like Dr. Martin Luther King, is revered as much for his nonviolent philosophy as for the social leadership he provided. A tough-thinking political pragmatist, however, must necessarily consider the possibility that these nonviolent rationales are splendid clothing for the lack of naked power available to their authors. It will not come as a surprise to a fight tactician to hear that Gandhi changed his rationale when he was in different circumstances some years later. When independent India and independent Pakistan were confronting each other in Kashmir, Gandhi said he had been "an opponent of all warfare. But if there was no other way to secure justice from Pakistan . . . the Indian Union would have to go to war against it."[12]

"THERE IS A POSITIVE AND NEGATIVE TO EVERY SITUATION"

Every cloud has a flip side and so does every silver lining. You may not immediately see them both but they are there. Keep turning a situation around and around until they both stand out. Then you can exploit the positive and be on guard for the negative.

The apathy of the Indians, and decency of the British toward them, must appear at first glance to be negatives for Gandhi. It's difficult to arouse an apathetic people, particularly if the colonial government is not all bad. Yet Gandhi discovered the positives in these factors and used them to his advantage.

Imagine the several steps required by a savings bank to open an account: an interview, a form to fill, a minimal $1.00 deposit, a stamped bank book and a signature. To stop a savings account requires similar steps in reverse order. This process is a positive for the bank since it provides firm and orderly control. Turn this around and the negative shows up: the complexity and expense of opening and closing a $1.00 account. That negative for the bank might be a positive for an organized group fighting the bank's policies. What if they opened 50 new $1.00 savings accounts on Monday, closed them on Tuesday and repeated this over and over? Just imagine it!

"MEN WON'T MOVE EXCEPT UNDER THE THRUST OF THREAT"

Particularly in fight situations, men will move when they believe that something worse will happen to them if they don't move. "Do it, or else." Design your fight tactics to be seen by the opposition as punishing to their self-interest. Then threaten to use them. It's a stick-up, pure and simple, and it's popular in all circles.

In 1969 a Mississippi senator threatened to withhold his important support for President Nixon's missile program unless the integration processes in his home state were slowed down. Only the threat was made, but Nixon believed it enough to acquiesce. Only threats were made by the United States to Mexico and by the Cornell students to the University. They were believed; that was enough.

It is better to threaten than to fight because it is less costly, but bluffs work only so long. You *can* fool all the people much longer than is generally thought (illusions being so widespread and untested), but you can't do it all the time. You have power only so long as the opposition believes you can and will do what they say you'll do. Be ready, therefore, to back up your threats. If you are challenged and can't deliver, your opposition will correctly see you as an impotent empty threat. To reduce the possibility of being challenged, it is worthwhile to fight easy fights just to "prove" you can, and will, deliver. This makes threatening easier at a later time.

Alinsky says, "You've heard it said that it's better to light a candle than to curse the darkness, but *I'm* telling you its better to light a candle and apply it to the tenderest portion of your enemy's anatomy." And when your enemy will believe you, it is easier just to light the candle.

"COMMUNICATE WITHIN THE EXPERIENCE OF YOUR ALLIES AND OUTSIDE THE EXPERIENCE OF YOUR OPPOSITION"

Clear communication is essential, of course, in uniting your allies in trust and common action. To be understood, you must talk and act in ways that are already familiar to them. That's why an organizer tries to discover the local leaders—they can communicate and interpet for him. Any teacher or speaker knows he must provide illustrations familiar to his listeners. The Training Director of a large company offered to double my fee if I would shave my beard before working with his department. He was right; a beard was outside the experience of his men and would prevent communication. When Gandhi asked his people to sit on the tracks, that was something they understood and trusted. It was within their experience.

With your opposition, however, design your tactics to be outside their experience. Surprise or shock them. Violate their expectations or do something they have never seen before—it will make them confused, frightened and irra-

530   *Violence and Coercion as Strategies of Social Intervention*

tional. They may even withdraw, but they definitely wont be able to cope with the problem. This is just what a fighter wants in his opponent.

General Sherman had tried for weeks to catch and destroy the Confederate army of General John B. Hood, "but he had not had much luck, and he complained bitterly, if illogically, that the real trouble was Hood's eccentricity: 'I cannot guess his movements as I could those of (General) Johnston, who was a sensible man and did only sensible things.' "[13] Apparently Hood could move outside of Sherman's experience. Sherman soon gave up the pursuit entirely and made plans for his march to the sea, "the strangest, most fateful campaign of the entire war, like nothing that happened before or afterward."[14] By moving outside the confederate experience, the march created panic.

My white-haired mother is a bishop's wife and a "Boston brahmin." In the deep South she is recognized as a "lady," though she is a Yankee to her breezy soul. In April, 1964, she lunched with a black lady in a restaurant in St. Augustine, Florida. Their purpose was to help Martin Luther King give high visibility to the town's segregationist practices. Since St. Augustine depended largely on tourists, it could ill afford bad press, especially on the eve of its 300th anniversary. It was outside the experience of the local citizenry for a "lady" to eat publicy with a Negro, and it confused them into making the serious mistake of jailing her. Once in jail, she was news, and the very *type* of person St. Augustine was hoping to lure to its expensive hotels was now pictured across the nation receiving another kind of hospitality. Having a "lady" in jail was *entirely* outside their experience, and the local white leaders became frantic. Some of them told me, "For God's sake, get that lady out of jail and take her home!" With her purpose splendidly accomplished, she flew home to her delighted family.

Picketing and demonstrations used to be effective, but now they are a familiar sight and rarely excite the opposition. At a big-city antipoverty agency there are black police officers on regular duty, city commissioners assigned regular days for meeting with the demonstrators on their frequent visits, and a room kept ready for the purpose. It is all very relaxed. The familiar tactics don't work. New and unfamiliar tactics need to be designed.

MASS JUJITSU

"Design your tactics to use the strength of your opponents to advantage, and you can count on them as your greatest 'ally.' Work outside his experience. Confuse him. Goad him to react irrationally—then use what he does! *The real action is in the reaction.*"

When Saul Alinsky rose to speak in a Texas city, he was confronted by a large delegation of the Klan which filled up the front rows in the auditorium. As he reported it, "There were so many sheets around, I thought there was a white sale." A tasteful powder-blue sheet indicated the Klan leader. As he spoke, Alinsky continued to wonder what his opponent's strength really was. Deciding that it was their racial bigotry (a negative for Alinsky), he designed a jujitsu tactic to turn the situation into a positive. Interrupting his speech, he said in effect, "You know, I took physical anthropology years ago. Among other things, we studied the facial characteristics of the different races. Now I've been looking carefully at the face of that man in the powder-blue sheet, and I could *swear* that he is a Negro." There was a shock among the Klansmen as Alinsky continued his speech, but they began to stare fixedly at the Klan leader. In their irrational, bigoted eyes, he was somehow already becoming a Negro. The strength of the opposition was now being used against itself. Suddenly the leader folded his tent, rose and left with a few Klansmen straggling after him.

In the Spring of 1969, SDS students were leading a mass meeting in the Harvard Yard. They were trying to enlist the sympathies of the moderate students—the great majority of those present at the meeting. The University strength was represented by large numbers of police. SDS successfully goaded the police into such punitive action that the moderates were shocked. Their sympathies were immediately aroused against the University, and SDS had won the day. Without the help of their University "ally," they could not have done so well. The action was in the reaction.

"WHEN YOU ACT, GO 100 PERCENT"

No issue is absolutely clear, with 100 percent right on one side and 100 percent wrong on the other. There are so many positives and negatives, that it is usually around 52 percent to 48 percent. "The mark of a free man is that gnawing doubt about whether or not he is right" (Learned Hand). No one can be absolutely sure. But once you have decided to move into action, the task is no longer to decide but to mobilize your strength; now you are "completely sure" and you create the illusion among allies and opponents alike that you are 100 percent right. There can be no doubts showing.

There was nothing objective about the Declaration of Independence.[15] Honest thought was not intended. It was a manifesto whose tactical purpose was to arouse Americans to arms. The difficult decision to fight had already been made, and it was time for action. It declared that the purpose of the King of Great Britain was to establish "an absolute tyranny over these States," and submitted "Facts" to a "candid World." The "Facts" reported the King's activity in the colonies:

"quartering large Bodies of Armed Troups among us," not mentioning the fact that the troups sometimes provide helpful protection; "imposing taxes on us without our Consent," not mentioning that some of these taxes were channelled back for the support of the colonies.

The Declaration laid it on thick: "He has plundered our Seas, destroyed our Coasts, burnt our Towns and destroyed the lives of our People."

When it is time for action, let the trumpet blow a certain blast.

Notes

1. Richard Beckhard. *Organizational Development: Strategies and Models.* New York: Addison-Wesley, 1969.

2. Arthur Schlesinger. *A Thousand Days*. Boston: Houghton Mifflin, 1965.

3. Theodore Sorensen. *Kennedy*. New York: Harper and Row, 1965.

4. Saul Alinsky is a professional community organizer, and Executive Director of the Industrial Area Foundation in Chicago. He wrote *Reveille for Radicals* over twenty years ago, and is currently completing *Rules for Revolution*, to be published by Random House. Much of this paper is based on the things this author has learned as he travelled and studied with Alinsky.

5. Ronald Lippitt, J. Watson and B. Westley. *The Dynamics of Planned Change*. New York: Harcourt, Brace and Co. 1958.

6. Jack Gibb. "Some Dimensions of Group Experience," lecture delivered at the National Training Laboratories, Bethel, Maine, July 18, 1962.

7. Harriet Van Horne, *New York Post*, October 10, 1969.

8. Saul Alinsky. *Reveille for Radicals*. Chicago: University of Chicago Press, 1946. Chapter 10.

9. J. William Fulbright. *The New York Times Magazine*, May 15, 1966.

10. Since these tactical guidelines are Alinsky's, they are reported as his quotations.

11. Alinsky discusses Gandhi's situation in detail in "Of Means and Ends," *Union Seminary Quarterly Review*, 22 (January, 1967).

12. Arthur Koestler. "The Yogi and the Commissar," *New York Times Magazine*, October 5, 1969.

13. Bruce Catton. *This Hallowed Ground*. Garden City, N.Y.: Doubleday, 1956, 354.

14. *Ibid.*, 356.

15. Alinsky. "*Of Means and Ends*."

PART SIX

Nonviolence and Direct Action as Strategies of Social Intervention

When one thinks of the use of nonviolence as a strategy for social change, many contemporary images may come to mind: strikers marching in front of a store or industrial plant; civil rights demonstrators "sitting-in" at a lunch counter or a building lobby; or pacifists refusing military service. Further reflection on the subject of nonviolence will lead one to recall that nonviolent action has a long and distinguished history. Civil disobedience, one form of nonviolent resistance, was practiced by Socrates over two thousand years ago. In the Far East, centuries ago, creditors fasted on debtor's doorsteps until they were paid. Many of the techniques practiced by Christ and his disciples conform to the guidelines of nonviolent activities. The American colonists tossed English tea into Boston Harbor to protest British taxes. In the nineteenth century, here in the United States, that intrepid Yankee, Henry David Thoreau, clearly stated his philosophy of civil disobedience, one which still serves as inspiration for nonviolent action. During that same century, the people of Hungary nonviolently defied the attempts of Austria's Franz Josef to tax, conscript, and rule the Hungarian populace.

Twentieth-century examples are also readily available. Much of the available literature focuses on particular campaigns and their inspirational leaders, most notably Mahatma Gandhi. In addition to a number of insightful biographies into Gandhi the man (Erikson, 1969; Bolton, 1934; Fischer, 1951; Radhakrishnan, 1949; Tendulkar, 1952), there is also an ample literature on his philosophy (Andrews, 1930; Bose, 1947; Bondurant, 1958; Dhawan, 1946; Diwakar, 1946; Shridharani, 1939) and his own accounts of his activities (Gandhi, 1940, 1932, 1942; Chander, 1945). Many of these volumes, and contemporary periodicals, record his efforts with other Indians for equal rights in South Africa, and his 26-year struggle against British rule for Indian independence. Nonviolent techniques were also used in recent times by the Danish and Norwegian people against Nazi invasion prior to World War II (Friedman, 1957; Gregg, 1959). Finally, recent American history is replete with examples from the civil rights and anti-war movements. The major civil rights figure, the late Martin Luther King, was catapulted to fame by his leadership of the 1956 Montgomery, Alabama, bus boycott (King, 1958; Miller, 1969). A counterpart to Dr. King in the anti-war effort was A. J. Mustie (Hentoff, 1963, 1967; Liberation, 1967).

While these activities and many more may seem diverse, they have all been grouped under the general heading of nonviolence and nonviolent action. One wonders, therefore, what *is* nonviolence, and how is it to be defined? What are the underlying philosophies and assumptions that characterize nonviolent action? What are the necessary psychological and sociological prerequisites for a successful nonviolent change effort? What strategies and tactics are employed to change the opponent, and what psychological and sociological mechanisms mediate these tactics? How effective has nonviolent action been, and what criteria can be used to evaluate successes and failures?

A DEFINITION OF NONVIOLENCE

Defining nonviolence is not as simple as it may seem initially, and the problem of doing so has sparked intense debate among the many students of nonviolence. Bondurant (1958) refers to nonviolence through the Hindu-Buddhist term "ahimsa," meaning "action based on the refusal to do harm." Sharp and Roberts, as reported in a book by the American Friends Service Committee (1967) indicate that " . . . nonviolence refers to (1) abstention from violence on the basis of a moral or religious principle or belief system or (2) the behavior of people abstaining from the use of violence in a conflict situation." A quite straightforward definition is offered by Naess (1958), which is quite simply that any ethic containing a norm against violence, is, by definition, a nonviolent ethic.

It is clear that the three definitions offered above (and others that are available) are ambiguous and contradictory. At least three questions may be raised immediately:

(1) Does nonviolence imply an abstinence from both physical and psychological violence? Naess (1958) argues that his definition implies the exclusion of both elements in the change agent's orientation; yet Bondurant and others (Galtung, 1959) only refer to an abstention from physical violence. The guidelines for determining physical injury are easy to agree upon, but "psychic terror" is a more elusive phenomenon. When does a strong influence for attitude or behavior change become terroristic? Are successful economic boycotts or mass demonstrations violent because they lead to inconvenience, loss of face, and even economic or political ruination for the target groups? The weight of current evidence indicates that actions which do not employ physical aggression should be categorized as nonviolent.

(2) Should the definition of nonviolence only refer to the change agent's behavior? Naess' definition is a normative one, based on an observer's perception of nonviolent acts; but one man's violence is another man's nonviolence. When demonstrators sit in a doorway, physically blocking access to a building, or when a demonstration prevents access to food, the question of physical violence is obviously debatable. Complicating this problem even further is the fact that one's perception of a nonviolent action will be altered by his role in the act. For example, whether one is the change agent, or the victim, or a bystander, or a historical scholar of nonviolence will influence his perceptions of the action, including its perceived legitimacy and success.

(3) Is nonviolence only a strategy for successful change which may be used by any change agent? Or is it also a way of life which severely limits those who may use it? This is a distinction that continually weaves through the literature on nonviolence. It is integral not only to a definition of nonviolence, but to the development of particular strategies, to the choice of certain tactics, and to the evaluation of successes and failures by actors, targets, and audiences. Many authors have chosen to define nonviolence as an integral element in a personal or religious value system, from which the strategy and tactics naturally evolve. Examples of this approach include writers on Gandhian *satyagraha* (Andrews, 1930; Bose, 1947; Bondurant, 1958; Dhawan, 1946; Diwakar, 1946; Shridharani, 1939; Chaigne, 1961), pacifism (Galtung, 1959; Hentoff, 1963, 1967) and Christian nonviolence (Miller, 1966; King, 1958, 1963). On the other hand, nonviolent tactics may be used by persons whose choice of the tactic evolves from its expected strategic advantages for change. In these instances, nonviolence is not a necessary element in a personal value system, and violence *may* be used in other circumstances. Examples of the "purely tactical approach" include Oppenheimer and Lakey (1964), De Crespigny (1964), Zinn (1964) and Bell (1968).

Stiehm (1968) believes that the "life-style" and the "tactical" approaches to nonviolence are intertwined and often confused in the American practice of nonviolent action. She sees the two as reflecting both different beliefs about the nature of conflict and its resolution, and the requisite strategy for changing the adversary. "Conscientious" nonviolence involves a deep commitment to human values, is usually practiced by an individual rather than a group, and seeks to convert the adversary to the actor's point of view. "Pragmatic" nonviolence, on the other hand, is more typically practiced by a group; the intent is to coerce an adversary to comply with the actor's demands. Lidz (1968), commenting on this article, suggests that the two approaches are really different phases of a social intervention model: A "conscientious" phase is likely to predate a "pragmatic" phase, and any movement is likely to employ the techniques of either or both phases for certain change conditions.

Rather than dealing with the problems posed by attempting a comprehensive definition of nonviolence, several authors have tried to develop a taxonomy of nonviolence by observing, recording, and then classifying all types of nonviolent action into a comprehensive category system. Some of the typical classification dimensions are the following three:

(1) *Focal Issue Around Which the Conflict has Developed.* Sharp (1970), in a forthcoming work, classifies eighty-three separate cases of nonviolent action into eight categories, based on the *issue* surrounding the protest—anti-war, oppression of minorities, religious oppression, long established undemocratic rule, new attempts at undemocratic rule, exploitation and economic grievances, particular injustices and administrative excesses, and communal disorders. Most case studies of nonviolence are based on this approach, and examples too numerous to cite exist for each type of issue. However, the case-study approach does not permit easy cross-case comparisons, particularly to identify successful assumptions, strategies, and tactics that might be used in a variety of settings.

(2) *Action Tactics and Methods Used.* This has been the most common approach, and several systems are available. Sharp (1959) developed a category system that includes nine "generic types of nonviolence": non-resistance, active reconciliation, moral resistance, selective nonviolence, passive resistance, peaceful resistance, nonviolent direct action, *satyagraha* and nonviolent revolution. Sharp has elaborated on his work (1968 and 1970) to include an unbelievable 146 distinctively different methods.

Other typologies based on tactical approaches and methods are found in De Crespigny (1964); Oppenheimer and Lakey (1964); Hare and Blumberg (1968). For example, tactics may be classified as active or reactive (initiating change vs. responding to pressures from the opponent), and as individual-centered vs. group-centered (*e.g.*, individual fasting or self-immolation vs. collective strikes, boycotts, or marches).

(3) *Influence Attempts.* Several authors have attempted to develop a typology of nonviolent techniques on the basis of their approach to the changing individual attitudes or behavior of their opponents. Galtung (1959) subdivides techniques into those that employ either positive or negative influence attempts. Lakey (1963) classifies particular techniques and assumptions into those that attempt to change by converting the opponent, by persuading the opponent to change, or by

Introduction 537

coercing the opponent. Similar distinctions are presented by Sharp (1970). The dynamics mediating the effect of these different influence strategies will be discussed more thoroughly later in this chapter.

There are some rather obvious advantages and drawbacks to classification schemes, particularly when they are meant to be definitional substitutes for a concept. Categorization helps us to take any particular element, and to decide whether that element fits into the scheme at all, and whether it fits into a particular part of the scheme. If a classification of nonviolence serves as the operational definition of the concept, it provides a technique for assessing whether particular acts are nonviolent or not. Yet there are also drawbacks. First, schemes are often unidimensional (for example, tactics), and we have shown that any definition of nonviolence is multifaceted. For example, the classification schemes ignore the distinctions between nonviolence and violence, and do not consider whether nonviolence requires a religious, philosophical, or utilitarian base to be effectively used. Second, even if all of the classification schemes were compiled into one grand network, the systems are still at the most primitive level of scientific analysis; they describe nonviolent phenomena, but do not begin to explain how and when it works, or to predict its success. These are the issues that are critical to the interventionist considering a nonviolent strategy.

THE DYNAMICS, STRATEGY, AND TACTICS OF NONVIOLENCE

Most types of nonviolent action can be characterized as seeking to change the power relations between the change agent (and his group) and the opponent, presumably in order to increase the relative power of the change agent's group. These are typically permanent changes, not just temporary ones. Sharp (1970) indicates that the choice of nonviolent strategy and tactics can reflect either an indirect or a direct approach to the opponent's power. The indirect approach is characterized by a decision to meet the violent style of the opponent with nonviolence. Theoretically, nonviolence disconfirms the enemy's expectation of the conflict situation by using nonviolent weapons. The enemy discovers that he cannot use weapons against an unarmed man; this internal conflict may actually lead him to disarm himself (Gregg, 1959; Hare and Blumberg, 1968). The direct approach is represented by the strategic upsetting of the opponent's political bases of power-ideology, and attitudes, availability of resources, public image, and opinion of third parties. The conflict is external to the opponent, not internal.

Any clear understanding of the efficacy of nonviolence requires an analysis of both approaches. The following section will examine the data, both pro and con, on the efficacy of these perspectives.

THE INDIRECT APPROACH
A major assumption shared by nonviolent change agents is that the amount,

duration, and intensity of violence is *minimized* by nonviolent change tactics. A number of arguments may account for this tendency. Gregg (1959) suggests that using nonviolence against a violent attacker acts like a "moral jujitsu"; the nonviolent behavior throws the attacker off guard, and exhausts him through an internal conflict between his needs to vent aggressive behavior and the situational inappropriateness of attacking a passive other. Sorokin (1954) cites evidence with children and college students that "love begets love and hate begets hate." Gandhi's statement of *satyagraha* indicates that violence coerces, but does not overcome, while nonviolence converts one's enemies.

Despite the popularity of this assumption, it is not always supported by the reality of the situation. There are a variety of reasons for this:

First, communication with the opponent, even verbally (rather than in action techniques) is often met with resistance and rigidity, and may increase rather than decrease the pressures against change. Even as this is being written, President Nixon is saying that he will not be influenced by peace demonstrations against the Vietnam War.

Second, while there is an indication that the casualties are considerably less than would occur in a violent approach, the risks of both psychological and physical harm are still present. Savage beatings of student demonstrators by police at Columbia, Berkeley, and Harvard are one example; the murder of civil rights workers Schwerner, Chaney, and Goodman is another.

Third, research conducted by experimental social psychologists to examine the efficacy of *simulated* nonviolent strategies in bargaining games has not supported these views (Solomon, 1960, Bixenstein and Wilson, 1963; Lave, 1965; Shure, Meeker and Hansford, 1965; Deutsch, Epstein, Canavan and Gumpert, 1967; Lewicki, 1969). The experiments indicate that subjects who are exposed to a nonviolent other will consistently exploit the others' nonviolence. It makes little difference whether the nonviolence is grounded in explicit religious and moral beliefs. Nonviolence may work, however, when the other has reformed from a violent strategy, or when the other is willing to defend himself against aggression but not to counter-aggress (Deutsch *et al.*, 1967). In all cases, the other's nonviolent behavior is seen as peculiar—the other subjects believe he does not understand the rules, and thus behaves in a pleasant but foolish and inappropriate manner.

Finally, Sharp has indicated that nonviolence is selected as a strategy because it tactically disconfirms the opponent's expectations of violence. The opponent, in his disconfirmed state, will now be responsive to a nonviolent strategy and agree to play the game "in kind." However whether the opponent actually responds this way will depend on a myriad of factors. Some of these are as follows.

If the Nonviolent Behavior is Seen as Appropriate. The nonviolence research cited above indicates that subjects easily dismiss nonviolent behaviors as inappropriate. "Appropriate behaviors" are those which conform to situational norms; nonviolence, particularly when used as a strategy to express dissent, will be deemed inappropriate by those who endorse other norms and support the controversial policy. If the perceived norms are to support one's government while it is at war, then anti-war protests are likely to be dismissed as inappropriate. Moreover, social-psychological research has clearly demonstrated that once behavior is deemed inappropriate, it is regarded as deviant, the actor is maligned, and his influence is negated.

If the Nonviolent Tactic is New. Disconfirmation of expectations can only occur if the opponent does not expect nonviolence. For disconfirmation to work, therefore, it cannot be repeatedly used. As police and power sources learn how to break up nonviolent demonstrations nonviolently, the effect of nonviolence diminishes. One way that interventionists might overcome this is to develop a myriad of tactics to outwit the opponent and the police.

If the Nonviolent Action is Seen as Resulting from a Strategy or a Way of Life. If the opponent perceived the actor's nonviolence as based in a nonviolent style of life, there may be a greater tendency to be responsive to his behavior than if he is using nonviolence as a strategy only. In short, as a way of life, nonviolent action becomes credible. Yet if the nonviolent actor's way of life arouses strong ethnocentric reactions in his opponent (for example, feelings that all pacifists are traitors), this may lead to continued or increased violence. In terms of the efficacy of nonviolent strategies, the target conditions that warrant actors with nonviolent life styles (as opposed to those merely using nonviolent tactics) are currently unclear. Particularly when using aspects of the direct approach, interventionists do not have to believe in a nonviolent way of life to induce measurable change.

If the Opponent can Trust the Nonviolent Actor. There is some research to indicate that aggressive and exploitative behavior increases the tendency to expect similar behavior from others (Deutsch *et al.*, 1967; Lewicki, 1969). It can be expected that the violent opponent would remain on his guard toward the nonviolent demonstrator, and that considerable communication, influence, and action is required to reduce his defensiveness and increase his trust.

If the Nonviolent Actor is Valued as a Human Being. History records repeated failures of nonviolent actions because the opponents did not perceive the actors as worthy human individuals. In part, the failure of passive resistance among black South Africans resulted from white perception of the Negroes as less-than-equal beings. Similarly, many nonviolent acts by the Jews in Nazi Germany could not have worked; the Jews were seen as *untermenschen*, "less than men," and hence unfit for the respect due other men. Sharp (1969) does not agree. He points out that there were many instances in which the Jews could have used tactics of noncooperation long before World War II began—for example, refusing to register or refusing to wear the identifying "J". In addition, governments such as Bulgaria, Norway, and Denmark nonviolently refused to comply with German policy in their treatment of Jews; hence, they minimized the number of exterminations in those countries.

It seems evident that the success of an indirect approach is highly speculative, particularly in light of the number of factors that could make it fail. Gregg (1959) and others are almost naive in their description of the "ideal" indirect approach;

clearly, they make no attempt to specify the conditions under which this "moral jujitsu" will tame the opponent rather than enrage him.

THE DIRECT APPROACH

There are two major factors involved in the direct approach—techniques of attitude change and the use of third parties. Both are used to manipulate the political position of the opponent, as well as to change his behavior and/or attitudes toward the issues.

Attitude Change. Sharp's article here proposes three basic mechanisms of attitude change—conversion, accommodation, and nonviolent coercion. (Other descriptions of the basic mechanisms may be drawn from Kelman, 1958; Lakey, 1963; Perloe, Olton and Yaffee, 1968). *Conversion* occurs when the opponent changes both his attitudes and his behavior toward the nonviolent actor. It would include situations in which the opponents are attitudinally persuaded by a variety of messages, as well as situations of identification with the nonviolent actor. Exemplary tactics fall into the category of "nonviolent protest" (Sharp, 1970): declarations, petitions, vigils, pickets, teach-ins, marches.

Accommodation, as Sharp defines it, is a mild form of coercion; it is a willingness to go along with the nonviolent demonstrators without measurably changing one's attitude. This behavior change without attitude change is much like Kelman's *compliance,* and occurs when the change agent has successfully manipulated the forces of social evaluation that control the opponent. Sample tactics include acts of self-retribution and hunger strikes; the tactic is successful when the suffering of the participants becomes intolerable to the opponent or third party witnesses.

Coercion differs from accommodation in that the opponent has no choice about his compliance. He is forced to behave in a certain manner by the change agent whether he likes it or not. The tactic will sustain change only when the threat of continued or renewed action is present, or when new laws may support the change. It is interesting to note that while this technique of change is the most tenuous (in terms of its stability and the consent of the target to be changed), the number of coercive tactics in use far outnumber the other two categories combined. Of the 146 tactics listed by Sharp (1970), over 70 per cent are coercive—strikes, boycotts, refusal to pay taxes, civil disobedience, sit-downs, occupations, and sit-ins.

The large proportion of coercive nonviolent tactics, and the frequency of their use, reveals two attractive arguments for an interventionist implementing these tactics. First, coercion induces behavior change, but without the initial consent of the target to be changed. One clear advantage of accommodation and coercion tactics is that they can create dramatic social change without a felt need for change by the target; this is not possible with many of the other intervention strategies discussed in this volume. Second, tactics of nonviolent coercion avoid many of the deleterious side-effects of violent coercion—physical harm, property destruction, and escalation of confrontation to an uncontrolled conflict. Therefore, nonviolent coercion is and can be more precise and more controlled than violent coercion, while applicable to many situations that would not be responsive to organizational development or individual change strategies.

Evaluating each of these three approaches to attitude change, and the tactics involved, is beyond the scope of this volume. Perloe, Olton, and Yaffee (1968) enumerate a number of factors that affect the success of a particular attitude change effort—credibility and prestige of the source, factors in the message being communicated, immunization of the audience to influence, and the function of the attitudes to the opponent's behavior. One major point may be summarized from their work: In nonviolent action, the role of attitude change will be small, most change efforts will require coercion, and change should be accomplished with a minimal amount of force to engineer the desired changes.

Third Parties. The role of third parties often has a dramatic effect on the success of a nonviolent strategy. Their impact is based on several factors: (1) their own attitudinal position and its correspondence to the attitudes of demonstrators or the opponent; (2) their communication to the opponent about his behavior; and (3) their availability to maintain surveillance over agreed-upon changes by either party.

The first factor is relatively clear: Prestigous third parties who lend their support to the demonstrators are likely to increase the perceived pressures on the opponent to change. Even under those conditions when third parties support the goals but not the tactics of a demonstration, the impact of the third party evaluation lends support to the demonstrators. Similarly, prestigous third parties who support the opponent's position will probably decrease the likelihood of change.

There are two interesting facets to third-party communication: messages to the opponent that his response to the demonstrators made him look foolish; and messages that the third parties support the nonviolent demonstrators. An opponent could be made to look foolish by acquiescing to the demonstrators or by responding inappropriately (for example, with violence). Parties in conflict situations who are informed that they acted foolishly are likely to increase their violent, competitive behavior toward the demonstrators, in an attempt to save face (Brown, 1968).

Communication that supports the nonviolent demonstrators is particularly effective when an opponent has responded violently to the nonviolence. This violence is likely to evoke a tirade of castigation from other sympathetic third parties, resulting in guilt feelings and accommodation by the opponent. Numerous examples are available from cases of police–demonstrator conflict in Southern civil rights marches, university sit-ins and political gatherings. The embittered cry of violently beaten protesters at the 1968 Chicago Democratic Convention—"The whole world is watching!"—amply illustrates this power.

The third factor, "surveillance power," is particularly effective in accommodation and coercion strategies. Changes brought about by these behavior-change approaches require impartial third parties to monitor the future actions of both sides in the conflict. The responsibilities of third parties in this context include clarifying terms and working arrangements of an agreement, public declaration of agreement violations by either side, and perhaps acting as a mediator or arbitrator in the settlement. The role of third parties in these respects is delineated by Stevens (1963), Walton and McKersie (1965) and others.

TACTICS, TRAINING, AND NONVIOLENT CAMPAIGNS

Numerous references have been made throughout this chapter to nonviolent tactics. The selection by Oppenheimer and Lakey in this volume reviews the more popular tactics in detail, as do other sources previously mentioned. It must be stressed here that a change agent should *not* expect to achieve success with nonviolent tactics unless he has made provisions for sufficient *training* in their use, and *planning* in their application and execution. A cognitive understanding of nonviolent tactics is not sufficient. They must be rehearsed extensively with those who will be involved in the action.

Extensive personal and group training is necessary to practice the techniques, to build solidarity with other demonstrators, and to experiment with simulated confrontations. Gregg (1959) has analogized this discipline to military training itself. Oppenheimer and Lakey (1964) propose "scenario *workshops*," in which the participants role-play the primary characters in the confrontations. The participants then talk about their feelings and behavior, both as demonstrators and targets of the change. Disciplined training is also necessary to contend with counterdemonstration actions, such as police violence, tear gas, fire hoses, police dogs, and hostile mobs. While it is true that many nonviolent demonstrations have accomplished their ends with unskilled and untrained activists, the probability of tactical failure is also significantly higher. Unskilled activists are more likely to be provoked to verbal or physical violence, will not follow their leadership effectively, and do not fully understand how to use nonviolent tactics to achieve maximum effectiveness.

It should also be stated that this training is as necessary for the leadership of the nonviolent action as it is for their followers. In fact, a second major purpose of training is to build effective leadership for a nonviolent campaign. Organizations to achieve this goal are described in detail by Oppenheimer and Lakey (1964), Bondurant (1958), Gregg (1959), Miller (1966), and Sharp (1970). The characteristics of an effectively managed campaign parallel those of any effective organization practicing social intervention and change: understanding of the issue, adequate diagnosis of the community and the opponent, selection of appropriate tactics, participative decision-making with the active members, effective member education, recruiting, and publicity to build community support. Many recent scholars have argued that campaign organizations tend to follow general tactical patterns of increased confrontation, coercion, and manipulation of third party support (Bell, 1968; Zinn ,1964; Bondurant, 1958). As would be expected, the response of the opponent also moves through stages, from indifference to antagonism and perhaps eventually to negotiation and settlement.

SUMMARY

The interventionist considering nonviolent strategy and tactics must ask himself several critical questions. First, does he understand what nonviolence is, and can he separate it into ideological and action-oriented components? Is he aware that it is possible to practice nonviolent action effectively without adhering to a particular ideology or world view? Has he considered all of the potential uses (and pitfalls) of the indirect and direct approaches to nonviolent change? Is the primary change expected through forces to directly change the opponent, or through moral jujitsu and manipulating the evaluation of third parties? If the interventionist intends to rely on the direct approach, has he considered whether the situation requires a conversion, accommodation, or coercion strategy? If so, do the tactics systematically evolve from this approach to change? Finally, is there sufficient impetus for systematically planning a nonviolent campaign, and the time and opportunity for training *activists*? If the interventionist can answer all of these questions affirmatively, he will be well on the way to exacting the desired change.

OVERVIEW

The papers that follow in this section focus on a limited scope of the critical issues raised in this chapter. They primarily examine the direct approach to nonviolent change, highlighting the processes, strategy, and tactics that evolve from this method.

In the first article, Gene Sharp discusses the three major mechanisms of change in nonviolent direct action—conversion, accommodation, and coercion. Each of these mechanisms is defined, the theoretical process of change is described, and the factors which influence the "successful" or "unsuccessful" outcome of the particular mechanism are enumerated in detail. Sharp also directs attention to the factors which influence the overall success of nonviolent action struggles—those that are related to the actions of the nonviolent group, the opponent, third parties, and the characteristics of the social situation. While Sharp only summarizes these factors, other references are available to explore them in more detail.

The second article, "Direct Action Tactics" by George Lakey, is a chapter from his book with Martin Oppenheimer, *A Manual for Direct Action*. Lakey's book was directed primarily at organizers involved in civil rights demonstrations, although the tactics he reviews (under the general headings of demonstration, non-cooperation and intervention) are applicable to many social-change phenomena. The guidelines he develops for thinking about new tactics are helpful for those considering untested tactical approaches.

Morton Deutsch's article, "Conflicts: Productive and Destructive" is drawn from a longer article of the same title. Deutsch points out that certain nonviolent and violent techniques may induce change, but do not lead to a future cooperative relationship between the parties. Deutsch feels that these techniques are dysfunctional because they will not lead to better relations between the parties in subsequent interactions. This has implications for many of the tactics derived from coercive strategies of nonviolent (and violent) change. Potential interventionists must examine whether they seek to merely induce change, or whether they would like to improve the future of the relationship between the parties as well.

The final article, by Virginia Olds, reports a case study of a frequently used tactic of the civil rights campaign—freedom rides. Examined as a social movement and social change process in the broader framework of the civil rights movement, she discusses the functions of the freedom rides and the critical factors that were integral to their success for the participants and for effecting change.

References

American Friends Service Committee. *In Place of War: An Inquiry Into Nonviolent National Defense.* New York: Grossman Publishers, 1967.
Andrews, C. F. *Mahatma Gandhi's Ideas.* New York: Macmillan, 1930.
Bell, Inge Powell. *Core and the Strategy of Nonviolence.* New York: Random House, 1968.
Bixenstein, V. E. and K. V. Wilson. "Effects of Level of Cooperative Choice by the Other Player on Choices in a Prisoner's Dilemma Game," *Journal of Abnormal and Social Psychology*, 67 (1963): 139–147.
Bolton, G. *The Tragedy of Gandhi.* London: Allen and Unwin, 1934.
Bondurant, Joan V. *The Conquest of Violence: The Gandhian Philosophy of Conflict.* New Jersey: Princeton, 1958.
Bose, N. K. *Studies in Gandhism* (2nd ed.). Calcutta: Indian Associated Publishing Co., 1947.
Brown, Bert. "The Effects of Need to Maintain Face on Interpersonal Bargaining," *Journal of Experimental Social Psychology*, 4 (1968): 107–122.
Chaigne, H. "The Spirit and Technique of Gandhian Nonviolence," *Cross Currents*, 11 (1961): 117–136.
Chander, J. P. *Teachings of Mahatma Gandhi.* Lahore: The Indian Printing Works, 1945.
DeCrespigny, A. "Nature and methods of nonviolent coercion," *Political Studies*, 11 (1964): 256–265.
Deutsch, M., Y. Epstein, D. Canavan and P. Gumpert. "Strategies of Inducing Cooperation: An Experimental Study," *Journal of Conflict Resolution*, 11 (1967): 345–360.
Dhawan, G. N. *The Political Philosophy of Mahatma Gandhi.* Bombay: The Popular Book Depot, 1946.
Diwakar, R. R. *Satyagraha: Its Technique and History.* Bombay: Hind Kitabs, 1946.
Erickson, E. H. *Gandhi's Truth.* New York: Norton, 1969.
Fischer, L. *The Life of Mahatma Gandhi.* London: Jonathan Cape, 1951.
Friedman, P. *Their Brothers Keepers.* New York: Crown, 1957.
Galtung, J. "Pacifism from a Sociological Point of View," *Journal of Conflict Resolution*, 3 (1959): 67–84.
Gandhi, M. K. *An Autobiography of the Story of My Experiments with Truth.* Translated from the original in Gujarati by Mahadev Desai. (2nd ed.) Ahmedabad: Navajivan, 1940.
Gandhi, M. K. *India's Case of Swaraj: Being Select Speeches, Writings, Interviews etcetera of Mahatma Gandhi in England and India.* (2nd ed.), Waman P. Kabodi (ed.). Bombay: Yeshanand, 1932.
Gandhi, M. K. *Non-Violence in Peace and War.* Ahmedabad: Navajivan, 1942.
Gregg, R. B. *The Power of Nonviolence.* New York: Fellowship Publications, 1959.

Introduction

Hare, A. P., and H. Blumberg. *Nonviolent Direct Action*. Washington, D.C.: Corpus Books, 1968.
Hentoff, N. (ed.). *Peace Agitator*. New York: Macmillan, 1963.
Hentoff, N. (ed.). *Pacifism and Class War: The Essays of A. J. Mustie*. New York: Bobbs Merrill, 1967.
Kelman, H. C. "Compliance, Identification and Internalization: Three Processes of Attitude Change," *Journal of Conflict Resolution*, 2 (1958): 51–60.
King, C. S. *My Life with Martin Luther King*. New York: Holt, 1969.
King, M. L. *Stride Toward Freedom*. New York: Ballantine Books, 1958.
King, M. L. *Why We Can't Wait*. New York: Harper, 1963.
Lakey, G. *Nonviolent Action: How It Works*. Pennsylvania: Pendle Hill Pamphlet 129, 1963.
Lave, L. B. "Factors Affecting Cooperation in the Prisoner's Dilemma Game," *Behavioral Science*, 10 (1965): 26–38.
Lewicki, R. J. "The Effects of Cooperative and Exploitative Relationships on Subsequent Interpersonal Relations" (unpublished doctoral dissertation). New York: Columbia University, 1969.
Liberation, September–October, 12 (1967): 6–7.
Lidz, V. "A Note on Nonviolence is Two," *Sociological Inquiry*, 38 (1968): 31–36.
Miller, W. R. *Nonviolence: A Christian Interpretation*. New York: Schocken Books, 1966.
Miller, W. R. *Martin Luther King*. New York: Avon Books, 1969.
Naess, A. "A Systematization of Gandhian Ethics of Conflict Resolution," *Journal of Conflict Resolution*, 2 (1958): 140–155.
Oppenheimer, M. and G. Lakey. *A Manual for Direct Action*. Chicago: Quadrangle Paperbacks, 1964.
Perloe, S. I., D. S. Olton, and D. L. Yaffee. "The Effects of Nonviolent Attitudes on Social Attitudes," in Hare and Blumberg (eds.). *Nonviolent Direct Action*. Washington, D.C.: Corpus Books, 1968, 407–446.
Radhakrishnan, S. *Mahatma Gandhi: Essays and Reflections on His Life and Work*. (2dn ed.) London: Allen and Unwin, 1949.
Sharp, G. "The Meanings of Nonviolence: A Typology (Revised)," *Journal of Conflict Resolution*, 3 (1959): 41–66.
Sharp, G. "How Nonviolent Action Works" (unpublished manuscript). June, 1967.
Sharp, G. "Types of Principled Nonviolence," in Hare and Blumberg (eds.). *Nonviolent Direct Action*. Washington, D.C.: Corpus Books, 1968, 273–313.
Sharp, G. *The Politics of Nonviolent Action*. (Manuscript in preparation.) Boston, Massachusetts: Harvard University, 1970.
Shridaharani, K. *War Without Violence: A Study of Gandhi's Method and Its Accomplishments*. New York: Harcourt, Brace, 1939.
Shure, G., J. Meeker, and E. A. Hansford. "The Effectiveness of Pacifist Strategies on Bargaining Games," *Journal of Conflict Resolution*, 9 (1965): 106–117.
Sibley, M. Q. *The Quiet Battle*. Chicago: Quadrangle Books, 1963.
Solomon, L. "The Influence of Some Types of Power Relationships and Game Strategies on the Development of Interpersonal Trust," *Journal of Abnormal and Social Psychology*, 61 (1960): 223–230.
Sorokin, P. A. *The Ways and Power of Love: Types, Factors and Techniques of Moral Transformation*. Boston: Beacon Press, 1954.
Stevens, C. M. *Strategy and Collective Bargaining Negotiation*. New York: McGraw-Hill, 1963.
Stiehm, J. "Nonviolence is Two," *Sociological Inquiry*, 38 (1968): 23–30.
Tendulkar, D. G. *Mahatma*. Bombay: Jhaveri and Tendulkar, 1952.
Walton, R. E. and R. B. McKersie. *A Behavioral Theory of Labor Negotiations*. New York: McGraw Hill, 1965.
Zinn, H. *SNCC: The New Abolitionists*. Boston: Beacon Press, 1964.

GENE SHARP

Mechanisms of Change in Nonviolent Action

*a*s a technique of social and political conflict, nonviolent action is still comparatively unstudied. Academic exploration has recently revealed that nonviolent action is a form of struggle with a vast history. The technique is manifested in at least 146 specific methods, including protest, economic boycotts, boycotts of social relations, strikes, political noncooperation and nonviolent intervention.

The ways in which this type of struggle "works" are proving to be much more complex than previously thought; they are particularly more diversified and complicated than comparable processes in political violence. Nonviolent action disproves the popular assumption that only a violent response can be effective against violent repression. On the contrary, maintenance of nonviolent discipline and steadfast resistance (despite violent repression) causes psychological, social, and political repercussions, weakening the violent regime by political *jiujitsu*. This process is important in producing the mechanisms of change that are described in this paper. This material is based on a more detailed analysis to be presented in *The Politics of Nonviolent Action*, prepared by this author.

No two cases of nonviolent action are ever exactly alike. They will differ in many respects: the influences and pressures wielded by the nonviolent actionists, the response of opponents, and the nature of the conflict situation. Nevertheless, it is possible to distinguish three general mechanisms of change that operate in nonviolent action, and to identify the factors that may determine the outcome of the struggle. This paper will explore these two important aspects in the operation of the nonviolent technique.

© Copyright, Gene Sharp, 1970.

MECHANISMS OF CHANGE

The three mechanisms of change in nonviolent action are *conversion, accommodation,* and *nonviolent coercion*.[1] Nonviolent actionists may seek to induce change by previously specifying one of these mechanisms or a particular mechanism may operate without advance choice. The technique can potentially use any one, or all three mechanisms to induce change; this is particularly important for understanding both the nature of the technique and its political potentialities.

CONVERSION

"By conversion we mean that the opponent, as the result of the actions of the nonviolent person or group, comes around to a new point of view which embraces the ends of the nonviolent actor."[2] This change may be influenced by reason, argumentation and other intellectual efforts, although it is doubtful that only intellectual efforts will produce conversion. Conversion in nonviolent action is also likely to involve the opponent's emotions, beliefs, attitudes and moral system. If this mechanism has been preselected, the nonviolent group deliberately seeks to convert the opponent so that he eventually grants their request, but also wants to grant it *because* he has come to feel that it is right to do so.

In conversion attempts, the self-suffering of the actionists may play a major role. This suffering is the major vehicle used to convert the opponent, by appealing to his emotions. Difficult problems of perception may be involved. Nevertheless, the self-suffering is regarded as a means of bridging the social distance between the two groups; the opponent changes his view of the actionists and the wider grievance group, seeing them now as fellow human beings. It may take a considerable period of time to achieve this goal, if it ever does happen. In time, this change of image may make it possible for the opponent to "identify" with the suffering nonviolent actionists: there is evidence that this can happen despite initially extreme social distance between the groups.

The psychological effect of this suffering on the opponent is achieved by initiating the forces for change without the conscious awareness of the opponent; only after this process is well underway does the opponent realize that he may be changing. There are several ways in which this process may be initiated. Awareness that third parties are moved by this suffering, and are repelled by the opponent's violence against the nonviolent actionists, may induce uncertainty in the opponent and *indirectly* stimulate changes in his attitudes, emotions or convictions. Such suffering may also be a *direct* stimulus to change, particularly when the social distance between the groups is not great or when it can be overcome over a long period of time. A complex of strong emotions, which may swing between opposite poles, is another factor facilitating conversion; this complex makes possible sudden rushes of admiration, remorse, compassion and shame. In addition, the opponent may become ashamed of the violence of his repression, while still thinking his *policies* are right; finally, he may progressively come to regret the policies which stimulated the nonviolent action.

The willingness to engage in sacrifice to further their beliefs or objectives will strongly demonstrate the sincerity of nonviolent actionists. If the opponent recognizes their sincerity, this may lead to respect for them, and to reconsidering his views of the group, their ideas and aims. Gandhi believed that the opponent's development of respect for the nonviolent actionists was a milestone that heralded approaching success. He argued that as this stage was approached, the nonviolent actionists must conduct themselves with special care. One possible consequence of this respect is that the opponent will unconsciously imitate them, and lessen his violence. Or, he may change his image of the actionists and the wider "grievance group" on whose behalf the struggle has been launched.

Repeated behavior which refutes the opponent's image of these people may help to create a new, more accurate, image. With increased recognition of the actionists as fellow human beings, the opponent may become more willing to reconsider and alter his controversial policies. "If you want to conquer another man," wrote Richard Gregg (author three decades ago of *The Power of Nonviolence*) "do it . . . by creating inside his own personality a strong new impulse that is incompatible with his previous tendency."[3] This inner conflict may be increased as the opponent discovers that his old outlook on life, his commitment to violent responses and his time-tested ways of responding to subordinates and to crises now seem to be inadequate. In the face of nonviolent action, these ways fail to produce the expected results. With both his objectives frustrated and his means of action ineffective, the opponent's response is uncertain. He may pursue his objectives and sanctions more ruthlessly. Or, he may become receptive to new ideas and ways out of the crisis.

The factors influencing the *conversion* mechanism can be divided into those which are "external" factors (inherent in the conflict situation and outside the direct control of the nonviolent group) and "internal" factors (which are directly under its control). The external factors include:
(1) the relative conflict of interest between the groups;
(2) the social distance between the groups (whether the subordinates are regarded as fellow human beings and members of a common moral order);
(3) the personality structure of the opponents;
(4) the degree to which the two groups share common beliefs and norms of behavior; and
(5) praise or condemnation by third parties.

The "internal" factors include:
(1) refraining not only from physical violence but also from personal hostility to the opponent;
(2) attempting to gain the opponent's trust, as by openness concerning intentions, etc.;
(3) refraining from humiliating the opponent;
(4) making visible sacrifices for their cause;
(5) carrying on constructive work, including improvements in the lives of the nonviolent actionists, the grievance group, and wider humanitarian activities;

(6) maintaining personal contact with the opponents, as by discussions and letters;
(7) demonstrating trust of the opponent; and
(8) developing empathy, good will and patience toward the opponent personally.

For a variety of reasons, efforts to convert an opponent by nonviolent self-suffering may be ineffective and fail to produce the desired result. Some nonviolent actionists may reject conversion as undesirable, unnecessary or impossible. Hence they may have sought change by the mechanism of accommodation or of nonviolent coercion. In most situations, the outcomes are likely to result from pressures produced by the three mechanisms. The most "successful" application of nonviolent action may involve their wise and deliberate combination.

ACCOMMODATION

Accommodation, as a mechanism of nonviolent action, takes an intermediary position between conversion and nonviolent coercion. The opponent is neither converted nor nonviolently coerced; yet there are elements of both involved in his decision to grant concessions to the nonviolent actionists. Lakey has suggested that this is the most common mechanism of the three in successful nonviolent campaigns.[4] In accommodation, the opponent resolves to grant the demands of the nonviolent actionists without fundamentally changing his mind about the issues involved.[5]

Accommodation is similar to nonviolent coercion, in that both mechanisms bring success by changing the social situation. In both, action is "directed toward... a change in those aspects of the situation which are regarded as productive of existing attitudes and behavior."[6] This means that the actionists

... operate on the situation within which people must act, or upon their perception of the situation, without attempting directly to alter their attitudes, sentiments or values. The pressure for a given type of behavior then comes either from (a) revealing information which affects the way in which individuals visualize the situation, or from (b) actual or potential alteration of the situation itself.[7]

In nonviolent coercion, changes are made when the opponent no longer has an effective choice between conceding or refusing to accept the demands. In accommodation, although the desired change is also made in response to the changed situation, it occurs while the opponent still can make an effective choice and before significant nonviolent coercion has occurred. The degree to which the opponent accepts this change as a result of influences which might have converted him, or influences which might have coerced him will vary; both types of influences may be present in the same case.

Through the conversion elements of accommodation, the opponent may become convinced that continued repression is inappropriate. Although not converted, the suffering of nonviolent actionists may have moved the opponent to see them as fellow human beings, against whom the continued infliction of violence is no longer tolerable. The opinions of third parties may also be important to him, so that he acts in order not to "lose face" still more. Sometimes the opponent may grant some or all of the demands to the actionists simply because he regards the group as a nuisance, which can be eliminated by making concessions to them. Thus, although he is perfectly capable of continuing the repression and still does not agree with the demands, the opponent may find that "the campaigner is not really so bad after all and that, all things considered, it 'costs too much' to suppress the campaigner."[8] He may thus resolve the inner conflict induced by the nonviolent struggle.[9]

One consequence of nonviolent action is the creation or deepening of internal dissension and actual opposition within the opponent's own group. This discord is most likely to focus on the contested policies or the repression of nonviolent actionists. It often, however, appears in the guise of conflicts over personalities or other policies. Aware of this fact, the opponent may wish to cut the ground from under his critics by settling the conflict through accommodation to the demands. In economic struggles, accommodation may arise from a desire to minimize the financial and material losses, especially from strikes and economic boycotts.

Through the coercion influences of accommodation, the opponent may concede because he perceives that if the struggle continues he will eventually be defeated; therefore, he tries to avoid the humiliation of defeat, and perhaps more severe losses, by accepting change gracefully. In some cases the social and political situation may have changed so much that while the opponent has not been nonviolently coerced, he could not easily pursue an earlier intended course of action.

The opponent may also decide to accommodate to the demands while he still has freedom of action; this will largely depend on his anticipation of the development of the conflict. In spite of what he says publicly, if he anticipates that the nonviolent movement will grow in strength, he may be inclined to accede to the demands voluntarily. The specific immediate issues at stake may seem to be of less importance than the possible consequences of a protracted struggle, particularly if the populace learns the power it can wield through nonviolent action. A face-saving formula may be important in a settlement resulting from accommodation.

The following factors will be influential to deciding whether a nonviolent action struggle is settled by accommodation:
(1) the degree of conflict of interest;
(2) all of the factors that influence the conversion mechanism;
(3) the actual and potential degree of sympathy and support for the nonviolent actionists, or for their cause, in the opponent's own group;
(4) the actual and potential degree of sympathy and support for the nonviolent actionists among third parties;
(5) the degree of effectiveness or ineffectiveness of repression and other countermeasures;
(6) the presence and extent of economic losses, direct or indirect;
(7) the estimated present and future strength of the nonviolent actionists;

(8) the estimated chances of victory and defeat and their consequences.
These factors will vary from case to case, both in the degree to which they are present and in their differing proportions and combinations.

In many situations, neither conversion nor accommodation will be achieved, for some opponents will remain unwilling to grant any demands to the nonviolent actionists. If attempts to achieve conversion or accommodation fail when tried, or if they seem highly unlikely to succeed, then a third mechanism of change remains open to the actionists: nonviolent coercion. Through this mechanism, it is possible to win demands against the will of the opponent and without his consent.

NONVIOLENT COERCION

"Nonviolent coercion" may be produced in any of three ways. The defiance may become too widespread and massive to be controlled by repression.[10] Second, noncooperation and defiance may make it impossible for the social, economic and political system to continue to operate unless the actionists' demands are achieved. Finally, even the opponent's ability to apply repression may be undermined and at times dissolved. In any of these circumstances, or in any combination of them, despite the opponent's determination to refuse to change his policies or system, he may find that he is unable to defend or restore them in the face of determined and widespread nonviolent action.

Coercion is not limited to the threat or use of violence, as is commonly thought; two theorists of nonviolent action have clarified this:

Coercion is the use of either physical or intangible force to compel action contrary to the will or reasoned judgement of the individual or group subjected to such force [11]
Coercion ... is taking away from the opponent either his ability to maintain the *status quo* or his ability to effect social change.[12]

There is, however, a vast difference between "nonviolent coercion" and "violent coercion." While the latter involves the deliberate intention to inflict physical injury or death, the former arises from a refusal of the nonviolent group to submit in the face of violent repression, from the noncooperation and defiance, and from a willingness to suffer the opponent's violence.

Nonviolent coercion occurs under two conditions. First, it happens when the opponent's will is blocked by noncooperation and defiance of the nonviolent actionists and grievance group, despite the opponent's continued efforts to impose his will. For example, changes from the *status quo* are made even though the opponent rejects the changes, or changes he desires are prevented from occurring while he still applies pressures and sanctions on their behalf. This frustration of his efforts is usually directly proportionate to the massiveness of the actionists' noncooperation and defiance. Second, nonviolent coercion occurs when the opponent's ability to implement his will is destroyed. This immobilization of his capacity to act is usually achieved by the breakdown of support and obedience on his own side, as when his soldiers and police mutiny, his bureaucracy refuses assistance, or population withdraws authority and support. The first of these conditions for nonviolent coercion is most common;

the second may or may not accompany it. This is not an inevitable pattern, however, and might be reversed. In all cases of nonviolent coercion, nonviolent action has so altered the social and political situation that the opponent can no longer wield his power contrary to the wishes of the nonviolent group.

Nonviolent action thus makes possible "coercion through non-participation."[13] It becomes coercive when the actionists succeed in withholding significantly the necessary sources of the opponent's political power. There are six major sources:

(1.) *Authority*: the extent of the regime's authority (accepted right to lead, command or rule) among the citizens.

(2.) *Human resources*: the number and proportion of persons in the population who accept the regime's authority, obey, assist and cooperate with it.

(3.) *Skills and knowledge*: the types of skills and knowledge possessed by the persons accepting the regime's authority, and the relation of these factors to the regime's needs.

(4.) *Intangible factors*: psychological and ideological factors, such as habits, attitudes toward obedience and submission, presence or absence of a common faith, a common sense of mission, etc.

(5.) *Material resources*: the degree to which property, natural and financial resources, the economic system, communication, transportation, etc., are under the control and at the disposal of the regime.

(6.) *Sanctions*: the type and extent of sanctions at the regime's disposal, for use against its own subjects and in conflict with other governments.

These sources of the opponent's power are all potentially vulnerable to direct or indirect control by the nonviolent group using a widespread, qualitative attack through nonviolent action. Changes in the availability of these sources will determine the degree of the regime's political power. The precise ways in which the availability of these sources is severed will vary. Not only will there be differences in the specific methods that are used; variation also occurs in *who* severs the sources of power: the nonviolent actionists, third parties, or disenchanted members of the opponent's own group. There will also be variations in the directness of the withdrawal of cooperation which curtails the power sources, ranging from open refusal and defiance, withholding of new support while continuing old forms, to inefficiency in carrying out orders. The strategy, tactics, and methods used will be among the factors which determine which power sources will be affected, and the degree to which they are reduced or severed.

Nonviolent action may reduce the availability of each of the sources of political power in the following ways:

(1.) *Authority*. The nonviolent challenge to the opponent offers a clear demonstration of the degree to which his authority is *already* undermined. The struggle may help to *alienate more people* who have previously supported the opponent; by focusing attention on the opponent's undesirable policies and by repression against the nonviolent volunteers. At times there will be a clear *transfer of loyalty* from the opponent to a rival authority. This may be a religious or moral system, a political or social principle, a political ideology, or movement or party. In extreme cases, it may even be a rival parallel government. Difficult tactical problems occur when a parallel government emerges and the old one continues to exist. When this new government is supported by significant genuine strength, it could be the final blow in destroying the old system.

(2.) *Human Resources.* Widespread nonviolent action may also reduce or sever the human resources necessary to the opponent's political power, by withholding the general obedience and cooperation of masses of subjects who maintain and operate the system. The sheer numerical multiplication of non-cooperating, disobedient and defiant numbers of the grievance group creates severe enforcement problems for the opponent. In addition the struggle may lead to a related withdrawal of consent by the opponent's traditional supporters reducing his power further. The withdrawal of human resources will also affect other needed sources (skills, knowledge, and material resources). Thus, the opponent requires greater power at the very time that his enforcement capacity is being reduced. If his resistance grows while his power weakens, eventually the regime becomes powerless. Nonviolent action in the political arena may produce comparable results to an effective strike in the industrial arena. Noncooperation of members may paralyse the system.

(3.) *Skills and Knowledge.* The availability of skills and knowledge necessary to the opponent is rarely the same as the percentage of the populace supporting the regime. Certain people or groups possess special skills or knowledge of particular importance; these include special administrators, officials, technicians and advisors. Just as their continued assistance significantly aids the opponent, withdrawal of their assistance disproportionately weakens his power. In addition to outright refusal, *reduced* assistance may also be important. Internal conflicts within the regime—which may be caused or accentuated by nonviolent action—will also weaken the opponent's power.

(4.) *Intangible Factors.* Habits of obedience and commitment to authority may also be threatened by widespread nonviolent action. Destroying the habit of unquestioning obedience does not necessarily mean increased disobedience, but it does involve more *conscious* choice to obey or disobey, based on an increased willingness to evaluate the regime's policies before supporting them. The nonviolent action may reflect the development of an outlook which challenges the official one. In other cases the struggle may cause people to question the established beliefs. Events may refute dogmas.

(5.) *Material Resources.* Nonviolent action may regulate the availability of material resources to the opponent: control of the economic system, transportation, means of communication, financial resources, raw materials, etc. A large proportion of nonviolent action methods are variations of the strike or economic boycott. The history of the labor movement demonstrates the considerable power that can be wielded by these types of economic noncooperation. Economic boycotts and refusal of revenue may reduce the economic benefits of the opponent's political domination. International action by trade boycotts and embargoes may assist the nonviolent actionists.

(6.) *Sanctions.* Even the opponent's ability to apply sanctions may on occasion be influenced by nonviolent action. His supply of arms may be threatened by a foreign country's refusal to sell them, or by strikes in the munitions factories and transportation system. In some cases the numbers of agents of repression—police and troops—may be curtailed as men decline to volunteer and potential conscripts refuse duty. Police and troops may carry out orders inefficiently or may refuse them completely (mutiny). Mutiny appears to be more likely during nonviolent struggle than when policemen and soldiers face personal attacks from violent resisters or from enemy troops. Against the nonviolent actionists, police and troops may face moral and psychological dilemmas resulting from carrying out acts of severe repression against a nonretaliating, but determined group of resisters. As a result, these agents may experience lowered morale and begin to question the justice of the orders and political policies they are executing. This may lead to a laxity in obeying orders and perhaps to open mutiny, though mutiny is likely only under special circumstances. Mutiny or deliberate inefficiency will occur when the troops or police experience conversion, while the leaders of the opposition remain unmoved. The *conversion* of the troops and police on a large scale may produce the nonviolent *coercion* of the opponent. A major mutiny of troops and police, or significant laxity in orders is bound to alter radically the power relationships. It will reduce the opponent's capacity to refuse the demands of the nonviolent group, or to maintain the objectionable policy or system.

A variety of factors operate to produce nonviolent coercion. Variation will exist in the sources of power affected, and degree to which they are severed. Depending on the pattern producing the nonviolent coercion (mutiny, massive defiance, or, economic or political paralysis), some or all of the following factors will be influential in determing the outcome:

(1) the numbers of nonviolent actionists (numerically, and their proportion in the general population);
(2) the degree of the opponent's dependence on the nonviolent actionists for the sources of his power;
(3) the skill of the nonviolent actionists in applying the technique, including the choice of strategy, tactics and methods, and their ability to implement these;
(4) the length of time that the defiance and noncooperation can be maintained;
(5) the degree of sympathy and support for the nonviolent actionists by third parties;
(6) the means of control open to the opponent and used by him to force a resumption of cooperation and to induce consent, and the reaction of nonviolent actionists to those means;
(7) the degree to which the opponent's subjects, administrators, aides and agents support or refuse to support him, and the action that they may undertake to support the nonviolent actionists; and
(8) the opponent's estimation of the probable future course of the nonviolent action movement.

FACTORS INFLUENCING THE OUTCOME OF NONVIOLENT ACTION STRUGGLES

The factors influencing the outcome of struggles may be classified into four groups: those related to the nonviolent group, the opponent, third parties, and characteristics of the social situation. Social system characteristics are relatively stable; they must be taken as the given limitations within which nonviolent action must operate. It may be possible to change some of these in the long run but such change during the course of the struggle cannot be relied upon. The other factors (related to the nonviolent group, the opponent, and third parties) are highly subject to change during the course of the struggle. These changes seem much greater than occur in violent struggle. *These three groups of factors will vary constantly during the struggle. The only question is whether these variations will strengthen relatively the nonviolent actionists or their opponent.* As the campaign proceeds, both the absolute and the relative strengths of both sides are subject to constant and considerable change. Not only do the dynamics of this technique depend on these changes; the technique works in special ways which produce them. Consequently, nonviolent discipline is crucial for producing the desired power shifts. In this special conflict situation, the factors determining the opponent's power are therefore less under his own control, and more subject to the direct and indirect control of the nonviolent actionists than if the latter were instead using political violence. This is one of the most important qualities of the dynamics of nonviolent action.

FACTORS IN THE SOCIAL SITUATION

Such factors include the degree of conflict of interest between the two groups, the social distance between them, the degree of shared common beliefs and norms, and the degree to which the grievance group (and sometimes, too, the opponent group) consists of an atomized mass of individuals with effective power highly concentrated, or, instead, consists of a more vital society of more self-reliant social groups and institutions which share and wield power.

FACTORS ASSOCIATED WITH THE OPPONENT GROUP

These include: a) the degree of the opponent's dependence on the noncooperators for the sources of his power; b) the degree of noncompliance that the opponent can tolerate without his position being seriously endangered (the less nonconformity and dissent he normally allowed, the greater will be the challenge when it does occur); c) the degree to which the opponent and the opponent group believe that their policies are right or necessary; d) the means of repression and control used to defeat the nonviolent challenge; e) the degree of conviction by the opponent and opponent group that the means of repression and control used against the nonviolent actionists are right and just; f) the length of time that the opponent can maintain his position and power in the face of nonviolent action, influenced by the degree of support he receives from his agents of repression, administrators, etc., and the general population; g) the opponent's estimate of the future course of the movement, the chances of its victory or defeat, and the possible consequences of each.

FACTORS ASSOCIATED WITH THIRD PARTIES

These involve their attitudes and actions. These factors include the degree to which third parties become sympathetic to either the opponent or the nonviolent group. The importance of such shifts will be influenced by what importance each group may place on such sympathy and approval. If opinions change, third parties may move from a noninvolved position to active support for, or to noncooperation with, either of the contending groups. The effectiveness of this action will depend on whether the contending groups are assisted by this support or hindered by the noncooperation actions.

FACTORS ASSOCIATED WITH THE NONVIOLENT GROUP

These factors are much more numerous partly because the technique gives this group major control over the development and outcome of the conflict. The first factor is the opportunity and ability to organize nonviolent action (or the ability to conduct effective spontaneous nonviolent action). A second factor is the degree of confidence of the nonviolent group and the grievance group in their cause and in nonviolent struggle to achieve their objectives. *How* the group acts is obviously a third factor: choice of the specific methods of nonviolent action, whether these are symbolic or involve noncooperation and intervention, whether the strategy and tactics are sound and are within the ability of the nonviolent actionists to execute. Success is more likely when the demands of the nonviolent group are within their capacity to achieve them. The relative ability to apply the technique will depend on several specific aspects: a) the voluntary acceptance of discipline within the nonviolent group (which will influence whether the plans are carried out with clarity and unity of action), b) the numbers of nonviolent actionists, within the context of the quality of the movement and the change mechanism employed, and c) the help or hindrance offered to the actionists by the general grievance group (on whose behalf they may be acting). Several factors are also relevant to the actionists' *continuance* of the struggle:

(1.) The balance between the degree of repression and terror the opponent is able and willing to use, and the determination of the nonviolent group to act regardless of sanctions.
(2.) The length of time that the nonviolent actionists are able and willing to continue the struggle.
(3.) Their ability to keep the struggle nonviolent.
(4.) The actionists' ability to maintain openness and nonsecretiveness in their actions under normal circumstances.
(5.) The existence and quality of an effective leadership group (formal or informal).
(6.) As an alternative to.
(7.) The ability of the nonviolent actionists to act with unity, discipline, and

with the choice of wise strategy, tactics and methods without a distinguishable leadership group.
(8.) Where conversion or accommodation are relevant, the actionists' ability to act in ways which help convert the opponent.
(9.) Where accommodation or nonviolent coercion are relevant, the nonviolent actionists' ability to maintain control over their own sources of power. The outcome of the conflict will be determined by the direction and degree of change in these various factors during the course of the struggle.

CONCLUSION

There are several other processes that are integral to the dynamics of nonviolent struggle. Crucial among these is the actionists' ability to meet violent repression with continued nonviolent struggle, thereby causing the opponent's violence to backfire politically and to weaken his power position. This has been called "political *jujitsu*." Due to the variety of processes involved in the workings of nonviolent action, the differing mechanisms of change, and the multiplicity of factors that influence the outcome of nonviolent struggle, the dynamics of this technique are extremely complicated. Indeed, nonviolent action may be far more complex than violent action. Major attention is needed to study the dynamics of nonviolent action more intensively; there are major gaps in our present knowledge, and a better understanding may be a prerequisite to major substitutions of nonviolent action for violence in political conflicts.

Notes

1. This roughly parallels a similar discussion by George Lakey, except that I have used a different term for the second process and modified its description. See George Lakey, "The Sociological Mechanisms of Nonviolent Action," Unpublished M.A. Thesis in Sociology, University of Pennsylvania, 1962, p. 23. The analysis of mechanisms of change is developed and documented in much greater detail in Sharp, *The Politics of Nonviolent Action*. Philadelphia and Boston: Pilgrim Press, 1970, Chapter 12.
2. *Ibid.*, 20.
3. Gregg, *The Power of Nonviolence*, Second Revised Edition. New York: Schocken, 1966, 53.
4. Lakey, *op. cit.*, 21.
5. *Ibid.*, 22.
6. Robin M. Williams, *The Reduction of Intergroup Tensions*, New York: Social Science Research Council, 1947, 14.
7. *Ibid.*, 17.
8. Lakey, *op. cit.*, 23. See also M. K. Gandhi, *Satyagraha*, Ahmedabad: Navajivan, 1961, 121.
9. Lakey, *op. cit.*, 36.
10. This refers to repression employed to achieve submission of the subjects. An attempt deliberately to exterminate a whole population is a very different process, and requires separate investigation.
11. Theodor Paullin, *Introduction to Nonviolence*. Philadelphia: Pacifist Research Bureau, 1944, 6.
12. Lakey, *op. cit.*, 18.
13. E. T. Hiller, *The Strike: A Study in Collective Action*. Chicago: University of Chicago Press, 1928, 125.

MARTIN OPPENHEIMER AND GEORGE LAKEY

Direct Action Tactics

One catalog of nonviolent action lists some sixty-four different methods which have been used throughout history.[1] We are taking from this list those which seem most significant for the current civil rights struggle.

DEMONSTRATIONS

Demonstrations are primarily expressions of a point of view, and do not of themselves change the power structure as vigorously as non-cooperation or direct intervention might. Nevertheless, they do go beyond verbal protest and are considered sufficiently threatening by many authorities to provoke harsh reprisals.

1. MARCHES AND PARADES

Technically, the difference between a march and a parade is that a march has a destination of symbolic or immediate importance to the cause, whereas a parade route is chosen for convenience or potential impact on a neighborhood. Both may be short or long. Mass marches and parades can express the solidarity of the campaigners and be an important morale-booster.

A common way of discrediting marches and parades is to describe them as disorderly and violent. You can take two steps to eliminate the validity of this charge:

(a) Have either silence, or singing in unison. Both make a powerful impression of unity and dignity. Slogan-shouting and conversation build an impression of disunity and disorder.

(b) Set up a system of leadership. Experience shows it is helpful to have a marshal and a number of line leaders who, once policy is set, follow the directions

Reprinted by permission of Quadrangle Books from *A Manual for Direct Action* by Martin Oppenheimer and George Lakey, copyright © 1964, 1965 by Martin Oppenheimer, George Lakey, and the Friends Peace Committee.

of the marshal. The leadership helps in two ways: keeping discipline and building the morale of the marchers. In addition, more efficient decisions can be made in the event of police interference, etc. Leaders should be clearly designated and should set an example for others to follow.

A long march is often called a walk. The best known civil rights walk is the one postman William Moore began through the South, which others continued when he was killed. The Committee for Nonviolent Action has organized two walks for peace and freedom through the South which had to contend with cattle-prods and the like. The effect of a walk can be somewhat like that of the Freedom Rides—to dramatize an issue and give a morale boost to the movement in the towns through which the walkers go.

2. PICKETING AND VIGILING

The difference between picketing and a vigil is that a vigil is longer and held in a meditative spirit. Often a vigil is held around-the-clock for several days, or it may be daily for weeks or even months. It is also customary for participants in a vigil to stand rather than walk, as in picketing. In a culture like ours where religion is held in high esteem, a vigil is sometimes more effective than picketing; however, it is slightly more wearying and requires more self- and group-discipline. The remarks about orderliness apply here, to both picketing and vigiling.

SAMPLE PICKET OR VIGIL DISCIPLINE[2]

We will try to maintain an attitude of good will at all times, especially in face of provocation.

If violence occurs against us, we will not retaliate but will try to practice forgiveness and forbearance.

We agree that one person is in charge of specific actions and agree to abide by the decisions of the person in charge, even if at the time we do not fully agree with or understand the decision.

If in good conscience we cannot comply with this decision, we will not take contrary action but will withdraw from that phase.

In the event of arrest, we will submit with promptness and composure.

We will try to be prompt in our appointments and to carry out responsibly the tasks we have been assigned.

Here are some suggestions which will help you to organize an effective picket line.[3]

(1.) Assemble somewhere other than the place where the picket line will be, then go to the place in a group; this avoids confusion and gives the leader a chance to pass out printed copies of the discipline (see sample in Figure 36-1) as well as to conduct registration.

(2.) Ask participants to refer questioners, press, or police to the marshal or information officer.

(3.) Expect participants to walk erectly and not slouch, call out, laugh loudly, or use profanity; smoking may be ruled out in some situations.

(4.) Assign two leafleteers to each location, so leafleting can go on if one leafleteer gets involved with a questioner.

(5.) Instruct leafleteers on how to answer very briefly when asked "What is this

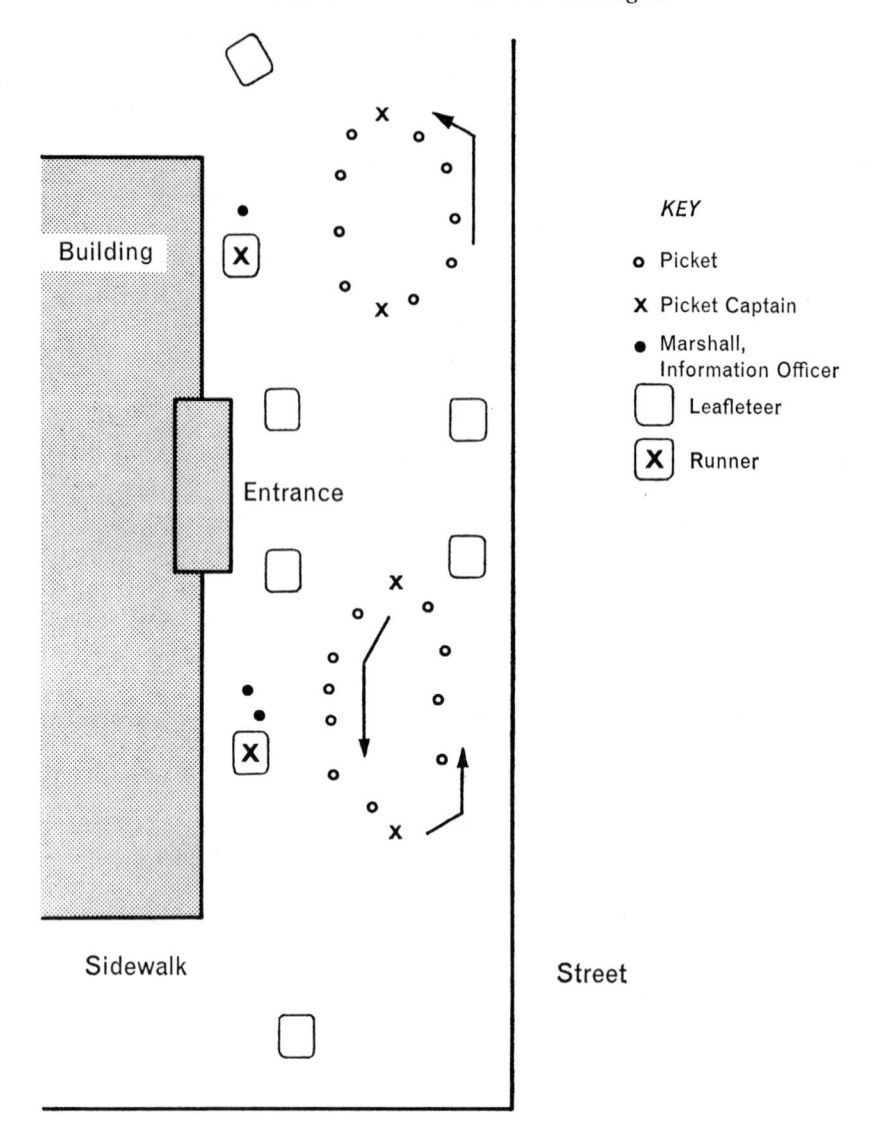

Figure 36.1.   An Organized Picket Line

all about?" or "Who's doing this?" or "Why don't you people go back to Russia?" or other questions.
(6.) Ask leafleteers to pick up all discarded leaflets (to avoid legal entanglements and to show good will).
(7.) Keep leaflets in a plastic bag in rainy weather.
(8.) Avoid unnecessary scurrying about.
(9.) Give instructions in a clear and authoritative voice, but avoid a domineering approach.

(10.) Remember that your conduct sets an example for others.

3. FRATERNIZATION

This technique has been used in countries occupied by a foreign power, as well as in this country. The idea is to go out of the way to talk with the police or other opponents in a friendly way and to try to persuade them that one's cause is just. Where it has been tried it has on occasion been amazingly effective, as some instances in Norway under the Nazi occupation testify. But it is not easy.

In the summer of 1964 a group of pacifists conducted a direct action project at a missile site in Quebec Province, Canada, including vigiling and civil disobedience. One of the techniques which they used to communicate was to pass out leaflets addressed "to our brothers in the armed forces," and "to our brothers in the police force." They also made impromptu speeches when soldiers and police were near, explaining their motivation and purpose. As a result, there was some breakdown in military discipline as soldiers went out of their way to join the pacifists in a prayer meeting at the conclusion of the vigil.

4. "HAUNTING"

This is a means of reminding officials of the immorality of their behavior—volunteers follow them everywhere they go. In India during the Gandhian struggles arrests were made, but the volunteers were replaced by others who "haunted" the authorities until officials were sick of it.

5. LEAFLETING

Leafleting can do several things for the cause: (a) provide the people with more accurate information than they get in the newspapers; (b) give more people more personal contact with the campaigners (in large communities many people never actually see demonstrators); (c) involve children and others who otherwise might not actively participate in the struggle.

6. RENOUNCING HONORS

There can be some symbolic impact when campaigners renounce honors given them in the past. For example, Negro veterans might send back medals of honor; a Negro "Woman of the Year" might refuse the award from an institution which is part of the power structure; Negro students might send back their American Legion School Awards.

Some of the techniques which come under the heading of demonstrations may become civil disobedience if the city declares them illegal. Injunctions may be issued by courts forbidding marches or picketing. Where the Constitution is in operation, however, these methods do not usually involve breaking the law.

NON-COOPERATION

This general category involves methods of direct action in which the campaigners withdraw their usual degree of cooperation with the opponent. The methods may be legal or illegal, depending on local laws.

1. STRIKE

The strike is one of the best known of all forms of direct action. It has not, however, been used very often in the civil rights struggle. It would be most potent in those areas where Negroes form a very large part of the population or of some economic concern which is important to the area. A form of the strike which might be experimented with is the "token strike." In a token strike all those sympathetic to the cause go off the job for a brief time—perhaps one day or a few hours. This is a way of showing solidarity and seriousness of purpose.

2. HARTAL

The Indians under Gandhi developed this device extensively, but it was also used in Budapest at the beginning of the 1956 Hungarian revolution. A Hartal involves staying at home for a full day or more, leaving factories, streets and places of amusement totally empty. In addition to reducing the chances of "incidents," the stay-at-home may serve to demonstrate to the opponent the degree of unity and self-discipline among the people. In a campaign which stresses religious aspects, the day can be seen as a time for meditation and purification.

3. CONSUMERS' BOYCOTT OR SELECTIVE BUYING

From the Montgomery Bus Boycott on, the consumers' boycott has played an important role in the civil rights struggle. This method has its roots in the American Revolution and even further back in history, and has been used throughout the world. Its effectiveness depends on how much the businessman needs the campaigners' patronage for his economic survival.

Here are the advantages of the boycott: (a) it minimizes violence; (b) it promotes solidarity; (c) it does not usually involve civil disobedience. On the other hand, it usually requires a good deal of unity on the part of the protesting community.

4. RENTERS' BOYCOTT (RENT-STRIKE)

The refusal to pay rent because of grievances against a landlord may be for a short period (token boycott) or indefinitely. Irish peasants in 1879 were often evicted for refusing rents to rich English landlords. Whether or not eviction takes place depends partly on the number of persons participating and on the nature of the local laws.

In the current civil rights struggle, workers go from house to house, apartment to apartment, talking with people about the injustice of their situation. They invite tenants to an area or house meeting, where the possibilities of united action are stressed. Those who will commit themselves at the meeting begin to strike at once—there is little to be gained by setting a date in the future for the beginning of the action. The action of the few who first volunteer will hopefully begin a wave of others joining the strike.

Guidelines for organization include: being realistic in explaining to the tenants what may happen (no one can guarantee major repairs); staying in close contact with the tenants to offset intimidation; and planning to put the rent money "in escrow," or into a special fund set aside for this purpose. The fund should be carefully accounted for.

Local regulations differ as to eviction possibilities. It is important to get legal counsel, for often constables themselves break the law in the process of eviction. In addition to countering eviction by legal action, picketing the constable and living on the sidewalk in front of the house are direct action tactics which may be tried; numbers of tenants can also obstruct constables' access to the house, thus preventing eviction. This is generally against the law, of course.

5. SCHOOL BOYCOTT

One of the advantages of the school boycott is that it involves the children in a struggle which will result in their eventual benefit, while still not involving them in a front-line confrontation with its accompanying dangers. The setting up of freedom schools for teaching the young can be a valuable exercise for those in the Negro community who are otherwise difficult to involve.

6. TAX REFUSAL

This is a drastic tactic, yet it has often been used in struggles in the past in various parts of the world. It can be partial, such as withholding school taxes, or complete. The money which would otherwise go for taxes can be given to the movement for distribution to needy campaigners. Generally opponents feel this tactic more deeply than almost any other, for if the refusing population is large it threatens the very survival of the government. Harsh reprisal may therefore be expected. Despite this, the strong moral appeal involved ("Why pay the police who are beating you?") and the strength of the tactic has made tax refusal effective in some campaigns.

INTERVENTION

Direct nonviolent intervention consists of physical confrontation rather than withdrawal of cooperation or demonstrating. It carries the conflict into the opponent's camp and often changes the status quo abruptly.

1. SIT-IN

The sit-in has been used in the U.S. mostly in restaurants and at lunch counters. Generally campaigners progressively occupy a large number of all of the available seats and refuse to leave until the Negro members of the group are served, the restaurant closes, the group is arrested, or a certain fixed period of time has gone by. This method can also be used in other situations such as on buses and trains, as in the Freedom Rides. There have been sit-ins in the offices of notables such as mayors and business executives in order to obtain appointments or to symbolize the blocking of freedom in which the official is participating. Legislative halls can be used similarly. Often the sit-in is a perfectly legal activity.

NONVIOLENT DISCIPLINE OF THE 1960 NASHVILLE
STUDENT SIT-IN MOVEMENT

Don't strike back or curse if abused.
Don't laugh out.
Don't hold conversations with floor workers.
Don't leave your seats until your leader has given you instruction to do so.
Don't block entrances to the stores and the aisles.
Show yourself courteous and friendly at all times.
Sit straight and always face the counter.
Report all serious incidents to your leader.
Refer all information to your leader in a polite manner.
Remember love and nonviolence.
May God bless each of you.

Allied methods are the stand-in, where people line up for admission to a theater or similar place; the wade-in, in which campaigners attempt to swim at a segregated beach; and the kneel-in, in which Negroes try to worship at a church which excludes them.

2. THE FAST

The fast was used as a method of psychological intervention by, among others, Danilo Dolci[4] when he led 1,000 unemployed fishermen in a twenty-four-hour mass fast on a beach in Sicily. The fast can be of heightened effectiveness when undertaken by persons of high status, such as ministers. Gandhi, the best-known faster, considered this the most difficult of all techniques and emphasized that it should be thought through carefully. This is especially true of the fast unto death. Experience with the fast in Albany, Georgia, by peace walkers, indicates that clarity of purpose and realistic time periods are important. Efforts must be made to overcome the misunderstanding which comes in a society where "good living" is prized and self-denial is looked down upon.

Gandhi believed that fasting is most effective when there is a close relationship between the faster and the opponent.

3. REVERSE STRIKE

This method has been found effective in various situations—e.g., agricultural workers have done more work and worked longer hours than they were paid for, in support of their demand for pay increases. The unemployed in Sicily in 1956 voluntarily repaired a public road that was badly in need of repair in order to call attention to the severe unemployment in the area and the government's failure to deal with it. Although this method looks harmless enough at first glance, it has in practice been regarded as a sufficient threat so that reverse-strikers have been arrested, imprisoned, and even in some cases shot by police attempting to stop them from working! Clearing an unused lot for a playground, despite the fact that the lot belongs to someone else, or to the city, might be a current example. This may involve breaking the law.

4. NONVIOLENT INTERJECTION AND OBSTRUCTION

This involves placing one's body between another person and the objective of his work. Civil rights workers in this country have used it at school and other construction sites, to protest the building itself or discrimination in hiring the construction workers. Striking hosiery workers in Reading, Pennsylvania, in 1957, lay down on the sidewalks at the factory gates making it necessary for non-strikers to walk over them to get into the factory, or else stay away from their jobs. In early 1964 at a Cleveland construction site several actionists lay down in front of a bulldozer; a minister, Rev. Bruce Klunder, seeing that the operator might reverse direction, lay down behind the bulldozer and was killed. We should remember that in a confusing situation the operator might not look in both directions before moving machine.

There is more danger of injury or death when one or a few persons engage in interjection than when a great many participate. An example of the latter case, called obstruction, occurred in Japan in 1956 when 10,000 people physically occupied a site intended for a U.S. air base. After several days of obstruction the plans for building the air base were abandoned.

Even while this manual is being prepared some individual or group is probably devising still other forms of nonviolent direct action. One of the elements of non-violence is the creativity which it stimulates, and the reader will probably want to experiment with new forms of nonviolent struggle. Not all of them will be really effective, and some will collapse as did the World's Fair "stall-in" in April, 1964. In evaluating a new tactic before trying it out, the thoughtful civil rights worker will ask:

(1.) Is it clearly related to the issue?
(2.) Are the people it will inconvenience really the people heavily involved in the injustice?
(3.) Is there chance of direct confrontation between the campaigners and the opponent?
(4.) Does the tactic put a major part of the suffering which is inevitable in social change upon our shoulders, rather than upon innocent bystanders?
(5.) If direct action, especially interjection and obstruction, involve violation of the law (civil disobedience), are demonstrators prepared to accept the penalties in order to make the point?

If the answer to these questions is "yes," the tactic may be worth trying.

Notes

1. Gene Sharp, *Methods of Nonviolent Action*, Institute for Social Research, Oslo, Norway.
2. Slightly revised from Charles C. Walker, *Organizing for Nonviolent Direct Action*.
3. This listing is based on Charles Walker's *Organizing for Nonviolent Direct Action*.
4. Dolci, sometimes called "the Italian Gandhi," is a pioneer in applying direct action to community organization.

MORTON DEUTSCH

Conflicts: Productive and Destructive

Editor's Note: The following contribution by Morton Deutsch is taken from a longer paper, "Conflicts: Productive and Destructive," presented as the Kurt Lewin Memorial Address to the American Psychological Association, September 1, 1968. In the early parts of his paper, not reproduced here, Dr. Deutsch defines the terms "productive" and "destructive," and discusses the factors that lead to destructive conflict escalation or productive conflict resolution. The following section represents the author's thoughts on a recurring contemporary problem: what actions can a low power group take to induce a higher power group toward a mutually cooperative relationship?

CHANGING THE COURSE OF CONFLICT

i believe that a *mutually* cooperative orientation is likely to be the most productive orientation for resolving conflict. Yet it must be recognized that the orientations of the conflicting parties may not be mutual. One side may experience the conflict and be motivated to resolve it; the other side may be content with things as they are and not even aware of the other's dissatisfaction. Or both may recognize the conflict but one may be oriented to a win-lose solution while the other may be seeking a cooperative resolution.

The usual tendency for such asymmetries in orientation is to produce a change toward mutual competition rather than mutual cooperation. It is, after all, possible to attack, overcome, or destroy another without his consent but to cooperate with another, he must be willing or, at least, compliant.

How can party A induce party B to cooperate in resolving a conflict if B is not so inclined or if B perceives his interests as antagonistic to A's? There is, obviously, no single answer to this question. What answer is appropriate depends

Reprinted by permission of The Society for the Psychological Study of Social Issues from *The Journal of Social Issues*, Vol. XXV, No. 1, pp. 29–41.

upon such factors as: the nature of the conflict, the relative power of A and B, the nature and motivation of B's noncooperation, the particular resources and vulnerabilities of each party, and their relationships to third parties. However, it is evident that the search for an answer must be guided by the realization that there are dangers in certain types of influence procedures. Namely, they may boomerang and increase open resistance and alienation or they may merely elicit a sham or inauthentic cooperation with underlying resistance. Inauthentic cooperation is more difficult to change than open resistance because it masks and denies the underlying alienation.

Let me offer some hypotheses about the types of influence procedures which are likely to elicit resistance and alienation:

(1.) *Illegitimate techniques* which violate the values and norms governing interaction and influence that are held by the other are alienating (the greater the violation, the more important and the more numerous the values being violated, the greater will be the resistance). It is, of course, true that sometimes an adaptation level effort occurs so that frequently violated norms lose their illegitimacy (as in parking violations); at other times, the accumulation of violations tends to produce an increasingly negative reaction.

(2.) *Negative sanctions* such as punishments and threats tend to elicit more resistance than positive sanctions such as promises and rewards. What is considered to be rewarding or punishing may also be influenced by one's adaptation level; the reduction of the level of rewards which are customarily received will usually be viewed as negative.

(3.) Sanctions which are *inappropriate* in kind are also likely to elicit resistance. Thus, the reward of money rather than appreciation may decrease the willingness to cooperate of someone whose cooperation is engendered by affiliative rather than utilitarian motives. Similarly, a threat or punishment is more likely to be effective if it fits the crime than if its connection with the crime is artificial. A child who breaks another child's toy is punished more appropriately if he has to give the child a toy of his own as a substitute than if he is denied permission to watch TV.

(4.) Influence which is *excessive* in magnitude tends to be resisted; excessive promise or reward leads to the sense of being bribed, excessive threat or punishment leads to the feeling of being coerced.

These factors summate. Illegitimate threat which is inappropriate and excessive is most likely to elicit resistance and alienation while an appropriate legitimate reward is least likely to do so. Inauthentic cooperation, with covert resistance, is most likely when resistance is high and when bribery or coercion elicits overt compliance.

WHAT ACTION INDUCES COOPERATION?

I have, so far, outlined what one should *not* do if one wants to elicit authentic cooperative conflict resolution. Let me turn now to the question of what courses of action can be taken which are likely to induce cooperation. In so doing, I wish to focus on a particularly important kind of conflict: conflict between those groups who have considerable authority to make decisions and relatively high control over the conventional means of social and political influence and those groups who have little decision-making authority and relatively little control over the conventional means of influence.

Although there have always been conflicts between the ruler and the ruled, between parents and children, and between employers and employees, I suggest that this is the characteristic conflict of our time. It arises from the increasing demand for more power and prosperity from those who have been largely excluded from the processes of decision-making, usually to their economic, social, psychological and physical disadvantage. The racial crisis in the United States, the student upheavals throughout the world, the revolutionary struggles in the underdeveloped areas, the controversies within and between nations in Eastern Europe, and the civil war in South Vietnam: all of these conflicts partly express the growing recognition at all levels of social life that social change is possible, that things do not have to remain as they are, that one can participate in the shaping of one's environment and improve one's lot.

ROLE SATISFACTION . . .

It is evident that those who are satisfied with their roles in and the outcomes of the decision-making process may develop both a vested interest in preserving. the existing arrangements and appropriate rationales to justify their positions These rationales generally take the form of attributing superior competence (more ability, knowledge, skill) and/or superior moral value (greater initiative, drive, sense of responsibility, self-control) to oneself compared to those of lower status. From the point of view of those in power, lack of power and affluence is "little enough punishment" for people so incapable and so deficient in morality and maturity that they have failed to make their way in society. The rationales supporting the status quo are usually accompanied by corresponding sentiments which lead their possessors to react with disapproval and resistance to attempts to change the power relations and with apprehension and defensiveness to the possibility that these attempts will succeed. The apprehension is often a response to the expectation that the change will leave one in a powerless position under the control of those who are incompetent and irresponsible or at the mercy of those seeking revenge for past injustices.

If such rationales, sentiments and expectations have been developed, those in power are likely to employ one or more defense mechanisms in dealing with the conflict-inducing dissatisfactions of the subordinated group: *denial*, which is expressed in a blindness and insensitivity to the dissatisfactions and often results in an unexpected revolt; *repression*, which pushes the dissatisfactions underground and often eventuates in a guerrilla-type warfare; *aggression*, which may lead to a masochistic sham cooperation or escalated counter-aggression; *displacement*, which attempts to divert responsibility for the dissatisfactions into other groups and, if successful, averts the conflict temporarily; *reaction-formation*, which allows expressions of concern and guilt to serve as substitutes for action to relieve the dissatisfaction of the underprivileged and, in so doing, may temporarily confuse and mislead those who are dissatisfied; *sublimation*, which attempts to find substitute solutions—e.g., instead of increasing the decision-making power of Harlem residents over their schools, provide more facilities for the Harlem schools.

WHAT CAN A LESS POWERFUL GROUP DO?

What can a less powerful group (A) do to reduce or overcome the defensiveness of a more powerful group (B) and to increase the latter's readiness to share power? Suppose, in effect that as social scientists we were consultants to the poor and weak rather than to the rich and strong, what would we suggest? Let me note that this would be an unusual and new position for most of us. If we have given any advice at all, it has been to those in high power. The unwitting consequence of this one-sided consultant role has been that we have too often assumed that the social pathology has been in the ghetto rather than in those who have built the walls to surround it, that the "disadvantaged" are the ones who need to be changed rather than the people and the institutions who have kept the disadvantaged in a submerged position. It is not that we should detach ourselves from "Headstart," "Vista," and various other useful training and remedial programs for the disadvantaged. Rather, we should have an appropriate perspective on such programs. It is more important that the educational institutions, the economic and political systems be changed so that they will permit those groups who are now largely excluded from important positions of decision-making to share power than to try to inculcate new attitudes and skills in those who are excluded. After all, would we not expect that the educational achievements of black children would be higher than they are now if school boards had more black members and schools had more black principals? Would we not also expect that the occupational attainment of blacks would be higher (and their unemployment rate lower) if General Motors, A.T. and T., and General Electric had some black board members and company presidents as well as white ones? Again, would we not expect more civil obedience in the black community if Charles Evers rather than James Eastland were chairman of the Senate Judiciary Committee and if the House had barred corrupt white congressmen as well as Adam Clayton Powell? Let us not lose sight of what and who has to be changed, let us recognize where the social pathology really is!

ATTENTION, COMPREHENSION, ACCEPTANCE

But given the resistance and defensiveness of those in high power, what can we recommend to those in low power as a strategy of persuasion? As Hovland, Janis and Kelley (1953) have pointed out, the process of persuasion involves obtaining the other's *attention, comprehension* and *acceptance* of the message that one is communicating. The process of persuasion, however, starts with the communicator having a message that he wants to get across to the other. He must have an objective if he is to be able to articulate a clear and compelling message. Further, in formulating and communicating his message, it is important to recognize that it will be heard not only by the other, but also by one's own group and by other interested audiences. The desirable effects of a message on its intended audience may be negated by its unanticipated effects on those for whom it was not intended. I suggest that the following generalized message contains the basic elements of what A must communicate to B to change him and, in addition, it is a message which can be overheard by other audiences without harmful consequences. Admittedly, it must be communicated in a way which elicits B's attention, comprehension and acceptance of its credibility rather than in the abstract, intellectualized form in which it is presented below. And, of course, the generalized objective of equality must be detailed in terms of specific relations in specific contexts.

I am dissatisfied with our relationship and the effects it has. I think it can be improved in ways which will benefit you as well as me. I am sufficiently discontent that I can no longer continue in any relationship with you in which I do not participate as an equal in making the decisions which affect me as well as you, except as a temporary measure while we move toward equality. This may upset and discomfort you but I have no alternative other than to disengage myself from all forms of inauthentic cooperation: my dignity as well as pressure from my group will no longer allow me to engage in this self-deception and self-abasement. Neither coercion nor bribery will be effective; my self-respect and my group will force me to resist them. I remain prepared to cooperate with you as an equal in working on joint problems, including the problems involved in redefining our relationship to one another. I expect that changing our relationship will not be without its initial difficulties for both of us; we will be uncertain and perhaps suspicious, we will misunderstand and disagree and regress to old habits from time to time. I am willing to face these difficulties. I invite you to join with me to work toward improving our relationship, to overcome your dissatisfactions as well as mine. I believe that we both will feel more self-fulfilled in a relationship that is not burdened by inauthenticity.

It would take too long to detail all of the elements in this message and their rationales. But essentially the message commits A irreversibly to his objective—self-esteem and social esteem are at stake; he will be able to live neither with himself nor his group if he accepts an inferior status. This is done not only in words but also by the style of communicating which expresses a self-confident equality and competence. It provides B with the prospect of positive incentives for changing and negative ones for not changing; A maintains a cooperative stance—throughout and develops in action the possibility of at rue mutual exchange by expressing the awareness that dissatisfactions are not one-sided. It also inoculates against some of the expected difficulties involved in change. It should be noted that A's statements of the threats faced by B if change is not forthcoming (the instrumental threat of noncooperation, the moral threat that the status quo violates important social norms concerning human dignity and authenticity, the threat of resistance to coercion) are neither arbitrary, illegitimate, coercive nor demanding to B—i.e., they are not strongly alienating.

RAGE OR FEAR HANDICAPS...

Rage or fear in the low power group often makes it impossible for them to communicate a message of the sort that I have described above. Rage leads to an emphasis on destructive, coercive techniques and precludes offers of authentic cooperation. Fear, on the other hand, weakens the commitment to the steps necessary to induce a change and lessens the credibility that compliance will be withdrawn if change does not occur. Although it is immediately destructive, rage is potentially a more useful emotion than fear since it leads to bold actions which are less damaging to the development of a sense of power and, hence, of self-esteem. And these latter are necessary for authentic cooperation. Harnessed rage or outrage can be a powerful energizer for determined action and if this action is directed toward building one's own power rather than destroying the other's power, the outrage may have a socially constructive outcome.

In any case, it is evident that when intense rage or fear are the dominant emotions the cooperative message that I have outlined is largely irrelevant. Both rage and fear are rooted in a sense of helplessness and powerlessness: they are emotions associated with a state of dependency. Those in low power can overcome these debilitating emotions by their own successful social action on matters of significance to them. In the current slang, they have got to "do their own thing," it cannot be given to them nor done for them. This is why my emphasis throughout this discussion has been on the sharing of power, and thus increasing one's power to affect one's fate, rather than on the sharing of affluence. While the sharing of affluence is desirable, it is not sufficient. In its most debilitating sense, "poverty" is a lack of power and not merely a lack of money. Money is, of course, a base for power but it is not the only one. If one chooses to be poor, as do some members of religious or pioneering groups, the psychological syndrome usually associated with imposed poverty—a mixture of dependency, apathy, small time perspective, suspicion, fear and rage—is not present.

AUTHENTIC COOPERATION

Thus, the ability to offer and engage in authentic cooperation presupposes an awareness that one is neither helpless nor powerless, even though one is at a relative disadvantage. Not only independent action but also cooperative action requires a recognition and confirmation of one's capacity to "go it alone" if necessary. Unless one has the freedom to choose not to cooperate, there can be no free choice to cooperate. "Black power" is, thus, a necessity for black cooperation: of black cooperation with blacks as well as with whites. Powerlessness and the associated lack of self and group esteem are not conducive either to internal group cohesiveness or to external cooperation. "Black power" does not, however, necessarily lead to white cooperation. This is partly because, in its origin and rhetoric, "black power" may be oriented against "white power" and thus is likely to intensify the defensiveness of those with high power. When "black power" is primarily directed against "whitey" rather than for "blacks" it is, of course, to be expected that "whitey" will retaliate. The resulting course of events may provide some grim satisfaction to those despairing blacks who prefer to wield even short-lived destructive power rather than to be ineffectual and to those whites who prefer to be ruthless oppressors rather than to yield the psychic gains of pseudo-superiority.

However, even if "power" is "for" rather than "against" and provides a basis for authentic cooperation, cooperation may not occur because it is of little import to the high power group. It may be unaffected by the positive or negative incentives that the low power group control; it does not need their compliance. Universities can obtain new students; the affluent nations no longer are so dependent upon the raw materials produced in the underdeveloped nations; the white industrial society does not need many unskilled Negro workers.

WHAT CAN THE GROUP DO FOR ITSELF?

What can the low power group do in such situations? First of all, theoretically it may be possible to "opt out" more or less completely—to withdraw, to migrate, to separate so that one is no longer in the relationship. However, as the world and the societies composing it become more tightly knit, this option becomes less and less available in its extreme forms. Black communities can organize their own industries, schools, hospitals, shopping centers, consumer cooperatives and the like but only if they have resources, and these resources would be sharply curtailed if their relationship with the broader society were completely disrupted. Similarly, students can organize their own seminars, their own living communes, their own bookstores, but it would be difficult for them to become proficient in many of the sciences and professions without using the resources available in the broader academic community. Self-imposed "apartheid" is self-defeating. "Build baby build" is a more useful slogan than "out baby out" or "burn baby burn."

Through building its own institutions and developing its own resources a low power group makes itself less vulnerable to exploitation and also augments its power by providing itself with alternatives to inauthentic cooperation. In so doing, it increases the likelihood that those in high power will be responsive to a change: the positive incentives for changing and the negative incentives for not changing take on greater value. Moreover, such self-constructive action may help to reduce the fears and stereotypes which underlie much of the defensiveness of high power groups.

In addition to the strategy of developing one's own resources and building one's own institutions, there are still other strategies that can be followed by a low power group in the attempt to influence a reluctant or disinterested high power group. The various strategies are not incompatible with one another. I list several of the major ones:

(1.) Augment its power by collecting or activating subgroups within the high power group or third parties as allies.

(2.) Search for other kinds of connections with the high power group which, if made more salient, could increase its affective or instrumental dependence upon the low power group and thus change the power balance.
(3.) Attempt to change the attitudes of those in high power through education and moral persuasion.
(4.) Use existing legal procedures to bring pressures for change.
(5.) Use harassment techniques to increase the other's costs of adhering to the status quo.

The effectiveness of any strategy of influence is undoubtedly much determined by the particular circumstances so that no strategy can be considered to be unconditionally effective or ineffective. Nevertheless, it is reasonable to assume that low power groups can rarely afford to be without allies. By definition, a low power group is unlikely to achieve many of its objectives unless it can find allies among significant elements within the high power group or unless it can obtain support from other ("third party") groups that can exert influence on the high power group. There is considerable reason to expect that allies are most likely to be obtained if:

(1.) They are sought out rather than ignored or rejected.
(2.) Superordinate goals, common values and common interests can be identified which could serve as a basis for the formation of cooperative bonds.
(3.) Reasonably full communication is maintained with the potential allies.
(4.) One's objectives and methods are readily perceived as legitimate and feasible.
(5.) One's tactics dramatize one's objectives and require the potential allies to choose between acting "for" or "against" these objectives and, thus, to commit themselves to taking a position; and
(6.) Those in high power employ tactics, as a counter-response, which are widely viewed as "unfitting" and thus produce considerable sympathy for the low power group.

CIVIL DISOBEDIENCE

There is no time here to elaborate on procedures and tactics of building allies; this is what politics is all about. However, let me just comment about the nonviolent, civil disobedience, confrontation tactics which have been employed with considerable success by civil rights and student groups. These methods have tended, with continuing usage, to have less effect in arousing public response and sympathy for the low power groups involved. In part, this is because many of those in high power have learned that to employ coercion as a response to a nonviolent tactic of civil disobedience is self-defeating; it only serves to swing much of the hitherto uninvolved public behind the demonstrators. This is, of course, what happened in Selma and Birmingham as well as at Columbia University and Chicago when unfitting force was used. These techniques also have become less effective because repeated usage vulgarizes them; a measure which is acceptable as an unusual or emergency procedure becomes unacceptable as a routine breeder of social disruption. Let me note parenthetically that I have discussed "nonviolent confrontation" tactics as a method for gaining allies and public support rather than as a procedure for directly changing the attitudes of those in high power who are strongly committed to their views. I have seen no evidence that would suggest it has any significant effects of the latter sort.

Finding allies and supporters is important not only because it directly augments the influence of a low power group but also because having allies enables the low power group to use each of the other change strategies more effectively. I shall not discuss the other strategies in detail but confine myself to a brief comment about each. A low power group can increase the dependence of a high power group on it by concentrating its power rather than by allowing it to be spread thinly. Thus, the political power of the Negro vote could be higher if it were able to decide the elections in a half-dozen states such as New York, California, Pennsylvania, Illinois, Ohio and Michigan than if the Negro vote were less concentrated. Similarly, their economic power would be greater if they were able to obtain over certain key industries and key unions rather than if they were randomly dispersed.

Education, moral persuasion and the use of legal procedures to bring about social change have lately come into disrepute because these strategies do not bring "instant change" nor do they produce as much *esprit de corps* as strategies which give rise to direct action techniques. Nevertheless, it would be a mistake to underestimate the importance of beliefs, values and the sense of legitimacy in determining individual and social action. Similarly, to engage in anti-intellectualism or to ignore the significance of intellectual work in establishing true knowledge is an error. Truth threatens arbitrary power by unmasking its unreasonableness and pretensions. Anti-intellectualism is a tool of the despot in his struggle to silence or discredit truth. Also, it would be a mistake to ignore the tremendous changes in beliefs and values concerning human relationships which have occurred during the recent past. Much of the evil which now occurs is not a reflection of deliberate choice to inflict such evil but rather the lack of a deliberate choice to overcome self-perpetuating vicious cycles. Obviously, a considerable educational effort is needed to help broaden the understanding of conflict and to accelerate growth in the ability to include others in the same moral community with oneself even though they be of rather different social, economic and ethnic background.

HARASSMENT

Harassment may be the only effective strategy available to a low power group if it faces an indifferent or hostile high power group. Although sharp lines cannot be drawn, it is useful to distinguish "harassment," "obstruction," and "destruction" from one another. "Harassment" employs legal or semilegal techniques to inflict a loss, to interfere with, disrupt or embarrass those with high power; "obstruction" employs illegal techniques to interrupt or disrupt the activities and purposes of those in high power; "destruction" employs illegal, violent techniques to destroy or to take control over people or property. Obstructive and destructive techniques invite massive retaliation and repression which, if directed against harassment techniques, would often seem inappropriate and arouse sympathy. However, a clearly visible potential for the employment of obstructive and destructive techniques may serve to make harassment procedures both more acceptable and more effective.

There are many forms of harassment which can be employed by low power groups: consumer boycotts; work slowdowns; rent strikes; demonstrations; sit-ins; tying up phones, mail, government offices, businesses, traffic, etc. by excessive and prolonged usage; ensnarling bureaucratic systems in their own red tape by requiring them to follow their own formally stated rules and procedures; being excessively friendly and cooperative; creating psychological nuisances by producing outlandish behavior, appearances and odors in stores, offices and other public places; encouraging contagion of the ills of the slum (rats, uncollected garbage, etc.) to surrounding communities; etc. Harassment, as is true for most procedures, is undoubtedly most effective when it is employed to obtain well-defined, specific objectives and when it is selectively focussed on key persons and key institutions rather than when it is merely a haphazard expression of individual discontent.

IN CONCLUSION

As I review what I have written in this last section, where I have functioned as a self-appointed consultant to those in low power, I am struck by how little of what I have said is well-grounded in systematic research or theory. As social scientists we have rarely directed our attention to the defensiveness and resistance of the strong and powerful in the face of the need for social change. We have not considered what strategies and tactics are available to low power groups and which of these are likely to lead to a productive rather than destructive process of conflict resolution. We have focussed too much on the turmoil and handicaps of those in low power and not enough on the defensiveness and resistance of the powerful; the former will be overcome as the latter is overcome.

Is it not obvious that with the great disparities in power and affluence within nations and between nations that there will be continuing pressures for social change? And is it not also obvious that the processes of social change will be disorderly and destructive unless those in power are able or enabled to lower their defensiveness and resistance to a change in their relative status? Let us refocus our efforts so that we will have something useful to say to those who are seeking radical but peaceful social change. Too often in the past significant social change in the distribution of power has been achieved at the cost of peace; this is a luxury that the world is no longer able to afford.

References

Coleman, J. S. *Community Conflict*. Glencoe: The Free Press, 1957.
Coser, L. *The Functions of Social Conflict*. Glencoe: The Free Press, 1956.
Deutsch, M. "Cooperation and Trust: Theoretical Notes," in M. R. Jones (ed.). *Nebraska Symposium on Motivation*. Lincoln: University of Nebraska Press, 1962. (a)
Deutsch, M. "A Psychological Basis for Peace," in Q. Wright, W. M. Evan, and M. Deutsch (eds.). *Preventing World War III: Some Proposals*. New York: Simon and Schuster, 1962. (b)
Deutsch, M. "Conflict and Its Resolution," Presidential address before the Division of Personality and Social Psychology of the American Psychological Association, September 5, 1965. (a)
Deutsch, M. "A Psychological Approach to International Conflict," in G. Sperrazzo (ed.). *Psychology and International Relations*. Washington, D.C.: Georgetown University Press, 1965. (b)
Deutsch, M. "Vietnam and the Start of World War III: Some Psychological Parallels," Presidential address before the New York State Psychological Association, May 6, 1966.
Deutsch, M. *The Resolution of Conflict*. New Haven: Yale University Press (in preparation).
Festinger, L. "The Psychological Effects of Insufficient Reward," *American Psychologist*, 16 (1961): 1–11.
Fisher, R. "Fractionating Conflict," in R. Fisher (ed.). *International Conflict and Behavioral Science: The Craigville Papers*. New York: Basic Books, 1964.
Hovland, C. I., I. L. Janis, and H. H. Kelley. *Communication and Persuasion*. New Haven: Yale University Press, 1953.
Rokeach, M. *The Open and Closed Mind*. New York: Basic Books, 1960.
Stein, M. I. *The Creative Individual* in manuscript, 1968.
Tomkins, S. S. and C. C. Izard (eds.). *Affect, Cognition, and Personality*. New York: Springer Publishing Co., 1965.

38

VICTORIA M. OLDS

Freedom Rides: A Social Movement as an Aspect of Social Change

The struggle for equal opportunity for the Negro people is not a recent development, but it has gained acceleration and more forceful impact since the 1954 Supreme Court decision that separate facilities for Negroes are not equal. However, the 1961 report of the U.S. Commission on Civil Rights indicates that although much progress has been made there is much more yet to be accomplished before Negroes are afforded status as first-class citizens.[1] The wide gap between the democratic principles of the United States and current practices in race relations has been lessened with the aid of Constitutional amendments, court decisions, legislative acts, executive orders, administrative rulings, local ordinances, and activities of private agencies and Negro interest groups. Nevertheless, a gap still remains between the commitments and guarantees officially made by the government to all citizens and the realization of these promises of civil rights for Negroes.

The federal courts have been active in prosecuting injustices with regard to discrimination in the use of bus terminals in interstate travel, mostly in the deep southern states of Alabama, Louisiana, Mississippi, Georgia and South Carolina. The Supreme Court in 1960 declared illegal any racial segregation in services provided for interstate travelers. In 1961 it decreed that the operation of a private restaurant in space leased from a public agency could not be conducted on a discriminatory basis.[2]

In that same period token desegregation of schools was begun in all but

Reprinted with permission of the author and the National Association of Social Workers, from *Social Work*, Vol. 8, No. 3 (July, 1963), pp. 16–23.

three of the states in the Deep South. The extent of school integration can be seen in Table 38-1. In Georgia, which was not due to begin desegregation until 1961–1962, Negro students were admitted to the University of Georgia earlier, an indication that, in some states, there may be less resistance to desegregation at the college level. However, this was certainly not the case in Mississippi in 1962.

The slow, uneven, painstaking process of correcting racial discrimination has been welcomed by segregationists who are eager for loopholes that will further delay the social change involved. But many groups, both white and Negro, felt frustrated by the lack of the "deliberate speed" that had been ordered by the Supreme Court. The "sit-ins" were the beginning of a non-violent

Table 38-1. *Integration of Students in Public Schools in the Southern States, 1960–1961**

STATE	SCHOOL ENROLLMENT	NEGRO STUDENTS Total	Percent	NEGROES INTEGRATED Total	Percent
South Carolina	612,894	258,667	42	0	0
Mississippi	566,421	278,640	49	0	0
Florida	1,919,792	212,280	20	27	.013
Alabama	787,269	271,134	34	0	0
Georgia	921,632	295,255	32	0	0
Louisiana	693,202	271,021	39	1	.0004
Texas	2,129,540	288,553	13	3,500	1.21
Virginia	879,500	211,000	23	208	.099
Arkansas	422,183	105,130	25	113	.107
Tennessee	828,000	152,352	18	376	.247
North Carolina	1,140,000	307,800	27	82	.026
Border States					
Delaware	81,603	14,973	18	6,783	45.3
Kentucky	635,432	41,938	6.6	16,329	38.9
Maryland	598,088	136,882	23	45,943	33.6
Missouri	842,000	84,000	10	35,000	41.7

* Data from *Education*, 1961 U.S. Commission on Civil Rights Report, Book 2 (Washington, D.C.: U.S. Government Printing Office, 1961), p. 238.

protest movement to demand implementation of civil rights that had not been achieved effectively by other methods.[3] Subsequent demonstrations at churches by "kneel-ins," at beaches by "wade-ins," at bus terminals by the Freedom Rides dramatize the determination and vigor of a more aggressive minority group.

The 1961 report of the U.S. Commission on Civil Rights gives recognition to the direct action of private citizens by noting:

Partly as a result of the sit-ins, there has been a marked change, for the most part unpublicized and without drama, in many southern cities. Racial barriers have been removed not only in areas where the law of the land supported the claim for equal treatment—as in publicly operated facilities and interstate transportation terminals—but also in many areas of private concern where no legal compulsion has been held to exist. By the close of 1960, for instance, variety store chains had opened lunch counters in 112 southern and border cities to Negro patrons.[4]

The social phenomenon of the Freedom Rides is dealt with in this paper on three different levels: (1) The Rides are viewed as important events in their own right in the struggle to extend civil rights to Negroes. (2) They are studied as a social system and as a type of social movement. In this latter context an effort is made to define and describe a social system and a social movement according to patterns developed by some of the leading theoreticians in the field and to see how closely these patterns can be fitted to the social entity of the Rides. (3) The Rides are considered in the light of their contribution to social change. Social workers have been concerned with social change from the earliest efforts to deal with poverty, but only in more recent years has the profession become articulate about the importance of understanding the processes of social change. Before social workers can be effective as participants in the formulation of policy directed toward positive social change, as indicated in the revised statement of curriculum policy adopted by the Council on Social Work Education in October 1962, it is essential that they acquire the technical competence and sophistication to understand the dynamics of social change.

WHAT IS A FREEDOM RIDE?

The Freedom Rides were developed in 1961, following the sit-ins, which were at their height in 1960. They arose out of the need to end segregation at lunch counters in bus terminals, as well as in other facilities essential to the intercity traveler. Participants were recruited by the Congress of Racial Equality (CORE) and trained carefully in the self-discipline required in a program of nonviolence. Sociodramas were used to enact situations that might arise. CORE had also been active in training and co-ordinating the persons active in the sit-ins.

The nonviolent direct action technique requires that a participant not strike anyone, not even to save himself or a group member from a beating. He must not push anyone or carry a weapon, must keep his hands unclenched and at his sides even if struck, must show no anger, regardless of provocation. He must not be antagonistic, sarcastic, or flippant. He must not willingly allow segregation.

Groups were assigned to different bus routes and each had a leader designated to make decisions in event of emergency. Comprising these groups were teams composed of three persons, two of whom were assigned to integrate the facility, whether it was a lunch counter, rest room, or waiting room at a terminal. These two persons, one white and one Negro, were observed closely by the third member of the team, whose task was to remain inconspicuous, warn of the approach of a hostile mob, witness any violence (which did occur, especially, in the smaller towns), and get help, as needed, from doctors or lawyers. Refusal of service and mob violence are law violations, and as such were reported to the Department of Justice and the Interstate Commerce Commission. A trip was considered successful when it resulted in establishing service in the facility on an integrated basis. Once the facilities were integrated, the local chapter of the National Association for the Advancement of Colored People (NAACP) could follow through to see that integrated service was continued.

In summary, the purpose of the Freedom Rides was to test existing laws and to demand that they be enforced. The Freedom Riders were an integrated group of highly motivated, well-disciplined, dedicated people. The Freedom Rides were effective as a demonstration of strength, a source of leverage for influential coalitions, and a means for focusing public attention on the issue of civil rights. Eugene Rostow, dean of the Yale University Law School, has pointed out that inasmuch as the South is not making rapid progress in securing civil rights for Negroes, outside intervention is needed to help those Southerners who believe in enforcing the Constitution to overcome the resistance of those who are opposed.[5]

ELEMENTS OF SOCIAL CHANGE

Before analyzing the elements of the social change processes embodied in the Freedom Ride movement, it is useful to note the changes in our national and international ways of life. The United States economy has adopted automation, intensifying the need for flexibility, adaptability, and mobility in the labor force, and for white-collar workers and skilled technicians, as well as for all types of professional workers. Greater stress has been placed on education and training of workers. The movement from farms and small towns to the cities and suburbs has accelerated. Means of mass transportation and the mass communication media have multiplied. The pressure is toward conformity and homogeneity throughout the entire country. All sections of the country are so interdependent that problems in one area create repercussions throughout.

For these reasons the continuation of the Southern pattern of an obsolete one-crop economy with a plantation psychology became dysfunctional and deleterious to an expanding national economy and to the international prestige of the country. The emergence of the independent nations in Africa created a new image of a dark-skinned people who had high status, important political power, and access to the elite centers in the United States and in other countries. As the "cold war" got under way, it became clear that the United States, as the champion of the underdeveloped countries, could not tolerate discrimination and inequalities within its own borders. American democracy had to demonstrate for the entire world that, in fact, all Americans were free and equal. These were additional pressures that made outside intervention in the South necessary when it became evident that there was too great resistance to permit adaptation to the changing conditions and demands in the national and international scenes.

Loomis has formulated some elements of social change that have applicability toward an understanding of the movement of the Freedom Rides, both as a social system and as a force for social change. He stated that change may come as a result of internal forces or from factors in the environment.[6] In the case of the Freedom Riders, the internal forces can be thought of as the restlessness of the Negroes because of the delay in realizing the benefits of the civil rights decisions, and the discrepancy between the treatment they see being given to white people and the discriminatory treatment they receive. Other internal forces might include the growth of the Negro middle class, which, because of improved education and better living standards, is able to be more assertive in making claims on society. External forces are the economic, social, and political changes in the United States and in the world. These categories of internal and external are not mutually exclusive but interact continually. The development of external factors creates a favorable climate for collective action. For example, one of the internal forces might be the availability of skilled leadership within the Negro group, without which effective collective action might not materialize.

FREEDOM RIDES AS A SOCIAL SYSTEM

The paradigm developed by Loomis, in which he lists nine elements as units of social interaction,[7] could also be applied to analysis of the Freedom Rides as a social system. Each element has an articulating process.

The first element is *belief* or *knowledge*. This would refer to the knowledge of the Freedom Riders of the condition of Negroes in the South as compared with those who live in the North, of civil rights legislation as compared with actual practices, of the cultural patterns of the communities to be visited and what behavior to expect from their inhabitants. "Belief" would extend to their ideals of human relations, their concepts of the "good life," and their sense of responsibility for helping to extend the benefits of this society to Negroes and to correct inequities. The process related to this element is *cognitive mapping* and *validation*. This has stemmed from the educational background, religious and ethical convictions, and empirical testing of the participants in relation to their beliefs in the equality of man.

Another element is *sentiment*, or the morale of the group and the liking of the participants for one another. Within the group there is a high degree of solidarity. Common ideals and the high ethical plane of the motivating factor create strong bonds. The dedication of the group to its goals despite the difficulties and even the dangers involved, and the fact that the beneficiaries are persons not known to the group are indications of high morale.

The processes involved are *tension management* and *communication of the sentiment*. Tension management is handled by the discipline imposed as a requirement for joining the group. Communication takes place daily through the structured inspirational evening meetings en route. Conformity to the *norms* or standards of good sportsmanship and to the rules of the game are structured in the training in nonviolence that precedes the trip. This is an interesting aspect of the Freedom Ride movement, because these norms are at variance with the usual norms of the larger society. Passive resistance, which is reminiscent of both Christ and Gandhi, has served to confound the belligerent opposition while at the same time heightening the group's solidarity. It also serves as a device for boundary maintenance, in that it sets the group apart from the ordinary man, since it demands unusual self-control and discipline. The group's ability to remain nonviolent evokes admiration and dramatizes the *goals* of the group.

Because of the difficulty involved in submitting to aggressive acts, there are structural devices used to facilitate mastery of this method. One such device is the daily *evaluation*, during which each member derives support from the group and encouragement for the next day's efforts. Another is the arbitrary separation of husband and wife, so that no group member will be exposed to the possibility of seeing his spouse harmed, and thus run the risk of violating the nonviolence rule.

The element of *sanctions*, the rewards and penalties that are used to motivate the participants, is more or less internalized with each participant, since this is a volunteer activity, each participant paying his own expenses. The rewards come from inner satisfaction, as well as from public recognition by civic-minded individuals and organizations.

The final element in Loomis's plan is that of *effective facilities*. The facilities used to achieve the ends of the Freedom Riders consisted of intangibles such as their personalities, skill in the nonviolent method, morale, and enthusiasm, and the skill of their leaders in planning the program and in using help from other groups.

Social change is facilitated if linkages can be set up between two social systems so that they act as a unit on specific issues. This development has been termed *systemic linkage* and defined by Loomis as the articulation of one or more of the elements of social interaction.[8] It is suggestive of Truman's discussion of the coalition of "interest groups."[9] An example of such linkage is that of the NAACP and CORE. Similar linkages exist with student nonviolent groups on college campuses, the American Civil Liberties Union, the Urban League, the Southern Regional Council, and others.

Other processes in this social system include the *socialization* of the members of the group by means of the training sessions, in which the trainers serve as role-models, and *institutionalization*, which is reflected in the formal classes in nonviolence that are offered in various places by CORE, the Peacemakers, the Southern Christian Leadership Conference, and the School of Religion of Howard University.

OPPOSITION TO SOCIAL CHANGE

It is important to keep in mind that while there are dynamic forces, such as those represented in the Freedom Rides, pushing for social change, there are also competing forces operating to maintain the status quo. For example, the White Citizens' Councils arose to maintain white supremacy and to oppose all efforts directed toward desegregation. There were also active supporters of the status quo in the ranks of state and local government officials, and opportunists among the Negro middle-class and professional groups.[10] The power of the regressive forces had to be countered by the greater power of the federal decisions to integrate the armed forces, to refuse contracts to firms that used discriminatory hiring policies, and to admit Negroes into the higher grades of the civil service.

The struggle for Negro rights can be viewed as a bid for power by a minority group and as a demand made upon the dominant group to admit the minority group into the circles where community decisions are made. The legitimate power invested in the government is reinforcing this demand by appointing Negroes to positions of authority and by attempting to extend the political power of the Negro by freeing the Negro vote. The economic power of the Negro is being improved by greater access to better jobs and higher wages and by access to better education. These factors will make for more rapid progress in the removal of discriminatory practices.

The analysis of the Freedom Rides as a social movement and a factor in social change can be clarified further by consideration of Heberle's emphasis that the function of a social movement is to bring about a basic change in the social order, especially in the relationship between labor and property, a change that will affect the distribution of income and wealth and the relative power positions of the classes.[11] Evidence of this change can be seen in the redefinition of the status and role of the Negro in the South and elsewhere. The shift is from low-status menial positions and second-class citizenship to open access to high-status preferred positions. Social situations must be altered to enable this movement to take place.

The processes of social change often are inseparably linked with crisis and conflict. King discusses the utility of crisis situations for provoking concrete action.[12] Coser develops this concept further and makes it clear that conflict is not only inevitable, but necessary to achieve social change.[13] Proponents of social change are usually those who envision an improvement, while the opponents are those who anticipate a loss by the change or who fear the change will worsen rather than improve conditions. Resistance to change, when forced out into the open as was done by the Freedom Riders, can lead to active conflict. In this instance, the conflict can be viewed as salutary and leading to social health, much as surgery that removes a cancer can be viewed as leading to physical health.

The Freedom Rides can be categorized as a reform rather than a revolutionary movement, in accordance with the distinctions made by Blumer[14] and others. A reform movement seeks no radical change in the social structure: The scope of objectives is limited to change in specific behaviors. The participants accept the prevailing mores and code of ethics. The movement is respectable and can make legitimate claims on the existing institutions of school, church, press, government, and social organizations. It appeals to the middle class and seeks a favorable public reaction. Its primary function is to reaffirm the ideal values of society. Aspects of all these criteria can be seen in the Freedom Ride movement.

The sponsorship of a movement is important. The closer the sponsorship is to the existing power structure, the more respectable is the movement and the greater is the chance for its success. This applies also to the tactics used. If the methods are unacceptable and frowned upon by the community, the objectives of the movement will be jeopardized. In the case of the Freedom Riders, the strategy of nonviolence has generally been approved, even though direct action methods seem unbecoming to many middle-class and professional groups. Coser points out that among sociologists as a group there is a tendency to avoid conflict and to want to maintain a state of equilibrium.[15] Conflict situations are viewed as negative, disorganizing, or even destructive, while the optimum condition is seen as one of harmony and equilibrium. Perhaps this observation may be made of social workers also, as a group that tends to underestimate the growth potential inherent in conflict situations.

PRINCIPLES OF SOCIAL ACTION

To apply the casework model of study, diagnosis, and treatment may seem too clinical an approach to the presentation of social action implications in this analysis of the processes of social change. It seems pertinent, however, to emphasize the first step in making a study. Before decisions can be made as to strategies and plans of action, it is essential to have a thorough knowledge of many facets of the situation. The problem itself needs to be clearly understood. What caused it? How long and in what ways has it manifested itself? How extensive is it? Who are the people affected? What are they prepared to do, if anything? How disturbing to their way of life is the problem? What are the linkages—to social institutions, to other groups in the population, to the power structure?

The area to be involved needs study. How is it to be encompassed or delimited? What are the sources of influence? What are the available resources in finance, personnel, alliances with other groups? What are the risks? What are the legal intricacies? What are the long-range and the immediate goals?

The activists in a social action program must be knowledgeable in many areas. The know-how is often gained in the course of a struggle, but, however acquired, the leadership must have knowledge of the community, its structure, its history, value system, patterning of power groups, points of leverage for various kinds of changes, the official and the unofficial positions of civic and social and religious groups on related issues. A friendly alliance with the mass media and avenues of communication are also necessary.

Because the indigenous groups in the South were subject to intimidation and reprisals, it was necessary to draw upon outside leadership and the strength of national organizations. These groups were able to set up linkages with other groups and institutional forces. With this help, and with the help of a charismatic leader like Martin Luther King, it was possible to develop local leadership in some instances and to strengthen the church group in the South and enable them to give leadership. It is important to educate the participants as to the issues, the lineup of opposing forces, the available resources, and the methods of collective action.

Continuity of leadership is needed because of the changing participants in the movement, with frequent turnover of demonstrators. The protest activities must be kept under control according to the pattern set, in order to be effective and to avoid loss of support from coalition groups. At the same time it is important to have a continuing evaluation of tactics, to facilitate refocusing when indicated, because of the unpredictability of outcomes. It is also important to be alert to expressions of interest and support from various sectors of the larger community, to present the issues to the public, and to keep people informed. Dramatic presentations are effective, also special pleas for recruitment of persons with high status who will make known their support of the movement.

CONCLUSION

After investigating some of the theoretical formulations regarding social movements and the processes of social change, it is important to focus attention again on the urgency of the civil rights issues and the further steps needed to insure the realization of equal opportunity for Negroes. The course of events favors desegregation forces, but there are many problems ahead. The changes that brought about the imbalance—economic, political, and social—in the South are being felt throughout the rest of the country, as Negro workers migrate into cities and towns in search of better job opportunities.

The increased mobility demanded of all workers presents special problems for Negro workers because of the blocked mobility resulting from racial visibility. Consequently, in place of segregation *de jure*, there may develop a segregation *de facto*, as the Negro is denied housing in the suburbs to which the white families move. Grodzins points out that already a polarization has taken place in large urban centers, with the central city containing the Negro population and the suburban fringes predominantly occupied by whites.[16] If such an ecological patterning should persist, there would be many serious social, economic, and political consequences for the greater metropolitan areas and for the country as a whole. What is needed is freedom of movement, so that Negroes as well as whites can select housing and neighborhoods according to their individual life-styles.

The Freedom Rides exemplify one aspect in the processes of social change. As a social movement, they act as a safety valve to release the pressure of unrest in the larger social system. They also test our commitment to basic humanitarian values and strengthen our pluralistic democratic system. The imbalance is righted, but only to go on to create a new imbalance.

Notes

1. *Civil Rights*. Washington, D.C.: U.S. Government Printing Office, 1961, ix.
2. *Ibid.*, 3.
3. Victoria M. Olds, "Sit-ins: Social Action To End Segregation," *Social Work*, 6, No. 2 (April 1961): 99–105.
4. *Op. cit.*, 4.
5. "The Role of the Outsider," *Current*, No. 16 (August 1961), 48.
6. Charles P. Loomis, "Toward a Theory of Systemic Social Change," in Irwin T.

Sanders (ed.). *Interprofessional Training Goals for Technical Assistance Personnel Abroad.* New York: Council on Social Work Education, 1959, 165.

7. *Social Systems: Essays on their Persistence and Change*, New York: D. Van Nostrand Co., 1960, 5–30.

8. *Ibid.*, 32–34.

9. David B. Truman. *The Governmental Process.* New York: Alfred A. Knopf, 1953, 251.

10. Oliver C. Cox, "Leadership Among Negroes in the United States," in Alvin W. Gouldner (ed.). *Studies in Leadership.* New York: Harper and Brothers, 1950, 260.

11. Rudolf Heberle, *Social Movements.* New York: Appleton-Century-Crofts, 1951, 6.

12. C. Wendell King, *Social Movements in the United States.* New York: Random House, 1956, 63.

13. Lewis A. Coser, *Functions of Social Conflict.* Glencoe, Ill.: The Free Press, 1956, 126.

14. Herbert Blumer, "Social Movements," in A. M. Lee (ed.). *Principles of Sociology.* New York: Barnes and Noble, 1951, 212.

15. *Op. cit.*, 29.

16. Morton Grodzins, *The Metropolitan Area as a Racial Problem.* Pittsburgh, Pa.: University of Pittsburgh Press, 1958, 5.

Index

Academic Market Place, The (Caplow and McGee), 332
Action-research intervention, 355, 378
Actions as target for change, 15, 21-22
Adams, D. W., 267, 268, 270-85
Administering Changes (Ronken and Lawrence), 191
Adorno, T. W., 445
Affiliated change agents, 5, 256-64
   initiatory aims and, 257
   pragmatic aims and, 257
Affluent Society, The (Galbraith), 332
Aggression, On (Lorenz), 469
Agnew, Spiro T., 454, 491
Alcoholics Anonymous, 333
Alinsky, Saul, 452, 465, 521-31
   See also Community organization, Alinsky's model for
Allen, V. L., 78
American Civil Liberties Union, 582
American Friends Service Committee, 534
American Youth Festival, 510
Analytic model, 4, 10-13
Anarchism, 512-19
   as an attitude, 512
   individualism and, 517-19
   violence and, 513-16
Andrews, C. F., 534, 535
Architectural Research Lab, 253
Ardrey, Robert, 445, 469
Arendt, Hannah, 452
Arensberg, C. M., 151, 152, 191, 345, 351
Argyle, M., 235, 239
Argyris, Chris, 18, 25, 26, 31-42, 63, 81-82, 84, 86, 150, 208, 346, 347, 351, 353, 354, 387, 394
Arnold, Matthew, 365
Asylums (Goffman), 332
Atkins, Stuart, 27, 43-59
Attitudes as target for change, 15, 19-20

Authoritarian personality theory of cause of violence, 445
Axelrod, W., 17
Azrin, N. H., 471

Bachman, J., 345
Back, K., 148
Bales, R. F., 236
Balkin, J. L., 17
Bamforth, K. W., 164
Bandler, R. J., 20
Bandura, Albert, 445, 446
Barnes, L. B., 72, 115
Basic group, 103
Bass, B. M., 77, 81, 86, 235
Baumgartel, H., 78, 79
Bavelas, A., 135, 235
Beatles, 509
Bechtel, R. B., 240
Becker, S. W., 235
Becker, W. C., 445
Beckhard, Richard, 145, 154, 213-22, 244, 267, 268, 286-93, 346, 347, 350, 389, 395, 396, 421-39
Beer, M., 73, 80
Beerbohm, Max, 365
Behaviorist model, 4, 13-14
Bell, G. B., 21
Bell, Inge Powell, 535, 542
Bem, Daryl, 20
Benedict, B. A., 345
Benjamin, L., 332
Benne, K. D., 62, 135, 314n, 351
Bennett, Edith B., 101, 345
Bennis, W. G., 62, 63, 64, 65, 75-76, 82, 100, 244, 250, 251, 310, 344, 345, 351, 353, 354, 357, 361-72, 387, 394, 398, 399n, 419n
Berkowitz, Leonard, 445, 464, 468-75
Berlew, D. E., 100

587

Bernard, Jessie, 456
Berzon, B., 64
Bienen, Henry, 442, 443, 444, 448, 452
Bim, W. R., 12
Biological theory of cause of violence, 445
Bion, W. R., 83, 103, 106
Bixenstien, V. E., 538
Black Panther Party, 2, 490-91
Black power, 477, 491, 571
Blake, Robert R., 19, 24, 27, 64, 72, 74, 79, 86, 113-20, 345, 351, 352, 353, 354, 355, 356, 383, 387, 390, 391, 395, 396, 397, 401-20, 418n, 461-62
Blumberg, H., 536, 537
Boettger, C. R., 355, 377n
Bolton, G., 534
Bondurant, Joan V., 534, 535, 542
Bonnot Gang, 517-18
Bose, N. K., 534, 535
Boulding, Kenneth, 500
Bowers, D., 345
Bowers, S., 244
Boycott, economic, 553, 562-63
Boyd, J. B., 67, 68, 69, 71, 84, 91
Bradford, L. P., 62, 63, 66, 134, 135, 314n, 351
Brehm, J. W., 152
Brezezinski, Zbigniew, 465, 502-6
Brown, Bert, 541
Brown, "Rap," 451
Brunstetter, P. H., 74, 387
Buchanan, P. C., 63, 66, 74, 357-58, 386-400
Buckley, William, 485
Bugental, J. R. T., 86
Bunker, D. R., 26, 27, 67, 69, 84, 91, 92, 344
Burckhardt, D., 238
Bureaucracy, 362-63, 368, 372
  gherao movement and, 496-97
Burke, H. L., 75
Burke, W. W., 353, 355, 357, 373-85
Burtt, H., 20

Calder, P. H., 310-15
Calico Printing Company, 158-83
Callahan, D. M., 310-15, 345
Calvinism, 2
Campbell, D. T., 21, 239, 240, 256, 260
Campbell, John P., 25, 27, 60-89, 78, 84, 344, 351, 352
Canavan, D., 455, 538
Canter, R. R., 297-98
Canter-Tyler studies, 297-98
Caplan, Gerald, 10, 12-13
Caplow, T., 332
Carmichael, Stokely, 451, 473, 510
Carr, S., 247
Caudill, W. A., 333
Caute, David, 491

Chaigne, H., 535
Chander, J. P., 534
Change, organizational
  bureaucracy and, 362-63, 368, 372
  comparison of managerial change and, 373-84
  crucial issues of, 386-99
  forecast of, 369-72
  goals of, 370
  idea of, 361-62
  intellectuals and, 364-66
  managerial philosophy and, 366-69
  problems of, 367-69
  rate of, 362
  reasons for, 363-66
  staff requirements and, 379-81
  structure and, 370-71
  time frame of, 379
  See also Change process; Organizational development
Change process
  anthropological analysis of, 185-94
  confrontation meeting for handling, 213-22
  corrective action for, 189
  detecting and assessing deviations in, 187-89
  helping a group with planned, 286-93
  implementation of, 192
  long-run, 191
  in rural communities, 270-84
  stability and, 186-87
  understanding social organization and, 294-308
  validation of, 192
  See also Change, organizational
Chapple, E. D., 149
Chein, I., 332, 355
Child, Irvin L., 445
Child-rearing practices theory of violence, 445-46
Chowdry, Kalma, 21
Christie, L. S., 144
Christie, Richard, 445
Civil disobedience, 483, 492, 533
  gherao movement and, 493-500
  justification of, 484-85
  in productive conflicts, 573-74
  rioting and, 476-86
  See also Nonviolence and direct action
Civil protest
  power and, 521-31
  See also Civil disobedience; Confrontation politics; Nonviolence and direct action; Violence and coercion
Civil rights movement
  freedom rides and, 559, 564, 577-85
  methods of, 534

Index

survey methods and, 216-29
See also Nonviolence and direct action
Clark, Colin, 365
Clark, J. V., 314*n*
Clark, K. B., 265
Clark, M. K., 265
Class conflict and violence, 453-54
"Classroom" human relations training and organizational feedback, 206-8
Client system, change process with, 286-93
Cline, V. B., 22, 66
Coch, L., 134, 145, 260, 345, 350, 354, 355
Coercion, *see* Violence and coercion
Cohen, A. R., 152
Cohen, M., 332
Collins, M. E., 152
Colman, A., 248
Colombia, change strategy in rural communities of, 270-84
Committee on Civil Rights in East Manhattan (CCREM), 316, 317, 320, 324, 325, 328
Committee for Nonviolent Action, 559
Community organization, Alinsky's model for, 523-31
  action strategies for, 526-31
  goals of, 525
  initial move for, 524-26
Comparison Study of Personal Managerial Styles, A (Scientific Methods), 117
Conant, Ralph W., 444, 464, 476-86
Conflicts, productive and disruptive, 566-75
  civil disobedience in, 573-74
  cooperation and, 567-68
  persuasion strategy and, 569-70
  rage or fear in, 571
  tactics of, 573-75
See also Nonviolence and direct action
Confrontation meeting, 213-22
  action plans for, 214-18
  conditions for, 214
  definition of, 214
  potential problems of, 219-20
  results of, 218-19
  structure of, 220-22
Confrontation politics, 487-92
  anti-democratic elitism of, 489-90
  fascism and, 488
  necessity of, 507-11
  New Left and, 487-88
  polarization and, 488-89
Congress on Racial Equality (CORE), 579, 582
Conversion through nonviolent action, 547-49
Cook, S., 355
Coons, A. E., 68
Cornell University, black students at, 521
Coser, Lewis, 443, 447-48, 461, 498, 583-84

Council on Social Work Education, 579
Crawford, M. P., 344
Critical mass problem, 26
Crockett, W. J., 355
Cronback, L. J., 22, 66
Crow, W. J., 22
Crowd behavior, 456-57
Cultural change, *see* Organizational development

Dahrendorf, R., 453, 454
Dalton, Melville, 196-97
Data-based strategy, 2, 5, 255-68, 355
  affiliated change agents in, 5, 256-64
  survey feedback and, 258-60
  unaffiliated change agents in, 5, 256-57
Data feedback
  meetings and, 312-13
  process analysis and, 313-14
  rationale of, 310-14
Davies, James, 472
Davis, S., 244
De, Nitish, 455, 465, 493-501
Dean, J., 235, 239
Debray, Regis, 458, 460
Decision making
  experience and 123-26
  feedback and, 124, 125-26
  participation in, 145, 146
  training for, 122-33
  use of model company for, 126-33
Declaration of Independence, 531
DeCrespigny, A., 535, 536
deFleur, M. R., 19
Delgado, Marion, 509
Demonstrations as nonviolent tactics, 558-61
Dennis, Jamie, 387, 388, 389, 394, 395, 396
Denny, R., 80
Deutsch, M., 146, 152, 443, 447, 455, 456, 464, 538, 539, 543-44, 566-76
Dewey, John, 15
Dhawan, G. N., 534, 535

Eastland, James, 569
Eckstein, Harry, 443
Ecology
  psychological, 147-48
  small group, 234-42
  transactions with environment and, 246-47
Education and organizational change, 364-66, 369-70
Efron, D., 241
Ego and His Own, The (Stirner), 517
Elkin, L., 237, 239
Ellis, B. R., 353, 355
Elliss, J. D., 67, 68, 69, 71, 84, 91

Emotions
   denial of, 32-33, 40, 104
   in T-groups, 46-59
Epstein, Y., 455, 538
Erikson, E. H., 534
Esser, A., 240
Etzioni, A., 3n
Evaluation of T-groups in management training, 61-87
Evers, Charles, 569
Exline, R. V., 21, 76
Experience as training for decision making, 123-26
Experimental social innovation, 330-40
Eysenck, H. J., 445

Fairweather, G. W., 17, 257, 258, 259, 263, 268, 330-41
Fanon, Frantz, 443, 447, 448, 452, 500
Fantani, Mario D., 399n
Fasting as nonviolent action, 564
Feedback
   "classroom" human relations training and, 306-8
   in decision making training, 124, 125-26
   meetings and, 312-13
   process analysis and, 313-14
   rationale of, 310-14
   in relationships between superiors and subordinates, 301-6
Feelings as target for change, 15, 16-17, 46-59
Feierabend, I. K., 472
Feierabend, R. L., 472
Felipe, N., 148, 236, 239
Festinger, L., 19, 20, 148, 152, 350
Fiedler, F. E., 22, 146, 154, 223-33
Fisch, E., 345
Fischer, L., 534
Fishbein, M., 20
Fisher, D., 19
Flacks, Richard, 456
Fleishman, Edwin A., 20, 298, 300, 344
Fleishman-Harris studies, 298-301
Force Field Analysis, 354
Ford, D. H., 14
Forman, James, 491
Franklin, M., 150
Freedom Rides, 559, 564, 577-84
French, R. R. P., 134, 145, 260, 345, 350, 354, 355
Frenkel-Brunswik, Else, 445
Freud, Sigmund, 15, 238, 445, 471
Friedman, P., 534
Frustration-aggression theory of cause of violence, 446, 448
   laboratory studies of, 468-75
Fugs, 509
Fulbright, J. William, 527

Gage, N. L., 21, 66, 76
Galanter, E. H., 21
Galbraith, John Kenneth, 144, 332
Galtung, J., 535, 536
Gamson, William A., 456
Gandhi, Mahatma, 528, 529, 538, 548, 562, 564, 581
Gardner, J. W., 352
Garfinkel, H., 239
Gassner, S., 75
Gherao movement in India, 493-500
   characteristics of, 493-96
   as technique for social intervention, 496-500
Gibb, J. R., 62, 314n, 351, 524
Gibb, Lorraine, 524
Gibbon, Edward, 363
Gilbert, E., 19
Gilchrist, J. E., 144, 145
Ginsberg, Allen, 509
Glazer, N., 80
Goffman, E., 332
Goldstein, J. W., 78, 79
Goldwater, Barry, 512
Good, L., 253
Goodman, P., 238
Goring, William, 465, 512-20
Government in Indian weaving shed, 167, 183
Graham, H. D., 443-44
Gramsci, Antonio, 499
Greer, F., 21
Gregg, R. B., 534, 537, 538, 539, 542, 548
Greiner, L. E., 72, 115, 387, 390, 391, 394, 395, 399n
Grimshaw, Allen, 454, 455
Group incentive systems, 198-211
   employee initiated action and, 198-99
   Rucker plan of, 201, 206-7
   Scanlon plan of, 201, 203-5, 207
   See also Incentive systems
Grusky, O., 237
Guerrilla warfare, 458, 462, 508, 568
Guest, Robert H., 387, 391, 394, 395, 396, 397, 399n
Guetzkow, H., 145
Guevara, "Che," 458
Gumpert, P., 455, 538
Gurr, T. R., 443-44, 448-50

Haire, M., 74, 114
Hake, D. F., 471
Hall, Calvin S., 445
Hall, E. T., 234, 236, 238, 241, 246, 252
Hall, H. E., 21
Hall, J., 344
Hall, Milton, 305
Hamilton, Alexander, 522
Hamilton, Charles, 451

Hamilton, E. L., 395, 399*n*
Hammond, K. R., 22
Hampden-Turner, C. H., 86
Hansford, E. A., 538
Hare, A. P., 236, 536, 537
Hare, R. D., 19
Harris, E. F., 20, 300
Harrison, Roger, 15, 77, 79, 83
Harvey, J. B., 355, 377*n*
Harvey, O. J., 445
Harwood Corporation, 260-61
Hastorf, A. H., 14
Havens, A. E., 267, 268, 270-85
Hawthorne studies, 196
Hayden, Tom, 488-89
Hearn, G., 147, 235
Henderson, C., 237
Henry, Emile, 514-15
Hentoff, N., 534, 535
Herzberg, F., 354, 356
Hickerson, G. X., 17
Hierarchy
  of management, 164
  status as, 146-47
Hislop, M. W., 19
Hites, R. W., 21
Hobbs, N., 14, 101
Hoffman, F. R., 259
Hollingshead, A. B., 332
Holmberg, Allan R., 395, 399*n*
Holt, H., 238
Homans, G., 313, 344
Hood, John, 530
Hook, L. H., 148, 236, 239
Hornstein, H., 145, 146, 310-15, 345
Horowitz, M. J., 238
House, R. J., 66
Hovland, E. I., 266, 569
Howe, Irving, 465, 487-92
Howells, L. T., 235
Human Relations Program of the Institute for Social Relations, 301
Hundley, James R., 478, 482
Hungarian Revolution, 453-54, 562
Hutchins, Robert, 368
Hutchinson, R. R., 471
Hyman, H. H., 258, 259

Incentive system, 195-211
  employee initiative and, 198-200, 204-5
  group based, 198-99
  monetary sharing as, 210-11
  participative management and, 201-4
  piecework as, 195-98
  profit sharing as, 210-11
  Rucker plan as, 201, 206-7
  Scanlon plan as, 201, 203-5
Indian weaving shed, 190

acceptance of reorganization in, 175-76, 180, 183
government in, 167, 183
job specialization in, 168
management hierarchy in, 164, 183
productivity and social organization in, 157-83
small work groups in, 168-69, 175-76, 183
status differences in, 174
work organization of, 159-64
Individual change strategy, 2, 4, 9-27, 343-44
  analytic model for, 4, 10-13
  behaviorist model for, 13-14
  social-psychological model for, 13
  targets for change and, 15-23
  Tavistock approach to, 10, 11-12
Individual distance, 238-40
Industrial Revolution, 362-63, 372
Initiation of action by employees, 198-200, 204-5
Initiatory aims, 5
Intellectuals
  attitudes towards, 364-66
  revolution and, 503-4
Intergroup interventions, 355-56
Introducing Social Change: A Manual for Americans Overseas (Arensberg and Niehoff), 152
"Invisible hand," 2

Jacob, Marius, 516-17
Jacob, Philip, 18-19
Jahoda, M., 258, 260, 262, 263, 445
James, J. W., 239
Janis, I. L., 23, 569
Janowitz, Morris, 452
Jaques, Elliot, 387, 388, 394, 395, 396, 397
Jenkins, D. H., 354
Job engineering, 223-33
Johnson, Chalmers, 444, 457-58, 460
Johnson, Lyndon, 362, 524
Jones, Maxwell, 333
Jungle, The (Sinclair), 265

Kahn, Herman, 455
Kahn, R. L., 3*n*, 13, 150, 163, 345, 346, 347
Kassarjan, H. H., 80
Katz, D., 3*n*, 13, 18, 150, 163
Katz, I., 332
Katz, P., 347
Kelley, H. H., 146, 150, 456, 569
Kelley's Role Constant Repertory Test, 77
Kelman, Herbert, 485, 540
Keniston, Kenneth, 445, 454
Kennedy, John F., 523, 524
Kepner, C. H., 23, 26, 27, 122-33, 355, 356, 378

Index

Kernan, J. P., 80
Kerr, Clark, 366, 368
King, G., 239
King, Martin Luther, 1, 2, 482, 510, 528, 530, 534, 583, 584
Kircheimer, B. A., 17
Kleisath, S. W., 73, 80
Klubeck, S., 235
Klunder, Rev. Bruce, 565
Knowles, E. S., 344
Krasner, L. P., 14, 19
Kroes, Robert, 453-54
Kropotkin, Peter, 513
Kruskal, W. H., 239
Kuethe, J. L., 238
Kuriloff, A. H., 23, 27, 43-59

Labor movement, *gherao* tactic in, 493-96
Laboratory education, 31-42, 62, 356
　analysis of change from, 93-94
　comparative study of, 91-101
　See also T-groups
Lakay, George, 484
Lake, Dale G., 351, 352, 358, 421-39
Lakey, G., 535, 536, 540, 542, 543, 548-65
Lambert, Wallace, 455
LaPierce, R. T., 19
Lasswell, H. D., 399n
Lattey, Christine, 19
Lave, L. B., 455, 538
Lawrence, P. R., 191
Leach, Edmund, 470
Leader-member relations, change of, 225-26, 233
Leadership styles, 223-33
　determination of needed, 225-26
　leader-member relations and, 225-26, 228
　position power and, 226, 233
　task structure and, 226, 227, 233
　training and, 298-301
Leavitt, H. J., 144, 235, 398, 399n, 425
Le Bon, Gustav, 456-57
Leipold, W. D., 239
Lemberg Center for the Study of Violence, 476, 482
Lenin, V. I., 452, 458, 491
Lesieur, F. G., 357, 389
Lester, Julius, 491
Levinson, Daniel J., 445
Lewiki, R. J., 538, 539
Lewin, Kurt, 13, 26, 83, 134, 145, 151, 332, 345, 350, 354, 356
Lewis, H. B., 150
Lewis, J. B., 353
Liberation, 534
Lidz, V., 536
Lieberson, Stanley, 478
Likert, R., 25, 145, 345, 350, 419n

Lincoln Electric Company, 200
Lindgren, H. C., 22
Lindzey, Gardner, 445
Lipkin, S., 117
Lippit, R., 135, 145, 262, 332, 345, 347, 350, 352, 387, 523
Little, K. B., 237, 238
Loomis, Charles P., 580-81, 582
Lorenz, Konrad, 445, 469-70, 471, 473
Lovaas, O. I., 446
Lubin, B., 83
Lynch, K., 247
Lynd, Staughton, 490
Lytle, William O., 387, 389, 395, 396, 397

Maccoby, N., 20
Machiavelli, Niccolò, 452
Machlup, Fritz, 366
Madaras, G. R., 20
Madge, J., 333
Mahler, W. R., 296
Maier, Norman, 23, 24, 26, 27, 133-42, 303
Maitron, Jean, 519
Management
　attitude toward work supervision of, 114-21
　changing philosophy of, 366-69
　confrontation meeting for, 213-22
　development of, 373-84, 421-39
　education of, 364
　effects of team development on, 421-39
　habits of, 202
　participative, 200-2, 204
　planning change of relationships within, 286-93
　problems of, 213, 376-77
　relationship with subordinates of, 301-6
　See also Manager; Supervisor training
Manager
　analyzing recurrent changes and, 190-91
　assessment of deviations by, 187-89
　corrective action by, 189
　implementation of change by, 191-92
　leadership styles of, 223-33
　process of change and, 185-86, 192-93
　as target for change, 373-84
　See also Management; Supervisor training
Managerial grid, 114-21, 351-52, 354, 383, 384, 390, 396, 401-17
　concepts of change and, 402-6
　corporate culture and, 406-11
Managerial Grid, The (Blake and Mouton), 117
Mann, Floyd C., 258, 259, 268, 294-309, 351, 353
Mann, Horace, 14
Mann, J. H., 19

Index

Mann, L., 23
Mannheim, B. F., 117
Manual for Direct Action, A (Lakey), 543
Mao Tse-tung, 452, 458-60
March, J. G., 3n
Martin, H. O., 67
Maslow, A. H., 25
Massie, J. L., 346
Mathis, A. G., 83
Maynard, Robert, 490-91
McBride, G., 239, 240, 241
McCarthy, Eugene, 507
McGee, R. J., 332
McGregor, Douglas, 18, 74, 252, 347, 354, 355, 364, 366
McGuire, W., 18
McKersie, R .B., 541
McLeish, John, 448
Meeker, J., 538
Menninger, K., 29
Mental health consultation, 12-13
Mental Hospital, The (Stanton and Schwartz), 333
Merton, R. B., 399n
Merton, R. K., 100
Midpeninsula Observer, 490
Miles, M. B., 26, 63, 67, 69, 91, 92, 100, 258, 259, 262, 310-15, 387, 389, 394, 395, 396, 397, 424
Milgram, Stanley, 457
Miller, N. E., 64, 446
Miller, W. R., 535, 542
Miner, J. R., 78
Monroe, W. H., 296
Montagu, Ashley, 445
Moore, William, 559
Morris, Desmond, 445
Morse, N. C., 145
Motivation and organizational change, 371-72
Mouton, Jane Srygley, 19, 24, 27, 65, 72, 79, 86, 113-20, 345, 351, 352, 353, 354, 355, 356, 383, 387, 390, 391, 396, 401-20, 461-62
Mowrer, O. H., 446, 472
Multiple Role Playing (MRP) as training technique, 134-41
Mustie, A. J., 534
Mutiny as nonviolent action, 554

Nader, Ralph, 2, 256, 265
Naess, A., 534-35
National Advisory Commission on Civil Disorders, 451, 462
National Association for the Advancement of Colored People (NAACP), 580, 582
Neff, F. W., 312

Negroes, 491
   discrimination against, 216-29, 530
   freedom rides and, 559, 564, 577-85
   integration of, 578
   nonviolent action by, 534, 561
   rebellion by, 472, 473-74, 476
   sit-ins by, 563-64, 578
New Industrial State, The (Galbraith), 144
New Left, confrontation politics of, 487-92
Newcomb, T. M., 18, 21, 151
Nieburg, H. L., 452, 454
Niehoff, A. H., 151, 152, 345, 351
Nietzsche, Friedrich, W., 517
Nixon, Richard M., 529
Nondirective leadership, 224-26, 228-33
Nonviolence and direct action, 2
   accommodation through, 549-51
   campaigns of, 542-43
   coercion and, 551-54
   conflict and, 566-75
   conversion through, 547-49
   definition of, 534-37
   demonstrations as, 558-61
   economic boycott as, 553
   freedom rides, 559, 564, 577-85
   harassment as, 573-74
   intervention as, 563-65
   mechanisms of change in, 546-57
   mutiny and, 554
   non-cooperation as, 561-63
   outcome of, 555-57
   satyagraha and, 535, 536, 538
   strategy of, 2, 6, 7, 533-44
   See also Civil disobedience; Civil rights movement; Violence and coercion
Nordlie, P. G., 21
Northrup, Herbert R., 197
Norum, C. A., 147, 237, 239
Nunn, H. L., 201, 207
Nunn-Bush Shoe Company, 200

Olds, Virginia, 544, 577-86
Olshansky, S., 333
Olson, Mancur, 499
Olton, D. S., 540
Oppenheimer, Martin, 460, 535, 536, 542, 558-65
Organizational development, 2, 5-6, 343-58
   comparison of managerial development with, 373-84
   crucial issues in, 386-99
   physical settings and, 244-53
   technology of, 353-57
   See also Change, organizational
Orth, C., 151
Orwell, George, 490
Osborn, Alex T., 229
Oshry, B. I., 77
Osmond, H., 240

Parkinson's Law, 188
Parsons, T., 3*n*
Participation in decision making, 145-46
    gherao movement and, 499-500
Participative management, 200-2
    management habits and, 202
    in Scanlon plan, 204-5
Paul, W. J., 356
Peabody, George, 452, 465, 521-32
Peacemakers, 582
Pepinsky, H. B., 68
Perceptions as target for change, 15, 20-22
Perloe, S. I., 540, 541
Personal Feeling Scales, 17
Physical settings and organizational
    development, 244-53
Picketing and nonviolent action, 554-61
Piecework incentive system, 195-98
    automation and, 196
    restriction of output and, 196-97
Pitney-Bowes Company, 211
Planned Change (Lippit et al.), 523
Polak, Fred, 500
Politics of Nonviolent Action, The (Sharp), 546
Population growth, 361-62
Position power, change of, 226-27, 233
Possessed, The (Dostoevsky), 490
Powell, Adam Clayton, 569
Power, 521-31
    action strategies for, 526-31
    measure of, 521
    organization building and, 524-26
    self-interest and, 522-23
Power of Nonviolence, The (Gregg), 548
Pragmatic aims, 5
Problem solving, training for, 122-33
Profit sharing as incentive, 210-11
Program of Business Effectiveness, 397
Psychiatric Hospital as a Small Society, The (Caudill), 333
Psychoanalytic theory of cause of violence, 445
Puckett, Elbridge S., 209, 210
Pyramidal values, 32-33

Quarantelli, E. L., 452

Radhakrishnan, S., 534
Rand, Ayn, 517
Rationalists, 2
Ravachol, François-Claudius, 513-15, 516
Reagan, Ronald, 489
Red Guards, 506
Redlich, F. C., 332
Reference Groups (Sherif and Sherif), 333
Reformers and revolution, 505-6
Reimer, E., 145

Resistance to change
    by individuals, 10-11, 19
    by organizations, 185
Revolution
    anarchism and, 513-19
    conditions for, 503
    counterrevolution and, 502-6
    economic causes of, 448-52
    errors of established authorities dealing with, 504-6
    errors of revolutionaries and, 505
    insurrection and, 483
    political causes of, 448-52
    reformers and, 505
    rising expectations and, 472
    typology of, 457-60
    Yippie concept of, 507-11
    See also Violence and coercion
Rice, A. K., 11, 27, 102-12, 147, 148, 149, 150, 153, 157-84
Richards, J. M., 22
Richardson, F. L. W., Jr., 188
Ricks, D. F., 17
Riecken, H. W., 259, 313
Riesman, D., 80
Rim, Y., 114
Road to H., The (Chein), 332
Robertson, K. B., 356
Robinson, Jaqueline, 22
Roethisberger, F. J., 344-45
Rokeach, Milton, 445
Ronker, H. O., 191
Ross, Dorothea, 446
Ross, Sheila A., 446
Rostow, Eugene, 580
Rothbard, Murray, 512
Rubin, I., 344
Rubin, Jerry, 2, 465, 507-11
Rucker, Allen W., 200, 206
Rucker plan, 201, 206-7, 211
Rural communities, change strategy for, 270-84
    See also Socio-economic research and change strategy for rural communities
Russian Revolution, 470, 506
Rustin, Bayard, 452, 489

Salisbury, Harrison, 365
Sanford, Robert N., 445
Sayles, L. R., 149, 153, 185-94
Scanlon, Joseph, 203
Scanlon plan, 201, 203-5, 207, 210, 211, 357, 389
Schacter, S., 16, 148
Schein, E. A., 20, 62, 63, 64, 65, 100, 310, 344, 351, 387, 394, 399
Schiavo, R. S., 310-15
Schmidt, W. H., 353, 357, 373-85

Index

Schroeder, Harold M., 445
Schultz, W. C., 78
Schutz, W., 151
Schwartz, M. C., 332
Schwartz, R. D., 240
Sears, R. R., 446
Seashore, D., 244
Sechrist, L., 240
Self-interest and power, 522-23
Selltiz, C., 256-57, 268, 316-29
Sensitivity training, *see* T-groups
Serge, Victor, 517, 520
Shannon, William V., 448
Sharp, G., 534, 536, 537, 539, 540, 543, 546-57
Shaw, M. E., 144, 145
Shepard, H. A., 351, 353, 354, 356, 387, 461-62
Sherif, Carolyn W., 333
Sherif, Muzafer, 241, 333, 455, 460-61, 463
Shridharani, K., 534, 535
Shure, G., 538
Sibley, W. B., 151-52
Siegel, L., 68
Silverman, Arnold, 478
Siman, H. A., 3n, 145
Simmel, Georg, 447
Simon, R., 333
Sinclair, Upton, 265
Skills as target for change, 15, 22-23
Skinner, B. F., 256
Slater, P., 244, 250
Slesinger, J., 345
Sloan School of Management, 364
Sloma, R., 355
Small groups
  ecology of, 234-42
  work and basic groups as, 103-4
Small work-groups, creation of in Indian weaving mill, 168-69, 175-76, 183
Smith, C., 345
Smith, D. G., 145
Smith, H. C., 60
Smith, P. B., 78
SNCC (Student Non-violent Coordinating Committee), 490-91
Snow, C. P., 264
Snyder, Glenn, 455
Social Class and Mental Illness (Hollingshead and Redlich), 332
Social influence problem, 26
Social innovation, experimental, 330-40
Social learning theory of cause of violence, 446-47
Social norms and techno-structural interventions, 150-53
Social organization, change and understanding of, 294-308

"classroom" human relations and, 306-8
feedback and, 301-6
interpersonal relations and, 295-301
supervisor training and, 295-301
Social problems, methodology for research of, 331-34
Social psychological model, 4, 13
Social Psychology in Treating Mental Illness: An Experimental Approach (Fairweather), 334
Social subsystem, 334-35, 338
Socio-economic research and change strategy for rural communities, 270-84
  change introduction and, 282-83
  decision-making processes and, 280-81
  economic structure and, 277-79
  physical conditions and, 272-73
  political structure and, 276-77
  problem identification and, 281-82
  social patterns and, 273-76, 279-80
Socio-technical system of Indian weaving shed, 157-83
Socrates, 533
Socratic-rational model, 4, 14-15
Sofer, Cyril, 387, 399n
Solomon, L. N., 64, 455, 538
Sommer, R., 147, 148, 154, 234-43, 252
Sorensen, Theodore, 523
Sorokin, P. A., 538
Southern Christian Leadership Conference, 582
Spatial relations, 147-48
  leadership and, 235-37
  organizational development and, 244-53
  small group ecology and, 234-42
  task and location in, 237-38
Specialization of labor in Indian weaving mill, 168
Srivasta, R., 240, 253
Stability and change in organizations, 186-87
Stanley, Julian C., 256, 260
Stanton, A. H., 332
State as institutionalized violence, 519
Status
  hierarchy and, 146-47
  in Indian weaving mill, 174
Steele, F. I., 100, 154, 244-54
Steiner, I. D., 21
Steinzor, B., 234, 235
Stevens, C. M., 542
Stevenson, Adlai, 507, 522-23
Stiehm, I., 535
Stirner, Max, 517
Stock, D. A., 66, 76
Stodgill, R. M., 68
Storr, Anthony, 445
Stratton, L. D., 238

Street Corner Society: The Social Structure of an Italian Slum (Whyte), 333
Strodbeck, F. L., 148, 235, 239
Strupp, H. H., 17
Student Non-violent Coordinating Committee (SNCC), 490-91
Study group, 104-13
  See also T-groups
Suchman, E., 258, 259, 263
Sullivan, H. S., 12, 238
Supervision
  in Indian weaving mill, 176-77
  union and management attitudes towards, 114-21
Supervisor training
  Canter-Tyler studies of, 297-98
  changing interpersonal relations through, 295-301
  for decision making, 122-35
  Fleishman-Harris studies of, 297-98
  multiple role playing in, 134-41
  See also Management; Manager
Survey feedback method, 316-29, 378, 388-90, 422
Survey methods in campaign against discrimination, 316-29
Synanon House, 333

T-groups (training groups), 15, 18, 20, 21, 25, 26, 27, 31-38, 100-1, 314, 358
  assumptions of, 65
  consultant in, 110-11
  criteria for evaluating, 66-85
  effectiveness of in managerial training, 61-87
  elements of successful outcome of, 44-45
  individual differences in, 82-83
  managerial grid and, 412-16
  needed research for, 85-86
  problem of mimicking in, 37
  pyramidal values and, 32-33
  role of educator and, 35-37
  study groups as, 104-13
  for a work team, 44-59
Talland, G. A., 21
Tannenbaum, A. S., 145, 345
Tannenbaum, R., 63
Task structure, change of, 226, 227, 233
Tavistock Institute, 150, 158, 190
  approach of, 10, 11-12, 15, 24
Taylor, F. C., 74
Team development, 355, 378
  communication and, 432-34
  effects of, 421-39
  long-term results of, 436-39
  production and, 427-29
  strategies of, 421-24
  turnover and, 429-34

Technological change, social repercussions of in an Indian cotton mill, 157-83
Techno-structural strategy, 2, 5, 143-55, 343-44, 355, 378
  in Indian cotton mill, 157-83
  participation in decision making and, 145-46
  psychological ecology and, 147-48
  social norms and, 150-53
  status hierarchy and, 146-47
Tendulkar, D. G., 534
Territorial Imperative, The (Ardrey), 469
Terrorism, 513-16
Theory Y, 252
Therapeutic Community, The (Jones), 337
Thibaut, J. W., 146, 150, 456
Thoreau, Henry D., 534
Toch, Hans, 457
Tocqueville, Alexis de, 361, 372, 448
Tools of Social Science, The (Madge), 333
Torbert, Frances, 154, 195-212
Toynbee, Arnold, 536
Training group, see T-group
Transference cure in individual therapy, 11
Tregoe, B. B., 23, 26, 27, 121-32, 355, 356, 378
Trist, E. L., 147, 149, 157, 164, 183n, 354
Truman, Harry, 523
Twain, Mark, 522
Tyler, B. B., 297-98

Ullman, L., 14, 18
Unaffiliated change agents, 5, 256-57, 264-67
Underdeveloped countries, socio-economic research in, 270-72
Underwood, W. J., 71, 84
Unions
  gherao movement of in India, 493-500
  leaders' attitudes toward supervision, 114-21
  in participative management plans, 207-8
U.S. Commission on Civil Rights, 577, 578-79
Unsafe at Any Speed (Nader), 265
Urban, H. B., 14
Urban riots, 462, 464
  civil insurrection and, 482-83
  frustration-aggression theory of, 468-75
  phases in, 479-81
  precipitation of, 469, 474, 477-78, 479-80
  preconditions of, 476-79
  social control of, 481-82
  use of police in, 474-75
  See also Violence and coercion

Valiquet, I. M., 67, 68, 69-70, 71, 91
Values as target for change, 15, 18-19
  laboratory education and, 31-42

Index

T-groups and, 31-38
work and, 370
See also Change, organizational
Van Alta, E. L., 68
Vernon Company, 286
Violence and coercion
  anarchism and, 513-16
  causes of, 444-47
  class conflict and, 453-54
  confrontation politics and, 487-92
  crowd behavior and, 456-57
  definition of, 443-44
  economic theories of, 448-51
  effects of, 461-64
  exercise of power and, 521-31
  functions of, 447-48
  gherao movement and, 493-500
  goal attainment and, 456
  power and, 456
  social psychological variables leading to, 454-60
  social-structural variables leading to, 448-53
  state institutionalization of, 519
  strategy of, 2, 6, 441-65
  See also Nonviolence and direct action; Revolution; Urban riots

Walker, Charles R., 198
Wallace, George, 488-89
Wallace, W. P., 239
Wallach, M. S., 17
Walters, Richard H., 445
Walton, R. E., 541
War Manpower Commission, 303
Watson, Goodwin, 11
Watson, J., 387, 523
Webb, E. J., 240
Weber, Max, 363
Weight, A. R., 399*n*
Weinstein, Gerald, 399*n*
Wessman, A. E., 17
Westie, F. R., 19
Westley, B., 387, 523
White, R. K., 134, 155, 262, 332, 350
White Citizen's Councils, 582
Whitehead, Alfred North, 369
Whyte, William, 197, 333, 395, 399*n*
Williams, J. L., 239
Williams, M. S., 344
Williams, Whiting, 196
Wilmer, H. A., 238
Wilson, K. V., 538
Winick, C., 238
Wogan, M., 17
Wolin, Sheldon, 443
Wolpe, J., 14
Wolstein, B., 11
Work group, 103-4
  T-group for, 44-59
Wright, C. R., 259

Yablonsky, L., 333
Yaffe, D. L., 540, 541
Yippies, 491, 507-11

Zand, Dale E., 387, 394, 395, 396, 397
Zeigarnik, B., 150
Zerfoss, Lester F., 23, 133-42
Zetterberg, H., 264
Zigler, Edward, 445
Zinn, Howard, 535, 542
Zuleika Dobson (Beerbohm), 365